'Professor Ronald Dworkin was that rarest of birds: a professor of jurisprudence who influenced profoundly leading judges and lawmakers throughout the world. Although born and trained in the United States and domiciled mostly in England, he was a cosmopolitan citizen of all countries and all legal systems. He contested the formalistic positivist legal philosophy that predominated in most common law countries. He advocated a moral interpretivist approach to constitutional and legal adjudication. For him, the law was inescapably a moral discipline. Deny it as they might, judges and lawyers could not escape the moral dilemmas inherent in their job. He favoured expanded judicial review and a search for the "right answer" to all important legal dilemmas. He was thus the defender of creative Indian judges like V.R. Krishna Iyer and P.N. Bhagwati and their counterparts in other countries. For judges like me, he was a paragon, inspiration and friend. This book explains why.'

Michael Kirby AC CMG,
Justice of the High Court of Australia (1996–2009)

'Human dignity is a much cherished principle in our constitutional jurisprudence. Dworkin famously said, "because we cherish dignity, we insist on freedom. Because we honour dignity, we demand democracy". Rendering human rights sacrosanct and inviolable has been at the heart of the Dworkinian way of living life. This book aptly divided into four parts, beautifully details the essence of Dworkin's theories through the lens of lawyers, scholars, and professors of law and philosophy.'

K.K. Venugopal,
Attorney General of India

'Ronald Dworkin's tall presence pervades twenty-first century jurisprudential landscape and comparative judicial action. This fine volume critically engages aspects of a theory of 'supra virtue' of dignity. Compelling remain critical exploration of 'interpretive' idea of law and the complex 'moral reading' of the law and constitution. Do 'unbridgeable pluralism' and defence of hate speech mark the global 'exit' of Dworkin's Hercules?'

Upendra Baxi,
Emeritus Professor of Law, University of Warwick, England

'An internationally distinguished group of authors contribute insightful and provocative essays on Ronald Dworkin's views on how the concept of human dignity must inform our understanding of a wide range of legal and policy issues. The collection is essential reading both for those interested in the concept of human dignity and those interested in Dworkin's work.'

Mark Tushnet,
William Nelson Cromwell Professor of Law,
Harvard Law School, USA

'The authors have done a great service to those who are curious to understand the philosophy underlying the principles embedded beneath rules which we call law. There are few who can match Dworkin in illumining such elemental underpinnings and the authors' selections and analysis does justice to that intellectual giant.'

Abhishek Singhvi,
Member of Parliament and National Spokesperson
for Indian National Congress

Dignity in the Legal and Political Philosophy
of Ronald Dworkin

Dignity in the Legal and Political Philosophy of Ronald Dworkin

edited by

Salman Khurshid
Lokendra Malik
Veronica Rodriguez-Blanco

OXFORD
UNIVERSITY PRESS

OXFORD
UNIVERSITY PRESS

Oxford University Press is a department of the University of Oxford.
It furthers the University's objective of excellence in research, scholarship,
and education by publishing worldwide. Oxford is a registered trademark of
Oxford University Press in the UK and in certain other countries.

Published in India by
Oxford University Press
2/11 Ground Floor, Ansari Road, Daryaganj, New Delhi 110 002, India

© Oxford University Press 2018

The moral rights of the authors have been asserted.

First Edition published in 2018

ISBN-13: 978-0-19-948417-1
ISBN-10: 0-19-948417-1

Typeset in Adobe Garamond Pro 11/13
by The Graphics Solution, New Delhi 110 092
Printed in India by Replika Press Pvt. Ltd

Contents

Foreword

Ronald Dworkin taught with notable clarity and firmness that laws, and a community's life under law's rule, need to be understood from 'the internal, participants' point of view', grasping 'the argumentative character of our legal practice by joining the practice and struggling with the issues of soundness and truth participants face'. Those issues of truth could never properly be fended off, or circumvented, by appeal to some fact or facts of convergent practice, convention, belief, or other consensus. The end of an enquiry or argument about law could only be some principle directing choices, some value. So his theory of law could not be other than integrated with a theory of political principle and philosophically warranted morality. The range of the contributions to this memorial volume manifests the range, depth, and energy of Dworkin's thought on these issues of truth in practical reasoning.

We were colleagues in Oxford for three decades, and together with Joseph Raz held seminars in jurisprudence and political theory for much of the first two of the decades, after which Dworkin's interests in political and moral theory, and in wider philosophical topics and discussions, led him to focus his Oxford teaching on, for the most part, other collaborations. (For much of those three decades we also participated in a weekly term-time philosophical-legal discussion group originated and hosted by H.L.A. Hart but later organized by the philosopher Derek Parfit, held in the jurist Tony Honoré's rooms, and dominated, or at least focused, by Dworkin's ever-ready, articulate penetration of problems and grasp of argumentation.) The three of us held strongly diverging views on some fundamental issues, not to mention topical legal and political developments. But the commonalities derived both from our overlapping interests in extending Hart's engagement with legal and social theory and with liberal political principles, and from the shared Oxford and wider culture of independence and civility, meant that the seminars we conducted could always be stimulating without heat or rhetoric. Dworkin's presence in a discussion—indeed, even the prospect of his presence—strongly tended to stimulate thought focused on deep questions. So it is a privilege to be able to share in the enterprise of this book.

During the years we taught together, Ronald Dworkin's concern with human dignity was articulated predominantly in the principle demanding equality of concern and respect. And that is the case, again, in the last of his 2011 lectures at the University of Bern, revised and published very shortly after his death early in 2013, the lecture in which his enquiry into reality's deepest make-up is brought to bear on the legal-political question of liberty of religious practice and expression. 'The egalitarian ideal of ethical independence' is his summation of our dignity's most immediate bearing on our rights, and the ideal or principle issues in his last book's political-legal judgment—this principle was being flouted by certain Swiss and Turkish restrictions on freedom of public expression of religious belief. He rested that final application of principle squarely on what he judged to be the actual motivations and factual presuppositions of those supporting and imposing the restrictions.

Reading this fine collection of reflections and enquiries about law and dignity, assembled in memory of Ronald Dworkin, one will join the editors and authors in honouring him if one keeps constantly in mind that the truth of human dignity, and the entailed equality of entitlement to respect and concern, will ground *right* answers in politics and law when, and only when, applied with clear-sighted resolve to *fit*—and soundly interpret—the facts, facts about the human condition (with its complex needs and interdependencies, not least of children and their parents) and facts about the motivations both of those who make laws and of those whom they direct. Dworkin's admirable zest for open discourse and debate, like his fruitful concern that there be in our polities at least one secure *forum* of principle, had its roots in keen and constant awareness that every instance of practical reasoning depends for its soundness on its first premises, about value and principle, but also on its second premises about facts past, present, and to come.

John Finnis
University of Oxford, UK

Acknowledgements

The book is the product of collective efforts of a number of persons who admired the scholarly contribution of Ronald Dworkin. Some words of thanks are must for all those who became the part of this unique project.

First of all, we are deeply grateful to eminent legal philosopher John Finnis for writing an erudite Foreword to this volume. We are equally grateful to Hon'ble Justice A.K. Sikri of the Supreme Court of India for writing an insightful Afterword. Both these contributions have enhanced the value as well as the beauty of our work.

We would like to place on record our sincere gratitude to all the distinguished contributors for their scholarly contributions despite their busy engagements. Jonathan Crowe, James E. Fleming, Linda C. McClain, Alexander Brown, Trevor R.S. Allan, Imer B. Flores, Pritam Baruah, Allen W. Wood, Barbara Baum Levenbook, Isabel Trujillo, David A.J. Richards, James Allan, Lorenzo Zucca, George Pavlakos, Erin Daly, Suhrith Parthasarathy, Mark Bennett, and Petra Butler deserve our sincere thanks.

We would also like to acknowledge the contribution of some of our friends and well-wishers who encouraged us a lot to bring out this volume. Professor Upendra Baxi, Professor M.P. Singh, Fali S. Nariman, and Justice Michael Kirby truly deserve our thanks.

We are sincerely thankful to the team at Oxford University Press for their valuable assistance during different stages of this volume.

Last but not least, we pay our sincere tribute to Professor Ronald Dworkin through this collection of essays in his memory and honour.

Salman Khurshid, Lokendra Malik,
and Veronica Rodriguez-Blanco
New Delhi

Ronald Dworkin

Life and Works

Lokendra Malik

Ronald Dworkin was an eminent legal philosopher of his generation. He was a great academic lawyer who continues to inspire many academics and has encouraged many of them to participate in a constructive morality-based legal discourse aiming at transforming the state of affairs in the jurisprudential world remarkably. His unique scholarly ideas, expressed in many books and journals, developed a powerful scholarly interpretation of the law and expounded critical comments not only on Anglo-American issues but various legal issues globally as well. He was a great advocate of human rights and dignity who developed an interesting scholarly combination of the law and expounded issues of contemporary importance and public concern, including the question as to how the law should deal with the contemporary socio-legal issues such as race, abortion, euthanasia, free speech, and equality in ways that are accessible to the ordinary people. His legal arguments were concise solutions to specific problems of a classic liberal philosophy, which in turn was grounded in his conception that law must derive its recognition from morality.[1] His key belief was that the law should be grounded in moral integrity, understood as the moral idea that the government should act on principle so each member of the community is treated as an equal. He was behind some of the most influential theories of law and morality in modern jurisprudence and overwhelmed his opponents with his ferocious debating skills. He was a committed Democrat and believed strongly in liberalism, equality, human rights, and dignity.[2] Indeed, he was a highly influential scholar of international reputation.

Ronnie, as he was popularly known, was considered to be one of the main critics of the famous Oxford Professor H.L.A. Hart, a great pioneer of theory of legal positivism.[3] He gave an alternative theory in opposition to Hart's positivist theory of law which had received a visible recognition among the legal scholars and philosophers globally, particularly in the Anglo-American jurisprudential world. Professor Hart was a renowned figure in British political and legal philosophy. He was Dworkin's predecessor at Oxford chair of jurisprudence. He had dominated legal theory and philosophy for a long period by propounding legal concepts in his well-known book titled *The Concept of Law*.[4] Dworkin strongly dissented with Hart's theory and focused more on the morality-based principles. He opined that legal reasoning is a form of moral reasoning and law without morality is nothing but a myth. He was recognized as one of the leading philosophers on moral and political philosophy who gave an alternative to Hart's theory of law by focusing on morality. The traditional theory of positivism, as advanced by Hart, intends to separate the law from morality. It reflects that there is a master test, which Professor Hart calls a rule of recognition that will identify those standards which are rules of the legal system. This ultimate rule is itself simply a social convention and its identification needs no appeal to moral or political rules. Professor Dworkin strongly argued against the existence of a rule of recognition and the alleged separation of law and morals.[5] His morality-based theory was ultimately recognized on a large scale.

Not only the Anglo-American world, but many other countries like India equally benefited from Professor Dworkin's scholarly contributions in many significant ways as is evident from his quotations finding a place in some of the landmark judgments of the Supreme Court of India.[6] On many significant issues like affirmative action, apartheid, equality jurisprudence, women rights, and minority rights and so on, the judicial tribunals across the globe cited his views generously in their judicial pronouncements.[7] He was the most cited legal philosopher of the contemporary times. In fact, he was an intellectual giant whose writings have truly graced the juristic world.

In the present chapter, the author intends to go through various phases of Professor Dworkin's life and his journey towards scholarly contributions, juristic thoughts, and theses.

Early Years

Ronald Myles Dworkin was born in Providence, Rhodes Island in the United States of America on 11 December 1931 in a Jewish-American family. His father, David W. Dworkin, had migrated from Lithuania to the United States of America during his early childhood. Following his parents' divorce, he was brought up by his mother Madeline Talamo, who was a piano teacher. His mother remarried but unfortunately her second husband died of a heart attack in a very short span of their married life. This tragedy put her in a very difficult situation. However, despite facing such a difficult time, she raised her three children on her own through her small earnings from piano classes.[8] Ronald was the middle child among his siblings. His sister, Fern Cohen, was five years elder to him and lives in New York. His younger brother, Alan, is a lawyer in Rhode Island (Liptak 2013).

Education

Ronald Dworkin went to a public school along the lines of the Boston Latin School and performed very well in his studies. After completing his schooling, he got a scholarship from Harvard University for his graduate studies where he achieved straight A's in all his four years' classes (Hodgson 2013). He earned the degree of B.A. in philosophy from the Harvard University in the year 1953. Thereafter, he went to the Oxford University as a Rhodes Scholar and obtained his masters' degree (MA) in Jurisprudence (Liptak 2013). At Oxford, he was taught by many eminent professors such as Sir Rupert Cross.[9] It not only encouraged him in voicing his thoughts extensively but also helped in shaping himself well and ultimately becoming a scholar and a philosopher of international repute. He had opted for law but he spent most of his time with philosophers as the study of philosophy had always been very close to his heart. He played a lot of bridge, much of it with his lifelong friend Guido Calabresi, later Dean of the Yale Law School and an appeal court judge in Connecticut, New York, and Vermont. 'His Oxford finals' papers were as impeccable as the Harvard ones: straight alphas, after straight As' (Hodgson 2013). Indeed, Oxford University became the heaven of his scholarly activities throughout his life and he became a role model for the Oxford scholars.

In 1955, Ronald Dworkin returned to the Harvard University to earn an American degree in law and graduated with top position in 1957. The Harvard Law Faculty recommended his name for clerkship to Judge Learned Hand. Hand was an internationally known American judge. Dworkin impressed

Hand with his work. By all accounts, at Oxford and Harvard, Dworkin turned out to be an outstanding student who not only influenced but also left an indelible mark on the minds of his teachers as well as classmates with his deep understanding of academic issues and strong sense of learning. He had a magnetic force in his orations and writings which also made him a centre of attention among the legal academics.

It is pertinent to mention that the Oxford University officially invited Professor H.L.A. Hart to evaluate Dworkin's final year's dissertation.[10] Professor Hart was highly impressed with his findings in the dissertation. He found him to be an intellectually intimidating student who scored the highest marks in every single examination that he appeared in (Lacey 2004). It was Professor Hart who subsequently recommended his name for the famous Chair of Jurisprudence at Oxford as his successor. That Chair had previously had an American holder, Professor Arthur Goodhart, who held it for some years until Professor Hart occupied it in 1952. English jurisprudence was then in the doldrums (Guest 1991: 2). However, as stated earlier, in due course of time, Professor Dworkin turned out to be a well-known critic of Professor Hart's juristic thesis of positivism which invited the attention of many scholars and the Hart-Dworkin debate became a famous jurisprudential show globally. In his book *Taking Rights Seriously*,[11] Dworkin contentiously attacked Hart's theory of positivism.

Marriage

Adam Liptak, Dworkin's magazine biographer, states that Dworkin met Betsy Ross, the daughter of a rich New Yorker, during the last days of his clerkship with Judge Learned Hand in 1958, and married her. Betsy was born in Manhattan to Walter and Adelaide Ross. She was a beautiful lady who became his life partner. After completing his law clerkship, Dworkin joined a New York-based law firm, namely, Sullivan and Cromwell, and served there from 1958 to 1962, just for four years. However, soon he realized that his interest is elsewhere and not in continuing as a hard-core courtroom lawyer. His work gave him many opportunities to travel abroad also. However, since his family was rooted in the United States, his wife persuaded him to return to America and consider joining academia. He recalled getting a telegram from her in Stockholm, wherein he was working on a deal. He had failed to deliver on a promise to be home by his birthday. 'By next year', the telegram said, 'you will have a new job or a new wife.'[12] And by the next year, Dworkin got a new job as a law faculty at Yale. It appears God had made him for academics.

Betsy Ross had studied history and literature at Radcliff, was a Fulbright scholar in Paris and had two masters' degrees, one in the history of fine arts from the Harvard University in 1957, and another in social policy from the London School of Economics and Political Science (Liptak 2005: 18). She went on to become a writer on the staff of the Metropolitan Museum, an Associate Editor of Art news and managing editor of a sister publication, the quarterly portfolio. In 1962, she moved to New Haven, where she helped run a poverty eradication programme in the public-school system. In 1969, she moved to England, where in 1972 she earned a second masters' degree in social policy from the London School of Economics and Political Science. From 1972 to 1989 she taught at Chelsea and University colleges.[13] She encouraged Dworkin to continue his scholarly journey particularly in Britain and the United States of America. Sadly, after 41 years of their marriage, she died of cancer in the year 2000. It was indeed a big loss for Dworkin. She was a great source of inspiration and support to him.

After Betsy's death, Dworkin married Irene Brendel, who was the ex-wife of the pianist Alfred Brendel.[14] Irene Brendel, popularly known as Reni, gave him a new lease of life and a new love which deeply encouraged him to continue his scholarly contribution till his last days. He dedicated his famous book *Justice for Hedgehogs*[15] to Reni who was a close companion of Dworkin.

Law Clerkship with Judge Learned Hand

After earning his law degree from the Harvard University in 1957, Dworkin joined Judge Learned Hand as a law clerk on the recommendation of the Harvard Law Faculty.[16] Judge Hand was one of the most influential American judges of his times who held the position of judge of the United States Court of Appeals for the Second Circuit in Manhattan.[17] He told Dworkin that he did not need him to draft his opinions as generally judges used to ask their law clerks in those days. 'I do not know how you write', the great man said, 'I write very well' (Hodgson 2013). He asked him to read his Holmes lectures that he had prepared for delivery at the Harvard University in which he questioned whether the United States Supreme Court had correctly decided *Brown v. Board of Education, Topeka Kansas*.[18] In this judgment, the United States Supreme Court had observed that racially segregated education was necessarily unconstitutional and violative of Equal Protection Clause of the Fourteenth Amendment of the Constitution. This is what the Court had observed in its judgment: 'To separate students from others of similar age and qualifications solely because of their race generates a feeling of inferiority as to their status in the community that may affect their hearts and minds in a way unlikely ever to be undone.'[19] This verdict was globally appreciated but Judge Hand did not like it. However, Dworkin dissented with Hand on this ruling and appreciated it.[20] It was indeed a courageous move on the part of Dworkin. Judge Hand was fond of Dworkin, who in turn respected Hand a lot (Dworkin 1996: 340).

Days with Sullivan and Cromwell

In 1959, Dworkin passed the Bar examination and joined the New York-based prominent law firm, Sullivan and Cromwell.[21] He worked there for four years from 1958–62 and handled cases pertaining to international business transactions. He could not show interest in becoming a litigation lawyer but was more interested in research, teaching, and legal philosophy. After leaving the law firm he joined the faculty of Yale Law School. It is worth remembering that at one point of time he declined the offer of doing clerkship with Justice Frankfurter, a judge of the United States Supreme Court, though he subsequently regretted his decision in these words: 'This was a very serious mistake and I cannot actually put together why I made it. I was just anxious to get started. I later learned that many lawyers thought it one of the great advantages of clerking for Learned Hand that they might get to work for Felix Frankfurter. That is how it worked. Obviously, it was a crucial missed opportunity. I missed a great opportunity' (Liptak 2005: 18).

Judge Learned Hand was fond of Dworkin and thus, called him to join as his law clerk and beat all law clerks (Liptak 2013: 81) with his intellect and in turn, Dworkin too would admire Judge Hand as an enormously influential mentor who guided many to successful careers (Dworkin 1996: 340).

Academic Career

Yale Law School

In 1962, Dworkin joined the Yale Law School as Professor of Law as Wesley N. Hohfeld Chair of Jurisprudence during the deanship of Professor Rostow.[22] He taught basic courses, and also taught a course together with Robert Bork on economic theory and the law. Subsequently, it is worth noticing that he opposed Bork's nomination to the United States Supreme Court.[23] He believed that Bork's nomination to the Supreme Court was against the fundamental principles of the Constitution. This academic appointment gave him an opportunity to marry his two passions, namely law and philosophy. This position also provided him the freedom to work on issues he found interesting such as race, justice, freedom, civil liberties, and so on; based on his intellectual interests and quest laying down the foundation of a creative jurisprudence based on moral values. For him, Yale was a place full of stars and he extensively enjoyed his tenure as the law school provided a rich intellectual environment. It was a great beginning of a great teaching career that subsequently made many landmarks in different phases of his constructive life.

Oxford University

After serving the Yale Law School for about seven years, Dworkin joined the Oxford University in 1969 and served it till 1998 as a joint faculty. He became a very popular lecturer at Oxford and held a prestigious Chair of Jurisprudence that had once been held by renowned jurist, H.L.A. Hart, whose views he critically analysed subsequently. He was also elected as a fellow of University College, Oxford. His crowded lectures at Oxford were very popular. He was a great model of an Oxford scholar, having clear arguments and strong convincing power. Richard H. Fallan Jr., who had attended some of his lectures at Oxford during his student days, recalls that Dworkin was a gust of fresh air blowing through Oxford during his two years there. He said that to make his point Dworkin would use vivid, often funny examples.[24] Usually, he targeted Hart's thesis in his lectures and writings many times. He was said to be generous in his dealing with students which made him a popular teacher in the university. He recalls his Oxford days in these words: 'I adored Oxford..... I loved the life of the philosophical community. Endless talk over wine, over dinner, long walks in the meadows' (Liptak 2005: 19).

University College of London (UCL)

From Oxford, Ronald Dworkin went to University College of London as Quain Professor of Jurisprudence where he subsequently became the Bentham Professor of Jurisprudence. He made landmark achievements in legal and political philosophy at the UCL. For many years, he chaired the high profile colloquium in social and legal philosophy at the UCL, an integral component of their academic course of Masters of Arts (MA) in legal and political theory. The University College of London immensely benefited from his scholarship as also from his stimulating and enlightening ideas.

New York University Law School

Dworkin joined the New York University Law School as a joint faculty in 1975, after rejecting the offer from Harvard Law School, his own *alma mater*.

The New York University Law School was not much known in the academic circles during those days. Today, however, it is amongst the most famous law schools not only in the United States of America but across the globe. It is commonly believed that during those days it was considered as a sleepy place having no colloquia or regular workshops, and the programmes were also poorly attended by students. Dworkin changed the dull atmosphere of the school and brought a wave of rejuvenation in the University.[25] He conducted a colloquium in legal, political, and social philosophy, for 25 years at the law school that changed its environment totally, providing a forum for the vigorous discussion and exchange of ideas that consequently attracted the numerous scholars from different parts of the world.

Dworkin's NYU colleague, Professor Thomas Nagel played a key role in conducting the colloquium and making it a grand success. Both of them used to invite scholars, from different places, to present their papers for debate and analysis on specific topics that were shared with other participants in the open forum. The colloquium became a wonderful platform for developing constructive ideas in the form of books and monographs for many renowned scholars who utilized it to present their scholastic thesis. Professor Thomas Nagel's *Equality and Partiality*, Scanlon's *What We Owe to Each Other*, Professor Kamm's *Morality, Mortality*, and Bernard William's *Shame and Necessity*, to name a few, were inspired and originated from his colloquium deliberations at the NYU. His last books—*Justice for Hedgehogs*, and *Religion without God*—were also conceived in the colloquium deliberations (Kornhauser 2014: 8).

Dworkin was a great orator who delivered many prestigious lectures, such as, the *Oliver Wendell Holmes Lecture* at Harvard, the *Storrs Lectures* at Yale, the *Tanner Lectures on Human Values* at Stanford, the *Scribner Lectures* at Princeton, the *Einstein lectures* at the University of Bern in 2011, and so on. In June 2011, he joined the professoriate of the New College of the Humanities, a private college in London. Indeed, he had a remarkable academic journey that truly inspires all his followers, admirers, and students placed in different parts of the world.

Academic Contribution and Honours

During his long academic journey Dworkin authored dozens of books and hundreds of papers on different topics pertaining to law, politics, and philosophy particularly related to American jurisdiction. *Taking Rights Seriously*,[26] *The Philosophy of Law*,[27] *A Matter of Principle*,[28] *Law's Empire*,[29] *Life's Dominion*,[30] *Sovereign Virtue: The Theory and Practice of Equality*,[31] *Freedom's*

Law: The Moral Reading of the American Constitution,[32] *Justice in Robes*,[33] *Justice for Hedgehogs*,[34] and *Religion without God*[35] are some of his prominent books that made him an illustrious academic figure.

Among all his books, *Taking Rights Seriously* was Dworkin's first famous book that was intended to be a strong reaction to Professor H.L.A. Hart's positivist theory. In fact, it was a modified version of his papers published in the *New York Review of Books*.[36] The book made him a very influential law professor of his times. His other books were equally influential not only in the law schools in the United States but also across other jurisdictions. His books set the agenda of the need for morality-based legal interpretation of laws.

Dworkin's numerous other scholarly contributions like articles and papers published in different journals spread over a long period, gave him the recognition of being a distinguished jurist of the intellectual world. In fact, it is believed that his writings made him an Emperor of the legal world. The author sincerely believes that his books and other works have made him immortal and would continue to inspire the legal scholars in the years to come.

In a survey published in 2000 in the *Journal of Legal Studies*, three of his books were amongst the eleven most cited legal books published since 1978: *Taking Rights Seriously* (1978), and *A Matter of Principle* (1985); two collections of seminal essays, and, at number two, *Law's Empire* (1986), his masterwork on the nature and role of adjudication (Liptak 2005). Charles Fried, a Harvard professor, states that 'Dworkin was the exemplification of good life and living well. He lived high but never for a moment hesitated to argue passionately for policies and parties that would surely have cut deeply—*a la Francois Hollande*—into his ability to live that way. His writing style was pithy and memorable. Arguments had a nerve. Proposals were on offer. And sentences and paragraphs built to a crescendo in a rhetorical but also a logical finale'.[37] The author endorses these scholarly views.

Contribution for the *New York Review of Books*

Professor Dworkin continued to engage many scholars on difficult issues facing the community particularly the Anglo-American society for a long time. He never avoided difficult issues, and rather gave them a voice through his erudite essays in the *New York Review of Books* that became very popular particularly in the Anglo-American world. He had a long association with the *Review* beginning since 1968 till his last days and published hundreds of essays and commented extensively in the *Review* that gave him a unique recognition globally.

Robert B. Silvers, the Editor of the *New York Review of Books*, recalls as to how in his 6 June 1968 issue, when the Vietnam war was at its height and groups of young men were burning their draft cards in Central Park, Dworkin posed in his first sentence the following question: 'How should the government deal with those who disobey the draft laws out of conscience?'[38] And he disagreed with Erwin Griswold, the Solicitor General of the United States and former Dean of Harvard Law School, who called for universal prosecution of all who carried out civil disobedience, saying, 'that organized society cannot endure on any other basis'. Silvers states that Dworkin argued to the contrary, if the issue is one touching fundamental, personal, and constitutional rights, and it is seriously arguable that the view of the Supreme Court was mistaken, then a person may be within his rights in acting on that possibility. In reply, Erwin Griswold—himself greatly respected for his defence of Great Society legislation, among many other accomplishments—wrote it to the effect that as a result of that article having been published in a non-professional forum, Ronnie had lost the respect of his peers, Robert Silvers states. Further Robert states that Dworkin's essay aroused intense support from many well-known lawyers and professors and it soon was followed by a special supplement to the Review of some 10,000 words, called *Taking Rights Seriously*, in which he argued that the very institution of rights represents the majority's promise to the minority that their dignity would be respected, and that if the law is to work, this promise should also apply to conscientious objectors.[39] Indeed, a great defence of human rights during a crucial time! This is how Robert Silvers recalls Dworkin's association with the *Review*:

> It was in 1967, soon after we began, that I had a call from Stuart Hampshire, who was teaching philosophy at Princeton, and he'd become, since our beginnings, a kind of shadow editor of the Review. And that morning he said, 'If you need someone to write on law and the philosophy of law, there's a young professor at Yale Law School who knows more about philosophy than a lot of the people you are using, and he writes better about it', and he gave me Ronnie's name. (Silvers 2014: 22)

Indeed, the *New York Review of Books* gave a great platform to Dworkin to express his scholarly thoughts which influenced people across the globe. Professor Dworkin addressed many important issues pertaining to American society in his essays over the years. Various issues such as affordable health care, Clinton's impeachment, affirmative action, Bork's nomination, euthanasia, abortion, and so on, were addressed by him in depth in his contributions for the *Review*. His writings benefited many other jurisdictions as well. In 1984, his theory of adjudication was given prominence by Professor Raymond Wacks of the University of Natal in Durban. He delivered a public lecture in which he argued that the South African legal order was 'quintessentially unjust', and that judges who shared this view and were concerned about the moral dilemma of having to apply apartheid laws should resign. In his speech, he referred extensively to *Taking Rights Seriously*, seeking support there for his conclusion. This speech gave rise to a heated debate in the press and to a formal reply by Professor Dugard. The debate captures the tension inherent in the role of a judge under apartheid.[40] This debate even influenced some liberal judges to resign rather than enforcing unjust laws in South Africa which violated even most basic human rights. But unfortunately, no judge resigned and unjust laws were strictly imposed. His reports from Argentina on the human rights trials and on the regime of Margaret Thatcher were highly appreciated putting him in the category of leading public philosophers of his times.[41] Professor Laurence H. Tribe admires his great teaching personality in these words:

> The mark of a great teacher is to ask questions that drive the listener into a lifelong search for answers. Ronald Dworkin was a great teacher as well as a great legal philosopher. He taught that none of us can be either without at least aspiring to be the other. And he did more; he not only taught us what questions to ask; he also left some tantalizing hints of what the answers might resemble.[42]

During his whole academic journey, Dworkin remained associated with many reputed academic bodies in different places across the globe. He was a fellow of the British Academy as well as the American Academy of Arts and Sciences. He was honoured for his work by numerous institutions and organizations, receiving many honorary degrees and the highest accolades in law and philosophy. Two of the most prestigious were the Ludvig Holberg International Memorial Prize (2007) for 'his pioneering scholarly work' of 'worldwide impact', and the Balzan Prize for Jurisprudence (2012), for his 'fundamental contributions to Jurisprudence, characterized by outstanding gifts of sharpness, originality and clarity of thought'. His alma mater, the Harvard University, also awarded him an honorary degree in 2009. He also delivered the famous Holmes Lectures at the Harvard University. The Holmes lectures are the most prestigious talks honouring the most reputed legal scholar at the Harvard University. The lecture series was established in 1954, as a result of the 1861 bequest of Oliver Wendell Holmes Jr., an HLS graduate and associate justice of the United States Supreme Court from 1902 to 1932.

***

On 14 February 2013, at the age of 81, Professor Ronald Dworkin passed away after a valiant battle with leukaemia in a London hospital. His death came as a big shock for the entire juristic world. The eloquent speaker, writer, and above all a great human being left us all with his legacy, leaving for posterity, scores of scholarly books and other invaluable material including hundreds of papers that truly made him immortal in the memory of all his friends, colleagues, students, and admirers. Media, his friends, colleagues, and fans poured their tributes in abundance. Some prominent law schools, such as Harvard and New York University Law School published their law reviews in his honour and memory. Many of his colleagues, friends, and students also poured their sincere tributes in these reviews.

Paying his tribute to Dworkin, Richard H. Fallon, Jr. stated that in the study of American constitutional and statutory interpretation, Dworkin, in his estimation, has no serious rival as the most incisive and fertile theorist of the past four decades.[43] Professor Charles Fried of Harvard Law School said that no account of Dworkin and his work can omit mention of, indeed must dwell on, the elegance of his writing style, of his argumentation, of his person.

Dworkin uniquely transformed the intellectual environment through his erudite writings for a long time by writing pieces for the general public addressing difficult issues pertaining to law, politics, and society in lucid terms for more than a half-century that would have far-reaching impact on the academic psyche. He was a great gift to the juristic world whose role as a theorist and a public intellectual cannot be underestimated for a long time. His influential writings encouraged many people to participate in the constructive public discourse pertaining to contemporary legal and political issues such as abortion,[44] medically-assisted suicide,[45] freedom of speech,[46] judges' nomination to the Supreme Court, pornography,[47] national security, war, and so on for a long time.

As stated earlier, Dworkin's countless writings, in the form of books and articles contributed to the *New York Review of Books* and other journals, persuaded many democratic institutions in different jurisdictions to introspect on some key issues that affected the life of the people deeply. It is well-known as to how he influenced the thinking process of American people relating to Bork's nomination to the US Supreme Court. Subsequently, Bork was rejected by the Senate during the confirmation proceedings.[48] Bork had taught law with him at Yale in 1960s. Professor Minow states that Dworkin drew other talented thinkers into the debate and action. A case in point is *The Philosophers' Brief*; he organized six distinguished moral and political philosophers to write and submit a brief and to share it with the public when the US Supreme Court considered the constitutionality of government prohibitions against assisted suicide.[49]

Professor Dworkin did not confine himself to a particular jurisdiction but also addressed many global issues that largely affected humanity like human rights' violations in Argentina, South Africa, and so on.[50] His timely interventions made a visible impact on the jurisprudential thinking in many ways. Beginning from Harvard to New York University via Oxford, the academic journey of Dworkin is extremely impressive and insightful. He was a born scholar, a scholar inextricably wedded to legal philosophy and academics who greatly defended human rights and dignity through his scholarly writings. He was the pre-eminent legal philosopher of the past half century whose contribution is everlasting and memorable.

Not only the western jurisprudential world took note of his scholarly views, but many other top courts of the world including the Supreme Court of India also quoted him in many landmark cases such as *Indra Sawhney*,[51] *S.R. Bommai*,[52] *SEBI v. Sahara India Real Estate Corporation*,[53] and so on which changed the course of constitutional dialogue in the country. His writings are highly relevant in constitutional interpretation by the Judiciary. It seems that the Supreme Court of India was influenced with his juristic thesis of liberal interpretation in the *NALSA*[54] case while on the other hand the Court ignored it in the *NAZ Foundation case*.[55] The Court missed a great opportunity to provide justice to the homosexuals in the country in this case. Long back, in 1980s, the legendary Justice V.R. Krishna Iyer of the Supreme Court of India had also cited him in his famous *ABSK Sangh v. Union of India*[56] judgment. Besides these cases, the Supreme Court of India also took a serious note of his jurisprudential thesis in its more pronouncements as and when required. Recently, in *Binoy Viswam v. Union of India*[57] (Aadhar card case), the Supreme Court has again cited the hard case theory of Ronald Dworkin. The legal and political conditions of the country perfectly demand the import of liberal juristic principles during the process of adjudication and Dworkin' theory is fully relevant in our land also. This is why Dworkin is fully relevant for India too. He was one of the most important philosophers of the last 100 years.[58] He was indeed a philosopher par excellence who made his place secure in the academic world by producing high-quality writings which would inspire generations to come.

The philosopher's life may now be over, but the life of philosophy he evolved is not going to fade and the outstanding academic work that remains would continue to inspire generations to come. His legacy for the human rights and dignity will always remain alive. The thousands of law students whom he taught at Oxford, Yale, UCL, NYU, and so on would carry that legacy forward to transform the quality of legal discourse aiming to protect human dignity. His ideas would always continue to inspire us to understand the law through the lens of morality and human dignity.

Notes and References

1. Godfrey Hodgson. 2013. 'Ronald Dworkin Obituary'. *The Guardian*, 14 February.
2. Marcus Williamson. 2013. 'Professor Ronald Dworkin: Legal Philosopher Acclaimed as the Finest of his Generation'. *Independent*, 15 February.
3. Ronald Dworkin. 1969. 'Morality and the Law'. *New York Review of Books*, 22 May.
4. H.L.A. Hart. 1961. *The Concept of Law*. Oxford University Presss.
5. Marshall Cohen. 1983. *Ronald Dworkin and Contemporary Jurisprudence*. New Jersey: Rowman and Allanheld. p. viii.
6. *S.R. Bommai v. Union of India*, (1994) 3 SCC 1.
7. Arthur Chaskalson. 2003. 'From Wickedness to equality: The Moral Transformation of South African Law', *International Journal of Constitutional Law* 1(4). pp. 590–609. 4 November.
8. Adam Liptak. 2013. 'Ronald Dworkin, Scholar of the Law, Is Dead at 81', *New York Times*. 14 February.
9. Stephen Guest. 1991. *Ronald Dworkin*. Stanford: Stanford University Press. p. 2.
10. Nicola Lacey. 2004. *A Life of H.L.A. Hart: The Nightmare and the Noble Dream*. New York: Oxford University Press. p. 186.
11. Ronald Dworkin. 1978. *Taking Rights Seriously*. Cambridge: Harvard University Press. p. 22.
12. Adam Liptak. 2005. 'Tribute to Ronald Dowrkin'. *The Transcendent Lawyer*. New York: New York University School of Law. p. 18.
13. 'Betsy Dworkin, 66; Taught Social Policy'. 2000. *The New York Times*, 28 April.
14. Matt Schudel. 2013. 'Ronald Dworkin Influential Legal Theorist, Dies at 81', *The Washington Post*, 14 February 2013.
15. Ronald Dworkin. 2011. *Justice for Hedgehogs*. Cambridge: Harvard University Press.
16. Martha Minow. 2013. 'In Memoriam: Ronald Dworkin', *Harvard Law Review* 127(2). p. 506.
17. Ronald Dworkin. 1994. 'Mr. Liberty', *New York Review of Books*. 11 August.
18. 347 U.S. 483(1954).
19. 347 U.S. 483(1954) p. 494.
20. Ronald Dworkin. 1996. *Freedom's Law: The Moral Reading of the American Constitution*. Cambridge: Harvard University Press. p. 340.
21. Marcus Williamson. 2013. 'Professor Ronald Dworkin: Legal Philosopher acclaimed as the finest of his generation'. *Independent*. 16 February.

22. Laura Kalman. 2006. *Yale Law School and the Sixties: Revolt and Reverberations*. United States: University of North Carolina Press. p. 49.
23. Ronald Dworkin. 1987. 'The Bork Nomination', *New York Review of Books*. 13 August.
24. Richard H. Fallan Jr. 2013. 'Ronald Dworkin'. *Harvard Law Review* 127(2). p. 489.
25. Lewis A. Kornhauser. 2014. 'Ronald Dworkin', *New York University Law Review* 89(1). p. 6.
26. Ronald Dworkin. 1978. *Taking Rights Seriously*. Cambridge: Harvard University Press.
27. Ronald Dworkin. 1977. *The Philosophy of Law*. New York: Oxford University Press.
28. Ronald Dworkin. 1985. *A Matter of Principle*. Cambridge: Harvard University Press.
29. Ronald Dworkin. 1989. *Law's Empire*. Cambridge: Harvard University Press.
30. Ronald Dworkin. 2011. *Life's Dominion: An Argument about Abortion, Euthanasia, and Individual Freedom*. New York: Knopf Doubleday Publishing Group.
31. Ronald Dworkin. 2000. *Sovereign Virtue: The Theory and Practice of Equality*. Cambridge: Harvard University Press.
32. Ronald Dworkin. 1996. *Freedom's Law: The Moral Reading of the American Constitution*. Cambridge: Harvard University Press.
33. Ronald Dworkin. 2006. *Justice in Robes*. Cambridge: Harvard University Press.
34. Ronald Dworkin. 2011. *Justice for Hedgehogs*. Cambridge: Harvard University Press.
35. Ronald Dworkin. 2013. *Religion without God*. Cambridge: Harvard University Press.
36. Ronald Dworkin. 1970. 'A Special Supplement: Taking Rights Seriously', *New York Review of Books*. 17 December.
37. Charles Fried. 2013. 'Remembering Ronald Dworkin', *New Republic*. 18 February.
38. Ronald Dworkin. 1968. 'On Not Prosecuting Civil Disobedience', *New York Review of Books*. 6 June. p. 14.
39. Robert B. Silvers. 2014. 'On Ronald Dworkin', *New York University Law Review*. 89(1). April. p. 22.
40. Arthur Chaskalson. 2003. 'From Wickedness to equality: The moral transformation of the South African Law', *International Journal of Constitutional Law* 1(4). pp. 590–609, p. 592.
41. Ronald Dworkin. 1986. 'Report from Hell', *New York Review of Books*. 17 July.
42. L.H. Tribe. 2014. 'Ronald Dworkin', *Proceedings of the American Philosophical Society* 158(2). June. p. 160.
43. Richard H. Fallan Jr. 2013. 'Ronald Dworkin'. *Harvard Law Review* 127(2). p. 490.

44. Ronald Dworkin. 1993. 'Feminism and Abortion', *New York Review of Books*. 10 June.
45. Ronald Dworkin. 1997. 'Assisted Suicide: The Philosophers' Brief', *New York Review of Books*. 27 March.
46. Ronald Dworkin. 1992. 'Freedom of Speech and Its Limits', *New York Review of Books*. 19 November.
47. Ronald Dworkin. 1993. 'Women and Pornography', *New York Review of Books*. 21 October.
48. Linda Greenhouse. 1987. 'Bork's Nomination is Rejected, 58–42; Reagan "Saddened"', *The New York Times*. 24 October.
49. Brief for Ronald Dworkin et al. as Amici Curiae in Support of Respondents, *Washington v. Glucksberg*, 521 U.S. 702 (1997), and *Vacco v. Quill*, 521 U.S. 793 (1997) (Nos. 95–1858, 96–110). The six were Ronald Dworkin, Thomas Nagel, Robert Nozick, John Rawls, Thomas Scanlon, and Judith Jarvis Thomson. Dworkin observed that he knew of no 'other occasion on which a group has intervened in Supreme Court litigation solely as general moral philosophers'. Ronald Dworkin. 1997. 'Introduction to Assisted Suicide: The Philosophers' Brief', *New York Review of Books*. 27 March. p. 41, 41 n 2., cited in Martha Minow. 2013. *Harvard Law Review*. 127(2). December. p. 506.
50. Ronald Dworkin. 1986. 'Report from Hell', *New York Review of Books*. 17 July.
51. *Indra Sawhney v. Union of India*, AIR 1993 SC 477.
52. (1994) 3 SCC 1.
53. (2016) 1 SCC 48.
54. *National Legal Services Authority of India v. Union of India*, (2014) 5 SCC 438.
55. *Suresh Kumar Kaushal v. Union of India*, (2014) 1 SCC 1.
56. *ABSK Sangh v. Union of India*, (1981) 1 SCC 246.
57. Writ Petition(Civil) No. 247 of 2017, decided on 9 June 2017.
58. Cass Sunstein. 2013. 'The Most Important Philosopher of Our Time', *Bloomberg View*. 15 February.

Introduction

There is no doubt that Kant champions an appealing concept of dignity, though the clear understanding of the concept with all the nuances of Kant's texts is not a minor philosophical task of interpretation. Crudely put, there might be two key interpretations of the idea of dignity within the Kantian lines of argumentation. First is the idea of dignity as connected to autonomy, and what we choose as a life worth living. According to this constructivist view, human beings have dignity because they ought to be respected and, therefore, dignity is not a transcendental value independently of our choosing and respecting others. Second, dignity stands for an intrinsic and transcendental value that guides our actions and our choosing. Thus, within this objective reading of Kant, dignity is prior to our choosing and guides our respect of others.

In addition to the Kantian possible readings of dignity, we have the historical use of the term, which includes elevation or rank[1,2] the place of man in the universe and in relation to the divine[3,4] and dignity as a condition or role (Waldron 2012).

Dworkin advances an interesting conception of dignity close to the Kantian view, where self-respect and authenticity play a key role and he adds the novel element that dignity is an attitude towards ourselves. However, the complexity of his view can be easily overlooked if we do not understand his proposal concerning value holism and his interpretative position of ethical and moral concepts.

This volume celebrates the thoughts of Ronald Dworkin on dignity. The contributors have critically engaged with all the different perspectives of

Dworkin's thoughts of dignity, especially the most elaborated view advanced in *Justice for Hedgehogs*. The aim is to shed light on juridical and moral contemporary conundrums, such as, the role of dignity in constitutional contexts in India; the understanding of dignity as either a foundation of human rights or as a supra value that illuminates other values and rights.

The volume is divided into four parts. In the first part, titled 'Integrity, Values, Interpretation, and Objectivity', the focus of the authors is on Dworkin's interpretive methodology and examines the way his value holism relies on his interpretative methodology. The second part of the volume 'Dignity, Responsibility, and Free Will', concentrates in elucidating the complex relationship between dignity, human will, and responsibility in Dworkin's moral, legal, and political philosophy. In the third section of the volume, 'Freedom of Speech, Right to Privacy, and Human Rights', the authors use Dworkin's philosophical moral framework and the interpretative methodology to shed light on his own views on freedom of speech and the language of rights, including human rights. The fourth part, 'Dignity, Constitutions, and Legal Systems' critically discusses Dworkin's interpretative methodology to understand dignity in the context of constitutions, State, and law beyond the State.

The first part begins with Jonathan Crowe's 'Integrity and Truth in *Law's Empire*' where he challenges Dworkin's view of integrity as intrinsic and defends an instrumental conception of integrity. Integrity has a value, Crowe tells us, due to the institutional role of the legal actors and the underlying institutional values. Crowe aims to show the role integrity plays in respecting basic values and the common good.

James E. Fleming and Linda C. McClain in their chapter 'Dworkin's Perfectionism' identify three gaps left by Dworkin's Constitutional Theory and advance a view on constitutional perfectionism to fill these gaps. The result is a mild form of constitutional perfectionism. According to the authors, Dworkin rejects John Rawls's neutrality and appeals to the integration of ethics, morality, and justice. Arguing against any form of liberalism that defend the idea that the State should remain neutral towards conceptions of the good, Dworkin also emphasizes governmental responsibility in the exercise of rights, and reflects on how government may encourage people to exercise their rights responsibly. However, as the authors tell us, Dworkin does not fully engage with civic virtues. Fleming and McClain aim to show that the distance between justice as respecting freedom and justice as cultivating virtues is not as some authors have attempted to demonstrate. For Fleming and McClain, Dworkin's moral and philosophical view on dignity advances a middle way between the aforementioned polarized views.

In his contribution 'Interpretation in Normative Domains', Alexander Brown aims to locate some key themes of Dworkin's legal and political philosophy in the context of the relevant literature on the topic. First, he aims to compare Dworkin's methodology and Rawls's idea of reflective equilibrium. He resorts to the views of William Lycan and Mark Timmons to better understand Dworkin's view on moral convictions. Second, the author scrutinizes Cohen's distinction between fact-dependent and fact-independent principles of justice to shed light on Dworkin's distinction between pre-interpretative and interpretative conceptions. Additionally, Brown argues that Dworkin's strong rejection of metaphysical commitments does not collapse into truth by coherence due to the idea that moral truth-seeing entails moral responsibility. Finally, Brown advances the point that the abstract egalitarian principle is fact-dependent in Cohen's sense. This is the case because, according to Dworkin, there are two basic principles of human dignity. First, every human life has objective value. Second, every human being has special responsibility for identifying and realising that value. This special responsibility is realized in specific institutions, rules and practices. The latter are justified by facts about contexts and interpretations, which serve to give a more concrete meaning to those facts.

In 'Justice, Integrity, and the Common Law', Trevor R.S. Allan discusses the tension between Dworkin's view on moral conviction and reflection and the idea that the law is firmly established to permit plausible disagreement. Allan examines two views that differ on the role of moral convictions. In the first perspective, a moral principle plays no role in adjudication unless it justifies acknowledged legal rules. In the second view, rules and principles are indistinguishable. Thus, a rule is a convenient summary of the weight of relevant principles in a specific context that can be changed by further moral judgments. Allan scrutinizes the role of judges' moral convictions. How judges do in fact or should strike out decisions that undermine their own standard of justice in liberal democratic regimes? Allan points out that judges' own standard of justice cannot diverge too far from those of the members of the community because otherwise he or she will be unable to provide an interpretive answer continuous with the institutional history. Allan shows that the interpreters' moral judgments are engaged throughout all the process of adjudication. The judges' moral convictions about 'fit' and settled rules are political and not mechanical. Therefore, there is no genuine threshold of fit that is detached from the judges' moral judgments.

Imer Flores's 'Taking (Human) Dignity and Rights Seriously: The Integrated Legal, Moral, and Political Philosophy of Ronald Dworkin' shows that Dworkin's interpretative methodology is truly innovative because it defends a theory of the nature of law that is constructive, interpretative, evaluative and integrative. He engages in explaining the innovative methodological turn advocated by Dworkin. Flores finalizes with a reflection on the idea of unity of value as shedding light on Dworkin's idea of dignity.

The first part of the volume finalizes with Pritam Baruah's 'Are There Any Interpretative Concepts?' In his piece, Baruah aims to challenge Dworkin's view that interpretative concepts have a special conceptual nature as concepts. Baruah distinguishes between conceptual nature and conceptual content. According to Baruah, Dworkin's argument that interpretative concepts are explicable by normative arguments alone is truly a position about the content of concepts and the phenomenon that the concept represents. According to Dworkin, the conceptual nature of all values is interpretative and this constrains the way we reason and think about values. Contra Dworkin, Baruah shows that an acceptance of interpretative concepts does not entail the special conceptual nature of values. Following Dworkin's view, Baruah offers theoretical accounts of what the paradigms of concept aim at and shows that this is an explanation about the determination of content, not a claim about what their content is. Baruah argues that it is burdensome to establish the special nature of some concepts based on the determination of their concepts. Dworkin defines what a concept is in *Justice for Hedgehogs*. A concept is interpretative when we share them, since our collective behaviour in using that concept is best explained by 'taking its correct use to depend on the best justification of the role it plays for us'. Baruah argues that concepts are mental particulars or objects of thought. The nature of concepts depends on how the phenomena is represented to us, and on what phenomena is being represented. Baruah concludes that Dworkin advances interpretative concepts as being about the nature of concepts, but they are concepts of interpretative phenomena and therefore a special manner of reasoning.

The second part of the volume *Dignity, Responsibility, and Free Will* begins with Allen Woods's 'Interpreting Human Dignity' where he advances an interpretive point on Dworkin's moral and legal philosophy. For Dworkin, Wood tells us, moral concepts as interpretative are the grounding to reject the idea that moral truth is different from scientific truth. Consequently, the realm of 'ought' is the realm of interpretative concepts and the activity of interpretation. Wood emphasizes that for Dworkin, acts of interpretation involve the taking of responsibility by the interpreter. Wood tells us that interpretation involves a special capacity or virtue, which for Kant is judgment. Determining judgment cannot be reduced to conceptual reasoning because if this is the case, then we can never reach the particular. Interpretive reasoning relates the interpretive concept to the whole of interpretation in which it is involved. Therefore, the Hedgehog Principle that all claims about value are holistic interpretation finds resonance in the Kantian idea of judgment. Dworkin, Wood tells us, starts with a central interpretive concept, which is human dignity. For Dworkin, ethics is about how we shall live, whereas morality is about the demands others make on us. We need to interpret morality from the interests that we should have. We need to integrate, Dworkin insists, morality and ethics. Dworkin thinks that it is living well that matters and to have self-respect is to take seriously the question of whether you have lived well. For Dworkin, authenticity entails the acceptance of responsibility. However, Wood argues that Dworkin's conception of human dignity grounded on self-respect and authenticity are problematic. As Dworkin describes them, they are attitudes towards oneself. However, Kant's idea of dignity requires that I treat others as having dignity whether or not they take those attitudes towards themselves. For Wood, therefore, Dworkin faces the following dilemma: either many people lack dignity and we do not need to treat them as if they had it, or self-respect and authenticity are something that everyone has trivially acquired, and they place no burden or responsibility on us. Wood rejects Dworkin's view that self-respect and authenticity are attitudes and argues that they are real and objective norms and that all human beings have the capacity to acquire them, and therefore the responsibility to do so. Wood asserts, 'Dignity is something from which we cannot be free.' Furthermore, Wood worries that Dworkin's ethics seems something too close to utilitarianism. According to Wood, Dworkin begins with concerns about aids and harms to others. Wood advances the superb point that in typical utilitarian discussions, like trolley problems, agency, and actions are presented in abstraction from dignity and rights. Wood emphasizes that there are 'no significant moral problems that concern only the distribution of goods and harms and our causal relation to it'. Human beings are not mere objects of moral deliberation. According to Wood, Dworkin faces conceptual problems since his idea of dignity begins with the value of a life and the person's attitudes towards oneself. In order to avoid the problem of justifying the dignity of others, Wood argues that the person's freedom and the person's free interactions with others should be at the centre.

In the essay 'Dworkin's Dignity under the Lens of the Magician of Königsberg', Rodriguez-Blanco explains that Dworkin sets himself the difficult task of integrating our ethical responsibilities, that is, values, personal projects, with our moral responsibility, that is, the demands that others impose on us. Dworkin uses the conception of dignity that focuses on self-respect and authenticity to show how this integration is possible. Rodriguez-Blanco argues that Dworkin's conception of dignity is not sufficiently robust to guarantee the desired integration between our moral and ethical lives. She advances the view that Kant's idea of the dignity of personality is as important as his idea of the dignity of humanity. When we act according to our personality, we act according to morality. Thus, personality is not about ends, but about moral action. By contrast, Dworkin refers to authenticity as the endorsement of who we really are and Rodriguez-Blanco resorts to two examples, Rousseau and Gauguin, where Dworkin's constructive model fails to achieve the desired integration because morality is pushed aside. She also defends the idea that an understanding of intentional action as future-directed process, which manifests the structure of practical reason, facilitates the view that our moral and ethical lives can be integrated and therefore, the dignity of our humanity and personality in our living well within the moral condition becomes apparent.

Barbara Baum Levenbook, in her contribution 'Does Dignity Help in Thinking about Paternalism?', argues that Dworkin's notion of dignity and constructive process, which has important parallels with reflective equilibrium, has little epistemic value regarding paternalism. Dworkin's conception of dignity, Levenbook tells us, is too inchoate to determine when paternalism is wrong. Paternalism entails imposing a decision on an individual, which is contrary to one's own sense of her or his own good. Ethical responsibility and dignity requires that we have a sense of our own good. Paternalism, according to Dworkin, can be permissible in certain circumstances, but it is wrong if it insults dignity. When we take away from the individual the capacity to choose, then the act is wrong. When we choose values, then ethical paternalism, according to Dworkin, is always wrong. By contrast, some other paternalism is not wrong, what Dworkin calls 'surface paternalism' in *Justice for Hedgehogs*[5](336). Levenbook shows through a number of key examples that Dworkin's idea of dignity cannot help us to demarcate the boundaries of justified and unjustified paternalism.

The second part of the volume finishes with Isabel Trujillo's 'Dignity, Rights, and Virtues in the Department of Values'. She aims to show that dignity is not an empty or redundant concept, but a key concept that adds something to other values and this is, Trujillo asserts, reflected in Dworkin's holistic approach to values and the centre role that dignity plays. Dignity for Dworkin, Trujillo tells us, is concerned with our lives and therefore includes the perspective of virtues. However, she also considers that values without dignity will lose a parameter for being ordered. She emphasizes that Dworkin's project is to transcend the language of rights to a new political perspective in which responsibility and virtues are crucial. Trujillo asserts that the core of morality is when our personal projects encounter the well-being and projects of other individuals. It seems inevitable that we need to put dignity at the core of the problem. Trujillo highlights the tension and the walk away from liberalism in Dworkin's *Justice for Hedgehogs*. Dworkin points out, Trujillo reminds us 'We need to understand happiness so that we can construct a good State, which is a State in which people are enabled and encouraged to lead good lives' (Dworkin 2013: 188).

David Richards' 'Dignity and Free Speech' is the first contribution of the third section 'Freedom of Speech, Right to Privacy, and Human Rights' of this volume. The author analyses Dworkin's arguments that dignity plays a key role in hate speech laws because the condemnation of hate free speech laws better realizes the underlying value of dignity. Richards argues that the right to conscience and speech protects the moral powers of 'rationality and reasonableness leading our lives as agents'. The protection of these moral powers ensures that we can have interpersonal relationships, including political relationships. Richards tells us that free conscience and speech is broader than political speech and includes creative arts, sciences, and erotic forms. The value of dignity, which grounds the rights of conscience and free speech, also grounds the principle of anti-discrimination that condemns racism, sexism, and homophobia. Eloquently, Richards maps the different forms of moral slavery that undermine autonomy or dignity, and destroy our moral powers of rationality and reasonableness.

James Allan in his work 'Ronald Dworkin and Free Speech' defends Dworkin's position on anti-hate speech laws against Waldron's view on the subject (Waldron 2005). Allan tells us that Dworkin defends freedom of hate speech based on the principle of legitimacy. For Dworkin and Allan, however, legitimacy is not an all-or-nothing. Legitimacy is a matter of degree, and depends on what is at stake. Waldron offers, Allan asserts, a consequentialist case against Dworkin's position concerning freedom of hate speech. Some legitimacy is a matter of degree, therefore, Waldron argues, there is a room for hate speech laws that do not undermine legitimacy, for example, hate speech laws that condemn the 'viciously vituperative end of the spectrum'. Good examples of these laws can be found in Canada and Australia. However, Allan shows that in some of these countries hate speech laws do not constraint themselves, contrary to Waldron's position, to the 'viciously vituperative end of the spectrum'. Finally, Allan discusses whether hate speech laws might deliver good consequences, for example how the laws reform the speakers and laws block what third party listeners get to her and stop them for being persuaded.

The last contribution of this section is Lorenzo Zucca's 'Exit Hercules: Ronald Dworkin and the Crisis of the Age of Rights'. In his chapter, Zucca aims to show that rights are part of another element of the moral horizon of societies and do not necessarily play a key role. Zucca asserts that for Dworkin, moral rights provide the ground to harmonize different political values. Zucca argues that after the end of the cold war, the liberal dogmas that centre on rights will show all its weaknesses and internal contradictions. Divisions arise in key domains, for example religious identity, sexual morality, and reproduction. Zucca tells us that the big value that could unite all plural values in the eyes of Dworkin is dignity. For Zucca, however, Dworkin's hopes of finding a common ground face the difficulties that arise from unbridgeable pluralism. Zucca also shows that the Supreme Courts of US and Italy together with the German Constitutional Court played a key role in the implementation of rights in the post-war. Additionally, Zucca advances the view that legal positivism has difficulties explaining how law is fully valid in cases where it contradicts our liberal convictions. Dworkin found Hart's legal positivism unsatisfactory for this and other reasons. Therefore, the idea that law is constituted by principles could better account for what the law is. Finally, Zucca highlights the tension between Dworkin's ideas of a harmonious unity of values as opposed to the force that rights have for each of us from our own perspective when we disagree with other's views on their rights.

The fourth part of this volume, 'Dignity, Constitutions, and Legal Systems', begins with George Pavlakos's examination of Dworkin's idea of associative obligations. In 'Revamping Associative Obligations', Pavlakos asserts that Dworkin's own view of associative obligations should be extended to boundaries beyond the State and coercive institutions in general. Pavlakos criticizes the voluntaristic conception of State and International Law. Furthermore, Pavlakos asserts that practices, conventions, and facts cannot be the grounds of associative obligations. On the contrary, principles and norms are the grounds of associative obligations and coercion only acts as a trigger of these grounding principles and norms. This new conception gives space to a new conception of global justice and associative obligations, which are at the heart of International Law. Like Dworkin, Pavlakos defends the idea that associative obligations bind us in an inevitable manner for the only feature of being human beings. He tells us 'a key congruence of non-voluntariness is that political obligation takes hold on citizens as a piecemeal approval of individual obligations, but instead as a general scheme of principle which ought to be presumed as forming a shared conception of legitimacy among the members of the political community'. Pavlakos argues that Dworkin's limited conception of associative obligation to the State is due to his starting point, which is his concern for showing that the political and legal institutions ought to provide a justification for the coercion of the State. The puzzle is that this limited view of political obligation would entail that special relations towards others is reduced to the narrow interpretation of 'proximity', which requires affinity, kinship, or tribal allegiance. However, Pavlakos asserts that the model reverses the order of explanation between associative obligations and feelings of responsibility. According to this model, we first 'come' about others and then we incur the relevant obligations. The feeling of responsibility, Pavlakos tells us, is the result of being subject to normative reasons that 'pull' us towards associative obligations. He argues that the coercive imposition of obligations is only a trigger forbinding associative obligation. Therefore, the scope of such associative obligations is determined by their grounding. Coercive facts, which are determined by the State, cannot explain the scope of political obligations.

Erin Daly's 'Dworkinian Dignity: Rights and Responsibilities of a Life Well Lived' highlights that Dworkin's first writings do not take dignity at central stage. Dworkin seems to recognize dignity, but not its complexity. In these first writings, dignity seems to be a 'super-right' and its importance lies in its inviolability. However, Dworkin also suggests that dignity is at the heart of human experience and individuals in the social dimension. In Dworkin's latter writings, dignity embodies each person's responsibility to live well. Hence, because we have dignity, there is an inescapable responsibility to act accordingly. Daly tells us that 'dignity requires respect for the importance of the lives of others and equal concern for their lives'. However, as Daly reminds us, we are not equal in physical attributes, capabilities, resources, or opportunities. Nevertheless, we treat others with equal concern when we allow them to pursue their own projects and plans of life. Dignity is preserved when everyone can decide how to live. Daly also highlights that neither in England, nor in the US does constitutional law resort much to the abstract concept of dignity. By contrast, a global perspective shows how constitutional courts of different countries illuminate Dworkin's concept of dignity as the capacity to choose one's fate, for example, South Africa, Italy, Germany, India, Colombia, Canada, Brazil, Peru, and México.

Salman Khurshid's 'Ronald Dworkin's Judge: Philosopher Master of Rights' examines Dworkin's theory of adjudication in *Taking Right Seriously*, to illuminate the different interpretations of Chapters III and IV of the Indian Constitution. According to Khurshid, there has been conflict in the interpretation of Chapters III and IV of the Constitution as reflected on a conflict between utilitarianism and principled readings of the Constitution. In *Kesavananda Bharati*, the majority of the judges advocated the view that their aimis to discover legal rights that exist, but are not apparent. Khurshid also defends adjudication by principles and judicial originality against two objections. First, the objection that rules and legislation should be created by an elected body. Second, the argument that suggests judicial originality entails retroactive legislation. Concerning the second objection, Khurshid argues that what is at stake is not the distribution of resources across the community, but rather a right that is of such character that it is not a matter for the majority to decide. On the contrary, judges are in a better position to engage in matters of rights and principles. The right thesis emphasizes that the rights already exist and therefore the adjudication process makes them explicit. Therefore, Khurshid's arguments indirectly show that there is no legal retroactivity *strictu sensu* in adjudication by principles. Khurshid finalizes his contribution with a scrutiny of the Indian cases *Naz Foundation, Kharak Singh v. U.P., Shreya Shinghal* and *Shyam Narayan Chouksey v. Union of India* to illustrate how Dworkin's focus on principles and rights should prevail in Indian judicial decisions.

Suhrith Parthasarathy's 'A Dworkinian Reading of the Indian Constitution' scrutinizes Dworkin's interpretive theory to shed light on how to interpret the Indian Constitution. According to Parthasarathy, Dworkin's moral reading of constitutions is a rational strategy to allow judges to interpret abstract constitutional principles in light of political morality. However, Parthasarathy reminds us integrity requires that when judges engage with the moral reading they also look at past judicial practice. Parthasarathy looks at the decisions of the Indian Supreme Court in *Maneka Gandhi v. Union of India* in which the court created an illusory conflict between liberty and equality. The author aims to show that had the judges in *Maneka* appealed to the Dworkinian principle of equal concern, then the interpretation of the constitution would have been consistent, harmonious, and unified principles. Parthasarathy tells us that for Dworkin, law is a 'branch of political philosophy, which is a branch of the more general theory of personal morality, which is in turn a branch of a yet more general theory of what it is to live well'. The author shows that liberty ought to be derived from equality and uses this conception to criticize the development of rights by decisions of the Supreme Court of India. His analysis begins with *A.K. Golapan v. State of Madras* and culminates with *Maneka*.

The last part ends with a joint paper of Mark Bennett and Petra Butler. In their joint piece, they have focused on Dworkininan right to privacy in New Zealand in the light of Dworkin's writings on the subject. Dworkin's different conceptual theses such as the unity of value, ethics and morality, politics and law, privacy, dignity and so on have been critically examined and analyzed in this section. The dignity finds a close linkage with privacy in their academic discourse.

There is no better way to celebrate the life of a philosopher and public intellectual than through a critical analysis of his work. All the contributors have excelled in the task of giving a charitable interpretation of the work of Ronald Dworkin on dignity, and showing the potential shortcomings of his views. The volume has also focused on analyzing the application of Dworkin's idea of dignity to legal problems, that is, rights of free speech and freedom of religion, and constitutional decisions in India. It is hoped that this volume will motivate younger legal philosophers and judges to take on the task of filling the gaps and improving our understanding of this crucial and important concept.

Veronica Rodriguez-Blanco
University of Surrey, UK

Notes

1. Jeremy Waldron. 2012. *Dignity, Rank and Rights*, Meir-Dan Cohen (ed.). Oxford: Oxford University Press.
2. Michael Rosen. 2012. *Dignity: Its History and Meaning*. Harvard: Harvard University Press.
3. Pico dellaMirandola. 1486/1956. *Oration on the Dignity of Man*. Chicago: Henry Regenry Company.
4. Cicero, *De officiis*. 2000. (On Obligations), P.G. Walsh tr. Oxford: Oxford University Press.
5. Ronald Dworkin. 2013. *Justice for Hedgehogs*. Cambridge: Harvard University Press.

PART I

INTEGRITY, VALUES, INTERPRETATION, AND OBJECTIVITY

1

Integrity and Truth in *Law's Empire*

Jonathan Crowe

Integrity is a central concept in Ronald Dworkin's theory of law. Dworkin treats integrity as a fundamental and distinctive political value. The importance of integrity lends normative force to his conception of adjudication as a process of finding the best interpretation of the legal materials. We care about finding the right legal answer because we care about integrity. Why, then, is integrity valuable? Dworkin treats integrity in both legislation and adjudication as holding *inherent* political value; that is, he argues integrity is valuable in and of itself. He supports this position primarily by appealing to our deep intuitions about the undesirability of legal practices that reject integrity.

My aim in this chapter is to contrast this approach with an alternative theory of the value of integrity, according to which integrity holds *instrumental* value as part of a legal framework that seeks to realize the basic values taken to underpin legal institutions. I suggest that my instrumental-value account explains the value of integrity more satisfactorily than Dworkin's inherent-value theory. I begin the chapter by introducing Dworkin's case for the value of integrity, focusing on the arguments advanced in *Law's Empire*.[1] I then introduce my alternative explanation and contrast it with Dworkin's account.[2] I conclude by considering the implications of both views for the truth conditions of legal propositions and the relationship between the grounds and force of law.

The Inherent-Value Theory

Dworkin's theory of law has developed significantly over time. I propose to focus here on the well known account of integrity found in *Law's Empire*. In that work, Dworkin famously analyses judicial decision-making as comprising three stages (Dworkin 1986: 65–8). The first is a *pre-interpretive* stage in which the standards that hold relevance for a specific case are tentatively identified. The second is an *interpretive* stage where the judge formulates a general theory of the motivations and rationales underlying the elements of practice identified in the previous stage. Finally, at the *post-interpretive* stage, the judge forms a view about what decision the prevailing social practice requires in the case, taking into account the general framework of justification posited at the preceding step.

Dworkin's account of adjudication, as summarized above, emphasizes the importance of reaching an outcome that is consistent with the legal materials. Indeed, he famously argues that judges should strive to reach the outcome that is *most* consistent with the materials. Why, then, should we care so much about this kind of consistency? Dworkin's answer to this question can be found in his theory of *law as integrity*. Dworkin treats integrity as a distinctive political value. He initially divides this concept into two parallel notions, corresponding to two different types of legal decision making: *integrity in legislation* and *integrity in adjudication*. Integrity in legislation requires the legislature to make the law coherent, bearing in mind a set of overarching values (Dworkin 1986: 176). Integrity in adjudication requires judges to treat the law 'as expressing and respecting a set of coherent principles' (217). The resulting theory depicts legal deliberation as containing both backward- and forward-looking elements. Legal practice is therefore seen as 'an unfolding political narrative' (225).

Dworkin's main example in favour of the value of integrity in legislation concerns 'checkerboard' laws that apply an arbitrary settlement to political disagreements (178–86). He frames the problem as follows:

> Do the people of Alabama disagree about the morality of racial discrimination? Why should their legislation not forbid racial discrimination on buses but permit it in restaurants? Do the British divide on the morality of abortion? Why should Parliament not make abortion criminal for pregnant women who were born in even years but not for those born in odd ones? (Dworkin 1986: 187)

Dworkin argues that there is something inherently dismaying about checkerboard solutions. The reason for rejecting such solutions, however, is not immediately clear; after all, we readily accept other types of political compromises. 'Why', Dworkin queries, 'should we turn our back on checkerboard solutions as we do?' (Dworkin 1986: 179) His answer is that integrity holds intrinsic political value. We object to checkerboard statutes simply because 'a state that adopts these internal compromises is acting in an unprincipled way' (183). In accepting checkerboard compromises, 'the state lacks integrity because it must endorse principles to justify part of what it has done that it must reject to justify the rest' (184).

Dworkin argues that integrity in legislation is 'so much part of our political practice that no competent interpretation of that practice can ignore it' (176). In this way, his claim about the political value of legislative integrity draws on an explanatory theory of our legislative practices—we can only satisfactorily explain these practices and the social attitudes that surround them if we credit integrity with inherent value. Dworkin proceeds to integrate this explanatory account of integrity into a broader interpretive theory of the political community. Integrity is consistent with a 'community of principle'—a 'genuine associative community' capable of sustaining a plausible claim to moral legitimacy—rather than a 'rulebook community', driven solely by power (214).

Dworkin's argument for the value of integrity in adjudication takes a similar form. It is primarily an argument about the best explanation for judicial practice. Dworkin contends that judicial interpretation of legal materials is structured by the notion of intention (228). The use of intention in legal interpretation, in turn, involves appealing to a set of general goals or principles in order to lend a coherent background context to particular legal rules (51–3). This interpretive theory of adjudication is then integrated into an overarching account of legal institutions as reflecting a particular notion of the legal community. It is at this more abstract level that the discrete principles of integrity in legislation and integrity in adjudication yield an overarching notion of law as integrity.

Dworkin seeks to illuminate the methodology associated with integrity in adjudication through his now notorious example of 'the chain novel' (228–38). We are asked to imagine an enterprise in which several authors cooperate to write a novel. Each author interprets the chapters she has been given in order to create a new chapter. The task of each author, Dworkin argues, is to contribute to making the novel 'the best it can be' (229). Each author will need to 'take up some view about the novel in progress, some working theory' about its plot, theme, characters, and so on (230). This will involve working out what possible interpretations 'fit' with the previous chapters of the book and judging 'which of these eligible readings makes the work in progress best, all things considered' (230–1). The authors of the chain novel will evaluate the various possible interpretations of the story based on a combination of 'formal and structural considerations' and aesthetic judgments (231).

The aesthetic element in the chain novel example is replaced in legal interpretation by what Dworkin calls 'political morality' (239). Dworkin describes his theory of law as 'relentlessly interpretive', insofar as 'it is both the product of and the inspiration for comprehensive interpretation of legal practice' (226). He does not claim that integrity has value regardless of the legal and political context. Rather, he sees it as possessing value within a particular type of political community—one founded on an Anglo-American common law system. The argument, then, is that 'our political practices accept integrity as a distinct value' (178)—that is, integrity 'is so much part of our political practice' that it cannot reasonably be ignored (176). Nonetheless, Dworkin sees integrity as *intrinsically* valuable in a community of this kind. We need posit no other conditions to see that it is worthwhile.

The Instrumental-Value Theory

Dworkin's theory in *Law's Empire* amounts to an inherent-value view of integrity. He presents integrity as valuable in and of itself, at least within a certain type of community. The alternative, assuming integrity has value at all, is an instrumental-value analysis, according to which integrity holds value as a mode of pursuing some other, more fundamental value or collection of values. Suppose I am engaged by a company to draft a mission statement. I am instructed that the document must be consistent with the aims and values of the organization, which are expressed to me in a general form. It seems clear that, in order to do the job well, I should do my best to ensure that my statement coheres with the values of the organisation; that is, I must pay attention to what Dworkin calls integrity. Coherence, in this situation, holds *instrumental* value—I must respect it in order to fulfil my brief of drafting a document that captures the values of the company.

We might imagine a parallel scenario where the directors of the company brief me to produce a document that will help them raise revenue from investors. They do not care whether it coheres with any particular set of underlying aims. In such a case, integrity lacks the instrumental value it holds in the situation imagined above. It might, nonetheless, hold some *inherent* value that I may wish to consider in approaching the task. However, that is a different question. We can, therefore, contrast the instrumental value of coherence in the example given above with Dworkin's account of integrity as a 'distinct political virtue' and an 'independent ideal' (1986: 176). Integrity, for Dworkin, is valuable in itself and not merely as a means to pursuing an underlying set of values.

Consider, for example, Dworkin's discussion of checkerboard legislation. He points out that we are inclined to reject statutes that enact unprincipled, arbitrary compromises on contested political issues; his conclusion is that integrity holds intrinsic political value. Dworkin's conclusion represents one possible explanation of our attitude to checkerboard solutions, but it is not the only one. We might posit that people generally view the legal system as furthering a particular set of underlying values (whether or not they feel confident about their ability to enunciate exactly what those values are). Integrity can then be viewed as instrumental to respecting the specific values at which the legal system is thought to aim. The latter explanation resembles the case of the company seeking a mission statement that reflects its values. It is as if the legislature had been briefed to draft laws that cohere with a particular set of underlying goods.

How are we to evaluate these two different explanations of the value of integrity? The matter is complicated by the particular sense in which Dworkin sees integrity as holding intrinsic value. As we have seen, he restricts his claim to a particular type of legal community. Nevertheless, Dworkin systematically separates integrity from adherence to a particular framework of background values. For instance, he denies that our rejection of checkerboard solutions merely reflects 'our conviction that no one should actively engage in producing' a result she regards as unjust (181).

Dworkin's objection to such an explanation is that if each legislator votes for the checkerboard compromise in order to 'give the maximum possible effect' to the specific set of values she endorses, it is not clear how anyone has behaved irresponsibly (181–2). However, the instrumental-value approach to integrity sketched above does not propose that integrity is instrumental to the diverse moral views of individual legal actors, but rather that it is instrumental to respecting a particular set of basic goods that are taken to ground the entire legal system. The latter view is quite capable of motivating a generalized objection to the enactment of checkerboard statutes.

Dworkin advances a further reason for thinking that the value of integrity is not grounded in a particular set of underlying values, by pointing out two different ways that integrity and morality may seem to conflict. He argues first that integrity may sometimes override the demands of value, as when decisions in previous cases clearly support an outcome in a current case that the judge in that case finds morally objectionable (176–8). In a later passage, Dworkin canvasses the opposite possibility—moral values may sometimes override integrity. He suggests that the requirement of integrity may not always be 'absolutely sovereign over what judges must do at the end of the day', since 'other and more powerful aspects of political morality might outweigh this requirement in particular and unusual circumstances' (218–19). He claims that where integrity leads to what a judge sees as a deeply immoral result, the judge will have to either enforce the unjust rule, 'lie and say that this was not the law after all' or resign from the bench (219).

Dworkin seems to think that because integrity may sometimes conflict with underlying moral values, it is not reducible to the pursuit of those values. The possibility of conflicts between integrity and the deeper demands of value arises from what Dworkin perceives as the disjunction between the 'grounds' and the 'force' of law. The grounds of law concern the circumstances in which particular propositions about law should be taken as true, while the force of law relates to the power any true proposition about law holds to justify 'the use of collective power against individual citizens or groups' (109–10). Dworkin holds that any 'full political theory of law' will contain accounts of the grounds and force of law that are mutually supporting. Nevertheless, he holds that the two types of analysis are separable and the factors they raise may sometimes conflict (110–11; 218).

In this way, Dworkin's analysis of 'integrity in adjudication' attempts to distinguish conscientious judgments about how to act in particular circumstances from legal reasoning, which includes an institutional dimension of political morality. In a similar vein, Stanley Fish notes that Dworkin's position 'suggests that there are two types of reasons — personal ones and institutional ones'.[3] It is as if the judge displaces her 'personal' moral convictions in order to engage with law as integrity, then only reopens the moral status of the resulting decision under extreme conditions. The principle of integrity 'does not necessarily have the last word' in motivating action by legal agents, 'but it does have the first word, and normally there is nothing to add to what it says' (Dworkin 1986: 219).

Truth in Fiction and Law

Dworkin's analysis of the distinction between the grounds and the force of law suggests that what makes a proposition of law true may not correspond with what makes the corresponding norm legitimate. He therefore separates the value of integrity from the role of background values in supporting the normative claims of legal institutions. Integrity, he argues, has value irrespective of whether it is used in support of deeper normative aims. Its value, in other words, pertains to the grounds of law and not necessarily the normative factors that legitimize the use of legal power.

I wish to conclude this chapter by casting doubt on this conception of truth in legal reasoning. I will argue that the instrumental-value account of integrity yields a better theory of the grounds and force of law. It will be useful to return here to Dworkin's example of the chain novel. Dworkin argues that the chain novelists will have to take account of both fit and aesthetic considerations when drafting their chapters (230–1). He frames the issue of fit primarily in terms of consistency with the earlier chapters. However, this is not the only dimension of fit that will be relevant. Each author will have to make her contribution consistent with developments in the earlier chapters, but she will also have to make it consistent with certain features of the world external to the novel.

The classic discussion of this point comes from David Lewis.[4] Lewis points out that fictional narratives are read against 'a background of well-known fact' (Lewis 1978: 41). The content of the fictional work, therefore, does not come purely from the explicit statements contained in the work itself. Rather, it comes from a combination of 'the explicit content' of the story and 'the factual background' presupposed by readers (41). The Sherlock Holmes stories, to use Lewis's example, say that Holmes lives at 221B Baker Street. The stories never explicitly state that Holmes lives nearer to Paddington Station than Waterloo Station, but a map of London (as it exists in the world external to the story) shows Holmes's address is nearer to Paddington. Lewis concludes it is true that Holmes lives nearer to Paddington than Waterloo, even though the stories never explicitly confirm this (41).

Imagine a chain novelist who was given the canonical Holmes stories and was asked to write a later instalment.[5] Lewis's analysis suggests that such an author should strive for consistency not only with the explicit content of the stories, but also with background facts. An author who carelessly stated that Holmes lived nearer to Waterloo than Paddington would not be making her contribution to the narrative the best it could be. There are also, as Lewis points out, many other facts that seem to be assumed in the course of the Holmes stories, even though they are never directly discussed:

> I claim that it is true, though not explicit, in the stories that Holmes does not have a third nostril; that he never had a case in which the murderer turned out to be a purple gnome; that he solved his cases without the aid of divine revelation; that he never visited the moons of Saturn; and that he wears underpants.[6]

There could, of course, be stories—even stories about Holmes—where these assertions are false. However, the genre of the canonical Holmes stories encourages the reader to make certain plausible assumptions about the structural features of the universe that Holmes inhabits. An author of a Holmes story who abruptly departed from these assumptions would strike a false note. A fantasy novel, on the other hand, might feature third nostrils, purple gnomes, and trips to the moons of Saturn. However, even fantasy novels depend upon background factual assumptions that are continuous with the actual world. No novelist can create a whole universe out of new cloth. Every fictional world, no matter how rich, draws on background material.

Fiction is one thing and law is another. Both forms of discourse, however, draw on background assumptions about the world. Novelists can construct their fictional universes so that they depart from fact in certain ways. However, they are powerless to enact the complete closure of their fictional universe. There are always background assumptions in play. The same applies to law. Legal discourse has the ability to create norms of conduct that would not otherwise exist. However, these legal norms operate against a wider normative backdrop. They are interpreted by officials and citizens in light of social and moral norms that exist independently of legal institutions.[7]

Suppose there is a set of shared, basic values that humans characteristically use to order their conduct and organize their communities.[8] These values will form part of the background context against which legal norms are interpreted. A person deciding a dispute within the framework of legal norms will have reason to make her decision consistent not only with the applicable legal rules, but also with the basic values that underpin the system as a whole. An outcome that exhibits a minimal fit with the existing legal materials, but sits uneasily with the shared values of members of the community will not make the law the best it can be. This is because it will defeat the background assumptions that legal officials and citizens use when interpreting the law.

Law, like fiction, is continuous with the broader universe. This continuity applies to values, as well as facts. The author of a Holmes story who had Watson abruptly kill a stranger without any compunction or remorse would violate the assumptions of the Holmes universe just as much as if she had introduced a purple gnome. Fictions can contain amoral characters and legal systems can contain unjust rules. However, unless a fictional character is clearly amoral, readers will assume the character thinks there is something morally bad about killing other people. Similarly, a legal system that does not clearly depart from the basic values that humans use to structure their lives and communities will be assumed to be continuous with those normative foundations. A legal proposition may be rendered true or false by its coherence with these background values.

The Value of Integrity

The basic values shared by members of a community form part of the context interpreters use to evaluate the truth of legal propositions. A full account of the grounds of law will make reference to this background context. The role of basic goods in legal reasoning also helps to explain the value of integrity. Dworkin argues that integrity holds inherent value in both fiction and law. However, the analysis offered above suggests a more nuanced answer. Integrity holds value partly by virtue of the institutional role of the actors to whom it applies and partly due to other underlying values.

Let us begin with fiction. Suppose that a person gives you a set of facts and asks you to write a narrative incorporating them. There is no need to credit integrity with inherent value to understand why you should try to make your narrative consistent with the facts you are given. This dimension of 'fit' is built into your task. There will, of course, typically be multiple narratives that exhibit strict consistency with a particular set of facts. It may therefore appear that the requirement of fit is a fairly minimal constraint. However, it is worth remembering here that, as we saw above, the facts that underpin a fictional narrative are not limited to those that are explicitly included in the plot.

A participant in a chain novel is therefore more constrained than it may at first appear. She must achieve consistency not only with the earlier chapters, but also with the background assumptions of the readership. This will involve paying attention to genre in order to determine what is and is not assumed. Aesthetic considerations may also play a role in shaping the author's choices. Notice, however, that we can tell this story about the constraints on the chain novelist without appealing to the inherent value of integrity. The chain novelist who respects the integrity of the story is just doing what she has been asked to do by the other participants in terms of maintaining a coherent narrative, while also considering the independent value of aesthetic factors.

A similar analysis applies to law. Law serves as an important means of social coordination and judges play a key role in upholding this framework. It follows that judges generally have an obligation to apply the existing legal rules.[9] This obligation may arise not only where a rule has independent moral content, but also where it is a reasonable and salient response to a social coordination problem or where a refusal to apply the law would undermine the coordination function of law as a whole.[10] However, maintaining consistency with the legal materials is not the only constraint on the judicial role. Judges, like legislators, also have reason to consider the underlying normative assumptions reflected in the legal system. These will include basic human values. A decision that coheres with these values will be preferable to one that departs from them. This is not because of any inherent weight attached to integrity, but rather due to the importance of the values themselves. Integrity is instrumental to these background norms.

The dimension of fit, then, arises from the institutional role of judges, while the relevance of underlying principles is attributable to the normative weight attached to shared community values. This picture of integrity holds important advantages over Dworkin's account in *Law's Empire*. It strengthens his explanation of the value of integrity by placing it in a broader explanatory context. Dworkin appeals to the notion of integrity to explain legal practices. However, the value of integrity is simply posited as an intrinsic component of an idealized political community. An appeal to background normative goals, however, allows us to explain precisely *why* integrity in law is valuable—it is instrumental to the underlying aim of respecting basic values and the common good.

An instrumental-value account of integrity also avoids a puzzling implication of Dworkin's theory. We have seen that Dworkin thinks integrity may sometimes conflict with the demands of moral value, leading to a disjunction between the grounds and force of law. Dworkin's conception of integrity therefore requires morally incorrect principles to be preferred to morally correct principles where the former are more consistent with the legal materials.[11] However, it is difficult enough to explain why integrity holds independent value in the first place. Why should we believe that its value is robust enough to impose an obligation to promote morally incorrect principles?

This implication is avoided if we treat the practice of integrity as resting on background values common to moral and legal reasoning. Legal officials have reason to value integrity precisely because they have reason to act consistently with the basic values underpinning the community. These background values are relevant to both the grounds and force of law. Integrity, then, does not come from nowhere. It comes partly from the institutional role of legal officials and partly from the normative assumptions that guide legal practice. Its value is instrumental, not inherent. It follows that we should uphold integrity in law, but only insofar as it furthers these aims. Integrity in the service of unjust principles is not something we have reason to value.

Notes and References

1. Ronald Dworkin. 1986. *Law's Empire*. Cambridge, MA: Belknap Press.
2. I draw here on arguments developed in Jonathan Crowe. 2007. 'Dworkin on the Value of Integrity', *Deakin Law Review*. 12(1). p. 167.
3. Stanley Fish. 1987. 'Still Wrong After All These Years', *Law and Philosophy* 6(3). pp. 401, 411.
4. David Lewis. 1978. 'Truth in Fiction', *American Philosophical Quarterly* 15(1). p. 37.
5. Many authors have, of course, done exactly this. See, for example, Adrian Conan Doyle and John Dickson Carr, *The Exploits of Sherlock Holmes* (Gramercy, 1999).
6. Lewis, 'Truth in Fiction', p. 41.

7. For further discussion, see Jonathan Crowe. 2009. 'Levinasian Ethics and the Concept of Law', in Desmond Manderson (ed.), *Essays on Levinas and Law: A Mosaic.* Palgrave Macmillan; Jonathan Crowe. 2011. 'Pre-Reflective Law' in Maksymilian Del Mar (ed.), *New Waves in Philosophy of Law.* Palgrave Macmillan; Jonathan Crowe. 2013. 'The Role of Contextual Meaning in Judicial Interpretation', *Federal Law Review* 41(3). p. 417.

8. For a discussion of the nature and origins of these basic values, see Jonathan Crowe. 2014. 'Natural Law and Normative Inclinations', *Ratio Juris* 28(1). Compare John Finnis. 1980. *Natural Law and Natural Rights.* Oxford University Press. Chapters 3–4.

9. This obligation is, however, far from absolute. For discussion, see Crowe, 'The Role of Contextual Meaning in Judicial Interpretation'. pp. 440–41.

10. For further discussion, see Jonathan Crowe. 2007. 'Natural Law in Jurisprudence and Politics', *Oxford Journal of Legal Studies.* 27(4). pp. 775, 786–91; Jonathan Crowe. 2011. 'Natural Law Beyond Finnis', *Jurisprudence* 2(2). pp. 293, 301–3; Jonathan Crowe. 2011. 'Five Questions for John Finnis', *Pandora's Box.* 18. pp. 11, 15–16; Jonathan Crowe. 2012. 'Clarifying the Natural Law Thesis', *Australian Journal of Legal Philosophy* 37. pp. 159, 162–4.

11. Compare Larry Alexander and Ken Kress. 1977. 'Against Legal Principles', *Iowa Law Review* 82. p. 739; Denise Réaume. 1989. 'Is Integrity a Virtue? Dworkin's Theory of Legal Obligation', *University of Toronto Law Journal* 39. p. 380.

2

Dworkin's Perfectionism

James E. Fleming and *Linda C. McClain*

Ronald Dworkin: A Eulogy

Ronald Dworkin is widely and rightly viewed as the most important legal philosopher and constitutional theorist of our time and as one of the leading figures in moral and political philosophy. In the words of Marshall Cohen, Dworkin's jurisprudential writings 'constitute the finest contribution yet made by an American writer to the philosophy of law'.[1] Cohen wrote those words when Dworkin published his first book, *Taking Rights Seriously*, in 1977. His many outstanding subsequent books and articles made good on that early, prescient assessment. Dworkin is unmatched and unrivaled in legal philosophy and constitutional theory.

In the words of T.M. Scanlon, Dworkin is 'our leading public philosopher'.[2] He regularly published essays on legal and political subjects in the *New York Review of Books* from 1968 through 2013. Like many readers, we eagerly opened each issue hoping to find a new piece by Dworkin. We shall miss that. Dworkin had the rare gift of being able to write abstractly in legal philosophy and constitutional theory yet also to write accessibly for the general educated citizen. He brought out the issues of moral and political principle at the heart of the major political and constitutional issues of the day. His writing not only bristles with brilliant insights but also exhorts and uplifts. Moreover, in courageous and spirited exchanges with leading conservatives, like Richard Posner,[3] Robert Bork,[4] and Antonin Scalia,[5] he gave as good as he got and then some!

Over the years, one of us (Fleming) has organized a number of conferences in constitutional theory and Dworkin was often the most appropriate keynote speaker. In conferences at Fordham University School of Law on 'Fidelity in Constitutional Interpretation'[6] and 'Rawls and the Law',[7] and at Boston University School of Law on his book, *Justice for Hedgehogs*,[8] Dworkin delivered powerful and eloquent keynote lectures. The readers of this book are likely familiar with the countless accounts of Dworkin's brilliance as a lecturer— of how he spoke without notes and with great flair, making it all seem so graceful and effortless. Even more impressive, in our experience, was how seriously he took his lectures and how energetically he responded to his interlocutors. In the conference at Boston University on *Justice for Hedgehogs*, held when Dworkin was 78-years-old, he demonstrated his characteristic energy by responding extemporaneously to all thirty-one commentators, one panel at a time, and elaborating those initial thoughts in a published response.[9] One of us had the privilege of writing the biographical entry on Dworkin in the *Yale Biographical Dictionary of American Law*, and closed that entry by stating, 'His work abounds with indefatigable energy, giving the impression that he will not stop making arguments until he has put the clamps of reason upon every rational being'.[10]

Dworkin's famous Colloquium in Legal, Political, and Social Philosophy at New York University (with Tom Nagel and sometimes Jeremy Waldron) set the standard for rigorous, vigorous, and constructive dialogue concerning important scholarship in those fields. Many other colloquia have been modeled upon it, but none has equaled it. Dworkin, Nagel, and Waldron gave incisive summaries of the works being presented, asked apt questions, and pressed probing and constructive criticisms. The command and vigor with which they did so was an inspiration to all who presented work in the Colloquium and to all who participated. One of us (McClain) benefitted both from the formative experience of being a student in the Colloquium and, years later, from receiving the generous input of Dworkin and Nagel when presenting a paper in the Colloquium.[11]

Dworkin's work in legal philosophy and constitutional theory was so powerful and fecund that it could inspire many careers wholly dedicated to building upon it and working out its implications. Dworkin (along with John Rawls) has been a powerful inspiration for our own work in constitutional theory. Fleming's *Securing Constitutional Democracy: The Case of Autonomy* puts forward a 'constitution-perfecting theory' that aims, in the spirit of

Dworkin, to interpret the American Constitution so as to make it the best it can be.[12] Sotirios Barbers's and Fleming's book, *Constitutional Interpretation: The Basic Questions*, is a response to Dworkin's call, in *Taking Rights Seriously*, for a 'fusion of constitutional law and moral theory'.[13] And our recent book, *Ordered Liberty: Rights, Responsibilities, and Virtues*, responds to charges that liberals like Dworkin 'take rights [too] seriously', developing a civic liberalism that takes responsibilities and civic virtues—as well as rights—seriously.[14]

Dworkin's successor as Professor of Jurisprudence at Oxford University, John Gardner, put it well when he said, 'The loss of Ronnie takes a bit of the sparkle out of life as a philosopher of law'.[15] But those who knew Dworkin and learned from his teaching and writing will never forget the thrill of engaging with him and building upon his work. His sparkling prose, the staggering ambition and monumental achievements of his works, and the flair and gusto of his arguments and insights will never cease to illuminate and inspire. We shall not look upon his like again. Ronald Dworkin made legal philosophy and constitutional theory the best they can be.

In this essay, we shall interpret Dworkin's constitutional theory in light of three varieties of perfectionism:

1. The idea that government should undertake a formative project of inculcating civic virtues and encouraging responsibility in the exercise of rights;
2. The idea that we should interpret the American Constitution so as to make it the best it can be; and
3. The idea that we should defend a 'constitution-perfecting theory' that would secure not only procedural liberties essential for democratic self-government but also substantive liberties essential for personal self-government.

We shall identify three gaps left by Dworkin's work and sketch how we have sought to fill those gaps in the spirit of his work through developing a mild form of constitutional perfectionism.

Taking Not Only Rights but Also Responsibilities and Virtues Seriously

First, there is perfectionism in political philosophy as it might be applied to constitutional theory. In criticizing perfectionism in constitutional theory, Cass Sunstein states that '[t]he perfectionist approach to constitutional law should not be confused with perfectionism in political philosophy', citing

John Rawls, *Political Liberalism*.[16] Rawls distinguishes between political liberalism and perfectionist liberalism (as well as perfectionist political philosophies more generally). Perfectionists of all stripes generally believe that statecraft is soulcraft, and that the state must inculcate civic virtues or even moral excellence in the citizenry. Despite Sunstein's remark, we should acknowledge the variety of constitutional perfectionism that brings perfectionist political philosophy to bear on constitutional theory. The two best examples are the work of Sotirios A. Barber[17] and that of Michael J. Sandel.[18] On Barber's view, we ultimately must face up to the challenge of 'supplying . . . the defect of better motives', not just by relying upon checks and balances and making '[a]mbition . . . counteract ambition'—James Madison's strategy in *The Federalist* No. 51[19]—but also by inculcating civic virtues that are necessary for responsible citizenship and for the success of the constitutional order. Similarly, Sandel argues not only that government should undertake such a formative project but also that in justifying constitutional rights like privacy, we should make recourse to substantive moral goods or virtues and a conception of justice as cultivating virtues. In our book, *Ordered Liberty*, we embrace a mild form of perfectionist constitutional theory along these lines.[20] Strikingly, although Dworkin rejected Rawls's political liberalism in favour of a comprehensive ethical liberalism, and he recognized considerable latitude for governmental encouragement of responsibility in the exercise of rights, he never fully developed a perfectionist theory of governmental responsibility to inculcate civic virtues.

Respecting Freedom and Cultivating Virtues

Dworkin, alongside Rawls, is the leading contemporary proponent of a liberal conception of justice.[21] As Sandel interprets these liberals, they think about justice in terms of *respecting freedom* as distinguished from *maximizing welfare* or *cultivating virtues*.[22] Sandel himself is the leading civic republican critic of such liberal conceptions of justice, interpreting them as holding, (a) that law should be neutral concerning competing conceptions of virtue or the best way to live and (b) that a just society respects each person's freedom to choose his or her conception of the good life (Sandel 2009: 9). And he is the most prominent civic republican proponent of conceiving justice in terms of cultivating virtues. Nonetheless, we want to point out some notable and unexpected affinities between Dworkin's and Sandel's conceptions of justice as put forward respectively in *Justice for Hedgehogs* and *Justice: What's the Right Thing to Do?*

First, in *Justice for Hedgehogs*, Dworkin rejects neutrality and criticizes Rawls's political liberalism for bracketing conceptions of the good life in arguments about justice.[23] Instead, Dworkin defends a comprehensive ethical liberalism and argues for the integration of ethics, morality, and justice.[24] He introduces two ethical principles that 'state fundamental requirements of living well':

> The first is a principle of self-respect. Each person must take his own life seriously: he must accept that it is a matter of importance that his life be a successful performance rather than a wasted opportunity. The second is a principle of authenticity. Each person has a special, personal responsibility for identifying what counts as success in his own life; he has a personal responsibility to create that life through a coherent narrative or style that he himself endorses.

He concludes, 'Together the two principles offer a conception of human dignity' (Dworkin 2010: 203–4). Dworkin develops two related political principles, arguing that '[n]o government is legitimate unless it subscribes to two reigning principles'—'First, it must show equal concern for the fate of every person over whom it claims dominion. Second, it must respect fully the responsibility and right of each person to decide for himself how to make something valuable of his life' (Dworkin 2010: 2). So, too, Sandel criticizes Rawls's political liberalism, arguing that we cannot separate arguments about justice from arguments about competing conceptions of the good life and of the virtues that a good society should promote.[25]

Second, in *Justice for Hedgehogs*, Dworkin is concerned to articulate the right process of moral reasoning. In doing so, he looks back to Aristotle for an example of a holistic approach to such reasoning and also looks to the relationship between questions of the good life and those of the good polity.[26] So, too, Sandel turns to Aristotle for a virtue–centered approach that integrates moral reasoning about justice with reasoning about moral virtues and conceptions of the good life.[27]

Third, in *Justice for Hedgehogs*, Dworkin explains that the 'idea of living well' means 'creating not just a chronology but a narrative that weaves together values of character—loyalties, ambitions, desires, tastes, and ideals' (Dworkin 2010: 244). Sandel has long criticized views like Dworkin's as forms of 'voluntarist' liberalism that conceive the person as a freely choosing, 'unencumbered self' who is the 'author' of his or her own ends and who can stand apart from relationships and commitments.[28] Yet in *Justice*, Sandel, like Dworkin, stresses the importance of a 'narrative quest that aspires to a certain unity or coherence' (Sandel 2009: 221) and contends that we are 'storytelling beings' and 'we live our lives as narrative quests'.[29]

Finally, in *Justice for Hedgehogs*, just as in *Life's Dominion*, Dworkin argues not only for taking rights seriously, but also for taking responsibilities seriously.[30] Dworkin stands in contrast to other forms of liberalism grounded in the idea that the state must be neutral between competing conceptions of the good life and the idea that rights insulate right-holders from moral judgments about their exercise. Rather, Dworkin argues that the state may encourage people to exercise their rights responsibly, short of compelling them to do what the government thinks is the responsible thing to do.[31] Sandel, much like Dworkin, has criticized those very liberal conceptions of neutrality and of rights as insulating right-holders from moral judgments.[32]

Are Dworkin's comprehensive ethical liberalism and Sandel's perfectionist civic republicanism as far apart as Sandel's criticisms of liberal conceptions of justice might suggest? The contrasts between justice as respecting freedom and justice as cultivating virtues may not be as stark as Sandel has put them. The work of some liberal political theorists, most prominently William Galston and Stephen Macedo, has narrowed the distance between these two conceptions. These theorists have developed attractive conceptions of civic liberalism, arguing persuasively that liberalism has a proper concern with cultivating civic virtues.[33] We too work on this terrain of civic liberalism in our book, *Ordered Liberty*.[34]

We shall suggest that the convergences between Dworkin, on the one hand, and the civic liberals and civic republicans, on the other, are closer with respect to recognizing considerable latitude for governmental promotion of responsible exercise of rights than they are with respect to recognizing the need for governmental inculcation of civic virtues. That is, Dworkin developed a theory of taking not only rights but also responsibilities seriously, but he for the most part eschewed developing a perfectionist project of cultivating civic virtues.

Taking Responsibilities as well as Rights Seriously

In *Life's Dominion*, Dworkin propounds a notably 'moralized' liberalism, making moral arguments for the right to procreative autonomy and the right to die while defending the authority of government to moralize concerning persons' exercise of these rights. He writes that America's political heritage is characterized by 'two sometimes competing traditions': 'The first is the tradition of personal freedom. The second assigns government responsibility for guarding the public moral space in which all citizens live'. Dworkin continues: 'A good part of constitutional law consists in reconciling these two ideas'. And he asks, 'What is the appropriate balance in the case of abortion?'[35]

This passage may have surprised many readers—both critics and allies—for two basic reasons. First, critics who associate liberals like Dworkin with exaltation of the tradition of personal freedom may be heartened that he acknowledges the legitimacy of the tradition that assigns government responsibility for guarding the public moral space. And allies who celebrate personal freedom may be alarmed that he sanctions governmental protection of the moral or ethical environment. (Scanlon, a friendly liberal ally, conceded that liberals including Dworkin have not talked very much about the latter tradition or about government promoting respect for intrinsic values like the sanctity of life. Indeed, he found Dworkin's reference to 'maintaining a moral environment' a slightly surprising phrase.)[36]

Second, critics and allies commonly associate Dworkin with the notion of 'rights as trumps' and thus with the idea that 'taking rights seriously' practically precludes reconciling rights with, or balancing rights against, governmental concern for guarding the public moral space.[37] Indeed, some readers might have expected a book by Dworkin on the right of procreative autonomy and the right to die to defend these rights solely on the basis of an argument about personal freedom. And they might have expected Dworkin to argue that these rights trump the very concerns regarding the moral or ethical environment that he here acknowledges as part of the American political heritage and constitutional law.

Dworkin's recognition of the place of the second tradition in the American political heritage is significant. Both as a matter of fit with American constitutional precedents and practice and as a plausible conception of government's proper authority, Dworkin is right to recognize that there are legitimate channels through which government may seek to promote the moral or ethical environment. At the same time, there is no denying that this tradition has been invoked to try to justify appalling deprivations of freedom and equality, for example, censorship of great works of literature and prohibition of interracial marriage.[38] For this reason, it is understandable that many liberals have sought to deny, avoid, or eradicate this tradition. Yet Dworkin is right to see that the risks of this tradition do not justify rejecting it entirely. Instead, he attempts to work with, and to work within, this tradition and to make it safe for liberals and for fundamental principles of freedom and equality, together with commitments to equal concern and dignity.

In *Justice for Hedgehogs*, in a passage concerning restricting liberty, Dworkin asks, 'Why should [the majority] not be permitted to protect the religious and sexual culture it favors...?' He answers,

> We need arguments like those of this book—the distinctions and interconnections among responsibility, authenticity, influence, and subordination that we have reviewed—properly to answer that question. The second principle of dignity makes ethics special: it limits the acceptable range of collective decision.

> We cannot escape the influence of our ethical environment: we are subject to
> the examples, exhortations, and celebrations of other people's ideas about how
> to live. But we must insist that that environment be created under the aegis of
> ethical independence: that it be created organically by the decisions of millions
> of people with the freedom to make their own choices, not through political
> majorities imposing their decisions on everyone. (Dworkin 2010: 370–71)

There clearly will be limits on government's protection of the ethical environment.

Dworkin's arguments for rights in both *Life's Dominion* and *Justice for
Hedgehogs* are grounded, not in governmental neutrality or in personal
autonomy, but in a deontology of state conduct. In other words, Dworkin
advances a theory that derives from a conception of the permissible bases
for collective decisions. His concern is with respecting limits on the grounds
for governmental decisions and with avoiding political majorities imposing
their decisions on everyone concerning questions such as how to live or how
best to respect the sanctity of life.[39] Dworkin specifically denied that he was
articulating a theory of rights that asks what our fundamental or especially
important interests are and what freedoms are necessary to secure or further
those interests.[40] For example, despite Dworkin's justification for a 'right of
procreative autonomy', his theory differs in important respects from a theory
of autonomy rooted in a conception of the person and what is necessary for
the development and exercise of moral powers or the like. In this respect, his
theory differs from the Rawlsian civic liberal theory of deliberative autonomy
that we have developed and applied in *Securing Constitutional Democracy*, *The
Place of Families*, and *Ordered Liberty*.[41]

This feature of Dworkin's theory in part accounts for why he contemplated
a relatively large space (compared to most liberals) for governmental moralizing. On his view, there is a large space between complete, hands-off non-
interference with liberty, autonomy, dignity, independence, or choice (of the
sort strong autonomy theorists advocate) and coercion. Furthermore, government need not, and should not, be neutral in that large space. It may moralize, encourage responsibility, and the like, so long as it does not coerce the
ultimate decision.[42] Likewise, citizens need not, and should not, be neutral.

At the same time, this feature of Dworkin's theory may help explain why
he did not develop a civic liberalism concerned to inculcate civic virtues or
to develop the moral powers or capacities for responsible democratic and
personal self-government. And why he did not put forward a theory of civic
education or of the roles of government and civil society in preparing persons for responsible citizenship and orderly social reproduction. In our book,
Ordered Liberty, we have elaborated a mild form of civic liberal perfectionism
that takes up these projects. It aims to take civic virtues along with rights

and responsibilities seriously. We think our view is not incompatible with Dworkin's ethical liberalism, even if he himself did not develop such a theory.

Making the Moral Reading of the American Constitution the Best It Can Be

Interpretive Perfectionism

Second, we distinguish perfectionism in the sense of a theory of constitutional interpretation entailing that we should interpret the Constitution so as to make it the best it can be.[43] On this view, as Sunstein puts it, constitutional interpretation is a matter of putting the existing legal materials 'in their best constructive light', or of making them 'the best they can be'.[44] Furthermore, it is the quest for the interpretation that provides the best fit with and justification of the constitutional document and underlying constitutional order.[45] This sense of perfectionism which we might call 'interpretive perfectionism' is famously associated with Dworkin. We embrace this sense.

Dworkin's interpretive perfectionism takes the form of the 'moral reading' of the American Constitution—the Constitution embodies abstract moral principles rather than laying down particular historical conceptions, and interpreting and applying those principles require fresh judgments of political theory about how they are best understood.[46] Dworkin's development of the moral reading makes it sound (a) more utopian and (b) more philosophical than it should. Therefore, he triggers objections that he propounds (a) a theory of the 'perfect constitution'[47] and (b) a theory that entails that judges should be philosophers.[48] To be fair to Dworkin, he does not claim that the moral reading is a moral realist reading—a reading that is prior to and independent of our own political and constitutional order and practice, and true to the moral order of the universe.[49] Rather, he contends that the moral reading is constrained by the requirements of fit and integrity. Thus it is bound to account for the legal materials of the existing constitutional order and practice.[50] And so, even if Dworkin's theory of constitutional interpretation aims to provide the best interpretation of these legal materials—to make the Constitution the best it can be—it is not unbounded.

Nonetheless, some critics charge that Dworkin's moral reading is utopian in two senses. One, it is a moral reading for a perfect liberal utopia—he would interpret the American Constitution to protect every right and produce every outcome that his liberal political philosophy would entail. And two, it is literally a theory for no place—he would give the same moral reading irrespective of the actual history and practice of the constitutional scheme, for example, the same for Britain as for the United States. We do not believe that such critics are right about Dworkin's moral reading, but they certainly are persistent and warrant a fuller response than simply directing them to read Dworkin more carefully.

When confronted with the 'perfect constitution' challenge,[51] Dworkin basically pleaded (we paraphrase): 'I do not believe the American Constitution is perfect. For example, while I do believe that justice requires welfare rights, I do not believe that the Constitution protects such rights. To continue our paraphrase: 'Your challenge applies to Frank Michelman, not me, because he, not I, believes that the Constitution does protect welfare rights.'[52] Beyond that, Dworkin was at pains to make clear, as noted above, that the constraints of fit and integrity entail that the actual Constitution is imperfect when measured against the standards of any normative political philosophy or conception of justice.

Our tack here for responding to the perfect Constitution challenge to Dworkin's moral reading is to show how Lawrence G. Sager's justice-seeking account of American constitutional practice helps meet the challenge, in particular, through its accounts of the thinness of constitutional justice, and more particularly, of the moral shortfall of judicially enforceable constitutional law. Sager argues that certain constitutional principles required by justice are judicially under-enforced, yet nonetheless may impose affirmative obligations outside the courts on legislatures, executives, and citizens generally to realize them more fully.[53] Sager's view is an important component of a full moral reading or justice-seeking account of the Constitution. For it helps make sense of the evident thinness or moral shortfall of constitutional law. For example, instead of saying that the American Constitution does not secure welfare rights—the move that Dworkin makes—Sager says that the Constitution does secure welfare rights, but it leaves their enforcement in the first instance to legislatures and executives.[54] Once a scheme of welfare rights and benefits is in place, courts have a secondary role in enforcing it equally and fairly.[55]

Furthermore, if Dworkin's moral reading of the American Constitution, though it embodies abstract moral principles, does not incorporate all of the important principles of justice, we need an account of the difference between the two. Dworkin does not offer such an account and may leave his readers wondering whether his theory entails that the American Constitution is a perfect liberal constitution. To be sure, the constraints of fit and integrity entail a gap between the Constitution and justice. But Dworkin says little about any such gap, and what he does say implies that the gap may be narrow. For example, he says that the Constitution is abstract, and therefore, it should come as no surprise that any right we can argue for as a matter of political morality, we can also argue for as a matter of constitutional law.[56] And where he does acknowledge a significant gap between the Constitution and justice, for example, with welfare rights, he does not provide a general account of why the Constitution—as he conceives it—does not incorporate elements of justice like welfare rights.

Sager's account of the domain of constitutional justice helps his regard. He distinguishes (a) judicially enforceable constitutional law from (b) constitutional justice, which he in turn distinguishes from (c) political justice and (d) morality generally.[57] Imagine a series of progressively thicker concentric circles representing these four domains. Dworkin's highly general formulation of the 'moral reading' may seem to blur the distinction between constitutional law and constitutional justice, as well as that between constitutional justice and political justice, and indeed that between constitutional law, on the one hand, and political justice and morality generally, on the other. His 'hedge-hogist' commitment to the integration of ethics, morality, and justice may further blur those distinctions. Sager's justice-seeking account underscores just how thin a moral reading of the Constitution has to be—as compared to our thicker conceptions of political justice and morality—in order to be credible as an account of American constitutional practice.

Sager's under-enforcement thesis may entail a conception of legislative responsibility congenial to the conception that Dworkin's early work promised but never fully provided. We refer to the 'doctrine of political responsibility' that Dworkin argued (in 'Hard Cases') is incumbent on legislatures as well as courts.[58] The doctrine of political responsibility implies that legislatures have an obligation to engage in coherent, responsible legislating with integrity (not precisely as coherent, responsible, and constrained as judging with integrity, but legislating with integrity nonetheless). And in *Law's Empire*, Dworkin spoke of 'integrity in legislation' as well as 'integrity in adjudication'.[59] Jeremy Waldron opens *The Dignity of Legislation* by suggesting that he aspires to do for legislation what Dworkin 'purports to [have done] for adjudicative reasoning'.[60] We interpret Waldron to mean that he aims to develop a conception of legislating with integrity, if not integrity in legislation.[61] Admittedly, Dworkin himself did not do this. Nor for that matter has Waldron fully accomplished it. We view Sager's idea of judicial under-enforcement, coupled with his notion that legislatures have the obligation to enforce constitutional norms and seek constitutional justice, as furthering Dworkin's unfinished business. For one thing, we should view legislatures as constrained by the Constitution outside the courts, not just as legislating in constitutionally gratuitous ways. For another, we should view legislatures as partners with courts in pursuing constitutional justice. Much work remains to be done in articulating a full-blown conception of legislating with responsibility and integrity as an aspect of the moral reading of the American Constitution.

Perfecting the Substantive Constitution

Third, we distinguish perfectionism in the sense of theories that interpret the American Constitution to secure or perfect the basic liberties that are preconditions for the legitimacy and trustworthiness of the outcomes of the political processes. John Hart Ely's 'process-perfecting' theory of reinforcing representative democracy, put forward in his book, *Democracy and Distrust*,[62] is the most famous version of such a theory. According to Ely's theory, the American Constitution's core commitment is to representative democracy, and judicial review is justified principally when the processes of representative democracy, and thus the political decisions resulting from them, are undeserving of trust. Ely argues that courts should reinforce or perfect the procedural preconditions for the trustworthiness of the outcomes of the political processes, but that they should eschew protecting substantive liberties.

Dworkin famously criticized Ely's theory for taking a 'flight from substance' to process,[63] including fleeing protecting substantive liberties like an individual's 'freedom to make ethical choices for himself'[64] to protecting only procedural liberties like the right to vote. And he developed a substantive conception of constitutional democracy—or a partnership view—as an alternative to Ely's procedural conception of majoritarian democracy. The partnership view of democracy holds that 'the people govern themselves each as a full partner in a collective political enterprise so that a majority's decisions are democratic only when certain further conditions are met that protect the status and interests of each citizen as a full partner in that enterprise.'[65] Majority support, just on its own, does not supply a 'moral reason' for what the majority supports; ideas drawn from political morality about 'justice, equality, and liberty' should inform our views about what is a democratic decision.[66] Thus, '[t]he partnership conception ties democracy to the substantive constraints of legitimacy'.[67] Dworkin is persuasive in contending that protection of, and respect for, rights that are the conditions for moral membership in our political community rooted in equal concern and dignity are themselves preconditions for the legitimacy of the outcomes of majoritarian political processes.[68] Here Dworkin, despite his criticism of Ely, appears to have taken a page out of Ely's book in conceiving our rights as democratic conditions and in arguing that courts protecting constitutional rights guarantee democracy rather than compromise it. But unlike Ely, Dworkin would include, among the conditions of democracy, certain substantive rights rooted in equal concern and dignity in addition to procedural rights.[69]

Dworkin has powerfully expressed the conditions of moral membership in our political community. But we would recast the architecture of his constitutional theory to differentiate it more sharply from that of Ely's process-perfecting theory. Characterizing all of our substantive and procedural rights as 'democratic conditions', as Dworkin does, may lead to unnecessary trouble and resistance. Many readers may resist his argument that substantive rights grounded in equal concern and dignity are 'democratic conditions'. They may suspect that Dworkin is pulling a fast one or being too clever by packing all of the substantive rights that constrain majoritarian political processes into the 'democratic conditions'.[70]

One of us has sought to develop a substantive *Constitution-perfecting theory* as an alternative to the *process-perfecting theory* advanced by Ely.[71] Such a theory would reinforce not only the procedural liberties (those related to democratic participation) but also the substantive liberties (those related to personal autonomy and ethical independence) embodied in the American Constitution and presupposed by its constitutional democracy. *Securing Constitutional Democracy* puts forward a guiding framework with two fundamental themes—first, securing the basic liberties that are preconditions for *deliberative democracy*, to enable citizens to apply their capacity for a conception of justice to deliberating about and judging the justice of basic institutions and social policies as well as the common good, and second, securing the basic liberties that are preconditions for *deliberative autonomy*, to enable citizens to apply their capacity for a conception of the good to deliberating about and deciding how to live their own lives. Together, these themes afford everyone the status of free and equal citizenship. They reflect two bedrock structures of deliberative political and personal self-government.[72] Unlike process theories, this Constitution-perfecting theory provides a firm grounding for rights of privacy and autonomy, along with liberty of conscience and freedom of association, as necessary to secure individual freedom and to promote a diverse and vigorous civil society. This theory also shows how basic liberties associated with personal autonomy, along with those related to democratic participation, fit together into a coherent scheme of basic liberties and constitutional essentials that are integral to the American Constitution and its underlying constitutional democracy. The architecture of such a Constitution-perfecting theory can comfortably house all of what Dworkin conceives as the conditions of moral membership in our political community without recasting substantive liberties constraining majorities as 'democratic conditions'. On this theory, we perfect the whole substantive Constitution, not merely the partial procedural Constitution.

Through offering this account of the moral shortfall of the moral reading and developing a substantive Constitution-perfecting theory, we aspire to make the moral reading of the American Constitution the best it can be.

Notes and References

1. Ronald Dworkin. 1977. *Taking Rights Seriously*. Cambridge: Harvard University Press, 1977. In this introduction, we draw from James E. Fleming. 2013. 'Ronald Dworkin: A Eulogy', *Balkinization*. Available http://balkin.blogspot.com/2013/02/ronald-dworkin-eulogy.html.

2. T.M. Scanlon. 1993. 'Partisan For Life', *New York Review of Books*. 15 July. (reviewing Ronald Dworkin's *Life's Dominion*).

3. Ronald Dworkin. 1998. 'Darwin's New Bulldog', *Harvard Law Review*. 111(7). p. 1718; reprinted in Ronald Dworkin. 2006. *Justice in Robes*. Cambridge, MA: Harvard University Press. p. 75.

4. Ronald Dworkin. 1996. 'Bork's Own Postmortem', *Freedom's Law: The Moral Reading of the American Constitution*. Cambridge, MA: Harvard University Press. p. 287.

5. Ronald Dworkin. 1997. 'Comment', in Antonin Scalia, *A Matter of Interpretation: Federal Courts and the Law*, Amy Gutmann (ed.) Princeton, NJ: Princeton University Press. p. 115.

6. Ronald Dworkin. 1997. 'The Arduous Virtue of Fidelity: Originalism, Scalia, Tribe, and Nerve', *Fordham Law Review* 65(4). p. 1249, reprinted in Dworkin, *Justice in Robes*, p. 117.

7. Ronald Dworkin. 'Rawls and the Law'. *Fordham Law Review* 72(5). p. 1387, reprinted in Dworkin, *Justice in Robes*, p. 241.

8. Ronald Dworkin. 2010. 'Justice for Hedgehogs', *Boston University Law Review* 90(2). p. 469.

9. Ronald Dworkin. 2010. 'Response', *Boston University Law Review* 90 (2010): p. 1059.

10. James E. Fleming. 2009. 'Ronald Dworkin', in Roger K. Newman (ed.), *The Yale Biographical Dictionary of American Law*. New Haven: Yale University Press. pp. 178–9.

11. That paper became Chapter 4, 'Marriage Promotion, Marriage (E)quality, and Welfare Reform', in Linda C. McClain. 2006. *The Place of Families: Fostering Capacity, Equality, and Responsibility*. Cambridge, MA: Harvard University Press, 2006), p. 117.

12. James E. Fleming. 2006. *Securing Constitutional Democracy: The Case of Autonomy*. Chicago, IL: University of Chicago Press. pp. 4–6, 73–4, 210–11.

13. Sotirios A. Barber and James E. Fleming. 2007. *Constitutional Interpretation: The Basic Questions*. New York: Oxford University Press. p. xiii (quoting Dworkin, *Taking Rights Seriously*, p. 149).
14. James E. Fleming and Linda C. McClain. *Ordered Liberty: Rights, Responsibilities, and Virtues*. Cambridge, MA: Harvard University Press. pp. 1–3.
15. John Gardner, quoted in Ronald Dworkin, 1931–2013, available https://www.law.ox.ac.uk/news/2013-02-15-ronald-dworkin-1931-2013.
16. Cass R. Sunstein. 2005. *Radicals in Robes: Why Extreme Right-Wing Courts Are Wrong for America*. New York: Basic Books. p. 254 n.9 (citing John Rawls. 1993. *Political Liberalism*. New York: Columbia University Press.
17. See Sotirios A. Barber. 2003. *Welfare and the Constitution*. Princeton, NJ: Princeton University Press. pp. 53–64, 118–42.
18. See Michael J. Sandel. 2009. *Justice: What's the Right Thing to Do?* New York: Farrar, Straus & Giroux.
19. *The Federalist* No. 51, 322 (James Madison), ed. Clinton Rossiter (New York: New American Library, 1961).
20. Fleming and McClain. *Ordered Liberty*. p. 209.
21. See John Rawls. 1971. *A Theory of Justice*. Cambridge, MA: Harvard University Press; Rawls, *Political Liberalism*. In this section, we draw from Linda C. McClain and James E. Fleming. 2011. 'Respecting Freedom and Cultivating Virtues in Justifying Constitutional Rights', *Boston University Law Review* 91. pp. 1311, 1312–14.
22. Sandel. *Justice*. pp. 6–10, 19–21, 140–66.
23. Ronald Dworkin. 2010. *Justice for Hedgehogs*. Cambridge, MA: Harvard University Press. pp. 263–4, 267–8.
24. Dworkin. *Hedgehogs*. pp. 1–19, 117–20.
25. Sandel. *Justice*. pp. 140–66, 246–51.
26. Dworkin. *Justice for Hedgehogs*. pp. 155, 186–8.
27. Sandel. *Justice*. pp. 9, 12, 184–207.
28. See Michael J. Sandel. 1998. *Liberalism and the Limits of Justice*, 2nd Edition. New York: Cambridge University Press. pp. 89–94, 175–83 (criticizing conception of the 'unencumbered self'); Michael J. Sandel. 1989. 'Moral Argument and Liberal Toleration: Abortion and Homosexuality', *California Law Review* 77. pp. 521, 522–25, 538 (criticizing liberal conceptions of autonomy as reflecting a 'voluntarist' conception of the self).
29. Sandel. *Justice*. p. 221. (citing Alasdair MacIntrye. 1981. *After Virtue*. Notre Dame, IN: University of Notre Dame Press).
30. See James E. Fleming. 2010. 'Taking Responsibilities as well as Rights Seriously', *Boston University Law Review* 90. pp. 839, 839, 844 (analyzing Dworkin's, *Life's Dominion*, and *Justice for Hedgehogs*); Dworkin. *Justice for Hedgehogs*. p. 482 n.7, and Dworkin. 'Response', 1078–9 (indicating that Dworkin carries forward the arguments about taking responsibilities seriously from *Life's Dominion* to *Justice for Hedgehogs*).
31. Fleming. 'Taking Responsibilities as well as Rights Seriously', pp. 839–40.

32. Sandel. 'Moral Argument and Liberal Toleration'. pp. 533–8.
33. See William Galston. 1991. *Liberal Purposes: Goods, Virtues, and Diversity in the Liberal State*. Cambridge: Cambridge University Press; William Galston. 2003. *Liberal Pluralism: The Implications of Value Pluralism for Political Theory and Practice*. Cambridge: Cambridge University Press; Stephen Macedo. 1990. *Liberal Virtues: Citizenship, Virtue, and Community in Liberal Constitutionalism*. Oxford: Clarendon Press; Stephen Macedo. 2000. *Diversity and Distrust: Civic Education in a Multicultural Democracy*. Cambridge, MA: Harvard University Press.
34. Fleming and McClain. *Ordered Liberty*. pp. 3–4.
35. Dworkin. *Life's Dominion*. p. 150. In this section, we incorporate portions of Fleming. 'Taking Responsibilities as well as Rights Seriously'. 840–3. See also Benjamin C. Zipursky and James E. Fleming. 2007. 'Rights, Responsibilities, and Reflections on the Sanctity of Life', in *Ronald Dworkin*. Arthur Ripstein (ed.). New York: Cambridge University Press. pp. 109, 127–30.
36. See Scanlon. 'Partisan For Life'. pp. 46–7.
37. See, for example, Dworkin. *Taking Rights Seriously*. pp. xv, 269; Robin West. 1990. 'Foreword: Taking Freedom Seriously', *Harvard Law Review* 104. pp. 43, 46–7 (criticizing Dworkin's liberal legalist strategy of 'taking rights seriously' and proposing instead a 'responsibility-based liberalism' that would 'take seriously not only the individual's demand for rights but also the burdens of his responsibility').
38. See, for example, *Loving v. Virginia*, 388 U.S. 1, 8 (1967) (describing one of the state appellate court's rationales for upholding Virginia's miscegenation statute as 'preserving the racial integrity of its citizens' (citation omitted)).
39. Dworkin. *Life's Dominion*. p. 151.
40. Ronald Dworkin. 1985. *A Matter of Principle*. Cambridge, MA: Harvard University Press. pp. 65–6; Dworkin. *Taking Rights Seriously*. pp. 272–3.
41. See Fleming. *Securing Constitutional Democracy*. pp. 61–85; Rawls. *Political Liberalism*. pp. 15–20, 29–35, 299–304. See also McClain, *The Place of Families*. pp. 4, 17–19, 64–7; Fleming and McClain. *Ordered Liberty*. pp. 3–4, 9–10, 94, 111, 151.
42. See Fleming and McClain. *Ordered Liberty*. pp. 62–8 (analyzing Dworkin's, *Life's Dominion*). Dworkin made these arguments with respect to the right to abortion and the right to die. It is not clear whether he would take the same view regarding governmental moralizing with respect to all constitutional rights, for example, freedom of speech and religious liberty.
43. Sunstein. *Radicals in Robes*. 32; see Fleming, *Securing Constitutional Democracy*, pp. 16, 211, 225.
44. Sunstein. *Radicals in Robes*. 32 (quoting Ronald Dworkin. 1986. *Law's Empire*: Cambridge, MA: Harvard University Press. p. 229).
45. Fleming. *Securing Constitutional Democracy*. pp. 5, 24, 63, 84; see Dworkin. *Law's Empire*. p. 239; Cass R. Sunstein. 2007. 'Second-Order Perfectionism', *Fordham Law Review* 75. pp. 2867, 2869–70, 2872–4.

46. Dworkin. *Freedom's Law*. pp. 1–38; Dworkin. *Life's Dominion*. pp. 118–47. In this section, we incorporate portions of James E. Fleming. 2005. 'Judicial Review without Judicial Supremacy: Taking the Constitution Seriously Outside the Courts', *Fordham Law Review* 73 (2005): pp. 1377, 1381–6.

47. See, for example, Henry P. Monaghan. 1981. 'Our Perfect Constitution', *New York University Law Review* 56. p. 353.

48. See, for example, Christopher L. Eisgruber. 2006. 'Should Constitutional Judges Be Philosophers?', in *Exploring Law's Empire: The Jurisprudence of Ronald Dworkin*. Scott Hershovitz (ed.) New York: Oxford University Press. p. 5.

49. For such moral realist accounts, see, for example, Sotirios A. Barber. 1993. *The Constitution of Judicial Power*. Baltimore, MD: Johns Hopkins University Press; and Michael S. Moore. 2001. 'Justifying the Natural Law Theory of Constitutional Interpretation', *Fordham Law Review* 69. p. 2087.

50. See Dworkin. *Freedom's Law*. p. 10–11; Dworkin. *Law's Empire*. p. 238–75.

51. See Dworkin. *Freedom's Law*. p. 36. In this paragraph we draw upon James E. Fleming. 2004. 'Lawrence's Republic', *Tulsa Law Review*. 39. pp. 563, 581.

52. See Dworkin, *Freedom's Law*. p. 36 (citing Frank I. Michelman, 'Foreword: On Protecting the Poor through the Fourteenth Amendment', *Harvard Law Review* 83 (1969): 7).

53. Lawrence G. Sager. 2004. *Justice in Plainclothes: A Theory of American Constitutional Practice*. New Haven, CT: Yale University Press. pp. 84–128.

54. Sager. *Justice in Plainclothes*. pp. 84–8.

55. Sager. *Justice in Plainclothes*. pp. 95–102.

56. Dworkin. *Freedom's Law*. p. 73.

57. Sager. *Justice in Plainclothes*. pp. 129–60; see also Lawrence G. Sager. 2004. 'The Why of Constitutional Essentials', *Fordham Law Review* 72. pp. 1421, 1423–9 (using concentric circles to illustrate these four domains).

58. See Dworkin. *Taking Rights Seriously*. p. 87.

59. See Dworkin. *Law's Empire*. pp. 167, 176–84, 217–28.

60. See Jeremy Waldron. 1999. *The Dignity of Legislation*. Cambridge: Cambridge University Press. p. 1.

61. See Jeremy Waldron. 2003. 'Legislating with Integrity', *Fordham Law Review* 72. pp. 373, 373 (distinguishing between legislating with integrity and integrity in legislation).

62. John Hart Ely. 1980. *Democracy and Distrust*. Cambridge, MA: Harvard University Press. pp. 73–104. In this section, we incorporate passages from James E. Fleming. 'The Place of History and Philosophy in the Moral Reading of the American Constitution', *Exploring Law's Empire: The Jurisprudence of Ronald Dworkin*. pp. 23, 27–30.

63. Ronald Dworkin, 'The Forum of Principle', *New York University Law Review* 56 (1981): 469, reprinted in Dworkin, *A Matter of Principle*, 33.

64. Ronald Dworkin. 2006. *Is Democracy Possible Here?* Princeton, NJ: Princeton University Press. p. 146.

65. Dworkin. *Is Democracy Possible Here?* p. 131. See also Dworkin, *Justice for Hedgehogs*, pp. 382–5.
66. Dworkin. *Is Democracy Possible Here?* p. 134.
67. Dworkin. *Justice for Hedgehogs.* p. 384.
68. Dworkin. *Freedom's Law.* p. 24; Dworkin. *Life's Dominion.* p. 123; Dworkin. *Justice for Hedgehogs.* pp. 384–5.
69. Dworkin. *Freedom's Law.* pp. 24–6, 349 n.5; Dworkin. *Is Democracy Possible Here?* p. 144, 146; Dworkin. *Justice for Hedgehogs.* pp. 384–5.
70. Sager has made a similar critique of the architecture of Dworkin's theory. See Sager. *Justice in Plainclothes.* pp. 132–7.
71. See Fleming. *Securing Constitutional Democracy.* pp. 19–36 (criticizing the process-perfecting theory defended in Ely, *Democracy and Distrust*).
72. Fleming. *Securing Constitutional Democracy.* pp. 3–4.

3

Interpretation in Normative Domains

*Alexander Brown**

A vast amount has been written about Dworkin's account of interpretation in the genre of law. I want to focus instead on his account of interpretation as it relates to the normative domains of politics, morality, and ethics. More specifically, I want to situate his account of interpretation as it relates to these normative domains within some of the relevant contemporary literature on moral epistemology, meta-ethics, and methodology in moral and political philosophy.

In the sections that follow I shall pinpoint three particular questions. First, what is the nature of Dworkin's account of epistemic justification or warrant in normative domains and how does it compare and contrast with other noteworthy views in the theory of moral knowledge including coherentist and naturalistic views as well as theories of epistemic responsibility? Second, what form does epistemic justification or warrant take in the case of interpretive normative judgments? Third, what implications does Dworkin's account of interpretation have for the methodological question posed by Felix Oppenheim about whether it is ever possible to perform conceptual analyses

* I am extremely grateful to Matthew Kramer and Andrea Sangiovanni for their critical commentaries on an early draft of this contribution.

of normative political concepts like justice, liberty, democracy, and so on, in ways that are themselves value-independent?

My exposition of Dworkin's accounts of epistemic justification and interpretation in normative domains shall not be devoid of arguments however, even if they are primarily arguments about how best to read Dworkin's position. To begin with, I argue that Dworkin is best understood as attempting to meet the epistemic challenge of explaining how normative judgments can be credible by converting the epistemic challenge into a moral challenge, to be met via the best light interpretation of the virtue of moral responsibility. Following on from that, I argue that the interpretation of normative concepts should be cast as an instance of the more general form of constructive interpretation of social practices. Next, I argue that the epistemic credibility of these sorts of interpretive–normative judgments also depends on meeting moral responsibilities. Finally, I argue that when Dworkin proposes that the right way to interpret the meaning of justice must appeal to a larger network of other values he means to refer not merely to other moral and political values but also to ethical values as well. In fact, the holistic integration of political, moral, and ethical values can be seen in evidence throughout his normative philosophy.

Meeting Epistemological Challenges in Normative Domains

A key question I want to ask about Dworkin's account of interpretation is how it connects with his account of epistemic justification or warrant in the normative domains of politics, morality, and ethics. At the centre of Dworkin's account of how it is that people's claims about justice, say, are epistemically justified or warranted is the contention that people do not merely set forth their normative commitments with conviction but also make the case for those convictions by drawing on other normative commitments of various kinds. As he puts it in *Justice for Hedgehogs*, 'any argument that either supports or undermines a moral claim must include or presuppose further moral claims or assumptions'.[1] In other words, 'morality is moral, all the way down' (Dworkin 2011: 131). By way of illustration, according to Dworkin, 'we believe that a government that respects liberty and equality in some way improves the lives of those whom it governs'.[2] In this way we seek to justify or make the case for what we believe about liberty and equality by drawing on further beliefs about what it means to improve the lives of citizens.

Sometimes Dworkin calls this reinforcing aspect of moral epistemology 'a kind of circularity' (2011: 100). But more often he describes the process of justifying one's normative beliefs and convictions in terms of embedding them in a larger, coherent 'system' (30, 441) or 'interlocking network'(117, 120, 154) or 'web'[3] of normative beliefs, convictions, arguments, principles, and so on. Whereas talk of 'circularity' ordinarily implies begging the question at hand and, therefore, a type of flawed reasoning or argumentation, talk of 'a complex web' of beliefs does not.

Dworkin also makes it clear, however, that *if* convictions are to operate as a basis for epistemically justifying our moral claims alongside as opposed to subordinate to coherence—Dworkin is clear that epistemic justification requires convictions as well as coherence and, what is more, that this mixed method is the best hope we have for achieving or grounding truth itself (Dworkin 2011: 120–1, 179–80)—then *not just any* convictions will do. The right convictions are those that we hold with such high levels of conviction that we can feel warranted in treating them as given. It is in this vein that he refers to the existence of particular interpretations of basic concepts in the domains of politics and morality that 'grip our soul' or that 'we cannot help believing' (Dworkin 2004: 18). That being said, he also accepts that even the most firmly held convictions are not fixed for all time but are subject to change. In the case of the social practice of courtesy, for example, we can imagine a day when the practice of men standing up to greet women when they enter a room is no longer considered courteous but instead 'the deepest possible discourtesy'.[4]

Nevertheless, if, as seems to be the case, Dworkin wants to say that we hold certain moral convictions with such high levels of conviction that we may be justified in taking them as given in our system of moral beliefs conceived as 'an integrated web of standards' (Dworkin 2011: 224), then this assumption seems to raise as many questions as it answers. The challenge is to explain how it is that we may be justified in taking certain convictions as given without relying on coherence to do the heavy lifting. The challenge is made even more difficult by the fact that Dworkin rules out an alternative, naturalistic account of the credibility of strongly held convictions. He rejects 'the causal impact hypothesis' according to which 'moral facts can cause people to form moral convictions that match those moral facts' (70). I shall not pause here to rehearse or critically examine Dworkin's reasons for this rejection.[5] Instead, I want to focus on the implications of this rejection for what Dworkin does want to say about epistemic justification and for how he meets the aforementioned challenge.

One possible response to the challenge might be to insist that human beings may at least claim a kind of credibility for their moral convictions under normal conditions, beyond the mere fact of coherence, even before they can provide a full blown epistemic justification for those convictions.

This is precisely the position defended by William Lycan in his 1988 book *Judgement and Justification*⁶—a book that went unnoticed by Dworkin. Lycan argues that certain moral convictions can be epistemically 'tenable' if they 'force themselves on us whether we will or no[t]', can survive initial inclusion into our system of beliefs without inconsistency or anomaly, and are weakly supported by a principle of conservatism that says 'one should hold on to any belief one has unless there is some positive reason to reject it' (Lycan 1988: 208). The nature of these 'spontaneous moral beliefs' (209) is such that human beings find them 'almost impossible to ignore or to write off' (170), 'save by extraordinary means' (211).

But even if both Dworkin and Lycan can accept that human beings possess certain moral convictions they cannot help believing, the question of full-blown epistemic justification remains a point of separation between them. For, Dworkin is far more parsimonious than Lycan about the nature of that helplessness viz-à-viz naturalistic analyses. Although Dworkin self-identifies as a moral realist (Dworkin 1996: 127–8) (albeit allied to various caveats as to the misleading and faulty assumptions built into labels in the field of meta-ethics⁷), he firmly dismisses what he calls 'the natural model' or 'the moral-field thesis', which posits the existence of fields of moral particles or 'morons' that impact human beings via a type of special moral faculty or sense.⁸ According to Dworkin, this possibility is 'barely intelligible' (1996: 128). Of course, not all naturalistic epistemologies posit the existence of morons—a point under-emphasized by Dworkin perhaps. And nowhere does Lycan say that he believes in the existence of morons (pardon the pun). Yet Lycan *is* nevertheless committed to the view that moral judgments are analysable in naturalistic, physical, and potentially causal terms. On Lycan's view, this is made possible because moral properties 'supervene on facts about utility, harm, degradation, or the like', which are themselves 'non-moral properties' or are involved in 'complex natural properties' (Lycan 1988: 297), and because '[f]or evolutionary reasons there may be a way [...] in which our brains register morally significant sociological properties of actions' (210). By analogy, '[m]oral intuitions can seem as hard to disdain or to write off as are perceptual sensings, and this sort of insistency is, in the case of perceptual sensing, felt to indicate the presence and activity of delivery mechanisms' (211). In this way, Lycan invites naturalistic, physicalist, and causal analyses—both of how we end up with a moral sense (for example, evolution by natural selection) and of the way this moral sense works (for example, as a psychological mechanism in which moral convictions are triggered as outputs in response to exposure to ordinary non-moral physical events or states of affair as inputs). And he thinks that these types of analyses or 'explanations' can be key to making the transition from having epistemically tenable moral beliefs to having epistemically justified moral beliefs. In fact, Lycan gives the following descriptions of what these analyses might look like. '[If] the mechanism that produces the belief was (as we say) a reliable one, in good working order', '[t]hen, I submit, our spontaneous belief is fully justified, and we may want to count it as an item of knowledge' (168). 'If our overarching total theory can explain not only one of our spontaneous beliefs but how it is produced in us, and if the latter explanation involved the truth of the belief, then the belief is fully justified, perhaps to the point of counting as an item of knowledge' (209). What is more, for Lycan, the very possibility of these types of analyses underwrites a sort of epistemological *I owe you* in the sense that it lends tenability to spontaneous moral beliefs even before they can be fully justified. As he puts it, 'spontaneous moral judgments are prima facie as worthy of respect as are perceptual judgments and wait only upon the discovery of a very diffuse sort of moral sense' (212). For Dworkin, by contrast, 'justifying a moral judgment never requires appeal to extraordinary modes of causation' (2011: 85). And I conjecture that Lycan's analyses are most likely 'extraordinary' by Dworkin's lights. This is because Lycan's descriptions of these analyses appear to presuppose the causal impact hypothesis, which Dworkin rejects as 'myth' (69–75, 438–9 n.3).

Nonetheless, we seem to have reached a stage in the discussion where the burden of argument has shifted onto Dworkin to show why conviction as well as coherence should be seen as crucial to epistemic justification in normative domains. Otherwise, the danger is that he is claiming the following. *The mere fact that we hold certain convictions with high levels of conviction must suffice to explain why it is fitting to take those convictions as given simply because the strength of these convictions is all we have to go on besides coherence itself and we need convictions to play a significant role in epistemic justification or warrant if we are to avoid the view that epistemic justification or warrant is purely a matter of coherence.* And this looks a lot like begging the question.

However, I believe that the above claim does not do justice to Dworkin's position. For, there is a proper argument lurking in the background here and it has to do with *moral responsibility*. According to Dworkin, acting as a morally responsible agent in the practice of figuring out what it means to do the right thing or act morally, including the practice of normative interpretation, means that agents 'act out of rather than in spite of their convictions' (2011: 103). Amongst other things, this means that a morally responsible agent takes various attitudes and inclinations which assail him or her on a daily basis (as in, 'emotions, preferences, tastes, and prejudices') and passes them through 'the filter of effective convictions' (108). If we are to be morally responsible agents (so the argument goes), then it is essential that 'we must find convictions that grip us strongly enough to play the role of filters when we are pressed by competing motives that also flow from our personal histories' (108). Dworkin explains that what he calls 'insincere convictions' and 'rationalizations' cannot play this role and are therefore ineffective convictions (107–8). Sincere convictions, convictions not born of self-interest, unbiased convictions, convictions held in a calm mind, or more generally, convictions produced via reliable mechanisms[9]— these, presumably for Dworkin, *can* be effective convictions. So Dworkin's claim is actually this. *Part of what it means to be a morally responsible agent on the best interpretation of that virtue is to find effective convictions that can act as filters on our affective states. And if we manage to be morally responsibly in this way, this gives us moral reasons to think that our effective convictions are epistemically credible.* And there is textual evidence for this reading (2011: 104–13). This is, in a nutshell, to pin epistemic credibility to moral responsibility.

Of course, Dworkin is not alone in thinking that *responsibility* holds the key to understanding credible moral convictions. However, for other writers in the literature the relevant sort of responsibility just is *epistemic responsibility.* In his 1999 book, *Morality Without Foundations,* for example, Mark Timmons proffers the following account of epistemic responsibility in normative domains.[10] According to Timmons, '[b]roadly speaking, being epistemically responsible has to do with such activities as: (a) gathering evidence, (b) considering and dealing with counter-possibilities, and (c) dealing with internal conflicts of belief' (195). In addition to this, he maintains that it is possible for an agent to be epistemically responsible whilst at the same time (d) possessing some moral beliefs that are not justified by evidence or by other beliefs.

He labels such beliefs 'contextually basic beliefs'—beliefs which are such that in certain contexts they do not need justification in order to be credible or to justify other beliefs that are non-basic (187). Timmons argues that when a member of a social community or group shares the 'moral outlook' of members of the group and does so as a result of undergoing 'a process of moral education', then the core moral assumptions that are constitutive of that moral outlook and that are acquired through moral education, say the assumption that under normal circumstances killing other human beings is morally wrong, are contextually basic beliefs (217–18).

Importantly, Timmons thinks that the extent and type of epistemic responsibility is set by goals of enquiry that are themselves epistemic, most notably having true beliefs and avoiding false ones. Thus, the challenge of being epistemically warranted is met by fulfilling epistemic responsibilities that serve epistemic goals (191–3). For Dworkin, by contrast, it is important to acknowledge that being epistemically warranted is *itself* resolutely an enterprise of moral reflection and argument. In other words, all epistemological challenges in the normative domains of politics, morality, and ethics are in the final analysis answered *as* normative challenges, met with further political, moral, or ethical claims or arguments. What we need, in other words, are *moral* reasons to think that the possession of effective convictions is essential to epistemic reliability in normative domains (Dworkin 2011: 108–9). So when people wish to argue that they are warranted in holding the moral beliefs they do it is not merely on the basis that they have fulfilled a set of epistemic requirements but also on the basis of interpretive claims or arguments about what it means to be an equal member of the political community or about what it means to fulfil one's moral duties toward other people or about what it means to live an ethical life or about all three, and the consequences of these meanings for how we understand what the operative standards of epistemic responsibility should be in given contexts (111–13). The position I am attributing to Dworkin is likely to be an instance of what Timmons calls 'normative contextualism', something he distinguishes from his own position, 'structural contextualism' (1999: 194–7).

Therefore, to conclude this section, earlier I said that Dworkinians face the not inconsiderable challenge of explaining the special epistemic status of certain convictions within complex systems of normative claims, convictions, arguments, principles, and so on, given the fact that Dworkin both affirms that epistemic credibility is not purely a matter of coherence and affirms that it is not the case that moral judgments are initially credible by virtue of the fact that they are somehow caused by moral facts. I said that this challenge is difficult to meet; I did not, however, say it was impossible. Dworkin's distinctive way of meeting that challenge is by arguing that effective convictions provide the necessary epistemic bootstrapping without relying on either strong coherentism or the causal impact hypothesis.

At this juncture, however, the picture is complicated by the fact that, for Dworkin, moral concepts are 'interpretive' (2011: 166). Dworkin believes that conceptual interpretation in the realms of politics, morality, and ethics will typically involve dispute, where different groups of interpreters compete to provide a successful interpretation of normative concepts, to find the single true meaning of the concept they share (160–70). So the question is: In what sense can interpretive moral judgements be epistemically credible? I shall attempt to answer this question in the next section.

Interpretation of Normative Concepts and Social Practices

Before enquiring about what makes interpretive moral judgement credible, let us first get clearer about the nature of interpretation itself. Dworkin proposes what he calls 'the value theory of interpretation'[11] according to which 'our standards for success in an interpretive genre do depend [...] on what we take to be the best light understanding of the point of interpretation in that genre' (2011: 153). This means that the interpreter has a responsibility to reflect critically about the point and purpose of artistic interpretation as opposed to legal interpretation as opposed to moral interpretation, and so on, and to factor this into the standards of success employed in these different forms of interpretation. In the genre of moral and political philosophy, for example, interpretation takes the form of conceptual interpretation—here the standard for success in interpretation is a matter of finding the meaning of a concept created by a community whose concept it is and which also includes the interpreter (136). In the genre of literary, artistic, and legal interpretation, by contrast, interpretation typically takes the form of collaborative interpreta-tion—here the standard for success in interpretation is a matter of assum-ing that the object of interpretation has an author or creator and that the interpreter collaborates with the author or creator in advancing the object of interpretation (135–6). According to the value theory of interpretation, these different standards for success in interpretation reflect what we take to be the best light understanding of the point and purpose of these different forms of interpretation.

Intriguingly, in his legal writings Dworkin draws parallels between concep-tual interpretation in the genre of moral and political philosophy and inter-pretation in the field of law, specifically the interpretation of legal practices. In both areas, the 'best light' interpretation of an interpretive practice or concept is one that makes it the best possible example of the type to which it belongs or that provides the best justification for it, perhaps because it realizes certain values or ideals that we all have reason to care about.[12] Take the concept of justice. This is a concept about which people think a great deal, a concept about which they employ certain language, a concept in virtue of which they act practically, and a concept about which they engage in disagreement, even though they share some basic understanding of it. This disagreement, according to Dworkin, takes the form of providing competing interpretations of justice, thus making it an interpretive concept (2011: 160–70). Dispute is unsurprising for various reasons. First is the abstract or vague nature of the political, moral, and ethical concepts at issue in these realms. Second is the fact that these concepts or values are characteristically used to regulate behaviour and appraise institutions or social practices, and when people are regulated and appraised in such ways they will inevitably form vital interests in the adoption of some interpretations rather than others.[13] A third potential reason, I think, is that it is part of human nature to not merely engage in the sort of intellectual reflection that embodies interpretation but to try to interpret things *in our own ways*, and this often means in contra-distinction to the interpretations of others. We may come to define ourselves by adopting interpretations that other people do not.

But what makes one interpretation superior to another? What makes an interpreter epistemically justified or warranted in affirming one interpretation rather than another? I have already explained how, for Dworkin, epistemic justification in normative domains depends upon finding as much conviction and as much coherence as we can command. Achieving epistemic justification in the interpretation of normative concepts like justice, liberty, democracy, and so on, is an instance of this more general rule. But what particular forms do the dimensions of conviction and coherence take in the particular case of interpretative judgments?

In order to answer this question it is important to recognize that conceptual interpretation is itself a kind of social practice, a practice of arguing about true meanings. 'People participate in social practices in which they treat certain concepts as identifying a value or disvalue but disagree about how that value should be characterized or identified' (2011: 160–1). This disagreement is a professional enterprise for moral and political philosophers. 'Much of the long history of philosophy is a history of conceptual interpretation' (157).

It is, however, possible to view the practice of conceptual interpretation in more general terms, as exemplifying a more universal form of interpretation. In his earlier work Dworkin gives the name 'constructive interpretation' to one such universal form. Constructive interpretation is about the interpreter imposing value on the object of interpretation, seeing that it has a point or purpose, or making it the best it can be. 'The constructive account', explains Dworkin, 'could perhaps provide a more general account of interpretation in all its forms' (1998: 53). 'We would then say that all interpretation strives to make an object the best it can be, as an instance of some assumed enterprise, and that interpretation takes different forms in different contexts only because different enterprises engage different standards of value or success' (53). If, therefore, we can understand conceptual interpretation as an instance of the more general category of constructive interpretation, then we might think that successful interpretation in the genre of conceptual interpretation is not so much a search for meaning as a search for *fit* and *justification*.

In the case of constructive interpretation, the requirement of fit demands that an interpretation of a normative social practice relating to a normative concept like justice can be successful or true only if it is supported by the relevant pre–interpretive data, that is, only if enough elements of the social practice are adducible in support of the interpretation being an interpretation of the social practice as opposed to an interpretation of something else. Consider a social practice of justice whose central elements include the government refraining (in the name of justice) from taxing the wealth produced by the industrious poor to give to the lazy rich (2011: 161–2). Suppose an interpreter of this social practice of justice suggests that the practice has value by dint of honouring the principle that a just distribution of wealth should be ambition-sensitive. To say that this interpretation achieves fit with the social practice of justice is to say that the pre–interpretive statement about the government refraining (in the name of justice) from taxing the industrious poor for the sake of the lazy rich can be adducible in support of this interpretation whereas it might not be adducible in support of other interpretations. This sort of minimal fit is not appropriate to interpretation as invention, of course.

The requirement of justification, by contrast, focuses more heavily on the requirement that an interpretation of a social practice should propose value for the social practice, which is to say, it must be capable of serving as a justification for it. Here, the interpretation justifies the social practice. Sticking with the above example, to say that the social practice honours the principle of ambition-sensitivity is to give the practice a point and purpose, a reason to think the practice is worth pursuing or valuable. Although ostensibly the conceptual interpretation of justice is about finding the single true meaning of justice created by the community, when conceptual interpretation is cast as an instance of the more general form of constructive interpretation one of the goals of interpretation becomes imposing value on the practice of justice or on the practices that employ the concept of justice. The imposing of value might take the form of saying that a particular practice of justice honours the principle of ambition-sensitivity. Or it might take the form of saying that a particular practice of justice realizes the abstract egalitarian principle that citizens have a right to equal concern and respect from their governments.

However, at this point it might be objected that conceptual interpretation does not lend itself to being recast as an instance of the more general form of constructive interpretation because in his writings Dworkin has a tendency to talk about the constructive interpretation of social practices as opposed to concepts.[14] However, I think it would be a mistake to think that the interpretation of concepts must be independent of or somehow removed from the interpretation of social practices—quite the reverse in fact.

First, even when philosophers are interpreting a concept like justice they are still looking at a social practice, the social practice of the concept, so to speak. By this I mean that the object of interpretation *is* the ways a community of people have of thinking about the concept, using the concept linguistically, acting on the concept practically, and disagreeing about the meaning of the concept. This is what Dworkin has in mind, I think, when he uses such locutions as 'the practice of justice' (1998: 75), 'justice is an institution we interpret' (73), and '[t]he practices that employ the concepts of justice, honesty, and the other concepts I called interpretive' (2011: 170).

Second, to think of the interpretation of concepts as an instance of the interpretation of social practices chimes with another thing Dworkin says about conceptual interpretation, namely, 'that the interpreter seeks the meaning of a concept, like justice or truth, that has been created and recreated not by single authors but by the community whose concept it is, a community that includes the interpreter as a creator as well' (1998: 136). Here, Dworkin is highlighting the potential impact of the interpreter on the object of interpretation: the interpreter who provides a new interpretation of a concept like justice and proceeds to use that concept accordingly 'will at least imperceptibly change the interpretive problem future interpreters face' (136). In other words, interpreters 'help in creating what they interpret' (157). This could only be true if the object of interpretation with which current interpreters are confronted is constituted by the sort of things to which previous interpreters might have contributed, and in my view social practices are prime candidates.

Third, my reading is supported by Dworkin's claim that conceptual interpretation is only possible because 'paradigms' of agreed usage obtain. These are broad consensuses among communities of people about what can and cannot be intelligibly said about and with interpretive concepts. These paradigms are important pre-interpretively, with respect to identification of the concept itself rather than the conception as it were: they help to ensure that interpreters are not simply talking past each other (Dworkin 1998: 74–5; 2011: 160–3). Historically the term 'paradigm' has been used by philosophers to connote a set of social practices.[15] And this seems to be exactly what Dworkin intends when he claims that paradigms of justice can be studied by philosophers 'or perhaps sociologists' (1988: 75).

Fourth, making a connection between the interpretation of concepts and the interpretation of social practices helps to render more plausible something else that Dworkin suggests about interpretation in general. I have in mind Dworkin's claim that one linking thread across all genres of interpretation is the fact that '[w]e find it natural to report our conclusions, in each and every genre of interpretation, in the language of intention or purpose' (2011: 125). At first glance, it seems problematic to apply this generalization to conceptual interpretation. For, it seems untenable to say that concepts have intention or purpose *in themselves*. Instead, communities of people have intentions towards or specific purposes in mind for concepts. Perhaps it is only by putting the emphasis on social practices of thinking about, using, and acting on concepts in certain ways that the aforementioned characterization of interpretation, in general, makes sense with respect to conceptual interpretation.

Finally, nothing essential is lost in the change of emphasis that I am proposing. An interpretation of the social practice of the concept of justice, say, is still likely to produce along the way an interpretation of the meaning of the concept, as would a more direct interpretation of the concept of justice. This is because it is an integral part of the complex social practice of justice that people think about and use linguistically the concept of justice, amongst other things. I should also like to make it clear, however, that by placing the emphasis on constructive interpretation of the social practices of concepts, this does not mean a move to 'conversational' or 'collaborative' interpretation.[16] On the contrary, the aim is not to find substantive fit with what the creators or authors of the practice took the point and purpose to be.

So what, more exactly, is involved in interpreting social practices involving concepts like justice? Dworkin argues that the constructive interpretation of social practices involves three stages.[17] In what follows I try to synthesize Dworkin's account of these three stages in *Law's Empire* (1998: 65–6) with a later statement found in *Justice for Hedgehogs* (2011: 130–9) in which Dworkin brings into the story the fact that interpreters are not merely engaging in interpretation of the object of interpretation but also of the very nature of interpretation in the relevant genre of interpretation.

First, an interpreter must identify the pre–interpretive data from which his or her interpretation is to be constructed.[18] In the case of a social practice, this includes the rules, standards, and modes of behaviour that embody the practice to be interpreted. At this stage, the interpreter will also appeal to certain background assumptions and values that help to define the nature of interpretation itself in the relevant genre of interpretation. In other words, 'we are also interpreting the practice of interpretation in the genre that we take ourselves to have joined' (Dworkin 2011: 131). This prior interpretation of interpretation will shape the judgements he or she makes about what things are or are not pre–interpretive data for the purposes of interpretation. Second, at the interpretation stage, the interpreter will posit an interpretation of the point and purposes of the social practice,[19] 'an argument why a practice of that general shape is worth pursuing' (Dworkin 1998: 67). This may involve positing that the social practice 'serves some interest or purpose or enforces some principle—in short, that it has some point – that can be stated independently of just describing the rules that make up the practice' (47). Dworkin makes it clear that the proposed point and purpose 'need not fit every aspect or feature of the standing practice, but it must fit enough for the interpreter to be able to see himself as interpreting that practice, not inventing a new one' (66). Third, at the post–interpretive or reforming stage, the interpreter must revisit the social practice in the light of his or her interpretation and may seek to reform those elements which do not serve the point or purpose posited. The interpreter may seek to establish some new exception to the rules, standards, and modes of behaviour identified in the pre–interpretive stage in order to realize the interpretation posited at the interpretation stage (Dworkin 2011: 131).

Having outlined the nature of interpretation, let us now return to the question posed earlier in this section: What makes an interpreter epistemically justified or warranted in affirming one interpretation rather than another? One answer is that it flows from finding interpretations that best serve the right purposes and standards of success for interpretation in the genre. But this raises a deeper question: What makes an interpreter's assumptions about the right purposes of and standards for success in the given genre of interpretation epistemically credible? It seems to me that one story that Dworkin might tell in answer to this question relies once again on the notion of effective convictions. In short, if we can plausibly see our assumptions about the right purposes of and standards for success in the given genre of interpretation as effective convictions, in the sense discussed in the previous section, we can begin to understand what it means to have epistemically credible assumptions. For, if these assumptions grip us strongly enough to filter out affective states which might mis-direct or taint or prejudice our judgments of successful interpretation, then we may have *prima facie* reason to see them as reliable. In the case of conceptual interpretation we might say that interpreters have effective convictions that the purpose of conceptual interpretation is to find meaning and that the right standards of success are those that help us to find meaning. If conceptual interpretation is cast as an instance of the more general form of constructive interpretation, we might say that interpreters have effective convictions about the right standards for success, namely, fit and justification in the interpretation of the practice of concepts. Indeed, when Dworkin describes the assumptions we have about the purpose of interpretation in given genres of interpretation he speaks as though these assumptions are given. 'Interpreters make or just have assumptions about these purposes and the values that support them' (2011: 153).

Moreover, Dworkin can say that what lends further credibility to these standards for success is the fact that they flow from or honour what we take to be the best light understanding of the responsibilities of moral interpretation (2011: 7, 113–17). Whenever Dworkin speaks of the moral responsibilities of interpreters in the genre of moral and political philosophy, for example, he makes it clear that part of the moral responsibility is to forge interlocking networks or complex webs of interpretations of normative concepts and social practices. Political philosophy 'must aim, first, to construct conceptions or interpretations of each of these values that reinforce the others—a conception of democracy, for example, that serves equality and liberty, and conceptions of each of these other values that serves democracy so understood' (2004: 17). 'We defend a conception of justice by placing the practices and paradigms of that concept in a larger network of *other* values that sustains our conception' (162). In other words, 'the epistemology of a morally responsible person is interpretive' (101).

I want to end this section by addressing two possible criticisms of Dworkin's account of interpretation. The first criticism is that the idea of justification contains an unhelpful ambiguity. At times Dworkin intimates that figuring out how well an interpretation justifies a social practice relative to another interpretation has to do with assessing *the comparative importance* of the purposes, values or principles that it attributes to that particular social practice. For example, 'If the raw data do not discriminate between these competing interpretations, each interpreter's choice must reflect his view of which interpretation proposes the *most value* for the practice' (1998: 52–3). In other words, it is then a matter of figuring out 'which one shows it in the better light, all things considered' (53). Sticking with the above example of taxation, in order for the requirement of justification to be satisfied it must be the case that the proffered interpretation of the government's practice as honouring the principle of ambition-sensitivity shows this social practice in a better light than other competing interpretations would—for example, better than an interpretation that depicts the government's practice as maximising sum utility. In other instances, Dworkin seems to suggest that these judgments have to do with looking at the general types or forms of social practice to which a particular social practice belongs and assessing *the comparative degree to which* the particular social practice exemplifies each of the types or forms put forward by the competing interpretations. For example, 'Roughly, constructive interpretation is a matter of imposing purpose on an object or practice in order to make of it *the best possible example of the form or genre to which it is taken to belong*' (52; emphasis added). The first reading implies that of two competing interpretations of a social practice the more successful interpretation is whichever one posits the most important purposes, values or principles, assuming that such comparisons are possible. The second reading suggests that the more successful interpretation is whichever one posits the most fully realized purpose, value, or principle.

I suspect that what Dworkin would say is that the mere fact justification can take different forms is not in itself a problem and may even reflect the value theory of interpretation. Suppose that the best interpretation of the point and purpose of interpretation in the genre of moral and political philosophy makes justification an important goal of enquiry (2011: 152–3). The question then becomes which of the two possible readings of justification mentioned above best advances the goal of enquiry.

In other words, the interpreter must consider how much weight to place on the issue of the comparative importance of the purposes, values or principles posited by the competition interpretations and how much weight to place on the comparative degree of realisation of the purposes, values or principles posited by the competition interpretations. The goal of enquiry requirement makes it clear to interpreters that whatever weight they assign to these different aspects of justification they must keep in mind the goal of making justification as good as it can be. This may not be an exact science, but keeping the goal of enquiry in mind may give interpreters a sound reason to make finely balanced judgments of weight such that neither comparative importance nor comparative degree of realisation are granted absolute weight over each other.

The second criticism has to do with circularity. Dworkin wishes to ground the epistemic credibility of effective convictions in a certain interpretation of moral responsibility: that a morally responsible agent is someone who possesses a dense web of effective convictions that is capable of filtering out his or her biases, prejudices, and other emotional responses. This argument is interpretive in the sense that it provides an interpretation of what it means to be a morally responsible agent, that is, an interpretation of something which is itself a normative concept or social practice. But what makes *this* second-order interpretive argument credible? Surely it must be none other than effective convictions about the standards of success in the interpretation of interpretive normative judgments about moral responsibility. Yet why should we think these effective convictions are credible? And so on.

Dworkin's answer here, I presume, is to grasp the nettle and accept that '[i]nterpretation is pervasively holistic' (2011: 154). It is to accept as a feature of interpretation the fact that any given interpretation of a normative concept or social practice depends on not merely a host of interpretations of other normative concepts and social practices but also an interpretation of the point of interpretation in the domain of moral and political philosophy as well as an interpretation of the meaning of moral responsibility. This network of interpretations provides reasons to think that our effective convictions are epistemically credible, but this methodology is itself also born of interpretations of the right moral epistemology. It is not surprising, then, says Dworkin, that we may lack absolute confidence about the epistemic standing of our interpretive normative judgments and about the effective convictions upon which they rest (155). But that is not the end of the story. For one thing, we feel the same lack of confidence when attempting to take seriously the idea that there is no such thing as moral knowledge (156). What is more—and here I am reading *into* Dworkin as opposed to reading *from* Dworkin—perhaps it is possible to possess confidence in thinking that finding interlocking networks or complex webs of interpretations and effective convictions is a better way of partaking in the practice of epistemic justification than other theories of moral epistemology would propose. This certainly seems to be a form of confidence Dworkin exemplifies in his work.

On the Point and Purpose of Political Philosophy

In this final section I wish to examine in more detail Dworkin's claims about the character of normative reflection and argument, as moral all the way down. In particular, I wish to interrogate his core message that the enterprise of interpreting normative political concepts like justice cannot and should not attempt to escape the realm of human values. At one stage Dworkin puts this message as follows. 'Philosophers of justice understand that they are taking sides: that their theories are as normative as the claims about justice and injustice that politicians, leader writers and citizens make' (2004: 8). On one level, this is itself a constructive interpretation of the social practice of interpretation in the domain of political philosophy. As such, I believe that it needs to be subjected to critical reflection and compared with other possible interpretations. The first part (the claim that philosophers of justice understand that they are taking sides) is innocuous enough. Very few philosophers are so solipsistic as to imagine that no other philosophers disagree with them. The second part (the claim that philosophers of justice understand that their theories are as normative as the claims about justice made by anyone else) is more controversial I think.

Part of what Dworkin is getting at is the thesis that interpreting moral and political concepts is itself laden with other moral and political concepts. 'We defend a conception of justice by placing the practices and paradigms of that concept in a larger network of *other* values that sustains our conception' (2011: 162). Yet it is plainly false to claim that *all* political philosophers would understand or constructively interpret the task of theorising basic political concepts in this way. The work of Felix Oppenheim immediately springs to mind. Consider this passage taken from his essay, '"Facts" and "Values" in Politics: Are They Separable?'.[20]

For the purpose of a scientific study of politics, we must at least attempt to provide basic political concepts with explications acceptable to anyone regardless of his normative and ideological commitments, so that the truth (or falsity) of statements in which these concepts (thus defined) occur will depend exclusively on inter-subjectively ascertainable empirical evidence.

Contrary to the proponents of the inseparability thesis, I believe that such a goal is not only desirable, but also attainable, at least in principle. Thus, in the case of the concept of social, political, or interpersonal freedom, the expression we must explicate is: 'With respect to B, A is free to do x'. This expression can be defined by, 'B makes it neither impossible nor punishable for A to do x'. Not only does this definition remain close to ordinary usage; it also is descriptive, and in two ways: the defining expression consists exclusively of descriptive terms, and it is 'value-free', in the sense that it can be applied to determinate states of affair by anyone independently of his political convictions. (Oppenheim 1973: 56)

Of course, it is one thing to think that it is possible to undertake conceptual analyses of the concept of freedom in ways that do not presuppose or harness other moral or political values (as part of the adequacy constraints that the analyses set forth as tests for identifying the single true conception of the relevant concept from among the field of competitors); it is quite another to think the same about the concept of justice.[21] Could the concept of justice ever be reduced to purely descriptive terms? But even when the concept of justice is at issue there may be *some* political philosophers who do hold out for value-independent analyses of a slightly different form. This, at least, is how Matthew Kramer reads Hillel Steiner's theory of justice. As Kramer explains, '[h]oping to rely exclusively on the compossibility test and a few other formal considerations for the vindication of his theory of justice, Steiner contends that a philosophical account of justice—and of connected phenomena such as liberty and rights—can and should be value-independent'.[22]

In the end Kramer argues that Steiner's compossibility test[23] cannot perform the work that Steiner intends it to perform because it is 'unhelpfully undemanding' (that is, the test is useless since it does not rule out any theories of justice that are not logically incoherent).[24] I do not intend to defend Steiner's theory of justice from that criticism. Instead, I want to pursue the implications of the *possibility* that that theory presupposes. For, the possibility of value-independent tests for identifying the single true conception of the relevant concept from among the field of competitors is not expunged by Kramer's particular critique of Steiner, even if accurate.[25] Of course, much depends on what is meant by 'value-independent tests' in this context. Yet it might be thought that there are plenty of tests we can use to judge successful interpretation of political concepts like justice that are *not* in and of themselves moral or political values. Arguably among the features that are likely to make for successful interpretation across various different genres of interpretation are that an interpretation is complete, systematic, simple, and even elegant. These are intellectual and aesthetic values, of course, but they are not, or do not need to be, moral or political values *per se*. Following this train of thought, it might be argued that Dworkin's interpretation of the practice of political philosophy is more controversial than he acknowledges. Since, it could be that a better interpretation of the practice of political philosophy is one in which the successful interpretation of normative political concepts like justice is not settled by the twin requirements of fit and justification after all, but instead by fit plus other intellectual and aesthetic values, for example, or by justification plus other intellectual and aesthetic values.

The story does not end there, however. Dworkin might retort that as an ethically responsible agent he possesses an irresistible conviction that fit and justification are indeed the stuff of best light interpretation in normative domains. He might also claim that choosing to employ intellectual and aesthetic values to judge interpretations of normative political concepts is itself a choice that cannot be motivated by relevant political and moral values.

This sort of claim about what it means to be an ethically responsible philosopher is certainly not lost on Dworkin. When he claims that political philosophers defend conceptions of justice by appealing to a larger network of *other* values he means to refer not merely to other moral and political values but also to ethical values as well.[26] As discussed earlier in this contribution, Dworkin believes that living well in the ethical sense not only means acting or being disposed to act in morally responsible ways, it also means pursuing coherence endorsed by conviction in figuring out what it means to do the right thing or act morally. According to Dworkin, there is a sense in which this responsibility falls particularly heavily, although not only, on moral and political philosophers. This is due in part to the fact that 'moral philosophy can influence people; it can make them more responsible as individuals'.[27] I would argue that the same goes for political philosophy. For, some people might take the normative position that because of the propensity of some policymakers and legislators to listen to political philosophers and because of the grave consequences for people's lives of interpreting basic political concepts in some ways rather than others, political philosophers owe it to society to measure the success of their interpretations of basic political concepts by giving more weight to the practical requirements of fit and justification than to intellectual and aesthetic values.

In fact, a holistic approach that integrates political, moral, and ethical values is manifest in different ways throughout Dworkin's normative philosophy. One manifestation is his claim in *Sovereign Virtue* that there ought to be 'continuity' between the ideas of personal responsibility that figure in our political principles of justice and the ideas of personal responsibility that we embrace in our ordinary ethical distinctions and practices.[28] A second is his suggestion in *Is Democracy Possible Here?* that 'the common ground we need in order to sustain' genuine debate about the true meaning of political values like justice, human rights, and democracy is encapsulated in two very basic principles of human dignity that are not 'distinctly political or even moral' but rather 'identify more abstract value in the human situation'.[29] The substantive connections between principles of human dignity across the domains of politics, morality, and ethics are further elaborated in *Justice for Hedgehogs*. There is a sense in which Parts 3, 4, and 5 of that book are all dedicated to the realization of the complex and momentous idea that coming to hold the ethical conviction that one's own life is objectively important points one in the direction of holding the moral conviction that everyone's life has the same objective importance and then towards the political conviction that all citizens should be treated by their governments as though the success or failure of their lives has equal objective importance.

Notes and References

1. Ronald Dworkin. 2011. *Justice for Hedgehogs*. Cambridge, MA: Harvard University Press. p. 99.
2. Ronald Dworkin. 2001. 'Do Values Conflict? A Hedgehog's Approach', *Arizona Law Review* 43. pp. 251–9.
3. Ronald Dworkin. 2004. 'Hart's Postscript and the Character of Political Philosophy', *Oxford Journal of Legal Studies*, 24 (1–37): 14; Dworkin, *Justice for Hedgehogs*: pp. 132, 192, 224.
4. Ronald Dworkin. 1998. *Law's Empire*, Reprinted edition. Oxford: Hart. pp. 72–3.
5. See, for example, Ronald Dworkin. 1996. 'Objectivity and Truth: You'd Better Believe It'. *Philosophy and Public Affairs* 25(87–139). pp. 103–5; Dworkin. *Justice for Hedgehogs*: pp. 70–6.
6. William G. Lycan. 1988. *Judgement and Justification*. Cambridge: Cambridge University Press.
7. Dworkin. 'Objectivity and Truth': 99–100. See also his *Justice for Hedgehogs*: pp. 9–11, 166.
8. Ronald Dworkin. 1977. *Taking Rights Seriously*. London: Duckworth: 159–60; 'Objectivity and Truth': pp. 104–5; *Justice for Hedgehogs*: p. 32.

9. T.M. Scanlon. 2002. 'Rawls on Justification', in S. Freeman (ed.), *The Cambridge Companion to Rawls*. Cambridge: Cambridge University Press.
10. Mark Timmons. 1999. *Morality without Foundations: A Defense of Ethical Contextualism*. Oxford: Oxford University Press. Chapter 5. In chapters 3 and 4 of the same book, Timmons defends moral irrealism, albeit as a special sort of moral irrealism that accommodates the idea that moral judgments can be true or false, by virtue of the fact that they are *assertoric* (they assert claims), just not true or false claims about moral facts. But in what follows I shall assume that his account of epistemic responsibility does not presupposes his moral irrealism and is not necessarily inconsistent with moral realism.
11. Dworkin, *Justice for Hedgehogs*: pp. 7, 131, 134, 141, 149, 153, and 175.
12. Dworkin, *Law's Empire*, p. 90. See also Ofer Raban. 2003. 'Dworkin's "Best Light" Requirement and the Proper Methodology of Legal Theory', *Oxford Journal of Legal Studies* 23(2): 243–64.
13. This reason partly has to do with Dworkin's distinction between 'criterial concepts' like *book*, which are the sort of concepts that communities of people simply use in their social practices (for example, the practice of visiting the library), and 'interpretive concepts' like *justice*, which people also use in order to make sense of or assess or critically evaluate other social practices (for example, the practice of giving full borrowing rights to some patrons and not others). *Justice for Hedgehogs*: pp. 158–9, 163–4, 166–70. See also his *Law's Empire*, 424–5 n.20.
14. See, for example, *Law's Empire*, 47, 50.
15. cf. Thomas Kuhn. 1962. *The Structure of Scientific Revolutions*.Chicago, IL: Chicago University Press.
16. Dworkin, *Law's Empire*, pp. 50–5, 64–5; Dworkin, *Justice for Hedgehogs*, pp. 135–8.
17. This is, of course, also an interpretive argument about the concept of interpretation.
18. It is worth emphasizing that although descriptions of pre–interpretive facts are supposed to be relatively uncontroversial, there may remain some degree of disagreement about even these facts in some cases. Thus, the difference between descriptions of social practices and constructive interpretations of those practices is a difference of degree as well as of kind. See Dworkin, *Law's Empire* (1998: 66). A similar point is made by Stephen Guest. 2012. *Ronald Dworkin*, third edition. Stanford, CA: Stanford University Press. pp. 66–7.
19. I intend the term 'point or purpose' to be read with a capacious meaning such that it could signify not merely that a social practice serves some purpose or enforces some principle but also that it respects or realizes some abstract value. As I shall explain below, central to Dworkin's political philosophy is the claim the that most successful interpretation of justice is whichever best demonstrates that this political ideal respects or realizes the abstract value of human dignity.
20. Felix Oppenheim. 1973. '"Facts" and "Values" in Politics: Are They Separable?', *Political Theory*. 54–68.
21. In the above cited article, for instance, Oppenheim does not seek to argue that the concept of justice can be defined in purely descriptive, value–independent terms.

22. Matthew Kramer. 2013. 'Conceptual Analysis and Distributive Justice', University of Cambridge, Legal Studies Research Paper Series, Paper No. 15. p. 15. Available at: http://papers.ssrn.com/sol3/papers.cfm?abstract_id=2277549 (accessed 1 June 2015).

23. For example: 'A set of rights being a possible set is, I take it, itself a necessary condition of the plausibility of whatever principle of justice generates that set'. Hillel Steiner. 1994. *An Essay on Rights*. Oxford: Blackwell. p. 2.

24. Kramer, 'Conceptual Analysis and Distributive Justice', p. 15.

25. I am not suggesting here that Kramer took himself to be extrapolating from his particular critique of Steiner in such a crude way.

26. For example: '[Political philosophy] must aim to construct these political conceptions, moreover, as part of an even more inclusive structure of value that connects the political structure not only to morality more generally, but to ethics as well.' Dworkin, 'Hart's Postscript', p. 17. And: 'My recommendation is similar to Rawls' method of reflective equilibrium, which aims to bring our intuitions and theories about justice into line with one another. The divergence with Rawls' methodology is more striking than the similarities, however, because the equilibrium, I believe philosophy must seek is not limited, as his is, to the constitutional essentials of politics, but embraces what he calls a 'comprehensive' theory that includes personal morality and ethics as well. If political philosophy is not comprehensive in its ambition it fails to redeem the crucial insight that political values are integrated, not detached'(18).

27. Dworkin, *Justice for Hedgehogs*, p. 110.

28. Ronald Dworkin. 2000. *Sovereign Virtue*. Cambridge, MA: Harvard University Press: 294–5, 323–4. cf. *Justice for Hedgehogs*, pp. 106–7.

29. Ronald Dworkin. 2006. *Is Democracy Possible Here?* Princeton, NJ: Princeton University Press. p. 9.

4

Justice, Integrity, and the Common Law

Trevor R.S. Allan

Part of the appeal of Ronald Dworkin's legal theory is its ability to illuminate the working of the ordinary common law—the manner in which judges reason on the basis of the principles that legal precedent exemplifies. Dworkin's account of interpretation exhibits the connections between legal rules and judicial decisions, on the one hand, and underlying moral and political principle, on the other. Legal reasoning and moral reasoning are closely connected. When legal decision-making satisfies the demands of Dworkinian integrity, it grapples with questions of *justification* and not merely the dictates of authority.[1] The common law judge cannot be a mere technician, deciding cases without regard for moral principle—his own personal moral and political convictions are necessarily engaged, if only as aids to understanding the tapestry of legal principle he is charged to administer. Dworkin's work is not only a stimulating challenge to legal positivism—especially positivist conceptions of adjudication—but, more particularly, a welcome corrective to positivistic accounts of the common law.[2]

This essay explores a certain tension, within Dworkin's legal theory, over the nature of that important connection between legal judgment and moral conviction. Although the theory navigates a distinctive course in legal philosophy, offering a highly nuanced account of the nature of law and adjudication, its view of the common law, in particular, is in some respects ambiguous. On the one hand, Dworkin gives pride of place to the reflexive and contentious character of common law reasoning—the vulnerability of its methods and ground rules to question and reappraisal in the very course of adjudication. On the other hand, it is often suggested that the law (on some specific matter) may be too well-established or firmly entrenched to permit plausible disagreement. And while the 'protestant' character of legal interpretation is a central feature of law as integrity, encouraging a fusion of legal judgment and moral conviction, Dworkin is nonetheless willing to contemplate moral dilemmas of the kind created by duties to obey or apply unjust—even gravely unjust—legal rules. For all its sophistication and complexity, it remains uncertain whether the theory can successfully bridge these fundamental divisions. Does the rule of law, correctly conceived, sometimes dictate serious—even radical—departures from justice in particular cases? Or are the relevant values of legality, integrity, and justice too closely intertwined to permit such occasions for moral regret?

In *Justice for Hedgehogs*, Dworkin records a change of attitude on his own part towards the connection between law and morality.[3] Whereas he had initially assumed that law and morals were different systems of norms, he subsequently rejected the 'two-systems picture', treating law as itself part of political morality. In the 'Model of Rules I', Dworkin had observed that, in addition to rules, law included justifying principles; in 'Model of Rules II', he denied that law and morality should be treated as wholly independent systems of norms.[4] He was not contending that 'the law' contains 'a fixed number of standards', including both rules and principles—he wished 'to oppose the idea that "the law" is a fixed set of standards of any sort' (Dworkin 1977: 76). Dworkin rejected, in particular, the idea that 'institutional support'—the statutes and precedents that may be taken to exemplify a purported legal principle— might amount to a 'rule of recognition' of the kind H.L.A. Hart defended.[5] While similar legal materials would feature in every lawyer's account of the requirements of law, their respective accounts would differ according to their divergent moral judgments. Each lawyer must develop a 'theory of law' that seeks to *justify* those legal materials; and each such theory would, in practice, be somewhat different from its rivals.

In an important respect, however, the amended version retains features of the 'two-systems' view, characteristic of legal positivism. Legal principles are those principles that serve to justify the adoption of 'all the rules that are plainly valid rules of law' in a certain jurisdiction, together with the 'explicit rules about institutional competence' invoked in identifying the other rules:

'a principle is a principle of law if it figures in the soundest theory of law that can be provided as a justification for the explicit substantive and institutional rules of the jurisdiction in question' (Dworkin 1977: 66). On this approach, the primary body of legal standards—those rules that all lawyers agree are valid, according to settled rules about institutional competence—enjoy a certain priority. A moral principle can have no claim to legal status—can play no legitimate role in adjudication—unless it is capable (in the view of the lawyer whose theory is pertinent) of justifying acknowledged legal rules. In any 'hard' case, in which the rules dictate no clear solution on their own, a judge must have resort to moral principles. He will not be free to exercise 'discretion' beyond the limits of the rules in the manner that legal positivists usually envisage.[6] But in ordinary cases, where the facts fall clearly within the terms of a legal rule, there will be little or no scope for moral judgment or controversy.

That general account of law and legal reasoning initially seems a good fit with the celebrated case of *Riggs v. Palmer*, on which Dworkin relies as a prime example.[7] Although in that case the principle that no one should be allowed to profit from his own wrong was applied to modify the literal terms of the Statute of Wills, in most cases the statute could be straightforwardly applied in accordance with its literal or ordinary meaning. Not only does a statutory rule have a canonical text, which lends it a precision that common law rules characteristically lack, but we may also suppose that only a quite unusual case will raise serious issues about whether an Act is subject to implicit exceptions, based on general moral principle: few cases will raise concerns as striking as those presented by the murdering heir. When our focus shifts, however, to the common law, by contrast with statute, Dworkin's stance looks more questionable—it is not so clear that we can identify uncontroversial rules whose meaning or scope is relatively detached from the moral principles that underpin and justify them. If common law rules are only summary generalizations of underlying general principles, subject to adaptation and revision in the light of fresh moral insight, the distinction between valid or accepted rules and morally justifying principles will all but disappear.

Certain passages in the 'Model of Rules I' support this latter approach, apparently undermining any real distinction between rule and principle. Dworkin asks us, for example, to consider what someone implies when he says that a particular rule is binding:

> He may imply that the rule is affirmatively supported by principles the court is not free to disregard, and which are collectively more weighty than other principles that argue for a change. If not, he implies that any change would be condemned by a combination of conservative principles of legislative supremacy

and precedent that the court is not free to ignore. Very often, he will imply both, for the conservative principles . . . are usually not powerful enough to save a common law rule or an aging statute that is entirely unsupported by substantive principles the court is bound to respect. (Dworkin 1977: 38)

On this view, a legal rule is only a convenient summary of the weight of relevant principles in a specific context, vulnerable to reassessment either in the light of (even small) changes to that context or in response to moral reappraisal. A rule is treated as 'nothing more than a device of convenience, a kind of *aide-memoire* for recording the perceived aggregate consequences of the various principles that bear on the resolution of a specific kind of dispute'.[8]

Stephen Perry interprets Dworkin's writing as the defence of a 'strong Burkean' conception of precedent, whereby a court is bound by a previous decision unless persuaded that there is a strong reason for overriding it. Lacking a canonical formulation, propositions of the common law are primarily determined by direct reference to underlying principles. They do not take the form of exclusionary rules, which possess a large degree of independence from their justifying reasons; nor is any previous formulation of underlying principles exclusionarily binding—the possibility of reconsidering the balance of justifying principles is typically left open.[9] The weight of any given proposition of law will be a function of many different factors, 'including the position in the judicial hierarchy of the courts that have relied upon the proposition in the past, the number of times that it has been so relied upon, and the age of the relevant precedents' (Perry 1987: 241). One should not conclude that the weight of a proposition is a determinate property fixed, at any given moment, independently of context: 'its weight is also relative to the position in the judicial hierarchy of whatever court is contemplating modifying it, as well as to the extent of the modification which is proposed' (Perry 1987: 242).

Perry helpfully distinguishes between the view of law as providing authoritative guidance by means of publicly ascertainable rules, characteristic of legal positivism, and the contrasting idea of law as 'the institutionalized adjudication and resolution of disputes in accordance with principles of justice or fairness' (215). While the expression 'the common law' may refer to the settled law as it currently exists, 'the more dominant and fundamental reference ... is to the dynamic, institutionalized process of rational dispute-settlement itself' (252). The body of settled law is only a 'by-product' of the common law process: 'it is never more than a weighted but nonetheless provisional approximation to those requirements of morality the determination and application of which constitute the ultimate obligation of the common law judge' (252). Perry suggests that this is the real basis for Dworkin's rejection of any picture of 'existing law' which treats it as a distinct collection of rules and principles, 'such that it is a sensible question to ask whether, at any given moment, a particular rule or principle belongs to that collection' (Dworkin 1977: 343).

In distinguishing between statute and common law, in his essay 'Hard Cases', Dworkin rightly gives pride of place to *precedent* as opposed to common law rules. It is the precedent decisions themselves—the outcome of specific legal disputes—that must be justified by recourse to general principle. He observes, in distinguishing common law adjudication from statutory interpretation, that 'judges often disagree not simply about how some rule or principle should be interpreted, but whether the rule or principle one judge cites should be acknowledged to be a rule or principle at all' (Dworkin 1977: 112). Even when both majority and dissenting opinions in a case recognize the same earlier cases as relevant, they may 'disagree about what rule or principle these precedents should be understood to have established' (112). Earlier decisions exert a 'gravitational force' on later ones, even when that force is controversial; such gravitational force is explained by the fairness of treating like cases alike: 'A precedent is the report of an earlier political decision; the very fact of that decision, as a piece of political history, provides some reason for deciding other cases in a similar way in the future' (113).

While an important dimension of political morality, the fairness of treating like cases alike may be offset, nevertheless, by contrary reasons. If that requirement of consistency is relatively weak, readily displaced by other considerations of justice, there is no real separation between law and morality—what may seem at first sight to be two distinct sets of norms are really only one, law being a (barely distinguishable) department of morality. If, on the contrary, the 'doctrine of precedent' is understood to place strong fetters on judges' freedom to depart from earlier decisions—to reach conclusions incompatible with the outcome of previous cases—then law and morality retain a real degree of separation. It is, of course, a matter of degree: even a relatively rigid doctrine of precedent would be likely to permit overruling in certain instances, if only by a higher court. Although a distinction of degree, it is nonetheless important. Does a common law judge attempt to do justice, as she understands it, treating precedent largely as an initial guide to correct decision? Or does she—or should she—rather attempt to make the best sense she can of previous decisions, even if that means invoking rules or principles she considers morally suspect? Is the requirement of consistency—like cases decided alike—simply a requirement of justice, whose weight varies according to any countervailing considerations of justice that may arise? Or is it rather an entrenched feature of common law practice that gives way to such countervailing considerations only in quite exceptional cases, perhaps when there is a strong judicial consensus that change or reform is urgently required?

Although statutory interpretation is distinguished by the existence of a canonical text, whose specific terms a court must construe, Dworkin identifies the law with the rule that emerges from consideration of the policies or principles that best explain and justify that text.[10] A hard case, at least, calls for an investigation of constitutional theory to explain the power of any statute to alter legal rights—a theory that will impose on the legislature certain responsibilities to advance the general welfare and respect individual rights. The correct interpretation of the statute is the one that best ties its language to the legislature's constitutional duties: 'It calls for the construction, not of some hypothesis about the mental state of particular legislators, but of a special political theory that justifies this statute, in the light of the legislature's more general responsibilities, better than any alternative theory' (Dworkin 1977: 108). Dworkin emphasizes how great a role the canonical terms of the statute play in the interpretative process—they 'provide a limit to what must otherwise be, in the nature of the case, unlimited' (109). But the moral and political convictions of the judge are plainly crucial: they serve to identify a meaning that makes sense of the statute as the product of a deliberative process aimed at fair and just governance (Dworkin 1986: 316, 377–47). Statutory interpretation can, then, be assimilated to the strong Burkean conception of common law reasoning.[11]

In *Law's Empire*, the focus is on *propositions* of law, rather than rules; and that terminology reflects the inherently controversial nature of legal argument, grounded in moral judgment.[12] Lawyers may agree about the grounds of law—the more general propositions in virtue of which specific legal propositions are true or false—but disagree about whether they are satisfied in a particular case (an 'empirical disagreement'). Or they may disagree about the grounds of law themselves—what Dworkin calls 'theoretical disagreement' (1986: 4–5). Legal practice is *argumentative*: 'Every actor in the practice understands that what it permits or requires depends on the truth of certain propositions that are given sense only by and within the practice; the practice consists in large part in deploying and arguing about these propositions' (13). If the judges disagreed in *Riggs v. Palmer*, it was not in consequence of any ambiguity or vagueness in the language of the Statute of Wills. They held different theories of statutory interpretation—different opinions about how to distinguish the 'real' statute from its official text: 'they disagreed about how to construct the real statute in the special circumstances of that case' (17).

Dworkin distinguishes, in *Law's Empire*, between a strict doctrine of precedent, which obliges a judge to follow earlier decisions (especially of higher courts) even if he thinks them wrongly decided, and a more relaxed doctrine, which 'demands only that a judge give some weight to past decisions on the same issue, that he must follow these unless he thinks them sufficiently wrong to outweigh the initial presumption in their favour' (24–5). Not only does opinion about the strength of this presumption vary from jurisdiction to jurisdiction, but it will vary within a jurisdiction: 'Differences of opinion about the character of the strict doctrine and the force of the relaxed doctrine explain why some lawsuits are controversial. Different judges in the same case disagree about whether they are obliged to follow some past decision on exactly the question of law they now face' (26).

It is reasonable to suppose that the demands of precedent will normally be thought more stringent for lower court judges, expected or bound to follow the guidance of higher court decisions. Even if the requirement of consistency is only a general requirement of justice, vulnerable to displacement by strong countervailing considerations of justice, that requirement is especially powerful at lower levels of the judiciary. It is important that, as far as possible, a litigant's chances of success should not depend on the outlook of the judge assigned to his case: a substantial degree of consistency is an aspect of genuine equality before the law.[13] Even a lower court judge can sometimes escape the fetters of established authority by distinguishing the current case; but the relevant distinctions must not (or not normally) threaten the coherence of existing doctrine.

From their privileged position in the hierarchy, however, higher courts can develop legal doctrine more freely, confident that any changes or adjustments will be followed by the courts below, preserving consistency at least for present and future litigants. Moreover, changes to legal doctrine can be justified as improving consistency of decision-making in the sense of overall coherence: modifications to one line of precedent are made to reflect developments in doctrine elsewhere. Cases have gravitational force, Dworkin explains, because the rights thesis holds: judicial decisions are justified by arguments of principle, which together impose a general scheme of justice. Hercules (Dworkin's model judge) must treat the law as if it were a seamless web: 'He must construct a scheme of abstract and concrete principles that provides a coherent justification for all common law precedents and, so far as these are to be justified on principle, constitutional and statutory provisions as well' (1977: 116–17).

—•—

For judges in higher courts, then, while precedent serves as a guide to correct decision-making, it will scarcely impel what seems to be a grossly unjust result in any particular case. If a pertinent line of precedent leads to unpalatable conclusions, it can usually be modified by reference to other, related areas of law where the applicable rules are a better reflection of moral principle. The more offensive is a dubious precedent to a judge's sense of justice, the larger the territory he can explore in order to distinguish or overrule it: it can be isolated as a deviant decision, making a rent in the seamless web. Hercules is entitled to disregard certain elements of institutional history as mistaken, even if a scheme of principle 'that designates part of what is to be justified as mistaken is prima facie weaker than one that does not' (Dworkin 1977: 122). That scheme of principle may still be stronger overall. If some previous decision, whether statute or precedent, is now widely regretted within the legal profession, it is vulnerable to review. Dworkin supposes that judges should defer, to a degree, to 'the community's own concept of fairness'; but considerations of fairness must ultimately yield to justice (122–3).

There is, however, a certain ambiguity in Dworkin's discussion. It is clear that a judge must be guided by statute and precedent, and in that sense find the law of his own community, correctly interpreted. In the process of interpretation, the judge will draw deeply on his own moral and political convictions: only his own moral compass can enable him to discriminate, as he must, between rival accounts of institutional history. What is less clear is whether a judge may (or must) repudiate previous political decisions that, in his considered view, cannot be justified by reference to any acceptable principles of justice. May he distinguish as vulnerable a particular decision, whether statute or judicial decision, on the ground that, though *not* widely regretted—either within the legal profession or outside it—it is gravely unjust by his own standards of justice? How far may a judge strike out on his own, challenging the general consensus?

It is part of Dworkin's thesis that, though legal rights and moral rights are not 'conceptually distinct', contrary to the positivist view, there can nonetheless be conflict between legal and moral rights, at least in despotic countries like Nazi Germany and the former South Africa, under apartheid (326). While 'background moral rights' are pertinent 'when the standard materials provide uncertain guidance', in some cases 'the institutional right is clearly settled by established legal materials, like a statute, and clearly conflicts with background moral rights'. Here the judge confronts a dilemma, which jurisprudence must faithfully report:

> In these cases the judge seeking to do what is morally right is faced with a familiar sort of conflict: the institutional right provides a genuine reason, the importance of which will vary with the general justice or wickedness of the system as a whole, for a decision one way, but certain considerations of morality

present an important reason against it. If the judge decides that the reasons supplied by background moral rights are so strong that he has a moral duty to do what he can to support these rights, then it may be that he must lie, because he cannot be of any help unless he is understood as saying, in his official role, that the legal rights are different from what he believes they are. (326–7)

The reference to despotic regimes suggests that such conflicts are unlikely to arise in a liberal democracy; but, if so, this may be a conceptual implication of Dworkin's thesis rather than a merely empirical observation. In a wicked system, which the judge deplores, the institutional right based on the 'standard materials' will presumably carry little if any moral weight. But in a generally just system, to which the judge is fully committed, that right will possess much greater moral force. That greater force, however, derives from the contribution of the relevant legal materials to a broadly just scheme; and that overall scheme will limit the scope for injustice within its integral parts. A purported rule giving rise, in any particular case, to grave injustice—something so offensive as to provoke a judge to question the limits of his official duty—would itself be suspect. It would arguably be a hard case, in which the judge would seek an interpretation (or re-interpretation) of law consistent with the standards of justice that endow the system with the moral authority he takes it to enjoy. Even if a lower court judge were constrained by precedent—perhaps a decision endorsing an interpretation of statute he deplores—his more senior colleagues would be free to deny that the law, correctly understood, authorized iniquity.

Of course, a judge's own standards of justice cannot diverge too far from those of other members of the community—especially, the legal community—or he would be unable to offer a recognizable account of institutional history. If too many decisions must be dismissed as mistakes, or be reinterpreted along radical lines that shocked judicial colleagues, the judge's good faith or competence would be called into question. Within those rather elastic limits, however, he may simply be more creative than his colleagues—more willing to test previous practice by reference to fresh moral insight (as Lord Denning was famously adept at challenging established precedent).[14] As Dworkin remarks, in respect of a judge's ability to expand the range of interpretation beyond the area of law immediately in point, sometimes 'the expansion will be deliberate and controversial' (1986: 246). Lawyers celebrate many decisions of that kind, 'including several on which the modern law of negligence was built'.

Dworkin says in *Law's Empire* that the 'brute facts of legal history' will limit the role a judge's personal moral convictions can play; but since any such facts obtain their significance via *interpretation*, that claim is very doubtful. The legal record will obstruct (rather than stimulate) a judge's moral deliberations about the present content of law only insofar as it threatens the possibility of any plausible interpretation, consistent with his loyalty to a morally decent regime. If institutional history inhibits the acknowledgement of any moral obligation of obedience—the system is too wicked to inspire allegiance—the judge is a sceptic, who denies the claims of integrity.[15] He is like Judge Siegfried in Nazi Germany, who (we imagine) despises the system in which he works:

> We might decide that the interpretive attitude is wholly inappropriate there, that the practice, in the shape it has reached, can never provide any justification at all, even a weak one, for state coercion. Then we will think that in every case Siegfried should simply ignore legislation and precedent altogether, if he can get away with it, or otherwise do the best he can to limit injustice through whatever means are available to him.[16]

An interpreter must have convictions about both fit and justification, which are relatively independent of one another: the former must not adjust too easily to the latter, which would allow justice automatically to override history. And an initial threshold requirement will eliminate otherwise preferable interpretations:

> Convictions about fit will provide a rough threshold requirement that an interpretation of some part of the law must meet if it is to be eligible at all. Any plausible working theory would disqualify an interpretation of our own law that denied legislative competence or supremacy outright or that claimed a general principle of private law requiring the rich to share their wealth with the poor. (Dworkin 1986: 255)

That 'rough threshold requirement' is clearly very weak: it appears to exclude only purported interpretations of the sort that suggests bad faith or gross incompetence. Moreover, different judges will set the threshold differently; they will have different convictions about the demands of fit.

Dworkin suggests that hard cases arise only when a judge's threshold test 'does not discriminate between two or more interpretations of some statute or line of cases'. 'Then he must choose between eligible interpretations by asking which shows the community's structure of institutions and decisions—its public standards as a whole—in a better light from the standpoint of political morality. His own moral and political convictions are now directly engaged' (Dworkin 1986: 256).

Admittedly, that engagement is complex, sometimes setting 'one department of his political morality against another': considerations of both justice and fairness must be appropriately weighed. Moreover, questions of fit arise

again 'because even when an interpretation survives the threshold requirement, any infelicities of fit will count against it . . . in the general balance of
political virtues' (256).

However, the threshold test, as Dworkin describes it, seems far too weak
to distinguish hard from easy cases in that way. Dworkin's analysis here suggests that moral judgment is necessary only in rather unusual cases, when
the 'brute facts of legal history' do not conclude the matter in a manner
that makes interpretation unnecessary. If, however, the threshold test excludes
only plainly ineligible interpretations—accounts of institutional history that
no one would for a moment treat seriously—moral and political convictions
will be in play from the outset. They will be an essential guide to the merits of
a range of possible readings of the legal record, all of which will pass any initial test of fit: moral judgment will exclude potential interpretations as readily
as criteria of fit. A construction of statute or precedent that does not represent
a close approximation, at least, to principles of justice—principles that the
interpreter recognizes and honours as genuine demands of morality—would
not be eligible for serious consideration. That unpalatable reading would be
excluded from the start. It would flout the very raison d'être of integrity—the
treatment of law as a scheme of justice capable of generating genuine moral
rights, which ought to be enforced.

Compare Dworkin's treatment of the distinction between hard and easy
cases, as one that might be thought to challenge the interpretative apparatus
of integrity:

> Law as integrity explains and justifies easy cases as well as hard ones; it also
> shows why they are easy. It is obvious that the speed limit in California is fifty
> five because it is obvious that any competent interpretation of California traf-
> fic law must yield that conclusion. So easy cases are, for law as integrity, only
> special cases of hard ones . . . (Dworkin 1986: 266)

If, then, easy cases are settled on the basis of any threshold requirement
of fit, it is only because alternative answers strongly suggest bad faith or
incompetence. The interpretative basis of the decision is assumed rather than
explored; and moral and political convictions can for that reason only lie
dormant. If a lawyer whose good faith and competence are not in question
does persuade us to reconsider our view, we engage with his arguments only
by recourse to our own moral and political convictions, which explain the
difference between our respective conclusions:

> We think the question whether someone may legally drive faster than the stipu-
> lated speed limit is an easy one because we assume at once that no account of

the legal record that denied that paradigm would be competent. But someone whose convictions about justice and fairness were very different from
ours might not find that question so easy; even if he ended by agreeing with
our answer, he would insist that we were wrong to be so confident. (Dworkin
1986: 354)

Contrary, then, to the initial impression given by Dworkin's talk of
threshold requirements of fit, the interpreter's moral judgment is engaged
throughout. If a specific account of statute or precedent (or of legislative or
judicial authority) is rejected, it will be because moral judgment excludes it:
the pertinent treatment of legal sources or powers is inconsistent with the
moral and political principles that (in our own view) animate and underpin
any plausible or acceptable interpretation. Easy cases are only those whose
solution most of us readily agree on in the light of our shared convictions
about the relevant political values. If we deny any scope for controversy, it is
because we *share* the consensus, not because (as Dworkin sometimes seems
to suggest) we are *bound* by the consensus, contrary to our own individual
moral convictions.

Dworkin readily concedes that 'the different aspects or dimensions of
a judge's working approach—the dimensions of fit and substance, and of
different aspects of substance—are in the last analysis all responsive to his
political judgment' (1986: 257). A judge's convictions about fit are 'political
not mechanical', expressing his commitment to integrity:

> [H]e believes that an interpretation that falls below his threshold of fit shows
> the record of the community in an irredeemably bad light, because proposing
> that interpretation suggests that the community has characteristically dishon-
> oured its own principles. When an interpretation meets the threshold, remain-
> ing defects of fit may be compensated, in his overall judgment, if the principles
> of that interpretation are particularly attractive, because then he sets off the
> community's infrequent lapses in respecting these principles against its virtue
> in generally observing them. (257)

But there is no genuine threshold of fit, detached from the judge's moral
judgment; so there can be no question of the community dishonouring 'its
own principles'. If an interpretation is ineligible on grounds of fit alone, it is
only because the legal record is so abysmal that it resists any morally attractive
construction. The interpreter is unable to propose an account that is both
faithful to institutional history and capable of supplying moral justification:
he is a sceptic, denying that the ideal of integrity applies. If an interpretation is
plausible, meeting minimum standards of fit, it exemplifies the community's

principles on that understanding. If it is *not* plausible because the legal record is quite abhorrent, then the principles dishonoured are those of the (would-be) interpreter, who deplores what he beholds.

———

I am not, of course, denying that an interpretation must apply independent criteria of fit and justification; a genuine interpretation must reflect the historical record as well as the interpreter's moral convictions. Any legal interpretation must be able to justify the results of many, if not most, of the leading cases, as well as showing how statutory enactments can be given a sense at least broadly consistent with the language they employ. Criteria of fit, however, are as much a matter of moral judgment as those of substantive justification: 'The constraint fit imposes on substance, in any working theory, is therefore the constraint of one type of political conviction on another in the overall judgment which interpretation makes a political record the best it can be overall, everything taken into account' (Dworkin 1986: 257). And Dworkin rightly adds that the mode of this constraint 'is not the constraint of external hard fact or of interpersonal consensus', even if his language elsewhere may sometimes suggest the opposite. It is, instead, 'the structural constraint of different kinds of principle within a system of principle, and it is nonetheless genuine for that' (257). But a system of principle, if it is one we can endorse, must preclude judicial decisions that would violate its moral foundations—*lex iniusta non est lex*.

These conclusions are strengthened by reflection on what Dworkin says about the role of paradigms—concrete examples 'any plausible interpretation must fit' (Dworkin 1986: 72). Argument against an interpretation (of a social practice) will usually try to show that it fails to account for a paradigm case, though even if successful such a critique is not conclusive: 'Paradigms anchor interpretations, but no paradigm is secure from challenge by a new interpretation that accounts for other paradigms better and leaves that one isolated as a mistake' (72). It follows that a competent lawyer may challenge any rule or doctrine, however well-established or deeply rooted, on the basis of a novel interpretation which, overall, provides an attractive account of institutional history and practice:

> Someone who denies that the traffic code is law does not contradict himself, nor does he speak thoughts no one can understand. We understand him only too well, and it is not inconceivable (though it is unlikely) that he will be able to defend his view through a radical reinterpretation of legal practice that is

otherwise so appealing that it persuades us to abandon what was formerly a cardinal paradigm (92).

If British lawyers agree that a duly enacted Act of Parliament necessarily determines the law, according to its plain terms, their agreement may reflect a consensus of conviction rather than convention; its basis lies in a shared sense of what political morality requires: 'The consensus will last only so long as most lawyers accept the convictions that support it' (136). Judicial attitudes to statutory interpretation and doctrines of precedent have changed significantly over time in response to arguments made within the context of adjudication. Unlike the rules of a game, which cannot normally be changed in the course of play, lawyers may question the demands of precedent or the nature of legislative intentions as part of their argument in court:

> The interpretive attitude needs paradigms to function effectively, but these need not be matters of convention. It will be sufficient if the level of agreement in conviction is high enough at any given time to allow debate over fundamental practices like legislation and precedent to proceed [as described] . . . contesting discrete paradigms one by one, like the reconstruction of Neurath's boat one plank at a time at sea. (138–9)

A lawyer may fail to persuade anyone that his own interpretation of law is correct; but he remains free to argue for his own position, confronting his colleagues with what he regards as the deficiencies of rival interpretations. Unless he succumbs to scepticism—abandoning the effort to defend an appealing account, adequate at least to justify continuing allegiance—he may continue to contest influential opinions, challenging their moral credentials as well as their technical competence. If he thinks either the prevailing consensus or an authoritative ruling on which it relies is intolerable—condemned by principles of justice he is unwilling to sacrifice—he will deny its truth or soundness. Its denial of justice, as he understands that value, destroys its authority as law.[17]

Dworkin's talk of 'thresholds' of fit and 'brute facts of legal history' are misleading insofar as they suggest—if only to the unwary—that an interpreter's recourse to his own judgments of political morality may be sharply constrained, whether by historical fact or prevailing consensus. While a lawyer whose convictions were radically at odds with the general ethos or spirit of legal practice would be driven to scepticism—denying the possibility of a morally acceptable construction—the committed interpreter defends an account of the legal record that does, in his own judgment, justify legal practice. And that account must deny the truth of egregiously unjust propositions of law, which would breach the first principles of the legal order, as the inter-preter understands it.

Legal practice may, of course, fall far short of perfection: it may authorize rules or decisions that justice condemns. No one can expect legal practice to conform precisely to his own conception of perfect justice: justice must give way (as Dworkin explains) to fairness, so that the law is a fair reflection of diverse opinions across the community. But justice gives way to fairness only to the extent that each interpreter thinks appropriate; integrity rests on find-ing an attractive accommodation between these competing values, according to context. Lawyers and judges will have different conceptions of fairness, as regards the role of other people's opinions about which principles of justice should be enforced; and they will have 'different higher-level opinions about the best resolution of conflicts between these two political ideals' (Dworkin 1986: 250). But no one is bound to defer to majority will in favour of a measure he deplores as irredeemably wicked. He would think such a mea-sure invalid on the criteria integrity supplies: considerations of fairness are overridden by those of justice, fundamental to (any plausible conception of) equal respect.

Integrity demands that everyone is treated with equal concern and respect: 'It requires government to speak with one voice, to act in a principled and coherent manner toward all its citizens, to extend to everyone the substantive standards of justice and fairness it uses for some' (165). A political society that endorses the ideal of integrity becomes thereby a genuine community, having the moral authority to deploy a monopoly of coercive force. Integrity denies that law is only a matter of 'negotiated solutions to discrete problems, with no underlying commitment to any more fundamental public conception of justice' (189). It seeks fusion between citizens' moral and political lives: 'it asks the good citizen, deciding how to treat his neighbour when their interests conflict, to interpret the common scheme of justice to which they are both committed just in virtue of citizenship' (189–90). When citizens interpret their mutual responsibilities in this way, those responsibilities qualify as genu-inely fraternal; people have associative obligations: 'The responsibilities a true community deploys are special and individualized and display a pervasive mutual concern that fits a plausible conception of equal concern' (201).

Departures from justice must, therefore, not be so great as to deny, in the interpreter's own opinion, any 'plausible conception of equal concern'. When very serious injustice is characteristic of a legal order, it will frustrate the con-struction of an account of law capable of justifying the state's deployment of coercion. No morally decent interpretation will fit. But even particular, if untypical, instances of serious injustice or oppression may threaten the coherence of an eligible interpretation. Either such instances are unlawful breaches of the fundamental principles that integrity protects; or, if legally authorized, they undermine the credibility of a morally attractive interpretation overall. They deny the plausibility of the relevant conception of equal concern. Occupying a 'moral middle ground' between mere consistency, on the one hand, and true justice, on the other, equal concern rules out the treatment of any person or group in a manner that no recognizable or tolerable account of justice would countenance.[18] It follows, contrary to Dworkin's view, that political obligation is *not* merely prima facie, capable of being overridden by independent considerations of justice.[19] In the context of integrity, associative obligation is normally conclusive: the relevant considerations of justice have already played their crucial role in guiding—and prescribing the conditions of—the interpretative construction of the content of law.[20]

Each lawyer, indeed each citizen, must take moral responsibility for her own determination of the content of law: 'Political obligation is ... not just a matter of obeying the discrete political decisions of the community one by one, as political philosophers usually represent it. It becomes a more protestant idea: fidelity to a scheme of principle each citizen has a responsibility to identify, ultimately for himself, as his community's scheme' (Dworkin 1986: 190).

That protestantism is scarcely consistent with subjection to a moral consensus that the citizen rejects. She can discharge her political obligation only by reflective adherence to a scheme of legal and moral principle whose merits (in her own opinion) *justify* her allegiance. Her ability to interpret that scheme as a broadly, if not perfectly, just legal and constitutional order is critical to her continued allegiance. The limits of that ability are themselves the boundaries of fit. If her best interpretative efforts fail to redeem a lamentable institutional record—too many political decisions must be dismissed as 'mistakes', infringing fundamental principles—she has perforce become a sceptic. There are no redeeming moral principles that fit.

In a wicked regime, where institutional rights have little or no moral force, such rights (if they exist) may depend on unjust principles, which morality condemns. No morally acceptable principle will satisfy the threshold test of fit; and Dworkin's general theory 'must endorse some unattractive principle as providing the best justification of institutional history, presenting the judge with a legal decision and also, perhaps, a moral problem' (1977: 342). Dworkin rejects the suggestion that legal principles are always sound or correct moral principles, though they must be moral principles in *form*, by contrast with, for example, 'prudential judgments or historical generalizations' (343). It is doubtful, however, whether that view is consistent with the idea of law as integrity, as Dworkin later develops it. We can offer what is only in *form* a moral principle, for example, 'the principle that blacks are less worthy of concern than whites'—to explain the conduct or attitudes of others. It might show why judges in a wicked regime behave as if there were institutional rights that required enforcement. But no such principle (or alleged principle) could provide even the smallest shred of *justification*; nor could it function within any interpretative theory we might apply, in the spirit of integrity, to the pertinent legal record. Within the interpretative enterprise of Dworkinian integrity, a legal principle must be a genuine moral principle—one that the interpreter embraces as affording real moral justification for the state's previous political decisions.[21]

A judge who administers law in a wicked regime that he despises is somewhat analogous to a lower court judge in a morally decent regime, when the latter is confronted by an offensive statute or precedent, incompatible (in his view) with the basic principle of equal concern and respect, but which a higher court nonetheless affirms. Either the lower court judge must insist on an understanding of legislative supremacy or *stare decisis* that allows him, perhaps exceptionally, to disagree; or else he must lie about the true content of law (or resign his office). If he thinks the statute or precedent too grossly unjust to follow, it is too unjust *in virtue of the principles of morality that lie at the foundations of the legal order*, when correctly understood. He dissents from his judicial colleagues, whether on the first-order legal issue or the second-order questions of authority, in the spirit of integrity—calling in aid the principles of justice critical to the legitimacy of the legal order.[22] The only other option is to abandon the internal point of view, becoming an external critic: his lies are those of an impostor judge—an 'internal' sceptic—not the actual moral conclusions of a real judge, who keeps faith with the system he administers.

If a common law judge must enforce the law according to 'inclusive' rather than 'pure' integrity, as Dworkin argues, the latter is nonetheless his lodestar: he seeks to do justice according to the principles that animate the tradition he serves.[23] Hercules is prevented from achieving pure integrity—coherence in the principles of justice that inform his interpretation of law—because he must defer, when appropriate, to principles of fairness and due process. Legislative supremacy may oblige him to enforce statutes that produce substantive incoherence; strict doctrines of precedent may stand in the way of overall coherence. And the doctrine of 'local priority' restricts his freedom of manoeuvre: his judgments about the boundaries of departments of law 'must in principle respect settled professional and public opinions that divide law into substantial areas of public and private conduct' (1986: 403). None of these various constraints, however, need be impenetrable barriers to fundamental justice—respect for the equal dignity of persons. Their force varies according to the gravity of the threat to basic human or constitutional rights. Inclusive integrity is only pure integrity adapted to take account of moral commitments to fairness and due process, according to their respective weights in all the circumstances.

***

Ronald Dworkin's exploration of adjudication provides fascinating insight into the complexity of the interconnections between law and justice. It obliges us to recognize the artificiality of any conception of adjudication that banishes moral judgment to the margins: we must affirm the centrality of moral judgment to any determination of the content of law in particular cases. I have argued, nonetheless, that Dworkin leaves unresolved an important tension between divergent understandings of that broader insight. While the dominant theme is that the content of law is a matter of moral conviction rather than convention, there remain discordant elements. Is legal judgment ultimately a matter of moral conviction, in the sense that an interpreter must adhere at all costs to her own understanding of the scheme of justice that lends the law overall coherence? Or must she sometimes compromise that scheme of justice in obedience to authoritative statute or precedent incompatible (in her own view) with fundamental requirements of equal respect and concern? Does adherence to integrity *permit* such compromise; and if not, must she sometimes override integrity itself? And can she retain her personal or professional integrity while infringing legal or political integrity—inclusive integrity, responsive to legitimate claims of fairness and due process?[24] A Supreme court judge enjoys a greater latitude with respect to precedent than his lower court colleague; there is more scope for reinterpretation or repudiation of unjust rules. If, however, law is ultimately a matter of moral conviction, it is hard to see why either judge—if committed to integrity—should ever have to lie about what, in his opinion, is the true content of the law.

Notes and References

1. The idea of integrity, as the characteristic virtue of law, is developed in Ronald Dworkin. 1986. *Law's Empire*. London: Fontana Press.
2. Compare A.W.B. Simpson. 1973. 'The Common Law and Legal Theory', in Simpson (ed.), *Oxford Essays in Jurisprudence*, 2nd series. Oxford: Clarendon Press. pp. 77–99 at 90: 'As a system of legal thought the common law . . . is inherently vague; it is a feature of the system that uniquely authentic statements

of the rules which, so positivists tell us, comprise the common law, cannot be made' (90). I treat legal positivism as the thesis that, being dependent on the contingent content of authoritative sources, law may not reflect the demands of moral principle: a legal rule may be both valid and gravely unjust.

3. Ronald Dworkin. 2011. *Justice for Hedgehogs*. Cambridge, Mass.: Harvard University Press. p. 402.

4. Ronald Dworkin. 1977. *Taking Rights Seriously*. London: Duckworth. Chapters 2 and 3.

5. For the rule of recognition, see H.L.A. Hart. 1994. *The Concept of Law*, 2nd Edition. Oxford: Clarendon Press. Chapter 6.

6. Dworkin denies that judges exercise discretion in the 'strong' sense of unrestricted choice, as opposed to 'weak' discretion in the sense of *judgment* (1977: 31–9).

7. *Riggs v. Palmer* 22 NE 188 (1889): a man who had murdered his grandfather in order to secure his inheritance was denied any right to receive it under the grandfather's will.

8. Perry, Stephen. 1987. 'Judicial Obligation, Precedent and the Common Law', *Oxford Journal of Legal Studies*. 7(2). pp. 215–57 at 225.

9. Perry considers in detail how far common law precedent is susceptible to an analysis in terms of Joseph Raz's idea of exclusionary rules, concluding that it resists such an analysis. For Raz's own account of adjudication, see Joseph Raz. 1979. *The Authority of Law: Essays on Law and Morality*. Oxford: Clarendon Press. Chapter 10.

10. For the distinction between policy and principle, see Dworkin 1977: 22 and Dworkin 1986: pp. 222–4, 242–4.

11. Compare Perry, 'Judicial Obligation, Precedent and the Common Law', p. 256: 'The univocal nature of *stare decisis* is thus accounted for, but without collapsing the theoretical distinction between statutory enactments and propositions of the common law: the former represent rules that have been created by particular legislative acts, whereas the latter represent direct judicial approximations of the requirements of justice and other relevant dimensions of morality'.

12. Perry observes, however, that judges characteristically speak of being bound by *cases* rather than propositions, which is 'consistent with the idea that second-order weighting principles ultimately apply not to propositions as such but to sets of first-order principles, where the actual degree of weighting is determined by what has been done in previous cases' (Perry 1987: 243).

13. The administration of justice according to a consistent and coherent body of principles is required by Dworkin's doctrine of political responsibility, which 'presupposes that articulated consistency, decisions in accordance with a program that can be made public and followed until changed, is essential to any conception of justice' (*Taking Rights Seriously*, p. 162).

14. See especially Lord Denning. 1979. *The Discipline of Law*. London: Butterworths.

15. Dworkin distinguishes between internal scepticism, which rejects the possibility of a successful (morally attractive) interpretation, and external scepticism, which

is a metaphysical theory about the philosophical standing of any interpretative claim: Dworkin, *Law's Empire*, pp. 78–85, 266–71.

16. Dworkin, *Law's Empire*, p. 105. Dworkin argues that, in some cases, we may think people do have legal rights, based on protected expectations, which 'survive rather than depend on our interpretive judgments of the system as a whole' (Dworkin, *Law's Empire*, p. 106). In such cases there is plainly no reliance on integrity: the rights enforced reflect, instead, what Dworkin calls 'conventionalism'.

17. For further argument, see Allan. 2009. 'Law, Justice and Integrity: The Paradox of Wicked Laws', *Oxford Journal of Legal Studies* 29. pp. 705–28.

18. Stephen Perry. 2006. 'Associative Obligations and the Obligation to Obey the Law' in Scott Hershovitz, *Exploring Law's Empire: The Jurisprudence of Ronald Dworkin*. Oxford: Oxford University Press. p. 199: 'Integrity . . . is not just a matter of sincerity or plausibility or coherence, but has genuine moral content. That content is provided by the concept of equal concern, which occupies a moral middle ground between simple consistency on the one hand, and true justice, on the other.'

19. While Dworkin connects the questions of political obligation and the concept of law, he also distinguishes between the 'grounds' and 'force' of law in a way that supposes (in the customary manner) that legal and political obligation may conflict in particular instances: see *Law's Empire*, pp. 108–13.

20. For detailed argument, see Allan, 'Law, Justice and Integrity', above. Dworkin's view that the Fugitive Slave Acts were part of antebellum United States law, despite their manifest iniquity, must be open to serious doubt (see *Law's Empire*, p. 219).

21. For a powerful argument that only correct moral principles have genuine weight, capable of justifying a judicial decision, see Larry Alexander and Ken Kress, 'Against Legal Principles', in Andrei Marmor. 1995. *Law and Interpretation: Essays in Legal Philosophy*. Oxford: Clarendon Press. Chapter 8. That view, if correct, sharply narrows the gap, if any, between integrity and justice (when justice takes full account of expectations generated by previous practice). But see also Stephen R Perry. 1997. 'Two Models of Legal Principles', *Iowa Law Review* 82. pp. 787–819, distinguishing between 'rationalization' and 'primacy' models of legal principles.

22. Compare Gerald J. Postema. 1997. 'Integrity: Justice in Workclothes', *Iowa Law Review* 82. pp. 821–55, identifying integrity with the 'justice-approximating principles' to which we are committed 'in virtue of our past collective decisions' (835).

23. For the distinction between pure and inclusive integrity, see Dworkin, *Law's Empire*, pp. 404–7.

24. Dworkin draws an explicit parallel between personal and political integrity in *Law's Empire*, p. 166. Dworkin argues, however, that integrity 'does not necessarily have the last word about how the coercive power of the state should be used' (219).

5

Taking (Human) Dignity and Rights Seriously

The Integrated Legal, Moral, and Political Philosophy of Ronald Dworkin*

Imer B. Flores

'So act as to treat humanity, whether in thine own person or in that of any
other, in every case as an end withal, never as a means only.'
    —Immanuel Kant, *Fundamental Principles of the Metaphysic of Morals*.[1]

'Taking (human) dignity and rights seriously' is at the core of Ronald Dworkin's
integrated legal, moral, and political philosophy. Dworkin developed an

* Revised and adapted version of a paper prepared to be presented at McMaster
Philosophy of Law Conference 'The Legacy of Ronald Dworkin', 30 May to 1 June
2014 in Burlington, Ontario (Canada), and published as I.B. Flores, 'The Legacy of
Ronald Dworkin (1931–2013): A Legal Theory and Methodology for Hedgehogs,
Hercules, and One Right Answer', *Problema. Anuario de Filosofía y Teoría del Derecho*,
9: 157–92. Later versions (or parts) were presented in Conferences and Seminars in
Brazil and in Mexico. I am grateful to Edgar Aguilera, Catarina Barbieri, Richard

original integrated theory with its distinctive first-order methodology, which not only has transcended the Natural Law and Legal Positivism dichotomy, but also has re-integrated law into a branch of political morality. He advocated a liberal theory based on (human) dignity and rights, appealed to the unity of value and shielded his theory from the foxy causes usually associated with scepticism, subjectivism, relativism, and pluralism.

In the first section, I will examine Dworkin's challenge to what appeared to be the 'ruling legal theory', which comprehends two parts, that is, a theory of 'what law is' and a theory of 'what law ought to be', and insists on their 'independence'. In the second section, I will reconsider the main legal theories and methodologies available for jurists following the distinctions not only amid general and particular but also between descriptive/explanatory and normative/justificatory, as well as the possibility of a more comprehensive or even integrated theory. In the third section, I will re-examine Dworkin's theory and his methodology, which can be characterized as: (a) constructive, (b) interpretive, (c) evaluative, and (d) integrative. In the fourth section, I will review Dworkin's conception of (human) dignity and rights, with a special emphasis on how he constructs—and even re-constructs—the ethical and moral analogues of two political principles and some of their applications; and, in the last section, as a way of conclusion, I will revisit a further variant of the drowning swimmer case.

Ronald Dworkin's Challenge

As advanced in the 'Introduction' to his celebrated *Taking Rights Seriously*, Dworkin aimed to 'define and defend a liberal theory of law' by being sharply critical of another theory widely thought to be liberal, that is, the 'ruling theory of law', which 'has two parts and insists on their independence'. The first part is a 'theory about what law is', that is, 'the theory of legal positivism, which holds that the truth of legal propositions consists in facts about rules that have been adopted by specific social institutions, and in nothing else'.

Bellamy, Thomas Bustamante, Enrique Cáceres, Jorge Fabra, Klaus Gunther, Kenneth E. Himma, Dimitrios Kyritsis, Ronaldo Macedo, Lokendra Malik, Daniel Mendonca, Alejandro Nava, Dan Priel, Gonzalo Ramírez, Luciana Reis, Verónica Rodríguez-Blanco, Ezequiel Spector, and Juan Vega, for their comments and challenging questions; to Roberto A. Cabrera y Rodríguez and Mariana Treviño for helpful research assistance; and, especially, to Ken Himma for his public commentary to the paper presented at McMaster, and Verónica Rodríguez-Blanco for her observations to the previous versions of this chapter. Whatever errors remain are still mine.

The second is a 'theory about what the law ought to be', that is, 'the theory of utilitarianism, which holds that law and its institutions should serve the general welfare, and nothing else'. Furthermore, he clarified not only that 'both parts of the ruling theory derive from the philosophy of Jeremy Bentham' but also that he was going to, in the critical portions of the essays, 'criticize both parts of the theory, and… the assumption that they are independent of one another'; and in the constructive portions to 'emphasize an idea that is also part of the liberal tradition, but that has no place in either legal positivism or utilitarianism', that is, 'the old idea of individual human rights', which Bentham called 'nonsense on stilts' (Dworkin 1977a; 1978: vii).[2]

Contrary to the insistence about the independence of both parts, he claims: 'A general theory of law must be normative as well as conceptual' (1977a and 1978: vii). Bear in mind that this claim will allow Dworkin to collapse the distinction between descriptive and normative (1977a and 1978: vii–viii). In a few words, he connects or even—as I will argue—integrates both parts, that is, the normative and the conceptual, not only within a general theory of law but also with other departments of philosophy. In his own voice:

> The interdependencies of the various parts of a general theory of law are therefore complex. In the same way, moreover, a general theory of law will have many connections with other departments of philosophy. The normative theory will be embedded in a more general political and moral philosophy which may in turn depend upon philosophical theories about human nature or the objectivity of morality. The conceptual part will draw upon the philosophy of language and therefore upon logic and metaphysics… A general theory of law must therefore constantly take up one or another disputed position on problems of philosophy that are not distinctly legal. (1977a and 1978: viii–ix)

In short, Dworkin challenged the ruling theory of law and its methodology,[3] which claimed to be general and descriptive or even indirectly evaluative but still morally neutral (Dickson 2001; Flores 2013a).[4] Thus, his conception of law as part of political morality resorts to a constructive interpretation, which entails persistent and pervasive disagreements regarding the questions what law is and what law ought to do (Priel 2014),[5] but that can still advocate for objectivity and in the process defend as a corollary 'the one right answer' thesis.

Legal Theories and Methodologies

H.L.A. Hart's clarification, in the 'Postscript' to *The Concept of Law*,[6] regarding the aims of his legal theory, as well as its basic methodological assumptions and presuppositions, is the following:

My aim in this book was to provide a theory of what law is which is both general and descriptive. It is *general* in the sense that it is not tied to any particular legal system or legal culture, but seeks to give an explanatory and clarifying account of law as a complex social and political institution with a rule-governed (and in that sense 'normative') aspect... My account is *descriptive* in that it is morally neutral and has no justificatory aims: it does not seek to justify or commend on moral or other grounds the forms and structures which appear in my general account of law, though a clear understanding of these is, I think, an important preliminary to any useful moral criticism of law. (Hart 1994: 239–40)

At the outset of the clarification, we can identify two basic methodological distinctions as applied to legal theories:

1. The distinction between *general* legal theories that respond to 'questions about what is common to all legal systems and cultures' and *particular* legal theories that respond to 'questions about what is specific to a legal system or culture';[7] and
2. The distinction between *descriptive* legal theories with explanatory aims that respond to 'questions about what the law *is*' or 'questions about *facts*'; and *normative*—or alternately *prescriptive*—legal theories with justificatory aims that respond to 'questions about what the law *ought to be*' or 'questions about *values*' (Figure 6.1).[8]

Furthermore, the clarification suggests that since there are there two axis—the one distinguishing *general* and *particular*, and the other *descriptive/explanatory* and *normative/justificatory*—there are four resulting quadrants that correspond to four initial possibilities: (1) *general* and *descriptive/explanatory*; (2) *general* and *normative/justificatory*; (3) *particular* and *descriptive/explanatory*; and (4) *particular* and *normative/justificatory*. Moreover, nothing

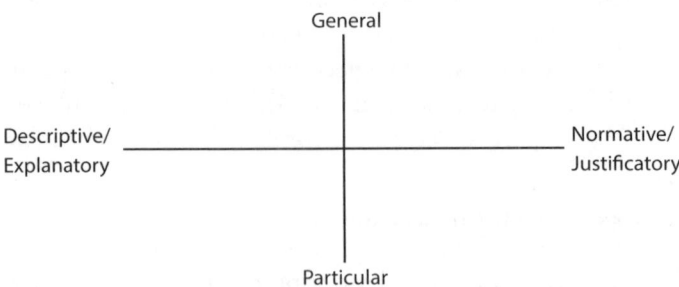

Figure 6.1   Two Axis
Source: Author.

	Descriptive/ Explanatory	Normative/ Justificatory
General	(1)	(2)
Particular	(3)	(4)

Figure 6.2   Four Quadrants
Source: Author.

precludes a more comprehensive legal theory that includes more than one quadrant and that corresponds to four additional possibilities combining: (1) and (2); (3) and (4); (1) and (3); and (2) and (4); and, even a much more comprehensive theory that integrates the four quadrants and a further possibility combining: (1), (2), (3), and (4) (Figure 6.2).[9]

Traditionally, *natural law theories* do accept and even embrace the *normative* dimension to the extent that they appear to be clearly *justificatory*, whereas *positive law theories* reject it by claiming to remain (purely or solely) *descriptive*, to the extent that they are *explanatory*.

On the one hand, additionally to Hart, John Austin, and Hans Kelsen as well as other positive law theorists, that is, legal positivists, are representative of (1). For example, Austin famously appealed:

> The existence of law is one thing; its merit or demerit is another. Whether it be or not be is one enquiry; whether it be or not be conformable to an assumed standard, is a different enquiry. A law, which actually exists, is a law, though we happen to dislike it, or though it varies from the text, by which we regulate our approbation and disapprobation. (1998/1832: 184)[10]

Analogously, Kelsen—at the beginning of both editions of his *Reine Rechstlehre*—asserted:[11]

> The Pure Theory of Law is a theory of positive law. It is a theory of positive law in general, not of a specific legal order. It is a general theory of law, not an interpretation of specific national or international legal norms; but it offers a theory of interpretation.
>
> As a theory, its exclusive purpose is to know and to describe its object. The theory attempts to answer the question what and how the law *is*, not how it ought to be. It is a science of law (jurisprudence), not legal politics.

On the other hand, Saint Augustine of Hippo and other classical natural law theorists are representative of (2), since they appear to hold that the normative exhausts the content and nature of the law—or alternately that the law is reduced to the prescriptive—to the extent that *iniustia lex, non est lex*, that is, 'unjust law is not law at all'.[12]

As already advanced, I am especially interested in the possibility of connecting (1) and (2), on the one hand, and (3) and (4), on the other hand, and even the possibility of contrasting (1) and (3), on one side, and (2) and (4), on the other. Therefore, a legal theorist can not only be fixated in either describing and explaining or prescribing and justifying, or both; but also be focused in either what is common to all legal systems and cultures or what is specific of a particular legal system and culture, or both.

Actually, following Bentham's distinctions, nothing prevents a legal theorist from exposing first what is specific of a particular legal system or culture (3) and censoring it later (4). Analogously, also following Bentham, nothing precludes a legal theorist from exposing first what is common to all legal systems or cultures (1) and censoring it later (2) (Bentham 1996/1789: 293–300). However, in the remainder of this section, we will bracket the former possibility and will focus on the latter possibility, that is, the connection or not between (1) and (2).

In that sense, most legal positivists—following Austin, Kelsen, and Hart—have insisted in the independence between (1) and (2) and have been claiming to be committed exclusively to (1) by suggesting that whenever the normative/justificatory dimension appears, it is no longer law but morality what is at stake; and, hence, law can remain morally neutral (Marmor 2001;[13] Raz 1994;[14] Shapiro 2011)[15] or indirectly evaluative (Dickson 2001); and so have been labelled as 'hard' or 'exclusive legal positivists'. Similarly, even those that admit that there are contingent relationships between (1) and (2) seem to subordinate (2) to (1), due to the fact that it is the law, which includes or incorporates references to morality (Coleman 2001;[16] Waluchow 1994[17]), and even can be reduced accordingly to a mere or pure conceptual analysis without normative/justificatory aims (Himma 2008;[18] Leiter 2007;[19] Marmor 2013[20]), and so have been labelled as 'soft', 'inclusive legal positivists' or 'incorporationists'. Moreover, some legal positivists have conceded to different extent by recognizing the possibility (Schauer 1996;[21] Vermeule 2008[22]) and even the necessity (Campbell 1996;[23] MacCormick 1985;[24] Murphy 2001;[25] Waldron 2001[26]) of connecting both (1) and (2). Finally, some natural law theorists, following Saint Thomas Aquinas dictum *Non lex, sed legis corruptio*[27] seem to be adopting a form of weak natural law theory that connects both (1) and (2).

To conclude this section I would like to advance a dual claim: Dworkin's model is neither fixated in describing/explaining or prescribing/justifying,

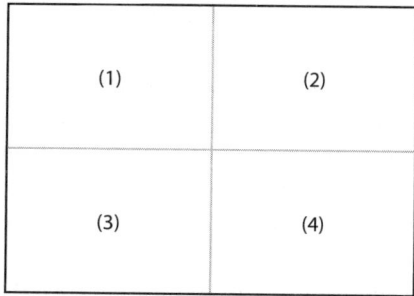

Figure 6.3   Blurring Dividing Lines
Source: Author.

nor focused in what is common to all legal systems and cultures or what is specific of a particular legal system and culture, but devoted to an integration or even more precisely re-integration of the different features. Let me clarify that Dworkin integrates (1), (2), (3), and (4) into a much more complex legal framework by conflating the different possibilities or more precisely by blurring the lines dividing them (Figure 6.3).[28]

Dworkin not only blurs the lines dividing the different possibilities, that is, general and particular, descriptive/explanatory and normative/justificatory but also collapses the distinctions between creation and application, between legislation and adjudication, and most notably between theory and practice. For example, in *Law's Empire*, Dworkin affirms: on one side, 'Jurisprudence is the general part of adjudication, silent prologue to any decision at law';[29] and, on the other, 'Interpretative theories are by their nature addressed to a particular legal culture, generally the culture to which their authors belong'.[30]

Dworkin's Theory and Methodology

In this section, I will like to revisit some features of Dworkin's model, which we characterize as being: (a) constructive, (b) interpretive (and even argumentative), (c) evaluative, and (d) integrative.

Constructive

Ever since the publication of his book review on John Rawls' *A Theory of Justice*[31] in 1973 (Dworkin 1973)[32] and all the way to his *Justice for Hedgehogs*,[33] Dworkin distanced himself from a 'natural' model and endorsed a 'constructive' one. The 'natural' model presupposes a philosophical position that describes an objective moral reality, which is not created by human beings, but rather discovered by them, as the laws of physics: 'Moral reasoning or philosophy is a process of reconstructing the fundamental principles by assembling concrete judgments in the right order, as a natural historian reconstructs the shape of the whole animal from the fragments of its bones that he has found'. On the contrary, the 'constructive' model 'treats intuitions of justice not as clues to the existence of independent principles, but rather as stipulated features of a general theory to be constructed, as if the sculptor set himself to carve the animal that best fits a pile of bones he happened to find together'. In his own voice:

> This 'constructive' model does not assume, as the natural model does, that principles of justice have some fixed, objective existence, so that descriptions of these principles must be true or false in some standard way. It does not assume that the animal it matches to the bones actually exists. It makes the different, and in some ways more complex, assumption that men and women have a responsibility to fit the particular judgments on which they act into a coherent program or action, or, at least, that officials who exercise power over other men have that sort of responsibility. (Dworkin 1977a and 1978: 160)

Interpretive

Later on, in his exchange with Stanley Fish on legal viz-à-viz literary interpretation (Dworkin 1982,[34] 1983;[35] Fish 1982,[36] 1983[37]) and throughout his works, but especially in *Law's Empire* (1986), Dworkin reinforces not only that the model is constructive and to some extent creative but clarifies that it is not inventive but interpretive of the practice. In other words, since law is an 'interpretive concept' the proper method requires a 'constructive interpretation' of the practice. In that sense, on the one hand, Dworkin is adamant in his criticism of 'semantic theories of law' which he labels as 'the semantic sting', because they appear to consider the concept of law as a 'criterial concept' (Dworkin 1986: 31–44; 2011: 158–9)[38] and even a 'natural kind concept'[39] with necessary and sufficient conditions, whereas it is an 'interpretive concept'.[40] On the other, firstly, defines, "[C]onstructive" interpretation is a matter of imposing purpose on an object or practice in order to make of it the best possible example of the form or genre to which it is taken to belong.'[41] Second, he delineates three stages of constructive interpretation:[42]

> First, there must be a 'pre-interpretive' stage in which the rules and standards taken to provide the tentative content of the practice are identified [...] Second, there must be an interpretive stage at which the interpreter settles on some

general justification for the main elements of the practice identified at the pre-interpretive stage [...] Finally, there must be a post-interpretive or reforming stage, at which he adjusts his sense of what the practice 'really' requires so as to better to serve the justification he accepts at the interpretive stage. (Dworkin 1986)

And, third, he insists that its nature is interpretive rather than inventive, 'The justification need not fit every aspect or feature of the standing practice, but it must fit enough for the interpreter to be able to see himself as interpreting that practice, not inventing a new one'.[43]

Evaluative

Although in 'How Law is Like Literature' Dworkin seemed to diminish the evaluative as well as the descriptive in the process of emphasizing the interpretive, at the end it was clear that he has been endorsing a moral reading of the practice, which requires references to value and even value judgments that are not necessarily subjective but objective.[44] Dworkin affirmed, 'propositions of law are not merely descriptive of legal history, in a straightforward way, nor are they simply evaluative in some way divorced from legal history. They are interpretive of legal history, which combines elements of both description and evaluation but is different from both' (Dworkin 1985: 147). He also clarified (with the 'rules of courtesy' as example) that the 'interpretive attitude' has two components, that is, an assumption that it has an objective value (or point) and a further assumption that it is sensitive to it. In Dworkin's voice:

> The first is the assumption that the practice of courtesy does not simply exist but has value, that it serves some interest or purpose or enforces some principle—in short, that it has some point—that can be stated independently of just describing the rules that make up the practice. The second is the further assumption that the requirements of courtesy—the behaviour it calls for or judgments it warrants—are not necessarily or exclusively what they have always been taken to be but are instead sensitive to its point, so that the strict rules must be understood or applied or extended or modified or qualified or limited by that point. Once this interpretive attitude takes hold, the institution of courtesy ceases to be mechanical; it is no longer unstudied deference to a runic order. People now try to impose *meaning* on the institution—to see its best light—and then to restructure it in the light of that meaning. (1986: 47; emphasis original)

Integrative

In *Law's Empire* Dworkin advanced his conception of 'law as integrity', which is highly dependent on the idea of coherence and fit,[45] but in 'Hart's Postscript and the Character of Political Philosophy',[46] Dworkin—by criticizing Hart's defence of an Archimedean jurisprudence—developed an argument against a detached conception of values and for an integrated conception of values. In a few words, Dworkin commences by affirming that 'It would make a little sense to treat the political values... as detached values' (2006a: 158); continues by announcing that 'political values are integrated rather than detached' (159) and by asserting that 'Law is a political concept' (162); and, concludes by avowing that this project 'must find the place of each value in a larger and mutually supporting web of conviction that displays supporting connections among moral and political values generally and then places these in the still larger context of ethics' (168).[47]

This claim, that is, integrated values, defends the thesis of the unity of value, which was somehow advanced in the 'Introduction' to *Taking Rights Seriously*[48] and proclaimed at the beginning of *Justice for Hedgehogs*, 'This book defends a large and old philosophical thesis: the unity of value' (2011: 1), and is Dworkin's response to the causes usually associated with foxes, that is, value scepticism, subjectivism, relativism, and pluralism. Nevertheless, let me reiterate that this thesis, in my opinion, was already implicit in his distinction between principles and rules, and so can be traced all the way back to the early publication of 'The Model of Rules I' in 1967: '[Principles] have a dimension that rules do not—the dimension of weight or importance' and 'principles rather hang together than link together [as rules do]'.[49]

Furthermore, in the process of reinforcing his argument, Dworkin makes a dual claim for 'independence of morality from science and metaphysics' (David Hume's principle) and for 'interdependence of morality and ethics' (Immanuel Kant's principle) (Dworkin 2011: 19). In a few words, Dworkin attacked the Archimedean epistemology and defended an integrated epistemology: 'Our moral epistemology—our account of good reasoning about moral matters—must be an integrated rather than an Archimedean epistemology, and it must therefore be itself a substantive, first-order moral theory' (Dworkin 2011: 100).[50] Likewise, he appealed not only to 'the character of interpretation and of interpretive truth and the independence of both ethical and moral truth from science and metaphysics' but also to an 'interpretive integration of ethics and morality' (Dworkin 2011: 14).[51] Hence, Dworkin stipulates and uses 'ethical' and 'moral' in a special way, 'Moral standards prescribe how we ought to treat others; ethical standards, how we ought to live our lives for ourselves. We can—many people do use either "ethical" and "moral" or both in a broader sense that erases the distinction, so that morality includes what I call ethics, and vice versa' (2011: 191).[52] Notwithstanding, let me clarify that according to Dworkin, 'If the connection [between ethical and moral] is to serve any useful purpose in our interpretive project, it must be a matter of integration, not simply incorporation' (2011: 202).

Finally, regarding law and morality, Dworkin, in an autobiographical paragraph in chapter 19 'Law' of his *Justice for Hedgehogs*, acknowledged—or more precisely confessed:[53]

> When more than forty years ago I first tried to defend interpretivism, I defended it within this orthodox two-systems picture. I assumed that law and morals are different systems of norms and that the crucial question is how they interact. So I said… that the law includes not just enacted rules, or rules with pedigree, but justifying principles as well. I soon came to think, however, that the two-systems picture of the problem was itself flawed, and I began to approach the issue through a very different picture. I did not fully appreciate the nature of that picture, however, or how different it is from the orthodox model, until I began to consider the larger issues of this book. (2011: 402; internal references omitted)

So, instead of considering law and morality as two separate systems, Dworkin has replaced it with a one-system picture, which now treats 'law as a part of political morality' and recalled the aim of the book: 'Our aim has been to integrate what are often taken to be separate departments of evaluation: we can easily place the doctrinal concept of law in that tree structure: law is a branch, a subdivision, of political morality' (2011: 405). What's more, Dworkin recognizes the existence of a difficult question and hints into its answer: 'The more difficult question is how that concept [that is, law] should be distinguished to show one as a distinct part of the other. Any plausible answer will centre on the phenomenon of institutionalization' (405).[54] Similarly, let me clarify, specially, to my friends in both sides of the inclusive 'positivism' v. inclusive 'non-positivism' divide,[55] that according to Dworkin it is not that law may simply include or incorporate references to morality, but that law must integrate—and actually do integrates—references to morality (Flores 2009a: 43).

Dworkin's (Human) Dignity and Rights Theory

Let me start this section by reminding that Dworkin offers a 'Baedeker', at the beginning of his *Justice for Hedgehogs*, where he affirms that the book 'defends a large and old philosophical thesis: the unity of value', and alleges, 'No government is legitimate unless it subscribes to two reigning principles. First, it must show equal concern for the fate of every person over whom it claims dominion. Second, it must respect fully the responsibility and right of each person to decide for himself how to make something valuable of his life' (2011: 1–2).

He announces, 'We must cherish our dignity' and 'we must explore dignity's dimensions', which correspond to the 'two fundamental principles of politics: a requirement that government treat those it governs with equal concern, and a further requirement that it respect... its subjects' ethical responsibilities'. Additionally, he asserts that the concept of dignity has been debased by a 'flabby overuse in political rhetoric... But we need the idea, and the cognate idea of self-respect, if we are to make much sense of our situation and our ambitions'. He provides the travel guide for the book and advances, in chapter 9 'Dignity': 'I construct the ethical analogues of these two political principles. People must take their own lives seriously: they must accept that it is objectively important how they live. People must take their ethical responsibility seriously as well: they must insist on the right— and exercise that right—to make ethical decisions finally for themselves'. Furthermore, he clarifies: 'I offer part of what is needed in Chapter 9, but the application of the two principles in later chapters... furnish much more detail' (13–14). Finally, after making explicit his reliance on Kant's thesis that 'we cannot adequately respect our own humanity unless we respect humanity in others' (14),[56] he stresses 'the last chapter is epilogue: it repeats the claim, now through the lens of dignity, that value has truth and that value is indivisible' (15).

In what follows we will revisit Dworkin's conception of (human) dignity and rights as presented in chapter 9 'Dignity' and developed in the following chapters.

First of all, after reiterating that he uses the terms, 'ethical' and 'moral' in what may seem a special way that not merely includes or incorporates one into the other but that integrates both of them (Dworkin 2011: 191–5), Dworkin distinguishes between 'having a good life' and 'living well'. And so, following the 'relation between the value of what is created and the value of the acts of creating it', he introduces a further distinction between 'product value' and 'performance value'. The former corresponds to 'having a good life' and is 'adjectival', whereas the latter to 'living well' and is 'adverbial' (195–99); and, insists: 'The final value of our lives is adverbial, not adjectival' (197). To reinforce such priority, after recalling not only the idea of 'moral luck'[57] but also the distinction between 'being bad' and 'bad moral luck' (200–2), Dworkin stipulates following Rawls: 'the value of living well is lexically prior to the value of a good life'.[58]

Afterwards, as promised, Dworkin constructs—or more precisely re-constructs—the ethical analogues of the two political principles:[59]

The first is a principle of self-respect. Each person must take his own life seriously: he must accept that it is a matter of importance that his life be a successful performance rather than a wasted opportunity. The second is a principle of authenticity. Each person has a special, personal responsibility for identifying what counts as success in his own life; he has a personal responsibility to create that life through a coherent narrative or style that he himself endorses.

Together the two principles offer a conception of human dignity: dignity requires self-respect and authenticity. (2011: 203–4)

On the one hand, the 'principle of self-respect', 'insists that I must recognize the objective importance of my living well'. But Dworkin does not mean simply that each person's life has intrinsic and equal worth, which is usually understood not as an ethical principle but as a moral principle about how people must be treated, by insisting that all human lives are inviolable and that no one should be treated as if his life were less important than anyone else's. On the contrary, for him 'it describes an attitude that people should have toward their own lives: they should think it important that they live well. The principle of self-respect requires each of us to treat his own life as having that kind of importance' (Dworkin 2011: 205).

On the other hand, the 'principle of authenticity', which according to Dworkin 'is the other side of self-respect. Because you take yourself seriously, you judge that living well means expressing yourself in your life, seeking a way to live that grips you as right for you and your circumstance' (209). Moreover, after bringing into attention the distinction between 'responsibility as a virtue' and 'responsibility as a relation between people and events', he adds: 'The second principle of dignity demands both that I be responsible in the virtue sense and that I accept relational responsibility when appropriate. I do not treat an act as my own, as issuing from my personality and character, unless I regard myself as judgmental responsible for it' (210; 102).

By the same token, 'Authenticity has another dimension: it stipulates what dignity demands we try to establish in our relations with other people. We must strive for independence' (211). However, he clarifies 'That does not mean trying to escape influence or persuasion'. 'We cannot escape influence, but we must resist domination'. In short, 'Authenticity demands that, so far as decisions are to be made about the best use to which a person's life should be put, these must be made by the person whose life it is'. In Dworkin's own voice:

So authenticity is not autonomy... [A]utonomy requires only that some range of choices be left open by the sum of circumstance, whether these be natural or political. A person's autonomy is not threatened, on this view, when government manipulates its community's culture so as to remove or make less eligible certain disapproved ways of living, if an adequate number of choices remain so that he can still exercise the power of choice. Authenticity, on the other hand, as this is defined by the second principle of dignity, is very much concerned with the character as well as the fact obstacles to choice. Living well means not just designing a life, as if any design would do, but designing it in response to a judgment of ethical value. Authenticity is damaged when a person is made to accept someone else's judgment in place of his own about the values or goals his life should display.

Later on, Dworkin proceeds to the applications of the two principles of dignity and begins by calling into attention the shift of focus in chapter 11 'From Dignity to Morality': 'We hope, remember, to integrate ethics and morality, not simply by incorporating morality into ethics but by achieving a mutually supportive integration of the two in which our thoughts about living well help us to see what our moral responsibilities are'.[60] Next, he considers the implications for morality of the first principle of dignity, that is, the principle of 'self-respect', according to which you must treat the success of your own life as a matter of objective importance. In a similar fashion, he applies the first principle in chapter 12 to 'Aid' cases (Dworkin 2011: 271–84); and, the second principle in chapter 13 to 'Harm' cases.[61]

In a very straightforward fashion and following Kant's principle, Dworkin declares, 'a proper form of self-respect—the self-respect demanded by that first principle—entails a parallel respect for the lives of all human beings'.[62] As already noted, Kant's principle changes the subject:

> [I]t speaks not to well-being as a goal but to attitude as a guide. We must treat other people consistently with accepting that their lives are of equal objective importance to our own. Failing to help is not necessarily inconsistent with that attitude... So I may recognize the objective importance of the lives of strangers without supposing that I must subordinate my life and interests to some collective or aggregate interest of them all, or even to any single one of them whose needs are greater than my own. (2011: 273–4)

As Dworkin clarifies, 'However, there is a limit to how far I can consistently ignore something that I claim has objective value' (274). This is especially true in 'rescue' cases, such as the drowning swimmer cases, where any plausible test will make room for three factors, 'the harm threatened to a victim, the cost a rescuer would incur, and the degree of confrontation between victim and potential rescuer'.[63] We will return to a variant of this case later.

Regarding the second principle of dignity, that is, the principle of 'authenticity', which 'assigns each of us a personal responsibility to act consistently with the character and projects he identifies for himself' (2011: 261), Dworkin states, 'The second principle insists that you have a personal responsibility for your own life, a responsibility you must not delegate or ignore, and Kant's principle requires you to recognize a parallel responsibility in others' (287). In order to reconcile these parallel responsibilities he distinguishes between two kinds of harm, an apparent harm labeled as 'bare competition harm', and a real harm as 'deliberate harm':

> No one could even begin to lead a life if bare competition harm were forbidden. We live our lives mostly like swimmers in separate demarcated lanes. One swimmer gets the blue ribbon or the job or the lover or the house on the hill that another wants. Sometimes, when one swimmer is drowning and another can save him without losing much ground in the race, the latter does have a duty to cross lanes to help…But each person may concentrate on swimming is own race without concern for the fact that if he wins, another person must therefore lose… It is part of our personal responsibility—it is what makes our separate responsibilities personal—that we accept the inevitability and permissibility of competition harm.
>
> Deliberate harm—crossing lanes not to help but to hurt—is a different matter. We need the right to compete to lead our own lives, but we do not need the right deliberately to injure others. On the contrary, if our responsibility for our own lives is to be effective, we each need a moral immunity from deliberate harm by others.

After extending the principle to cases of 'unintended harm' from which a liability responsibility generates (290–1), Dworkin recognizes not only that 'We have so far concentrated on our responsibility not to harm others in pursuit of our own interests', but also 'a different puzzle: whether and when we may injure some people in order to protect or benefit others' (293), such as in the 'trolley cases',[64] and proceeds to the discussion of 'the principle of double effect':

> It is permissible to let someone die when that is the necessary consequence of rescuing others. So it is permissible for the doctor to save one of two patients who each needs a liver, or for you to save one of two drowning swimmers, even though as a result the other patient or swimmer dies. But it is not permissible to kill someone or even to let him die when this is not just a consequence of your rescuing others but a means you adopt to that end. So it is not permissible to kill the old heart patient who is anyway dying, because the point of killing him—or not saving him—would be that he dies so that his liver is available.

Keep in mind that for Dworkin: 'People have a right, in all these cases, that nothing be done to them that supposes that they are not the final judges of how their bodies are best used' (2011: 295). Hence, for him, the implication in these cases is:

> The second principle does not forbid any act, like choosing a patient for a liver transplant, that saves one life and dooms another. Or any act, like diverting a trolley, that puts a life in peril that was formerly safe. It forbids such acts only when they are based on a usurping judgment that the best use of one person's body is to save another's life... Aiming at death is worse than just knowingly causing it, because aiming at death is a crime against dignity. (295–6)

What's more, Dworkin introduces a variant of the drowning swimmer cases to reinforce not only the distinction between bare competition and deliberate harm but also between letting nature take its course and interfering with it:

> Suppose you and I, shipwrecked, are equidistant from a bobbing life jacket. We do not let nature take its course, which would mean both drowning. We race for the life jacket. If I lose, it is the presence of a rescuer trying to save another person—you trying to save yourself—that leads to my death. Why does it matter if your rescuer is not you but a third party who is a better swimmer—your wife?—tossing you the jacket instead of me? The harm I suffer then is only competition harm—only my bad luck. But if your wife shoots me so that you will get to the life jacket first, then this is not just my bad luck. She has usurped my right to decide whether my life should end immediately. (299)

A further set of applications is developed in chapter 14 'Obligations'. Dworkin commences by recalling that, 'We seek concrete interpretations of our two principles of dignity—that we must respect the equal importance of human lives, and that we have a special responsibility for our own lives—that allows us to live in the light of both without compromising either' (300).

Furthermore, he recognizes, 'The crucial role of convention and social practice in fixing obligation poses a philosophical difficulty. Conventions are only matters of fact. How can they create and shape genuine moral duties? [...] They seem alchemy: making something moral out of nothing moral'. And points out: 'moral responsibilities... do vary as facts vary. Whether you have a duty to try to rescue [a drowning swimmer] depends on whether you can swim, have a lifeline, and so forth' (302). Hence, 'It is not magic. The conventions are parasitic on underlying and independent moral facts' (309). In the following paragraphs Dworkin specifies the cases of lying and of promising.

On one side, 'Dignity explains why: any lie (except in circumstances, like some games, in which lying is permissible) contradicts the second principle, because lying is an attempt to corrupt the base of information through which people exercise their responsibility for their own lives' (305). On the other, 'Promising is not an independent source of a distinct kind of moral duty. Rather it plays an important but not exclusive role in fixing the scope of a more general responsibility: not to harm other people by first encouraging them to expect that we will act in a certain way and then not acting in that way'.[65]

Dworkin makes explicit one further and very important implication, 'Social practices create genuine obligations only when they respect the two principles of dignity: only when they are consistent with an equal appreciation of the importance of all human lives and only when they do not license the kind of harm to others that is forbidden by that assumption. They demand special treatment for certain people, but they cannot license hatred or murder' (315). However, social practices cannot be '*only* matters of convention… exhausted by the scope of consensus' (316).

What's more, Dworkin points out to the paradox of political obligation:[66]

[W]e usually have an independent moral reason to do what the law requires and not to do what it proscribes. Laws condemn murder, and murder is wrong. But the question of political obligation arises when we have no other reason to do what law requires… I can accept that I have a standing obligation, in principle, to obey the laws of my community and yet think that some particular law is so unjust or so brutally unwise that I am justify in disobeying it… [T]he moral permissibility of disobedience… is an exception to a more general principle that requires obedience even to the laws they disapprove but do not think wicked.

In that sense, he confirms, 'The challenge the paradox poses is, once again, interpretive. We must develop our conception of what dignity requires further than we yet have, so that we can identify a politics that is consistent with it. We have already accepted that the second principle of dignity—that we must take responsibility for our own lives— permits us, under certain conditions, to share that responsibility with others'. It is clear that 'Collective coercive government is essential to our dignity. We need the order and efficiencies that only coercive government can provide to make it possible for us to create good lives and live well… But coercive government also threatens to make dignity impossible'.[67] For that reason, 'governments have a sovereign responsibility to treat each person in their power with equal concern and respect. They achieve justice to the extent they succeed' (Dworkin 2011: 321). In short, governments 'can be legitimate if their laws and policies can nevertheless be interpreted as recognizing that the fate of each citizen is of equal importance and that each has a responsibility to create his own life' (321–2).

The remaining chapters, corresponding to Part Five 'Politics', shift the problem from 'personal morality' to 'political morality', from 'duties' and 'obligations' to 'rights', and identify not only a further abstract problem but also its solution: 'coercive government destroys dignity without partnership' (324). The more concrete problems and solutions regarding political morality have been explored, elsewhere, in *Life's Dominion*, *Sovereign Virtue*, and *Is Democracy Possible Here?*,[68] which are integrated into *Justice for Hedgehogs* by reference (328). Dworkin explains and justifies the shift of focus in the following terms (328):

> We studied ethics and personal morality through the concept of responsibility—what people must do for their own sake or for others—rather than the often corresponding idea of a right: what people are entitled to have. Responsibility is a particularly suitable focus for ethics, because it is more natural and accurate, when judging what it is to live well, to think of what we are responsible for doing than of what we have a right to demand. We might have studied morality through the idea of rights. We might have asked, for example, what aid we all have a right to have, even from strangers, or what help friends or lovers or citizens are entitled to expect from one another. When we come to political morality, however, rights plainly provide a better focus than duties or obligations, because their location is more precise: individuals have political rights, and some of those rights, at least, are matched only by collective duties of the community as a whole rather than of particular individuals.

In the next passages, Dworkin recalls the nature and force of political rights. In short, '[P]olitical rights are trumps over otherwise adequate justifications for political action' (329). And summarizes his conclusion of the previous discussion:

> A political community has no moral power to create and enforce obligations against its members unless it treats them with equal concern and respect; unless, that is, its policies treat their fates as equally important and respect their individual responsibilities for their own lives. That principle of legitimacy is the most abstract source of political rights. Government has no moral authority to coerce anyone, even to improve the welfare or well-being or goodness of the community as a whole, unless it respects those requirements person by person. The principles of dignity therefore state very abstract political rights: they trump government's collective policies. We form this hypothesis: All political rights are derivative from that fundamental one. We fix and defend particular rights by asking, in much more detail, what equal concern and respect require.
>
> That hypothesis explains the capital importance in contemporary political theory of certain interpretive concepts, including the concepts of equality and

liberty. In mature democracies people almost all recognize, as an abstract the-sis, that government must treat those it governs with equal concern and must allow then the liberties they need to define a successful life for themselves. We disagree, however, about what more concrete rights follow from these abstract ones. (330)

Actually, he even points out that in the following chapters he attempts to produce a 'substantive theory of political rights' by constructing and defend-ing conceptions of these master interpretive concepts, namely equality and liberty: 'We aim, remember, to interpret the two fundamental principles of dignity so that no compromise between the two is necessary; so that each complements and reinforces the other. So, we must reject the opinion now popular among political philosophers that liberty and equality are conflicting values. We hope to define equality and liberty together: not only as compat-ible but as intertwined' (331).

Let me clarify that, in what remains of this section, I do not intend to review exhaustively his 'substantive theory of political rights', but I pretend merely to recall how Dworkin interconnects and distinguishes them as a genre from both 'legal rights' and 'human rights' as some of their species.

On the one hand, 'legal rights' are 'political rights', but must be distin-guished from other 'political rights'. A 'legal right' is 'a right enacted by a legislative body of a legitimate government to be enforced on the demand of individual citizens through the decisions, if necessary, of an adjudicative institution like a court'. In that sense, 'a legal right may be designed to give effect to a pre-existing political right' to the extent that certain 'political rights' correspond to 'legislative rights', whereas 'legal rights' correspond to 'adjudicative rights' (331–2).

On the other hand, 'human rights' are 'political rights', but must be dis-tinguished from other 'political rights'. After pointing out the flaws of other conceptions, that claim that 'human rights are those that trump not merely collective national goals but also national sovereignty' and as such seem to justify economic sanctions and military interventions, or that suggest that 'human rights are in some way particularly important', but 'All political rights are particularly important' (332–4), Dworkin suggests a different strategy, 'We must therefore insist that though people do have a political right to equal concern and respect on the right conception, they have a more fundamental, because more abstract, right. They have a right to be treated with the attitude that these debates presuppose and reflect—a right to be treated *as* a human being whose dignity fundamentally matters' (335). Hence, 'a government's overall behaviour is defensible under an intelligible, even if unconvincing, conception of what our two principles of dignity require'. On one side, 'Nothing could be a plainer violation of the first principle of dignity than acts that exhibit blatant prejudice—assumptions of supposed superiority of one caste over another or of believers over infidels or Aryans over Semites or whites over blacks'. On the other, the second principle of dignity 'supports the traditional liberal rights of free speech and expression, conscience, political activity, and religion that most human rights documents include'. Thus, 'Governments that forbid the exercise of any but a designated religion or that punish heresy or blasphemy or deny in principle the right of free speech or of the press violate human rights for that reason. So do governments that intimidate or kill or torture people because they hate or fear their political opinions' (335–6).

***

To conclude, I will like to return yet to another variant of the drowning swimmer cases, but it is necessary to reiterate first that Dworkin's commitment to the unity of value implies objectivity and includes the one right answer thesis.[69] Briefly, in *Justice for Hedgehogs*, Dworkin distinguishes between indeterminacy and uncertainty: 'But in all these aspects indeterminacy differs from uncertainty. "I am uncertain whether the proposition in question is true or false" is plainly consistent with "It is one or the other", but "The proposition in question is neither true nor false" is not' (Dworkin 2011: 91).[70]

In a few words, Dworkin by differentiating indeterminacy from uncertainty is able to separate the lack of certainty, that is, a final demonstration or proof, from the claim for determinacy, that is, a pre-existing one right answer for every legal question being already somehow 'out there'. Let me clarify that 'out there' in Dworkin's model means that the answer is, on the one hand, not to be discovered (or deducted) but to be constructed, from the already pre-existing legal materials; and, on the other hand, not to be invented (or created and even changed) but to be interpreted (and even argued for), again from the already pre-existing legal materials. Similarly, the one right answer thesis can be constructed and interpreted from the already pre-existing legal materials because their objective value is evaluated according to the underlying principles, including moral ones, which not only justify the practice but also are integrated into law.[71]

Against the critique that the pre-existing legal materials may appear to be contradictory and even incommensurable, Dworkin provides an interpretation following his unity of value thesis that reconciles values by showing that moral conflict requires a deeper form of collaboration to solve the apparent conflict and even to figure out a point of comparison or contrast, to the extent that somehow the one right answer will despite all still be available even in very crazy cases.[72]

For that purpose, Dworkin develops a variation of the drowning swimmer cases, in which he first poses the problem and later reflects upon it:

> One person clings to a life preserver in a storm that has wrecked her boat; sharks circle her. Two other passengers cling to another life preserver a hundred yards away; sharks circle them as well. You have a boat on shore. You can reach one life preserver in time, but then not the other one. Assuming all three are strangers, do you have a duty to save the two swimmers and let the lone swimmer die?
>
> But if we approach the decision in another way—by concentrating not on consequences but on rights—it is far from plain that we should automatically save the greater number. We might think that each victim has an equal antecedent right to be saved, and we might therefore be tempted by a lottery in which each shipwreck victim has at least one-third chance to be saved. (The sharks agree to circle while the lottery is conducted.) (Dworkin 2011: 280–1)

Although most people will appear to be automatically inclined to save two, due to the bare fact that they are more than one, it is far from clear that is is the correcct answer. Actually, saving the greater number may seem to be the right answer from a consequentialist approach, but not according to a conception based on (human) dignity and their corresponding rights and even responsibilities. According to the latter, each person has an equal antecedent right to be saved and must be treated with equal concern and respect by those carrying the rescue mission.

In sum, as we have seen, Dworkin not only defended and elaborated these ideas throughout his works and thoroughly in *Justice for Hedgehogs*, but also completed and fulfilled the project advanced back in 1970 with the very early publication of 'A Special Supplement: Taking Rights Seriously':[73]

> Anyone who professes to take rights seriously, and who praises our government for respecting them, must have some sense of what that point is. He must accept, at the minimum, one or both of two important ideas. The first is the vague but powerful idea of human dignity. This idea, associated with Kant, but defended by philosophers of different schools, supposes that there are ways of treating a man that are inconsistent with recognizing him as a full member of the human community, and holds that such treatment is profoundly unjust.
>
> The second is the more familiar idea of political equality. This supposes that the weaker members of a political community are entitled to the same concern and respect of their government as the more powerful members have secured

for themselves, so that if some men have freedom of decision whatever the effect on the general good, then all men must have the same freedom. I do not want to defend or elaborate these ideas here, but only to insist that anyone who claims that citizens have rights must accept ideas very close to these.

Notes and References

1. This quote corresponds to the second formulation of the categorical or practical imperative, Section II 'Transition from Popular Moral Philosophy to the Metaphysic of Morals', in Kant (1949a/1785): *Fundamental Principles of the Metaphysic of Morals*. Thomas K. Abbot tr. New York: Macmillan Publishing. p. 46, and has different versions, for example, Kant (1949b/1785). 'Metaphysical Foundations of Morals', in Carl J. Friedrich (ed.), *The Philosophy of Kant. Immanuel Kant's Moral and Political Writings*. Carl J. Friedrich tr. New York: The Modern Library. p. 178: 'Act so as to treat man, in your own person as well as in that of anyone else, always as an end, never merely as a means'; and, 1983/1785: 'Grounding for the Metaphysics of Morals', in Immanuel Kant, *Ethical Philosophy*. James W. Ellington tr. Indianapolis: Hackett Publishing. p. 36: 'Act in such a way that you treat humanity, whether in your own person or in the person of another, always at the same time as an end and never simply as a means'.
2. Ronald Dworkin. 1977a. *Taking Rights Seriously*. Cambridge, MA: Harvard University Press & London: Duckworth and Ronald Dworkin. 1978. *Taking Rights Seriously*, 2nd Edition. Cambridge, MA: Harvard University Press & London: Duckworth: p. vii.
3. Ronald Dworkin. 1974. 'Hard Cases', *Harvard Law Review* 88: pp. 1057–109 (reprinted in Dworkin [1977a and 1978]). See, for the early version Dworkin (1967, 1972, 1974, 1977a, and 1978); for the later version, Dworkin (1986); and, for the latest version Dworkin (2011).
4. Julie Dickson. 2001. *Evaluation and Legal Theory*. Oxford & Portland: Hart Publishing and Imer B. Flores. 2013a. 'The Problem about the Nature of Law viz-à-viz Legal Rationality Revisited: Towards an Integrative Jurisprudence', in W.J. Waluchow and S. Sciaraffa (eds), *Philosophical Foundations of The Nature of Law*. Oxford: Oxford University Press.
5. Dan Priel. 2014. 'Jurisprudential Disagreements and Descriptivism', *Problema. Anuario de Filosofía y Teoría del Derecho*. 8: pp. 483–512.
6. H.L.A. Hart. 1994. *The Concept of Law*, 2nd Edition, 'with Postscript'. Oxford: Oxford University Press.
7. The distinction between 'general and particular jurisprudence' can be traced all the way back to John Austin. 1998/1832. 'The Province of Jurisprudence Determined', in *The Province of Jurisprudence Determined and The Uses of the Study of Jurisprudence*. Indianapolis: Hackett Publishing: 'Particular [or National] Jurisprudence is the science of any actual system of law, or of any portion of it'. 'The proper subject of General or Universal Jurisprudence... is a description of

such subjects and ends of Law as are common to all systems' (372). See, for reference, Jeremy Bentham. 1996/1789. *An Introduction to the Principles of Morals and Legislation*. Oxford: Oxford University Press. (referring to the different branches of jurisprudence and using the parallel distinctions between 'universal and internal, local, national, particular or provincial jurisprudence'. pp. 293–300).

8. I am not only following Dickson (2001: 1–28 and 29–49), but also adapting Hart's distinction between 'descriptive/explanatory and normative/justificatory legal theory' (1994: 239–40; and 1982: 1–2, 41 and 137), which is parallel to Bentham's distinction between 'expository and censorial jurisprudence' (1996/1789: 293–4). Also see Jeremy Bentham. 1988/1776. *A Fragment on Government*. Cambridge: Cambridge University Press. 'A book of jurisprudence can have but one or the other of two objects: (a) to ascertain what the *law* is; (b) to ascertain what it ought to be. In the former case it may be styled a book of *expository* jurisprudence; in the latter, a book of *censorial* jurisprudence' (emphasis original); and (7): 'There are two characters, one or other of which every man who finds any thing to say on the subject of Law, may be said to take upon him—that of the *Expositor*, and that of the *Censor*. To the province of the *Expositor* it belongs to explain to us what, as he supposes, the Law *is*: to that of the *Censor*, to observe to us what he thinks it *ought to be*. The former, therefore, is principally occupied in stating, or in enquiring after *facts*: the latter, in discussing *reasons*.' (emphasis original)

9. Let me advance that for the purposes of this paper, I am especially interested in the possibility of connecting (1) 'general descriptive/explanatory legal theory' and (2) 'general normative/justificatory legal theory, on the one hand, and (3) 'particular descriptive/explanatory legal theory' and (4) 'particular normative/justificatory legal theory', on the other hand, and even the possibility of contrasting (1) and (3), on one side, and (2) and (4), on the other. The only two options that I do not consider feasible because they will turn out to be logically fallacious are connecting: (1) and (4); and (2) and (3); and, hence, they are completely ruled out.

10. John Austin. 1998/1863. 'The Uses of the Study of Jurisprudence', in *The Province of Jurisprudence Determined* and *The Uses of the Study of Jurisprudence*. Indianapolis: Hackett Publishing.

11. Hans Kelsen. 1967/1960. *Pure Theory of Law*, 2nd ed. Translated by Max Knight. Berkeley: University of California Press. p. 1 (emphasis original); and Hans Kelsen. 1992/1932. *Introduction to the Problems of Legal Theory*. Translated by Bonnie Litschewski Paulson and Stanley L. Paulson tr. Oxford: Oxford University Press. p. 7: 'The Pure Theory of Law is a theory of positive law, of positive law as such, and not of any special system of law. It is general legal theory, not an interpretation of particular national or international legal norms. As theory, the Pure Theory of Law aims solely at cognition of its subject-matter, its object. It attempts to answer the questions of what the law is and how the law is made, not the questions of what the law ought to be or how the law ought to be made. The Pure Theory of Law is legal science, not legal policy.'

12. Saint Augustine of Hippo. 1993. *On Free Choice of the Will*. Thomas Williams tr. Indianapolis: Hackett Publishing. pp. 387–9 and pp. 391–5: 8: 'an unjust law is not law at all'. See, for reference, Saint Thomas Aquinas. 2002/1265. *On Law, Morality and Politics* (selections of *Summa Theologica*). Richard J. Reagan tr. Indianapolis: Hackett Publishing. p. 54): 'Augustine says in his work *On Free Choice*: "Unjust laws do not seem to be laws".'

13. Andrei Marmor. 2001. *Positive Law and Objective Value*. Oxford: Oxford University Press.

14. Joseph Raz. 1994. *Ethics in the Public Domain*. Oxford: Oxford University Press.

15. Scott J. Shapiro. 2011. *Legality*. Cambridge, MA: Harvard University Press.

16. Jules Coleman. 2001. *The Practice of Principle. In Defense of a Pragmatist Approach*. Oxford: Oxford University Press.

17. Will Waluchow. 1994. *Inclusive Legal Positivism*. Oxford: Oxford University Press.

18. K.E. Himma. 2008. 'Reconsidering a Dogma: Conceptual Analysis, the Naturalistic Turn, and Legal Philosophy', in R. Harrison (ed.), *Law and Philosophy: Current Legal Issues*. Oxford: Oxford University Press.

19. Brian Leiter. 2007. *Naturalizing Jurisprudence. Essays on American Legal Realism and Naturalism in Legal Philosophy*. Oxford: Oxford University Press.

20. Andrei Marmor. 2013. 'Farewell to Conceptual Analysis (in Jurisprudence)', in W.J. Waluchow and S. Sciaraffa (eds), *Philosophical Foundations of The Nature of Law*. Oxford: Oxford University Press.

21. Frederick Schauer. 1996. 'Positivism as Pariah', in R.P. George (ed.), *The Autonomy of Law: Essays on Legal Positivism*. Oxford: Oxford University Press.

22. Adrian Vermeule. 2008. 'Connecting Positive and Normative Legal Theory', *University of Pennsylvania Journal of Constitutional Law* 10. pp. 387–98.

23. T. Campbell. 1996. *The Legal Theory of Ethical Positivism*. London: Ashgate.

24. Neil MacCormick. 1985. 'A Moralistic Case for A-Moralistic Law', *Valparaiso Law Review*. 20. pp. 1–41.

25. Liam Murphy. 2001. 'The Political Question of the Concept of Law', in J.L. Coleman (ed.), *Hart's Postscript. Essays on the Postscript to the Concept of Law*. Oxford: Oxford University Press.

26. Jeremy Waldron. 2001. 'Normative (or Ethical) Positivism', in J.L. Coleman (ed.), *Hart's Postscript. Essays on the Postscript to the Concept of Law*. Oxford: Oxford University Press.

27. Saint Thomas (2002/1265–74: 54): 'And a human law diverging in any way from the natural law will be a perversion of law and no longer a law'. See John Finnis. 1980. *Natural Law and Natural Rights*. Oxford: Oxford University Press. And also, John Finnis. 2011. *Natural Law and Natural Rights*, 2nd Edition. Oxford: Oxford University Press.; and, M.C. Murphy. 2013. 'The Explanatory Role of the Weak Natural Law Theory', in W.J. Waluchow and S. Sciaraffa (eds), *Philosophical Foundations of The Nature of Law*. Oxford: Oxford University Press.

28. I am grateful to Dan Priel who pointed out to me the importance of emphasizing the blurring of the lines dividing the different possibilities.

29. Ronald Dworkin. 1986. *Law's Empire*. Cambridge, MA: Harvard University Press. p. 90; and D. Kennedy. 1997. *A Critique of Adjudication (fin de siècle)*. Cambridge, MA: Harvard University Press. pp. 30–8.

30. Dworkin (1986: 90). Also see Ronald Dworkin. 1985. *A Matter of Principle*. Cambridge, MA: Harvard University Press; and Ronald Dworkin. 1987. 'Legal Theory and the Problem of Sense', in Ruth Gavison (ed.), *Issues in Contemporary Legal Philosophy*. Oxford: Oxford University Press.

31. John Rawls. 1971. *A Theory of Justice*. Cambridge, MA: Harvard University Press.

32. Ronald Dworkin. 1973. 'The Original Position', *University of Chicago Law Review*, 40: pp. 500–33 (reprinted as 'Justice and Rights' in Dworkin [1977a and 1978]).

33. Ronald Dworkin. 2011. *Justice for Hedgehogs*. Cambridge, MA: Harvard University Press. pp. 63–6; (p. 63): 'moral judgments are constructed, not discovered: they issue from an intellectual device adopted to confront practical, not theoretical, problems'.

34. Ronald Dworkin. 1982. 'Law as Interpretation', *Critical Inquiry* 9: pp. 179–200 (reprinted in *Texas Law Review*, 60: pp. 527–50; and, in W.J.T. Mitchell (ed.), *The Politics of Interpretation*. Chicago: Chicago University Press).

35. Ronald Dworkin. 1983. 'My Reply to Stanley Fish (and Walter Benn Michaels): Please Don't Talk about Objectivity Any More', in W.J.T. Mitchell (ed.), *The Politics of Interpretation*. Chicago: Chicago University Press.

36. Stanley Fish. 1982. 'Working on the Chain Gang: Interpretation in Law and Literature', *Critical Inquiry* 9. pp. 201–16 (reprinted in *Texas Law Review* 60: pp. 551–67; and, in W.J.T. Mitchell (ed.), *The Politics of Interpretation*. Chicago: Chicago University Press).

37. Stanley Fish. 1983. 'Wrong Again', *Texas Law Review* 61: pp. 299–316.

38. And also, Ronald Dworkin. 2006a. *Justice in Robes*. Cambridge, MA: Harvard University Press. pp. 9–12

39. Dworkin (2006a: 10; and, 2011: 158–9).

40. Dworkin (1985: 146–8; 1986: 45–96; 2006a: 10–2; and, 2011: 160–3 and 403–5).

41. Dworkin (1986: 52); and Dworkin (1986: 90): 'constructive interpretations… try to show legal practice as a whole in its best light, to achieve equilibrium between legal practice as they find it and the best justification of that practice.' In that sense, Dworkin's interpretive model is not merely applicative but argumentative as well: I.B. Flores. 2016. '(Un)Chaining Prometheus: Is Law an Applicative Model?', *Problema. Anuario de Filosofía y Teoría del Derecho*, 10: pp. 167–91.

42. Dworkin (1986); I.B. Flores. 2012. 'Natalie Stoljar's Wishful Thinking and One Step Beyond: What Should Conceptual Legal Analysis Become?', *Problema. Anuario de Filosofía y Teoría del Derecho*. 6. pp. 81–105).

43. Dworkin (1986: 66–7): 'He also needs convictions about how far the justification he proposes at the interpretive stage must fit the standing features of the practice to count as an interpretation of it rather than the invention of something

new'; and, Dworkin (2006a: 15): 'Any lawyer has built up, through education, training, and experience, his own sense of when an interpretation fits well enough to count as an interpretation rather than as an invention.'

44. Dworkin (1985; 1986). Ronald Dworkin. 1996a. *Freedom's Law: The Moral Reading of the American Constitution*. Cambridge, MA: Harvard University Press. pp. 1–38. (2006a and 2011); and I.B. Flores. 2008. 'The Living Tree: Fixity and Flexibility. A General Theory of (Judicial Review in a) Constitutional Democracy?', *Problema. Anuario de Filosofía y Teoría del Derecho*. 2. pp. 285–305; 2009a. 'Legisprudence: The Role and Rationality of Legislators—viz-à-viz Judges—towards the Realization of Justice, *Mexican Law Review* 1(2). pp. 91–110; 2009b. 'The Living Tree Constitutionalism: Fixity and Flexibility', *Problema. Anuario de Filosofía y Teoría del Derecho*. 3. pp. 37–74.

45. Dworkin (1986: 94–6; especially 96): '[Law as integrity] argues that rights and responsibilities flow from past decisions and so count as legal, not just when they are explicit in these decisions but also when they follow from the principles of personal and political morality the explicit decisions presuppose by way of justi-fication'; Dworkin (1986: 176–224 and 225–75, especially 176): 'We have two principles of political integrity: a legislative principle, which asks law makers to try to make the total set of laws morally *coherent*, and an adjudicative principle, which instructs that the law be seen as *coherent* in that way, so far as possible' (emphasis added); Dworkin (1986: 225): 'Law as integrity denies that statements of law are either the backward-looking factual reports of conventionalism or the forward-looking instrumental programs of legal pragmatism. It insists that legal claims are interpretive judgments and therefore combine backward- and forward-looking elements; they interpret contemporary legal practice seen as an unfolding political narrative. So law as integrity rejects as unhelpful the ancient question whether judges find or invent law; we understand legal reasoning, it suggests, only by seeing the sense in which they do both and neither'; Dworkin (1986: 406): 'We hope that our legislature will recognize what justice requires so that no practical conflict remains between justice and legislative supremacy; we hope that departments of law will be rearranged, in professional and public understanding, to map true distinctions of principle, so that local priority presents no impediment to a judge seeking a natural flow of principle throughout the law'; and I.B. Flores. 2005. 'The Quest for Legisprudence: Constitutionalism v. Legalism', in Luc J. Wintgens (ed.), *The Theory and Practice of Legislation: Essays on Legisprudence*. London: Ashgate. pp. 35–8 and pp. 43–7; Flores 2007. 'Legisprudence: The Forms and Limits of Legislation', *Problema. Anuario de Filosofía y Teoría del Derecho*. pp. 257–60 and pp. 264–6; 2008: pp. 100–6 and pp. 106–109; and, Flores 2013a: pp. 115–23)

46. Ronald Dworkin. 2004. 'Hart's Postscript and the Character of Political Philosophy', *Oxford Journal of Legal Studies* 24. pp. 1–37 (reprinted as 'Hart's Postscript and the Point of Political Philosophy', in Ronald Dworkin [2006a]).

47. Dworkin (2006a: 160): 'must try to understand them holistically and interpre-tively, each in the light of the others, organized not in a hierarchy but in a fashion of a geodesic dome.'

48. Dworkin (1977a and 1978: XV): 'That promise of *unity* in political theory is indistinct in these essays, however. It must be defended, if at all, elsewhere. In particular it must be shown how the same conception of equal concern that justifies the trade-offs characteristic of economic collective goals also justifies exemption, in the form of economic rights, for those who suffer most from those trade-offs.'

49. Dworkin (1977a and 1978: 26 and 41); and, I.B. Flores. 2010. 'Ronald Dworkin's Justice for Hedgehogs and Partnership Conception of Democracy (With a Comment to Jeremy Waldron's "A Majority in the Lifeboat")', *Problema. Anuario de Filosofía y Teoría del Derecho*. 4. pp. 65–103; and I.B. Flores. 2013b. 'Proportionality in Constitutional and Human Rights Interpretation', *Problema. Anuario de Filosofía y Teoría del Derecho*. 7: 83–113.

50. And also Dworkin (2011: 82): '[W]e must make assumptions about what is true in order to test theories about how to decide what is true.'

51. Also see Ronald Dworkin. 2013. *Religion Without God*. Cambridge, MA: Harvard University Press. p. 90).

52. And Ronald Dworkin. 2006b. *Is Democracy Possible Here? Principles for a New Political Debate*. Princeton: Princeton University Press. p. 21: 'Our ethical convictions define what we should count as a good life for ourselves; our moral principles define our obligations and responsibilities to other people'.

53. Also see Ronald Dworkin. 1967. 'The Model of Rules', *University of Chicago Law Review* 35. pp. 14–46 (reprinted as 'Model of Rules I' in Dworkin [1977a and 1978]) and Ronald Dworkin. 1972. 'Social Rules and Legal Theory', *Yale Law Journal* 81. pp. 855–90 (reprinted as 'Model of Rules II' in Dworkin (1977a and 1978)).

54. And, Dworkin (2006: 34–5): 'We might treat law not as separate from but as a department of morality. We understand political theory that way: as part of morality more generally understood but distinguished, with its own distinct substance, because applicable to distinct institutional structures. We might treat legal theory as a special part of political morality distinguished by a further refinement of institutional structures'.

55. Waluchow 1994 and 2007. *A Common Law Theory of Judicial Review: The Living Tree*. Cambridge: Cambridge University Press; Coleman (2001); K.E. Himma. 2002. 'Inclusive Legal Positivism', in Jules Coleman and Scott Shapiro (eds), *The Oxford Handbook of Jurisprudence & Philosophy of Law*. Oxford: Oxford University Press; and Robert Alexy. 2002/1994. *The Argument from Injustice*. Bonnie Litschewski Paulson and Stanley Paulson tr. Oxford: Oxford University Press; 2012. 'Law, Morality, and the Existence of Human Rights', *Ratio Juris. An International Journal of Jurisprudence and Philosophy of Law* 25: 2–14. and 2013/2012. 'Between Positivism and Non-positivism? A Third Reply to Eugenio Bulygin', in J. Ferrer Beltrán et al. (eds), *Neutrality and Theory of Law*. Dordrecht: Springer.

56. Dworkin (2011: 19): 'A person can achieve the dignity and self-respect that are indispensable to a successful life only if he shows respect for humanity itself in all

its forms.' Dworkin (2006b: 16): '[I]t is impossible to separate self-respect from respect for the importance of the lives of others. You cannot act in a way that denies the intrinsic importance of any human life without an insult to your own dignity… [R]espect for our own humanity means respect for humanity as such; Kant insisted that if you treat others as mere means whose lives have no intrinsic importance, then you are despising your own life as well.'

57. Bernard Williams. 1984. *Moral Luck*. Cambridge: Cambridge University Press. pp. 20–40.

58. Dworkin (2011: 202); and, Rawls (1971: 214–21).

59. It is worth to mention that Dworkin constructed in slightly different terms the two dimensions of human dignity in (2006b: 9–10): 'The first principle—which I call the principle of intrinsic value—holds that each human life has a special kind of objective value. It has value as potentiality; once a human life has begun, it matters how it goes. It is good when that life succeeds and its potential is realized and bad when it fails and its potential wasted… The second principle—the principle of personal responsibility—holds that each person has a special responsibility for realizing the success of his own life, a responsibility that includes exercising his judgment about what kind of life would be successful for him… These two principles—that every human life is of intrinsic potential value and that everyone has a responsibility for realizing that value in his own life—together define the basis and conditions of human dignity, and I shall therefore refer to them as principles or dimensions of dignity.'

60. Dworkin (2011: 255; and 255–70).

61. Dworkin (2011: pp. 285–99)

62. Dworkin (2011: 255); and (2011: 260): 'The first principle of dignity, recast to make plain the objective value of any human life, becomes what I called Kant's principle. Your reason for thinking it objectively important how your life goes is also a reason you have for thinking it important how anyone's life goes; you see the objective importance of your life mirrored in the objective importance of everyone else's.'

63. Dworkin (2011: 274–5; 275–6; 276–7; and 277–80).

64. J.J. Thompson. 1984. 'The Trolley Problem', *Yale Law Journal* 94: pp. 1395–415; and F.M. Kamm. 2001. 'The Trolley Problem' in *Morality, Mortality*, Vol. 2: *Rights, Duties, and Status*. New York: Oxford University Press. 2006. *Intricate Ethics: Rights, Responsibilities, and Permissible Harm*. Oxford: Oxford University Press.

65. Dworkin (2011: 304); and, (2011: 310): 'promising is not a self-contained practice that generates obligations automatically, but is instead parasitic on the much more general duty not to harm others.'

66. Dworkin (2011: 318); and (1977a and 1978: 17): 'In a democracy, or at least a democracy that in principle respects individual rights, each citizen has a general moral duty to obey all the laws, even though he would like some of them changed. He owes that duty to his fellow citizens, who obey laws that they do not like, to his benefit. But this general duty cannot be an absolute duty, because

even a society that is in principle just may produce unjust laws and policies, and a man has duties other than his duties to the State. A man must honour his duties to his God and to his conscience, and if these conflict with his duty to the State, then he is entitled, in the end, to do what he judges to be right'.

67. Dworkin (2011: 320); and (2006b: 21): 'The principle of personal responsibility (which is more or less equivalent to the principle of authenticity) allows the state to force us to live in accordance with collective decisions of moral principle, but it forbids the state to dictate ethical convictions in that way'.

68. Ronald Dworkin. 1993. *Life's Dominion. An Argument about Abortion, Euthanasia, and Individual Freedom.* New York: Knopf; 2000. *Sovereign Virtue: The Theory and Practice of Equality.* Cambridge, MA: Harvard University Press. 1996b. 'Objectivity and Truth: You'd Better Believe It', *Philosophy and Public Affairs.* 25: 87–139.

69. Dworkin (1977a and 1978: 279); 1977b: 'No Right Answer?', in P.M.S. Hacker and J. Raz (eds), *Law, Morality and Society: Essays in Honour of H.L.A. Hart.* Oxford: Oxford University Press. 84; Dworkin 1985; and, 1996b: 136.

70. I.B. Flores. 2011. 'H.L.A. Hart's Moderate Indeterminacy Thesis Reconsidered: In Between Scylla and Charybdis?', *Problema. Anuario de Filosofía y Teoría del Derecho.* 5: 150–1, fn 3.

71. See, Stephen Guest. 1992. *Ronald Dworkin.* Stanford: Stanford University Press. Although Guest used to emphasize that Dworkin's 'one right answer' thesis was 'purely defensive', I will like to suggest that Dworkin's defence became part of his offense as both the adagio 'The best offense is a good defence' and the proverb *a meilleur défense c'est l'attaque,* i.e. 'attack is the best defence'. (137–47, especially 145): 'Dworkin's thesis is… a defensive thesis to the criticism that there cannot be right answers in hard cases where there is no "proof" or demonstration'; and, Stephen Guest. 2013. *Ronald Dworkin,* 3rd edition. Stanford: Stanford University Press. pp. 135–43.

72. Dworkin (2011: 120; and, 1993); L.L. Fuller. 1999/1949. 'The Case of the Speluncean Explorers', *Harvard Law Review.* 112: 1859–75.

73. Ronald Dworkin. 1970. 'A Special Supplement: Taking Rights Seriously', *New York Review of Books,* December 17 (reprinted as 'Taking Rights Seriously', in Dworkin (1977a and 1978)); and (1977a and 1978: 198–9).

6

Are There Any Interpretative Concepts?*

Pritam Baruah

Ronald Dworkin proposes that moral values such as dignity, truth, responsibility, and equality are interpretive concepts. The idea of interpretive concepts has consistently occupied a central place in Dworkin's work on legal and moral philosophy.[1] As he says in *Justice for Hedgehogs*, '[D]ignity like so many of the concepts that figure in my long argument, is an interpretive concept.'[2]

In this paper, I offer a critique of Dworkin's characterization of moral values as interpretive concepts. My conclusion is that given the literature on the nature of concepts, an argument for interpretive concepts having a special conceptual nature is unsustainable. By conceptual nature I mean that Dworkin's claim amounts to saying that certain concepts have a special nature as *concepts*. In his own words, 'I suggest that we treat certain concepts as special by designating them as interpretive concepts whose nature cannot be explicated except through normative argument' (Dworkin 2010: 102). Note that the designation claim is about the nature of special *concepts* and not the phenomena that they are concepts of. Such concepts are special because they are interpretive—a quality all such concepts possess. The justification for such a claim then lies in explaining what it means to be interpretive, and how that is a property of

* I thank James Penner and Jeff King for critical comments on a very early draft of this paper.

a class of concepts. Dworkin's work must have offered an explanation of what concepts are, and how the nature of concepts allowed for them to be interpretive. I saddle his theory with this burden. As there is in philosophy, psychology, and cognitive science extensive literature on what concepts are. On my argument, the fundamental premises of that literature do not allow interpretive concepts to be a kind of concept on the basis of their conceptual nature.

Distinct from *conceptual nature*, though related in many ways, is a question about *conceptual content*. It is evident from Dworkin's view of interpretive concepts, that he thinks their nature to be explicable by normative argument alone. I argue this to be a distinct claim making sense about the content of concepts and the phenomena that the concepts represent. Indeed, this claim does hold valuable insights about how the *content* of concepts is determined, and it is this claim that motivates Dworkin's prescription of how we ought to reason with interpretive concepts. I critically examine that claim elsewhere. The claim about content however, is not an argument about how we should understand the conceptual nature of interpretive concepts. I establish this by first pointing out some mistakes about how Dworkin is commonly understood. I then argue that he has a picture of interpretive concepts that is logically prior to his claims about why normative argument is required to understand such concepts. My argument in this paper is that this prior picture is unsustainable if one were to hold a plausible view about what concepts are. One way of looking at the critical argument in this paper is that it is aimed at a general strategy of characterizing values as special kinds of concepts by attributing a special conceptual nature to them. Interpretive concepts are a contemporary paradigm of such a strategy.[3] An illustrious predecessor is W.B. Gallie's idea of Essentially Contested Concepts, which Dworkin recognized in one of his early works.[4] Gallie characterized the special nature of some values as essentially contested.[5] Likewise, Dworkin characterizes the conceptual nature of all values as 'interpretive'. He additionally claims that the peculiar nature of interpretive concepts controls how we ought to reason with values.[6] The first claim is an account of what interpretive concepts are, while the second claim about reasoning with values is a prescription of how one ought to reason with such concepts.[7] This paper focuses on the first claim to argue that the idea of interpretive concepts does not amount to a claim about the special *conceptual nature* of values.[8]

Understanding Interpretive Concepts

Dworkin offers several values including DIGNITY, TRUTH, LEGALITY, RESPONSIBILITY, EQUALITY, FRIENDSHIP, and COURTESY as examples of interpretive concepts.[9] Multiple claims contribute towards explaining why such concepts are interpretive concepts. These include claims about their having a deep structure,[10] that structure being normative (Dworkin 2007: 155), the concepts themselves being integrated (156–9), and interpretation of those concepts being a conceptual matter (155). The background against which he brings up the proposal of interpretive concepts also involves more than one influential theory in law and political philosophy. In particular, he employs interpretive concepts to explain how his theory of law and his characterization of moral and political philosophy differ from Hart's claims to a descriptive theory of law, and Isaiah Berlin's value pluralism. Given the several claims that Dworkin makes about interpretive concepts, I will pick out three distinct attempts at conceptualizing interpretive concepts which are found in three of his most influential works. The latest and the clearest conceptualization is found in *Justice for Hedgehogs*, where Dworkin defines what interpretive concepts are. Earlier attempts are in *Law's Empire*, where he explains interpretive concepts through the idea of constructive interpretation, and in *Justice in Robes*, where he lists some constitutive elements of political concepts, which he thinks are interpretive. I will examine these conceptualizations in chronological order.

Interpretive Concepts in *Law's Empire*: Moral Reasoning through Paradigms

In *Law's Empire*, Dworkin employed the idea of interpretive concepts to defend his account of theoretical disagreement in law. His strategy was to extrapolate the question from the realm of law and frame it in terms of disagreement generally. The resulting project was aimed at demonstrating that genuine disagreement about a concept was possible even in the absence of clear criteria defining the concept. He thus set out to explain how people could disagree about what a concept is, and what it requires, and still be sure that they are talking about the same concept, that is, they have a genuine disagreement.[11] The answer he proposed relied on the function of paradigms—since participants directed their interpretations at the same paradigm cases, they could be sure that they were speaking about the same concept (Dworkin 1998: 46). It is important to note that in *Law's Empire* despite invoking the term 'interpretive concepts' Dworkin claimed that his theory aimed at explaining interpretive social *practices* and *structures* (49). Perhaps this explains the idea of being interpretive as something that participants in a practice do, rather than being a property of concepts. Allow me to reserve my examination of this issue for a discussion of interpretive concepts in *Justice for Hedgehogs*, where Dworkin develops his thinking more along these lines. I point this out now since Dworkin employs the term interpretive to characterize both concepts and practices, and employed these two terms interchangeably.

In *Law's Empire*, Dworkin argued that to understand disagreements that arise in interpretive practices like law, one must abandon criterialism—the view that the correct use of a concept depends on the shared criteria that participants hold about the concept (Dworkin 2007: 151). Genuine disagreement could ensue in the absence of settled criteria about the concept due to the existence of common paradigms, and in offering contesting views of the concept, participants engaged in constructive interpretation mediated by paradigms. Participants postulate a point and purpose to the concept/practice,[12] and examine which interpretation of the concept best justified this point and purpose, and also its paradigm cases. He sometimes labels this point and purpose 'the concept', and the candidate explanations as 'conceptions' (Dworkin 1998: 71). At other times he calls it the value that justifies the practice (66).[13] Despite the varied terminology, in effect he proposes a two-stage ascent in the reasoning of participants when they engage in constructive interpretation. The stages are represented in Figure 7.1.

In this scheme, no paradigm is safe from revision since it is the concept that participants seek to develop an understanding of (Dworkin 1998: 72). The paradigm is instrumental. It is an instance that represents the concept/value, and provides a common point of access to that value. Perhaps in Platonic terms, the paradigms are cases that represent hypotheses about what the concept is, and participants must ascend to the level of understanding to realize what these paradigms really are by exercising their power of reason.[14] To use one of Dworkin's examples, the paradigm cases of courtesy are actually about respect, and the various practices of courtesy that we have, are therefore, about respect (1998: 71). To determine what courtesy requires, we must understand what respect is. The role of paradigms here is that through them, participants try

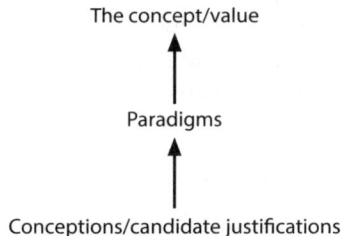

Figure 7.1 Constructive Interpretation in *Law's Empire*
Source: Author.

and access the reasons that are a true understanding of the concept of respect. Their own conceptions in turn are their best effort at discovering this truth.

In the process of constructively interpreting our practice, one dimension of proof is that of fit with paradigms. This occurs at a time when the paradigms are not yet proven to be mistakes. Here, accounts of values that fit the paradigm will be more convincing than others. However, evidence of fit is not proof of having arrived at the truth of the matter (Dworkin 2010: 131).[15] When we have some view of the values that are in operation in explaining the paradigms, we are in a position to reason with the values themselves and thus transcend the limits of the paradigm. Once we are past the paradigms and in the realm of values, Dworkin thinks that we will discover a moral value that justifies the practice. It is this value that will guide us in thinking about what it requires of us. Such a value might turn out to be a contested concept, and we will have to depend on our own moral convictions and reasoning to determine what it requires (Dworkin 1996: 101–3).

In this picture of constructive interpretation, note that Dworkin has not made any claims about the nature of interpretive concepts. He provides us an account of *how* we should, and on his account, do, reason with such concepts. That however does not explain *why* we should reason that way with those concepts. If such concepts do warrant constructive interpretation, something must be said about the nature of these concepts that requires such interpretation. The account of interpretive concepts in *Law's Empire* is silent on this matter. Rather its value lies in describing how genuine disagreement is possible due to paradigms, and in prescribing how one embarks on constructive interpretation. It does not explain how moral reasoning mediated by paradigms is required by the nature of concepts involved. Though it might be true that in several practices that Dworkin labels as interpretive, participants do engage in constructive interpretation; that does not make a case for certain *concepts* being interpretive in nature. Perhaps Dworkin realizes this inadequacy and therefore offers us an account of the nature of interpretive concepts now found in *Justice in Robes* (Chapter 6). Here he proposes some constitutive elements of interpretive concepts. This account, therefore, holds more promise in explaining how the idea of interpretive concepts enables us to understand the nature of moral and political values, and how that warrants reasoning with them in a special manner.

Constitutive Features of Interpretive Concepts

Dworkin spells out three constitutive features of interpretive concepts. First, that they have a deep structure (2007: 154–5). Second, that at the heart of this structure is a normative core (154–5). Third, that to share such concepts participants in a practice must take the correct use of the concept to be the best justification of the role that it is supposed to play for them (2010: 158). In this section I will examine the first two claims. The third feature turns out to be a definition of what interpretive concepts are, and I examine that closely in the following section. The objective in this section is to examine if the first two claims make out a strong case for some concepts to be understood as interpretive, and whether the notion of being interpretive in this sense furthers our understanding of how participants in a practice reason with interpretive concepts.

That interpretive concepts have a 'deep structure' is a relatively new argument from Dworkin's armory. It closely connects his interpretivism to Nicos Stavropoulos's work on semantics and substantive disagreement. The argument rests on an analogy with natural kind concepts; the claim being, that interpretive concepts are similar to natural kinds to the limited extent of both having deep structures as their cores. Dworkin offers a skeletal account of the deep structure argument when taken on its own. But situating it in the context of the views he challenges brings out the major philosophical claims that he thinks it supports. So let me first reconstruct the argument with Dworkin's statements and then situate it in the context of other views that he develops.

Dworkin claims that *political* concepts have a deep structure. I read this as being a claim that *interpretive* concepts have a deep structure. This is so because Dworkin does not clearly state what political concepts are. Rather he lists many of the concepts that he thinks are interpretive, to be political concepts. In this he does not distinguish between political, legal, or moral concepts. Perhaps it is a fair reading of his work to say that interpretive concepts, including political ones have a deep structure. The case for this reading becomes stronger with his claim in *Justice for Hedgehogs* that all our concepts of value are interpretive (2010: 166). Since most of the political concepts he lists, for example, justice, freedom, and liberty, are concepts of values, it is more than safe to assume that Dworkin's claim about deep structure applies to all interpretive concepts.

Dworkin claims that political concepts such as justice, freedom, and liberty have a deep structure, similar to the deep structure of natural kind concepts such as water or gold. Their deep structure explains other characteristics of political concepts just as the deep structure of a natural kind explains its other features (Dworkin 2007: 154). The deep structure of a concept is therefore, fundamental to its nature. However, on Dworkin's view, unlike the deep structure of natural kind concepts, which is physical, the deep structure of political concepts is normative (155). Being normative does not make the deep structure of interpretive concepts any more elusive than that of natural kinds. Dworkin believes that '...just as a scientist can aim, as a distinct kind of project, to reveal the very nature of a tiger or of gold by exposing the basic physical structure of these entities, so a political philosopher can aim to reveal the very nature of freedom by exposing its normative core' (155).

Notice that the deep structure argument makes a case for the existence of objectivity in the realm of political values. This fits well with Dworkin's views on objectivity in law and morals that critiqued an Archimedean view of morality generally by denying the possibility of external scepticism (Dworkin 1996: 25).[16] The deep structure argument develops a novel dimension of critiquing Archimedianism about political concepts by attacking the criterial semantics on which it rests. In brief, the Archimedean view holds that political values can be described in a neutral manner without engaging in substantive normative arguments about what they are (Dworkin 2007: 145–50). It holds that even if we disagree about what such concepts require, or even what they are, there is a threshold agreement on what we take them to be before we have disagreements about them (148). Dworkin alleges that holding such a view permits philosophers like Isaiah Berlin to claim that the meaning (content) of a concept, say liberty, can be established by conceptual analysis that does not involve 'normative judgment, assumptions or reasoning' (146). Archimedeans believe such analysis to be purely descriptive and therefore neutral among the controversies that are involved in the practice (137).[17] In opposition, Dworkin cites evidence from the practice of applying political concepts as contradicting the Archimedean view. He argues that participants in a practice that involves political concepts do not disagree merely on whether a particular concept, say democracy, is important or not, but they disagree on what democracy *is* (Dworkin 2007: 148).[18] Their arguments about what democracy *is* are normative arguments. They are normative arguments about a *value* that democracy tries to capture. Participants contest the description of democracy by others with their own; the bone of contention being, which description best captures or realizes the value.

I take it that it is this value that is the normative core that Dworkin thinks constitutes the deep structure of interpretive concepts (2007: 156).[19] Participants hold different descriptive senses of a political practice because they differ in their beliefs about which description best justifies the value. In such disagreements participants dispute each other's descriptions of political concepts such as Justice, Democracy, and Dignity. Dworkin thinks that in such disagreement we try and provide an account of the value that lies at the core of the concept. This I think might be true. When we disagree about what justice is, it is not to say that we do not have the concept of justice, rather we have different beliefs about what justice stands for. Traditionally situations of different beliefs about the same concept have been spoken in terms of concepts and conceptions (Dworkin 1998: 71). The central question has been about whether the conceptions are about the same concept.

Dworkin has at least three answers to this question all of which anchor disagreement in prior agreement, the first of which we have examined in considering agreement as pre-interpretive materials in the form of paradigms. The second answer was agreement on the criteria required for sharing an interpretive concept (2010: 158). And the third is the fact of the existence of a deep structure which roots our disagreement in common ground. The last is not an answer that Dworkin expressly provides for the question about agreement. It is a possible answer—since there is a deep structure of interpretive concepts that can be elucidated by philosophers, our differing beliefs are those about the deep structure.

I will consider these answers in turn in light of Nicos Stavropoulos's explanation of substantive disagreement on the basis of K-P semantics, which he thinks is compatible with Dworkin's interpretivism. Stavropoulos's K-P semantics that purportedly supports Dworkin's theory of law is an argument for substantive disagreement in law. His account also provides a detailed account of a deep structure of political concepts which is probably what Dworkin has in mind too.

K-P Semantics, Deep Structure, and Paradigms

The question of disagreement about what a practice *is*, has been variously understood, sometimes as the debate on substantive disagreement, or as theoretical disagreement in law, or rational disagreement in philosophy. The central question is about how we understand disagreements where participants argue over what a practice is, without characterizing it as radical disagreement. David Plunkett and Tinothy Sundell have argued that Dworkin's characterization of such disagreement is mistaken.[20] My intuition is that their criticisms are sound. In this paper however, my focus is not on the mis-characterization of such disagreements as theoretical disagreement. My attention is directed at how answers to the question of theoretical disagreement can be anchored in a question about concepts, as Stavropoulos does. That answer however, does not make a case for some concepts being interpretive concepts.

Dworkin and Stavropoulos have argued that positivist theories of law are unable to explain theoretical disagreement except as cases of radical disagreement. Positivists are destined to such a conclusion due to the criterial semantics, or criterialism, they adopt (1998: 45–6).[21] Criterialism is the view that the determining factor for the correct use of concepts depends on their conformity to certain shared criteria that users hold (Dworkin 2007: 151). It holds that the extension of a concept is determined by criteria that is conventionally determined by users, and when there are cases in which the agreement among users that underlies the standard cases break down, then there will be indeterminacy over the application of the concept.[22]

Dworkin attributes criterialism to Hart and other legal positivists.[23] On this view, if participants in a practice disagree over what a concept is, then they probably hold different criteria for the meaning of the concept. Their disagreement, therefore, is not intelligible since they are not disagreeing about the same concept. In contrast, Dworkin argues that participants in practices like law routinely engage in disagreement about what the law is, or what the grounds of law are. Positivists would have to take all such disagreements to be radical ones.

As an alternative, Dworkin proposes that political concepts, including law, are interpretive. Their correct use does not depend on any agreed criteria that users of the concept hold. This proposal is supported by at least two distinct arguments, one advanced by Nicos Stavropoulos and the other by Dworkin himself. Until the publication of *Justice in Robes* and *Justice for Hedgehogs*, it appeared that Dworkin's criticism of criterialism supervened on Stavropoulos'. Now it appears that Dworkin adheres to criterialism of some sort as he posits a criterion to be shared by participants that generates the agreement required for meaningful disagreement about political concepts, including law. Let me first take up the chronologically prior view that is argued for at length by Stavropoulos.

In his book *Objectivity in Law*, Stavropoulos relied on Saul Kripke and Hilary Putnam's work on meaning (K-P Semantics) to criticize criterialism, and consequently legal positivism. His work made positions in the theory of meaning (semantics) central to debates in legal philosophy, especially the Hart-Dworkin debate. Stavropoulos' semantics also made concepts the principal unit of semantics, as opposed to words.[24] Adopting K-P semantics, he argues that the meaning of concepts does not depend on any criteria that the community of users might hold as the meaning of the concept.[25] Rather like in the case of natural kinds like water and gold, the meaning of other concepts is also in the referent, which is an objective property in the world. Reference is object-dependent. Stavropoulos then transfers this argument to what he calls *legal concepts*. I will take this to mean that K-P semantics can apply to non-natural kind concepts. This is his crucial cognitivist move that does not require a commitment to strong realism.[26] Borrowing from McDowell's views on objectivism, Stavropoulos adopts the position that for such properties to be objective they need not be 'queer' mind-independent properties.[27] He then makes the core claim that drives the rest of his book, and in this he follows Tyler Burge's anti-individualism about meaning, constrained by Davidson's 'Principle of Charity'.[28] Stavropoulos explains the claim first in the context of propositional attitudes like thoughts, beliefs, and intentions. The claim is that mental contents are not autonomous (world-independent). They are individuated by their object. Objects here are not to be construed as physical mind-independent properties. Rather they are to be explained by taking into consideration the 'subject's purposes and actions', along with 'objective factors affecting his relation with the environment' (Stavropoulos 2000: 42). 'Hence what thought will be attributed to the subject depends on the most coherent story available concerning the subject' (42). There is however a bootstrapping allegation that Stavropoulos anticipates to his argument. In order to be able to attribute thoughts, beliefs, or intentions to a subject, we must rely on some characterization of the subject's actions, and on the meaning of the language used. Such attribution and meaning itself is dependent on relevant propositional attitudes again, and thus the bootstrapping allegation. To overcome the allegation Stavropoulos introduces the principle of charity as a *constitutive non-optional* constraint—that we assume that the speaker is rational in a *substantive* way by ascribing natural contents to her—that she believes in certain truths, has sensible desires, uses language properly, and so on. Without these assumptions we will be unable to view the subject as a subject (43). This principle of charity does not imply indubitable truths about the ascriptions we make to the subject. Rather it leaves room for error in the form of Davidson's two interpretive devices. The first is an evaluation of how well placed and equipped the subject is to observe aspects of her environment. The second is the evaluation of her connections among the beliefs attributed to her with special emphasis on her epistemic beliefs, that is, belief in sentences whose truth she counts as supporting the truth of others.

Burge's non-individualism coupled with Davidson's principle of charity thus supports a view of the meaning of concepts that is compatible with K-P semantics' object dependence. In the case of non-natural kinds, the object that is the referent of the concept is to be found in the manner in which a community *in fact* uses a concept, not on what criteria the community thinks to be the correct meaning of the concept. Meaning is thus not conventional. Even for concepts that are theoretical, say for example the meaning of 'phlogiston' is dependent on complex ways in which we have cognitive access to the world (45–6). In the case of theoretical concepts, the properties described in introducing such terms are 'reference-fixing devices liable to be amended as more information is available concerning the physical property they are really meant to capture' (45, 88). They are *targeted* on nature. Thus, phlogiston is about combustion, and as we come to know more about combustion we may revise our beliefs about phlogiston.

But in the case of theoretical concepts that do not clearly refer to physical properties in the world, how do we determine the content of a concept, other than by turning to what the community takes to be the fact of the matter, the best evidence of which is the criteria that it takes to be correct? Stavropoulos answers that we must construct a theory based on paradigms of what that property is. We try and construct the best coherent account we can, of the property that collects for us the paradigms of the concept (46, 146). Our theories are *targeted* at the property which exists in nature (88). This demonstrates the semantic depth of the theoretical concept—it is not merely theoretical stipulations, but stipulations targeted at properties in the world which act as data constraints. For Stavropoulos, the meaning of theoretical concepts is determined both by mental states of concept holders, as well as their relationship to properties in nature, in the manner I described above (146).

Can Stavropoulos' account sustain a claim about the deep structure of interpretive concepts? What the account does do is anchor questions about substantive disagreement to question about conceptual content. If the content of theoretical concepts (read interpretive concepts) is determined partly by properties in nature, then perhaps that is the deep structure that Dworkin might be referring to. On Stavropoulos' account however, the content of concepts being fixed to referents in the world is a theory of content in general applicable to all concepts. What is special about interpretive concepts then? If interpretive concepts are theoretical concepts, then arguably, their content is also to be determined in part by mental states of concept holders in that they construct theories about the property that collects the paradigms of the concept. This takes us back to the circularity of Dworkin's constructive interpretation. Indeed, Stavropoulos takes this circularity to be inevitable (146). To repeat, it is unclear as to whether the property collects the paradigms for us, or whether the paradigms are all we have in taking a shot at the property that the concept represents? Be that as it may, my intention here is to point out that Stavropoulos' view is one about conceptual content and not the special conceptual nature of some concepts. Even if we were to admit that theoretical concepts were special due to the special manner in which their content was determined, it certainly does not amount to saying that they have a deep structure as concepts, which can be elucidated. If the claim is, that when we apply such concepts we offer theoretical accounts of what the paradigms aim at, then that is a claim about how the content of concepts is determined, not a claim about what their content is. Neither does it explain why content need be determined in this manner. If the answer was indeterminacy, then all indeterminate concepts would be interpretive concepts.[29] Dworkin however, refrains from admitting this clearly and ends up offering a novel ground for designating some concepts to be interpretive. I discuss this in the following section.

The lesson to be drawn from the discussion in this section is threefold. First, that Dworkin does not offer a clear picture of what the deep structure of interpretive concepts is. Second, Stavropoulos' attempts at explaining substantive disagreement through K-P semantics is a theory of conceptual content that does not immediately make out a case for the special conceptual nature of certain concepts. Indeed, his is a view that relies partly on K-P semantics and partly on particular forms of holism as theories of both conceptual content and the content of mental states. I fear that the aspects of his theory that rely on holism are fraught with problems if applied to questions of conceptual content.[30] They are more suited for explaining the content of mental states. Since I do not take up these issues here, let me point out that Stavropoulos' views are not a view about the nature of concepts that is, they do not answer the questions, 'What is a concept?' and 'What are the different kinds of concepts?' Neither do his views support a view that there is a deep structure of interpretive concepts that is normative. Indeed, the content of theoretical concepts is akin to that of natural kinds in that mind-world relations figure in both. Both kinds of concepts are linked to referents in nature.

The third lesson to be drawn from this section is that it is unduly burdensome to establish the special nature of some concepts on the basis of how their content is determined. For that one must propose a theory of content determination of some concepts that is peculiar to them. Theories of conceptual content generally hold that the content of all concepts is determined in a similar manner. For instance, holism holds that the content of concepts is determined by their relationships with other concepts;[31] theories about inferential role hold that the content of concepts is determined by their inferential relations to other concepts;[32] while information-atomism holds that the content of concepts is determined by law-like relationships that mental particulars have with properties in the world.[33] If the manner of content determination cannot establish that certain concepts have a special nature, then what else can? Dworkin perhaps needs an account of what concepts are and how they are individuated to claim that interpretive concepts are a special kind of concept. In the following section I test that claim by examining if his latest description of interpretive concepts can discharge that burden.

Interpretive Concepts in Theories of Concepts

In *Justice for Hedgehogs*, Dworkin defined interpretive concepts on the basis of criteria to be satisfied for sharing them, 'We share an interpretive concept when our collective behaviour in using that concept is best explained by taking its correct use to depend on the best justification of the role it plays for us' (Dworkin 2010: 158).[34] In the literature on concepts in cognitive science, there is a debate on whether the question of *having/sharing* a concept, is prior to the question of what a concept is.[35] That I take it is not Dworkin's concern, and presumably he thinks that there are some concepts that are interpretive in nature, and being interpretive turns on how we share such concepts.

How we come to *share* concepts however may not be a tenable basis for identifying *kinds* of concepts on the basis of the nature of concepts. If it were, then it would have to be on the premise that the manner of sharing concepts holds the key to the nature of concepts. Such a view would be at great variance with the literature on concepts in psychology, philosophy, and cognitive science. In these disciplines, the nature of a concept depends on how it represents phenomenon to human minds, and it may not even make sense to talk about kinds of concepts on the basis of their conceptual nature. To start with, and in simple terms, concepts are mental particulars or objects of thought.[36] They represent a *token* phenomenon to our minds that enables us to think about such phenomenon.[37] As I will explain below, what concepts *are* neither depends on how we share them, or even on what beliefs we have about them. What concepts are, depends on knowing what enables us to think about the things they are concepts of.

There is of course a different sense in which we can speak of *kinds* of concepts. Concepts can be sensibly classified on the basis of kinds of the kind of phenomenon they represent, or on the basis on how they are acquired or more controversially, on the manner in which they represent phenomenon. The most prevalent basis of individuation is the first of the three. On that basis concepts could be concepts *of* natural kind objects, or concepts *of* values, or concepts *of* artifacts.[38] What distinguishes one concept from the other here is the subject matter that the concept represents and not the nature of concepts themselves. Claiming that there are different kinds of *concepts* on the basis of the nature of concepts would mean that there are natural kind concepts, or value concepts, or say artifact concepts on some basis other than the kind of subject matter they represent. Traditions of thinking about the nature of concepts in the three disciplines demonstrate that the nature of concepts depends on *how* they represent phenomena to us and not on *what* phenomenon is being represented. How concepts represent phenomenon to us is closely related to how we acquire concepts.[39] A brief detour into the literature of concepts will demonstrate why speaking of kinds of concepts irrespective of the phenomenon they represent, and irrespective of the manner in which we acquire them, does not generally make sense.

Concepts in Psychology: The Problem with Concepts as 'Bodies of Knowledge' and the Concept-belief Distinction

The literature on concepts can be broadly divided into the disciplines of psychology on the one hand, and philosophy and cognitive science on the other. There are considerable overlaps between the disciplines and there have been efforts at distinguishing their respective projects, especially between philosophy and psychology.[40] For most psychologists concepts are bodies of knowledge stored in long term memory that are used by default in processes underlying our higher cognitive processes (Machery 2009: 12, n. 73). There are theories in psychology that oppose this view, the prominent grounds being that concepts are stored in short-term memory, and that concepts are categorization devices (Machery 2009: 25–9). Despite this opposition, the fact that concepts store bodies of knowledge is not widely disputed. There is also wide agreement about the central questions that psychologists seek to answer about concepts: (a) the kind of knowledge stored in concepts, (b) the format of concepts—do they store knowledge as definitions, prototypes, exemplars or some other form, (c) their use in cognitive processes, that is, how they figure in thinking (d) their manner of acquisition and (e) their neural localization (18).

Saying that concepts store 'bodies of knowledge' is however problematic for philosophers and cognitive scientists, for many of whom the term would presumably be too broad. 'Bodies of knowledge' would suggest that a concept would not only store information about the thing that it is a concept of, but also beliefs about that thing that can later be retrieved from memory when we are faced with instances where the concept has application. Cognitive scientists would point out that there is a difference between the concept itself and beliefs about it. For example you and I might both have the concept TIGER, but may have different beliefs about it. Your beliefs might be true, while mine false, yet we could both have the concept. The fact that both of us can entertain beliefs about tigers proves that we have the concept TIGER, about which we form beliefs. The term 'body of knowledge' does not allow maintaining this distinction. Rather it suggests that a concept, say TIGER stores all the knowledge we have about tigers in our memory, including beliefs about them, and when we have an instance of a tiger before us, we retrieve that knowledge including beliefs about tigers in order to think and/ or act in that situation. This view collapses the concept-belief distinction that is dear to cognitive scientists and philosophers.[41] It is of course possible to overcome this difference between the disciplines if one were to read the term 'bodies of knowledge' narrowly. The term could be restricted to the view that a concept (say TIGER) stores only that information that makes it possible for us to entertain thoughts, including beliefs, about tigers. This implies that concepts only do enough to enable us to entertain thoughts, whether correct or incorrect, about things they are concepts of, and taking such a view would allow psychologists to maintain the concept-belief distinction. Despite this possibility I would not hold a brief for psychologists like Machery on this point since knowledge includes belief and the narrow interpretation might be stretching it too far. However, it is also true that psychologists like Machery accept that concepts can be of the kind that philosophers and cognitive scientists say they are, without perhaps realizing that this causes tensions with the use of the term 'bodies of knowledge'. The view I adopt is that concepts are not bodies of knowledge and to that extent I do not subscribe to Machery's view. However, given Machery's acceptance of the prevalent views in philosophy and cognitive science, I will test the possibility of Dworkin' interpretive concepts as being a kind of concept under Machery's view to that extent.

Concepts Are Mental Representations That Are Constituents of Thought

In philosophy and cognitive science, there have been two central questions: (a) what it means to *have* a concept and (b) what *is* a concept. Answers to (a) have generally been of the form that having a concept of x means the ability to have propositional attitudes towards x. For example, to have the concept TIGER means the ability to have propositional attitudes like beliefs and desires about tigers. To say that this precedes the question of what concepts are is controversial, given the dispute over the priority of (a) and (b) above—which question comes first, what *is* a concept, or what it means to *have a* concept. The cognitive scientist and philosopher, Jerry Fodor thinks that this is a methodological question that rests on a preference.[42] For him, those thinking that the question of concept possession is prior, have some kind of pragmatism in mind. Such pragmatism however does not dispense with the need to answer the question about what a concept is.[43] Answers to this dispute about the priority of the two questions do not affect the argument I am advancing here. Contemporary cognitive scientists, psychologists, and philosophers of concepts, generally agree on what I draw upon from the literature of concepts, and the question I will concern myself with is about what a concept *is*.

There are four major theories about what concepts are: the classical view that concepts are definitions, the prototype theory, the theory-theory, the neo-classical theory, and conceptual atomism.[44] I may be excused from elaborating on each of these theories as the point I want to drive home is not dependent on the content of each theory, but on the nature of the question that they seek to answer. To be answering the same question requires that there is some agreement on what these theories consider to be their subject matter. The agreement here seems to be that concepts are mental particulars, which are constituents of thought.[45] For most theories, including the atomist one that I incline towards, concepts are mental particulars in the form of mental representation. Mental representations, simply put, are representations of things (physical or abstract) that our minds store, enabling them to think about those things. Concepts, thus, are mental representations *of* things that enable us to think of those things. Amongst the many things that concepts enable us to do is to have propositional attitudes towards things, and compose complex concepts using other concepts. For example if we had the concept CONCEPT, we can have beliefs about concepts, say by combining them with other concepts like DRY, (UN)EXCITING, and IMPORTANT. We could then believe that concepts are dry and unexciting things, but they are important nevertheless. Or we could compose more concepts like DRY CONCEPTS, and UNEXCITING CONCEPTS.

Given the agreement on concepts as mental representations, most theories of concepts inevitably seek to explain the nature of concepts by explaining the nature of mental representations. The dominant method is to explain the structure of mental representations, except for Conceptual Atomism that argues that they have none.[46] There is no disagreement however about concepts being mental representations. The general agreement I point out can also be inferred from the fact that psychologists, philosophers and cognitive scientists converge, even if only to criticize, on what they take to be the dominant theories of what concepts are. The classical paradigm of thinking about the nature of concepts is that concepts are definitions.[47] This view holds that concepts are structured mental representations in the form of *conditions* that need to be satisfied to identify an instance of the concept in question. These conditions include sensory and perceptual ones. For example, I can identify grass if it looks like a blade, is green in colour, and smells the same as when I first acquired the concept. Concepts are thus definitions. Later views argue that concepts are either prototypes, exemplars, theories, or to take another traditional but not definitional view, that concepts are mental particulars that are constituents of thought.[48] Holders of one theory generally deny the others. The classical paradigm held that *all* concepts were definitions; prototype theorists hold that *all* concepts are prototypes and so on. None of these views generally allow that concepts can be of any other kind. There are of course exceptions. For example, Jerry Fodors' conceptual atomism allows for complex concepts to be definitions.[49] Fodor, however, denies the classical theory generally, and also denies that concepts are either prototypes or theories. Let me expand this a bit given I take Fodor's theory to be the most appealing. For Fodor, concepts are not prototypes because being a prototype denies compositionality, which, on his account, explains how concepts are productive and systematic. In brief, compositionality means that complex concepts inherit their contents from those of their constituent ones. For example, the concept of a BROWN COW, is composed of the concepts BROWN and COW. This explains how concepts are productive and systematic—we can produce complex concepts from simpler one in a systematic manner, just as we produced BROWN COW from the constituent simpler concepts. Fodor rejects the prototype theory as prototypes deny compositionality. Many complex concepts do not have prototypes, and conversely many prototypes cannot be understood in terms of their constituent prototypes. Thus, prototypes do not compose and therefore, are not a good explanation of what concepts are.[50] Similarly, Fodor argues that those holding the 'theory' of concepts, do not have a positive account of concept possession/individuation. In brief, the theory of concepts is the view that concepts are mental representations whose structure consists of their relations to other concepts as specified by a mental theory.[51] Thus, my concept of say DIGNITY depends on what role it plays in some theory in which DIGNITY figures or the inferences that one can draw about DIGNITY from the other constituents of that theory. Fodor thinks that if one were to agree with the theory, theorists that concepts are embedded in theoretical inferences, it remains to be explained which inferences are to count towards proving that one possesses a concept.[52]

Apart from Fodor's exception for some concepts also being definitions, it is Edouard Machery who holds the view that concepts can be definitions, prototypes, exemplars or theories. His views, as explained earlier are contrary to most philosophers and cognitive scientists, but Machery nowhere denies that concepts are mental representations of phenomena.

Interpretive Concepts as a *Kind* of Concept

Since concepts are mental representations, it is only within this constraint on the nature of concepts that theorists individuate concepts. Some available options for individuation, therefore, are to categorize concepts on the basis of what they represent, how they are acquired, and probably how they figure in mental processes. A claim about a particular *kind* of concept is thus a claim of this sort. A claim about there being interpretive concepts, as a special kind of concept, thus has to be a similar claim. Dworkin however seems to suggest that interpretive concepts are a special kind of concept on some other grounds. First he thinks that there is something special about the nature of these concepts. Second, he thinks that part of the reason why some concepts are interpretive is the manner in which we share them. Third, he thinks that interpretive concepts are special because their nature can only be explicated by normative argument. The first claim is unsustainable since a claim about the nature of concepts is a claim about the nature of mental representations. The claim about interpretive concepts is not a claim of this sort. To be so would require arguing that some interpretive concepts represent phenomenon to us in a special manner. The second and third claims tie up with other claims that Dworkin makes which have wider implications. Let me therefore, first dispense with one support base that Dworkin might seem to have in the literature on concepts in psychology. I will then return to the second claim and third claims later.

Interpretive Concepts and the Heterogeneity Hypothesis

In the literature in psychology, there is a view that might support interpretive concepts as a kind of concept on grounds other than the ones for individuating concepts. This view is Edouard Machery's heterogeneity hypothesis. The heterogeneity hypothesis allows that for the same phenomenon we may have different kinds of concepts. Kinds of concepts are identified by the manner in which phenomenon is represented to us, and stored in our long-term memory, for example, as prototypes, exemplars, or theories. The hypothesis proposes that information about the world is stored in all these forms in our long term memory and thus, it is better to eliminate the term 'concepts' from the vocabulary of psychology, and refer straightaway to prototypes, exemplars and theories. Notice that the heterogeneity hypothesis does not negate the argument I am advancing, rather it claims that concepts are about how information about the world is stored in our memory and then employed in cognitive processes. Machery suggests, given that there is evidence of the co-existence of all the different kinds of concepts suggested by existing theories, it is better to speak of the theories themselves and eliminate the vocabulary of concepts. In other words Machery suggests that definitions, prototypes, exemplars, and theories are *kinds* of concepts, that is, the manner in which information is stored in our memory. The term 'concept' then seems to refer to an amalgamation of ways in which information is stored, and thus, does not contribute independently to understanding our cognitive processes. The vocabulary of concepts could thus be done away with.

The heterogeneity hypothesis does not make a case for interpretive concepts, for, to establish such a case it must be argued that being interpretive is a way of how information is stored in our long-term memory and how that functions in the processes underlying our higher cognitive capacities. I do not think that Dworkin seeks to make any claim of this sort. Thus, if interpretive concepts are to be a *kind* of concept then it must be so in some other sense.

Sharing Interpretive Concepts

Dworkin's second claim that being an interpretive concept depends on how we share such concepts is also not about the nature of mental representations. In that sense therefore, it is not a claim about the nature of concepts; it is though a claim about the manner in which we share some concepts. Dworkin states that we share interpretive concepts 'when our collective behaviour in using that concept is best explained by taking its correct use to depend on the best justification of the role it plays for us'.[53] The claim here is about what we take the correct use of a concept to be. Indeed, Dworkin's statement above presupposes that people already have the concept in question, and his claim is about a further criterion that is to be met in order to identify whether we are employing the concept in the same sense, that is, as an interpretive one. The further criterion is that we must accept the correct use of the concept to depend on the best justification of the role that it plays for us. Now, this suggests that to share an interpretive concept the following must exist:

1. Agreement, even though loosely, on the role that it is to play for us.
2. Sharing the belief that the correct use of the concept is the best justification of that role.

Oddly, it appears, that for both these features to exist, we must already have the concept which is in issue. Otherwise we could not identify the role we were agreeing about, and about what we are to offer the best justification possible. Both of these involve having propositional attitudes towards the concept in issue, and that requires that we already have the concept. If that be the case, then his definition is surely not about what amounts to having an interpretive concept. For example, if DIGNITY is an interpretive concept, then it requires that we believe that the correct use *of* DIGNITY depends on the further belief *about* DIGNITY, that we offer our best justifications for its use. This requires that we already possess the concept DIGNITY in order to know that what is in issue is our use of *that* concept.

One might reply that Dworkin here is talking about the correct *use* of a concept, and evidence of correct use is what determines whether we *have* a concept or not. On this view, if someone were using the concept TIGER, and identified hyenas to be tigers, then we might as well say that she does not have the concept tiger. Thus, when Dworkin says that we must share a belief about the correct use of the concept, he is in effect speaking of what it means to have a concept.

This reply is misplaced. There is a difference between speaking about *a particular* application as the correct application of the concept, and a *belief* about what *sort* of application is the correct one. Let me first explain why the reply is mistaken because it moves too easily from an incorrect use of a word to a conclusion about not having a concept. In our example involving a tiger, we had concluded that employing the word tiger to identify a hyena was at least an incorrect use of the word tiger. We might demand reasons from such an applier as to why she used the word tiger in that manner. Such an enquiry might lead us to at least four conclusions: (a) we might either find out that she made an incorrect use of the *word* tiger even though she has the concept TIGER, (b) that she held false *beliefs* about tigers though she has the concept TIGER, (c) she does not have the concept TIGER, (d) she misapplied the concept TIGER. Let me explain how we might arrive at these conclusions in more detail.

For incorrect use of the word, we might realize that the applier used the word tiger to refer to hyenas, but when a real tiger appeared before her, she held the correct beliefs about it—she would know that it posed a danger to her, or that tiger cubs that are around might be those of the tiger and not the hyena's, or in case the person possessed updated scientific knowledge, she might identify the right DNA in the lab as belonging to the tiger and not to the hyena. She thus, has the concept TIGER as we have, but only a different word for it. She has the ability to form beliefs about tigers, and thus is able to use the concept.

For different beliefs about tigers, we might find out that she not only refers to the hyena as a tiger, but when a real tiger appears, she thinks that it would bark, eat biscuits, and if chased, would fly away using wings. In this case we know that the person has false beliefs about tigers, but the fact that she can identify tigers and form beliefs about them means that she has the concept TIGER. It might appear as if this is a case about not having the concept TIGER. That, however, would amount to collapsing the concept-belief distinction. The person in question is able to identify tigers, which is enough for her to have the concept TIGER and form beliefs about tigers, whether true or false.

For the third conclusion of not having the concept TIGER, we can be sure about it if she cannot identify TIGERS when they appear before her. It might turn out that she has no beliefs about the thing that we know as a tiger. In such a case we realize that the person not only has a different use for the word tiger (she uses it for hyenas) but also does not have the concept of TIGER that we have. Tigers do not figure in her world.

For the fourth conclusion of misapplying the concept TIGER, a case might arise in the following manner. We know that the concept applier has the concept TIGER and can identify tigers when they appear, even if she has a different word for the concept, say NIGER. Now we witness a case where she uses the word NIGER for a striped Great Dane. This means that she thinks that the dog is a tiger, probably because it is brownish-yellow and has stripes. We can enquire whether she attributes the same beliefs that she has for tigers, both true and false, to the dog. If she does, then we know that she has misapplied the concept TIGER. Wrongly applying a concept involves applying the concept to a thing that it is not. In other words, it means applying a mental representation to a thing that it is not a representation of. Evidence of wrong application may be holding wrong beliefs about the thing in question, and on further investigation we might establish that the wrong beliefs are being invoked because the concept applier is applying beliefs about some other concept to the thing in question, which she thinks is represented by the same concept. Misapplying a concept is therefore distinct—both from not having a concept, and wrongly using a word according to our linguistic usages.

The four conclusions above are about when a particular case is an incorrect use of a particular word, or holding wrong beliefs about a particular concept, or not having a particular concept, and cases of misapplication of a particular concept. In contrast to the four conclusions above, stands a claim about what *kind* of application of a concept is a correct one. In my view, Dworkin's criterion for sharing interpretive concepts is a claim of this sort. Such a claim is about stipulating the conditions under which a particular use is a correct use. In other words, it is a claim about a *procedure* that yields correct use. A need for such a procedure perhaps arises when there is disagreement over what the correct use of a concept is. In cases where there are no disagreements, reasons for establishing such a procedure may not arise. An example would be that we share a belief that in the process of determining the correct use of a *class* of concepts, say of animals, contesting users will provide the best imitation they can of the animal to demonstrate their familiarity with it and thus strengthening the probability that their use is correct. Holding such a belief does not demonstrate that we have the concept of a particular animal, but only that we have an agreed procedure to judge whether the candidate's applications of a concept are correct or not. We might of course say that when we hold such beliefs about some concepts then we call them 'imitative concepts'. But this naming does not prove whether we have a particular imitative concept or not. It only demonstrates that we have the concept IMITATIVE CONCEPT, which represents concepts to which we apply the decision procedure we have devised. The concept of IMITATIVE CONCEPT has come into existence by way of definition. To share this concept we must share the content of the definition. Notice that whether one has any particular IMITATIVE CONCEPT, that is, a concept that falls within that category—a particular animal in our example—does not depend on whether we have the concept IMITATIVE CONCEPT. It depends on whether we have had sensory stimulus about that animal whether direct (for instance sight, sound, touch, and so on of that animal) or indirect (read about it, or heard it being described). The IMITATIVE concept only kicks in when we have a disagreement about, say, whether the animal before us is an instance of a particular animal, and where we must decide on which of the candidate claims is correct. Therefore, holding a belief *about* the correct use of a class of concepts of the sort that Dworkin prescribes is not about *having* a concept about which the belief is. In sum, Dworkin's criteria for an interpretive concept is not about having some concept that is interpretive, but about having the INTERPRETIVE concept. This is a concept we have learned by way of Dworkin's *definition*. Thus, if dignity was an interpretive concept, the criteria for having the INTERPRETIVE concept does not help us in understanding what dignity is or what its correct use is, but it only informs us that if we have disagreeing uses of dignity then the correct one is the best justification for it.

Does this shed any light on the nature of dignity, or any other value over which we have persistent disagreement? For starters, we presumably already possess the concept DIGNITY if we are to speak about our beliefs of what is a correct use of DIGNITY. Secondly do we not offer best justifications for any concept we use? Why would we genuinely put forward something as the correct use of a concept unless we thought that our reasons were the best justification for it? If this is true, then all concepts are interpretive concepts whenever we have to provide justification for their use. Is it the case then that there are some instances of employing concepts that demand justification while others do not? The answer would be in the affirmative for the following obvious reasons. If a concept is employed unchallenged, there is no demand for justification. Challenges might arise due to disagreement on a particular application of the concept, or a demand for explanation for other reasons, for example, to develop a better understanding of why the concept is applied in a particular manner. Demands for justification on an application leads to explanations of the best possible justification for that application, albeit that the application is a genuine one, where we choose it on the basis of the best reasons available to us. This is when the concept employed becomes interpretive. In effect, an interpretive concept is any concept that we have disagreements about, or about which justification is warranted for any other reason. Interpretive concepts then presuppose disagreement, or a demand for justification. The idea of an interpretive concept does not provide leads to answers for why we have disagreement, or why there is a demand for justification when such concepts are involved. It describes a situation where people demand justification from each other and hold the belief that others will provide the best justification for their proposed use of the concept. In addition, they hold a further belief that this is how the concept is correctly used. Indeed, Dworkin himself indicates this when he says that 'concepts migrate' (Dworkin 2010). For him criterial concepts sometimes migrate and become interpretive concepts. The reason for this migration is that the criteria for determining the correct use of the concept is no longer settled. This view of Dworkin's reduces the idea of interpretive concepts to concepts about which there exist disagreements about their correct use. If this is what the concept of an interpretive concept does, then surely it does not answer questions about why we have disagreement on such concepts, apart from stating the obvious that the criteria for its use are unsettled. Dworkin also leaves us with another puzzle. If we agree with him that sharing an interpretive concept requires us to hold the belief that the correct use of any interpretive concept is the 'best justification of the role that it plays for us', then at first sight, all the candidate uses will be correct uses. Indeed, any genuine user will think her use to be the best, and therefore the correct use. Dworkin's criteria for interpretive concepts, therefore, are not a decision procedure, unlike in the case of IMITATIVE CONCEPTS. Yet, it is a claim about a sort of use that is a correct use. So how do we characterize what sort of claim it is? At best it appears that it is a description of the attitudes of users when concepts that Dworkin thinks are interpretive concepts at play.

This view of interpretive concepts found in *Justice for Hedgehogs* is a statement about the kind of belief concept appliers must hold in order for a concept to be interpretive. The belief is strikingly similar to W.B. Gallie's criteria V and VII for essentially contested concepts. The two criteria set out that opposing users of a concept accept others having intelligible reasons for disagreeing with their use; and all users believe that their disagreements will result in the concepts being used in an optimum fashion. These criteria are latent in Dworkin's account of interpretive concepts. First, without the user accepting the intelligibility of other's reasons for disagreement, it is impossible to recognize that others offer candidate best justifications for the role that the concept plays. To assess what is the best justification, the candidate's justifications must be intelligible. Secondly, without believing that their disagreements will result in the development of the exemplar (paradigm cases for Dworkin) in an optimum fashion, it would be impossible to agree that offering of best justifications is the correct manner of using the concept. A use that cannot make sense of the exemplar cannot be agreed upon as a justified use, as the exemplar generates agreement on what we are having a disagreement about.

What remains, thus, leads to the conclusion that by interpretive concepts Dworkin probably means concepts of interpretive phenomenon. That is a claim that I cannot subject to close examination here. For now, we have reason to believe that interpretive concepts are not a kind of concept in the sense that they say something about the nature of concepts, but only in the sense that they are concepts *of* interpretive phenomenon.[54]

The argument I have advanced might be thought to be trivial. It might be argued that it does not matter whether we say 'interpretive concepts' or 'interpretive phenomena' or 'interpretive practice'. Similarly, it does not matter if we speak of 'essentially contested concepts' or 'essentially contested practices/ phenomena'. The argument might proceed that the nature of important questions that these practices/concepts raise for human societies remains the same whether we refer to them as practices or concepts. We would still be concerned about how we ought to reason with them, how we ought to understand disagreements they seem to generate, and what would be a justified way of employing them in justifying authoritative decisions.

This objection is partly true. Even if we abandoned the terminology of concepts, it would not contribute to answering the issues that the terms 'interpretive concepts' or 'essentially contested concepts' are employed to raise. These issues center around understanding disagreement, and justifying our actions in the face of disagreement.[55] Admitting this truth does not blunt the argument about concepts I made, nor does it reduce its relevance. It was never the objective of the argument to offer resolutions for the issues that interpretive, or essentially contested practices, raise. Rather the argument serves the interests of clarity. It highlights and maintains the important distinction between a word for a concept, the concept itself, and the phenomenon of what it is a concept of. This traditional distinction is important to maintain and at least two reasons for its importance are worth citing. First, it brings clarity to the questions that are asked. For example, to say that there is something peculiar about how political concepts are conceptualized, because they are interpretive concepts, would be a claim about a special manner in which political practices are represented to our minds. For psychologists, it would be a claim about the special manner in which knowledge about political practices are stored in long term memory, which in turn will demand explanations of the ways in which they will figure in our cognitive processes. In contrast, a claim about a political practice will focus our attention on the features of the practice without having to think about any special manner of how they are represented to our minds. No fresh investigation into the literature of concepts is necessary to explain what these practices are.

Second, maintaining the distinction might do more justice to the distinctions there might be between various political and moral concepts. It will also provide added opportunity for the literature on concepts to provide fruitful insights into understanding the nature of many such practices that the concepts capture. For example, it might be the case that most of the concepts in our political practices are accessed by way of learning existing theories about them, and for that reason we might want to call them theoretical concepts. Other concepts might be acquired on the basis of paradigms. Some might be complex concepts, with their constituent concepts being acquired in ways more than one. Investigating how we have acquired a concept of a practice and how that affects our beliefs about the practice might go a long way in shedding more light on questions about the practice. In contrast, if we assumed that our concepts of certain practices, say political ones, belonged to a special kind of concept, clarity of thought will demand that we provide an explanation of how this kind of a concept is different from a prototype, a stereotype, an exemplar, a theory, or some other kind of mental particular. Indeed this draws focus away from the real questions. It does not appear that Dworkin's or Gallie's view on concepts discharges such a burden, and thus it might be the best to leave it open whether our political concepts are acquired in the same way or not, and whether, if the heterogeneity hypothesis is true, all our political practices belong to one kind of concept or not.

***

I have argued that the literature on concepts in other disciplines do not allow interpretive concepts to be a special kind of concept. Dworkin's argument for interpretive concepts requiring constructive interpretation does not establish that it is their interpretive nature that requires constructive interpretation. If the fact of constructive interpretation itself designates concepts subjected to it as interpretive concepts, then interpretive concepts do not denote a special kind of concept, but a manner of reasoning. If it is the case that some concepts require such reasoning then such a case has not yet been made out apart from the claim that all indeterminate concepts are interpretive concepts.

Dworkin's claim about the deep structure of interpretive concepts is also under-described. Neither is it clearly supported by Nicos Stavropoulos's account which is perhaps suited to describing the content of mental states rather than conceptual content. Holist theorists of conceptual content might build bridges between interpretive concepts and Stavropoulos's account. Such a claim would however be about how conceptual content is determined in general rather than about special kinds of concepts.

The claim about interpretive concepts that they depend on how we share such concepts also turns out to be implausible, given the literature on cognitive science, philosophy, and psychology. What remains is that Dworkin's claim is not about how some concepts have a special nature, but about how we should reason with moral and political values in an interpretive manner. That would be a claim about determining the content of such values—not because such concepts are special kinds of concepts that warrant such reasoning, but because of the independent merits of such reasoning in determining content. I think that such a picture exists in philosophy as a holist account of conceptual content. Such accounts do not restrict themselves to special kinds of concepts but purportedly apply to all concepts. Dworkin does not explicitly embrace it, but I suspect that it might sustain a plausible view of interpretive reasoning. This deserves close attention on its own. The aim of this paper was to examine if there were other ways in which interpretive concepts could be made sense of. At least as a special kind of concept, it does not.

Notes and References

1. Several of Dworkin's interpreters take interpretation and interpretive concepts to be central to his work. See for example, Stephen Guest. 2013. *Ronald Dworkin*. 3rd ed. Stanford University Press. pp. 66, 76.
2. Ronald Dworkin. 2010. *Justice For Hedgehogs*. Belknap Press. p. 204.
3. I have previously criticized other such attempts at characterizing values as Essentially Contested Concepts and as placeholders. See Pritam Baruah. 2014. 'Human Dignity in Adjudication: The Limits of Place holding and Essential Contestability Accounts', *Canadian Journal of Law and Jurisprudence* 27(2): 329.
4. Ronald Dworkin. 1996. *Taking Rights Seriously*. Universal Book Traders (Indian Reprint). p. 103.
5. W.B. Gallie. 1955. 'Essentially Contested Concepts'. *Proceedings of the Aristotelian Society* 56(1): p. 167.

6. I mostly rely on Dworkin's explanation of interpretive concepts in *Law's Empire* and *Justice for Hedgehogs*, with references to *Justice in Robes* and *Taking Rights Seriously* to trace how the idea has developed.
7. I examine this claim in another paper. Pritam Baruah. 'Dworkin's Value Holism' (unpublished paper on file with the author).
8. Dworkin clearly reserves the name conceptual for his account. See *Justice for Hedgehogs* Chapter 8.
9. In keeping with the tradition of writing about concepts in cognitive science, I shall refer to concepts in capitals, properties represented by concepts in italics, and words standing for properties in single quotes. For instance, DOG (concept), *doghood* (property), and 'dog' (word).
10. Ronald Dworkin. 2007. *Justice in Robes*. Universal Law Publishing (Indian Reprint). p. 154.
11. Ronald Dworkin. 1998. *Law's Empire*. Hart Publishing. pp. 46, 73.
12. Dworkin uses the word practice as he does not maintain a distinction between concepts and practices.
13. Here Dworkin speaks of a value that justifies the practice as a justification for an interpreters 'sense' of what the practice requires.
14. Here I refer to Plato's metaphor of the line in *The Republic*. In Plato's line paradigms can be analogized to hypotheses in the third section of the line. It is in the realm of understanding, but only as starting points for philosophical reflection. G.R.F. Ferrari (ed.), Translated by Tom Griffith. 2000. *Plato: The Republic*. Cambridge University Press. pp. 217–19.
15. See generally *Justice for Hedgehogs* Chapter 8 (for Dworkin's account of why conceptual interpretation is also moral through and through.)
16. Ronald Dworkin. 1996. 'Objectivity and Truth: You'd Better Believe It', *Philosophy and Public Affairs* 25(2): p. 87.
17. Nicos Stavropoulos launches an attack on a similar view prevalent in the debate on thick concepts. The view claims that concepts like cruelty have a non-evaluative component independent of evaluative considerations. Nicos Stavropoulos. 1996. *Objectivity in Law*. Clarendon Press Oxford. p. 94. In contemporary literature on thick evaluative concepts such a view figures in debates over the 'disentangling problem'.
18. Dworkin employs the same question in his attack on positivists in *Law's Empire*. There he points out through the hard cases he cites, that lawyers routinely disagree on what the law *is* on an issue.
19. He indicates this by taking the important question about political concepts to be how to identify a 'value's value'.
20. David Plunkett and Tim Sundell. 2013. 'Dworkin's Interpretivism and The Pragmatics of Legal Disputes'. *Legal Theory* 19(3): p. 242.
21. Dworkin labels this inability, the semantic sting.
22. Stavropoulos, *Objectivity* (n. 39) p. 3. Many theorists have pointed out that Stavropoulos' errs in ascribing criterialism to Hart, even though his account of

semantics is sound. See James Penner. 1997. Book Review: Objectivity in Law by Nicos Stavropoulos. *Modern Law Review* 60(5): p. 747.

23. Dworkin, *Justice in Robes*, Chapter 6.
24. Anne De Moor. 1998. 'Nothing Else to Think? On Meaning, Truth, and Objectivity in Law by Nicos Stavropoulos', *Oxford Journal of Legal Studies* 18(2): pp. 345–6.
25. I use the term 'meaning' for concepts as it often figures in the literature I refer to. The term however properly applies to 'words'. For concepts the proper term is 'content'. Words have meaning, while concepts have content.
26. Iain Law. 2000. Review of Nicos Stavropoulos's *Objectivity in Law*, *Mind* (NS) 109(435) 650–3.
27. Stavropoulos, *Objectivity in Law* (n. 39) pp. 40–4.
28. Stavropoulos, *Objectivity in Law* (n. 39) pp. 36, 43.
29. Dworkin does indicate that this is what he means when he says that concepts migrate. See Dworkin, *Justice for Hedgehogs*. pp. 164–5.
30. I discuss this in a yet unpublished paper on file with the author. Pritam Baruah, 'Dworkin's value Holism' (n. 8).
31. Peter Pagin. 2006. 'Meaning Holism', in Ernest Lepore and Barry C. Smith (eds), *The Oxford Handbook of The Philosophy of Language*. Oxford University Press. p. 213.
32. Jerry Fodor and Ernest Lepore. 1992. *Holism: A Shopper's Guide*. Basil Blackwell. p. 163.
33. Jerry Fodor. 1998. *Concepts: Where Cognitive Science Went Wrong*. Oxford University Press. Ch. 1.
34. It might be thought that using the term 'criteria' to explain interpretive concepts is a mistake, given Dworkin's arguments against criterial concepts. However the definition that he provides does seem to be criteria for identifying interpretive concepts.
35. For a distinction between the two see Jerry Fodor, *Concepts* (n. 67): 3.
36. See Jerry Fodor, *Concepts* (n. 67): 3; Eric Margolis and Stephen Laurence. 1999. 'Concepts and Cognitive Science', in Eric Margolis and Stephen Laurence (eds), *Concepts: Core Readings*. MIT Press. pp. 5–6 (for a discussion of why concepts are mental particulars).
37. Fodor, *Concepts* (n. 67), Ch. 1.
38. I am grateful to James Penner for pointing this out. James Penner, 'Interpretive Concepts: What is the Disagreement About?' (unpublished paper on file with author).
39. There are of course theories that take concepts to be non-representational. Those theories however have not gained much currency. See Edouard Machery. 2009. *Doing Without Concepts*. Oxford University Press. Ch. 1.
40. For attempts at such distinction see Christopher Peacocke. 1992. *A Study of Concepts*. MIT Press 1992. Ch.7, and Machery, *Doing Without Concepts* (n. 73): 38–9.

41. See for example Fodor, *Concepts* (n. 67): 7–9.
42. Fodor, *Concepts* (n. 67): 3. See also Jerry Fodor. 1994. 'Concepts: A Potboiler', *Cognition*. 50: 95, 100.
43. Fodor, *Concepts* (n. 67): 3.
44. See Eric Margolis and Stephen Laurence. 1999. 'Concepts and Cognitive Science', in Eric Margolis and Stephen Laurence (eds), *Concepts: Core Readings*. MIT Press. Chapter 1 (for an overview of theories of concepts). Perhaps the only exception is the view that concepts are abilities. The view has lost favour amongst philosophers and cognitive scientists. See Eric Margolis and Stephen Laurence. 2014. 'Concepts', *The Stanford Encyclopedia of Philosophy* (Spring Edition), Edward N. Zalta (ed.), available http://plato.stanford.edu/archives/spr2014/entries/concepts/. (accessed on 14 July 2016.)
45. Fodor,*Concepts* (n. 67), Chapter 1.
46. All theories of concepts assume that concepts have a structure except conceptual tmoism that concepts are like atoms (in the 1990s) that do not have structure.
47. Laurence and Margolis, *Concepts: Core Readings* (n. 70): 8. Machery, *Doing Without Concepts* (n. 73): 78; Fodor, *Concepts* (n. 67): Ch. 3 and 4; Jerry Fodor, 'Concepts: A Potboiler' (n. 79) at pp. 101–5. The view that concepts are definitions is traced back to Aristotle, and sometimes to Plato. However, Plato gave a subsidiary role to definitions, unlike Aristotle. For Plato the first amongst the necessary conditions for possession of a concept is prior apprehension of a corresponding form of the object that the concept is about. A definition of the essence of the concept comes further down the scale as a condition for possession of the concept. For a discussion of Plato's implicit theory of concepts, see Morris Weitz, 1988. *Theories of Concepts*. Routledge: London. Chapter 1.
48. It is important to note that there are different versions of each of these paradigms.
49. Fodor, *Concepts* (n. 67): Ch. 3.
50. Fodor, p. 100.
51. Margolis and Laurence, p. 47.
52. Fodor, p. 119. Machery, pp. 100–6, for a description and criticism of the theory theories of concepts.
53. Ronald Dworkin, *Justice For Hedgehogs*, p. 158.
54. A similar but not so detailed argument is made by Joseph Raz when he says that concepts stand between the objects in the world they represent and the words we use to refer to them. They capture properties of the world for us. In this sense when Hart speak of *The Concept of Law*, or Gilbert Ryle writes about *The Concept of Mind*, they are speaking of the nature of law, and the nature of the mind. See Joseph Raz. 2004. 'Can There Be a Theory of Law?' in Martin P. Golding and William A. Edmundson (eds), *The Blackwell Guide to the Philosophy of Law and Legal Theory*. Blackwell. p. 324.
55. Susan Hurley provides a clear statement of how these issues are primarily about disagreement. See Susan Hurley. 1999. *Natural Reasons*. Oxford University Press. Chapter 3.

PART II

DIGNITY, RESPONSIBILITY, AND FREE WILL

7

Interpreting Human Dignity

*Allen W. Wood**

Justice for Hedgehogs is a whimsical title for a very substantial book. It provides a larger frame of reference for a lot of Ronald Dworkin's other work on ethics, rights, and the philosophy of law. The basic framework is Dworkin's thesis of the independence of value and his theory of interpretation as the way in which reasoning about value is to be carried out. But the fundamental value is human dignity. It is from this foundation that Dworkin develops his theory of aid and harm, political legitimacy and human rights, politics, and law. My aim in this essay is to discuss Dworkin's concept of human dignity by situating it within his more general view that values, ethics and morality are all *interpretive* enterprises. A lot more could be said than I will try to say here about the way Dworkin develops the idea of human dignity as the foundation of ethics and morality. But I will try to achieve a basic understanding of his conception of human dignity and how he means to develop it. My exposition of Dworkin is largely sympathetic, but I will offer some questions and criticisms, and even some suggestions as to how his project might have been more firmly grounded and more successfully executed.

* I am grateful for thoughtful comments on a draft of this paper by Ariel Zylberman and Marilia Espirito Santo.

The Independence of Value

The playful title of Dworkin's very serious book is derived from the saying of the Greek poet Archilochus (made popular by Isaiah Berlin) that while the fox may know many things, the hedgehog knows one big thing (Dworkin 2011: 1).[1] For Dworkin, the one big thing is *value*. But Dworkin's view of value does not make it as big a thing as it could be (or as I suspect it actually is). Dworkin insists that value is independent of fact, that 'ought' is independent of 'is'. This is a thesis he calls 'Hume's Principle': 'No amount of empirical discovery about the state of the world—no revelations about the course of history or the ultimate nature of matter or the truth about human nature—can establish any conclusions about what ought to be without a further premise or assumption about what ought to be' (Dworkin 2011: 17). But this could well be questioned. To begin with, David Hume himself is a very peculiar authority to cite on behalf of 'Hume's Principle', since the 'ought'-claims of his own ethics are clearly based on 'is'-claims about human nature.[2] Hume's Principle, as Dworkin understands it, may perhaps best be interpreted as rejecting the attempt to ground judgments of value on a conception of the 'factual' which, on closer examination, turns out to be questionable or even self-undermining.

Moral Skepticism: External and Internal

We can see this very point in Dworkin's own cogent rejection of 'external moral skepticism' (2011: 40–4). External moral skepticism is the meta-ethical position that all moral claims are lacking in truth conditions, so that they must be interpreted as not making truth claims at all, but instead as expressions of emotion, preference or approval, or as imperatives disguised as assertions of fact. Dworkin rejects external skepticism as self-undermining because, he says, it can be interpreted only as itself a moral position—but one that either contradicts itself or talks nonsense (44–68). Dworkin regards as coherent (whether or not they are correct) various forms of 'internal' moral skepticism, that challenge the *content* of moral values, or even reject 'moral' values as a whole when it comes to leading one's life. But they do so on the basis of *other* values. One finds internal moral skepticism in such radical contrarians as Friedrich Nietzsche, Max Stirner, or the Marquis de Sade. External moral skepticism, however, is a very different animal—in fact, a chimaera (that is, it is self-defeating or incoherent). As an agent, the external moral skeptic asserts moral claims just as everyone else does, but then as a theorist the external moral skeptic says these same claims are not true and could never be true. We should not be distracted by the semantic diversions through which external moral skeptics attempt to conceal the self-contradiction. They propose to accept morality as agents but to reject it as theorists. As theorists, however, they always remain agents too. Meta-ethical realism could be interpreted as merely a trivial affirmation of what the realist holds about value. But anti-realism about value could never be anything but a direct denial of what the theorist actually believes (no matter what that might be).

The basic problem, as Dworkin sees, is that there can be no questions *about* moral judgments that do not themselves *involve* moral judgments (67). He therefore, argues that meta-ethics itself rests on a mistake and concludes that all the standard meta-ethical options—realism, error theory, expressivism, constructivism, if they are supposed to be answers to theoretical questions of that form—are equally answers to questions that cannot be asked. They try to investigate the nature of value without presupposing any commitment to the reality of value. That cannot be done. Internal moral skeptics—even radical ones—do it no more than the defenders of conventional morality. They merely have different views—from *within* human thinking and discourse about value.

Dworkin sees this conclusion as following from Hume's Principle, but I would sooner see it as *discrediting* Hume's Principle, at least in the (anti-Humean) form in which Dworkin and others are wont to state it. 'Of course' Dworkin concedes, 'there are interesting questions of anthropology and of personal and social psychology that are second-order in the sense that they are about moral judgment but do not themselves call for moral judgment' (2011: 67). This could be true, however, only if we could separate moral judgment from other kinds of value—such as the values of self-understanding and cultural understanding that underlie the enquiries of anthropology and psychology. These are cognitive values, not moral ones, but if we accept what we might call 'Dworkin's Hedgehog Principle': 'Value is one big thing', then can we engage in these enquiries without committing ourselves to values that impinge on, or even presuppose, certain moral values? Perhaps this can be made to sound plausible in the case of fields like mathematics and physics. But we can do that only as long as we ignore the moral values that underlie the practices of enquiry, argument, and the enterprise of science—which forbid the plagiarizing of mathematical results,[3] the falsification or deliberate misinterpretation of empirical data, or the basing of our conclusions on our interests, wishes, and prejudices rather than on reason and evidence. And we haven't a ghost of a chance in anthropology, or in history—where the great historian David Hume himself would have been among the first to passionately reject such a separation. 'The writers of history', he says, 'as well as the readers, are sufficiently interested in the characters and events, to have a lively sentiment of blame or praise; and, at the same time, have no particular interest or concern to pervert their judgments'.[4] Even if we can effect a separation of cognitive from specifically moral values in a given context, the local independence of cognitive or scientific from moral value would have to be based, in Dworkin's own view, on an interpretive enquiry about the relation of these values within the one big thing—value. So we should sooner reject meta-ethics by appealing directly to Dworkin's Hedgehog Principle, and leave 'Hume's Principle' altogether out of it.

The result for meta-ethics, however, is the same. The only forms of realism, anti-realism or skepticism that make any sense are what Dworkin calls 'internal'—part of value enquiry, even if they question accepted moral values, even quite fundamental ones. Spinoza, for instance, thought that attitudes of indignation and repentance are always bad and contrary to reason.[5] Friedrich Nietzsche claimed that all sympathy with the weak is both pointless and sick, that all value systems resting on human equality are harmful and dangerous. When Nietzsche said, 'there are altogether no moral facts' (Nietzsche 1954: 501),[6] he took this to be a radical rejection of conventional morality, and an invitation to a 'transvaluation of all values'—a radical revision (even an inversion) of the Christian (and post-Christian humanist) values. Whatever we may think of Nietzsche's proposals, they were, in Dworkin's terminology, forms of *internal* skepticism about what is and is not really valuable. They would be answerable to the kinds of argument of which all value questions admit. Spinoza's and Nietzsche's claims were radical skeptical proposals about *what* is to be considered valuable. They were not engaging in an *external*, supposedly 'objective,' or 'merely factual' enquiry that tries to state truths *about* moral (or any other) value that supposedly hold entirely independently of all substantive value questions, and presupposes no objective truths about them.

Many practitioners of meta-ethics, however—especially skeptical or anti-realist ones—appeal to this kind of externality or 'value-independence' whenever it is suggested that their position might commit them to the rejection of common sense and moral conclusions. Theirs is, they say, a merely second-order, meta- or theoretical enquiry about the nature of value and valuation, which supposedly leaves first-order ethical issues just where they were. In order to confirm this, some of them offer ingenious 'quasi-realist' accounts of the semantics and psychology of ordinary moral evaluation, showing that their purely external skepticism about the reality of value is entirely consistent with the internal acceptance of moral values asserted by common sense, and (so they say) permits them to 'talk the talk' as well as 'walk the walk.'

It is symptomatic of the self-undermining character of their project, however, that some of these very same practitioners of anti-realist meta-ethics also in effect concede Dworkin's point, whether or not they fully realize it. Simon Blackburn, for example, argues that Derek Parfit's meta-ethical realism is allied with, or even committed to endorse, such odious cultural phenomena as political absolutism and Western imperialism.[7] Blackburn associates meta-ethical anti-realism with a benign Humean ethics of passions and sentiments and opposed to the wicked 'rationalism' of Kant those who have fallen prey to his malign influence. These charges, however, amount to the admission that meta-ethical issues cannot be separated from substantive value judgments—in other words, that Blackburn's own skepticism is *internal* rather than *external*. If it is, then we can argue with his anti-realism on obvious ethical grounds—it is a form of ethical *nihilism*. We can accept, or else quarrel with, the ethical judgments Blackburn makes, but reject (as inconsistent with these) the meta-ethical anti-realist (or 'quasi-realist') gloss he wants to put on such statements. For then his 'meta-ethics' becomes part of moral argument, like the critical reflections of Spinoza, Nietzsche, or Sade on common sense morality. But if the basic claim of antirealist meta-ethics is nihilistic—that there are no truths or truth-conditions for assertions about value—then that undermines all of the value assertions they themselves make, such as that their view is tolerant and democratic, in contrast to the wicked colonialist and authoritarian views of realists.

Interpretation

Value, according to Dworkin's Hedgehog Principle, is *One Big Thing*. We can make assertions about it and justify them. But of what kinds of arguments do value questions admit? An important part of Dworkin's ambitious project turns on his answer to this question. According to Dworkin, both in everyday life and in philosophy, ethical thinking is *interpretive*. In Chapter 7 of his book, Dworkin provides a wide-ranging discussion of the nature of interpretation in general—of actions and events in history, of actions or practices in social science, of documents and statutes in law, of creative works in literary studies and art criticism, of scriptures in religion. He might have added, to please people like me, that internal to philosophy is the ongoing interpretation of classic texts in its history. But he does hold that philosophy itself deals essentially in the interpretation of contested concepts (Dworkin 2011: 123).

Genres of Interpretation

One important thesis Dworkin holds here is that there is no such thing as interpretation in general (2011: 124). Every interpretation belongs to a particular genre, and its value as interpretation depends on the standards appropriate to the genre. Dworkin thinks there can be true interpretations, but concedes that we are often uncomfortable speaking of interpretations as true or false, preferring to think of them as better and worse (2011: 125–8). Why is this? Dworkin's preferred explanation for it is what he calls the 'value account': 'We are reluctant to call interpretations true or false because interpretations have different purposes. Many interpretations, moreover, have simultaneously more than one purpose, and what serves one purpose better may serve another worse. This makes us justifiably reluctant to apply the stark bivalent notions of 'true/false' to any given interpretation. Further, few interpreters have (or even need) a clear conception of what the purpose (or purposes) of an interpretation are, and the practitioners of a given genre of interpretation may not agree about what these purposes are, or about the priority among them' (2011: 130–4). Arguments about these purposes, and how the truth/falsity or superiority/inferiority of interpretations, are all internal to the activity of interpretation.

Dworkin contrasts interpretation with science (2011: 152). This seems to be the real meaning for him of Hume's Principle. Both interpretation and science, at a superficial level, can be said to seek *truth*. But the way they strive for it, and even what truth is in regard to the two sorts of enquiry, is for Dworkin radically different. Science may have purposes—practical or technological ones, for instance—in addition to *finding the truth*. But those other purposes are quite distinct from the scientific search for truth, and scientific truth serves them solely in the relation of means to end. Interpretation, however, is fundamentally driven by purposes, often multiple purposes, whose relation to one another is part of what interpretation itself tries to sort out—not, however, in general, but in each given context for each given task of interpretation. What counts as truth in interpretation is equally contextual and purpose-driven. An interpretation is good, or better, or even true, only to the extent that it realizes the multiple and contested values involved in these multiple purposes. The standard of truth in interpretation is nothing beyond the way it serves the purposes of interpretation better than its rivals (2011: 153). Strikingly, however, Dworkin seems to hold this for truth too (2011: 173). If he does, then that erases his distinction between interpretation and science, and thereby directly undermines 'Hume's Principle' as Dworkin understands it.

The background of any interpretation is *first*, a shared practice or tradition in which it stands, and *second*, a set of assumptions (usually inexplicit, vague, and disputed) about the purpose of the practice. Any proposed interpretation claims to realize these purposes better than its alternatives (134). The difference in general purposes of interpretation enables Dworkin to distinguish three species of interpretation: *Collaborative* interpretation, which assumes that the interpreted object has an author, and seeks to advance the project begun by that author; *explanatory* interpretation, which assumes that the object or event has a certain significance for a target audience addressed by the interpreter, and attempts to explain the object to the audience; and *conceptual* interpretation, whose objects are concepts shared by a community and attempts to understand that concept (135–6). In this third case the distinction between creator and audience disappears. We all belong simultaneously to the collective creator community and to its collective audience. Moral thinking and moral philosophy both belong to this third species—conceptual interpretation.

Kinds of Concepts

Conceptual interpretation applies to a certain class of concepts—*interpretive* concepts. Some concepts, Dworkin says, are *criterial*—we possess and share them to the extent that we agree on the criteria for identifying instances of them. 'Equilateral triangle' is such a concept. So is 'bald' (2011: 158). If we disagree about whether a friend of ours is bald without disagreeing about how much hair he has on his head, then our disagreement is merely verbal or even spurious. A second class of concepts is *natural kind* concepts. Natural kinds are assumed to have a fixed reference in nature, though we may undertake enquiry in order to determine what nature fixes its reference (2011: 159). Sometimes natural kind concepts can be rendered criterial by a better understanding of the natural kind. Criterial and natural kind concepts have in common that genuine disagreement about their application is ruled out once all the pertinent facts are agreed upon (2011: 160). Both are therefore fit concepts to use in clear, deductive procedures based on some 'analysis' of the concept that is accepted by those to whom the reasoning is addressed.

It is altogether different, Dworkin argues, regarding *interpretive* concepts. Their use requires that we agree sufficiently about their application that we can propose theories that purport to explain their use. These theories typically take their origin from paradigm cases, since these can help to establish that we are arguing about the *same* interpretive concept. We then proceed to give an account of why the concept applies in paradigm cases, and also why it should apply (or should not apply) to cases that are controversial or disputed. But these theories do not consist in the kind of 'analysis' that operates in the case of criterial or natural kind concepts. They are instead interpretations of the concept in question; they are to be judged by the way in which they serve the purposes for which we use the concept. Applications of the concept, and also these purposes, are possible or even necessary objects of dispute, since the aim of the interpretation is to decide disputed cases, to explain the cases that are not disputed, and also to fix the purposes for which we use the concept and also offer competing interpretations of it.

Moral Concepts as Interpretive Concepts

It is Dworkin's contention that moral concepts are typically interpretive concepts. I suggest that it is really this, and not any version of what Hume might have had in mind early in Book III of the *Treatise*, that explains Dworkin's endorsement of what he calls 'Hume's Principle'. Dworkin rejects, namely, the idea that moral truth could be gotten at through enquiries fundamentally aimed at the kind of truth that science seeks. This is supposedly a truth independent of values or purposes of interpretation, or a truth that can be formulated in natural kind concepts or criterial concepts. Thus, 'ought' enquiry is independent of factual or 'is' enquiries, if the latter are based on merely criterial or natural kind concepts and the kinds of reasoning appropriate to their use. I question only whether Dworkin himself can, consistently with his other views, acknowledge that science itself falls outside the one big thing that is the subject of his Hedgehog Principle.

But Dworkin rejects views that assume there are ethical truths falling outside interpretation. Thus, he rejects those forms of neo-Aristotelian naturalism and eudaimonism that appeal to criterial or natural kind concepts of virtue, happiness, or self-realization—such as a concept of virtue or vice that would identify them with the objects of certain natural human sentiments. Here we see how Dworkin's appeal to 'Hume's Principle' undercuts Hume's own ethics. Moreover, as we will see presently, Dworkin also offers a very different interpretation of Aristotle himself from this neo-Aristotelian naturalistic one. If that sort of truth is thought of as the realm of 'is', then the ethical realm—the realm of 'ought'—must be independent of it, because the realm of 'is' is not governed by interpretive concepts and the standards of interpretation appropriate to them, but is a realm in which interpretive questions are regarded as already settled or else trivial. The realm of 'ought', by contrast, is dominated by interpretive concepts and the activity of interpretation.

This point is related to the fundamental way interpretive concepts differ from other kinds of concepts, especially criterial concepts. We can reason from criterial concepts, or even from natural kind concepts (once a theory is supplied describing the criteria for the natural kind), by way of formally valid deductions. From interpretive concepts, however, we must proceed not by way of deduction but by way of what could be called 'specification' and 'judgment'. That is, we move from higher level to lower level principles by providing an interpretation, governed by a set of purposes (as Dworkin would emphasize, this is always an essentially vague and contested set of purposes), of what the higher order principle requires under a given set of circumstances. This act of interpretation requires a skill that can never be precisely codified. It involves the taking of *responsibility* by the interpreter for the act of interpretation.

This last point explains why Dworkin introduces the entire section of the book that deals with interpretation through a chapter on responsibility (2011: 99–122). Dworkin's many writings on the law and legal reasoning argue at length for the idea that judicial pronouncements are interpretive rather than criterial and deductive. In Dworkin's view, it is an evasion of responsibility for jurists not to recognize that they must *interpret* laws in applying them, rather than pretending to deduce their pronouncements from laws or legal precedents formulated as if they were framed in terms of criterial concepts. The attempt to reduce interpretive concepts to criterial concepts in this way is always question-begging and doomed to failure. It is a cowardly abdication of our responsibility as moral beings.

In the application of concepts or principles to particular cases, interpretation ultimately also involves a special capacity or virtue. Aristotle calls it φρόνησις (*phrónēsis*; practical wisdom, translated into scholastic Latin as *prudentia*). Kant calls it 'judgment' (*Urteil, Beurteilung, Urteilskraft*). This is the ability to relate general concepts or principles to a particular case. Kant distinguishes *determining* judgment, which moves from the general to the particular, from *reflective* judgment, through which the mind forms a concept that unites a manifold of instances into a single consciousness.[8] Kant argues that determining judgment cannot, on pain of a vicious regress, be reduced to conceptual or discursive reasoning. For if we apply concept C_1 through deducing from it a less general concept C_2, and then apply C_2 through a still more specific concept C_3, we can never even in principle reach the particular through this process. At every point we merely invoke further general concepts and remain forever at a distance from their individual instances. Judgment is therefore, a distinct capacity or skill, partly inborn and partly developed through experience, which is required for the application of general concepts to their instances.

Kant's point would, of course, hold of all concepts, not only of interpretive ones. But if Dworkin is right, a related capacity is involved not only in their ultimate application to particulars, but at every level at which they are employed. Reasoning that uses them is never merely deductive, but always distinctively *hermeneutical*. It relates the interpretive concept to *the whole of interpretation* in which it is involved. Dworkin's Hedgehog Principle thus turns out to be equivalent to his claim that all claims about value involve *holistic* interpretation. This makes value claims different from claims that might be settled using criterial or natural kind concepts, and reasoning about value different from reasoning in those fields where criterial or natural kind concepts predominate.

There are two basic features, on Dworkin's account, of our use of interpretive concepts, which apply especially to moral concepts. *First*, as I've already said, the use of interpretive concepts is always *holistic*. 'Interpretation', Dworkin asserts, 'is pervasively holistic' (2011: 154). To think about an interpretive concept, or to apply it, always involves other related interpretive concepts. In morality some concepts are 'thinner', more general and abstract ('right' and 'wrong', 'good' and 'bad') while others are 'thicker'—an act can be wrong because it is 'treacherous, inconsiderate, cruel, dishonest, indecent, niggardly, unreasonable, cheap, unworthy, unfair' and a good character can be good because it is 'generous, courageous, noble or selfless'. 'In either case', says Dworkin, whether we are using thinner or thicker concepts, 'more concrete or more abstract judgments are waiting in the wings, even if they never appear' (183).

Plato and Aristotle

Dworkin illustrates the pervasive holism of moral theory by citing Plato and Aristotle as instances. Many of the early Socratic dialogues of Plato seem to assume that typical virtue concepts—temperance (in *Charmides*), courage (in *Laches*), piety (in *Euthyphro*)—are criterial. The entire discussion in these dialogues is aporetic precisely because it founders on this false assumption, since no successful 'definition' or 'analysis' of the concept is ever found (or ever could be found). By contrast, Dworkin argues, Plato's positive account of justice (and the other virtues) in *Republic* is both holistic and interpretive. It relates justice to the other accepted virtues: courage, wisdom, temperance, and all of them to happiness (εὐδαιμονία) as the encompassing good of the soul (184–6). Aristotle too, Dworkin argues, treats the virtues, and their relation to happiness, interpretively and holistically. We understand happiness as the exercise of virtue, and the particular virtues in their relation to one another and to the good life (186–8). 'Naturalistic' neo-Aristotelian ethics—if it treats happiness or virtue as criterial or natural-kind concepts—is therefore not authentically Aristotelian.

The *second* basic feature of moral concepts as interpretive concepts is their involvement with human *practices*. It is in our social and political activities that we employ, and also interpret, concepts like justice, honesty, virtue, good and bad, right and wrong, and all their thicker children, nephews and nieces, and cousins (however far removed). Interpretation in general, as Dworkin presents it, is itself a social practice. Any genre of interpretation belongs to a *tradition*. Every tradition has its own aims and purposes. But these too are complex, treated holistically and always up for dispute through the activity of interpretation. Both every day and theoretical thought about morality, law and politics are part of the common life that people live, share, argue about—they are entwined with our practical agreements and disagreements. Philosophy and common sense are both practical as well as interpretive.

Interpretation and Integrity

John Rawls distinguished the *concept* of justice from different *conceptions* of justice—for example, his own conception of 'justice as fairness'.[9] Dworkin in effect extends this distinction to all ethical and all moral concepts. The starting point for interpretation is a concept (of justice, of a good life, of living well, etc.); different interpretations of the concept yield different (perhaps rival) conceptions (of justice as fairness, justice as maximizing welfare, of the good life as the life of wealth, or moral virtue, or philosophical contemplation, etc.). The aim of ethics, then, is to integrate one's interpretations of different interpretive concepts, one's conceptions of value, into a whole by which one can live responsibly, with integrity and authenticity. The task of conceptual interpretation for Dworkin is holistic. Dworkin does not use the terms 'system' and 'systematicity', but he seems to me to be agreeing with a long tradition of philosophers (including Kant and the post-Kantian idealists, who for me represent the paradigm of great philosophy) in insisting that the proper approach to philosophy, especially to ethics, is always a *systematic* approach.

Nietzsche famously said, 'The will to system is a lack of integrity' (Nietzsche 1954: 442). Like many of Nietzsche's famous sayings (often quoted by his admirers with a supercilious air of fatuous superiority), this one is obviously false. Any thinking person can see this easily after only a moment's reflection. Dworkin's account of the correct way to engage in ethical enquiry shows why it is. The aim of interpretive enquiry is always the systematic integration of our different interpretations. It is founded on an ethical commitment—the commitment to *integrity*. 'Interpretation knits values together. We are morally responsible to the degree that our various concrete interpretations achieve an overall integrity so that each supports the other in a network of value that we embrace authentically' (Dworkin 2011: 101). This commitment to integrity, according to Dworkin, is what provides moral enquiry with its 'epistemology'. Moral epistemology consists solely in integrity or responsibility in seeking overall coherence among interpretations (2011: 447). Yet Nietzsche's paradoxical *bons mots*, however silly they may be when taken literally, usually make a valid point. That is true of this one as well. For systematic philosophers do often betray a lack of integrity when they *fail* to achieve coherence and integration but nevertheless dishonestly pretend to have done so. Nietzsche's saying becomes true when applied to these philosophers (or pseudo-philosophers). Dworkin, however, regards the integration of interpretations as an ongoing process which is never complete, 'To the extent that we fail in our interpretive project—and it seems impossible wholly to succeed— we are not acting fully out of conviction, and so we are not fully responsible' (101). Integrity thus requires (the very point on which Nietzsche is correctly insisting) that we acknowledge our failure when we fail. At the same time, Nietzsche could not be more wrong—for the *will* to system—the *endless quest* for complete systematic integration among our interpretations—is the only thing that integrity or responsibility could ever consist in.

Relativism

Dworkin considers the challenge that this makes his interpretive account of morality 'relativistic' in a bad sense of that term (170–1). Relativism is the position that different people can use the same concept (for example, 'justice'), make conflicting judgments using it, and yet all be correct in these opposed judgments. Dworkin's response is to offer relativism a dilemma, from which he believes it cannot escape. If he's right, it shows that no coherent view, including his own, could ever be committed to relativism. Suppose it is claimed that *justice*, for instance, is different in different societies. Some societies think that discrimination and privilege based on birth or sex is wrong, while others think this is not only right, but even belongs to the foundations of any just social order. Dworkin points out that posing the problem this way assumes that both societies have the same concept—here, the concept 'justice'—and that each has the unilateral authority to determine what this concept means or implies. Each makes judgments using this authority, with which the other society, using its equally valid authority, disagrees.[10]

Such a position is subject to the following dilemma: On the one hand, we might interpret the different societies as having *different concepts*. The word we translate as 'justice' might refer to a different concept in that different society. In that case, our judgments do not really disagree, because they are not about the same thing. This would have to be so, for instance, if we could not agree with them even about the paradigm instances of the concept that enable us to treat our claims and our theories as interpretations of the same concept. On the other hand, if we do agree sufficiently on the paradigms that we can treat their judgments and ours as (conflicting) judgments about the same thing, then this puts *all* of us in a position to question the authoritativeness of *any* of the conflicting judgments. We can question their judgments and they can question ours. We can both employ interpretations of the common concept, and of other related concepts that we might share, in determining what judgments about justice are correct and incorrect—perhaps ours are, perhaps theirs, or perhaps both are partly right and partly wrong. We can therefore keep the part of relativism that says each side is authoritative only if we give up the part that says they disagree, and we can keep the part that says they disagree only if we abandon the part that says each is authoritative.[11]

According to Dworkin, you can't have it both ways. If each has the authority to interpret its own concept as it pleases, then there can be no genuine disagreement, but only an incommensurable difference in concepts. If we disagree, however, then we are using the same concept—we can communicate and there is a right and wrong, even if nobody has found it. Either way, any coherent representation of the situation will reject relativism. If relativism is never a real threat, then Dworkin may persist in the doctrines that might mistakenly be thought to lead to it. As we noted a bit earlier, he applies these doctrines even to the concept of truth itself (172–8). 'We can understand truth as an interpretive concept' (173). Different theories of truth can be understood as different interpretations of it in light of the purposes of enquiry, and different theories of truth may be better for some domains of enquiry than for others. Truth in ethics is to be understood as success in the employment of the method most appropriate to that genre of interpretation (179). Dworkin would be more self-consistent if he had acknowledged the same thing about science, and given up on 'Hume's Principle'. But he's quite right in saying that 'nothing in this argument even hints that truth is up to us. That is already ruled out by the most abstract formulation of truth as success in inquiry... Nor are we talking past each other in our philosophical arguments over truth. We really do disagree' (180).

The Value of a Life

This brings us at last to the starting point of Dworkin's interpretive enterprise in ethics. Of course, since the enterprise is interpretive, and interpretation is pervasively holistic, we could in principle start anywhere, with any ethical concept. But it usually makes sense to start with an interpretive concept that we will recognize as central to ethics and also as basic as any concept can be within the interdependent whole of interpretation. This is why Plato chose justice and why Aristotle chose happiness. In setting forth a modern ethical conception, Dworkin begins with the concept of *human dignity*. Even here, however, he wants to show that the starting point is not arbitrary, and that it can be defended against its chief modern rivals.

Dworkin understands 'ethics' to concern the question—How shall we live? 'Morality' is about the demands others may make on us. One basic issue then is—How are moral values to be integrated interpretively into ethical values? He presents an argument (191–2) that we should not choose self-interest, even generalized self-interest, as our starting point in pursuing this task, because this cuts us off from the basic moral conviction that we should do what is right even when it is not in our interest or even when doing wrong is in everybody's interest. Nor should we start with the contrasting view (which Dworkin calls the 'austere' view) that moral convictions form a closed system cut off from other values. For then we are prevented from integrating moral values into other values, and also from offering any non-trivial answer to the question, 'Why be moral?' (192–3). Nor can we even ground morality in desires and interests we find we do have—as Thomas Hobbes does with our interest in survival, and Hume does through a broader and more humane conception of what we in feel, or are inclined to approve (194). We need to interpret morality not in terms of the interests we *do* have, but rather in terms of the interests we *should* have (195). What we need most fundamentally, Dworkin argues, is a way of *interpretively* knitting 'morality'—the justified demands others may make on us—together with 'ethics'—the question how we should live in order to realize value in our life and live a meaningful life (13–14).

Dworkin distinguishes three types of value we can realize in our lives. First, there is having *a good life* (what we can call the *adjectival* value of a life). He admits, or rather he insists, that it is a matter of controversy (a question of interpretation) what a good life is. 'Is it plausible', he asks, 'to suppose that being moral is the best way to make one's life good? It is wildly implausible if we hold to popular conceptions of what morality requires and what makes a life good' (195). But there is a second, distinct concept, that of 'living well' (the *adverbial* value of a life) (196–7). Dworkin clearly thinks that moral conduct is part of living a good life. But this is not to be a trivial truth. It is to be vindicated through the way the concept of living well is interpreted in relation both to moral concepts and to other value concepts. Someone can *live well*, but—due to misfortune—not have a *good life*. Moreover, it is at least a possible view that one can have a *good life* without *living well*. Perhaps someone can have a *good life* precisely because he has *lived badly*—getting the means for a good life through cheating and wrongly taking advantage of others (202). Dworkin also distinguishes the *product* value of a life—what it effects, achieves, or accomplishes (197). A person can have lived badly, and even had a bad life, but their life might still *produce* something of value. An artist, for example, might have produced good works of art even though he lived badly—was a morally despicable human being—and also suffered a wretched life. (This might even be one sort of person Nietzsche would admire: the genius who defies morality, suffers a life of misery, but creates great works.)

Dignity

Dworkin holds the recognizably Aristotelian view that of these three kinds of value a life can have, it is *living well* that matters most, 'The final value of our lives is adverbial, not adjectival' (197). But as we have seen, he might dissent from Aristotle's doctrine that you cannot have a truly good life without living well. This emphasis on the adverbial value of a life rests on two principles, which Dworkin calls 'self-respect' and 'authenticity'. To have *self-respect* is to take seriously the question whether you have lived well. You respect yourself if you consider it a matter of importance whether your life is a successful performance or only a wasted opportunity (203). *Authenticity* consists in the acceptance of personal responsibility for identifying what counts as success in your own life, and also for striving to achieve it. Authenticity appears to encompass accepting responsibility not only for living well, but also for achieving—or at least striving for—both a good life and a life with significant positive product-value. Together, self-respect and authenticity constitute the *dignity* of a human being. 'Dignity requires self-respect and authenticity' (204). Later on, it will become clear that Dworkin regards the recognition of one's own dignity as committing you to recognize the dignity of others as well. This extension of dignity from oneself to others is something Dworkin finds in Kant's Formula of Humanity as End in itself. He gives to it the name 'Kant's Principle' (19, 260, 264–77).

Dworkin's conception of human dignity, however, remains unclear and troubling. Here's the problem—Self-respect and authenticity, as Dworkin describes them, are *attitudes toward myself.* They are supposed to *constitute* my dignity. If I take these attitudes toward myself, I have dignity. But what if I do not? Do I then *lack* dignity? Or is it instead the case that *I have dignity* but merely *do not recognize* the dignity I have, or *do not live up to* my dignity? If we take Dworkin at his word, then it might seem he is committed to the former view. For if dignity *consists* in leading my life so that I actually exhibit self-respect and authenticity, then if I lack these self-directed attitudes, I appear to lack dignity. But Kant's Principle appears to require me—or at least to require all those who think of themselves as having dignity—to treat others as having dignity whether or not they take these attitudes. That seems to imply that they—and perhaps I myself as well—do have dignity even if they do not take the attitudes toward oneself on which Dworkin seems to hold that dignity depends. How can Dworkin defend this?

Prima facie or superficially—and as we will see presently, in its actual history— 'dignity' seems to refer to some sort of social status. In discussing the concept of legal status and social status in status-based societies, Jeremy Waldron distinguishes 'sortal-status' from 'condition-status'.[12] In a society based on fundamental differences in status, sortal status depends on the basic sort of person you are—a patrician or a plebeian, an aristocrat or a commoner, a man or a woman (where women have a lower status than men), or a white, black, or coloured person (as in apartheid South Africa). Condition-status, by contrast, is a status that can be acquired or lost depending on what you do, or what happens to you (for example, marriage, bankruptcy, legal incompetence, being a member of the military, or being convicted of a felony). In these terms, if whether I have dignity depends on whether I display self-respect and authenticity, then it is a concept denoting a condition-status. Dworkin is then presupposing that among humans there is only one *sortal status*, namely the sort *eligible to acquire* dignity as a condition–status.

Perhaps Dworkin could defend the view that dignity is (in these terms) an acquired condition–status by arguing that no one could *entirely* lack dignity; no one could *coherently* take an attitude toward life that *totally* eschews self-respect and authenticity. Then he could say that everyone does take an attitude that includes them and so acquires the condition of dignity. About a person who says, 'I don't in fact care about living well. I care only about enjoying myself as far as I can', Dworkin remarks, 'There is a well-known difficulty with that reply. Enjoyment in most cases is not a freestanding state of mind like hunger. It is normally an epiphenomenon of the conviction that we are living as we should' (2011: 206). Or again, Dworkin considers someone who just wants what they want for no further reason. He doubts that this makes sense, and argues with such a person—'Don't you have an over-all self-image?... Self-images...play the critical role they do because they are constructed not of what we just find we like but of what we admire and think appropriate' (207–8). More generally—'You want your life to be successful because you think its success is important, not the other way round' (206).

I don't disagree with Dworkin here, but he isn't addressing the crucial question. For if dignity consists in self-respect and authenticity, then what he needs to show, if he is to claim that we all have dignity, is that we all actually do care about our lives—that those who think, say, or act as if they don't, do in fact respect themselves, even if they don't realize it. Instead, however, he seems to be arguing with them, trying to convince them that they *should*. But if dignity depends on our *actual* attitudes, that's not to the point. The problem for Dworkin is that there really are people—a great many people, in fact—who really do not care whether they live well or achieve anything of value, and even people who do not care whether they have a good life. If they are aware that their lives are worthless, they do not assume responsibility for it but blame someone else—their parents, or 'society'. Or they think so little about their lives that even the issue of taking responsibility for themselves never arises. They simply do not care. At least that's how they act; sometimes it is even what they say about themselves. We can quite easily find such talk in popular culture, perhaps even from some contrarian philosophers.

Dworkin argues that such people are guilty of thinking incoherently. He may be right, but that is still not to the point. For it is sadly possible for people (even for people who consider themselves highly successful) to live stable lives based on thinking incoherently and lying to themselves. It is possible even for whole societies to live incoherently and self-deceptively. This is true, for instance of our own society, with its conception of 'the American dream', based on obsessive greed and competitiveness unbridled by either morality or prudence. The incoherence is clearly a ground for criticizing American values, but not for claiming that Americans do not really think (incoherently) and live (badly). The hard question for Dworkin is: Do such people have dignity or don't they? If dignity is a condition-status, acquired through actual attitudes of self-respect and authenticity, then it would seem that they lack dignity, and there would be no reason why anyone should treat them as if they did have dignity. Kant's principle, however, holds that we should treat *all* our fellow humans as beings with dignity—the bad and the shallow as well as the good and the thoughtful. I think Dworkin wants to agree. But it is not clear how he can defend that position.

Perhaps Dworkin would argue that the minimal measure self-respect and authenticity sufficient to acquire dignity belongs to everyone *precisely because* it is incoherent to think of living well as unimportant, or to fail to take some responsibility for your life. Perhaps Dworkin's claim is that everyone, even the most thoughtless and irresponsible person, has some self-respect and authenticity, hence has acquired *some* dignity after all. But in that case I must worry whether Dworkin's conceptions of self-respect and authenticity could possibly mean what they were supposed to mean. They looked like serious demands on us, challenges it would take effort and commitment for us to meet. But if it would be incoherent to suppose that anyone did not meet them, then we begin to wonder why Dworkin thinks they are so important.

If Dworkin's position is that dignity is a condition–status belonging only to those who actually have self-respect and authenticity, then he faces a dilemma—Either many people lack dignity, and we need not treat them as if they have it; or else self-respect and authenticity are something everyone has trivially acquired, and they place no burden even on the most thoughtless person to care more about how they live, or to take any more responsibility for it than they already do. Both horns of this dilemma seem unacceptable.

Dignity, Objective Value, and Radical Freedom

Let me suggest a rescue from this dilemma by offering an alternative inter-pretation of Dworkin's conceptions of dignity, self-respect, and authentic-ity—Let's take these as referring *not* to attitudes people *actually do take* toward themselves, but instead to *real and objective norms* to which people are subject and with which they are responsible for complying, whether they comply or not, whether they recognize the norms or self-deceptively flee from their responsibility under them. Non-human entities—a tree or a beast—are not *capable* of caring about whether they live well, or of taking responsibility for having a good or a productive life. All normally functioning human beings, however, do have this *capacity*, and therefore this *responsibility*. That is the foundation of their dignity. All people, then, possess dignity simply because all people (at any rate—all normally functioning human adults) are subject equally to the same *norms* demanding self-respect and authenticity. They have the responsibility whether they acknowledge it or not, and whether or not they comply with the norms under which it places them.

Dworkin tends to confirm this interpretation when he asks, concerning the responsibility involved in the principle of authenticity, 'Responsibility to whom?' and responds that it is misleading to say 'responsibility to our-selves'. For those to whom we are responsible can normally release us from the responsibility, but nothing and no one can release us from the responsibil-ity to live well, to care about how well we live and whether we have made anything meaningful out of our lives (Dworkin 2011: 196). This suggests that the norms in question are *real* or *objective*. Our dignity is not consti-tuted, then, by the fact that it is simply important — *really and objectively important*—that we live well and take the responsibility for our lives (196,

211–18). That real and objective importance, and not any attitude we may or may not take toward it, is what constitutes our dignity.

There is, however, a serious cost to interpreting Dworkin this way, which is also a reason for doubting that Dworkin would accept my sympathetically intended interpretation. For if dignity belongs to any being that stands under objective norms of self-respect or authenticity, whether or not they meet these norms, then what we must say about human dignity is the same as what Sartre says about radical freedom, it is something from which we cannot flee, no matter how hard we try. Moreover, it seems clear that human dignity has this property in common with radical freedom because they refer to the very same thing. We shortly see that it belongs to the history of the concept of human dignity that it is associated with this same radical freedom. The demand that one live well and be responsible to oneself for what one is presupposes the capacity to determine one's identity in a radical sense, one's place in creation. It depends on a radical freedom that resists being fit comfortably into the causal structure of the universe.

Dworkin, however, takes a 'compatibilist' view about freedom (219–52). Like most compatibilists, he wants to trivialize the whole issue of freedom, seeing it as an issue only about blame and punishment—about responsibility to others. They thereby totally miss the point, beause the issue of free will is always first and foremost an issue about *dignity*—dignity in precisely Dworkin's sense of the term. It's about being someone who has the capacity and also the burden of being in charge of your own life, rather than being a mere object of science or of engineering—that is, a mere thing to be investigated, explained, predicted, and pushed around or manipulated. Dignity requires ascribing to ourselves a freedom that resists being 'naturalized'—that is, fit comfortably into the causal structure of nature as science necessarily understands it. All this remains the case even if—as I myself would pointedly insist—religious or supernaturalist views of freedom are untenable on the ground that there is no credible evidence whatever for the supernatural. Freedom is something we have no choice but to presuppose we have, even if it is forever unintelligible to us in either natural *or supernatural* terms. The point is rather that even to take the standpoint of natural science, and investigate the causal structure of the world, we must place ourselves beyond it, because we must engage in a collective communicative enterprise through which we *interpret* nature, our relation to nature, the objective norms of knowledge, and action and even come to understand ourselves as knowers and agents in relation to one another.

Dworkin could accept all this, if he chose, by emphasizing the way that dignity, incompatibilist freedom, and objective value all resist being 'naturalized' because they are all part of the 'One Big Thing' that the wise hedgehog knows. But I interpret several things in Dworkin's position—his compatibilism, his insistence on 'Hume's Principle', and also his presentation of self-respect and authenticity as attitudes toward oneself that constitute dignity—as the choice not to take that route. Dworkin wants dignity to rest on mere contingent facts about the way we think of ourselves. I see why he might make this choice, but then I have to insist that doing so confronts him with a serious dilemma—If dignity is an acquired condition–status, then many (perhaps most) people lack it and we need not treat them as if they had it. But if self-respect and authenticity are so easily acquired that we can assume everyone has them, then it is hard to see why they, or the dignity that rests on them, should matter as much to us as Dworkin insists.

The Concept of Human Dignity: Its History and Meaning

At this point I would like to look more broadly at the concept of human dignity and its history. Most basically, the word 'dignity' refers to a kind of *value*. Its etymology derives from the Greek δοκειν—to seem or to show, a cognate of the Latin *decus*—ornament, distinction, honour, glory. In Roman usage, the dignity of a person is based on their conformity to what is fitting (*decus*), manners characteristic of the upper classes. In Boethius and Aquinas, 'dignity' is equated with 'person'. A *person* (in social or legal contexts, or even in Trinitarian theology) is a *hypostasis proprietate distincta ad dignitatem pertinente*.[13] The social background of this is the assumption that persons are arranged in ranks, with some superior and some inferior. For much of its history, the concept of dignity was in fact associated with that of social rank, especially high rank by birth. Hobbes identified the dignity of a human being with the price others set on him.[14] Even Kant, whose ethical theory is grounded on the principle of the equal dignity of all rational beings, refers to offices within the state as 'dignities'.[15]

But eventually—even in the ancient world, but especially in modernity—the thought arose that *all human beings equally have dignity*. The earliest versions of this thought involved treating human beings as enjoying a special rank within creation.[16] Pico Della Mirandola thought the special dignity of human nature lies in human freedom, which enables the free and rational being to *choose* what rank it occupies among creatures.[17] Pico's claim was anticipated even earlier by Cicero:

> From this we see that sensual pleasure is quite unworthy of the dignity of man (*non satis esse dignam hominis praestantia*). [...] And if we will only bear in

mind the superiority and dignity of our nature (*quae sit in natura excellentia et dignitas*), we shall realize how wrong it is to abandon ourselves to excess and to live in luxury and voluptuousness [...]. We must realize also that we are invested by Nature with two characters (*personis*), as it were: one of these is universal, arising from the fact of our being all alike endowed with reason and with that superiority which lifts us above the brute. From this all morality and propriety are derived, and upon it depends the rational method of ascertaining our duty.[18]

Waldron's Approach

Let's try to put this traditional conception of *human* dignity in Waldron's terms by saying that all human beings, as free agents, have the same sortal-status.[19] The egalitarian aspect of this thought is that this status belongs *equally* to *all* human beings, even though the glaringly obvious social implications have been grasped by our dismal species only slowly, reluctantly, and haltingly. People are not in fact treated in our social institutions as though they have equal dignity, which is glaringly obvious.

This shows the big problem with Waldron's approach. By consigning human dignity to the social economy of honour and esteem, this would make it dependent once again (as Hobbes did) on the price placed on persons by others, or by society. If a society fails to acknowledge human dignity, does dignity then not exist? That would not be Kant's or Fichte's view, or Pico's, or Cicero's either. I fear that, despite his intention to treat modern conceptions of dignity as a 'transvaluation' of the traditional concept, this is what inevitably happens in Waldron's handling of the notion. It seems more accurate to treat the modern notion of human dignity as a subversion (or transvaluation) not merely of the traditional inequalities of sortal status, but of the whole concept of status—both sortal and condition status—in other words, of the entire conceptual framework in terms of which Waldron wants to understand the concept of dignity.

Overuse and Abuse of the Concept of Human Dignity

Dworkin warns us that the concept of human dignity is overused and misused (2011: 204). He prefaces his discussion of its application to morality with this warning, and with a declaration of his intention to supply, through his principles of self-respect and authenticity, an interpretation of human dignity that can be useful in moral reasoning. It is worth reflecting, I believe, in light of the history of the concept as I have just briefly sketched it, on why the concept of human dignity is so open to over-use and misuse.

All talk of 'human dignity' has a tendency to sound pompous and empty. It sounds pompous partly because of the aristocratic background of the term. It sounds empty because its rejection of the honour-based social conception is framed in terms of that very conception. If, within a culture of status and honour, all human beings have the same dignity, then dignity cannot mean much after all. It then seems to be true of 'human dignity' what Hegel says about the term 'person'—it is a term of greatest honour and simultaneously something wholly ordinary, sometimes even a term of contempt.[20]

For just this reason, the most effective presentation of the idea of human dignity is often ironical. Human dignity shines most brightly through its exhibition when the human condition is presented comically, as one of poverty, absurdity, and humiliation, as happens in Samuel Beckett's play, *Waiting for Godot*. We see our human dignity best when attention is directed to the condition of the poor and despised, to human hunger and want, to the absurdity of all our lives, to our inevitable mortality, to our pitiful vulnerability to all-powerful and all-cruel nature, to our nakedness, our shame, our sexual inadequacies, our excretory functions. Perhaps only a human dignity that can survive this sort of presentation is authentic and real. For if all human beings really do possess dignity, then in the real world where we live, all beings with dignity are finite, mortal, and subject to humiliation. In fact, most of those very beings who possess dignity do live in conditions of utter degradation at the hands of other beings, also with dignity, who constantly disgrace their own dignity through the satisfaction they take in degrading other beings who have dignity. For this is the race of beings—so sublime, pitiful, abominable, cosmically so improbable, to itself so incomprehensible—to which we all belong.

People sometimes use the notion of human dignity to prop up beliefs that offend outrageously against any meaningful conception of how beings with human dignity ought to be treated. The chief representative of the notion of dignity in modern philosophy is Kant. But we know that Kant approved of social arrangements that treated women as dependents; he even developed an influential theory of race that both reflected the reality of white supremacy and could be used to offer a defense of it.[21] The dignity of personhood is a theme on which Roman Catholic moral theology exhibits much heartfelt reflection. But Catholic doctrine corrupts the concept of personhood at its root by extending that status to groups of cells within the body of a woman, claiming these cells, since they constitute a potential person, have coercively enforceable rights against that very woman herself. Where it is enforced, this doctrine effectively deprives half the human race of the basic right over one's own body. Dworkin points out that some even abuse the idea so far as to argue that it is an insult to human dignity for physicians to attempt to repair disease or deficiency in a fetus (2011: 204). In our day, attempts to redistribute wealth in order to protect the rights of the poor have been attacked on the ground that they violate human dignity in the same way slavery did. In the sixteenth through the nineteenth centuries, Catholic bishops in the American South, and in those countries that promoted the slave trade, even defended slavery itself by appealing to the Church's conception of human dignity.

With friends like these, human dignity hardly needs any enemies. Moreover, the empty use of the notion in human rights campaigns and political manifestos of all stripes creates in people's minds the easy impression that *of course* everyone believes in the dignity of all human beings. One can proclaim it and then go on supporting whatever one likes, including the most backward and inhuman institutions. When we see this happen, we are tempted to turn away from the idea of human dignity out of boredom, weariness, even disgust.

Against these thoughts, it is worth making an important point—that it is inevitably the best and most essential moral ideas that are the soonest abused. As Jason Stanley has recently argued, propaganda itself typically takes the form of representing oneself as supporting a value while in fact undermining that same value.[22] Propagandists naturally choose the best ideas as targets for this self-subversion, for the most effective conceivable weapon against the good is subversion of the best. The idea of human dignity is especially vulnerable to this kind of abuse, because it is so abstract and yet so basic to modern ethical values. It is important to realize that there are no ideas or values that ideology and propaganda cannot twist, abuse, misapply, and misinterpret. Those who might want to do moral or political philosophy by searching for certain privileged ideas that are immune to abuse will be drawn to other ideas—perhaps even the opposites of the true ideas, and will therefore be drawn only to bad ideas—often, the diametrical opposites of good ideas. Radicals of the left and the right have both offered illustrations of this point.

What follows is that no one can make any intelligent contribution to moral discussion by advocating some otherwise intellectually dubious idea on the ground that it is immune to abuse or by criticizing a widely accepted idea—for example, the idea of human dignity—solely on the ground that it can be and has been abused. Unfortunately, such argumentative interventions have also been all too common. Dworkin is therefore right to choose human dignity as the central idea in his interpretive project. The aim should be to rescue the idea both from its apparent emptiness and from its many modes of abuse. The method of rescue should be an interpretation of the idea that relates it to other moral and ethical ideas and values that can serve as ways of giving it substance and protecting it from abuse.

Essential to this method would be to emphasize two ideas—both closely connected with Dworkin's account, but not sufficiently emphasized in his conception of human dignity. The *first* is freedom of the will, the rational capacity to determine your own identity rather than have this determined for you by causal processes. The *second* is the capacity to communicate with others about living well, having a good life, right and wrong, the meaning of our lives both individually and together. This presupposes that we are all free, that as beings with self-respect we are co-deliberators in all ethical choice and not merely passive objects to be moved about (whether benefited or harmed) by the results of deliberation. It presupposes that our interactions are governed by reasons rather than determined by causes. It belongs to Dworkin's conception of ethics as an interpretive enterprise that we have the capacity for this kind of communication, since he conceives the interpretation of interpretive concepts as a collective enterprise. But in Dworkin's execution of his project, I see both these crucial elements of his own view overshadowed by themes more characteristic of the utilitarian or consequentialist approach he explicitly rejects. An ethics of freedom and communication gives way to an ethics of welfare—of aiding and harming. Even the theme of human rights, which has been central to Dworkin's thought from the beginning, is distorted by this emphasis.

Human Dignity and Moral Principles

Dworkin's basic principle, then, in his treatment of morality in the last half of *Justice for Hedgehogs* is 'acts are wrong if they insult the dignity of others' (2011: 204). This is based on what Dworkin calls 'Kant's Principle': *You should think about the lives of others in the same way you think about your own.* If you ascribe human dignity to yourself, you must ascribe it equally to every other human being (2011: 19, 260). But this sets up two different perspectives on human dignity: Your concern with living well yourself and taking responsibility for your life, and your concern with the lives of others. The two perspectives might come into conflict; Dworkin argues that the conflict must be resolved not by compromise but by interpreting human dignity from each perspective so that the two do not come into conflict, and uniting the interpretations into a single perspective which each of us can take (261–4).

Human Dignity vs. Maximizing Consequentialism

In developing a morality based on human dignity, Dworkin is especially concerned to reject maximizing consequentialist theories. Such theories are sometimes understood in a way that requires impartial concern for all. Dworkin insists that this is the wrong interpretation, and agrees with what he takes to be Kant's position, 'we claim no right in ourselves that we do not grant to others and suppose no duty for them that we do not accept for ourselves' (2011: 266). Taken literally, however, this seems neither plausible nor authentically Kantian. People are individuals, different from one another. They have different rights and different duties, depending on their social roles and situations. It is also still too close to impartialist ethics to be authentically Kantian. For better or worse, Kantian ethics are not ethics of abstract, impartial, well-wishing or well-doing, in which persons are morally interchangeable. Kant recognizes that we have duties to particular people—to our friends, our family, our neighbours—duties we do not have to strangers. In a rational society, this would not conflict with their fundamental equality as beings with dignity. But I fear that Dworkin's position retains too much of the 'impartiality' of standpoint and 'in-principle–interchangeability of persons' that are often wrongly associated with Kant, but are actually more characteristic of maximizing consequentialism. Kant's ethics recognize the uniqueness of every person's perspective in the second of his three rules for the use of reason:

1. Think for yourself.
2. Think from the standpoint of everyone else.
3. Think consistently.[23]

The second principle here might seem like a form of impartiality, but it is really just the opposite—for it emphasizes the distinctiveness of each person's unique perspective. Depending on my relation to specific others (as family members, friends, or fellow citizens, or in my role as a member of a profession) I may well have both duties and rights in relation to these specific others that other people do not have. I don't think Dworkin means to deny any of this, but it is denied when Kant's Principle is associated with ideas drawn from maximizing consequentialism, such as like impartiality and the interchangeability of persons.

There simply is no general obligation to be either partial or impartial in the way we treat people. It is a misinterpretation of the idea of human dignity to associate it with this false notion. As a genuine moral requirement, impartiality holds only contextually, and depends on the special nature of other obligations. As a parent, I am not merely permitted but required to be partial to my own children as regards providing for their welfare and education. But if I am a judge in a school contest, it is wrong of me to be partial to my own child, and also wrong of me in making political decisions regarding education to favour policies that would benefit my child at the expense of other children. The extreme form impartiality takes in maximizing consequentialism is a result of its tendency to oversimplify everything, and reduce all decision making to a means–ends calculus instead of considering (as Dworkin would surely insist) that principles must reflect the proper interpretation of a wide variety of different values and different perspectives.

A second way in which Dworkin rejects maximizing consequentialism is by insisting, that 'a person's well-being is not a commodity that can be measured' (2011: 273). The same is true of the values of living well or having a good life. None of these can be reduced to pleasure or the absence of pain, or to desire satisfaction or preference satisfaction. A fortiori, these are not the kinds of goods that could be summed up or conceived as a collective quantity to be maximized.

A third point emphasized by Dworkin is that the sense in which Kant's Principle requires treating the lives and interests of all as equally important is not one that requires or even permits us to promote the good of others in ways that compromise their self-respect or their responsibility for their own lives. The danger in many consequentialist theories is that they would operate on the assumption that we must try to act toward others in ways that presuppose that we know better than they do what their interests are, or what living well or having a good life means in their case (276). Qualifications of this dangerous assumption are often defended only on it as a basis—we allow others to govern their lives only because doing so turns out to be the most effectively consequence-maximizing way for *us* to govern their lives. Human dignity, if it means anything at all, involves the utter rejection of that whole way of thinking.

Virtues and Vices of Consequentialism

My own view is that these caveats about consequentialist theories apply only conditionally. They depend on certain mistakes to which maximizing consequentialists may be susceptible, but which they might also avoid if they proceeded with good moral judgment. Consequentialist theories are often good at clearly formulating the best ways to achieve the ends we bring to them, but become shallow, trivial (or worse) when they try to justify claims about what our ends should be. Pleasure, for instance, is usually valued because we independently value that in which we take pleasure. These values are derived interpretively from the one big thing, about which consequentialism has nothing distinctive or interesting to say. Wise consequentialists would realize this.

When consequentialist theories are developed with wisdom, however, then they often cease to be interestingly different from other theories. Some of the initial distinctive appeal of consequentialist theories will then be seen to vanish, because it is based on true but simplistic ideas (for example, that we should choose what is best, that we should seek efficient means to our ends, that each should count for one and none for more than one). In the minds of some consequentialists, these trivial truths often combine in the wrong-headed thought that these simple ideas can cut through the complexity of moral reasoning and offer us some sort of radical enlightenment in contrast to the murkiness of traditional moral ideas. The most wrong-headed idea of all was the anti-enlightenment idea that a few experts ('scientists', 'social engineers', 'technocrats'), should be trusted to make decisions for other people. Here, human dignity grounded on radical freedom is the antidote. For if human dignity means anything, it is that because persons are free agents, in all moral reasoning they must be regarded as co-deliberators, not objects to be deliberated about—even, or especially, for what the experts determine to be 'their own good'.

Dworkin's Focus on Welfare

For much of the twentieth century, it was widely supposed in Anglophone philosophy that some form of utilitarianism has to be the final truth about both ethics (how to live) and morality (how to treat others). This complacent supposition was rightly challenged late in the century, beginning with John Rawls' *A Theory of Justice* (1970) and Onora O'Neill's *Acting on Principle* (1975) but also with the work of other important moral philosophers, including Dworkin. It is nevertheless striking that even these philosophers often seem strangely susceptible to parts of utilitarianism that one might have hoped they had outgrown. I think this claim can be documented regarding even Rawls himself, but the present context makes it important to see how it is true of Dworkin.

When Dworkin begins to apply his conception of human dignity in conjunction with Kant's Principle, his first approach is to deal with the topics of 'aid' (271–84) and 'harm' (285–99). This starting point strikes me as distressingly ill-motivated. One would have thought that welfare for Dworkin is to be interpreted as one important aspect (but not the only one) of the *adjectival* value of a life—whether it has been a *good life*. People condemned to want and poverty often have bad lives as a result. But some lives can be bad even though abundantly supplied with welfare-goods—or even precisely because they are *too* abundantly supplied with them—while other lives can be good even though the supply of such goods in them, though adequate, has been quite modest. The difference, as Dworkin should be the first to point out, often lies in the *adverbial* value of a life—whether the life has been well lived—the very value on which Dworkin's conception of dignity lays primary stress. This should lead to a set of thoughts that lead us away from the centrality of issues about 'aid' and 'harm' and to a very different orientation.

A Better Way to Look at Dignity, Living Well, and Happiness: A Collective or Inter-subjective Way

A person who lives well can have a good life even if they are supplied with quite limited resources and enjoy only modest satisfactions, while some people who live badly have bad lives because they have wasted the opportunities afforded to them by abundant supplies of resources and have instead spent their time enjoying shallow, worthless or meaningless pastimes and satisfactions. The goodness of someone's life often depends most of all on how they relate to those around them. What truly makes a life best is that the one who lives it has successfully devoted him or herself to making the lives of *others* better, while also benefitting from the caring, sharing and benevolence of others. This is the chief way in which living well, and especially being part of a community of people who live well, is also the only way that all can have good lives. Dworkin is at times aware of this, or at least of the badness of its opposite: 'In America and many other places [the rich] use their wealth politically, to persuade the public to elect or accept leaders who…like the rich, think they live better when they are richer… [But] there are no winners in this macabre dance of greed and delusion' (422).

I think Dworkin should have made this point far more central to his conception of the good life than he has. One might have hoped that Dworkin, given his conception of dignity as the combination of self-respect and authenticity would pay chief attention to how we might contribute to giving others the opportunity—especially the freedom—to live well, and to take responsibility for their own lives. No doubt it is also morally significant, as regards our contribution to help others live well and take responsibility, how we aid or do not *aid* others, and whether we *harm* them. So it is not surprising that Dworkin would sooner or later deal with these topics. But why did he have to take them up *first*, and give them a kind of foundational status in respect of other moral topics—especially the topic of the freedom to lead one's own life not subject to the domination of others? This privileging of aid and harm is a symptom of the lingering utilitarianism in Dworkin's view. Moreover, several specific things Dworkin says in these discussions of aid and harm strike me as highly questionable. I will restrict myself to two instances.

Trolley Problems

Many who now do ethics discuss so-called 'trolley problems'; Dworkin eventually gets around to discussing them too, and he appears to agree with the majority view that it would be permissible to turn a runaway trolley toward one hapless person, killing him, in order to save five others (2011: 293). In our world—the real world, rather than the abstract, theoretical world of trolley-problem ethics—there would be strict rules for those employees of the trolley service as to how they could permissibly manipulate the switches in emergencies. It would not be up to them to choose between one life and five. Further, no mere bystander could legally touch the switching points of a trolley, and anyone who caused a death in this way would have committed a crime.[24] Of course in considering trolley problems, we are supposed to be abstracting from these inconvenient facts. For we are supposed to accept this because we are supposed to thinking that there could be significant moral issues that are about nothing except the distribution of benefits and harms and how these distributions are brought about. But that very thought is abhorrently false. There ought to be something offensive to us already in the very idea that somebody should be placed in a position to decide between one life and five lives, or that those who might happen to have the power might, merely by observing certain fussy distinctions drawn by trolley-problem philosophers, choose without qualm to kill innocent people in the name of the greater good. For this whole way of thinking once again treats human beings as mere objects (whether victims or beneficiaries) of moral deliberation carried on entirely by others.

Promising, Harming, and Wronging

A second instance is Dworkin's curious treatment of the obligation created by a promise. He bases this obligation on a general responsibility 'not to harm other people by first encouraging them to expect that we will act in a certain way and then not acting in that way' (2011: 304). This curious linking of the obligation of promise to harm (to a loss of welfare) seems to me to get the matter exactly backwards. When we promise someone to do something, and then fail to keep the promise, we thereby *wrong* the person. Wronging is more basic than harming, especially in cases like that of a lying promise. A bit later, Dworkin seems to see the basic point when he defines lying as 'an attempt to corrupt the basis of the information through which people exercise their responsibility for their own lives' (305).[25] The wrong consists in the way we deprive them of the freedom to live up to the value Dworkin calls 'authenticity', for which each of us bears objective responsibility. This, however, is quite independent of any *harm* we may cause the person to whom we lie, or whom we *wrong* by breaking our promise.

It might happen that by breaking my promise to you, I cause you no harm at all—if, for instance, by lucky accident the welfare value to you of my keeping my promise is supplied by some other source entirely independent of me. This good luck does not, however, alter the fact that by breaking my promise I have *wronged* you. Even if I have done you no harm, I have wrongfully interfered with your choices about how to lead your life, which is central to your human dignity in a way that neither harming nor aiding is central to it. Wronging is independent of harming precisely because wronging most directly and essentially affects not your welfare but your *freedom*. And it is your freedom to direct your life that is the basis of your dignity. Aiding or harming may contingently or indirectly promote or obstruct your self-respect and your authenticity, but your dignity is *directly* affected negatively if you are *wronged*.

Human Dignity and the Structure of Obligation

By setting up morality in the way he does, Dworkin poses a set of interpretive problems with a certain structure. He proposes to base the most general moral concepts, values, and requirements—morally good and bad action, moral right and wrong, and moral obligation—on the interpretation of human dignity. Dworkin begins with your own dignity—the importance you must attach to your own living well and your responsibility for your life. Then, by way of Kant's Principle, he proposes to extend this to the dignity of others and the moral demands it makes on you.

In setting up his project this way, Dworkin has posed a certain set of problems and set forth a way of solving them. I find it unclear how Dworkin proposes to do two things he must do in order to solve these problems in this way. On the one hand, he must draw inferences from premises about the way I value my own human dignity to conclusions about what I must do in order to value the human dignity of others. On the other, he must account for the structure of moral obligations in relation to the value of human dignity, and must consider the meaning of human dignity in light of that structure. Dworkin's interpretive project must succeed in relating the concepts of dignity, self-respect, and authenticity to the kinds of relationships between people, and the kinds of duties, that make actions right or wrong, and also make it the case that some actions wrong assignable others, whose dignity gives them a ground for claiming specific rights in relation to specific other people.

I remain unsure whether he has given himself sufficient interpretive resources to accomplish these two tasks. I will end my discussion by raising questions about these matters.

First, it is not clear how we are to move from valuing our own human dignity to valuing the dignity of others. Can this be done merely by drawing valid inferences from what is to be done in respecting oneself and taking authentic responsibility for one's own life to conclusions about what is required in the case of others? One supposes not, given Dworkin's insistence that ethics is an *interpretive* enterprise. But does the interpretive *ethical* concept of *one's own* human dignity offer sufficient resources for the interpretation of what is required of us *morally* by the dignity of others? Or does this also require the introduction of what Stephen Darwall has called a 'second-person standpoint'?[26] In addition to looking at human dignity in terms of my own attitude toward *my* self-respect and authenticity, do I not also need to consider the attitudes of others toward *their* dignity, and also the demands they may rightfully make on *me* from their standpoint, which is distinct from my own? If Darwall is right, our own human dignity does not give us enough to enable us to provide a correct interpretation of our moral obligations to others based on *their* human dignity.[27]

Second, there are conceptual distinctions between the kinds of value judgments that will be needed for a morality grounded on the claims of human dignity—especially the claims that one specific person may address specifically to another person. If I begin solely from *my own standpoint on my own dignity*, it is not clear how I can interpret *my* dignity in a way that justifies these claims.

Consider the following set of distinctions (Table 8.1) between value judgments and deontic judgments that has been proposed by Ariel Zylberman:[28]

Table 8.1   Table of Value and Deontic Judgments

Value judgments	Non-relational deontic judgments	Relational deontic judgments
It is good that *X* happen.	It is right/permissible for *A* to do *Y*.	*A* has a right against *B* that *A/B* (not) do *Y*.
It is bad that *X* happen.	It is wrong/forbidden for *A* to do *Y*.	*B* has a duty to *A* to (not) do *Y*.
It is indifferent that *X* happen.	It is a duty/obligatory for *A* to do *Y*.	*B* wrongs *A* in (not) doing *Y*.

Source: Ariel Zylberman, 'Why Human Rights? Because of *You*'.

As Zylberman points out, each of these three types of judgment forms a distinct inferential network. Some judgments falling in each column imply or conflict with others. But there is no direct or non-controversial way to get from one network to either of the others. This is especially true if we are trying to get from one network to one that in this presentation is arranged *to its right*. Instrumentalist or utilitarian accounts try to get from value judgments to deontic judgments (to move from the left-most column to the center column), but such attempts are always questionable, for the simple reason that right and wrong is not about *welfare* but about *freedom*, and freedom goes deeper than welfare because it is more intimately connected to human *dignity*.

Dworkin, of course, does not begin from 'value judgments' of the kind listed above—judgments attaching to happenings or *states of affairs*—but he does begin with value judgments attaching to *human persons*—namely, their human dignity. Specifically, he begins with the dignity that each of us must value in him—or herself. This gives him an advantage over welfare-based accounts. But Dworkin's attempt to get from this special kind of value judgment to moral judgments—to non-relational deontic judgments is troubled (as we have already seen) by the way he begins with issues of welfare (aid and harm) rather than with issues of right and wrong. That is because of the way he reverted to a pattern of thinking more characteristic of welfare-consequentialism than of the wiser ethical path on which he set out.

Dworkin faces a further problem, however, which could not be avoided merely by declining to make welfare—aid and harm—basic. This is that it is at least as questionable to try to get from the central column to the right-most column—from non-relational to relational deontic judgments—as to get from the leftmost column to the central column—from value judgments to non-relational deontic judgments. If human dignity is to ground some conception of human rights and the duties to which they give rise, and the judgments involving these rights and duties are relational deontic judgments, then it seems to Zylberman that the basic or original structure of the concept of human dignity must itself be *originally relational*. The value represented by human dignity must from the ground up correspond to a certain kind of second-person respect for that value on the part of others, and the relation between human dignity and that specific concept of respect must be reciprocal. Our basic conception of human dignity itself will not be complete without the specification of what kinds of relational deontic judgments (rights and duties) this dignity demands, and the concept of these deontic judgments will not be well grounded without reference to that specific conception of human dignity. Viewing the matter in Dworkin's terms, this will be a task of interpretation. I don't mean to suggest otherwise. But it is a quite specific task, and one that Dworkin does not address in *Justice for Hedgehogs* or in any other writings of which I am aware. And it is not clear how he can address it in the terms set forth in that book, for the reasons just presented.

Thus, Dworkin faces more than one serious problem in moving from value judgments about *one's own* dignity to the *relational deontic judgments* involved in the human rights that are based on human dignity. There are legitimate worries about the transition from value judgments to deontic judgments, and from non-relational to relational deontic judgments. The basic problem for utilitarians is that an act is *bad* does not entail that it is *wrong*. But for Dworkin this is even more problematic because if act *does wrong*—for instance, polluting the environment—does not entail that it *wrongs any assignable person or persons*. Here again, Dworkin's beginning with value—the value of a life, the dignity of a person as the object of that person's attitudes toward self—leaves out some important things: the person's freedom, and the person's free interactions with others. These are every bit as fundamental to human dignity as the adverbial, adjectival, or product valuations we place on our lives.

It is worth pointing out that Zylberman's worries about these matters are not based on anything like the idea that these transitions must be deductive, or must employ methods appropriate to what Dworkin calls criterial or natural kind concepts. Zylberman appears to agree with Dworkin that to move from even a relational conception of human dignity (involving both a conception of dignity and a corresponding conception of respect) to specific relational deontic judgments about human rights and duties is to engage in an interpretation (or what Zylberman prefers to call a 'specification') of the concept of human dignity in terms of a relational conception of it. It would fit well into Dworkin's conception of ethics as a collective, interpretive enterprise to bring out the inter-subjective dimension of dignity, as founded on the free interactions of free persons. The problem is that Dworkin has begun with a conception of human dignity as a *value* conception (and a conception of *one's own value* rather than of a second-personal conception applicable to the dignity of others). By ignoring the radical freedom on which human dignity is based, and leaving out the inter-subjective dimension essential to the concept of human dignity, Dworkin may not have put himself in a position successfully to complete his own interpretive project in ethics and morality. Certainly the manner in which he pursues this project in *Justice for Hedgehogs* (Chapters 11–14 and beyond) seems problematic for reasons I have tried to indicate in the last few pages.

***

Dworkin's great accomplishment in *Justice for Hedgehogs* is to have established a fundamentally interpretive conception value, and of ethical and moral concepts, and to have made a convincing case that the concept of human dignity should play a pivotal role in the interpretive enterprise of ethics—both in philosophy and in ordinary ethical and moral reasoning. Dworkin has long been known as one of the leading political philosophers and philosophers of law of the late twentieth and early twenty-first centuries. The strength of his position in those fields is the way he has related legal and political concerns to ethics and morality. In *Justice for Hedgehogs*, he provides the systematic reflections on ethics that underlie his entire legal and political philosophy. The ways in which I have suggested at various points that he might have developed his project differently are attempts to advocate variations on what he has accomplished that would make it richer and more defensible. In that way, I hope this essay has helped to make at least a qualified case for the soundness of Dworkin's project.

Notes and References

1. πόλλ' οἶδ' ἀλώπηξ, ἀλλ' ἐχῖνος ἓν μέγα (The fox knows many things but the hedgehog knows one big thing; Archilochus) is the basis for the title of Isaiah Berlin. 1953. *The Hedgehog and the Fox: An Essay on Tolstoy's View of History*. London: Weidenfeld and Nicolson. But this page reference, and unless otherwise noted, all page references below will be to Ronald Dworkin. 2011. *Justice for Hedgehogs*. Cambridge: Belknap Press of Harvard University Press.

2. David Hume belongs to that long list of great historical philosophers who are famous for asserting things they in fact denied. What could Hume himself have meant by his famous remarks about 'is' and 'ought' in the final paragraph of *Treatise* Book III, Part I, Section I? It can't possibly be what Dworkin and many others have taken him to mean. In the paragraph just prior to that one, Hume asserts, 'When you pronounce any action or character to be vicious, you mean nothing, but that from the constitution of your nature you have a feeling or sentiment of blame from the contemplation of it.' See David Hume. 1888. *Treatise of Human Nature*, ed. Selby-Bigge. Oxford: Clarendon. p. 469. That is a blunt statement of the thesis that what counts as vicious (clearly an 'ought' statement) *can* be inferred from *facts* (what *is* true) about the constitution of our human nature. In the sentences following the one just quoted (including the famous 'is/ought' sentence) Hume's actual point was that we become acquainted with these moral truths not by reason only but also through engagement of our feelings and sentiments. But the rationalist in me cannot resist interjecting here that this is not anything an intelligent rationalist would want to deny. For thoughts and feelings are intertwined: we get at each through the other. What rationalism holds is that *thoughts*—such as Hume's own perceptive thoughts about

the sentiments pertaining to human nature—do a better job than our *feelings* of enabling us to *understand why* things are good or bad, virtuous or vicious. Rational thoughts, therefore—which (as Hume rightly observes) are thoughts at least partly *about* our feelings—are what enable us to see *how we can* infer 'ought' from 'is'—as Hume himself validly does in this very passage. Hume's statement could of course also be interpreted as saying that when you pronounce an action to be vicious, you merely *express* the feeling or sentiment in question. But that's not a defensible reading of Hume. For if only that much were what you were doing, then your act of expression alone (your mere growl of disapproval) would not contain the thought that the sentiment you are expressing arises from the constitution of your nature (rather than merely from your momentary peevishness). Without this additional 'is' thought, what Hume says could not represent a plausible account about *what we mean* when we pronounce an action vicious. For such an account must refer somehow to a *good reason* for your attitude of blame. To pronounce an action vicious is *never* merely to evince an attitude (a grumble of disapproval), but must also somehow involve the thought that the action has *some property that justifies* that attitude. Hume's reference to the fact that your sentiment of blame arises from the constitution of your nature is the only thing that could do this. So to leave this out of Hume's account, and to treat him as a mere 'expressivist' about blame, is to misread him, and to substitute an indefensible account of blame in place of the one Hume is actually offering.

3. As was supposedly recommended (Боже мой!) by the great mathematician Nicolai Ivanovich Lobachevsky in a wonderful Tom Lehrer song available: https://www.youtube.com/watch?v=gXlfXirQF3A.

4. David Hume. 1987. *Essays, Moral, Political, and Literary*, ed. Eugene F. Miller, Revised Edition. Indianapolis: Liberty Press. p. 568.

5. Benedict de Spinoza. 1991. *Ethics: Treatise on the Emendation of the Intellect and Selected Letters*, Samuel Shirley tr. Indianapolis: Hackett. pp. 144, 179–80, 182, 184.

6. Friedrich Nietzsche. 1954. *The Portable Nietzsche*, ed. and tr. Walter Kaufmann. New York: Viking.

7. See Simon Blackburn. 2011. 'Morality Tale', *The Financial Times*. August 6. Availablehttp://www.ft.com/cms/s/2/2bf7cf30-b9e1-11e0-8171-00144feabdc0. html#axzz1WKy5LqRt.

8. Immanuel Kant. 2000. *Critique of the Power of Judgment*, tr. Paul Guyer and Eric Matthews. Cambridge University Press. pp. 66–7.

9. John Rawls. 1970. *A Theory of Justice*. Cambridge: Harvard University Press. p. 5.

10. In the real world, relativism looks most appealing to those who are trying to protect the right of cultures, subcultures, and individuals to determine their own judgments and ways of life when these rights are threatened by the aggressive incursion of other dominant cultures, subcultures, or individuals. The dominant rationalize their imperialistic invasion of the lives of others on the pretext that they represent not naked power but rather 'justice and truth'—in other words, the universal and omnilateral authority of communicative reason. The danger

that the powerful will rationalize their unjust coercion using this fraudulent pretext is often very real. It is usually supported by ignorance or self-deception on the part of the powerful oppressor, which is then inflicted on the oppressed in the form of a dominant ideology, which the oppressed can often be induced, coerced, or manipulated to accept. Relativism, however, is a self-defeating way to combat such oppression. Relativism tries to erect a sort of Maginot-line of unilateral cultural authority by which the weaker party can supposedly protect itself. Fearing to challenge the powerful imperialist head-on, the relativist strategy allows the conqueror to keep his own convictions, conceding that they are 'true for him'—based on his own unilateral authority. In return for this concession, it claims for the colonized weaker party a like unilateral authority to protect its own convictions and preserve its own way of life. But the supposed authority possessed by the weaker party, by the relativist's own account, cannot be rationally justified to either side. The fraudulent bargain offered to the powerful imperialist is obviously disadvantageous to him—there is no reason why he should accept it. It also rests on a deception just as flagrant as his own—the fiction that each side possesses unilateral authority to define truth or validity for itself without any need to submit its claims to common standards of reason that could be shared by all. The relativist's line of defense will always be easily overrun simply on the unilateral authority relativism grants to the more powerful invader. The relativist's only hope is that the relativist's lie will be more persuasive to the powerful than their own lies rationalizing their unjust hegemony. This is doomed to be a forlorn hope. For it is bankrupt of rational merits and utterly powerless to alter the unequal relations of power through which the oppressor can always enforce his own unjust dominance with impunity.

11. When relativism is not a sad, ineffectual attempt to defend the weak against domination by the strong, it may be an honest, if confused response to a very real intellectual problem followed rapidly by an equally confused but dishonest response to the very same problem. When we see that others appear to disagree with us and that they have their own systematic understanding of the world—even their own way of life, which we can't share or agree with—then we are rightly confused and uncertain. We do not understand what is going on. How is it possible that they reject what seems to us so self-evident? Do we really disagree with them? Are we even using the same concepts? Or are we using the same concepts and just not fully understanding their reasons for their position? At this point do we even understand any longer our own way of life and our own reasons for it? This state of confusion is an honest reaction to the situation. Those who stubbornly reject this part of 'relativism' are 'absolutists' in a bad sense: they are dogmatic, complacent, intolerant, and closed-minded. If relativism went only that far, I would myself subscribe to it, since when dealing with cultural difference and apparent disagreement, I share the confusion and don't pretend to get entirely beyond it, even though I have no choice but to go on resolutely leading my own way of life while trying (probably forever failing) to understand that of others. What I can't subscribe to is the next step: the dishonest but confident

claim that they have resolved the problem by saying 'their views are right for them' and 'ours are right for us'. This claims incoherently that the different sides disagree and yet that all are right. That claim is dishonest because it makes no sense but it pretends to make sense. At that point relativism has become its own confused, incoherent form of dogmatism.

12. Jeremy Waldron. 2012. *Dignity, Rank and Rights*, ed. Meir-Dan Cohen. Oxford: Oxford University Press. pp. 57–9.

13. See Mette Lebech. 2002. 'Towards a Definition of Human Dignity', *La cultura della vita: Fondamenti e dimensioni, Supplemento al volume degli Atti della VII Assemblea Generale 1–4 marzo 2001*, eds Vial Correa and Sgreccia. Città de Vaticano: Libreria Editrice Vaticana. pp. 87–101. Cf. Thomas Aquinas, *Summa Theologiae* IaIIae 29, 3.

14. Thomas Hobbes. 1994. *Leviathan*, ed. Edwin Curley. Indianapolis: Hackett. Chapter X, p. 52.

15. Immanuel Kant. 1902. *Metaphysics of Morals*. Academy edition. Berlin: Walter de Gruyter. Vol. 6: p.328.

16. A treatise attributed to St. Ambrose, but probably authored much later by Alcuin, was entitled *De conditione dignitatis humanae*. *Patrologia Latina* 17, 1106/ 40, 1213 – 4/ 100, pp. 565–8. See also, *Clavis Patristica Pseudegraphicum Medii Aevii IIB, Corpus Christianorum*, Series Latina, (Turnholt: Brepols, 1990–4), p. 683, no. 3008 and John Marenbon. 1981. *From the Circle of Alcuin to the School of Auxerre*. Cambridge: Cambridge University Press. pp. 30–43 and pp. 144–63.

17. Pico della Mirandola, *De Hominis Dignitate* (1486). The point is often made that this title was not Pico's, nor does the phrase 'human dignity' even occur anywhere in his famous oration. But the crucial thought—that human beings occupy a special place in creation owing to their freedom—is clearly expressed in it. There is a latter-day, post-Kantian echo of the same thought found in Fichte's brief, inspirational lecture *On Human Dignity* (1794), which locates that dignity in the freedom of the I, its absolute independence of everything outside it. Johann Gottlieb Fichte. 1988. *Fichte: Early Philosophical Writings*, ed. and tr. Daniel Breazeale. Ithaca: Cornell University Press. pp. 83–6.

18. Marcus Tullius Cicero. *De officis* (1898) I.xxx. pp. 106–7.

19. For the version of this thought that seems to have inspired Waldron, see Gregory Vlastos. 1984. 'Justice and Equality', *Theories of Rights*, ed. Jeremy Waldron. Oxford: Oxford University Press. pp. 41–76, and Waldron, 'Dignity and Rank', p. 17. Available https://www.brown.edu/Research/ppw/files/dignity%20 and%20rank5%20WALDRON%20Brown.pdf.

20. Georg Wilhelm Friedrich Hegel. 1991. *Elements of the Philosophy of Right*, ed. A.W. Wood, tr. H.B. Nisbet. Cambridge: Cambridge University Press. 35A; Cf. 1977. *Phenomenology of Spirit*, tr. A.V. Miller. Oxford: Clarendon Press. pp. 477–80.

21. The literature about Kant on this topic is complex, and full of controversy. For my own discussion of it, see Allen W. Wood. 2008. *Kantian Ethics*. New York: Cambridge University Press. pp. 6–15, 228–39, 275–6.

22. Jason Stanley. 2015. *How Propaganda Works*. Princeton: Princeton University Press.
23. Immanuel Kant. 2001. *Critique of the Power of Judgment*, tr. Paul Guyer and Eric Matthews. New York: Cambridge University Press. p. 174.
24. Frances Kamm thinks these objections miss the point. She thinks they can be answered simply by changing the examples so that the specific moral factors to which I appeal become irrelevant. See Frances Kamm. 2015. *Trolley Problem Mysteries*, ed. Eric Rakowski. Oxford: Oxford University Press. Chapter 1, Note 4. That's because she thinks they *always are already* irrelevant. But she thereby misses *my* point. Of course if you change the examples then you change what a sensible person would say. But other moral factors besides goods and harms and our causality in relation to them—factors concerning people's rights and what we are entitled to do in the newly devised bizarre circumstances—will then *always* also be present in some different form, and these factors will *always* expose the superficiality of theories based solely on the considerations with which trolley problems are concerned. My point is that *there are no significant moral problems that concern only the distribution of goods and harms and our causal relation to it.* Human dignity, in one form or another, is always the nasty little gremlin that mucks things up. Beings with dignity must always be among those whose choices determine the distribution; they may never be mere recipients of what others decide for them. See my comments, Allen W. Wood. 2011. 'Humanity as End in Itself', in Derek Parfit ed, *On What Matters*, Vol 2. Oxford: Oxford University Press. pp. 66–82. For a broader challenge to Dworkin's acceptance of the principle of double-effect, see my book Allen W. Wood. 2014. *The Free Development of Each*. Oxford: Oxford University Press. Chapter 10, especially pp. 243–6.
25. Not all falsehoods would do this. Those told under conditions where there is no expectation of an obligation to be truthful would not. But those falsehoods would also not involve any wrong. It is not usually appreciated that this is the view of lies and wrongs taken by Kant: *Metaphysics of Morals*, Academy edition, 6:238. That misunderstanding is why Kant's views about veracity are commonly thought to be so unreasonable. See also my book Allen W. Wood. 2008. *Kantian Ethics*. New York: Cambridge University Press. Chapter 14.
26. Stephen Darwall. 2006. *The Second Person Standpoint*. Cambridge: Harvard University Press; Darwall has since developed themes from this book in two others: *Essays in Second-Personal Ethics*, Volume 1: *Morality, Authority and Law* and Volume 2: *Honor, History and Relationship* (Oxford: Oxford University Press, 2013).
27. Darwall's intended claim, however, is far more radical: He thinks the basic concept of dignity is second-personal. Dworkin might be right to reject that, finding a basic value in our capacities for self-respect and authenticity, and our being subject to the normative requirements they impose, that can be appreciated from either a first-person or a third-person standpoint. My worry here is only that Dworkin's interpretive treatment of dignity has not developed the second-person implications of the concept to the degree required for its moral use.

28. Ariel Zylberman. 2015. 'Why human rights? Because of *You*', *Journal of Political Philosophy*, 5 November. pp. 1–23. Two related writings by Zylberman are: 2016. 'Human Dignity', *Philosophy Compass*. pp. 1–10 and 2015. 'Review of Stephen Darwall, *Essays in Second-Personal Ethics*', *Ethics: An International Journal of Social, Political, and Legal Philosophy*. 125(3). April, 2015) pp. 862–7. See also Michael Thompson. 2004. 'What Is It to Wrong Someone? A Puzzle about Justice', in R. Jay Wallace, P. Pettit, S. Scheffler, and M. Smith (eds), *Reason and Value: Themes from the Moral Philosophy of Joseph Raz*. Oxford: Clarendon Press.

8

Dworkin's Dignity under the Lens of the Magician of Königsberg

Veronica Rodriguez-Blanco

Ronald Dworkin discusses his view on dignity in the context of providing an interpretive construction that integrates our moral and ethical responsibilities.[1] In our ordinary lives, moral and ethical conceptions seem to pull us in opposite directions. We engage in personal projects, and have values and commitments that contradict and clash with our moral judgments or with what we ought to do categorically. Personal projects, values, and commitments are subject to conditions, for example, talents, wealth, intelligence, socio-economic status, and so on. By contrast, the demands of morality are unconditional. We cannot avoid acting according to a moral demand by excusing ourselves in terms of our circumstances. We can realize certain projects and participate in values if we are motivated to do them and if we have the talents, resources, or intelligence to be able to do them. They are contingent on our psychological make-up, that is, on our inclinations, desires, judgments of value, and circumstances. They do not apply universally and we cannot demand categorically their realization. By contrast, moral values do not depend on our desires or inclinations, socio-economic status, talents, or intelligence. Consequently, every human being can realize and participate in a moral life. Our personal tragedy as human beings arises from the awareness that a successful life, which entails the realization of our personal projects, values, and commitments, does not *necessarily* mean that we have led a moral life. We cannot show that morality is essential to having a good life. In other words, that having a good life is being moral, or perhaps vice versa, that a moral life will ensure a good life. Disintegration of the relationship between morality and ethics seems inevitable. In an attempt to swim against this current, Dworkin aims to show that integration between morality and ethics, that is, having a good life, is possible. According to him integration is possible if we seek moral responsibilities that will be construed in terms of, and therefore, determined by, our ethical responsibilities. As part of this endeavour Dworkin attacks what might be called 'the independent view'. The independent view cannot integrate morality and ethics because our moral responsibilities are presented as being fixed. According to this view, morality can only be determined by morality itself and therefore ethics is necessarily excluded. By contrast, Dworkin advances what we might call the 'construc-tivist view'. According to the latter, morality is an interpretive concept and the correct interpretation of what it requires involves interpreting our ethical responsibilities, that is, personal projects, values, and commitments, within certain limiting conditions. However, these limiting conditions cannot be formulated in terms of our duties to others. The key concept that establishes the bridge between our moral and ethical responsibilities is living well. Living well 'means striving to create a good life, but only subject to certain constraints essential to human dignity'. We search for personal projects, commitments, and values that will give us a good life; there are limiting conditions, however, for instance, authenticity and self-respect. Dworkin advances the view that the two principles of authenticity and self-respect give content to the *idea of dignity*. Authenticity entails that you lead a life that suits your situation and values and that you live your life according to them. Self-respect requires that you take yourself seriously; it requires engagement with the idea of 'living well' and that you recognize its importance.

At first glance one could assert that there is a Kantian theme in Dworkin's construction of the idea of dignity. According to Kant free will in accordance to rational nature, which is the unconditional and ultimate objective value, is the source of the dignity of humanity and personality.[2] According to Dworkin, living well is manifested in activities and performances. Our activities and performances have value because we are the source of them and our activities are manifested through our authenticity and self-respect. Thus, we strive and we take ourselves seriously. Our dignity is reflected in our activi-ties, whose ultimate source is us. The problem lies in how to understand the 'us' of the previous sentence. Unlike Kant, Dworkin does not mention that our rational nature is the source of our dignity. On the contrary, he wishes to establish a distance between his view and the Kantian one. For example, he makes it clear that autonomy and authenticity differ. Let me quote him in full:

> So authenticity is not autonomy, at least as some philosophers understand the protean concept. They suppose that autonomy requires only that some range of choices be left open by the sum of circumstances, whether these be natural or political. A person's autonomy is not threatened, on this view, when government manipulates its community's culture so as to remove or make less eligible certain disapproved ways of living, if an adequate number of choices remain so that he can still exercise the power of choice. Authenticity, on the other hand, as this is defined by the second principle of dignity, is very much concerned with the character as well as the fact of obstacles to choice. (Dworkin 2011: 212n1)

I will argue that Dworkin's limiting condition of dignity, whose defining pillars are self-respect and authenticity, cannot establish the required boundaries to guarantee a place for morality in the ethical domain. As a result the 'constructive model' does not offer a genuine integration between morality and ethics. On the contrary, morality is pushed aside and the remaining space is for ethical responsibilities alone. In Dworkinean language what is left is 'living well', that is, striving to have a good life *without* limiting conditions. In this paper the core argument that I advance is that under Dworkin's constructive model, the 'source' of the performance and activities in our striving to live well is not *necessarily* our rational nature. This is why there is *no room* for morality in Dworkin's constructive model.

In the second section of this chapter, I discuss Dworkin's idea of dignity and his constructive model with the aim of overcoming the separation between morality and ethics. In the third section, I contrast Dworkin's notion of dignity with the Kantian notion of dignity and show that my reading of the Kantian conception of dignity provides opportunity for the integration of ethics and morality. I also discuss a possible objection to my proposal.

Dworkin's Dignity and the Constructive Model

The ideas of self-respect and authenticity give content to Dworkin's conception of dignity, which is the limiting condition in our striving to live well. Self-respect, according to Dworkin, is not a moral claim. It is not the idea that every human being has intrinsic value. It is rather a *normative* claim about attitudes towards ourselves. We should care about our living well, that our activities and performances have an importance. We recognize our status as beings that perform and act, and this is why we feel miserable when we think that we have not lived well. We have ideas about how to live and we *try* to live up to those ideas. The value is not in the result but in the performance itself. Thus, for example, the value of reading a book is not that the book has been read, but in the reading itself.[3] The value of love lies not in being loved, but in the act of loving. In other words, what counts is the journey rather than the result, that is, the process of doing something and the manifestation of our capacities and limitations in the doing of the thing. The enjoyment is not *merely* the state of mind of being satisfied by the performance.[4] If it were there would be no enjoyment in the doing of thing; we would feel enjoyment only when we succeeded or obtained a result. The enjoyment is also in the recognition that living our lives according to our ideas is important and significant because we value these ideas. The importance to me, for example, of living well is reflected in my self-conception as a person who values, and disregards, certain things and activities. I value and find it appropriate to eat certain foods; to entertain friends in specific ways; to educate my child with certain values; and to read and study specific subjects. I want to do things and activities in *this way* rather than *that* and these ways define my personal identity. Since the endorsement of these values is from the practical point of view,[5] questions about their objectivity or subjectivity, which belong to the theoretical domain, are irrelevant to their importance in our engagement with the world and values. Authenticity, according to Dworkin, refers to the endorsement of who we really are. It is the recognition of our unique individuality and the values and projects that are our own. It is unfolding your life according to what you recognize as your values and appropriate situation. In this way, there is no alienation since you recognize yourself in the results and product of your activities and performances. Your activities and performances are not determined by following conventions, by what ought to be done, or by mere tradition. On the contrary, they are determined by the endorsement of values and situations as appropriate.

Dworkin aspires to integrate morality and ethics by resorting to the idea of living well, in other words, to engaging with a performance *in* life that will be limited by dignity, that is, self-respect and authenticity. (To help clarify) Let us image these two different examples.

Gauguin Borrowing Money from a Friend (Gauguin)

Gauguin has been asked by his wife and children to leave the family home. The family feels that he does not share their values anymore. He has decided to become a full-time painter after failing to establish a career as salesman in Denmark and provide for his family. He needs money to buy canvasses, brushes, and paints, and decides to borrow some money from a friend. He knows that he cannot repay the money but despite this he promises his friend that he will pay the money back next month. He borrows the money and never pays it back.

Rousseau Abandoning his Family (Rousseau)

Rousseau is living a precarious life and fears that his five children will not have a good education. He decides to leave them for good at a Foundling Hospital where they will have a better future. This gives him the freedom to dedicate his life to philosophy and to write important philosophical works.

Can we say that Gauguin and Rousseau satisfy the constructive model advanced by Dworkin, where morality and ethics are meshed together by the notion of 'living well' within the limiting conditions of self-respect and authenticity? In the first example, Gauguin takes his life seriously, he gives importance to aesthetic values, and he explores new techniques and innovative ideas on what art truly is. Every day he engages in the activity of painting and he produces performance-value. He tries to succeed in bringing about a new way of representing humans, nature, and our understanding of it. He takes himself seriously as a painter and creator of new ways in art. He respects himself and his performance. Gauguin is also authentic since he recognizes and endorses as unique and true to himself the values and appropriate situations of his living as a painter. In the second example, Rousseau takes his life as a philosopher seriously. He engages in thinking and searching for truth and he gives significance and importance to his living well as philosopher. He engages in performance-value and tries to succeed in his philosophical work. He is also authentic because he lives according to values that he endorses and recognizes as unique and true to himself. We see that Rousseau and Gauguin satisfy Dworkin's constructive model, where Gauguin and Rousseau live well within the limiting conditions of dignity, whose content is determined by self-respect and authenticity. It is arguable, however, that neither Gauguin nor Rousseau act morally and in these two cases, therefore, morality and ethics fail to be successfully integrated. Thus, the constructive model, in these examples, does not succeed. I am not resorting here to the philosophical account of morality but to our common conception of morality. When Gauguin makes a false promise to a friend, we would say that he has breached the trust that his friend has put in him. We would say that Gauguin has used his friend for his own purposes without giving his friend the possibility of choosing how to act. Gauguin's act of lying takes away from his friend the freedom of choosing whether to lend the money or not. Rousseau's abandonment of his children is a renunciation of his moral obligations as a father. We would say that a father has an obligation to *try* as hard as possible to fulfil the basic needs of his children, for example, by providing education, food, protection, care and love, and that Rousseau has failed in his parental obligations. I am not arguing that always being truthful and taking our parental responsibilities seriously are the only right possible actions according to a specific moral philosophy. My argument is that our common sense morality will consider the actions of Gauguin and Rousseau immoral. We could say, therefore, that Dworkin's constructive model cannot explain the integration between ethics and our common sense morality. The puzzle of integration arises precisely at the level of common sense morality where we cannot reconcile our ethical personal projects, commitments, and values with our common sense morality. In Dworkin's constructive model, morality has been pushed aside.

Is there an alternative way of making the integration project feasible? In the next section I offer a reading of Kant's idea of dignity that can provide a platform for a possible integration between ethics and morality.

Acting According to Ends, Freedom, and Dignity in Kant: The Integration Project

The standard discussion of Kant's moral philosophy and his view on dignity aims to understand the relationship between his four key notions, that is, the formula of universal law, the formula of autonomy, the formula of humanity, and the formula of the kingdom of ends. In recent interpretations, privilege has been given to the formula of humanity and the formula of the kingdom of ends over the other formulas.[6] However, the discussion is centred on how best to understand the idea that good will is the unconditioned value that grounds moral action and freedom. Kant distinguishes between the categorical imperative and the hypothetical imperative.[7] In the former case we choose a maxim that we are willing to endorse universally and therefore, our empirical conception of ourselves and the world seems irrelevant for the requirement of universalization. The universalization is unconditional, that is, it does not depend on our personal projects, commitments, desires, or what we value. The categorical imperative is the mark of a moral action. By contrast, the hypothetical imperative is characterized by a condition, namely our personal projects, values, and desires. The idea is that if we aim to pursue an end and we understand that this end can only be achieved through certain means, then it is rational to choose these means to achieve the desirable end. This picture makes more acute the integration problem. A moral action is possible because of the unconditional good will that is capable of universalizing a maxim of action. If the good will is conditioned empirically, which involves an engagement with personal ends and projects, then the good will is unable to universalize subjective maxims of action and unable to act morally. The possibility of reconciling our moral and ethical responsibilities within this reading of the Kantian framework seems almost impossible. Paradoxically, Kant emphasized our humanity and the *dignity of our humanity*. For Kant, humanity is our capacity to establish our own ends and act according to them. Kant also underscores the *dignity of personality*.[8] Personality seems to be in continuity with our humanity and therefore, presupposes it. When we act according to our personality, we act according to morality. It is, therefore, not an action that is determined by our personal projects and values only. In *Groundwork*[9] Kant refers to both humanity and personality as interchangeable; however, in the *Critique of Practical Reason* he advances the view that personality is not only about our ends, but about moral action. The key issue is whether we can reconcile the realization of our ends and personal projects, our humanity, and our capacity to set our own ends, with the realization of actions that have a moral character, that is our personality. I will argue that the correct way of integrating morality and ethics is *via* an argument that shows that the categorical imperative and the universalization requirement *underpin* our intentional actions, which involve the pursuing of ends and the commitment to personal projects. Consequently, our dignity lies in our capacity to set our own ends, but to set these ends within the limiting conditions of our moral judgments according to the categorical imperative. In this way, the Kantian theoretical framework can reconcile our ethical and moral responsibilities. For a better understanding of this reading of Kant's moral philosophy we need to understand intentional action and the way the categorical imperative underlies the structure of both our intentional action and practical reason.

There has been a predominant conception of intentional action as a mental state that hinders our understanding of the way that *moral requirements can underlie intentional action construed as future-directed actions towards an end*. I now turn to explain the non-standard conception of intentional action which illuminates the relationship between the categorical imperative and actions that are performed to achieve an end.

Understanding the Structure of Intentional Action and Practical Reason

An intentional action is an action that is directed towards ends. Intention is not merely a mental state about the desired end. On the contrary, an intentional action has a future-directed structure that reveals the underlying practical reasoning of the agent. For example, Gauguin intends to paint some canvasses according to his own understanding of the importance of light, colours, and contemporary explorations of human figures and expressions. He intends to paint some canvasses in Tahiti, where the light is intense and where human expression is different. In order to get to Tahiti he needs to make arrangements to travel there by boat; and he needs to buy canvasses, brushes, and paints. He needs a suitable suitcase for all his painting equipment and so on. However, he does not have any money to do what he intends to do. He, therefore, decides to borrow money from a friend and goes to visit his friend. Let us imagine the following dialogue between a bystander and Gauguin:

Enquirer: Why are you knocking at your friend's door.

Gauguin: To enter into his house and talk to my friend.

Enquirer: Why do you want to talk to your friend?

Gauguin: To borrow some money.

Enquirer: Why do you want to borrow some money?

Gauguin: In order to buy a boat ticket to travel to Tahiti and to buy brushes, canvasses and paints to use there.

Enquirer: Why do you want to travel to Tahiti and paint over there?

Gauguin: Because the light is unique, and I can discover and paint new forms of human expression.

Enquirer: Why do you want to discover and paint new forms of expression?

Gauguin: Because I can transcend myself through art.

Enquirer: Why do you want to transcend yourself through art?

Gauguin: Because this gives meaning to my life and art, and aesthetic experience is the highest value of human beings.

The only way to identify the will and whether it is involved in the action is to understand the action in terms of the description provided by the agent himself. We elicit such a description when we ask 'why'[10] such and such an action is performed. This way of eliciting the description of the action is called the why–question methodology and is Anscombe's central device in *Intention* for elucidating the connections between the different parts of an action and (our) practical reasoning.[11] There are a number of considerations that need to be taken into account to fully grasp this methodology:

1. An intentional action is, paradigmatically, a successive series of actions directed towards the final end of the action.

2. We know that the explanation finishes because the last step is described in terms of good-making characteristics that make intelligible and illuminate as a coherent whole the successive steps of the action.
3. We do not have different actions but only one action unified by the final intention as a reason for action formulated in terms of good-making characteristics.
4. It is a reason that is given to *others* in a genuine way within a framework of justification, but it is also the reason that the agent gives to *herself/ himself*.

Taking these considerations into account, let me now explain the why-question methodology.

Anscombe begins *Intention* by stating that the subject of the book should be studied under three headings: expression of an intention, intentional action, and intention in acting[12] and that all these should be understood as interdependent. Thus, an expression of an intention cannot be understood as a prediction about my future acts nor as an introspective explanation of an intention such as desires, wants, etc. Anscombe tells us, however, that people formulate expressions of intentions that are about the future and that *they turn out to be correct*.[13] How is this possible? In order to answer this question she tries to understand how we can identify intentional actions and demarcate them from non-intentional actions. The logical step is to understand what it means when a person says, 'I have acted with an intention'. Anscombe identifies acting intentionally with acting for a reason or 'reasons for actions' and such acting involves the view that the question *why* applies.[14] In other words, when we act for reasons, we act intentionally and therefore, we are sensitive and responsive to a justificatory framework. If we perform an action 'Φ' and the answers to the *why* questions are either of the following: 'I did not know I was doing Φ'; or 'I was not aware I was doing Φ', then we neither have an intentional action, nor an action performed and guided by reasons. We might have a voluntary action but it is not an intentional one.[15] But if the response has, for example, either of the following forms: 'in order to Φ' or 'because Φ', then we might have a prima facie case for an intentional action or an action done for reasons. In other words, reasons, so to speak, show themselves in intentional action and indicate, by 'showing themselves', how they are able to operate and be part of the agent's practical reasoning.

Do we have any control over the truthfulness of the answer prompted by the question 'Why?' Anscombe points out that we have a set of contextual conditions that enable us to say whether or not the person has expressed his genuine intentions.[16] For example, if someone is poisoning a river with toxic substances and we ask him, 'Why are you doing this?', his response might be 'I am just doing my job', we can verify whether this is part of his routine job, but if it is not we have reason to think that his response is not genuine.

Intentional action or an action done for reasons involves a successive number of steps or actions and subsequently a successive number of reasons that explain each step, but when do we know that the explanation provided by the agent can stop? Anscombe tells us that the explanation and justification stop when the end of the action is described in terms of what is good or desirable. The final end of the action is something, that is, a state of affairs, events, facts, objects that *seem or appear* to be good or desirable to the agent. The state of affairs, event, fact or object is believed to be a good sort of thing by the agent. In some ways, this is the most common sense and *naive* explanation of our actions.

For example, when I collect you at the train station I do not say that I collect you because I am in the mental state of desiring to collect you at the train station and have the mental state of believing and remembering that this is that kind of action. On the contrary, *in order to pick you up at the train station* I start my car, drive down the road, park my car at the train station and get out of my car and enter the train station. The successive steps of action find unity and intelligibility in my *reason* as a good-making characteristics that, for example, you are my friend and it is good to welcome friends at the train station. Gauguin intends to borrow money *in order to* buy tickets to go to Tahiti and buy canvasses, brushes, and paints, and he does this *in order to* discover new ways of human expression, and he intends to discover new ways of human expression because he finds aesthetic experiences the most valuable kind of experiences. Aesthetic experience as a value is the good-making characteristic that makes intelligible his successive series of actions.

The core motivation behind the why-question methodology is to pay attention to the structure or articulation of an intentional action.[17] The action is *not given* and therefore, the issue is not to discover the propositional attitudes, that is, beliefs and desires, that will explain the action. The issue is to unveil the structure of the intentional action to understand whether there is an action or not.

In Anscombe, evaluation and motivation do not separate. I ask, from the deliberative viewpoint, '*What* should I truly do?' and '*Why* should I do this or that?' The answers to these questions involve both an apprehension and an evaluation of the state of affairs or facts of the world and this entails, so to speak, a theoretical engagement with the world. In some way we might say that the question is formulated from the deliberative point of view, but the answer should be given as if it were a theoretical question.

We also say that the agent knows the reasons for his actions without observation. This means that the reasons for actions are transparent to the agent. An expression of an intention, according to Anscombe, is not mainly from the third-person perspective.[18] The knowledge that we have about our body's position is not known *mainly* by observation; it might be *aided* by observation, but I do not need to take a theoretical or observational stance to know that my legs are crossed whilst I sit typing on my laptop. Anscombe thus, tells us that intentional action is a 'sub-class of non-observational knowledge'.[19]

Gareth Evans in *The Varieties of Reference* refers to the phenomenon of 'transparency' that characterizes beliefs:

> In making a self-description of belief, one's eyes are, so to speak, or occasionally literally, directed outward—upon the world. If someone asks me 'Do you think there is going to be a Third World War?', I must attend, in answering him, to precisely the same outward phenomena as I would attend to if I were answering the question 'Will there be a Third World War?' I get myself in a position to answer the question whether I believe that p by putting into operation whatever procedure I have for answering the question whether p. (Evans 1982: 225)[20]

Ludwig Wittgenstein asserts:

> 477 What does it mean to assert that 'I believe p' says roughly the same as 'p'? We react in roughly the same way when anyone says the first and when he says the second; if I said the first and someone didn't understand the words 'I believe', I should repeat the sentence in the second form, and so on.

> 478 Moore's paradox may be expressed like this: 'I believe p' says roughly the same as 'p'; but 'Suppose I believe that p...' does not say the same as 'Suppose p...'

> 490 The paradox is this: the *supposition* may be expressed as follows: 'Suppose this went inside me and *that* outside'; but the assertion that this is going on inside me asserts: this is going on outside me. As suppositions the two propositions about the inside and the outside are quite independent, but not as assertions. (1980)[21]

For both Evans' and Wittgenstein's answers about whether I 'believe p' are outward-looking. I cannot answer the question whether I believe that it is raining, for example, without looking through the window, or reading the weather forecast. To answer such a question in terms of my introspective states seems absurd. We do not need to look inward at our states of mind to know whether or not it is raining.

Following in the steps of Evans and Wittgenstein, Richard Moran explains transparency as follows:

> With respect to belief, the claim of transparency is that from within the first-person perspective, I treat the question of my belief about P as equivalent to the question of the truth of P. What I think we can see now is that the basis for this equivalence hinges on the role of deliberative considerations about one's attitudes. For what the 'logical' claim of transparency requires is the deferral of the theoretical question 'What do I believe?' to the deliberative question 'What am I to believe?' And in the case of the attitude of belief, answering a deliberative question is a matter of determining what is true. When we unpack the idea in this way, we see that the vehicle of transparency in each case lies in the requirement that I address myself to the question of my state of mind in a *deliberative* spirit, deciding and declaring myself on the matter, and not confront the question as a purely psychological one about the beliefs of someone who happens also to be me. (2001: 62–3)[22]

We can take the idea of transparency and see how it applies to reasons for actions. If I act intentionally I act according to reasons for actions, therefore I *believe*[23] that I am acting intentionally for reasons as good-making characteristics, but if the transparency condition is sound, I do not need to look at my mental state to know whether I have the belief in my intentional action for reasons that for *me* are good-making characteristics, I just look outward to the facts, objects, and state of affairs of the world. In this way, my belief that I am acting intentionally and that I have reasons for acting as good-making characteristics is transparent. The idea of transparency in terms of reasons for actions can be formulated as follows, 'I can report on my own reasons for actions, not by considering my own mental states or theoretical evidence about them, but by considering the reasons themselves which I am immediately aware of.'

When I say that I intend to get up at six o'clock tomorrow morning to drive you to the train station because you are my friend and one should always help friends even in little ways, I know that I intend to act for such reasons. I do not need to look at my mental state to know that I have such reasons, I look outward to the world, my car, your presence in my house and the fact that it takes ten minutes to drive to the train station from my house. I have *groundless* knowledge of my reasons for action. It is not incorrigible.[24] Let us suppose that I discover that you are not truly my friend and that, therefore, my reason of driving you to the station because you are my friend is a mistaken one. However, the way I attain knowledge of my reasons for action does not depend on an inference from my observations or other data about myself. This entails that we have certain capacities, not only conceptual, but also practical.

I am also able to exercise control over my actions because I can direct myself towards the end of my action as described by the reasons for actions as good-making characteristics and I can change the movements of my body if I discover, aided by observation, that I am not doing what I intended to do (Theophrastus Principle). Thus, let us suppose that I am making an espresso and mistakenly find myself about to pour milk into the cup, then I do not say 'I am not making an espresso after all, I am actually making a latte, that's all right.' On the contrary, I change my movements and stop my action of pouring the milk into the cup. The world fits my intentions, I transform the state of affairs through my actions to fit what I intend and am committed to perform, whereas in theoretical knowledge my beliefs fit the world. In this way, I do not need observational knowledge to know that I intend to make an espresso, but I can be aided by observation to know the results of my intention.

Groundless knowledge of our reasons entails not only the capacity to act for reasons, but also includes *knowing how* to act intentionally according to reasons for actions in the specific context. Following legal rules entails *know how* about how to follow the legal rules because of their grounding reasons. But this does not mean that this groundless knowledge is not factual. On the contrary, it is knowledge about the world. Anscombe puts this as follows:

> Say I go over to the window and open it. Someone who hears me moving calls out: 'What are you doing making that noise?', I reply, 'Opening the window.' I have called such a statement knowledge all along; and precisely because in such a case what I say is true, I do open the window; and that means that the window is getting opened by the movements of the body out of whose mouth those words come. But I don't say the words like this, 'Let me see, what is this body bringing about? Ah yes! The opening of the window.'[25]

Our practical knowledge is also factual. When I intend to open the window and make the necessary movements with my hands, I know that I am opening the window and that I am actually opening the window.

Can we understand what we are doing *because* we *observe* what we are doing? If we take a theoretical stance towards our own actions then we might argue that there is a kind of alienation concerning the identity of ourselves and our actions;[26] in one sense the action is lost because we do not look at the goal or object towards which our actions are directed, but we look at ourselves doing the action. We do not look outwards, but inwards and we lose the object or goal that we aim to bring about. Imagine that I am making an espresso and begin to reflect on the movements of my hands; I see myself putting the coffee beans into the espresso machine, look at the coffee flowing into the cup, and smile at the thought of a fresh coffee. At some point it seems that I will lose the action of 'making an espresso'. It is impossible to be Narcissus. O'Shaughnessy asks whether this impossibility is really about the impossibility of doing two things at the same time, rather than a matter of the character of practical knowledge because if this is the case, then it is a quantitative matter and trivial. O'Shaughnessy argues that it is a matter of logic, 'Just as I cannot be going north and south at the same time, so I cannot be reading a book and playing tennis at the same time.'[27] Thus, pathological cases are explained as the separation of the acting and the observing self.[28]

Aristotle in *De Anima*[29] points out 'it is always the object of desire which produces movement, [and] this is either good or the apparent good' (433 a27–9), and in the *Eudemian Ethics* he establishes:

> The end is by nature always a good and one about which people deliberate in particular, as a doctor may deliberate whether he is to give a drug, or the general where he is to pitch his camp; in these there is a good, an end, which is the best without qualification; but contrary to nature, and by perversion, not the good but only an apparent good may be the end. (1227a19–22)[30]

How can values actualized in particulars provide reasons for actions? When we begin to deliberate about what to do, we begin by judging whether something, that is, an object, state of affairs or event, is good or not. We engage in the process of valuing things and we start to desire that this particular thing obtains. Values are instantiated by the good-making characteristics of objects and states of affairs and they become reasons for actions. Pure desires, by contrast, are passive and are not tied to our valuing processes. Pure desires are a pure state of the mind without object. For example, the pure desire for pleasure does not aim at a specific object, but at its own satisfaction or fulfilment and also at *eliminating* itself. When making valuations we have in our minds the object and the satisfaction of attaining the object. Therefore, as Watson has said, *desires are mute on the question of what is good.*[31] Values and pure desires are, hence, two independent sources of motivation.[32]

The Integration Problem under the Kantian View: Re-enacting Dignity

Our ethical responsibilities are shaped by what we value and our intentional actions are connected to our chosen values that provide the good-making characteristics of our actions. However, our moral responsibilities cannot be determined by our values. What we value is contingent upon who we are and what we care about. It is dependent on whether we endorse the valued thing wholeheartedly and on our constitution and character. By contrast, morality has an unconditional character. So, how we can make room for the high demands of the categorical imperative and the universalization requirement within the domains of the contingent self that values and pursues personal projects? The core idea that I aim to advance is that the notion of intentional action as construed in the previous section enables us to accommodate the integration of ethics with morality. We intend ends as good-making characteristics and these ends are the reasons that ground our actions. They are transparent to us and we engage in their realization in the world. However, *morality and ethics can be integrated* if the realization of these ends presupposes that we engage with maxims that we are willing to endorse in a universal way. We do not intend the maxims since we can only intend ends. Thus, the maxims operate as the *grounding* of the relevant practical judgment and are present and *manifested* in the execution of the intentional action. Let me illustrate this point using the examples of Gauguin and Rousseau. Gauguin intends to become a painter by profession, to buy a boat ticket to travel to Tahiti, and to buy canvasses, brushes, and paints. The limiting condition of the categorical imperative underlies his intentional action. He cannot lie to his friend about being able to repay the loan because 'lying to a friend' is not a maxim that he would be willing to endorse universally. If he lies to his friend he takes away his friend's freedom to choose. Thus, he *does not intend* the universal moral law but when he acts according to his intentional action and brings about the intended state of affairs, for example, a career as a painter and travelling to Tahiti, he performs his actions *in respect of* the moral law. Similarly, Rousseau intends to become a philosopher, he intends to write important books and in order to do this he needs to dedicate most of his time to thinking and writing. He cannot intend this by acting against a maxim that he is not willing to endorse universally. By abandoning his children he will breach his parental obligations and inflict emotional harm on his children. He should *try* to pursue his end of becoming a philosopher but, at the same time, act according to the underlying maxims that he is willing to endorse universally. Thus, for example, he should provide for his children's needs and, when he is not reading or writing, aim to spend time with his children.

The general idea is that we act intentionally, (that is, we have a future-directed intention that aims at an end which is transparent to us and is presented as having good-making characteristics) and underlying this structure of an intentional action are maxims of conduct that we should be willing to endorse universally. The latter provide the limiting conditions of the action.

So far I have argued in favour of a reading of Kant's moral philosophy that integrates our ethical and moral responsibilities. When we act intentionally we set our own ends and personal projects but their underlying maxims are under the scrutiny of a limiting condition, that is, a universalizing requirement. Dworkin might object that there is no genuine integration in this model that combines intentional action as future-directed actions towards good-making characteristics shaped by the categorical imperative. Thus, the concept of morality, Dworkin could object, remains fixed and therefore our ethical responsibilities, that is, our personal projects, values, and commitments, are determined by what is right. Therefore, the 'right' action trumps the 'good' action. In other words, what we want, that is, personal projects, personal commitments, values, is determined by what is morally correct. But this objection misunderstands the connection between underlying maxims of the structure of intentional action, the nature of intentional actions and its connections to our personal projects, values, and commitments. First, the limiting condition is a *formal* limiting condition and therefore it is not a substantively fixed moral judgment. The categorical imperative is not telling us what to do in any substantive form. On the contrary, it regulates our intentional actions and their ends, that is, personal projects, values and commitments. The categorical imperative *underlies and therefore regulates or grounds the maxims of conduct* of the structure of intentional action and practical reason. Second, it is misleading to present our moral requirements as clashing with our values, personal projects, and commitments. We intend the latter but we do not intend the categorical imperative. The categorical imperative as a limiting condition establishes the boundaries of what *is permissible* to intend. On my reading of Kant, the categorical imperative is a way of executing and realizing an intention and therefore, an end.[33] For example, imagine the moral dilemma of Gauguin. Gauguin is facing a dilemma between staying with his family and fulfilling his duty as a father, or travelling to Tahiti and becoming a painter. Fulfilling his duty as a father might involve renouncing his beliefs and convictions as a painter and would probably also involve trying to become a successful businessman in order to provide for his family. In the dilemma his personal project of becoming a painter clashes with his moral duty of providing for his children. For some critics of Kantianism, Gauguin needs to choose between either his ethical or moral duties. By contrast, on the reading of Kant that I have advanced, Gauguin can fully develop his personal project as a painter, but in his intentional actions he is limited by the categorical imperative. He needs to keep trying to experiment with painting (that is, through exploring new concepts of human expressions), but within the limitation of fulfilling his parental duties. Perhaps he could travel alone to Tahiti for few months while ensuring that the basic needs of his children are satisfied. His parental duties would involve communication, caring, and loving. He might need to convey to his family the importance of his new identity in art and his transformation as an artist. As Williams has clearly argued,[34] we cannot imagine a *human and rich* life without personal projects. It does not make sense to say that your intention is to be moral and that in all your actions you *intend to* follow the categorical imperative. This way of presenting the categorical imperative makes human agency poor and formalistic. The categorical imperative is a *form* and in the case of Gauguin, it would have no subject matter. It would be the conduct of a moral fetishist: an intention of the form *because of* the form itself. This cannot be what Kant was trying to convey. In my interpretation our intentions are multiple and varied. Our personal projects and therefore intentions might be to teach, to learn, to love, to paint, to think. In general, to have a good life which can only be defined by our chosen ends. For rational and free creatures such as human beings are, all these ends need to presuppose a limiting condition which is best formulated as the categorical imperative. The integration project is fully achieved under this reading of Kant because we can lead good lives that are limited by formal moral requirements. The formality of the moral requirements instead of being empty achieves a new force and appeal. The moral permissibility is constructed around our conception of good life. Human dignity is achieved because we set our own ends and in their realization we impose on ourselves limiting conditions. Individual dignity lies in the fact that individuals have the capacity to pursue personal projects respecting the moral law, and respect for the dignity of others is achieved through the recognition that others set their own personal projects that respect the categorical imperative. You also recognize the dignity of others who also have the capacity to set their own personal projects in ways that would respect the categorical imperative, that is, no degrading themselves to immoral acts. The dignity of humanity and personality is the corollary of recognizing our capacity to have a good life according to limiting moral conditions.

***

In chapter 9 of *Justice for Hedgehogs*, Dworkin sets himself the difficult task of showing that the integration of our ethical responsibilities, that is, values, personal projects, commitments, with our moral responsibilities is possible. The idea that we can live well within the limits of a conception of dignity that focuses on self-respect and authenticity is the key argument advanced by Dworkin to demonstrate the integration between ethics and morality. I have argued that Dworkin's conception of dignity is not sufficiently robust to guarantee the desired integration. Self-respect and authenticity cannot ensure that our rational nature will set the limits of our ethical actions in living well. Therefore, in Dworkin's 'constructive model', morality collapses into ethics. I have shown that there is a plausible Kantian reading of the relationship between action that pursues ends and the categorical imperative that can guarantee the integration of morality and ethics. However, the success of this reading of Kant requires a better understanding of the non-standard conception of intentional action. Intentional action is construed as a future-directed process that unfolds within time and manifests the structure of practical reason. It has been argued that when we integrate our ethical and moral lives, the categorical imperative underlies the process of intentional action and also manifests itself in the structure of practical reason. In this way, we recognize the dignity of our humanity and personality in our living well within moral conditions.

Notes and References

1. Ronald Dworkin. 2011. *Justice for Hedgehogs*. Cambridge, Mass.: Harvard: Harvard University Press. pp. 191–218.
2. Immanuel Kant. 2012. *The Metaphysics of Morals*, tr. Mary Gregor, Cambridge: Cambridge University Press. 6:387, 6:392, 6:420, 6:462); 2002. *Groundwork for the Metaphysics of Morals*. tr. Arnulf Zweig. Oxford: Oxford University Press, 4:435, 4:436; 1997. *The Critique of Practical Reason*. tr. Mary Gregor, Cambridge: Cambridge University Press, 5:71, 5:87, 5:88. According to Allen W. Wood. 2008. *Kantian Ethics*. Cambridge: Cambridge University Press, the dignity of humanity is the first step towards the most complete idea of dignity which is the 'dignity of personality'.
3. For an explanation of the distinction between process and result in action, see chapters 3 and 4, of my 2014 book. *Law and Authority Under the Guise of the Good*. Oxford: Hart-Bloomsbury Publishing.
4. See Gary Watson. 1975. 'Free Agency', *Journal of Philosophy*. 72(8): 205, for a rejection of the satisfaction model of desire in favour of the value-model of actions.
5. This crucial argument is overlooked by Dworkin but I think it is needed to make sense of his view on performance value and his attacks on all theoretical attempts to undermine objectivity in practical reason (see his discussion on Archimedeanism in 'Objectivity and Truth: You'd Better Believe It' (1996) *Philosophy and Public Affairs*. 87 and *Law's Empire*. 1986. Cambridge, MA: Harvard University Press. See also Dworkin (2011: 209). For a full discussion of this point see my book *Law and Authority Under the Guise of the Book*, above (n4).
6. Christine Korsgaard. 1996. *Creating the Kingdom of Ends*. Cambridge: Cambridge University Press, and 1996. *Sources of Normativity*. Cambridge: Cambridge University Press.

7. Kant, *Groundwork for the Metaphysics of Morals*, above (n2): 4:414 and 4:415.

8. Kant, *The Metaphysics of Morals,* above (n2), 6:462.

9. Kant, *Groundwork for the Metaphysics of Morals*, above (n2).

10. Moran and Stone explain the why-question methodology as follows: 'Hence all psychic forms are performance modifiers: insofar as they are employable in action-explaining answers to the question "why?", they express forms of being on-the-way-to-but not-yet having Φ-ed, of already stretching oneself toward this end'. See R. Moran and M. Stone. 2009. 'Anscombe on Expression of Intention', in Constantine Sandis (ed.), *New Essays in the Explanation of Action*. Basingstoke: Palgrave. p. 148.

11. Anscombe's exposition follows very closely Aquinas's explanation of intentional action. Anthony John Patrick Kenny. 1979. *Aristotle's Theory of the Will*. New Haven: Yale University Press, points out that Aquinas' model should be understood more as a *Gestalt* psychology. Recent work on Anscombe emphasizes the point that acting intentionally should be interpreted as a series of successive steps towards an action. See Moran and Stone. 2008. 'Anscombe on Expression of Intention' (n10 above) and Thompson. 2008. *Life and Action*. Cambridge, Mass.: Harvard University Press. pp. 85–119.

12. Moran and Stone in 'Anscombe on Expression of Intention' (n10 above) explain the transformation of these three headings in the post-*Intention* literature. Most of the authors ignore the heading 'expression of an intention' and conflate the other two subheadings: intentional action and the intention with which the action was committed. Consequently, intention becomes a mental state. 'Given the possibility of "pure" intending, it becomes hard to see how this category could fail to designate a mental state, attitude or disposition of some kind. So the division of 'intentions' now takes shape around the philosophical polestar of the division between mind and world: two notions of intentions find purchase only where there is behaviour causing things to happen; a third refers to a mental state, attitude or disposition which, though in some way is present in such behaviour, is also abstractable from it and capable of existing on its own' (p. 137).

13. Elizabeth Anscombe. 1957. *Intention*. Oxford: Blackwell (2nd Edition, 1963). pp. 3–4.

14. Anscombe, *Intention*. pp. 4–6.

15. Anscombe, *Intention*. p. 17.

16. Anscombe, *Intention*. p. 25.

17. Candace Vogler. 2001. 'Anscombe on Practical Inference', in Elijah Millgram (ed.) *Varieties of Practical Reasoning*. Cambridge, Mass.: MIT University Press.

18. Anscombe, *Intention*. pp. 2–3.

19. Anscombe, *Intention*. p. 8.

20. Gareth Evans. 1982. *The Varieties of Reference*. Oxford: Oxford University Press. See also Roy Edgeley. 1969. *Reason in Theory and Practice*. London: Hutchinson and Co.

21. Ludwig Wittgenstein. 1980. *Remarks on the Philosophy of Psychology*. Oxford: Blackwell.

22. Richard Moran. 2001. *Authority and Estrangement*. Princeton: Princeton University Press.

23. Setiya defines the connection between belief and acting intentionally as follows, 'When someone is acting intentionally, there must be something he is doing intentionally, not merely trying to do, in the belief that he is doing it'. K. Setiya. 2010. *Reasons without Rationalism*. Princeton: Princeton University Press. p. 41.

24. Keith S. Donnelan. 1963. 'Knowing What I Am Doing', *Journal of Philosophy*. 60. pp. 401, 403 argues that there is a difference between our knowledge of having a headache, being in anger, in pain and practical knowledge that is non-observational. In the latter case, the knowledge is corrigible whereas the former not. We revise the statements of our intentions and we can make mistakes about them. However, observation is not the basis of our knowledge, we cannot *infer* from our observations our intentions. What we correct is the *result* or purpose of our intentions.

25. Anscombe, *Intention*. pp. 28–9.

26. Moran, *Authority and Estrangement*, explores the nature of this theoretical stance towards our deliberative understanding of our actions. He makes an important connection between the Sartrean notion of 'bad faith'and the theoretical stance that we might take towards our actions (pp. 77–83).

27. Brian O'Shaughnessy. 1963. 'Observation and the Will', *The Journal of Philosophy*. p. 380.

28. See L. Bortolotti and M.R. Broome. 2008. 'Delusional Beliefs and Reason-Giving', *Philosophical Psychology*. p. 821.

29. Aristotle. 1968. *De Anima*. tr. D.W. Hamlyn. Oxford: Clarendon Press.

30. Aristotle. 1952. *Eudemian Ethics*. tr. H. Rackham, Loeb Classical Library. Cambridge, Mass.: Harvard University Press. See also Aquinas. 2006. *Summa Theologicae*. Cambridge: Cambridge University Press, paperback edition, Latin and English texts, edited by Gilby, 1a2ae,8,1.

31. Watson, 'Free Agency' (n5).

32. See Watson, 'Free Agency' (n5) for a contemporary defense of this platonic distinction between two sources of motivation. See also Plato *Phaedrus*, 237e–8e In: *Plato Complete Works,* John M. Cooper (ed.), A. Nehamas and P. Woodruff (tr.), Indianapolis: Hackett (1997).

33. My reading of Kant does have similarities with Barbara Herman's reading in *The Moral of Judgment*. Cambridge, Mass.: Harvard University Press (1993). However, my reading differs from hers on the fact that my focus in on action and the display of the activity. On my reading the categorical imperative is practical all the way through and is manifested in the action.

34. Bernard Williams. 1973. *Morality: An Introduction to Ethics*. Harmondsworth: Penguin.

9

Does Dignity Help in Thinking about Paternalism?

Barbara Baum Levenbook

It is fairly well known by now that Dworkin, in *Justice for Hedgehogs*, offers an analysis of an alleged virtue he calls 'dignity'. He elaborates two principles of dignity—self-respect and authenticity. Authenticity, in turn, is described in terms of ethical responsibility and ethical independence. Dworkin's master thesis in the book is that there is a unity, and thus, a coherence, of values. The values that he focuses on as examples of this unity come from two realms—what he labels as a personal 'ethics', which concerns living well (as opposed, he says, to living a good life), and what he labels as 'morality', which concerns our duties to others.

Dignity is a necessary, but not a sufficient, condition of living well, according to Dworkin. Dignity is also allegedly an important explanatory philosophical tool. Dworkin tells us that he is using 'the idea of dignity to help identify the content of morality' (2011: 204).[1] In doing so, Dworkin thinks he is illustrating a process, itself based on a theory of moral truth (264), that explains and justifies moral convictions on the basis of some alleged requirement or demand of self-respect or authenticity, itself arrived at by refining an initially 'inchoate' account of dignity in a sort of reflective equilibrium with convictions about the moral duty in question (368). What saves this process from vicious circularity is that the results about dignity and about morality, according to Dworkin, independently appear to be sound.[2]

Previous commentators have offered critiques along two broad lines. The first attacks the contention that some of Dworkin's moral convictions are independently sound. The second attacks his claims that particular moral convictions he advances can be explained and justified with the tools he produces, generally by attacking the dignity case Dworkin proffers for the moral convictions in question. I am going to add to this second line of attack. In this chapter, I will argue that Dworkin's dignity framework has little explanatory value for one moral topic for which Dworkin apparently thinks it is especially suited—paternalistic intervention by one adult with another. As the quotation about the identification of the content of morality suggests, Dworkin thinks the dignity framework has epistemic value for morality. I will argue that it has little epistemic value regarding paternalism. Dworkin's conception of dignity is too inchoate to help us to discover why and when individual paternalism is wrong, all things considered. It does somewhat better in illuminating why some types of individual paternalism are pro tanto wrong; but there are many other types of paternalism that are pro tanto wrong. Moreover, the conception of dignity cannot be refined the way Dworkin thinks it should be, by the process described above, and retain any epistemic value on this matter.

These results should be particularly troubling to Dworkin. There is a long tradition in Western philosophy of arguing against—and sometimes, restricted to certain circumstances, for—paternalism on the grounds of something called the 'autonomy' of the subject of paternalism. While Dworkin is at pains to point out that dignity, as he conceives it, is not autonomy (2011: 212), dignity is not a wholly unrelated notion. Moreover, Dworkin's idea of dignity seems to be a refined and elaborated version of what in *Sovereign Virtue* Dworkin calls 'ethical integrity'. There, he uses the alleged primacy of ethical integrity to undermine some alleged justifications for paternalism.[3] Hence, one would expect that a very natural—indeed, a central—use of the conception of dignity developed in *Justice for Hedgehogs* would be to explain and illuminate moral claims about paternalism. That Dworkin's conception of dignity largely fails to do so is, therefore, particularly important.

——— — ———

Dworkin is concerned to produce non-consequentialist accounts of moral convictions; hence, he does not treat dignity as a value to be maximized, or to be balanced against other values, or to be preserved in the future. Rather, 'dignity' is the name for a set of requirements (responsibilities), liberties, and, it turns out later, rights (288).[4]

Dworkin tells us, previewing his excursion into interpersonal morality, that his guiding assumption is that 'acts are wrong if they insult the dignity of others' (204). One might suppose paternalism turns out to be unjustified when it offends or is inconsistent with the requirements and rights of dignity of the person interfered with, and justified (or justifiable) when it is consistent with these normative elements.[5] Though earlier in his career, Dworkin did present an argument against paternalism;[6] he nowhere in *Justice for Hedgehogs* explicitly offers this or any other worked-out account regarding paternalism. However, he does make some remarks on the subject, and he makes claims that are applicable to paternalism in his accounts of other interpersonal moral duties and of rights people have against their political communities.

Dworkin defines 'paternalism' as 'imposing a decision on someone supposedly for his own good but contrary to his own sense of what that is' (2011: 361–2).[7] That puts Dworkin in a long tradition of defining 'paternalism' in terms of a motive or rationale. It is clear that Dworkin supposes governments to be capable of paternalism. There are several problems, some of them from metaphysics, some of them from Dworkin's own theory of the nature of law (in particular, his metaphysics for law), with the assumption that governments can practice paternalism when 'paternalism' is defined in terms of a motive or an intended justification. Instead of exploring these problems and their solution, I will concentrate on Dworkin's views on individual paternalism.

Recall that paternalism involves imposing a decision on someone contrary to the subject's sense of his or her own good. Having a sense of one's own good is essential for meeting the requirements of the ethical responsibility component of dignity. Dworkin gives various characterizations, not necessarily consistent, of this component—It is a responsibility to identify 'what counts as success in' one's life (2011: 204), to decide on 'a way to live that grips you as right for you and your circumstances' (209), to find 'values around which to live your life' (204) that you endorse, to commit to 'standards and ideals' (210), to choose 'values of character—loyalties, ambitions, desires, tastes, and ideals' (244), to fasten on a 'design' or 'style' for your life 'in response to a judgment of ethical value' (212). What is pertinent to paternalism is whether being free from 'imposed decisions' contrary to one's sense of good is also essential to dignity, according to Dworkin. Given what Dworkin previously wrote on the subject and what he says in this book, his answer seems to be—not always. He claims, 'In some very limited circumstances paternalism justifies others in seizing temporary control over my body—to stop me harming myself in a moment or hour of madness, for example' (289). Paternalistic policies and laws can be justified as well. Dworkin seems to think a mandatory seat belt law, which he regards as a paternalistic exercise by government, is permissible. His initial explanation is that it 'helps people achieve what they actually want in spite of moments of acknowledged weakness' (336). Compulsory education for children and teens, he suggests, is also a 'permissible [form] of paternalism' because it 'enhances rather than diminishes a person's capacity to take charge of his own life...' (336).

Recall that paternalism is wrong, on Dworkin's dignity framework, when it 'insults' dignity. If it doesn't always insult dignity, when does it? Let us set aside the attractive (and, I think, correct) idea, not raised by Dworkin, that intending to insult the subject of paternalism makes the paternalistic intervention at least pro tanto wrong. When does paternalism do this 'insulting' even in the absence of intentions to insult? Dworkin makes this early general claim—denying someone's 'freedom to choose values for himself' makes an act wrong (205). More specifically, this would be denying someone's freedom to choose what Dworkin would call *ethical* values for himself. Let us call this 'the Freedom Principle'. So when paternalism denies its subject's freedom to choose ethical values, it insults its subject's dignity and is, therefore, wrong.

Given Dworkin's remarks about paternalistic intervention in the hour of madness, such paternalism will not amount to denying the subject's freedom to choose values for himself. (Dworkin might be assuming that the subject values bodily integrity or continued life.) If so, this is a case where an agent adopts a means that does not, contrary to the agent's beliefs, serve an end the agent values. I will return to this particular example in the next section.

There is language in *Justice for Hedgehogs* (and also in *Sovereign Virtue*) to suggest that Dworkin thinks that if someone coercively intervenes with another individual to force that individual to act in ways that are intended to be inconsistent with an ethical value the second person endorses, the first person *is* denying the second's freedom to choose such values for his- or herself.[8] As I understand it, intervening to force another individual to act on an ethical value inconsistent with an ethical value the subject endorses allegedly for the subject's own good is what Dworkin calls 'ethical paternalism'. (Ethical paternalism involves 'ethical justification' by the paternalistic intervener.) Dworkin may assume that in such a case, the intervener has made a substitute judgment of ethical value for the subject, one antithetical to the value whose pursuit is being blocked. So Dworkin seems to be committed to the view that ethical paternalism is always wrong, whereas some other paternalism may not be wrong. This seems to be confirmed by other remarks that suggest his wholesale rejection of governmental ethical paternalism.[9] Note that he seems to be able to make this case—implicitly—on the basis of considerations about dignity.

How well does Dworkin do in this endeavor? The purpose of this and the next section is to argue that he does not succeed.

To begin, there is a problematically metaphoric quality to Dworkin's language in the Freedom Principle, 'den[ying the] … freedom to choose values for [oneself]' (2011: 205). What would be an example of choosing values for oneself? Would deciding that sadism, particularly practiced on the unwilling, is a very good thing be an example? Would an example be deciding that fleecing the part of the population one deems 'born suckers' adds value to one's life? Wouldn't choosing values like this include trying to act on them when one thinks one has the opportunity? It is reasonable to think that part of choosing values for one's life is forming a disposition to pursue them, which entails trying to act on them when one thinks one has the opportunity. If the answers to these questions are affirmative, there isn't any plausibility in thinking that merely denying people's freedom to choose ethical values is wrong, all things considered.

If the answers to the first two questions are affirmative but the answer to the last question is negative, it is difficult to view ethical paternalism as *denying* someone the freedom to choose ethical values for himself. He is free to choose all he wants. It is just that, on this or that occasion, we will coerce him into acting contrary to them (as in forcing someone to buckle a seatbelt), prevent him from acting on them (as when we dump the alcohol he has purchased and hidden down the drain), or otherwise frustrate his chosen end (as in stopping a suicide attempt).

The reader will note that choosing the values described above is making a choice that has direct implications about matters of interpersonal morality. So is it fair, one might wonder, in framing the Freedom Principle to think that these are the kind of ethical values Dworkin had in mind? My answer is that it is, because many other values for living well have such implications. Dworkin recognizes this point by offering two examples. He acknowledges that 'judg[ing] the life of a Samurai or Robin Hood ideal for me' has implications for 'physical violence and theft' (2011: 369), at least when I pursue that life. Moreover, choosing a religion is one of Dworkin's prime examples of choosing an ethical value; and it is clear that many religions—perhaps all of them—include strictures on how other persons—and sometimes other animals—are to be treated. If you value the religion, if you choose being a practitioner of that religion as one of your ethical values, you are committed to valuing living by its tenets (indeed, to living by them). If you choose to be a Hindu, you are committed to treating animals with compassion and to refraining from killing them under many circumstances. If you choose to be a Quaker, you are committed to refusing to go to war against other humans.

There are or were religions the choice of which required animal sacrifice, or human sacrifice, under various circumstances. Some sects of Christianity, or perhaps subgroups of such sects, in the United States interpret the Christian Bible to license marital rape by the husband (though they refuse to recognize it as such). Male practitioners are thus committed to permitting themselves the liberty of sexually forcing themselves upon their unwilling wives. Worse, still, from the point of view of rejecting ethical paternalism, some sects of Christianity teach their practitioners that they have a God-given duty to convert the heathen, which sometimes requires, in their view, paternalistic intervention to convert someone from a false religion to the true one.

So the Freedom Principle, as stated, seems false. There are two avenues that may rehabilitate it. Perhaps Dworkin means by the Freedom Principle that, if (and only if) the person's choice of ethical values is within the boundaries of what morality will permit that person to do, denying that person freedom to choose those ethical values is wrong. This makes good sense if one assumes that the freedom to choose such values entails the freedom to act on them, given the opportunity and the means. Since Dworkin uses 'fashioning one's life on the basis of one's ethical values' language in describing some of the 'responsibilities' of dignity, this second interpretation—if I may be pardoned for using "interpretation" in its original, non-Dworkinian sense—of the Freedom Principle looks initially promising.

But this interpretation is one he must reject, because it does precisely what he tells us he doesn't want—that is, if the Freedom Principle is alleged to fol- low from Dworkin's principles of dignity. The reason is this: in order to figure out the bounds of morality (in this case, the morality of ethical paternalism), this interpretation makes the bounds of dignity dependent upon the bounds of morality. Thus, it makes ruminations about dignity explanatorily useless for at least this portion of morality. It does this, that is, unless Dworkin is correct that he can derive the bounds of morality from considerations about dignity (and what he calls 'the Kantian Principle'—treat others 'consistently with accepting that their lives are of equal objective importance' to one's own [2011: 273] and consistently with accepting that they have equal ethical responsibilities [287]). I will return to his claim in the last section of this chapter.

At any rate, this first interpretation may not be plausible as a bi-condi- tional. Choosing an ethical value within the boundaries of what morality will permit a person to do may not be sufficient to make denying the freedom to do so wrong. Dworkin himself suggests—inadvertently, perhaps—possible constraints on the liberty to choose ethical values other than moral ones. He tells us (275) that the life projects you choose must not be too 'expensive' in terms of the resources you can 'expect to be at [your] disposal' if society is fair in its distribution of resources. This is a further specification of one of the responsibilities of authenticity Dworkin earlier outlined. Dworkin makes it clear that no one is under any duty to aid another in succeeding in 'expensive' projects or (in *Sovereign Virtue*) in indulging 'expensive' tastes. If, in addition, choices of such projects or of the pursuit of expensive tastes are not worthy of respect, even when morality would permit them, no one denying the freedom to make or do them is doing anything wrong.

There is a second way to rehabilitate the Freedom Principle—a pro tanto version. This version contends that paternalism is wrong, pro tanto, if it denies its subject the freedom to choose ethical values for him or herself. Of course, rarely does paternalism deny its subject the freedom to choose *all* ethical values for him or herself. For the principle to be relevant to an interesting class of paternalistic interventions, it ought to be recast as: Paternalism is wrong, pro tanto, if it denies its subject the freedom to choose *an* ethical value for him-or herself. To have any bite, this principle must be accompanied by the assumption that the freedom to choose entails the freedom to act on one's choice.

Even so, further refinement may be advisable. For instance, we might limit the principle to those who are competent to choose the ethical value. We will thus arrive at a principle that sounds good, but still has limited application. Governmental paternalism through the criminal law sometimes denies to its subjects the political freedom to choose to value what the law forbids—a life of getting high on cocaine, for instance. But often paternalistic law seems merely to deny its subjects the freedom to order ethical values in a certain way. As Wolfe, in an early commentary, pointed out, someone who does not want to go through a windshield when driving may also value the comfort and convenience of driving without buckling up.[10] The mandatory seat belt law denies its subjects the freedom to order comfort and convenience over personal safety while driving. Individual paternalism often does the same reordering. Think of preventing the medical missionary from risking her life to help victims of Ebola (where she does value her life, but not as much as being of service in trying to save the lives of others), or of the medical paternalism that forced Donald 'Dax' Cowart to undergo painful burn treatment for months in order to save his life. (It is arguable that Dax valued continued life, but not above avoiding a certain level and duration of pain.)

Note, too, that a biconditional pro tanto claim would not be acceptable. One might claim that those who choose 'expensive' life projects never had the ethical liberty to make those choices. The responsibility in authenticity may be to choose your ethical values and life projects within the bounds of the 'reasonably priced'. (Think of this analogy with employment: the architect's draftsmen are given the responsibility of designing the building so that its cost lies within the client's budget. In such a scenario, the draftsmen are not at liberty to design a building beyond that budget.) Perhaps not only are choices of 'too expensive' life projects not worthy of respect, no one who blocks acting on them is denying a freedom to choose them. But it doesn't follow that no paternalistic intervention counter to them is wrong.

Moreover, Dworkin thinks conditions limiting one's choices do not offend authenticity (212); and presumably, they do not deny one the freedom to make ethical value choices. But if this is so, then a proponent of paternalism can contend that some individual paternalistic interventions merely alter the conditions of its subject's action so as to block it (perhaps temporarily), as when one hides his cigarettes from a smoker who is not trying to quit, or the car keys from someone about to drive to a rendezvous of which one disapproves. Yet these paternalistic interventions, too, may be wrong.

To sum up, our reflections on the sufficient-condition pro tanto version of the Freedom Principle have revealed a modest role for some aspect of dignity in the moral issues surrounding paternalism. This freedom to choose ethical values is also an aspect of autonomy and of independent agency. So the suggested reason some paternalism is objectionable can be accommodated on other overlapping notions which are allegedly distinct from Dworkin's idea of dignity. Can Dworkin argue that considerations specific to dignity provide grounds for objecting to paternalism?

Recall that the principles of dignity impose a number of 'responsibilities' on an agent. Dworkin makes an inchoate appeal to usurping ethical decisions that he might use to object to paternalism. Dworkin declares, '… [A person] does not live authentically, no matter how great the range of options he is offered, if others forbid him some options otherwise available because they deem those options unworthy. The indignity lies in usurpation, not limitation…' (212).[11]

It is a short step to a condemnation of ethical paternalism if one claims that in ethical paternalism, the paternalist forbids the subject an option because the paternalist deems it unworthy and concludes that the paternalist usurps a decision.

Authenticity, the reader will recall, is only half of the conception of dignity Dworkin develops. He might make the same sort of objection on the basis of the other principle of dignity, self-respect. Dworkin claims, 'Self-respect…requires that you treat yourself as autonomous in one sense of that idea: you must yourself endorse the values that structure your life. That demand matches our second principle: you must judge the right way to live for yourself and resist any coercion designed to usurp that authority'

(265). It remains only to contend that ethical paternalism usurps the subject's authority in self-respect.

Dworkin has similar language about 'usurping a responsibility'. It is worth noting, however, that at one point he makes an odd claim about the *absence* of such usurpation: 'Prohibiting physical violence and theft makes it less likely that I will judge the life of a Samurai or Robin Hood ideal for me and much more difficult for me to pursue that life if I do. Taxation makes it less likely that I will judge collecting Renaissance masterpieces the ideal life. None of these laws denies my responsibility to define ethical value for myself, however, because none aims to usurp my responsibility to identify a successful life. Properly motivated laws of my community are part of the background against which I make my ethical choices. My own ethical responsibility for making those choices is not diminished by that background' (369–70).

This line of thought provides the proponent of paternalism with a wide opening. The paternalistic intervener no more imposes a decision on someone against her sense of the good than do laws coercing people to refrain from theft impose a decision on would-be Robin Hoods. So if the reason imposing a decision that removes an option for someone to act on her chosen ethical value does not usurp her responsibility to select ethical values is that she chooses against a 'background of properly motivated' laws, then it is open to someone to claim that the subject also chooses against a background of reasonable expectations about properly motivated interventions. It merely remains to contend that paternalistic interventions of various kinds are properly motivated interventions. The usurping or not usurping of responsibilities clearly will not settle the question of whether this contention is true.

It is, in any case, evident that usurpation is not a promising line to take against paternalism. 'Usurps' implies *illegitimacy*. One cannot explain why paternalism is wrong by saying it usurps something. Doing so is in part restating the claim that paternalism is wrong.

Let us, however, recast this line of argument. Consider the following: Paternalism is wrong when the intervener thereby undertakes a responsibility (or an authority) regarding a choice of ethical values belonging to its subject.[12] Let us call this 'the Responsibility Principle'. It only has bite if imposing a decision based on my own sense of what is good for someone is taking a responsibility. Let us assume it is. This principle is plausible only if the responsibility properly belongs to its subject *and no one else*. The scope of the Responsibility Principle thus depends on what those responsibilities (if any) are. Perhaps marriage and other intimate, committed unions create shared responsibilities for the shape of one's life, for one's life goals, and for many values one will endorse. Perhaps the responsibilities that properly belong to a subject are limited by other responsibilities—for example, a responsibility to develop one's talents and abilities (suggested by Kant), or a responsibility to choose a morally good life among a morally limited set of incommensurable ethical values.

Dworkin overstates the responsibilities in question. For example, he says, 'Authenticity is damaged when a person is made to accept someone else's judgment in place of his own about the [ethical] values or goals his life should display' (212).[13] But Dworkin can't mean this contention. Recall that he thinks that some paternalism is justified. In particular, he thinks that something he calls 'surface paternalism' is justified (336), where intervention can 'plausibly' be 'understood' as enhancing 'a person's capacity to take charge of his own life' or helping 'people achieve what they actually want in spite of moments of acknowledged weakness'. Recall, too, Dworkin's earlier claim that paternalistic intervention can be justified to prevent my harming myself in an hour of madness. I have assumed that Dworkin is thinking of cases where the subject irrationally (and temporarily) adopts behaviour that is inconsistent with a long-standing end the subject values. There are also cases where the subject chooses what he wrongly believes is a means to an end, but is in ignorance of how that choice will compromise reaching the end. In such cases, Dworkin seems to assume that the paternalist is not choosing values antithetical to the ones the subject has chosen. But that isn't always true. For instance, in an 'hour of madness', I may adopt a new value—suicide—and a paternalistic intervener will reject it. Further, as with the seat belt law, a paternalistic intervention can be making an ethical decision for a person who does value continuing life, because the imposition disvalues something the person values—comfort and convenience, or, for the suicide, the immediate cessation of pain. The same can be said about motorcycle helmet laws; some who want to live and to avoid massive brain damage have actually claimed that they value feeling the wind in their hair when riding a motorcycle. In all of these cases, the paternalist rejects an ethical value chosen by the subject or treats it as much less important. If Dworkin nonetheless insists on this broad contention about when authenticity is damaged, he must conclude that damaging authenticity is not always wrong, all things considered.

Returning to the Responsibility Principle, note that it does not follow that one does something wrong *all things considered* if one undertakes, temporarily, a responsibility belonging to another. Consider the store manager who, in disgust and under the pressure of time, takes over the responsibility of a subordinate that hasn't been met or has been met poorly. Let us suppose that subordinate cannot be found or persuaded to act. The responsibility belongs to the employee alone *in the first instance*, but because of the manager's responsibilities, and his/her liberties, and the other circumstances, this undertaking hardly seems wrong, all things considered.

So perhaps, one might think, it is the restriction to the responsibility *regarding choice of ethical values* that makes the Responsibility Principle plausible. However, ordering values seems to be a responsibility of authenticity that the intervener undertakes in the counter-examples of justified paternalism above. So the Responsibility Principle as formulated must be rejected.

Let us try, then, confining the Responsibility Principle to undertaking responsibilities to *introduce* (acting on a) value not endorsed by the subject. Still, this refinement will not produce a plausible sufficient condition for unjustified paternalism. Intervening with a subject who has never valued his own life, in order to get him professional help, may not be wrong, all things considered. Such a person, Dworkin might maintain, fails to fulfil his responsibility of self-respect, and thus, fails to meet a foundational responsibility of dignity. However, even in the case in which a person has fulfilled this and other responsibilities of dignity, paternalistic interventions of this sort are not necessarily wrong. Consider the person who has had so few options in his life, and so little exposure to the lifestyles and pursuits others enjoy, that he cannot conceive of them, and hence, doesn't value them—someone grown to adulthood in poverty in the inner city, for instance. Paternalistic intervention to get such a person who is not acquainted with, say, classical music, the seaside, or country air, an experience of it in the hopes that he will come to endorse the value of it is also not necessarily unjustified. (Much here might depend on whether he subsequently does endorse it, and by what causal mechanism.)

One way to handle the counter-examples of justified 'surface paternalism' discussed earlier is to modify the Responsibility Principle to say that paternalism is objectionable when the intervener assumes a responsibility to make a 'foundational' ethical choice for the subject. Dworkin describes foundational choices as 'about the basis and character of the objective importance of human life that the first principle of dignity [the one on self-respect] declares' (2011: 368). The counter-examples of ethical values adduced in the discussion of surface paternalism would not, presumably, be foundational.

A difficulty with this approach is that the distinction between foundational and subsidiary ethical choices can be manipulated to support contrary intuitions about particular instances of paternalism. Choice of religion would seem to fit the description of 'foundational ethical choice', particularly if the religion in question comes with a metaphysics that postulates a theologically-sourced soul that accounts for the value of persons and that views human life as objectively important only because it can serve the will of the Deity.[14] Consider forcing a blood transfusion onto an unwilling Jehovah's Witness. One can maintain that there is something foundational—in this case, the subject's choice of religion—that is being interfered with. So on the suggested view, this paternalistic intervention would be wrong. However, those who think this paternalistic intervention is justified can maintain that the intervener is merely serving a foundational ethical choice of the patient—to exist consistently with the value the Deity assigns the subject's life. The intervener merely needs to add that the value is too high to permit an easily avoidable death.

One would not want to maintain that assuming a responsibility to make a foundational ethical choice is *all* that makes paternalism objectionable. For such a view will justify too broad a range of paternalistic interventions. It will justify all sorts of paternalistic interventions and by whatever means for an adult son who has never adopted foundational values (but has other values). There are such people. Imagine a young man who drifts through life with little independent living skill, afraid to embrace life fully, going for the pleasure or whatever appears to be the easier way at the moment, failing to meet many of his responsibilities of dignity. (The young adult is exhibiting what is popularly known as a 'failure to launch.') The proposed view raises no objection to the domineering father paternalistically steering his son into a job, making the choice of living quarters for him, enforcing a particular diet, bullying his son into marriage with a woman the father has chosen, and so on.[15] Further, as Dworkin recognizes, much paternalism does not interfere with foundational values even though they are chosen by the subject. Not all of this sort of paternalism seems benign. Suppose someone who has been born with partial hearing loss—in the high registers—has adjusted quite nicely in his life. He has learned to speak, and so on. Now a doctor offers him the chance to increase his hearing range with a cochlear implant. The subject refuses. He does not know, the doctor says, cannot imagine, how a 'whole new world' will open to him after the change in hearing. In this, the doctor is correct. But the subject is adamant. He is not interested in running the risks of surgery and its possible complications, and in spending the time to learn to interpret the signals the implant produces, for what seems to him a gain of little importance. Since none of his ethical choices so far seem foundational, there is nothing left on the necessary condition view to make forcing the patient to undergo the surgery wrong.[16] But it may not be right—at least, not without subsequent consent caused in the right way.[17] Note, too, that the proposed account would justify paternalistic intervention whenever the subject believes that human life is only important when it is a good life, or aims at a good life, one that involves endorsing and pursuing what is objectively good and has sufficient 'weight,' and the intervener is correct on this matter.

Does the Responsibility Principle, foundational-value-version, provide a sufficient condition for unjustified paternalism? It's doubtful that it does. Dworkin has the seed of an argument from self-respect, an alleged component of dignity, that some foundational ethical choices are inconsistent with dignity. '[A]nyone who embraces projects that require him to ignore the suffering of others altogether', Dworkin claims, 'lacks self-respect...' (2011: 277). If dignity imposes a limitation on the choice of foundational ethical value, it is not evident that choices that violate that limitation ought to be respected. Why can't they be lightly devalued, even dismissed, by others?

As Dworkin might with justice claim that the person who chooses to value what blinds him to all other human suffering has a foundational value that violates morality, the same kind of question can be asked generally about foundational ethical choices that violate morality. It is arguable that a Satanist does not ignore the suffering of others, but in some cases actively seeks it for reasons he thinks is justified. If a Satanist thinks that the importance of human life lies in its serving and its capacity to serve pure evil, he has foundational ethical values that are immoral. One might choose to interfere, not for the good of others, as one would normally do, but for the Satanist's own good. The thinking may be that he will be happier in the long run, or a better candidate for Heaven, or more likely to form relationships with others that meet his most profound psychological needs. It does not appear to be objectionable *all things considered* to interfere, even paternalistically, with this kind of foundational ethical choice. No reason presents itself, save a prior sense that aspects of self-determination are especially weighty. But this is an opinion not everyone shares. It is not so firmly entrenched, so widespread or so appealing that it can be relied on without argument. Perhaps it's the idea of imposing, among a lot of other alternatives, a particular contrary choice that seems wrongful—for example, substituting pursuing (and thus valuing) philanthropy for the values of the Satanist. But if some choice must be imposed to prevent the subject acting on the choice that violates morality, it is not clear that doing so is wrong, all things considered.[18]

The same goes if someone shirks the responsibilities of dignity altogether or nearly altogether. The paternalist might with justice cry, 'Somebody has to do the job—at least, temporarily!' Indeed, the paternalistic intervention might be justified if the intervention has the consequence of stimulating the shirker to undertake his dignity responsibilities. Such might happen, for instance, if the father in the earlier example boots his son out of the house, refuses to let him live in it any longer, for his own good.

Suppose Dworkin concedes that it isn't necessarily morally objectionable to interfere (paternalistically) with a range of foundational choices that are inconsistent with dignity and maintains, further, that this class includes those inconsistent with morality. He thereby narrows his claim about interfering with foundational ethical choices. However, if Dworkin is correct that there is a unity of value, morality bounds ethics. Once again, in order to figure out the bounds of morality (in this case, the morality of ethical paternalism), Dworkin will have made the bounds of dignity dependent upon the bounds of morality. Moreover, recall that some foundational choices commit one to practice some ethical paternalism (for a holy cause, for example). Thus, to know what foundational ethical choices are consistent with dignity, we will first have to know when paternalism is justified. Dignity then plays no epistemic role.

Let us return to the Responsibility Principle applied to all ethical values chosen by the subject, and consider whether Dworkin would have better luck with a pro tanto version of this principle, to wit—Paternalism is wrong pro tanto when the paternalistic intervener thereby undertakes a responsibility (or an authority) regarding a choice of ethical values belonging to its subject.[19] Once more, this version might be best confined to subjects who are competent to meet that responsibility. One immediate difficulty is that this version of the principle appears to apply to few paternalistic interventions. It is stretching language too far to describe a single paternalistic intervention as involving *undertaking* a responsibility for choosing or ordering ethical values, as if the intervention sets for the subject some general standard for future occasions. It may merely be that on a particular occasion, the decision imposed on the subject displays or is in the service of a value, or an ordering of values, the subject doesn't endorse. The better view, and one that Dworkin may intend, is that the responsibility undertaken is to decide what ethical value will be served on a particular occasion in the subject's life.

The main problem with this version of the principle is that normally, undertaking a responsibility belonging to someone else is not pro tanto wrong. It can be a way of giving a gift to someone, as when in a traditional heterosexual household on Mother's Day the husband takes over the wife's duties to cook breakfast, or when a kindly neighbor wheels my emptied garbage bins back from the curb to their place beside the garage on collection day. Demanding a justification of such actions seems inappropriate in the absence of some other factor; for example, the wife takes anyone else cooking in her household as a slur on her cooking abilities, I resent technical trespasses on my property. Admittedly, in these cases, although the subject has the responsibility, he or she hasn't exercised it on the occasion of the paternalistic act. Since Dworkin defines 'paternalism' as requiring that the subject have a sense of his own good applicable to the occasion, it follows that the subject has exercised his responsibility to identify his own good on all paternalistic occasions. So the paternalistic intervener is not merely undertaking a responsibility the subject has; the intervener is duplicating (an exercise of) it, albeit in a contrary manner. If the responsibility is to decide what ethical value will be served on this occasion, however, that responsibility may not be being duplicated.

So it is the nature of this responsibility, and perhaps the added fact that the choice is contrary to the subject's sense of his good, that is alleged to make the moral difference in paternalism. That is, it is the fact that the responsibility undertaken is to decide *what ethical value* will be served on this occasion in some other person's life, or *what is good for* this person, (contrary to his sense of what is good for him), that is alleged to be pro tanto wrong.

I have already touched on a potential objection that can be raised at this point. Joseph Raz has maintained that autonomy contributes no value toward living well when the goals and projects chosen aren't objectively worthwhile.[20] The point may be illustrated with an example from Rawls, 'a life project of counting blades of grass'.[21] Dworkin provides his own example in *Justice for Hedgehogs*, 'a life project of collecting matchbook covers'. Raz's autonomy contention can be easily transposed to the dignity framework and the present discussion. The claim would be that it isn't always pro tanto wrong to undertake a responsibility to choose or to order ethical values belonging to someone else, because there is nothing wrong with doing so (within limits, perhaps) if that person has chosen 'values' from among the objectively worthless. This contention can be strengthened by adding the case of someone who has chosen to value a lifestyle that has immoral implications. Imposing a decision contrary to such a person's sense of the good for his own good need not be unjustified, it might be maintained, since his mere valuing, his deciding for himself, has no independent moral weight. On this view, one should note, the fact that the subject's values are worthless isn't treated as a justification for the intervention. Rather, at best this fact removes a presumption against the permissibility of the paternalism. So undertaking a responsibility (or an authority) regarding a choice of ethical values belonging to its subject isn't, on this view, pro tanto wrong. At best, it is prima facie a wrong-making characteristic.

Dworkin recognizes that the 'weight' of the values chosen contributes to the goodness of a life (420–1). Weight, however, is a consideration beyond dignity, as Dworkin acknowledges. Note that this objection applies not only to this pro tanto Responsibility Principle but to the pro tanto Freedom Principle.

Though I am sympathetic to the Razian view, I recognize that opinions differ on this point, and do not wish to press it. But it doesn't follow that we ought to acknowledge Dworkin's success with the pro tanto Responsibility Principle. Recall that the principle says that paternalism is pro tanto wrong when the intervener thereby undertakes a responsibility (or an authority) regarding a choice of ethical values belonging to its subject. Without the phrase, 'belonging to its subject', the principle as I have interpreted it becomes just a way of saying that paternalism by Dworkin's definition is pro tanto wrong because it is paternalism. (The principle would then be a bi-conditional.) It is evident that one cannot explain why paternalism is pro tanto wrong this way. Adding the phrase 'belonging to its subject' does tie the point to Dworkin's ideas about dignity and might be an explanation. However, for reasons cited above, adding this phrase alone does not add any credibility to this principle. One would need the independent claim that these responsibilities in particular (unlike many others) are such that it is pro tanto wrong for others to assume them, even temporarily. I have suggested that this contention isn't *obviously* 'independently sound'. It needs independent argument. More importantly, it will be reflections about the morality or immorality of paternalism (in particular, intuitions about whether it always needs a justification) that would be driving this claim. Dworkin thinks the circle here is not vicious; my point is that dignity is doing no epistemic work in that case.

Dworkin has an argument from rights that entails that the responsibilities assumed in paternalism are such that it is wrong for others to assume them, even temporarily. In discussing kinds of harm, he introduces the view that we have a 'right to ethical independence'. This right 'is compromised when others attempt to make ethical decisions for us...' (288). Later, in his discussion of political morality, he limits this right. He declares, 'People have a right to independence in ... decisions [on foundational ethical matters], provided that they do not threaten the like independence of other people. So government may not constrain foundational independence for any reason except when this is necessary to protect the life, security, or liberty of others' (369). Although he is writing about governmental restrictions, the point generalizes. Perhaps what is wrong with individual paternalism, when it is wrong, is that it violates this right to ethical independence.

For reasons rehearsed in this section, including Dworkin's view that some paternalism is justified, it should be clear to the reader that Dworkin cannot insist on the existence of such rights and also hold onto his view that rights are trumps. He cannot, that is, unless this right to independence has interestingly restricted boundaries. So all that the proposed line of thought provides is the idea that when individual paternalism is wrong, it is wrong because it illegitimately violates the right to independence. There is no guidance yet about when that occurs or what the boundaries of the right happen to be.

Can Dworkin at this point claim he has shown at least that dignity explains what is morally objectionable, pro tanto, with individual paternalism? Unfortunately, he cannot. For the 'rights' language appears suddenly; it is not in his initial characterization of the principles of dignity. Dworkin apparently draws an inference to the existence of such rights from his initial claims about responsibility in dignity. For example, he says that the 'assignment responsibility' involved in dignity 'must include a power of control—some power to select which acts are performed in the exercise of the purported assignment' (288). This quickly becomes a 'right of control', even though rights are not powers, and vice versa. The responsibility to 'strive for independence' from others, first introduced on page 211 of *Justice for Hedgehogs*, becomes a 'right to ethical independence' on page 288. There is no argument for the existence of such rights as claim rights, and one is needed. As F.M. Kamm has pointed out, claim rights do not follow from the existence of a responsibility.[22] She gives the following example: 'if one needs a car to fulfill a promise one has made, one may have no claim right to the car'.

Admittedly, one will not be able to discharge the various responsibilities of dignity *autonomously* without some independence from coercion and manipulation. Postulating a claim right to this independence seems a reasonable stipulation if 'ought' implies 'can'. But Dworkin's right to independence goes further, further even than a right to freedom from being compelled to act against one's will. It includes a right to be free from others making ethical decisions for one. This is a stipulation, pure and simple. Given my previous point that even a 'surface' paternalistic intervention can be contrary to an ethical value of its subject, stipulating this right as part of a conception of dignity amounts to begging the question about whether paternalistic intervention always stands in need of justification. There is no need to repeat points made earlier about the intuition that it does and what drives this intuition.

If dignity bestowed the alleged claim right, others would not have a liberty to make ethical decisions for us. If we want to maintain, as Dworkin does, that the father in the example used earlier does not have the liberty to take over the management of his son's life, it is better to say that the father lacks ethical standing. Presumably, the father did have this liberty when his son was too young to fulfil all the responsibilities of dignity. (I assume Dworkin would agree that it isn't plausible to hold that children, perhaps below a certain age, have the responsibilities that the two principles of dignity impose.) It is significant that a passing stranger did not have this liberty, even at that time—except, perhaps, in an emergency. A zealous neighbour who accosts stray children at random on a playground, to force, say, exposure to classical music or the playing of the violin (for their own good) in the hopes that they will grow up and love the musical life is an officious intermeddler at best. So standing seems to be an independent criterion, one that cannot be explained by proper respect for the principles of dignity.

———————

Switching attention from the act of paternalistic intervention and its motive to ancillary beliefs of the intervener yields two possibilities for redeeming the pro-tanto version of the Responsibility Principle and tying it to insulting dignity. One can insult dignity by failing to recognize that the subject of a paternalistic intervention has the responsibility to choose and act on ethical values in the first instance. Such a failure violates the Kantian principle and may amount to denying the subject's ethical responsibilities. As the example of the manager shows, merely assuming someone's responsibilities when he defaults or does it poorly does not deny he has the responsibility in the first instance. But such a denial is possible. These considerations suggest the following principle: A paternalistic intervener who undertakes ethical responsibilities for a subject without that recognition, or who refuses to make that recognition, is doing something pro tanto wrong.

The route to the second possibility begins by supposing, on the contrary, that a paternalistic intervener agrees with Dworkin that in the first instance, the subject has the responsibility to choose and act on ethical values.[23] If the paternalistic intervener recognizes that the subject has a sense of good contrary to the decision the intervener imposes, the intervener is undertaking the responsibility in this instance based on the belief that the subject isn't good at this responsibility (in this instance). We might distinguish two kinds of reasons the intervener holds this belief. The first is that the intervener recognizes factors affecting the subject that can be rectified—ignorance, strong emotion, drunkenness, cognitive bias, and so on. The second is that the intervener believes the subject is constitutively and irredeemably unable to carry out the responsibility of choosing and acting on ethical values. Suppose we hold that when the latter belief is false, or merely unjustified from his epistemic position, the paternalistic intervener is insulting the dignity of the subject. We might then maintain that paternalism is pro tanto wrong when it both assumes a responsibility to choose and apply ethical values and is based on the paternalistic intervener's false or epistemically unjustified belief that the subject is irredeemably incapable of living up to this responsibility (in the relevant area of life). (I hesitate to extend the claim to the case where the belief is true or epistemically justified.)

There is considerable plausibility in both principles. Note that for both, it isn't the act of paternalism that insults dignity, but rather acting on the accompanying beliefs or attitudes of the paternalistic agent. However, these principles apply to a very small range of paternalistic actions. Not many paternalistic interveners will hold these beliefs; and there are other grounds on which their paternalistic acts can be pro tanto wrong. Some of these grounds I have considered on behalf of Dworkin—intending to insult the subject by the paternalistic intervention, denying the subject the freedom to choose ethical values for himself in the first instance, undertaking a responsibility belonging to the subject to choose values from some objectively acceptable (and perhaps worthy and morally limited) list of incommensurables when the subject has made this choice. But there are still others—the paternalistic intervener is the one who is bad at determining what is in the subject's best interests (bad at exercising the responsibility undertaken), the expected consequences are appalling, the intervener lacks standing.

Note that there is much less plausibility if the second proposed principle is converted to an all-things-considered-wrong claim. The resulting contention would be that paternalism is all-things-considered wrong when it both assumes a responsibility to choose and apply ethical values and is based on the paternalistic intervener's false or epistemically unjustified belief that the subject is irredeemably incapable of living up to this responsibility. Consider, again, the case of Dax Cowart. Suppose his doctors, who imposed burn treatment against his protests for ten or so months,[24] did so on the basis of the combination of their knowledge that it was necessary to save his life and their belief that he was irredeemably incapable of making a good choice about what was in his own best interests in medical matters of this sort. Suppose that he wasn't incompetent, and that the doctors had not sufficient epistemic justification for thinking he was; suppose, that is, that Dax was fully competent to decide that continued life wasn't worth the length of excruciating pain the treatments involved. Suppose further that Dax afterwards lived and thrived, got married and started a family, started a career, and is currently enjoying his life. Then the paternalistic intervention by his doctors, though based on a deplorable attitude, may have been justified after all. Consequences matter, even in paternalism.[25]

The foregoing reflections on the sufficient-condition pro tanto version of the Responsibility Principle-plus-beliefs have revealed a further, very modest role for the idea of dignity in the moral issues surrounding paternalism. Once more, however, there is nothing to tie the wrong-making characteristics uniquely to Dworkin's conception of dignity. This is a further difficulty with the two new principles. On Dworkin's conception of dignity, the subject has a responsibility to *decide* (and pursue) what is good for himself by choosing from, presumably, a long list of possible goals, personal characteristics, tastes, ideals, lifestyles, pursuits, and so on. The paternalist ignores the choice, imposing some contrary choice to be applied in a particular instance. The insult, such as it is, comes from the paternalist's denial that the subject has this responsibility or from the paternalist's belief that the subject is irredeemably unfit to exercise it. But suppose Dworkin is wrong about the responsibilities of the subject. Note that the pro tanto wrongness does not disappear if we assume instead that the subject's responsibility is to *discover* (and pursue) what is good for himself, some objective moral truth independent of the subject's choice. In either case, the paternalistic intervener is acting on a rejection of the idea that the subject has a responsibility for his own well-being or is constitutively fit for this responsibility in general. The action on these beliefs constitutes the insult, and produces the reason why substituting a choice seems pro tanto to be usurping the responsibility in question. But in the second case, the insult is not an insult to *dignity*, as Dworkin conceives it. It is an insult to something much more general, the subject's status as an independent moral agent. It is, therefore, not clear that the specifics of dignity, as Dworkin conceives them, add anything to the explanation of the wrongness of paternalism by an agent who denies the subject's responsibility for his own well-being or his fitness to exercise it.

In addition to 'denying responsibilities' language, Dworkin uses 'diminishing responsibilities' language (Dworkin: 2011: 370). Consider the view that paternalism is wrong, at least pro tanto, when it diminishes its subject's ethical responsibilities. Though I think this principle is a rough approximation of the truth, it may also be of limited use. It is questionable how many of the wrongful acts of paternalism this contention captures. What is wrong with some individual paternalism, I suggest is that it discourages or stands in the way of its subject's developing or exercising the skills for autonomous living (See endnote 15). That is to diminish, not the responsibilities of dignity (how can that be done?), but the capacity to fulfil them or the opportunities to fulfil them (if the responsibilities include trying to act on them). Though Dworkin seems to agree that diminishing these capacities makes paternalism pro tanto wrong (recall his remarks about compulsory education, cited above), this line is perilously close to a consequentialist objection to paternalism.

Dworkin may at this point retreat to the claim that since we are tracing paternalism's effects on dignity, he will have a non-consequentialist objection to paternalism so long as dignity has non-instrumental value. He provides no argument for its having non-instrumental value, however, and one is needed. It is possible to argue that the root idea of dignity, self-determination, has only instrumental value.

The search for a non-consequentialist account of the wrongness of wrongful individual paternalism has revealed that Dworkin's dignity framework produces few and extremely limited pro tanto principles that are plausible. I have, moreover, expressed doubts about the role of specifics about dignity in these principles. Suppose, however, that these doubts are misconceived. Suppose, too, that my idea that paternalism can be wrong on grounds independent of dignity (such as standing) is unsustainable. The best case for the idea that dignity has *central* epistemic value for the moral issues surrounding individual paternalism is as follows: We are, in ethical paternalism, substituting our judgment about what is good for someone for the subject's, in the sense that we are relying on our judgment and discounting or rejecting the subject's. We are disvaluing the other person's ethical choices—to some extent. If, independently, Dworkin could show that the other person's ethical choices are not to be lightly devalued—if, in other words, their existence always puts a burden of justification on the paternalist—then, when that burden cannot be met, Dworkin may be able to say that dignity is insulted. It would follow that paternalism is wrong, and on dignity grounds.

This line of reasoning assumes that another person's ethical choices are always to be respected, such that ignoring them or disvaluing them calls for a justification. I have argued that this assumption is called into question by ethical choices that are 'too expensive', objectively worthless or have immoral implications. In addition, I have argued that delineating which value choices ought to be respected, or claiming that all of them ought to be, is driven by intuitions about when paternalism needs a justification. On this subject, dignity has no epistemic value.

Dworkin contends that the dignity framework will delineate when implications of a choice of value or lifestyle are immoral. But this is precisely what is to be shown with respect to practicing ethical paternalism. (Recall that there are persons whose life choices entail they must practice ethical paternalism.) So one cannot take his contention on faith without begging questions. Moreover, the claim is highly doubtful. It is difficult to see how Dworkin could use the principles of dignity (even when combined with the Kantian principle) to show the wrongness of pedophilia. Pedophilia cannot insult or offend the dignity of children, for reasons given at the end of the last section. As I noted at the beginning of this chapter, previous commentators have argued that Dworkin's claims for the dignity framework fail with respect to their moral convictions.

More important, if the justifications for paternalistic intervention cannot ultimately be traced to dignity—if such justifications rely on distinct and unrelated moral considerations—then dignity has little epistemic value for the morality of individual paternalism. (Indeed, if the moral considerations are distinct and unrelated, there is no unity of value.) Paternalistic acts will be wrong when and only when they have no justification. At best, dignity comes in only to explain why justification is needed in the first place.

This puts pressure on what these justifications are, and whether they can be tied in the right way to the dignity framework. Perhaps the burden of justification is met when the subject's choice of ethical value the paternalist is rejecting has immoral implications and the paternalist is not forcing or causing the subject to act immorally. (Recall the example of interfering with the Satanist, not to protect others but for the subject's own good—his happiness, his emotional security, and so on.) The main trouble for Dworkin then would be his difficulties explaining immorality in terms of dignity alone. Note that Dworkin cannot afford to argue that what makes implications immoral is that they require or license the subject to be insufficiently respectful of the *process* involved in 'authenticity'. For the twin assumptions that (a) a justification for paternalistic intervention is that the subject's ethical choices have immoral implications and (b) what makes the implications immoral is that they require or license the subject to be insufficiently respectful of the process involved in authenticity yield a paradox. Consider, once more, someone who practises ethical paternalism to convert others because his chosen religion mandates the conversion and offers a paternalistic rationale for it. Then he is doing something immoral, and his ethical choice of a religion has immoral implications. But our paternalistically interfering with him for his own good is both wrong (for the reasons that his paternalistic practices are) and justified (because his choice of ethical value has immoral implications).

Perhaps the burden of justification is met when the choice the paternalist is rejecting has irrational sources. This suggestion is consistent with Dworkin's remark about justifying seat belt laws in terms of overcoming momentary 'weakness' (presumably, akrasia) of drivers and passengers in vehicles. Recall, too, the case of someone choosing, out of irrationality or ignorance, a means that does not serve that person's chosen end. Dworkin, as I have said, apparently thinks paternalism in such a case is justifiable. However, as our discussion revealed, the justification here cannot simply be that the paternalist is *not* disvaluing an ethical value choice of the subject, for he may well be doing so. Will Dworkin now contend that such a subject has failed to meet the responsibilities of authenticity (because his value choices prove to be incompatible)? Or are such choices exceptions to the claim that other persons' ethical choices are not to be lightly devalued, and on grounds distinct from dignity?

Consider, next, the most extreme case of irrationality—the individual in question comes to make his ethical choices, not in the usual way, but because of a deep pathology. It is arguable that the pedophile is an example. Bernd

Brandes, who valued being eaten above life, health, bodily integrity, and human society (but did not appear to be otherwise suicidal) is another. In his case, the value was 'foundational'.[26] Perhaps Dworkin can make a case that such an individual has failed to meet the responsibilities of dignity, perhaps by failing to meet the first principle of self-respect and the Kantian principle. Will, then, paternalistic intervention to prevent such persons from successfully pursuing their values be justified, at least when there is little time for a lesser alternative? Or perhaps no justification is needed, and such choices are another exception to the claim that other person's ethical choices are not to be lightly devalued.[27]

The answers to these questions tell us how much weight to give the fact that someone has met the requirements of the principles of dignity, perhaps. Perhaps, instead, the answers tell us what the true principles of dignity are, modifying (Dworkin might say 'refining') Dworkin's conception considerably. Perhaps, that is, there is nothing to respect in the mere fact that someone has made decisions about how he or she is to live well. Perhaps it is false that people have a responsibility to try to fashion their lives around *whatever* their decisions on what is good for themselves have been, to pursue whatever they take as their ethical values. Their responsibility may be to pursue ethical values chosen under certain conditions only, or meeting additional restrictions. The point is, the principles of dignity have no epistemic value here. We need the answers to these questions on paternalism first.

Notes and References

1. In addition, he claims that the two principles of dignity he identifies are 'fundamental' to morality. Ronald Dworkin. 2011. *Justice for Hedgehogs*. Cambridge, Mass.: Harvard University Press. p. 330.
2. Given that some of Dworkin's convictions are controversial, as I shall argue below, there are problems with *to whom* they must appear to be sound to give this process any significant philosophical value, either constitutive or epistemic. On the possible constitutive and epistemic value of a Dworkinian integration of values, see Joseph Raz. 2016. 'A Hedgehog's Unity of Value', in Wil Waluchow and Stefan Sciaraffa (eds), *The Legacy of Ronald Dworkin*. Oxford: Oxford University Press. pp. 3–22.
3. Ronald Dworkin. 2000. *Sovereign Virtue: The Theory and Practice of Equality*. Cambridge, Mass.: Harvard University Press. pp. 268–74.
4. Dworkin finds at least two 'rights' in the second principle, authenticity: a 'right of control we must have to lead our own lives' and a 'right to ethical independence'. Ethical independence is a right against 'domination', among other things (2011: 212). See the discussion of ethical independence later in the chapter.

5. Alternatively, perhaps paternalism is justified when it promotes the exercise of or conditions for dignity. (Suggestion by Michael Pendlebury.) See the discussion in endnote 25.

6. Dworkin's earlier views on paternalism were largely anti-paternalist, particularly when it came to governmental paternalism forcing people to act in ways they do not think make their lives better. (See, for example, *Sovereign Virtue*, [2000: 268–74].) But he maintained that paternalistic intervention might sometimes be justified.

7. Notice that this definition differs from a definition of 'paternalism' as interfering with someone against his or her will for his or her own good. The difference might lead one initially to suspect that Dworkin is trying to narrow the field for paternalism, along the lines of a distinction he draws in an earlier work. As Dworkin points out in *Sovereign Virtue* (2000: 268), there is a difference between interfering against someone's will and interfering contrary to someone's ethical convictions. There he offers as an example of the former mandatory seat belt legislation, which coerces someone to fasten his seat belt against his will. We are to assume the person values the relevant harm prevention enough to justify restrictions. Dworkin offers as an example of the latter (interfering with conviction) forcing a homosexual to change his sexual behaviour, when the person in question regards the result as distinctly inferior to the life he prefers (218). One might suppose that in *Justice for Hedgehogs*, Dworkin is trying to confine paternalism to interferences against conviction, but his discussion of justified paternalism suggests otherwise.

8. Endorsement, which featured in Dworkin's earlier discussion of paternalism, is mentioned on p. 204 in connection with ethical responsibility. Dworkin adds in *Justice for Hedgehogs* (2011: 265): 'Self-respect [another component of dignity] also requires that you treat yourself as autonomous in one sense of that idea: you must yourself endorse the values that structure your life.' See also *Justice for Hedgehogs* (2011: 213).

9. For example, Dworkin says that government's motives in enacting a law can make a law violate ethical independence (369), especially when the government 'assumes the superiority of any ethical values controversial in the community'. If when the government disagrees with an individual about what end is worth seeking, the ethical value favoured by the government is controversial in the community, it follows that Dworkin rejects all strong paternalism by law. On the other hand, see *Justice for Hedgehogs* (2011: 370), where he declares a mandatory seat belt law is 'not ethical paternalism'.

10. Christopher Wolfe. 1994. 'Liberalism and Paternalism: A Critique of Ronald Dworkin', *The Review of Politics*. 56(4): 615–39, p. 625.

11. It is not clear what Dworkin would say in the case in which the others deem those options unworthy *because* they cause intentional harm to unwilling others or otherwise treat others immorally.

12. Suggested to me in private conversation by Michael Pendlebury.

13. On the same page, Dworkin also offers this claim: 'Authenticity demands that, so far as decisions are to be made about the best use to which a person's life should be put, these must be made by the person whose life it is.' A law requiring easy rescue in an emergency decides in part about the best use to which people's lives should be put—aiding others in an emergency. It would, thus, be contrary to the authenticity of its law subjects. Moreover, volunteers for the armed forces find themselves ceding the right to make decisions about the best use to which their lives should be put to military authorities, particularly in wartime. It would follow that they are ceding their authenticity.

14. Dworkin declares that medical paternalism isn't ethical paternalism and 'not an offense against authenticity' (2011: 370). It follows that medical paternalism doesn't interfere with the subject's foundational ethical choices. But of course it can, as the example of forcing a blood transfusion onto an unwilling Jehovah's Witness shows. Perhaps Dworkin meant medical paternalism doesn't *typically* interfere with such choices. (Suggestion by Michael Pendlebury.)

15. I'd suggest that what is wrong with this paternalistic behaviour is that it reinforces the message that the son is incompetent in life and discourages or stands in the way of his ever developing the skills for autonomous living. It stands in the way of his personal growth, preventing him from learning from his mistakes because it prevents those mistakes. I take up this point in the next section.

16. Dworkin would find it wrong. He argues that the responsibilities of dignity '[require] at a minimum that we be in sole charge of what happens to or in our own bodies' (2011: 288). He also remarks that dignity requires one to 'make for' oneself 'the decision what use is to be made of my body or my life' (2011: 295). As I indicated in endnote 13, it would be interesting to know how he would handle the case of volunteering for military service under combat conditions. Private foot soldiers rapidly discover they are not in sole charge of what happens to or in their own bodies, and that they have lost a considerable amount of liberty to decide what the use of their bodies or their lives is to be.

17. Point made to me privately by Robert Mabrito.

18. In discussing the responsibilities of dignity, Dworkin occasionally likes to use 'performance' language. For example: the principle of self-respect introduced, 'Each person must take his own life seriously: he must accept that it is a matter of importance that his life be a successful performance rather than a wasted opportunity' (2011: 203). Also, human lives lived well 'embody a performance: a rising to the challenge of having a life to lead' (2011: 197). See also 2011: 288. In response, one might claim that some performances are so poor, they are worth correcting.

19. Suggestion made to me in private conversation by Michael Pendlebury.

20. Joseph Raz. 1989. 'Facing Up: A Reply', *Southern California Law Review* 62: pp. 1153–235, 1228–9.

21. John Rawls. 1971. *A Theory of Justice*. Cambridge, Mass.: Harvard University Press. p. 432.

22. F.M. Kamm. 2010. 'What Ethical Responsibility Cannot Justify: A Discussion of Ronald Dworkin's *Justice for* Hedgehogs', *Boston University Law Review*. pp. 691–713, 700.

23. I owe the second suggestion to Robert Mabrito.

24. See https://en.wikipedia.org/wiki/Dax_Cowart.

25. Dworkin appears to recognize this point with his claim, cited in the second section of this chapter, that enhancing the capacity for dignity makes compulsory education a permissible paternalistic endeavour. Dworkin might think that paternalism is justified whenever it enhances the subject's capacity for dignity. Since paternalism is contrary to an exercise of dignity—namely, pursuing a chosen value in an instance—this enhancement must be for the long run. One might argue that saving Dax's life enhances his capacity for dignity, compared to the capacity that would have existed had Dax had his way on the burn treatments. However, if this is so, the principle that paternalism is justified whenever it enhances the subject's capacity for dignity is overbroad. It would justify any paternalistic intervention that saves or extends life, including frog-marching total strangers to annual medical and dental examinations.

26. See, for example, the account in *The Guardian* of 4 December 2003, available http://www.acrss.ca/blogs/ce10-cr/files/2012/09/Victim-of-cannibal-agreed-to-be-eaten-%EF%80%A7-World-news-%EF%80%A7-The-Guardian1.pdf. See also Peter Finn. 2003. 'Cannibal Case Grips Germany', *Washington Post*, 4 December section A p. 26; Tony Paterson. 2003. 'Cannibal Says He Was Lonely and Dreamt of 'Brother' to Disembowel', *Independent* (London), 4 December, at p. 15. See also follow-up accounts: Ben Aris. 2003. 'Self-Confessed Cannibal Is Ruled Sane by Psychiatrist', *Guardian* (London), 30 December, p. 11; Jeffrey Fleishman. 2003. 'Germans Get a Look at Dark Side of Cyberspace', *Los Angeles Times*, 31 December, section A, p. 3; Luke Harding. 2006. 'German Court Finds Cannibal Guilty of Murder', *Guardian* (London), 10 May, p. 16. Brandes appeared to believe that the value of his life consisted in his having the potential to be eaten by another human being. Perhaps he lacked foundational values because it isn't clear how he would have generalized to the value of others—as potential eaters, perhaps? It is interesting to note that the cannibal Meiwes, in court, allegedly echoed a line from Dworkin, declaring 'everyone should be able to decide what he wants to do with his own body', Roger Boyes. 2006. 'Cannibalism Is Murder—Even if the Victim Requests to Be Eaten' *Times* (London), 10 May, p. 3.

27. In *Sovereign Virtue*, in a discussion of paternalism changing the person to endorse new values, Dworkin remarks, 'We must distinguish acceptable from unacceptable circumstances of endorsement' (218). This remark cuts both ways: there may be unacceptable circumstances of a person's initial endorsement, such that they obviate the need to justify some paternalistic intervention contrary to the endorsed values.

10

Dignity, Rights, and Virtues in the Department of Value

Isabel Trujillo

This article regards Dworkin's contribution to the idea of dignity as the core of all 'department of value' (2011: 327). From the very outset it is worth noting that in the vast debate on dignity, two main meanings can be distinguished: dignity as a concern for human beings because of their equal value, and dignity as an ethical task or challenge for human beings. In his last works, Dworkin opts for the second one, even if his contribution on political morality is full of useful elements for highlighting also the first one. Besides, he tries to hold both meanings together.

After a premise about the role of dignity in the world of values, the article is divided in two sections, following the order contrary to Dworkin's *Justice for Hedgehogs*[1]—not from ethics to morality, but from morality to ethics. In the first section, the paper emphasizes how Dworkin's theory of dignity can enrich the current political paradigm dominated by liberal rights starting from his idea of dignity and the thesis of the continuity between ethics and morality, built precisely on the concept of dignity. He is opening new perspectives, (re)introducing elements coming from the Aristotelian tradition of the good life in a context in which the language of individual rights and the liberal equilibrium between individual freedom and state's coercion are dominating. These innovations will be presented here through the analysis of the different faces of dignity.

The second section is dedicated in more depth to the perspective of the good life from the point of view of ethics, where some problems arise if it is looked at from Dworkin's liberal political morality. According to Dworkin's teaching, the key concept in the first section will be that of 'rights', while the key concept in the second one will be 'responsibility'. The inversion of Dworkin's order is justified by the opinion that his proposals in the field of 'morality in continuity with ethics' are more persuading than his suggestions in the field of ethics. But this does not eliminate his worthy contribution to the complex and crucial topic of dignity.

Dignity as the Core of the Department of Value

Dignity means a kind of eminence, superiority, status worth to which due respect is ascribed. The problems raised by dignity are of two types: on the one hand, who is worthy and why—the identity question—and, on the other hand, what kind of treatment dignity requires—the normative question.

The idea of dignity as a task can be assumed in this last one, as long as it regards the enquiry on which behaviours are consonant with or due to dignity. In other words, which normative implications derive from dignity. They are two different enquiries, even if related to each other and difficult to divide completely. Nevertheless, in the wide political debate, it is easy to find separate disputes about one of these different questions when the other one has not yet been clarified. Both queries are crucial, but in some way dignity permits to proceed in the debate without eliminating disagreement in advance. This feature sometimes leads to say that dignity is one of the most elusive legal and political concepts, in particular for analytical minds in search of neat and clear notions.[2] However, concepts like these are needed because they facilitate the beginning of the dialogue and negotiation that constitutes the aim of Politics (Walzer 1994).[3] From this point of view—as well as rights, freedom, equality—dignity can be considered one of the possible current *endoxa* in the Aristotelian fashion—those common knowledge or opinions that can be the starting point of a deliberation process (Aristotle, *Topics* I, 100b).[4] Their being a common starting point is perfectly compatible with a wide disagreement about their nature, content, and implications. As a manifestation of concern for human beings, the reasons for disagreement about dignity include also the difficulty of limiting the respect for human beings to standard models, as well as the unpredictable situations in which that respect must be assured. Dworkin then properly considers dignity an interpretive concept, rather than a criterial one (2011: 158–63). Moreover, it is not only the particularity of the contexts that makes complex dealing with dignity, but also the indeterminacy of human actions and history—what in the language of classical morality would be called contingency as opposed to necessity. And human acts are certainly contingent.

Nonetheless, dignity is not an empty container for a discussion on what we owe to human beings, and how legal and political institutions must protect them. Apart from the agreement about the necessity of starting from there—that it is anyway remarkable in itself and it is better not to presuppose—there will be some arrangements clearly not compatible with dignity, to be prevented. The aim of deliberation and decision making in Politics is to progress in the task of realizing dignity. Dignity is not 'behind' but 'forward'.

Dignity is difficult to grasp also for another reason. It becomes intricate as far as its protection involves a plurality of values—autonomy and equality; needs and freedom, and so on. The two more notorious cases in which we can observe this feature are the social and legal practice of human rights, in which dignity interacts with human basic interests whatever they are (Tasioulas 2013),[5] and the legal experience of the rule of law, aiming to enhance dignity by ensuring individual autonomous agency through special forms and limits of power.[6] Nonetheless, the convergence in the concept of dignity of more than one value must not wonder. Otherwise dignity could just be replaced by the value with which it can be linked—it is the thesis of the stupidity or uselessness of dignity (Macklin 2003;[7] Pinker 2008).[8] According to this thesis, if dignity is recognized to autonomous subjects, there is no need to speak of dignity, it is enough to speak of autonomy. In others words, if dignity just stands for another concept, it is redundant. On the contrary, dignity reacts with other values producing certain kinds of normative implications in specific contexts (Barak 2015: 119).[9] Dignity adds something to those values, and this is the prominence of human beings. As we will see, in the case of rights, for instance, dignity is a reason for going beyond rights.

As a champion of bravery in the field of political morality (and also as a supporter of a rights' center theory from the beginning of his researches), Dworkin has faced the task of proposing a plausible notion of dignity, in spite of all the difficulties in defining it. In *Justice for Hedgehogs* and in *Is Democracy Possible Here?* (2006),[10] he is in search of a common background for Politics against skepticism and/or indifference. In continuity with the holistic approach of his legal works on integrity, he identifies dignity as the key of all the department of value, that is, at the center of ethics, morality, law, and Politics. According to Dworkin's thesis, dignity is not only the ground of rights, but also the key of our moral responsibilities. In this way, he is using the two meanings of dignity recalled above. From the point of view of its role in deliberation, dignity is also the standpoint for building a reasonable agreement in Politics.

More specifically, in *Justice for Hedgehogs* Dworkin's explicit interest is to show how dignity is the bridge between both personal and political morality, and not only the core of ethics and political morality separately. Dignity is the central concept of ethics as far as it is the ground of self-respect. At the same time, it is the basic value of political morality, so it serves to identify its content. This means that 'acts are wrong if they insult the dignity of others', and not that 'an act is an insult to dignity when and because it is morally wrong in some other way' (Dworkin 2011: 204, against Scanlon 2000).[11] In other words, dignity is the content of what we owe to each other. Dignity is not only referred to the practice of recognizing rights, but more generally it is concerned with our lives. From this last point of view, Dworkin's idea of dignity includes the perspective of virtues, in addition to a specific idea of justice and reciprocity, centered on equal concern.

Many perplexities can derive from this central role of dignity in the department of value. On the one hand, there is the problem whether dignity is complete only if it is thought in relation to justice and reciprocity, that are the keys of dignity in political morality or, on the contrary, a meaning of dignity in ethics can be isolated. On the other hand, Dworkin is undoubtedly trying to ground dignity on ethics. However, in more than one point, it is not clear which one comes before. In *Justice for Hedgehogs* chapter 12, for instance, Dworkin clearly says that his ambition is to locate morality in ethics (2011: 272). In order to establish what each one owes to other people, he seems to give more importance to personal ethics, '[w]e must show full respect for the equal objective importance of every person's life, but also full respect for our own responsibility to make something valuable of our own life' (2011: 272). This is the premise for introducing (subjective) limits in helping others even in situations of extreme bad luck: 'it would not be against our dignity to refuse to make admirable sacrifices' (2011: 274).[12] Definitely, one of the most intriguing points in the book regards in fact the relationship between ethics and morality, which is not very clear. But as long as the book defends the unity of value (2011: 1), the question of independent meanings of dignity in these different contexts and the problem of priority among the different fields would not be decisive. In addition, as far as dignity is never working alone, it is not difficult to imagine that the arduous equilibrium with other values is not the exception that proves the rule, but precisely the rule of practicing dignity, which is interacting with other values. From here it can be derived the challenging task of dealing with dignity. But, at the end of the day, all these elements are in favour of the unity of value, not only because dignity does not exclude the presence of other values, but also precisely because all those elements are positively related to dignity. Dignity without those values would probably be useless and meaningless. All those values without dignity would lose a parameter for being ordered, in attention to the eminence of human beings.

It is anyway relevant to say in this introduction that the main interest of this article is not to identify possible internal contradictions and inconsistencies in Dworkin's work, a risk hard to avoid in the ambitious enterprise of facing the key concept of all the department of value. Instead, the aim is to try to understand the keys of the last development of Dworkin's thought—the legacy of one of the most important Western political philosophers—taking seriously his suggestions regarding those central questions on ethics and political morality.

In particular, as it has been noted, in his last works Dworkin wishes to affiliate his views with those of Aristotle on the good life (Kamm 2010: 692, n.7),[13] putting this idea at the center of both personal and political morality. Doing this, he is introducing new crucial elements in his account of morality. Nonetheless, it is well-known that the issue of good life seems a crucial topic... for a vanished world (Taylor 1989;[14] Taylor 2002;[15] Viola 2000: 1–13).[16] And, in fact, the easiest line of criticism regards the incompatibility between Dworkin's liberal modern mentality and Aristotle's views on the good life. But this line would be too predictable. Instead, it is worth taking Dworkin's attraction to the paradigm of the good life seriously, and examining how and until what point his suggestions could reshape the field of political morality. The comparison with Aristotelian ideas of the good life will serve to highlight some Dworkinian suggestions for current questions of political morality, but also to notice what it is missing in his perspective. Rainer Forst has observed a sort of humanistic turn in Dworkin's liberalism—he moved from the standard neutrality of his liberal starting position, to a form of ethical liberalism compatible with a theory of the good life (Forst 2002: 56),[17] or even something more than that—a tentative political theory of a good life starting from dignity.

Before going into the field of political morality, there are two points that must be underlined. The first one is related to the unity of value. This thesis—unless from dignity's point of view—does not seem to imply the monolithic character of value, one and indivisible (even if sometimes it seems that for Dworkin the monolith is autonomy). Instead, the unity of value and the centrality of dignity mean that there is a common background for disagreement in morality and in Politics, that is, there is room for debates and deliberation.

The second point is that if there is a truth of morality, this truth is not a system of ideas, but it is a principle, or better, a manifold principle—what we call dignity. To say that a principle is true means something different from saying that a theory is true. To say that a principle is true means that the principle is adequately justified and it serves to guide human actions. For this reason, Dworkin states that it is worth being responsible when discussing principles, '[w]e cannot defend a theory of justice without also defending, as part of the same enterprise, a theory of moral objectivity. It is irresponsible to try to do without such a theory' (2011: 8). This is an important point and regards the practical character of the discussion. Looking at how post-modern feminists developing the priority of interpretations over facts trivialize important questions related to human rights, Catharine MacKinnon asks them, 'what are you doing?' (MacKinnon 2006: 63).[18] The very challenge is to reach that moral objectivity without confusing our personal ideas with what can be proposed as having a justification, and this is one of the aim of public deliberation. Moral objectivity, in fact, is a common and tentative enterprise.

Dignity and Morality: Creating Asymmetries

Rights, Duties, and Virtues

In general, dignity is a suitable standpoint for 'the age of rights' (Bobbio 1996)[19] to be understood as a general framework within which rights are the key concepts of morality. Rights' centrality in the current debate depends precisely on the concern for human beings. It is not then the case that dignity is recognized as the common ground for fundamental and human rights[20] in constitutions, declarations, and international agreements, even if that recognition does not solve—certainly not alone—the problems of identifying, interpreting, and implementing those rights. Dignity and rights form a complex project to be performed, and sometimes the difficulty of understanding the content and the role of dignity in the legal and political contexts seems an obstacle to the practice of protecting rights, because of dignity's vagueness and openness. It is not a concept that tends to simplify the controversies, but rather a guide for change, conflict, and revision. As said before, the very meaning of the couple dignity-rights is the prominence of human beings. The consequence of dignity is the protection of rights, then dignity plausibly goes 'beyond' rights. In the legal practice, for instance, dignity is very often the parameter against which some standard readings of rights appear to be insufficient from the point of view of individual's circumstances (McCrudden 2008).[21] In some way, this can be seen as an implication of the idea of rights as 'trumps'—trumps over the sovereignty of states, in the case of human rights (2011: 333); trumps over the general interest and public policies (473, n1), in the case of political rights.

The centrality of dignity as a ground for rights must not hide the idea that dignity can be observed from different points of view within the same perspective of rights, both in consideration of the subjects of dignity and in consideration of the way in which the worthy subject is characterized. In the context of the practice of rights, the subject of dignity is not only the rights' holder, but also an agent in a dynamic perspective—the responsibility to protect rights in a non-technical meaning.[22] Leaving aside the simple idea, deriving from dignity, that human rights look at empowering the rights holders promoting their agency, it can be said that there is also a dignity of those that are bearers of the corresponding duties. It is the dignity of those involved in making rights real as far as the very meaning of the practice of human rights is to defend others' rights, more than 'our own' rights. This clarification is motivated by the necessity of distinguishing the practice of human rights from the theories of natural rights.

As it is well-known, the long run in the history of human rights links them to the natural rights of natural law tradition at the beginning of Modern Age. Even if there are many similarities between them, human rights differ from natural rights from many points of view—their relationship with law; their being part of historical and cultural processes; the idea of human nature they involve.[23] It is possible to say that human rights seem to have acquired their very shape only after the Second World War (Moyn 2010),[24] when it became clear that human rights were others' rights to be protected. Being the outcome of a process of reacting to violations and discriminations against human beings, human rights engage others' commitment in avoiding those discriminations and violations. The relevant humanity—and then the dignity involved—in human rights then it is not only that of the rights holder, but it is to be referred also to those who have the duty to protect rights (Trujillo-Viola 2014: 1–10).[25] In order to make sense of this, the assumption is that the actors in the practice of human rights are not only the states (even if they are the main ones), or international organizations (even if they are necessary too), but more generally all those able to cooperate in this common enterprise of protecting human beings, including private citizens and the civil society (Sen 2004,[26] Trujillo-Viola 2014: 113–19).

Both perspectives on dignity—the holders of rights and the dignity of agents taking part in the practice with the role of duty bearers—are relevant in the current project of human rights. Nevertheless, it is interesting to notice that these two faces of human dignity are not symmetrical, not only because the normative priority must be attributed to rights as grounds for duties (Raz 1988: 170–1),[27] and then there will always be rights in search of duty bearers (otherwise the practice would not be normative), but also because dignity is not running out all its potentiality in the context of rights holders. As we will see, in his last works, Dworkin developed a different idea of agency, neither related exclusively to the holding of rights, nor just to the bearing of correlative duties, but rather to a more general idea of an agent responsible of her life, mastery of her destiny, that wants to live well and have a good life also in the context of a political community, performing noble aspirations. From this point of view, the language shifts from rights and duties to virtues and responsibilities, as far as 'it is more natural and accurate, when judging what it is to live well, to think of what we are responsible for doing than of what we have the right to demand' (Dworkin 2011: 328).

Dworkin's definition of dignity is then not simply devoted to squaring the circle of the normativity of individual rights through the identification of duty bearers, as sometimes happens with the proposal of the priority of duties in the context of theories of justice.[28] On the contrary, his aim is to design a more ambitious reading of moral agency in the political context. This turn transfers the contents and language of morality from the dominance of rights (and correlative duties) to a new political perspective in which responsibilities and virtues are crucial.

It is worth underlining that this is not a trivial change—something important has been added. If correct, in fact, it can be said that the main question of morality is not just how people ought to treat each other, but rather a question about the scope of our responsibilities. Morality is not only the field of relationships of justice, but it is also the scenario of personal projects, engagements, and aspirations.[29] The problem would be then how our projects interact with others' lives. Summing up, morality is neither only a question of rights, nor only a question of duties (linked to those rights). It is also the field of a different form of agency—the one in which our personal projects encounter the wellbeing of other people. On which basis is that meeting possible? It is doubtful how Dworkin can solve this problem, unless starting from dignity and grounding dignity on equality. In fact, our responsibility for a good life does not produce necessarily that result.

Commenting on Lon Fuller's approach to the morality of aspirations, Luban explains well the link between our aspirations and morality, being obvious that our aspirations belong to the field of ethics. Our aspirations have a moral dimension 'whenever other people's wellbeing depends on them' (Luban 2000: 183).[30] In this light, it can be saved, on the one hand, the belonging of dignity to morality, because it regards our relations with others and on the other hand the link with ethics through virtues and responsibilities. Is this what Dworkin wants to indicate with the prevalence of responsibilities?

The imbalance between rights and responsibilities is not necessarily an element to criticize. On the contrary, it can just be understood as the proof of an existing moral asymmetry where we usually see the symmetry of justice. This is also a crucial point because it implies a shift from the balanced logic of reciprocity—sovereign equality—to a different paradigm—the logic of aspirations that is necessarily imbalanced. There remains the problem of how to manage that imbalance in the field of morality. Is it possible to put together aspirations and justice? This is the point in which the calling for a good life is heard.

We can provisionally conclude observing that Dworkin seems to be proposing a way back to the ancient ideal of personal excellence but in favour of both the modern concept of duty and the current dominance of rights. But from this point of view, it cannot be forgotten the difficulties that this wayback implies, since it has become hard for us to even appreciate the idea of human goodness in the way the ancients understood it.[31]

Dignity, Agency, and the Rule of Law

Before analyzing the approach of dignity as personal excellence in details, it is useful to look at another existing political practice in which dignity is certainly operating—the rule of law. The point is whether the ideas of moral agency and dignity that Dworkin is proposing can take shape in this practice. More than the practice of rights, the rule of law involves a notion of moral agency that would have satisfied Dworkin's demand of commitment and responsibility.

There is neither room nor it is the case to discuss the very meaning and status of the rule of law. It has been transformed from a legal concept to a crucial political value, in part because of its link to dignity and rights. In fact, according to Dworkin, the rule of law is part of a 'true' theory of individual rights. In the debate about the formal or substantial rule of law's status (Craig 1997),[32] Dworkin adopts a rights' conception of the rule of law,[33] according to which it 'is the ideal of rule by an accurate public conception of individual rights. It does not distinguish [...] between the rule of law and substantive justice; on the contrary, it requires, as part of the ideal of law, that the rules in the book capture and enforce moral rights' (Dworkin 1985: 12).[34]

As a demonstration of the rich nature of dignity, the practice of rights and the practice of the rule of law are different even if both give form to the relationship between dignity and rights. The rule of law deals with the forms of exercising (public) powers.[35] Observed from the point of view of the subject to be protected (rather than as a device of controlling the public force) the rule of law is a mechanism for protecting dignity as agency. This result can be summed up in the difference between the managerial way of directing actions, and that form of guiding human action according to the rule of law. The latter involves a reasonable subject, a free and responsible agent, able to plan her life, who wants to act according to the law (Fuller 1969).[36] From this point of view, the rule of law is potently connected to human dignity (Luban 2010), because free and rational agency is at stake.

The most common strategy for distinguishing the practice of rights and the rule of law is to note that the protection given by the rule of law is only partial in terms of rights. The rule of law is in fact aimed at ensuring consistent treatment with dignity in relation to the exercise of authority and power, while human rights look to a global protection of the fundamental interests of human beings. In other words, from the perspective of a rights' conception of the rule of law, its purpose is not the protection of *all* human rights, but only of those that are necessary in the context of the exercise of authority. From this point of view, it has been noted that the rule of law protects mainly the negative liberties, or even rights in a libertarian fashion, or property rights (Luban 2010: 43). It is not difficult to replay to this criticism. On the one hand, things get a little bit more complicated if it is asked which rights are necessary to protect the human being as an autonomous agent, able to plan her own life and affairs, and then to comply with rules. Is it necessary to ensure minimal basic rights for the individuals to organize their life freely and independently? This is a pertinent question and an affirmative answer is plausible from many points of view—as it is known, rights tend to go together. More significantly, *dignity* holds all rights together. Quoting the enigmatic but stimulating Hannah Arendt's (1958)[37] formula, dignity is the right to have rights.

On the other hand, the focus of the rule of law is to protect human beings as able to plan their own life in a context of interdependence or interaction (Luban 2010). In general, by context of interdependence it is meant the field of collective decision making, those choices that affect the common life and the life of each one. In other words, the rule of law has to do directly with authority and coordination (also at the international level: Waldron 2011[38] and Besson 2011[39]). It is true that the object of the rule of law is the mode of decision making and not its content, and this mode responds to certain characteristics of the subjects involved. As it is well known, Dworkin's thesis is that the rule of law protects human beings assuring them *equal concern and respect* (Dworkin 2013: 29).[40] This idea is supported by the compatibility of liberty and equality in the framework of the unity of value. According to this view, they are not irreconcilable (Dworkin 2011: 331). From the point of view of the rule of law, to be treated with equal concern means to guarantee the same freedom from subordination to an arbitrary power.

It is in this context that is possible to understand Dworkin's strong position about an 'absolute truth at the basis of a theory of human rights'— the 'judgement about the conditions of human dignity and the threats that coercive power offers to that dignity' (2011: 338). Strong normative power limitations derive from dignity. This is the core of liberalism. There remains the problem of coordination as rule of law's task, if it is to identify completely with coercion or it means something different. Dworkin's focus on the rule of law is dominated clearly by the idea of the modern state, characterized by the monopoly on coercion. Sometimes it seems that he is presupposing some of the pillars of the modern state. For instance, he seems to accept as uncontroversial that '[c]oercion is plain when it is achieved or threatened by the criminal law or by other forms of state action. In other circumstances more subtle discrimination is needed to distinguish influence from subordination' (2011: 212). But it is difficult to think of plain common decisions, also in the field of criminal law.

Anyway, the rule of law admits the idea that free and rational agents comply willingly with rules, always backed by coercion. Nonetheless, even from a Hobbesian perspective, the intuitive idea is that coordination leads to coercion. In other words, coercion is needed because of the necessity of coordination, and not the opposite. It is then reductive that political association could be explained just in terms of coercion (324). It seems that the main problem with political community is in line with his liberalism—how far the necessary exercise of power can limit our freedom. Dworkin affirms that we have special relationships to our fellow citizens independently of any consent, because '[c]ollective coercive government is essential to our dignity. We need the order and efficiencies that only coercive government can provide to make it possible for us to create good lives and to live well' (320). The point is that in his last works he is clearly introducing a totally new idea: '[w]e need to understand happiness so that we can construct a good state, which is a state in which people are enabled and encouraged to lead good lives' (188). Every step towards a good state like this seems a step away from liberalism.

This impasse can be observed also from another point of view, through the question of political obligations that in Dworkin's account serve for the transition from ethics to political morality. Political obligations represent the hinge between our responsibilities (the key feature of ethics) and rights (the key feature of political morality as long as it looks at what we owe to each other when we act in and on behalf of articulated collective person as the state).[41] In the context of authority and decision making human dignity pushes for autonomy and liberty. There remains to prove if political obligations are 'thicker' than that.

In *Justice for Hedgehogs*, Dworkin brings back the question of political obligations to that of associative obligations. From this point of view the main problem is again why we should obey the law. The answer however, cannot be grounded on people's consent, otherwise anarchism is right. Moral responsibilities are neither always voluntary, nor only voluntary responsibilities are genuine. According to Dworkin, political obligations are a special case of associational obligations because there is a special relationship with our fellowships grounded in facts. Those facts do not count as history, but as they produce contemporary effects in the present time (2011: 319). In Dworkin's perspective, this is a strange explanation if it is not considered the moral dimension of facts. Those facts are indeed the roots of shared responsibilities through the rule of reciprocity (320). In this light, the approach is then functional—those facts producing responsibilities, at the roots of our political associations, are aimed at assuring a net of support and interaction. It is this reason to justify the convenience—but not the necessity—of maintaining those responsibilities. The problem of the demands of that fellowship and its scope remains nevertheless open. Facts and circumstances are elements of every moral relationship, and it is important to deal with them. But those facts and circumstances must be evaluated within a deliberation process—there can always be facts that overturn those facts prima facie justifying a commitment. In other words, political associations are pro tanto obligations—fellowships and borders cannot be assumed as unequivocal facts.[42] They have an objective relevance not because they are facts, but because of their justification. In the department of value reigns uncertainty. This is one of the pillars of virtue ethics, that for this reason—its tendency to moral particularism, as long as only the virtuous person judges everything rightly (Aristotle, *Nicomachean Ethics* 1113a 30)[43]—it is difficult to be accepted.

Different Paradigms of Dignity

Returning to the first enquiry on dignity, what has been called above the identity question, it can be said that the main common models of dignity in current political theory are two different ones: dignity as autonomy, and dignity as vulnerability. In a moral theory dominated by the centrality of rights and of the rule of law, these two paradigms seem to be prevailing. The link between autonomy and dignity, on the one hand, and between vulnerability and dignity, on the other hand, can be considered two competing—or complementary—views, able to explain the practice of protecting human beings. Both together remind the debate between the two more common accounts of rights—the choice theory and the interest theory (Waldron 1984).[44] These two approaches, sometimes considered two opposing theories, actually contribute together to highlight the complex practice of human rights that cannot be reduced to a theory (Trujillo-Viola 2014: xi–xiv). Dignity as autonomy has emerged in the context of the rule of law.

It is interesting to note that it is precisely the teaching of the classical heritage—and particularly Aristotle's contribution—to lead some authors, like Martha Nussbaum, towards a notion in which the link between dignity and vulnerability and fragility of the rights holders is crucial, even if within a framework in which freedom is also decisive. It is the case of the famous capabilities' approach (Nussbaum-Sen 1993),[45] in which rights are devoted to promoting agency meeting the basic needs for the exercise of freedom.

Moreover, the link between dignity and vulnerability is notoriously the key of Nussbaum's criticism against the abstract Kantian notion of dignity. The Kantian notion between liberty and dignity is the universal validity of rational legality, free from empirical and natural limitations. Nussbaum notices that in Kant, but also in Rawls, and perhaps in almost all the liberal tradition, dignity tends to be linked to our moral capacities—rationality and human freedom—and completely separate from the natural world, the world of natural necessities. 'Insofar as we exist merely in the realm of nature, we are not ends in ourselves and do not have a dignity; things in that realm simply have a price (as Kant puts it, *pretiumusus*). In so far as we enter the realm of ends, thus far, and thus far alone, we have dignity and transcend price' (Nussbaum 2006: 131).[46]

On the contrary, human dignity—or at least the human dignity of human rights holders in Nussbaum's theory—fits with the existence of vulnerable beings similar in many things to animals, not self-sufficient but rather dependent on others, subjected to luck and fragility. This is the very identikit of rights holders to whom dignity must be recognized, in contrast with the idea that human rights protect self-sufficient individuals that aspire just to not having interference from others (Taylor 1989: 11).[47]

The link between dignity and vulnerability and/or fragility is a crucial topic because it explains one of the implications of the complexity and the universality of the modern idea of dignity. Both these dimensions—complexity and universality—justify the recognition of dignity to every human being, independently of their qualities, performances, or merits. It is not a case that Dworkin recalls the distinction between appraisal respect and recognition respect (2011: 206). This distinction, introduced by Darwall (1977),[48] differentiates between the respect motivated by character and achievements from the respect deriving from peoples' status. Dignity in Dworkin's perspective of morality is of the second kind, that is, it is linked to a general status. However, it should be recognized not only as status and this is what the rule of reciprocity and the link with equality assure. Only in this way, dignity can be egalitarian; is a positive attitude of recognizing equal worth of others. It is not a quality possessed by some, but something that we can recognize in others.

The importance of this point comes out when we consider that the universality of dignity includes not only those who do not do anything worthy of being appreciated, but also those who positively do what is not worthy at all. Except in the case of the perspective of the theory of the intrinsic value, that is the more egalitarian account of dignity (Viola 2013),[49] there remains the problem of the dignity of those who are detestable because they wasted their lives or even because their lives are dedicated to wrongdoing—crimes, damages, and iniquities. It is interesting to observe how Dworkin deals with this specific problem. The opportunity is given by the controversy about the so called 'hate speech', where it is possible to notice the difference between the American and the European points of view on the topic. In the framework of the American Constitution, hate speech is permitted as part of freedom of speech (on the basis of arguments grounded on liberty: limitations of freedom will offend ethical independence), while in Europe the prohibition of hate speech is preferred, with heavy legal implications, because of the risks for safety (policies based argument) (Dworkin 2011: 372–3; 2006: 33).[50] But, at the end of the day, Dworkin's position is that hate speech within the framework of freedom of speech makes democracy possible. In other words, hate speech is a price to pay or a wrong to be tolerated because of a bigger good at stake, that is democracy. Nonetheless, this does not have anything to do with dignity—it is neither the respect for those that are wrong, nor for their right to do wrong. It seems more a sort of collateral effect to warrant democracy. On the contrary, in the perspective according to which dignity is proper of imperfect, vulnerable, weak, frail, fallible beings, the dignity of wrongdoers makes sense of its normative status. In other words, what is perfect, self-sufficient, achieved, successful does not need dignity, because it is eminent in itself. And in fact Dworkin reminds us that virtue is an award in itself. As we will see below, in the field of ethics performance value will be central, even if distinguished from product value. But this means that dignity is not egalitarian.

Differently than you might expect, Dworkin's emerging model of dignity seems to look neither at autonomy as rights entitlements, as his liberalism would imply, nor at needs as implied by a common approach grounded on rights. In particular, his approach to dignity is far from the connection with limits, needs, and vulnerability. Partially, the explanation is related to the Kantian idea of human beings as ends, but, more intensely, he is influenced by the Kantian categorical imperative (*Groundwork for the Metaphysics of Morals* 1785),[51] because of the link with equality. It is not by chance that from his concept of dignity it follows that people 'have a right to be treated with the attitude that these debates presuppose and reflect—a right to be treated as a human being whose dignity fundamentally matters. That more abstract right— the right to an attitude—is the basic human right' (2011: 335). Dignity is then the ground for a basic human right to an attitude of concern and respect. The question about what we owe to each other leads to a rule of equality, and this has to do with the relationship between dignity and justice. Dignity is not just the right to be respected, but rather the right to have the 'same' respect.

Dworkin's idea of dignity as a bridge between ethics and morality is related precisely to this rule of equality or reciprocity, but it cannot be reduced to that. He insists on the importance and salience that our lives must have as well as on the important roles that we can play in the world. Dignity is then also the content of projects and aspirations. It is a task and a challenge. At the same time, the importance of our lives is connected to the importance of others' lives—the reason for considering our lives important is the same for considering the importance of others' lives. From this point of view, dignity is neither a quality, nor a relationship,[52] even if it concerns our and others' lives. It is a rule of reciprocity or justice and in this form it connects the fields of ethics and morality.

For the influence of religious thoughts centered on the idea of every man as God's image and likeness, and even more for the Christian teaching of the value of each person redeemed by the Son of God, dignity has been transformed little by little in a general status to be recognized to all human beings, regardless of their merits, performances, actions, and even wrongdoings, although it maintained for a long time some of the classical characters such as the link to virtues.[53] The practice of human rights involves the maximum of inclusivity—dignity is recognized just because they are human beings. Before crossing the line of ethics, we can compare Dworkin's approach with a third model of dignity, coming also from Greek's philosophy—the paradigm of dignity as excellence. Dworkin in fact seems to be thinking of the dignity of those who spend their lives in a good way, in worthy activities, those who look at achieving a successful life. From this point of view his approach reminds us the perspective of 'virtue ethic', centered on the qualities of agents involved in important tasks.

In its classical version, the paradigm of dignity as excellence was linked to the honour ethic because the ground for any prominence was greatness in action. Dignity and honour—that is the respect bestowed upon those that have dignity—depend on virtues, and virtues look at excellence in activities. The notion of goodness is then related to the meaning of accomplishment, success, and execution. This notion introduces certainly a dynamic perspective in evaluating a life's worth—it regards one of the possible faces of moral agency.

It is well known that Aristotle confers special importance to the virtue of magnanimity, the quality of those who consider themselves worthy of great things and devote themselves to them. Interestingly, he insists on magnanimous people not caring of honour bestowed from others (otherwise they will fall in vanity).[54] In this perspective, dignity is not to be understood as reciprocal, and here there is a relevant difference with the Kantian notion. Magnanimity is a quality in the middle between vanity and pusillanimity—the first is the search for honour 'in itself', and it is an excess; the second is the lack of appraisal for the calling towards a high and noble destiny, and it is defective (*Nicomachean Ethics*, 1233, 5). In addition, magnanimity is nullified by envy because what really matters is the implementation of great actions and not the comparison with others.[55] In other words, dignity as excellence is not egalitarian.

An approach grounded on excellence, in fact, is inevitably elitist and hierarchical in itself, that is, it creates a distance between who deserves dignity and others (Vincenti 2009: 153–4).[56] Virtues imply superiority and they are rare (Taylor 2002) or at least unequally distributed because they depend on personal freedom. A model centered on *dignitas* is meritocratic and elitist. But the most interesting thing to emphasize is that it looks at the future—in fact, dignity is not an award for the past even if it is recognized to those who give proof of existing virtues. It is a task to perform. Dignity—as well as virtues—is connected to functioning to be developed. Virtue ethic requests also an others regarding attitude, precisely because virtue is connected to valid actions to the advantage of others. Magnanimity makes virtues commitments towards the social group, instead of projects oriented to self-respect (Viola 2000: 4). From this point of view the very modern heritage of the paradigm of *dignitas* could be Waldron's translation of dignity in terms of citizenship as a rank and office. Between the universality of dignity and the hierarchical idea of *dignitas*, Waldron's proposal is to link dignity to (active) citizenship. Because of the modern relevance of equality, citizenship is considered a leveling up form of parity for citizens (Waldron 2012),[57] but he has to distinguish the dignity of citizens from the human dignity.

In search of a plausible idea of dignity, the centrality of the political community is a good point from a classical perspective, because the *polis* was precisely the frame of human flourishing, not just as a context, but rather as a means for achieving the knowledge of rights and wrongs (Aristotle, *Politics* 1253a 1–20).[58] There is a clear difference between a political community understood on the one hand as a fair framework of rights in which each one pursues her own interests and values, and on the other hand as a society able to produce virtuous citizens or, even more, a political community in search of what is right and wrong.[59] Every step towards a political society like this is another step away from liberalism.

The distinction between citizenship and human dignity is controversial, even from the point of view of dignity as a task. A dignity with an universal scope as commitment is perfectly fitting with the importance of magnanimity at the crossroad of the modern Western identity—Descartes' générosité consecrated by the principle of Enlightenment's morality according to which 'we all should work to improve the human condition, relieve suffering, overcome poverty, increase prosperity, augment human welfare. We should strive to leave the world a more prosperous place than we found it' (Taylor 1989: 85). It is obvious that the forms of commitment in this different, wider context must be different and probably more difficult to be determined (but not impossible) than in the case of citizenship. In some way this difficulty is linked to the fact that the universal scope of dignity expands strongly moral asymmetries. But Greek philosophy knew also how to give form to this position through cosmopolitanism. Nowadays it represents an important challenge (Trujillo 2015).[60]

It is possible to conclude provisionally that dignity in the context of rights (even considering the peculiar position of the bearer of duties) and dignity in the light of virtues are two different things. It is not only the difference between a dynamic versus a passive dignity. A reading of dignity for rights holders does not make any sense of dignity as greatness in action. Dworkin tries to link these both meanings through autonomy interpreted as the responsibility of living well (Dworkin 2011: 196). It means that within the limits and the luck of our lives—that saves the adverbial final value of each life (197)—we have to look for realizing a critically good life. In some way, this dynamic dignity is reflected in the centrality of empowerment in the practice of rights. But the dignity linked to virtues depends on the freedom of agents once they are empowered.

Apart from the risks for his liberalism, it has been observed that Dworkin's analysis in political morality emphasizes one of the aspects of the normative question about dignity. It regards what the worthy agent can do beyond the strict symmetry of equality (and then presumably in favour of others). The equal treatment due to each one is only the premise for the development of personal excellence in the domain of our relationships. Partially, this active notion of dignity fits with the engagement in the practice of protecting rights, even if Dworkin tends to attribute this task to the states, as well as with the rational and free agency in the context of the practice of the rule of law. But dignity goes beyond all these dimensions as long as it is the ground of our political responsibilities. It increases the impression that political commitments are the scenario of flourishing lives, and not only the field of limiting interferences.

In the next paragraph we will consider why Dworkin insists on the good life and how he understands it in the field of ethics. We have to take our lives seriously and not to waste them. This calling seems to make appeal to individual magnanimity. But dignity in ethics is not only that. Paradoxically, in some points, it seems that Dworkin is assuming also the continuity between ethics and morality and not only between morality and ethics. The thesis of the unity of value works in both directions.

Dignity as Justice from the Point of View of Ethics

Dworkin's concept of human dignity in the field of ethics is composed of two principles: self-respect and authenticity. According to the first one '[e]ach person must take his own life seriously: he must accept that it is a matter of importance that his life be a successful performance rather than a wasted opportunity' (2011: 203). According to the second one, '[e]ach person has a special, personal responsibility for identifying what counts as success in his own life; he has a personal responsibility to create that life through a coherent narrative or style that he himself endorses' (2011: 204). Authenticity is the other side of self-worth. These two principles can be examined separately even if they converge on dignity.

Self and Mutual Respect and Justice as a Virtue

The first principle is linked to what Dworkin understands as the objective value of a good life. As it has been said, the respect due to human beings is not an appraisal but a recognition of respect, linked to a shared status. This means that it is not relevant the value of just one individual and her merits, but it is a respect to be recognized as well to all the other people. On the one hand, the dimension of recognition leads to cross the line of ethics. In this sense, the principle confirms the continuity between ethics and morality. On the other hand, from the rule of reciprocity at the root of recognition arises the problem of indeterminacy of the fellowship—what other people? All citizens? All human beings? All those similar to us? On which basis?

In the perspective of ethics, there is a way in which it is possible to understand this principle in abstract, according to a rule of universalization—as long as each of us attributes importance to our own life (my own self-respect), we have to recognize that others' lives are important too (respect for others). Dworkin's notion of self-respect seems to follow this rule of reciprocity or universality in the Kantian fashion. But the original element is my own self-respect. The kind of dignity deriving from this reading is a sort of indirect dignity—others are worthy because *I am worthy*. The question is then why *am I worthy*? Am I worthy because I respect myself? Or do I respect myself because I am worthy? Here there is the worry of a possible circularity.

In the perspective of morality (what we owe to each other) this circularity can be accepted because the starting point is equality, but no justification can produce a result without people's consent and endorsement. At the end of the day, what Rawls called an interest to justice is necessary in order to assure equal concern and respect. As it is well-known, even if justice is the main virtue of political institutions, Rawls has to accept that each system of justice needs an attitude, a personal choice, a rational but personal concern from the part of citizens. It is a sense of justice that can be taught, in the family context, as well as in the political community (Rawls 1999: 3 and 46).[61] In Rawls's perspective, the nature of this interest is difficult to establish. From this point of view, Dworkin's proposal is more outspoken, and this is possible precisely—as it has been said—because he is openly trying to link the level of morality with that of ethics. In other words, he is linking the theory of justice to personal projects, attitudes, and abilities, that is, to virtues. In the perspective of the first person—her qualities, her choices, her virtues involved in actions—it is possible to identify this interest with virtue—the main virtue of justice as an agent's quality. He is so resuming a long and important tradition that it would be worthy to recuperate, because institutions depend on human beings.[62]

Aristotle defines justice as a moral attitude consisting in taking the same part of goods and evils in the social distribution. It is not just moderation, even if it is linked to it, as long as it is the contrary of avidity. Aristotle would say that justice consists in the disposition of taking for ourselves what we assign to others. It is the attitude of those who recognize the same value to own and others' lives. The just person does not take more than one's due of good. The unjust person is the one who takes the larger share of goods or the lesser part of evils (*Nicomachean Ethics*, 1130a, 10–11): doing so, she does not respect equality. As it is evident now, it is the opposite of Thrasymachus' idea that justice is nothing but the advantage of the stronger (Plato, *Republic* 338c).[63] According to a basic meaning, self-respect and respect for others go together because of justice, and this is what we call dignity—our self-respect is linked to our virtues, and in particular to the virtue of justice.

But the link between dignity and justice as a virtue is more intriguing. In some way, we can say that dignity does not imply justice, but it *is* justice, both in terms of the moral attitude described above and as a rule characterized by reciprocity. Dignity is in fact a bridge between ethics and morality because it concerns our attitudes and the way in which we consider others.[64] The meaning of dignity emerging in this perspective is obviously linked to equality. Instead of embracing the common liberal thesis of the priority of the right over the good—and the consequent separation between ethics and morality—it is interesting to note that for Dworkin a discourse on virtues is always thick, it involves the good. In light of the unity of value, this perspective is not eccentric. His idea is that the distinction between thick and thin is not polar but one of degree (2011: 182). The stimulating point is that—in Dworkin's opinion—duties and obligations are 'thicker than the concept of the good' because to say that someone has a duty 'suggests a promise or undertaking or some special responsibility of role or status' (2011: 182). What in the Aristotelian practical approach is built on the teleological nature of virtues,[65] it is here proposed in terms of a link to duties and responsibilities. It is not the idea of the duty as a rational mean for a good, but an addition to the potentiality of the good in terms of possibility–necessity. If you can, you should. It is a very demanding perspective that can be explained only in terms of aspirations.

The Aesthetic Analogy and the Three Meanings of Responsibility

As it is well known, in the first book of *Nicomachean Ethics*, Aristotle states that arts, research, human actions, and human choices tend to the good—their objective is a good. In some way, then, the good is to be seen as a consequence, a result, or an outcome as it comes after the human action and not before, even if it stands before as an end to achieve. It is what Dworkin tries to explain through the concept of responsibility as a relation between people and event—it is the responsibility for performing a good. This is the first meaning of responsibility.

The aesthetic analogy serves to explain the dynamicity, context-specificity, and singularity of human actions. It could help the Kantian idea of reflective judgment (Ginsborg 2014).[66] Both the teleological and aesthetic judgments contain the goal, in Kantian terms, the rule of its excellence in themselves.

Its reflective character serves to highlight the modern idea of goal that is not given from outside, as a given order. The link between the work and its rule, and then to its fulfilment, comes from inside.

Nevertheless, according to Aristotle, the goal/outcome of human actions can be an activity or a work. In the latter case, the result is something other than the exercise of skills. It is the thing produced (the house for the building). Where there is no other result besides the exercise, the activity in itself is the result (the seeing for the seer). In this way he distinguishes immanent and transitive activities (Aristotle's *Metaphysics*, 1050a).[67] The first ones are those that make good human beings; the second ones are those that perform excellence in techniques. The analogy between art and virtues is in fact imperfect because in art the final product is worthy in itself, separate from its author. In an act performing a virtue the whole person is involved in terms of knowledge, choice, and character.

It is not possible to introduce further clarifications on what a teleological perspective would imply for the reading of human actions, even if this is the point in which any enquiry on Aristotle's influence must be decided. The idea—in ethical perspective—can be illustrated in terms of functions. Virtues are practical forms of completing a potential human orientation, similar to the idea of competence (Taylor 2002). The world of virtues is that of the correct way of knowledge (theoretical and practical), of using well material goods, of enjoying the right pleasures, of using strength for what is worthy, with courage and fortitude, and so on. There is also a potentiality of being just human (Aristotle, *Nicomachean Ethics*, 1178), that is, in realizing successfully our humanity. At the end of the day, an achieved life is the one that performs all these skills. In Dworkin's words, it is unsuccessful the one that wastes all those potentialities. It is not only a problem of choices, but of good choices, as we will see below when we will look at the difference between authenticity and autonomy. Virtues aim at some goods, and then they are grounded on thick arguments that could only be made within a certain culture and context. They generate also responsibilities related to the potentiality of the good pursued.

The second principle of dignity has two aspects: the principle of autonomy or ethical independence (Dworkin 2011: 211) in identifying what counts as good for us, and the principle of commitment or our responsibility as a virtue (210) in putting our project into effect. It is worth noting that Dworkin denies the identification between authenticity and autonomy (212), and this is the case because authenticity 'is very much concerned with the character as well as the fact of obstacle to choice. Living well means not just designing a life, as if any design would do, but designing it in response to a judgment of ethical value. Authenticity is damaged when a person is made to accept someone else's judgment in place of his own about the values or goals his life would display' (212). Authenticity implies then an autonomous judgment in the context of an objective value for our lives, '[w]e cannot escape influence, but we must resist domination' (212). Authenticity includes autonomy or ethical independence, but it is not reduced to it.[68] In fact, authenticity requests a personal commitment with a design of a good life, '[a]uthenticity is not a taste, but a necessary virtue' (213). The emphasis on virtue is related to the personal engagement, and this fits with the idea of virtues as deriving from namely, force and commitment. The dimension of commitment is in some way related to the idea of responsibility—responsibility as a virtue, its second meaning. Among virtues, together with justice or equality, authenticity seems to be particularly relevant for a good life. In his last works, the impression is that for Dworkin, not only equality, but also authenticity is a sovereign virtue. In part, this is because the principle according to which each one has a particular responsibility on her own life implies—in the field of morality—maximum rights to freedom. But in part it is also because only a personal commitment can lead to a good life.

The link between authenticity and dignity goes through the idea of personal judgment and commitment. It is not a good life, but *my good life*, the life for which I am responsible. Being my life means that I am responsible for it. This is important for establishing the goodness of our lives according to a subjective parameter; it depends on the first person's commitment. 'The value of our striving is adverbial; it does not lie in the goodness or impact of the life realized. That is why people who live and die in great poverty can nevertheless live well. Even so we must each do what we can to make our own life as good as it could have been. You live badly if you do not try hard enough to make your life good' (2011: 419–20).

Following the analogy between human acts and the aesthetic production, Dworkin states that the work of art is beautiful because it is the outcome of a value performance; it embodies a performance (197). Its value does not correspond to its product value but to its value performance. This is important for considering human lives as achievements, independently of their actual value. It is a result possible for all thanks to the adverbial value of a life lived well. Even in difficult circumstances, human life can be the upshot of a value performance. On the contrary, sometimes adverse circumstances make the performance more appreciable. But the more we insist on this subjective parameter, the less the objective parameter is relevant. As Philippa Foot explains, the difference between art and actions is that in the first case it is better a voluntary mistake than an involuntary one; in the second case the reverse is valid. In mistaking the spelling of a word it is better to know the correct way and not to do it, than the contrary. From the point of view of ethical behaviour it is better the contrary (Foot 1978: 7–8).[69] In the ethical field, ignorance exculpates.

What about morality? This is the very Achilles' heel in Dworkin's doctrine—when others are involved our ethical independence is limited. Not only because they can have a different point of view—because of pluralism, that is compatible with the unity of value—but rather because what is good for us can be different from what is right for me. In some way, we share a common destiny. For this reason the search on the good was, for Greek philosophers, a common enterprise. Moral autonomy is the premise for a good life, but it is not enough for a good state. And this probably is the weaker point in Dworkin's contribution.

Together with the two meanings of responsibility indicated, as virtue and as relation between people and event (2011: 102), there seems to be a third one— responsibility towards others. In fact, responsibility is a reactive attitude that arises from our interpersonal links and affiliations. This kind of responsibility assumes the existence of concrete others to which we have to respond. Dworkin is very keen to stress that it is misleading to say that we answer to ourselves (196). The third meaning of responsibility can be introduced by the second one—I can be responsible for something that happens to you. Otherwise, each swimmer stays better in her own lane (371). Why, then, would a moral and autonomous agent respond to others? There remains the same circular perplexity: am I worthy because responsible or responsible because worthy?

***

Dworkin's analysis of dignity is of paramount importance and interest. Apart from the audacious task of facing a controversial concept, choosing it as the key of the department of value, and even if he does not distinguish some of the different questions, meanings, and dimensions here separated (the identity question, the normative one; dignity as worth, dignity as a challenge; the different models of dignity), he points at its role as a starting point in deliberation, and he establishes it as the *fil rouge* that justifies the continuity between morality and ethics.

His reading on virtues and personal excellence introduces new perspectives in a political theory wholly colonized by rights and correlative duties. The symmetry of justice in fact erodes any possibility of complementary relationship between different agents. His different stand-point—dignity and responsibilities for a good life, inspired by Greek philosophy—paradoxically makes possible to maintain and develop a certain degree of asymmetry in morality. He is so emphasizing the challenge that each one faces—to perform a salient life in the context of what we owe to each other.

There remain strong perplexities deriving from his taken for granted endorsement of liberalism. His extraordinary appreciation of ethical independence explains the paramount value of liberty and his understanding of state and authority as related to the equilibrium between freedom and coercion. He perhaps forgets that Aristotle states that human beings are able to go into partnerships precisely because they are neither lower animals nor gods (*Politics* 1253a)—neither incapable of distinctions produced by freedom, nor self-sufficient in their good life.

Notes and References

1. Ronald Dworkin. 2011. *Justice for Hedgehogs*. Cambridge, Mass. & London: The Belknap Press of Harvard University Press.
2. The bibliography on dignity is vast and covers multiple areas of research, from constitutional to international law; from political to moral philosophy; from religion to bioethics. For an elaborate demonstration, see for instance, Marcus Düwell, Jens Braarvig, Rogerd Brownsword, and Dietmor Mieth (eds). 2014. *The Cambridge Handbook of Human Dignity: Interdisciplinary Perspectives*. Cambridge: Cambridge University Press.
3. Michael Walzer. 1994. *Thick and Thin: Moral Argument at Home and Abroad*. Notre Dame: University of Notre Dame Press. As it is well-known, Dworkin faces the difference between thick and thin discussing Williams' distinction (1985). This topic is explored later in the chapter. See Bernard Williams. 1985. *Ethics and the Limits of Philosophy*. Cambridge, Mass. & London: The Belknap Press of Harvard University Press.
4. Aristotle. 1984. 'Topics', in Jonathan Barnes (ed.), *Complete Works of Aristotle: The Revised Oxford Translation* Vol. 1. Princeton: Princeton University Press. pp. 167–277.
5. John Tasioulas. 2013. 'Human Dignity and the Foundations of Human Rights', in Christopher McCrudden (ed.), *Understanding Human Dignity*. Oxford: Oxford University Press. pp. 293–314.
6. David Luban. 2010. 'The Rule of Law and Human Dignity: Re-examining Fuller's Canons', *Hague Journal on the Rule of Law* 2: 29–47.
7. Ruth Macklin. 2003. 'Dignity is a Useless Concept', *British Medical Journal* 327: pp. 1419–20.
8. Steven Pinker. 2008. 'The Stupidity of Dignity', *The New Republic* 28 May: pp. 28–31.
9. Aharon Barak. 2015. *Human Dignity*. Cambridge: Cambridge University Press. Barak censures Dworkin's theory of dignity because of the idea of the unity of

value. He seems to understand that this notion is not compatible with the way in which constitutions deal with dignity, that is, in a pluralistic framework of values. As we will see, dignity—also in the light of Dworkin's thesis of the unity of value—is dealing with plural values.

10. Ronald Dworkin. 2006. *Is Democracy Possible Here? Principles for a New Political Debate.* Princeton: Princeton University Press.
11. Thomas M. Scanlon. 2000. *What We Owe to Each Other.* Cambridge, Mass. & London: The Belknap Press of Harvard University Press. It is plausible that what is against our self-respect will also be against our dignity, but the problem will then be the intrinsic link between responsibility and dignity.
12. In the quoted paragraphs Dworkin is facing the problem of how much we have to help others. As it is well known, from the Utilitarian approach it is difficult to establish a measure for personal sacrifices. Dworkin is solving this particular problem with the recourse to autonomous judgment. A good comparison between Dworkin and Peter Singer on this point can be found in Macario Alemany. 2015. 'Ricos y pobres: sobre el fundamento y alcance del deber de ayuda al prójimo', *Doxa. Cuadernos de Filosofía del derecho* 38: pp. 159–88.
13. Frances M. Kamm. 2010. 'What Ethical Responsibility Cannot Justify: A Discussion of Ronald Dworkin's *Justice for Hedgehogs*', *Boston University Law Review* 90: pp. 691–713.
14. Charles Taylor. 1989. *Sources of the Self: The Making of the Modern Identity.* Cambridge: Cambridge University Press.
15. Richard Taylor. 2002. *Virtue Ethics.* New York: Prometheus Books.
16. Francesco Viola. 2000. *Etica e metaetica dei diritti umani.* Torino: Giappichelli.
17. Rainer Forst. 2002. *Contexts of Justice: Political Philosophy beyond Liberalism and Communitarianism.* Oakland: University of California Press.
18. Catharine MacKinnon. 2006. *Are Women Human? And Other International Dialogues.* Cambridge, Mass. & London: The Belknap Press of Harvard University Press.
19. Norberto Bobbio. 1996. *The Age of Rights.* tr. Allan Cameron. Cambridge: Polity Press.
20. Fundamental rights indicate a form of rights' protection: through state tools. Human rights indicate the international covering of this practice. In a less technical meaning, the second includes the first one. Dworkin prefers the formula political rights when he speaks of rights against the state, as will be seen in the next section. But also human rights can be seen as rights against the states.
21. About the thesis according to which the variety of meanings and its context-specificity make dignity open to the risk of judicial manipulation, see Christopher McCrudden. 2008. 'Human Dignity and Judicial Interpretation of Human Rights', *The European Journal of International Law* 19 (4): pp. 655–724.
22. As it is well known the responsibility to protect in a technical meaning is a doctrine about the duties of states in protecting rights, developed after the Secretary General's Report on Implementing the Responsibility to Protect 2009,

regarding in particular collective acts of reaction to rights' violations through the so-called—ambiguously—humanitarian interventions.

23. It is interesting to note that natural rights were linked to the category of *dominium*, another way of indicating the eminence of human beings. Firstly, *dominium* means a status worth, a position of eminence. Second, it implies a reading of freedom and a relationship of power over other things. When at the beginning of the Modern Age some authors of the Second Scholastic formulated the question whether the Indians have *dominium*, they intended to establish if they had dignity, and then rights. See, Francisco de Vitoria. 1991. *Political Writings*. ed. Anthony Pagden, tr. Jeremy Lawrence. Cambridge: Cambridge University Press.

    A recent and useful comparison between natural rights and human rights in historical perspective can be found in Brett 2016. Annabel Brett. 2016. 'Human rights and the Thomist tradition', in Pamela Slotte and Miia Halme-Tuomisaari (eds), *Revisiting the Origins of Human Rights*. Cambridge: Cambridge University Press. pp. 82–102.

24. Samuel Moyn. 2010. *The Last Utopia: Human Rights in History*. Cambridge, Mass.: The Belknap Press of Harvard University Press.

25. Isabel Trujillo and Francesco Viola. 2014. *What Human Rights Are Not (or Not Only)*. New York: Novascience Publishers.

26. Amartya K. Sen. 2004. 'Elements of a Theory of Human Rights', *Philosophy & Public Affairs* 32(4): pp. 315–56.

27. Joseph Raz. 1988. *The Morality of Freedom*. Oxford: Clarendon Press.

28. It seems O'Neill's aim defending the thesis of priority of duties because of the imperfection of rights without them, see Onora O'Neill. 1996. *Towards Justice and Virtue: A Constructive Account of Practical Reason*. Cambridge: Cambridge University Press.

29. The morality of aspirations or the morality of excellence has become famous with Fuller's *The Morality of Law* (1969). It has been identified as the opposite to a morality of duties in which in order to establish if an act is right or wrong the criterion is the conformity to a duty. It has had a discrete diffusion in professional ethics, as long as the best professional behaviour does not correspond to the fulfilment of professional duties, but consists in search of professional excellence. This morality has to do with our efforts to make the best use of our lives.

30. David Luban. 2000. 'Natural Law as Professional Ethics: A Reading of Fuller', *Social Philosophy and Policy* 18(1): pp. 176–205.

31. Richard Taylor's thesis is that the change from the ancient ideal of personal excellence to a model of morality focused on duties and rules, followed also by the affirmation of the equal dignity of all individuals without distinction, has been determined by the influence of religions. According to Taylor's statements, even when their position is atheism, many contemporary thinkers still use to move within this paradigm, denying the foundations, but maintaining the framework (Taylor 2002).

32. Paul Craig. 1997. 'Formal and Substantive Conceptions of the Rule of Law: An Analytical Framework', *Public Law*. pp. 467–87.
33. About the no-rights conception of the rule of law see Evan Fox-Decent. 2008. 'Is the Rule of Law Really Indifferent to Human Rights?', *Law and Philosophy* 27(6): 533–81.
34. See Ronald Dworkin. 1985. 'Political Judges and the Rule of Law' in Ronald Dworkin, *A Matter of Principle*. Cambridge: Harvard University Press. pp. 9–32. As it is well known, on the contrary, the opposite position states that the rule of law 'is not to be confused with democracy, justice, equality (before the law or otherwise), human rights of any kind or respect for persons or for the dignity of man [...]. The law may, for example, institute slavery without violating the rule of law.' See Joseph Raz. 1979. 'The Rule of Law and Its Virtue', in Joseph Raz, *The Authority of Law: Essays on Law and Morality*. Oxford: Clarendon Press. pp. 210–32.
35. Rule of law is obviously linked to public powers, but it is open the question whether any form of norm building processes must be subjected to a similar mechanism.
36. Lon Fuller. 1969. *The Morality of Law*. New Haven: Yale University Press.
37. Hannah Arendt. 1958. *The Origins of Totalitarianism*. Cleveland: World Publishing Company.
38. Jeremy Waldron. 2011. 'Are Sovereigns Entitled to the Benefit of the International Rule of Law?', *The European Journal of International Law* 22(2): 315–43.
39. Samantha Besson. 2011. 'Sovereignty, International Law and Democracy', *The European Journal of International Law* 22(2): 373–87.
40. Ronald Dworkin. 2013. 'A New Philosophy for International Law', *Philosophy & Public Affairs* 41(1): 2–30.
41. This is the very meaning of Dworkin's notion of political rights: rights against the state.
42. I have defended the idea of the duty towards our fellowships as conditioned priorities in Isabel Trujillo. 2007. *Giustizia globale. Le nuove frontiere dell'eguaglianza*. Bologna: Il Mulino.
43. Aristotle. 1984. 'Nicomachean Ethics', in Jonathan Barnes (ed.), *Complete Works of Aristotle: The Revised Oxford Translation* Vol. 2. Princeton: Princeton University Press. pp. 1729–867.
44. Jeremy Waldron (ed.). 1984. *Theories of Rights*. Oxford: Oxford University Press.
45. Martha C. Nussbaum and Amartya K. Sen (eds). 1993. *The Quality of Life*. Oxford: Clarendon Press.
46. Martha C. Nussbaum. 2006. *Frontiers of Justice. Disability, Nationality, Species Membership*. Cambridge, Mass. & London: The Belknap Press of Harvard University Press.
47. It has been observed that the idea of rights as shields reminds us that rights are quasi-possessions of the agent to whom rights are attributed, and then dignity as a possessed quality.
48. Stephen Darwall. 1977. 'Two Kinds of Respect', *Ethics*. 88(1): 36–49.

49. Francesco Viola. 2013. *Lo statuto normativo della dignità umana.* In Angelo Abignente and Francesca Scamardella (eds), *Dignità della persona. Riconoscimento dei diritti nelle società multiculturali.* Napoli: Edizioni Scientifiche. pp. 283–95.

50. In *Is Democracy possible here?*, Dworkin compares American and European approaches to hate speech and he seems to say that prohibiting hate speech is wrong even if in good faith (Dworkin 2006: 38).

51. Immanuel Kant. 2012. *Groundwork for the Metaphysics of Morals*, Mary Gregor and Jens Timmermann (eds). Cambridge: Cambridge University Press.

52. As it is well known, Margalit (1996) has proposed an idea of dignity explained in terms of belonging to humanity. Each human being is an icon of humanity and from this point of view the individual performance in term of virtues and responsibilities is not relevant. See Avishai Margalit. 1996. *The Decent Society.* Cambridge, Mass. & London: The Belknap Press of Harvard University Press.

53. From Aquinas (*Summa theologiae* II–II, q. 63, a. 3c) to Thomas Hobbes (*De Homine* 1658, chapter 3) and John Locke (*The Reasonableness of Christianity, As deliver'd in the Scriptures* 1736). The Christian perspective on dignity involves always the dimension of the intrinsic value of human beings, together with that of a task to perform. At least, this seems to be the best reading of human beings as image of God, and it is clear in the connection between this likeness and their role as custodians of creation.

54. Richard Taylor writes, commenting on this point, that a proud man needs nothing from others, or nearly nothing, but he willingly renders service to others (2002, ebook pos. 1011). Aristotle explains that honour is the greatest of external goods, but it cannot be searched in itself (*Nicomachean Ethics* 1132b, 18–22).

55. As it is well known, Dworkin proposes the envy test as a device for distributive justice, even if recently he has recognized that the test fails because of the market (2011: pp. 356–7).

56. Umberto Vincenti. 2009. *Diritti e dignità umana.* Roma-Bari: Laterza.

57. Jeremy Waldron. 2012. *Dignity, Rank, and Rights.* Oxford: Oxford University Press.

58. Aristotle. 1984. 'Politics', in Jonathan Barnes (ed.), *Complete Works of Aristotle: The Revised Oxford Translation* Vol. 2. Princeton: Princeton University Press. pp. 1552–728. In his book on the honour code, Appiah deepens the engine of honour-shame as a means of moral progress of civilizations (2010). His way of conceiving the search of what is right and wrong through shame and honour is an interesting way of translating the ancient idea of the epistemological dimension of moral research. See Kwane A. Appiah. 2010. *The Honor Code: How Moral Revolutions Happen.* New York: W.W. Norton & Company.

59. This is what motivates the Communitarian approaches to Politics, with their limits: the idea that we need epistemological traditions for the research on justice. The problem in the background is what Charles Taylor (1989: 36–40) calls the perspective of identity, that is an unfamiliar problem for liberalism. We need horizons of goods against which our freedom has to be determined.

60. Isabel Trujillo. 2015. 'Cosmopolitanism and Human Rights', in Lorena Cebolla, Francesco Ghia (eds), *Cosmopolitanism: Between Ideals and Reality*. Newcastle upon Tyne: Cambridge Scholars Publishing: pp. 10–34.

61. John Rawls. 1999. *A Theory of Justice*. Oxford: Oxford University Press.

62. This can be applied to the problem of corruption: there can be institutions more or less easily influenceable, but without the personal engagement in justice of those that take part in them is difficult to prevent their deterioration.

63. Plato. 1968. *The Republic of Plato*. Allam Bloom (ed.). New York: Basic Books. (second edition).

64. Translating this idea in Finnis's vocabulary, it can be said that the notion of general justice (*Nicomachean Ethics* 1129b26–1130a13) indicates the maximum of practical reasonableness in dealing with our relationships. Finnis's explanation of virtues and vices in terms of practical reasonableness substitutes the reference to human nature (1980: VII, 2). See John Finnis. 1980. *Natural Law and Natural Rights*. Oxford: Clarendon Press.

65. It can be said simply that we are in the sphere of practical reason in which human acts are seen as having a finalistic structure caused by goals.

66. Hannah Ginsborg. 2014. 'Kant's Aesthetics and Teleology', in Edward N. Zalta (ed.), *The Stanford Encyclopedia of Philosophy*. Available at https://plato.stanford.edu/entries/kant-aesthetics/ (accessed on 17 August 2016).

67. Aristotle. 1984. 'Metaphysics', in Jonathan Barnes (ed.), *Complete Works of Aristotle: The Revised Oxford Translation* Vol. 2. Princeton: Princeton University Press. pp. 1986–2129.

68. As happens when dignity is identified with autonomy, the former becomes useless and stupid (Pinker 2008).

69. Philippa Foot. 1978. *Virtues and Vices and Other Essays in Moral Philosophy*. Berkeley & Los Angeles: University of California Press.

PART III

FREEDOM OF SPEECH, RIGHT TO PRIVACY, AND HUMAN RIGHTS

11

Dignity and Free Speech

David A.J. Richards

The value of dignity has played a prominent role in the understanding of basic human rights that Ronald Dworkin defended as the basis for the authority and legitimacy of the role constitutional judiciaries, including the United States Supreme Court, play in invalidating laws, state and federal, that abridge constitutionally guarantees of basic human rights, for example, the protections of liberties of conscience and speech in the First Amendment of the American Bill of Rights. It is a distinctive feature of the judicially enforced American conception of free speech that the hate speech laws, regarded as consistent with guarantees of free speech in other constitutional democracies, are unconstitutional.[1] Dworkin himself regarded the American view as the more defensible interpretation of the value of dignity that justifies the rights of conscience and speech as basic human rights as a matter of liberal political theory.[2] But, more recently, one of Dworkin's students, Jeremy Waldron, has argued, on the basis of the value of dignity to which both he and Dworkin appeal as the normative basis of human rights, that the American view is mistaken; as he puts it, the harm in hate speech (the injury to dignity) justifies such laws, which, properly understood, do not compromise but rather advance dignity, the value underlying free speech.[3] In this article, I address this question as a matter of liberal political theory in which, as both Dworkin and Waldron agree, the value of dignity plays the central role, and argue that Dworkin has the more defensible view as a matter of liberal political theory.

Dignity plays a role in liberal political theory in the justification, both of the principle of equal human rights that are constitutionally protected from majoritarian politics and the principle of non-discrimination that constitutionally condemns the political expression of the irrational prejudices of religious intolerance, racism, sexism, and homophobia. It is because dignity plays the role it does in the justification of both principles that we can best understand why, consistent with Dworkin's position, the expansive and muscular American understanding of free speech, one that condemns hate speech laws, better realizes the underlying value of dignity central to both principles. To understand why this is so, we must examine the role dignity plays in the justification of both principles, which are, I believe, closely connected in ways that are often not fully understood or appreciated.

I start with the justification of the principle protecting basic human rights, in particular, the rights to conscience and speech that are my central topic here. What these interconnected rights identify for protection are the higher order interests we have as persons in the twin moral powers of rationality and reasonableness in leading our lives as agents. By rationality, I understand the principles that we bring to bear reflecting both on our system of ends and the ways better to realize our ends. By reasonableness, I understand, following Kant and Rawls,[4] the principles we can accept and offer to one another as the ultimate standards that reasonably regulate all our lives on terms of equal respect for our sovereignty as persons over our ends.[5] Conscience and speech are basic human rights because they protect the exercise of these twin moral powers that make possible living a life from reflective normative conviction, both prudential and ethical, as embodied agents pursuing our system of ends on the integrated basis of experience, thought, and feeling in real relationship to other persons.

Human lives, from our vulnerable and fragile infancies on forward, are lived in relationship, learning to understand ourselves as we learn to read the human world around us on which we depend for care, growth, understanding, and support into an inter-subjective world of shared language and community, including intimate life, religion and philosophy, art, science, work, and politics. Both our rationality and reasonableness are nurtured and sustained and exercised in and through interpersonal relationships.[6] All our experience of the history of our common humanity shows, however, that some interpersonal relationships may not only frustrate our moral powers, but may war on them, as the aggressively inhuman totalitarianisms of the twentieth century clearly show,[7] pre-figured in the long history of violence keyed to creating and giving effect to dividing us from one another and our common humanity through unjust and anti-democratic hierarchies keyed to differences in religion, ethnicity, gender, and sexuality. It is because of such historically validated serious and sometimes deadly threats to our moral powers, as persons and moral agents, that we can understand the place and role and status of the principle of equal liberties of conscience and speech as basic human rights. Such rights are among the minimal ethical conditions for all interpersonal relationships and, in particular, those political relationships that define what counts as legitimate political power in all its forms. I focus here on the requirements these rights impose on what can count as any legitimate politics, whether democratic or not.

We understand better today, perhaps, than we ever have, the ways in which unjust political arrangements, through strategies of control and domination based on violence and intimidation and terror, may lead whole populations of putatively civilized peoples literally to lose any sense of the ethical responsibilities of care and respect owed other persons that arise from the free exercise of our moral powers. Such a politics of terror, based on aggressive violence aroused by any even imagined threat to its authority, leads its victims, sometimes the whole population, to identify with the demands of the aggressor, an identification that is certainly not a real relationship among equals, and indeed makes possible, through traumatizing the human psyche, the dehumanization of scapegoats, setting the stage for squalidly self-righteous genocide (Arendt 1968). Such politics, which has existed in some form in human societies throughout our recorded history, literally cuts our sense of humane connections to one another, the ability to read and respond to a human world of other persons that is one of our most important evolutionary strengths as a species capable of ethical thought and feeling.[8]

The urgent priority of rights to conscience and speech among other values makes sense against the background of such de-humanizing threats to our common humanity, not least because after the nightmare totalitarianisms of the twentieth century we now appreciate the ways in which such dehumanizing threats, when not resisted, make possible catastrophic violence. Rights to conscience and speech must be understood against this background as indispensable expressions of the appropriate and indeed demanded respect for our competence, each and every one of us as persons, for the free exercise of our moral powers, and thus of our dignity in living our lives from the rational and reasonable convictions, reflective thoughts and feelings, that enable us to give shape to our lives as agents in a moral community of real relationships based on freedom and equality.

Both the scope and limits of the principles of conscience and speech must be understood against this background. The scope of free conscience and speech, at least when understood as serving the background value of dignity, requires that politics is only legitimate when it expresses equal respect for all forms of conscience and their expressions in speech rooted in the exercise of authentically believed convictions rooted in the twin moral powers of rationality and reasonableness. While these principles constrain politics or what can count as legitimate politics, the scope of the principle of free speech is importantly not limited to political speech, as other theories of free speech sometimes mistakenly and disastrously assume. The free exercise of the twin moral powers is at the core of a well lived human life, and little of human life, including what is most valuable in the relationships central to a good life, is lived in politics or indeed has anything to do with politics. So, the scope of free conscience and speech is much broader than political speech, extending to the full range of the exercise of the convictions expressive of our moral powers, including the sciences and the imaginative creative arts in all their complex and sometimes erotic forms. What marks the core of protected speech is any and all expressions of conviction addressed to the public mind or heart of one's community, including expressions of conviction fundamentally critical of the values of one's community. Because the scope of free speech is thus rooted in expressions of conviction, it does not include speech that does not express conviction, for example, speech known or believed to be false by the speaker, which, of course, does not express belief and thus conviction (for example, fraud, or defamation of individuals, both believed to be false when spoken). Nor does the scope of free speech extend to the disclosure of those private, though true, facts in which there is no legitimate public interest, disclosures that compromise the value of control of one's private life that is also an aspect of the individuality central to respect for our dignity.[9]

Within the scope of speech that is within this principle (namely, conscientious expressions of conviction about matters of public interest aimed at one's community), the principle of free speech forbids the state to engage in forms of censorship that express the state's judgment of what counts as good or bad speech in the domain of conviction. The anti-censorship principle precisely forbids such state judgments because of a wholly legitimate skepticism that such judgments, as has been the history of censorship throughout human history, in fact not only preserves the state from legitimate criticism, but preserves as well from criticism of the sectarian religions and ideologies, whether majoritarian or not, that often use the state to enforce their unjust sectarian demands. What the principle of free speech thus centrally protects is the right of each and every person to hear the judgments of conviction of other persons, and to make its own judgments as to the worth or value of the speech in question, including coming to entertain reasonable doubts about otherwise hegemonic sectarian religions or ideologies.

The skepticism about exercises of state power in this domain of conviction extends and must extend, on the ground of the dignity of our twin moral powers, precisely to those expressions of conviction that give offense. Otherwise, the critical role of free speech, as an exercise of our moral powers in the criticism of dominant sectarian religions and ideologies, would be compromised precisely when it is most needed, as people continue to a life never critically examined, one that never engages their moral powers and indeed makes them vulnerable to violent ideologies whose violence is elicited precisely by any threat to the legitimacy of the ideology placed in doubt by such criticism. The principle of free speech, as a political principle, constrains only the power of the state. Indeed, part of its point is to remove the repressive role of the state in the domain of conviction, and open each and every person themselves to make judgments on the issues of conviction central to a life humanely lived from within, with a sense of responsibility for one's convictions and for the life that gives expression to those convictions.

Both the basic human rights of conscience and speech require the state to constrain its power in the domain of convictions for reasons of equal respect for the dignity of the free exercise of our moral powers. Neither right, however, extends to the sometimes harmful acts of violence rooted in conviction, nor to unjust acts similarly motivated. Even in the United States, with the robust and muscular protection of speech that I have, in part, here defended as the best understanding of political liberalism, the principles in question have not been applied to harmful or unjust actions, though such actions are sometimes rooted in conviction. The criminal law of homicide fully applies to murders rooted in conviction, and the anti-discrimination laws that forbid discriminatory actions on grounds of religion, race, gender, and sexual orientation are constitutionally legitimate.

Speech that allegedly incites to violence has, however, been constitutionally protected, but the principle has properly been limited to public conscientious speech (not threats targeted to some person on his property)[10] which can only be forbidden if the violence is very harmful, highly probable, and not rebuttable by opposing public debate.[11] The concern, consistent with the underlying value of dignity, is that the offensiveness of the speech itself should not be a ground for state censorship, usurping the critical powers of each and every person themselves to confront and question the speech with which they disagree. The American principle of free speech, which limits the power of the state to censor such speech, has empowered groups like the National Association for the Advancement of Coloured People (NAACP) and the

Anti-Defamation League to confront and criticize the racist and anti-Semitic speech they oppose, and they have sometimes been notably successful in the American court of public opinion, in part because state censorship plays no role in these matters and responsibility rests with a free people.

I turn now to the question of hate speech laws, but, before addressing that question, I want to frame that discussion by an account of how the same value of dignity, which grounds the human rights of conscience and speech, also grounds the principle of anti-discrimination that condemns the expression through law or policy of religious intolerance, racism, sexism, and homophobia. It is on the basis of this discussion that I hope to show the value of dignity justifies both the human rights of conscience and speech and the anti-discrimination principle, and, properly understood, neither principle can reasonably be understood to justify hate speech laws.

I earlier explained the urgency of the priority of the human rights of conscience and speech as responses to the nature of the dehumanizing threats to them and our common humanity, not least because after the nightmare totalitarianisms of the twentieth century we now appreciate the ways in which such dehumanizing threats, when not resisted, make possible catastrophic violence.[12] We have also come to appreciate something else, namely, that these dehumanizing threats express often deeply entrenched, irrationalist cultural prejudices and that these prejudices are properly condemned as violations of the principle of anti-discrimination. I have elsewhere explored in depth the cultural background of such prejudices in terms of what I called 'moral slavery'.[13] By moral slavery, I understand a longstanding cultural prejudice—whether an extreme religious intolerance like anti-Semitism, or racism, or sexism, or homophobia—all of which may reasonably be understood and explicated in terms of an entrenched culture that targets with hostility whole groups of persons in terms of insults to the dignity of their twin moral powers: first, the group in question is deprived of all the basic human rights accorded to other persons (not only the rights of conscience and speech but of intimate life and work); and second, such abridgement of basic human rights is rationalized in terms of dehumanizing stereotypes (whether anti-Semitic, or racist, or sexist, or homophobic) whose force depends, in a vicious circularity, on the abridgement of the basic human rights of the group. In the United States, for example, race has been regarded as the paradigm case of a suspect classification that may not be a basis for law and policy because American slavery, only constitutionally abolished in 1865 by the Thirteenth Amendment to the United States Constitution, was rationalized by racism—only people of colour, regarded as subhuman, could be held in slavery and therefore not eligible for the basic rights of conscience, speech, intimate life, and labour, all of which were abridged by American slavery. After the constitutional abolition of slavery in the wake of the American Civil War and a defeat which humiliated the proud people of the South, American racism, if anything, worsened as a virulent racism scapegoated the people of colour now emancipated from slavery. This was supported by a pervasive pattern of racial segregation, illegitimately validated by the Supreme Court in 1898 in *Plessy v. Ferguson*[14] that created a racist caste system quite foreign to American traditions, and enforced as well by the violent terror of the atrocities of lynching, all of which aimed to deprive or abridge the basic rights of conscience, speech, intimate life, and work now constitutionally owed people of colour by the anti-discrimination principle of the Equal Protection Clause of the Fourteenth Amendment of the United States Constitution, ratified in 1868.[15]

What is common as well to the irrationalist prejudices of extreme religious intolerance (anti-Semitism), sexism, and homophobia is a similarly entrenched, longstanding cultural tradition of moral slavery. In each case, an entire group of persons was dehumanized in terms of the two features of moral slavery: the group was deprived of the basic human rights (conscience, speech, intimate life, and work) all other persons enjoyed, and that abridgement was rationalized in terms of stereotypes that, in a vicious circularity, drew their force from the abridgement of the basic human rights, including conscience and speech, that would have empowered the dehumanized groups reasonably to resist and contest the stereotypes that dehumanized them. In the case of homophobia, gays, lesbians, and transgendered persons were, in contrast to other dehumanized groups, literally regarded as unspeakable, not accorded any acknowledged cultural space at all.[16]

What is, I believe, importantly common to all these cultural forms of moral slavery is something that has not, I believe, been sufficiently noted, let alone appreciated. All of them were enforced by forms of irrationalist violence, forms of terror (intimidating both thought and feeling) that held such groups of person in the abject position in which moral slavery subjected them. While I believe this case can reasonably be made with respect to all the irrationalist prejudices I have identified and discussed, the point can be most starkly illustrated through the American experience of African-American resistance to American slavery. What should strike us about such resistance—whether the advocacy of the NAACP or the pacifism of Bayard Rustin or the civil disobedience of Martin Luther King, Jr.—is the crucially important role non-violence played in such resistance. Both Rustin and King carefully studied the forms of public non-violent resistance developed and deployed by Mohandas Gandhi first in South Africa and later in British India.[17] It cut against much in the conventional understanding of manhood that resistance to injustice should not take the form of violent resistance, but rather men and women, themselves the victims of terrible injustice, should resist through disciplined, deliberative, collective strategies of non-violent resistance to injustice, including civil disobedience. What made these strategies so brilliantly successful both in India and in the United Sates is the ways in which Gandhi in India, trained in London as a British lawyer, and Martin Luther King, Jr., a brilliant student of both American Christianity and constitutionalism, understood, used, and sometimes expanded, in the case of Gandhi, the political liberalism of Great Britain and, in the case of King, the liberalism of the United States Constitution. Martin Luther King, Jr. is usually honoured for the role he played in mobilizing and leading a civil rights movement that culminated in two enduring milestones in the struggle against American racism, the Civil Rights Act of 1964 and the Voting Rights Act of 1965, both of which draw upon and expand the principle of anti-discrimination. But, King's non-violent resistance, precisely because of its disciplined non-violence, used and expanded the American understanding of free speech, including, as it now does, the conscientious speech that fundamentally criticizes American institutions.[18] It was, as a response to the pressure of King's non-violent resistance, that the Supreme Court of the United States was moved to embrace all forms of conscientious speech as protected speech, no matter how offensive to sometimes dominant and quite violent majorities in the American South. The Supreme Court made its point in *Brandenburg v. Ohio*, in which the Court, which had already embraced within the principle of free speech the speech of King, also embraced, as equally resting on dignity, the speech of the KKK.[19]

What is most important, for our current purposes, is to note what King's non-violent resistance so dramatically exposed to the American public mind, namely, that such non-violent resistance, grounded, as the Supreme Court was brought to acknowledge, on the basic principle of free speech owed all Americans, was met with mindless violence, culminating in the murder of King himself in 1968. What this reveals, I believe, is the fascist impulse to violence that motivates all the forms of irrationalist prejudice condemned by the anti-discrimination principle. Such violence, which defines fascism,[20] extends, I believe, to the irrationalist prejudices (for example, German anti-Semitism) to which it gave such monstrous political expression. Fascism and irrational prejudice monstrously feed on and rationalize one another through lies and violence. The point may be less obvious in some cases than in others, as, it may be urged, some defenders, say, of Christian homophobia (the so-called new natural lawyers) do make arguments which they advertise as having a secular, not a sectarian religious, basis. But, similar such arguments were once fashionably made in defense of anti-Semitism (T.S. Eliot's argument for the need for a homogeneously Christian British culture),[21] as well as racism and, of course, sexism, yet we now see such arguments as bad to the point of lacking any semblance of public reason, indeed deeply irrational and unreasonable. The defenders of homophobia, as I and Nicholas Bamforth have argued at length elsewhere, are, on critical examination, no better.[22] Their bad arguments masquerade as reason, clearly covering and masking what are sectarian religious arguments without any secular appeal whatsoever. There is a wilful violence here, more like throwing stones not making reasonable arguments. Its advocates thus speak of a culture war, as the reactionary forces arrayed against gay rights have self-consciously employed the rhetoric of being warriors, implicitly invoking the gender binary against their opponents. When non-violent ethical resistance is transmogrified into war, we know or should know that patriarchy has once again darkened our ethical intelligence.

How should we understand this fascist impulse to violent repression that, on examination, motivates all the irrationalist prejudices condemned by the principle of anti-discrimination? To understand the roots of such political violence, we must take seriously what James Gilligan has exposed as the psychological root of the violence he has so brilliantly explored in the psyches of America's most criminally violent men, a shaming of manhood that elicits violence.[23] Shame is, of course, one of the moral emotions central to our sense of ourselves as competent, arising from failures of competence, and expressing itself in the attempt better to exercise our sense of competence and mastery in future. It plays, like guilt, an important and necessary role in human development, including the development of the moral powers of rationality and reasonableness, and does not usually elicit violence in the way Gilligan found in the men he studied.[24] The experience of shame in these men has a very different character—the violence is often irrational corresponding to no real threat, and, if there is any threat, disproportionate. Such irrationalist shame requires explanation. Men are particularly vulnerable to such shame when, often through a history of traumatically violent abuse of them earlier in their lives, they have identified with the patriarchal conception of manhood of their abuser, identifying with the aggressor. Identification in such cases covers lack of caring relationships or the trauma arising from broken relationships. Such men invest their sense of personal competence in a self-image of patriarchal manhood marked by a strictly observed gender binary and hierarchy (men over women) in which their often fragile sense of manhood requires them strictly to confine themselves to what they take to be their male gender role, and the violence is triggered by any insult to this patriarchally defined sense of manhood.

What makes their sense of manhood psychologically fragile is that the gender binary is in fact false to experience (men have many of the features the gender binary deems feminine, and women, the features the gender binary deems masculine), and the idea of gender hierarchy is not only not in the nature of things, but condemned by the moral powers of rationality and reasonableness that men and women, as human and as democratic equals, share. The cultural power and appeal of patriarchal manhood and womanhood can be reasonably understood as yet another example of culturally entrenched forms of moral slavery that illustrate the two features of moral slavery, a dehumanization arising from the abridgement of the basic human rights of whole classes of persons, and rationalized by stereotypes that rest, in a vicious circularity, on the abridgement of such rights. The irrationalist vulnerability to shame of Gilligan's criminally violent men arises from the psychology of traumatic breaks in real relationships that leads these men to identify with the patriarchally imposed gender stereotypes of their oppressors.[25] What holds such cultural patterns in place is precisely the propensity to violence elicited by any challenge to these gender stereotypes. What the study of Gilligan's men illuminates is the larger political psychology of fascist violence that, as we have seen, underlies and indeed supports all the forms of irrationalist prejudice so far discussed: extreme religious intolerance (anti-Semitism), racism, sexism, and homophobia against any reasonable challenge or doubt. The key to all of them is some form of the patriarchally imposed gender binary and hierarchy that gives rise to a political psychology of identification with unjust stereotypes that arises from traumatic breaks in relationship.

The marks of trauma are both loss of memory and of voice,[26] and we can see this poignantly in Gilligan's men in which the fascist propensity to violence is made possible precisely by their loss of voice in relationship; indeed, violence replaces and covers a personal voice that cannot be heard or spoken. It is thus understandable how the humane therapy of a skilled psychiatrist like James Gilligan offers these men, often for the first time in their lives, an opportunity to find and speak in a personal voice, and that, when such voice is found and expressed, the propensity to irrationalist violence, resting on the repression of voice, much diminishes.

Yet another illuminating way to understand the fascist impulses to violence that support the forms of irrationalist prejudice here under study is to draw upon the therapeutic study by Jonathan Shay of the war trauma of Vietnam War veterans.[27] Shay identifies, describes, and explores what he calls moral injury to the character of these men arising from structures of authority that require these men in high stakes war situations of life and death to do things they know to be wrong, traumatically injuring moral character in ways that lead some such men to go berserk, wantonly injuring and killing innocent persons without any sense of limit or accountability to personal conscience. What therapy of these men requires is, like the comparable therapy of Gilligan, a care that enables these men to remember what they have suffered and find and speak in a voice that enables them communally to grieve for what they have lost, including sometimes the deaths of comrades in war they loved.

The cultural structures of moral slavery may, I have suggested, be plausibly understood in terms of the demands of patriarchy (enforcing the gender binary and hierarchy). Such patriarchal demands inflict moral injury on our twin moral powers of rationality and reasonableness in precisely the way Shay identifies and explores, namely, authoritative structures require us to do what we know to be morally wrong, and such injury to moral character expresses itself in an irrationalist shame arising from our identification with the gender stereotypes that patriarchy enforces. Any insult to our sense of patriarchal manhood thus elicits a violence that represses any voice that would challenge patriarchy. The internalized dimension of irrationalist shame enforces violence, intra psychically, against one's own ethical voice, a self-inflicted death, a suicide of the soul.

What has given moral slavery such power and appeal is that, when successful, it represses the moral voice not only of the oppressors, but of the oppressed, precisely through an internalization of the irrationalist sense of shame keyed to the gender binary and hierarchy that patriarchy enforces. The traumatized victims of irrationalist prejudice thus, sometimes, are ashamed of their religion or ethnicity or gender or sexual orientation, and, to the extent feasible, will cover their identities to avoid such prejudice and certainly not remember or want to remember the history of their unjust moral slavery, let alone give voice to resistance to such injustices.[28]

What made Gandhi and King's non-violent resistance to injustice so remarkable, revealing, and ethically empowering is that, against the background of the repressive violence on which moral slavery depends, these advocates of non-violence expressly eschewed violence and instead found and spoke in a resisting voice that challenged the racism that supported British imperialism and had deformed American constitutionalism since its founding. There is an intra-psychic dimension to such resistance, namely, its advocates had not internalized, or had overcome their internalization of, the irrationalist shame that is sometimes the consequence of the moral injury inflicted by moral slavery. De-stigmatizing what such shame irrationally condemns, including its conventional symbols of infamy (for example, the homosexual as abject and unspeakable), is the necessary psychological pre-requisite for the freeing of an ethical voice that had been buried, but was still very much alive in our sense of ourselves as human. I have elsewhere argued at some length that the ethical strength of both Gandhi and King can be traced to ongoing close relationships to maternal caretakers (neither thus experienced the traumatic breaks in relationship that patriarchy requires), which explains how and why in still highly patriarchal cultures these men not only did not respond violently to insults to their identities as men of colour, but innovated a strategy of resistance that implicitly questioned the two features of patriarchy, the gender binary and hierarchy, not only by calling for a non-violent resistance that combines both masculine and feminine features, but empowering democratic movements of resistance that included, among its agents of change, women and even children traditionally denigrated by patriarchy.[29] We should not underestimate the degree to which at least implicitly both Gandhi and King challenged dominant patriarchal images of manhood, and we can register the depths of their challenge in the fact that both were murdered by patriarchal men infuriated by their challenge to dominant conceptions of patriarchal manhood, showing once again the psychological logic of the fascist impulses to violence that enforce moral slavery and remain so alive everywhere.

Gandhi and King show us, writ large in the resistance movements they so brilliantly led, how much resistance to evils, as culturally entrenched as moral slavery, turns on overcoming the terroristic violence against resisting voice that enforces patriarchy. We better understand the remarkable achievements of such men when we understand their advocacy of non-violent resistance not as a general pacifist position (King, for example, was, following Reinhold Neibuhr, certainly not a pacifist),[30] but as a resistance particularly keyed to its object, the evil of moral slavery, an evil enforced by fascist impulses to violence against any resisting voice. It is when one takes this seriously, as Gandhi and King certainly did, that their advocacy of non-violent resistance makes such brilliant sense. It makes sense, of course, strategically as both Gandhi and King knew that violence would against the injustices of the British Empire or of dominantly white America not only be ineffective, but disastrously counter-productive. But, it makes a deeper sense, as the vehicle of moral and political transformation, if understood as a kind of therapy for the moral injuries inflicted on moral character not only on people of colour in India and America, but on the British and American people in general. Both Gandhi and King found a resonance for their advocacy not only among people of colour in India and in America, but among the British and American people generally. We can see this point quite clearly in the way King appealed to what he took to be the deeper ethical impulses within both American constitutionalism and its dominant religion, Christianity, and Gandhi, trained as a British lawyer, well-understood its strand of political liberalism and its

Christianity (indeed, the Sermon on the Mount of Jesus of Nazareth was one of Gandhi's acknowledged inspirations).[31] In both cases, it was through the non-violence of their resistance that both Gandhi and King found and spoke in the resisting moral voice that was to have such resonance among the British and American people, as a kind of therapy for the moral injury patriarchy had inflicted on both the British and American people. What made their non-violent advocacy so profoundly resonant and indeed revelatory was the reactionary response to it—the fascist violence that enforces patriarchy. The moral slavery that had been assumed by so-called civilized people to be in the nature of things was revealed to the public mind of democratic people for what it was, namely, as injustices enforced by violence against resisting voice.

It is this role of voice in resistance that is, I believe, the key to understanding why both the great structural principles of political liberalism (the priority of the human rights of conscience and speech, and the anti-discrimination principle) condemn hate speech laws. To see this point, we need to understand and coordinate how both principles rest on the value of dignity. The human rights of conscience and speech thus protect the free exercise of the twin moral powers of rationality and reasonableness, our dignity as persons, from threats to their free exercise, in particular, any form of state censorship of the exercise of these powers in the domain of conviction. The principle of anti-discrimination rests on the condemnation of the expression through law and policy of the irrational prejudices (extreme religious intolerance—anti-Semitism, racism, sexism, and homophobia), arising from a long entrenched culture of moral slavery. Since such irrational prejudices arise, as I have argued, from the de-humanization of whole classes of persons as lacking, inter alia, the moral powers of rationality and reasonableness, the principle of anti-discrimination condemns the expression through law and policies of these prejudices, and thus protects them from a denial of their dignity as persons. The principles are connected since moral slavery incorporates, in its conception of moral slavery, the abridgement of basic human rights, which include, of course, the principle of equal respect for conscience and speech. Indeed, on my account of moral slavery, violence against resisting voice is the heart of darkness of moral slavery, inflicting moral injury on the powers of rationality and reasonableness that make us human.

Hate speech laws enlist state power to criminalize what has sometimes been called group defamation, the imputation to whole classes of persons of false claims that they have negative qualities that make them inferior and even subhuman.[32] These laws differ fundamentally from the laws of individual defamation (libel and slander) that turn on a speaker's statement of false facts, often known to be false, about a private individual that may lead the audience of the statement to hold the individual in contempt, and thus no longer associate with him or her, causing damages like loss of business and friendship. Such statements, when known by the speaker to be false and about a private individual not otherwise able to defend him or herself, are not expressions of conviction and indeed infringe the right to privacy that is itself an aspect of dignity, and thus are not within the scope of the human rights of conscience and speech.[33] Group libel laws, in contrast, are directed against statements that not only express conviction, but conviction about evaluative matters of public interest (not about hard facts, or about particular private individuals) which are or should be the subject of ongoing debate among democratic equals in the domain of conviction, and interested groups may and do organize to question and rebut such evaluative claims. Group libel laws and hate speech laws generally thus violate the principle of free speech because they claim for the state a power to censor some statements in the domain of conviction from legitimate public debate, a power that, consistent with the human rights of conscience and speech, it does not and should not have.

Such laws may appear to be less questionable, or even to be defensible, on the ground of the anti-discrimination principle, understood as the prohibition on the expression through public laws and policies of irrational prejudices arising from a historically entrenched culture of moral slavery. This is indeed the standard defense of such laws, namely, that they are laws which do precisely what the anti-discrimination principle requires, namely, not express such prejudices but condemn them, in particular, forms of hate speech that dehumanize groups subject to such prejudices. But, there is a difference in basic liberal principle (coordinating the principle of equal respect for conscience and speech with the principle of anti-discrimination, both rooted in dignity) between state power over action (including, of course, harmful or discriminatory actions rooted in prejudice) and over education in a liberal society (imparting to the young the tradition of liberal democratic values) and state power over adults in the domain of conviction. It is perhaps obvious why the principle of equal respect for conscience and speech, rooted in dignity, condemns hate speech laws, and less obvious why the principle of anti-discrimination condemns such laws as well. But, both these principles rest on the deep value of respecting the dignity of our moral powers of rationality and reasonableness, and it is when we consider them in their different though coordinated relation to this value that we can see why both of them condemn hate speech laws.

The basis of the value of the human rights of conscience and speech is protection from threats to our moral powers of rationality and reasonableness. The principle of anti-discrimination, when understood against the background of moral slavery, also protects our moral powers, but here against the threat to our dignity of moral slavery which, precisely because it enforces a terroristic violence against any resisting voice to moral slavery, inflicts what I have called moral injury on oppressors and the oppressed alike. It is a wholly reasonable understanding of the anti-discrimination principle to regard it as justifying state action against harmful actions, including forms of violence and bullying, directed against groups with a history of moral slavery, for it is precisely unjust violence that is at the heart of what, properly understood, we condemn and should condemn in moral slavery. But, it is not a reasonable interpretation of the anti-discrimination principle to regard it as justifying a state power over censorship in the domain of conviction, for that is to endorse the legitimacy of coercion against conscientious voice that is precisely the evil at the heart of moral slavery.

It is a feature of what makes moral slavery such an evil that it uses patriarchy (enforcing a strict gender binary and hierarchy) to divide us from our common humanity, fostering, as we have seen, a psychology of irrational shame invested in patriarchy that, when challenged or placed in doubt, triggers sometimes horrific violence. But, it does not responsibly address this evil, but rather perpetuates and enforces it, to justify censorship in the domain of conviction that violates equal respect for dignity, which is what hate speech laws do, supposing some conscientious speakers do not share our common humanity. What such laws do, in the spirit of the moral slavery they claim to condemn, is to create scape-goats for a cultural evil which is much more profound and more broadly shared than many of us would like to believe.

It is surely remarkable how little attention advocates of hate speech laws give to what one might regard as an urgent empirical question about such laws, 'do they in fact lower the incidence of the forms of irrational dehumanizing prejudice they claim to combat?'[34] American experience without the benefit of such laws suggests they may not only not be useful in achieving that goal, but, if anything, might be counter-productive (as we shall shortly see). If, as I have argued, such laws violate the most reasonable understanding of basic liberal principles like free speech and anti-discrimination, it would seem more likely that such laws might be so resented, and not unreasonably, by these against whom such laws justify criminal sanctions that they would, if anything, exacerbate and inflame the underlying evil. By attempting to condemn such advocates through criminal sanctions, one makes a martyr of them, enflaming a sectarian polarization and, by abridging what they correctly regard as basic rights of citizenship, perhaps even encouraging the violence at the heart of moral slavery.

There is another perhaps more fundamental objection to hate speech laws on the ground of the value of dignity central to both free speech and anti-discrimination. Such laws enlist state power ostensibly to combat irrational prejudices that de-humanize, but it is the state itself that decides and interprets what counts as an irrational prejudice in the domain of principle, thus usurping what, on grounds of liberal principle, is the inalienable right of individuals themselves to decide and rebut in their own voice what he or she regards as irrational prejudice. In a working democracy, it is surely clear that such criminal laws will be enforced in terms most congenial to dominant groups in the society, as defined by the leaders, for example, of dominant religious or other ideological groups, so that it will be their sense of what counts as an insult to one's identity as, say, a Christian, that will determine what counts as an actionable form of hate speech. But, in enforcing what counts as dominant views of group identity, the state may be enforcing what are, in fact, the kinds of de-humanizing stereotypes that are one of the central features of moral slavery; historically, dominant religions and ideologies have often played such a role, and there is no reason today to regard this skepticism about group identity, as the enemy of authentic moral individuality, as any less justified. Quite the contrary. It is the enforcement of these stereotypes by coercion that represses resisting voice, and thus inflicts or further inflicts moral injury. However, as we have seen, it is only the freeing of resisting ethical voice that reparatively addresses moral injury, empowering leaders like Gandhi and King not only to find and speak in such a voice but to find a resonance in others who have suffered such injury, mobilizing them into resisting social movements that contest and change the practices and institutions that enforce moral slavery, including the internalized irrational shame that silences ethical voice.

There can be little doubt that, had hate speech laws been legitimately and fully in effect at the time of Gandhi's non-violent resistance in India and the comparable resistance of Martin Luther King, Jr., that it is precisely such resistance, however non-violent, that would have led the British authorities in India or the Southern states in the United States to use hate speech laws to criminalize such movements on the ground that they defamed the honour of the British or aroused race hatred against the Southern authorities. What is distinctive about the ethical voice of both these transformative ethical leaders is how much their ethical views challenged dominant religious and political ideologies in both India and the United States. Gandhi's syncretic ethics of nonviolence was thus as much an indictment of conventional Hinduism as it was of British Christianity, a fact shown by his murder by a Hindu zealot; and King in his remarkable 'Letter from Birmingham Jail' indicts the conventional

Christianity of white liberals as he indicts the failed promises of American constitutionalism (Richards 2005: 165–9). It was not conventional groups, religious or otherwise, that empowered their resistance, but the creative moral powers of these remarkable individuals who so brilliantly innovated a non-violent activism that exposed the lies and violence of moral slavery in ways it had never been exposed before. Group libel laws would have accorded a coercive power to conventional groups that would have crushed such move-ments and perpetuated the cycle of violence on which moral slavery depends. It was precisely such worries that led the Supreme Court of the United States to rule that such laws were constitutionally problematic in the United States, thus empowering the most ethically and politically important and effective movement of resistance in the history of the United States, laying the founda-tion, in turn, for the equally important and effective anti-war, feminist, and gay rights movements. The Court correctly grounded its views on the human rights of conscience and speech, but this view is grounded as well in a proper interpretation of the anti-discrimination principle for it is only such freeing of individual resisting voice through empowering the voice of individuals to challenge the unjust stereotypes that afflict them and disallowing the group libel actions that silence such voice that empowers challenge to the forms of moral slavery that rest on violence directed against such voice.

The point extends as well to the attempt to extend the argument for hate speech laws, ostensibly grounded in protecting dignity, to the allegedly de-humanizing effects of speech that insults women, for example, pornography.[35] The claim that our erotic interests and representations appealing to them are not of deeply human value will not bear examination, and the role that state censorship in this domain might play, in protecting women from insult, is at least as objectionable and probably more so as it is elsewhere, using coercion against the freeing of sexual voice (enforcing sexism and homophobia) that many feminists now argue is the key to ethical emancipation of both women, straight and gay, and gay men.[36]

Hate speech laws, ostensibly grounded in combating the de-humanization inflicted by the irrational prejudices of extreme religious intolerance, rac-ism, sexism, and homophobia, perpetuate and worsen such dehumanization because such laws enlist state coercion against voice. It is only when we take seriously the propensities to fascist violence that are the heart of darkness of moral slavery that we can understand how problematic, on grounds of the basic principles of political liberalism, such laws are. Moral slavery rests on a tangled political psychology of highly gendered irrational shame about failures in one's patriarchal manhood or womanhood, strictly construing authority in terms of a rigid gender binary and hierarchy. Its power arises from the way any challenge to patriarchal manhood elicits violence. We cannot release ourselves from the hold on us of moral slavery until we challenge the irrational shame culture of patriarchy that continues to sustain and support it. The problem, fundamentally, with hate speech laws is that they are symbiotically connected with and support such a shame culture. In claiming a state power coercively to repress hate speech, such laws endorse a gender hierarchy of good conviction over bad, friends over enemies, and enforce it through coercion, legitimating violence against voice. This kind of putatively legitimate war against conviction makes sense only within the framework of the propensities to violence of a patriarchal shame culture. It is no accident, if I am right, that such hate speech laws often exacerbate the violence they claim to combat, masking their own complicity with the continuing power of the culture of moral slavery they are not prepared responsibly to address.

If I am right about this as a matter of liberal principle, why is the point so difficult to see, let alone take seriously? We need, to understand this difficulty, to take more seriously the continuing hold on all of us, including liberals of good will, of the political psychology that has supported moral slavery for much too long in our common human history.

It illuminates such difficulties to end my argument with some reflection on the historical roots of political liberalism in the struggle for religious toleration, as it was made, seminally, by John Locke and Pierre Bayle, both deeply religious Protestant Christian,[37] and by Baruch Spinoza, a heretic from traditional Judaism,[38] all roughly in the same time and place, namely, the Netherlands of the late seventeenth century, a relatively liberal republican regime in the midst of the authoritarian and hostile absolute monarchies around it. What distinguishes all these pioneers of political liberalism is their arguments both identifying equal liberty of conscience as an inalienable human right if anything is and protecting it from coercive threats unsupported by any compelling secular justification in terms of general goods like life, liberty, or property (or, the pursuit of happiness, as Jefferson later put it) on which all reasonable persons could agree as the all-purpose goods all would want, whatever else they might want. What is of interest, from the perspective of the question of political psychology just put, is that even these defenders of universal toleration, notably Locke, compromise the universality of their argument by exempting from its protections intolerant groups who refuse to accept or respect the argument; for this reason, Locke exempts Catholics and atheists from liberal toleration because, in his view of them, neither could or would themselves extend toleration to forms of ethical conviction; Catholics because they were committed to the Augustinian defense of the persecution of Christian heretics, atheists because Locke wrongly thought ethics required

Judeo-Christian religious belief in a just God.[39] In contemporary terms, the historical tradition of political liberalism apparently would have endorsed something like hate speech laws, laws directed against those groups incapable of liberal tolerance and mutual respect.

Though I believe the Lockean and other arguments for a qualified scope of the principle of toleration are unjustified, it is psychologically understandable how and why the historical Locke and Bayle, who themselves suffered from unjust religious persecution (Bayle's brother, a Protestant, died in a French prison from such persecution, rationalized by the theory of Augustinian persecution that Bayle criticized so brilliantly),[40] would have found it difficult to appreciate arguments for a more universal scope to the principle of toleration. Such intolerance, an example of what I have called moral slavery, inflicts moral injury, and the legacy of such injury is an anger at and fear of the intolerant that understandably inflicts on them a coercive violence that responds commensurately, so it may be believed, to the violence one has unjustly endured.

What is of interest is that no group has historically been subject to greater persecution or unjust intolerance than Jews, who have suffered a long history of moral slavery that, in modernity, culminated in the catastrophic violence of the Holocaust.[41] Yet, Spinoza, who experienced persecution even from his fellow Jews, argued for a more universal scope for toleration than either Locke or Bayle,[42] suggesting a level of ethical and psychological intelligence that has been able to master even the most understandable impulses of anger and fear. It may be precisely because the persecution of the Jews placed them so far outside the institutions of Christian patriarchy, including its Augustinian contempt for human sexual love with all that means in the relationships central to human life, that their resistance to conversion would make possible a more radical and reasonable ethical independence, based in a more realistic and less disassociated sense of our embodied and relational minds and hearts.[43] What may have made this possible is that their longstanding resistance to patriarchal Christianity may have enabled some of them to be less subject to the moral injury of internalized shame that afflicted those who accepted the Church's authority and were ordered to do things they knew to be wrong, which, on Shay's view, gives rise to moral injury. Less subject to traumatic moral injury and the resulting disassociation, such persons may be less likely, unlike others still held in the sway of moral slavery, to endorse violence against ethical voice.

In American constitutional history, it is striking that the most robust and muscular defense of the principle of free speech, consistent with the argument offered here, was given by Justice Louis Brandeis, the first Jew appointed to the Supreme Court of the United States, in a case that involved the prosecution of a woman for her political advocacy.[44] What Brandeis offers is an argument clearly rooted in dignity, in particular, respect for the twin moral powers of rationality and reasonableness, one that calls for equal respect even for the convictions we find most hateful: '[t]hose who won our independence believed that the final end of the State was to make men free to develop their faculties, and that in its government the deliberative forces should prevail over the arbitrary.'[45] Brandeis clearly argues from within the experience of persecution, and, consistent with the argument I have here made, argues that we best express the value of dignity, which human rights protect, when we display a moral courage based on an ethical independence that masters our anger and fear, and does not allow the experience of moral slavery to remake its victims in the image of its unjust aggressors. When Brandeis writes in this way of the courage that free speech requires, he points to the need to master our fears of those with whom we fundamentally disagree in the domain of conviction, releasing ourselves from our vulnerability to the irrational shame of patriarchal manhood. The liberties that political liberalism respects call for more defensible ideals of personal competence, ones not wedded to the gender binary and hierarchy that patriarchy enforces, thus, separating us from one another and our common humanity.

Ronald Dworkin's work in legal and political philosophy is very much in this tradition, and his defense of a political liberalism that condemns hate speech laws bespeaks the same values of dignity that we honour in Spinoza and in Louis Brandeis, both of whom came, like Dworkin, from the most persecuted of religious groups. We honour him, as we do Spinoza and Brandeis, for upholding and defending liberal values during a long period when a reactionary conservatism in American politics sought to marginalize such values and reward its sycophantic apologists. Those who knew Dworkin well were always struck and instructed by the consistent and rigorous liberalism of his public life, which was at one with the embodied pleasure he took in living well and to the full in all its earthly and secular dimensions, public and private. There was never a less ascetic philosopher, and yet a great philosopher of law he certainly was, among, I believe, the very greatest. To have been touched by him was always to be challenged and always improved. He was, for many of us, a touchstone of integrity, a voice we always looked to test whether we had held ourselves to the highest standards of what it meant to stand on the values of dignity that make us human.

Notes and References

1. See, for example, *Brandenburg v. Ohio*, 395 U.S. 444 (1969) (holding unconstitutional an Ohio criminal syndicalism statute applied to KKK rally advocating violence against Jews and people of colour).

2. See, for example, Ronald Dworkin. 1996. *Freedom's Law: The Moral Reading of the Constitution*. Cambridge, Mass.: Harvard University Press. pp. 195–226.
3. Jeremy Waldron. 2012. *The Harm in Hate Speech*. Cambridge, Mass.: Harvard University Press.
4. For Kant's formulations of the Categorical Imperative, based on the value of dignity, see Immanuel Kant. 1959. *Foundations of the Metaphysics of Morals*. Lewis W. Beck tr. New York: Liberal Arts Press. (originally published, 1784); for Rawls's contractualist statement of Kant's position, see John Rawls. 1971. *A Theory of Justice*. Cambridge, Mass.: Harvard University Press.
5. For fuller defense and explication of rationality and reasonableness as moral powers, see David A.J. Richards. 1971. *A Theory of Reasons for Action*. Oxford: Oxford at the Clarendon Press.
6. See, for fuller discussion, David A.J. Richards. 2013. *Resisting Injustice and the Feminist Ethics of Care in the Age of Obama: Suddenly,…All the Truth Was Coming Out*. New York: Routledge.
7. The best general study remains Hannah Arendt. 1968. *The Origins of Totalitarianism*. Orlando: A Harvest Book.
8. See, for fuller discussion, Carol Gilligan and David A.J. Richards. 2009. *The Deepening Darkness: Patriarchy, Resistance, and Democracy's Future*. Cambridge: Cambridge University Press, 2009.
9. For fuller defense of these claims, see David A.J. Richards. 1986. *Toleration and the Constitution*. New York: Oxford University Press; David A.J. Richards. 1999. *Free Speech and the Politics of Identity*. Oxford: Oxford University Press.
10. See Justice O'Connor's opinion for the Court in *Virginia v. Black*, 538 U.S. 343 (2003), holding that a state statute criminalizing cross burning is not constitutional when it presumes all such burnings are intimidating; O'Connor draws the operative constitutional distinction between cross burning at a rally (which is constitutionally protected) from such cross burning targeted at a home (not protected). The statute in question was unconstitutional because it failed to make and observe this distinction.
11. See *Brandenburg v. Ohio*, 395 U.S. 444 (1969) (holding unconstitutional an Ohio criminal syndicalism statute applied to KKK rally advocating violence against Jews and people of colour).
12. The best general study remains Hannah Arendt. 1968. *The Origins of Totalitarianism*. Orlando: A Harvest Book.
13. For further discussion, see David A.J. Richards. 1998. *Women, Gays, and the Constitution: The Grounds for Feminism and Gay Rights in Culture and Law*. Chicago: University of Chicago Press.
14. *Plessy v. Ferguson*, 163 U.S. 537. 1896. (holding constitutional a Louisiana law that required separate railway cars for whites and people of colour).
15. For fuller exploration in some depth of these matters, see David A.J. Richards. 1993. *Conscience and the Constitution: History, Theory, and Law of the Reconstruction Amendments*. Princeton: Princeton University Press.

16. See, on this point, David A.J. Richards. 1999. *Identity and the Case for Gay Rights: Race, Gender, Religion as Analogies*. Chicago: University of Chicago Press.

17. For fuller discussion, see David A.J. Richards. 2005. *Disarming Manhood: Roots of Ethical Resistance*. Athens, Ohio: Swallow Press. On Bayard Rustin, in particular, see John D'Emilio. 2003. *Lost Prophet: The Life and Times of Bayard Rustin*. Chicago: University of Chicago Press.

18. See, on this point, Harry Kalven, Jr. 1965. *The Negro and the First Amendment*. Chicago: University of Chicago Press.

19. See *Brandenburg v. Ohio*, 395 U.S. 444 (1969) (holding unconstitutional an Ohio criminal syndicalism statute applied to KKK rally advocating violence against Jews and people of colour).

20. On the roots of fascism in violence, see Robert O. Paxton. 2004. *The Anatomy of Fascism*. New York: Vintage Books.

21. See Christopher Ricks. 1988. *T.S. Eliot and Prejudice*. London: Farber and Farber. pp. 40–1.

22. See Nicholas C. Bamforth and David A.J. Richards. 2008. *Patriarchal Religion, Sexuality, and Gender: A Critique of New Natural Law*. Cambridge: Cambridge University Press.

23. See James Gilligan. 1996. *Violence: Reflections on a National Epidemic*. New York: Vintage Books.

24. On shame and guilt, see Gerhart Piers and Milton B. Singer. 1953. *Shame and Guilt: A Psychoanalytic and Cultural Study*. Springfield, Ill.: Charles C. Thomas, Publisher.

25. I am indebted for the importance of the distinction between shame and guilt cultures, as well as for the irrational shame underlying patriarchal violence, to conversations with James Gilligan.

26. See, on this point, Bessel A. van der Kolk, Alex C. McFarlane, and Lars Weisaeth. 1966. *Traumatic Stress: The Effects of Overwhelming Experience on Mind, Body, and Society*. New York: The Guilford Press; Judith Herman. 1997. *Trauma and Recovery*. New York: Basic Books.

27. See Jonathan Shay. 1994. *Achilles in Vietnam: Combat Trauma and the Undoing of Character*. New York: Scribner. I am indebted for this point to Carol Gilligan, who immediately saw the connection of Shay's work to the psychology that supported patriarchy, and urged me to take it seriously in my thinking about moral slavery.

28. On covering, see Kenji Yoshino. 2006. *Covering: The Hidden Assault on Our Civil Rights*. New York: Random House.

29. See, on all these points, David A.J. Richards, *Disarming Manhood*.

30. On the development of King's interest in nonviolence, much under the influence of the work of the theology and morality in politics of Reinhold Neibuhr, but never taking the form of the pacifism of Tolstoy and Gandhi, see Richards 2005: 131–80.

31. See, on all these points, Richards 2005: 92–180. For Gandhi on the Sermon on the Mount, see Richards (2005: 95).

32. See, for an example of such a law, *Beauharnais v. Illinois*, 343 U.S. 250 (1952) (upholding group libel law in 5–4 opinion). But, see *Brandenburg v. Ohio*, 395 U.S. 444 (1969) (holding unconstitutional an Ohio criminal syndicalism statute applied to KKK rally advocating violence against Jews and people of colour).

33. See *New York Times Co. v. Sullivan*, 376 U.S. 254 (1964) (individual libel action held invalid but only when person defamed is public official); *Gertz v. Robert Welch, Inc.*, 418 U.S. 323 (1974) (individual libel action upheld but only where no strict liability and there are actual damages).

34. See, for example, Waldron 2011: 81, 154–5, where it is presumed that such law lessen racism.

35. See, for an example of this move, Waldron 2011: 73–4, 89–92, 180–1.

36. See, for fuller defense of this position, Carol Gilligan and David A.J. Richards, *The Deepening Darkness*.

37. See, on this point, Richards (1986: 89–98).

38. See, on this point, Gilligan and Richards (2009: 139–40).

39. See, on this point, Richards (1986: 95–8).

40. See, on Bayle's life, Elisabeth Labrousse. 1983. *Bayle*. tr. Deny Potts. Oxford: Oxford University Press.

41. See, on this point, Gilligan and Richards (2009: 129–37).

42. See Gilligan and Richards (2009: 139–40).

43. On the strengths of Jewish resistance to Christianity, see Gilligan and Richards (2009: 131–7).

44. See *Whitney v. California*, 274 U.S. 357 (1927) (conviction under state criminal syndicalism statute for membership in Communist Labor Party which, over defendant's objections, has endorsed terrorist tactics)

45. *Whitney v. California*, 274 U.S. 357, 375 (1927).

12

Ronald Dworkin and Free Speech

James Allan

Ronald Dworkin was one of the best lecturers I have ever heard. He came twice to give guest lectures in the William Twining jurisprudence course I was taking in London in 1985–6. And Dworkin was magnificent. Not a note in sight. Not a hint of a stumble or hesitation or pause or muttered 'hmm' or 'umh'. Rather he spoke in paragraphs, as it were, and covered incredibly difficult issues such as those related to theories of constitutional interpretation with an overall deftness and fluency that carried the listener along. And then he took questions with a remarkable and unnerving ease.

This was university lecturing at its finest. So in any commemorative book of essays such as this, it bears remembering that Ronald Dworkin was a wonderful speaker and conveyor of ideas. Indeed his skill in front of the class is doubly impressive in my particular case because on many—no most—substantive issues I myself am not a Dworkinian.

I think Dworkin is on the losing side of the arguments when it comes to the relative plausibility of moral realism versus non-cognitivism;[1] or the coherence and persuasiveness of 'one right answer' type claims emerging from the Herculean or integrity-fuelled interpretive process;[2] or the best, most defensible approach to constitutional interpretation;[3] or the on-balance benefits versus costs of strong judicial review, including whether its democratic credentials pass muster;[4] or what flows from that, whether a country such as the United Kingdom (or Australia, for that matter) ought—or ought not—to opt for a bill of rights;[5] or even whether the H.L.A. Hart understanding of the nature of a legal system is preferable and more illuminating than the Dworkinian one.[6]

On all these issues, and a few more besides, I do not find Dworkin's positions ultimately convincing. Insightful and thought-provoking, definitely, but they are not for me, persuasive. Hence that is just what I told the editor of this book of essays when he approached me to write an essay for this book in honour of Ronald Dworkin. I suggested that given the nature of this book, many others were more suitable than I to contribute. Yet when the editor, on receiving this reply, asked me nevertheless to think again, I did and I realized that there was perhaps one small topic on which I might be well-placed to write in honour of Professor Dworkin.

I refer in general terms to Dworkin's strong defence of free speech, his overall view that in a democracy the inroads and restrictions on what a person can say or write should be few and far between. Indeed the exceptions should be at most, really, what the Justices of the Supreme Court of the United States have carved out under their First Amendment jurisprudence—a small and limited collection of exceptions in such areas as sedition, obscenity, fighting words, defamation of private (or non-public) persons, and a few others.

This commitment to a robust degree of free speech protection places Dworkin squarely in the tradition of John Stuart Mill, though of course Mill's defence of that commitment was ultimately a utilitarian one while Dworkin's is rights-based, moving from a non-consequentialist equality starting point on to this free speech commitment (in part for legitimacy reasons, as the price society pays for enforcing laws on dissenters).

Now as readers may have inferred, I find this powerful Dworkinian commitment to comparatively unfettered free speech very congenial indeed. It is true that my reasons for sharing that strong commitment are at core Millian (and even Benthamite) rather than Dworkinian, but all the same there is a certain 'willingness to take my principles wherever they may lead and no matter who may disagree with me' in this full-blooded Dworkinian defence of free speech that I greatly admire.

In the rest of this short chapter I want to focus on one aspect of Dworkin's free speech commitment, namely his position on (or more aptly, against) hate speech laws. And I want to defend Dworkin's anti-hate speech laws position against the views of his former student at Oxford, Jeremy Waldron.

This defence of Dworkin against Waldron is, for me at least, somewhat ironic because on several of the substantive issues I mentioned above—and in particular on the undesirability of strong judicial review and on avoiding a bill of rights[7]—I am very much in the Waldron camp.[8] But not on this issue of whether an established and well-functioning democracy, one such as the US or UK or Canada or Australia or New Zealand say, ought to enact hate speech laws. On this I can be counted firmly in Dworkin's camp. Such laws should not be enacted.

Now in general terms I have elsewhere and already set out why I think that Waldron's hate speech position falls down.[9] Here I want to do something different. I want to lay out the basic case Waldron makes against Dworkin's anti-hate speech laws position, and then I want to defend the general thrust (though not every one of the specifics) of that Dworkinian position.

Here, then, is how Waldron sees the essence of Dworkin's opposition to hate speech laws. Waldron, correctly I would say, sees Dworkin's position as resting on two main planks—one being a fairness or principle-based opposition founded on legitimacy concerns and the other being a consequentialist argument or claim related to how much harm hate speech does, or does not, in fact cause to its intended victims. Waldron focuses on the first of these, the legitimacy argument, but I will consider both of the two prongs underlying Dworkin's opposition to hate speech laws.

Accordingly, let us see how Waldron attempts to deal with Dworkin's legitimacy concerns. Waldron starts by noting that '[a]ccording to Professor Dworkin, freedom for hate speech or freedom for group defamation is the price we pay for the legitimacy of our enforcing certain laws that hatemongers oppose'.[10] In other words, Dworkin is concerned with political legitimacy. Dworkin himself puts it this way, 'The majority has no right to impose its will on someone who is forbidden to raise a voice in protest or argument or objection before the decision is taken.'[11]

Waldron then spends nearly a dozen pages arguing that Dworkin's legitimacy point cannot be taken literally, in absolute terms, such that the enactment of any hate speech laws (whatever the circumstances or details) would in and of itself spoil the justification there otherwise would be for insisting that all people (even those silenced by the hate speech laws) must obey all the enacted laws. So even if silencing some few people on account of a hate speech enactment forecloses them from opposing certain other laws in the language and manner that they wish that cannot always and everywhere result in some sort of blanket taint of illegitimacy descending on all other laws. It cannot be, says Waldron, that in some all-encompassing sense that legitimacy is ruined by the passage of any sort of hate speech law, however crafted, bracketed, or focused.

And surely Waldron is correct about that. Or so it seems to me. Of course at the end of those dozen pages Waldron himself observes that '[m]aybe we should not take Dworkin's argument about legitimacy literally' (Waldron 2012: 186). Indeed Waldron suggests that the best understanding of Dworkin's position—what you have, as it were, when you seek the best fit with all of Dworkin's other settled positions and writings, in the way some mythical Hercules might—is that 'the legitimacy of any given law, for any person, is itself a matter of degree; and that, on a moderate version of Dworkin's argument, the enforcement of hate speech laws *diminishes*—or as he puts it, 'spoils'—the legitimacy of downstream laws without destroying their legitimacy altogether' (188).

It is this version of the argument, what Waldron calls 'a moderate version of Dworkin's argument' (188), that I want now to defend, not least because it is this moderate version that Waldron himself thinks 'is what Dworkin wants to say' (188). Hence, legitimacy is not an all-or-nothing matter. Instead, the legitimacy deficit can be larger or smaller, a matter of degree, depending on what else is in play—though there will always be something morally to regret when we silence people.

At this point Waldron offers up what is in effect a consequentialist case against this moderate Dworkinian anti-hate speech laws position. And as I am myself a consequentialist, it is here that I will attempt to defend Dworkin.

Waldron's claim, in effect, is that since legitimacy is a matter of degree, there is plenty of room for a hate speech laws regime to pass muster. After you throw into the consequentialist hopper the real harms on both sides of the ledger—what intended targets would suffer without such laws in place and what those silenced would suffer with them there—you might sometimes find that you come down for the former. And so if the hate speech laws could be kept well bracketed, so they were 'specifically tailored to prohibit only expression at the viciously vituperative end of [the] spectrum, it might be an open question whether [such bracketed and contained hate speech laws] would have anything more than a minimal effect on the legitimacy of [other laws]' (Waldron 2012: 191).

Waldron then tries to buttress this claim by pointing to the UK and Australia and Canada and arguing (implicitly if not explicitly) that the hate speech laws in existence there do not unduly undermine legitimacy. The overall Waldronian thrust is that these countries *do* aim their hate speech laws at 'the viciously vituperative end of [the] spectrum' (191), that hate speech laws in the real world of day-to-day life *can* be kept sufficiently bracketed and limited so as not to unduly affect issues of legitimacy. Indeed Waldron attempts to buttress his anti-Dworkin position by noting that 'most such laws bend over backwards to ensure that there is a lawful way of expressing something like the propositional content of views that become objectionable when expressed as vituperation' (190). And on top of all that, causal claims about the factual effects of hate speech laws 'are something for legislators to consider' (176–7).

So we can avoid hate speech laws over-reaching themselves; we can see such laws working perfectly (or at least tolerably) well in Canada and Australia and the UK; we know such laws just affect how one says what he or she wants, because almost always they leave room to make the same desired substantive point less vituperatively; and really this should all be left to the elected legislatures. Or at least so says Waldron. These are the points that form the core of his case against the moderate version of Dworkin's anti-hate speech argument.

Yet I prefer Dworkin's position. Yes, on the last of these points—that we should want the call on whether to have such hate speech laws made by elected legislators, not by unelected judges—I am with Waldron. But on all the others count me with Dworkin. More importantly, perhaps much more importantly, I am with Dworkin on the fundamental issue of whether to be optimistic or pessimistic about the capabilities and capacities of one's fellow citizens—the issue that unavoidably seems to me to underlie much of the disagreement about the desirability or otherwise of hate speech laws. I am with Dworkin in being optimistic. Meanwhile it seems to me that it is hard to understand Waldron's position without seeing him as a pessimist on this score, and if that is correct it also seems to me that such pessimism may well undermine some of his other substantive positions, including his opposition to strong judicial review and to bills of rights.

However let me work up to that more fundamental issue by starting with the specifics. Firstly, I simply do not agree that the hate speech law regimes in, say, Canada and Australia are aimed largely at 'the viciously vituperative end of [the] spectrum' (191). I made a broadly similar point elsewhere when questioning Waldron's hate speech position more generally. But what I said then bears repeating.[12] Let me start with Canada.

In his book Waldron makes repeated references to Canada and to the top court's decision there in *R. v. Keegstra*.[13] But it seems to me that Waldron leaves himself open to the charge that he has cherry-picked this example. Waldron refers to the *Keegstra* case, a more than two-decade old Supreme Court of Canada decision, in four separate parts of the book. And it certainly is an important and leading decision that upheld the constitutionality of *criminal* hate speech laws in Canada against attack on the grounds of *Charter of Rights'* freedom of expression.

Yet in Canada, or so it seems to me, the criminal law plays a small to insignificant role in the government's attempt to suppress hate speech. Most of the action, nay the vast preponderance of the action, takes place in administrative tribunals where truth is not even a defence, where complainants have all of their costs picked up by the taxpayer but accused do not, and where penalties include five figure fines *and* (I mean this seriously) tribunal-backed-by-the-court orders never to speak on certain matters again.[14]

It was in this non-criminal law realm that political commentator Mark Steyn was ensnared when the biggest selling Canadian news weekly magazine published an article that was an excerpt of a chapter of Steyn's *New York Times* Number One best seller *America Alone*. And in that article (and chapter, and book) Steyn pointed to unchallenged demographic trends related to high birth rates for Muslims but not for others and expressed grave concerns about their political, social, and cultural implications.

Steyn and that news magazine *McLeans* were accused of hate speech and dragged before three separate jurisdiction's tribunals, the Ontario Human Rights Commission, the British Columbia Human Rights Commission, and the Canadian Human Rights Commission by a serial complainant, an official of the Canadian Islamic Council. In some of these tribunals no accused had ever prevailed—not a single person ever—in the entire time of these tribunals' existence. Complainants had a 100 per cent success track record. Those accused of hate speech always lost.

Now the cases against *McLeans* were eventually dropped, not least because *McLeans* had deep pockets and the cases were embarrassing all sorts of people, but not before the defendants had spent in excess of $2 million on that defence.[15] So let us pause and ask ourselves if this sort of hate speech law regime in Canada looks anything like what might be described as one aimed largely at 'the viciously vituperative end of [the] spectrum' (Waldron 2012: 191).

Or perhaps we might first also consider the case involving the Saskatchewan Christian evangelist, Bill Whatcott, who was taken before a Saskatchewan equivalent tribunal and fined for his publications condemning 'sodomite' sex. Whatcott appealed all the way to the Supreme Court of Canada which in early 2013 decided unanimously against him and upheld the constitutionality of these civil hate speech laws, laws that do not even make truth a defence—indeed the Supreme Court of Canada in Whatcott explicitly said that 'truth may be used for widely disparate ends'.[16] Whatcott vows now to continue speaking, which means he will be imprisoned for contempt of court, in theory until his will is broken or for life.

And for what it is worth there are dozens and dozens and dozens of similar cases from Canada—hundreds if you count the many people who are accused of hate speech and who would like to fight but who opt on prudential grounds to make a perfunctory apology, pay a fine and get away.

So just to be clear, the criminal law route for limiting hate speech in Canada with its various built-in safeguards related to the burden of proof, to truth being a defence and to prosecutions needing the consent of the Attorney-General—has at a high level only one single successfully prosecuted case that I know of this past quarter century. That's *Keegstra*, the one Waldron repeatedly refers to in this book. Meantime speech-restricting laws that get a near daily workout in Canada—laws where truth is not a defence, complainants get their costs paid but not accused, just being offended comes close sometimes to seeming to be enough, and more—receive not a single mention from Waldron in this entire book when he looks beyond American shores to weigh up the costs and benefits of hate speech laws.

When it comes to Canada, in other words, the sort of hate speech laws that do the real work are by no means at all ones that look to me to be confined to the viciously vituperative end of the spectrum. Moreover, they very much do seem to me to raise real issues of legitimacy for the legal system as a whole, the very sort of thing that worried Dworkin and that (even on the moderate version of his position) led him to be a strong opponent of hate speech laws. Put differently, when one looks at Canada it seems to me that the well-bracketed and safeguard-laden criminal hate speech laws have vanishingly few effects— they do not accomplish anything like the volume of speech suppression that would be needed to make any difference at all to Waldron's consequentialist case—while the speech-suppressing administrative law-type anti-hate speech regime over-reaches itself in a noticeable and legitimacy-sapping way. Canada is anything but a jurisdiction in which hate speech laws work perfectly well.

And that goes a long way to explaining why Canada's federal parliament very recently repealed the federal non-criminal law (Section 13) of Human Rights Commission hate speech laws[17] (a democratic procedure for removing this law that I think to be a good procedure and which, I assume, Waldron also thinks is a good procedure, the substantive desirability of a law being a different matter).

Or turn to Australia. The main vehicle for attempting to suppress hate speech there is likewise not the criminal law. And as it happens before a recent election there the then opposition political party in their federal Parliament pledged to repeal this non-criminal hate speech law.[18] And that opposition party won the election and formed the government. So we will see, in Australia (where there is no national bill of rights of any sort), how the legislature responds in what is both Waldron's and my preferred turf. But even if we focus on the courts in Australia, and on this non-criminal law machinery, we see that the big, notorious case involving hate speech laws in Australia is the *Eatock v. Bolt* case.[19] That case involved a political pundit who commented that self-identifying Aborigines with mere traces of Aboriginal blood were scooping up too many affirmative action rewards. It is a case anyone familiar with the Elizabeth Warren saga in the US would immediately recognize.[20]

And the political commentator, Bolt, lost. He had to pay a small fine, make a pseudo-apology, remove the newspaper column in question from all websites, and avoid speaking on the same matter again. Based on the legislation the judge ruled that Bolt could have made his criticisms less stridently. A key pillar of the judge's reasoning was that he didn't like Bolt's tone!

Here again in Australia, as with Canada, the hate speech laws that do the real work do not look to me as though they are aimed only at the viciously vituperative end of the spectrum. They are certainly not the sort of highly contained and bracketed laws that have only 'a minimal effect on the legitimacy of [other laws]' (Waldron 2012: 191).

If that is my response on behalf of Dworkin to Waldron's specific claims about how hate speech laws need not over-reach themselves and how they work perfectly—or at least tolerably—well in the Canadas and Australias of the world, here is my reply to Waldron's specific claim that 'most such [hate speech] laws bend over backwards to ensure that there is a lawful way of expressing something like the propositional content of views that become objectionable when expressed as vituperation' (190). It is a two-part reply. The first part is to ask for what Waldron (in critiquing the non-moderate version of Dworkin's legitimacy argument) calls 'a reality check' (184). The sort of anti-hate speech administrative law regimes one finds in Canada and Australia do *not* seem to me to bend over backwards to let one express one's views. Who should be awarded affirmative action benefits is a pretty big issue of public policy and a tone dripping with sarcasm may well be precisely how one wants to frame his attack on, say, middle class, one-sixteenth of the required racial mix beneficiaries scooping up race-based benefits. Yes, a biting tone may well lie at the heart of the desired speech. The fact such a pundit could re-write the article to remove all the biting jibes that constitute the unfriendly tone and translate it into some boring, dull, management-speak prose does not seem, to me, to qualify under the rubric of 'bending over backwards to allow one to express one's desired propositional content'. It is more of a grudging allowance, if it is anything. And the same goes for Mark Steyn's writings about demographic trends. The particular laws invoked against him could not really be characterized as 'bending over backwards to let him make his point'. Indeed if you can suggest that with a straight face I think you ought to consider moving to Los Angeles and looking for acting work.

But even if you reject that first part of my reply there is a further response to be made here when someone claims that a speech-stifling law allows room for a re-worked way of making much the same point. And notice that I am responding here to Waldron's specific claim (when he is trying to counter a moderate version of Dworkin's dislike of hate speech laws) that the core goal of hate speech laws is not so much to block and suppress any particular set of ideas, however loathsome, but rather it is just to stop particularly nasty and crude articulations of those ideas. And my second response to that claim can perhaps be captured under the rubric of 'be careful what you wish for'. The 'just rephrase what you want to say in less epithet-laden terms' mandate seems to me to come perilously close to legislating in favour of smart people. Not nice people, with nice sentiments—but smart people. In other words, it works against the common man and woman. At which point I start wondering about unintended consequences. Would such a Waldron-mandated need to say things the 'proper way' sometimes have the unintended and undesired effect of making certain detestable views *more* persuasive and *more* effective than they otherwise would be—by, as it were, putting a clever and moderate-sounding new spokeswoman on an old National Front soap box (or the analogous claim in India, say, or wherever)? Who knows? But this is no implausible worry.

As for the last of Waldron's specific claims against Dworkin, I mentioned above that I am with Waldron in wanting the final decision on whether to have these hate speech laws lie with our elected legislators, not with our unelected top judges. But I did not then make plain that in two of the countries that Waldron points to as having at least tolerable well-working hate speech laws in existence the legislators in those jurisdictions at least partially seem to disagree. In Canada at the federal level the administrative law-type regime I discussed above has been repealed.[21] And in Australia the now governing party very recently made pre-election commitments to do the same.[22]

I hope that discussion of the specific sort of claims Waldron makes against the moderate version of Dworkin's anti-hate speech law case suffices to allow me to shift now to the more fundamental or general issue I mentioned above, and then put to one side. And this issue revolves around the view one takes of the capacities of one's fellow citizens. To see why, start with the question, 'How, precisely, do hate speech laws deliver the good consequences that is being claimed for them?'

I considered this question in some small amount of depth in the general review of Waldron's hate speech position (Allan 2013: 56). But in brief we can think that hate speech laws might deliver good consequences (in theory at any rate) because of the effects they would have on the intended victims of that hate speech (who with the laws in place would not have to hear what some few others think of them); or because of how these laws reform the speakers; or because these laws block what third party listeners get to hear and so stops some of the listeners from being persuaded. But the first two are very implausible and unpersuasive. The first might deliver a sense of security, but it is a false sense of security. And the second imagines that speakers of hate will have their beliefs reformed by the threat, or execution, of the law's penalties.

Though I do not agree with the third of these possibilities, it is the most plausible. And I think it is where Waldron sees the good consequences of hate speech laws delivering the goods. We see it in his general case in favour of hate speech laws (Allan 2013: 56). And we see it in his more specific reply to Dworkin, not least when Waldron talks in terms of '… if we leave hate speech alone, then we are leaving alone the poison that leads to violence and discrimination…' (Waldron 2012: 178). This metaphor seems premised on something like the idea that hate speech is dangerous—that it has bad consequences—because of its effects on listeners outside the target group. It persuades some of them. It changes opinions. The hate multiplies.

Now I have written elsewhere on why that argument seems unpersuasive to me (Allan 2013). And I have written in the same place on how it is an argument that is especially difficult for Waldron to make, given his other substantive writings (ones I agree with, be it noted) that lament over-powerful judges and that oppose strong judicial review precisely on the basis that much disagreement in society, even that related to rights disputes, is best seen as reasonable disagreement over which all of us, on more or less equal terms, have a right to participate in resolving it (Allan 2013: 68–9; 75).

I will not repeat all that here. Simply notice that the plausibility of the poison metaphor, and of this basis for thinking that hate speech laws might deliver a modicum of good consequences, really rests on taking a rather dim, pessimistic view of the capacities and capabilities of your fellow citizens. Oddly enough, it is here that Waldron seems to be the pessimist and Dworkin the optimist. Yet it is very much with Dworkin, the optimist, that I wish to stand on this matter. And not just stand with him but assert that Dworkin has the better of the argument. Indeed for me the whole of the moderate version of Dworkin's legitimacy argument, that enacting hate speech laws diminishes and spoils the legitimacy of other laws and makes their enforcement less fair, rests to a significant extent on an unspoken belief that one's fellow citizens will overwhelming see through the ranting of neo-Nazis and cross-burners and Holocaust deniers and peddlers selling hatred against homosexuals and misogynistic rap artists and what have you so that silencing carries a sort of unfairness to them, not just to the purveyors of such stuff. Indeed, without a hefty degree of optimism on that front, I am not clear on how one can oppose hate speech laws.

As it happens I think the facts are with Dworkin on that score. Or rather they are with Dworkin in the jurisdictions which lie at the heart of all his writings about the Herculean best fit or integrity-fuelled interpretive process, namely what I have called benevolent, liberal democracies (Allan 2011). It is in these jurisdictions, not in the North Koreas or Somalias of the world, that Dworkin's attempt to build a theory of law out of a theory of how best to interpret is most plausible and it is here that his view of a legal system fares best against a Hartian one. And I say that, as noted above, as one who does not ultimately find those Dworkinian theories persuasive but who can see where they do and do not work best.

Likewise, it is here that optimism as regards the capacity of one's fellow citizens to be immune to the 'poison' of hate speech is warranted. In the world's Rwandas and Yugoslavias that optimism is unwarranted and the case for hate speech laws is significantly and no doubt sometimes decisively greater. But for those of us lucky enough to live in a benevolent liberal democracy, the case for being optimistic about the capabilities and capacities of one's fellow citizens to see through hate speech is compelling. At least I think it is.

If that is correct, one can then go all the way back[23] to the other plank in Dworkin's anti-hate speech position, the one based on his scepticism that the harms of hate speech to the intended victims are anywhere near as great as some suggest—that many such 'claims are inflated' (Dworkin 2009: vi). This Dworkinian scepticism makes no sense at all in the context of the world's Rwandas. But take a country such as, say, the US and consider how a purportedly vulnerable group such as Muslims does (in a jurisdiction without any hate speech laws at all) compared to how it does in countries with such laws (perhaps Germany or France or the UK) and that scepticism seems eminently defensible to me. And that is so even after the attack on the Twin Towers. Add to that the danger of fostering identity politics and the benefits that flow when people have some incentives to develop a thick skin and Dworkin's scepticism is buttressed further. In other words, people tend to respond to incentives, including when these exist for seeing oneself as a victim, and that makes it hard to disentangle what is and is not something we want to count as a harm to be thrown into the consequentialist hopper.

So I think one can see the second plank or prong to Dworkin's opposition to hate speech laws as interlinked in this way to the first. Both require you to think that the case for optimism about the capacities of your fellow citizens can be made in your jurisdiction.

Let me finish this short paper by picking up that notion of Dworkin, the optimist, and suggesting that perhaps, in some way or other, it was just that sort of optimistic bent that made Ronald Dworkin one of the all-time best speakers I have ever heard. For without that view of his fellow citizens, it is less obvious why he would bother to lecture in the magnificent way that he did and why he would endeavour, as he also did, to influence public opinion as a public intellectual. Whatever one thinks of that speculation, I think that Dworkin got it right on the issue of hate speech laws.

Notes and References

1. See, for example, J.L. Mackie. 1977. *Ethics, Inventing Right & Wrong*. London: Penguin, and James Allan. 2001. 'Truth's Empire: A Reply to Ronald Dworkin's *Objectivity and Truth: You'd Better Believe It*', *Australian Journal of Legal Philosophy*. 26: 61.

2. See, for example, my favourite J.L. Mackie. 1985. 'The Third Theory of Law', *Persons and Values*, Volume II. Oxford: Clarendon Press.

3. See, for example, Grant Huscroft and Bradley W. Miller (eds). 2011. *The Challenge of Originalism: Theories of Constitutional Interpretation*. New York: Cambridge University Press.

4. See, for example, Jeremy Waldron. 1993. 'A Right-Based Critique of Constitutional Rights', *Oxford Journal of Legal Studies*. 13. p. 18 and Jeremy Waldron. 1999. *Law and Disagreement*. Oxford: Clarendon Press.

5. A subject dear to my heart, see, inter alia, James Allan. 1996. 'Bills of Rights and Judicial Power—A Liberal's Quandary? *Oxford Journal of Legal Studies*. 16. p. 337; 2003. 'A Modest Proposal', *Oxford Journal of Legal Studies*. 23. p. 197; 2004. 'An Unashamed Majoritarian', *Dalhousie Law Journal*. 27. p. 537; 2006. 'Portia, Bassanio or Dick the Butcher? Constraining Judges in the Twenty-First Century', *King's College Law Journal*. 17. p. 1; 2006. 'Thin Beats Fat Yet Again—Conceptions of Democracy', *Law & Philosophy*. 25. p. 533; and 2008. 'Jeremy Waldron and the Philosopher's Stone', *San Diego Law Review*. 45. p. 133.

6. See James Allan. 2011. *The Vantage of Law: Its Role in Thinking about Law, Judging and Bills of Rights*. Farnham, Surrey: Ashgate Publishing Co.

7. See endnotes 5 and 6.

8. I am *not* in that camp, though, as regards Waldron's flirting with the acceptability of a statutory bill of rights or when it comes to his position on constitutional interpretation. See James Allan. 2011. 'Statutory Bills of Rights: You Read Words In, You Read Words Out, You Take Parliament's Clear Intention and You Shake It All About—Doin' the Sankey Hankey Panky', in Tom Campbell, K.D. Ewing, and Adam Tomkins (eds), *The Legal Protection of Human Rights: Sceptical Essays*. Oxford: Oxford University Press. See too James Allan. 2012. 'Fantastic

Mr. Fox—A Review of Brian Simpson's *Reflections on 'The Concept of Law'*, *King's Law Journal*. 23. p. 331.

9. See James Allan. 2013. 'Hate Speech Law and Disagreement', *Constitutional Commentary*. 29. p. 59.

10. Jeremy Waldron. 2012. *The Harm in Hate Speech*. Cambridge, Mass.: Harvard University Press. p. 174.

11. Ronald Dworkin. 2009. 'Foreword', in Ivan Hare and James Weinstein (eds), *Extreme Speech and Democracy*. Oxford: Oxford University Press. p. viii.

12. See endnote 9. Much of the next two pages more or less follows the argument I made there.

13. [1990] 3 S.C.R. p.697 (Can.).

14. See *Lund v. Boissoin*, 2008 AHRC 6 (Can.), *rev'd*, *Lund v. Boissoin*, 2012 ABCA 300 (Can.).

15. This was told to me, in person, by Mark Steyn. I have no supplementary proof of this claim.

16. *Saskatchewan Human Rights Commission v. Whatcott*, 2013 SCC 11 (Can.). Of course it is also true that the Supreme Court of Canada read down the non-criminal hate speech law, severing concepts including dignity: '… However, expression that "ridicules, belittles or otherwise affronts the dignity of" does not rise to the level of ardent and extreme feelings constituting hatred required to uphold the constitutionality of a prohibition of expression in human rights legislation' *Id.* at p.18. And the Court also narrowed what hatred means, further than prior precedents, by saying it was an objective reasonable-person standard. In short, the Supreme Court of Canada 'upheld' the constitutionality of a different law, with one possible implication being that the Court doesn't want it used too much.

17. Canadian Human Rights Act, R.S.C., 1985, c. H-6, s. 13 (Can.); *See* Charlie Gills. 2012. Section 13: 'How the battle for free speech was won', *Maclean's*. 19 June. Available at http://www2.macleans.ca/tag/bill-c-304. The Bill to repeal it has been passed though the elected lower house and through the wholly unelected and appointed Upper House Senate. Royal Assent has also been given.

18. *See* Malcolm Farnsworth. 2012. 'Tony Abbott Speech on Free Speech', *Australian Politics*. 6 August. available at http://australianpolitics.com/2012/08/06/tony-abbott-speech-on-free-speech.html (Federal Opposition leader Tony Abbott addressed the Institute of Public Affairs about the importance of free speech and repealing Section 18(c) of the Racial Discrimination Act).

19. *Eatock v. Bolt* [2011] FCA 1103 (Austl.).

20. Garance Frank-Ruta. 2012. 'Is Elizabeth Warren Native American or What?', *The Atlantic*, May 20. available at http://www.theatlantic.com/politics/archive/2012/05/is-elizabeth-warren-native-american-or-what/257415.

21. See Waldron 2012: 191 (endnote 12).

22. See Waldron 2012: 190.

23. See the paragraph in the main text just after the one that contains endnote 9.

13

Exit Hercules

Ronald Dworkin and the Crisis of the Age of Rights

Lorenzo Zucca

The age of rights is in crisis. Particularly so, now that Ronald Dworkin has passed away—without him, rights lose their most successful spokesperson that incessantly tried to show their objectivity, independence, and deep harmony. It takes great faith and hope in human rationality to believe that we can come up with a single—right—answer based on rights to any ethical, moral, and legal dilemmas that our societies face. Ronald Dworkin attempted just that throughout his long career that just came to an end. He is the greatest of all the advocates of rights, and deployed all his vigour, sharpness, and rhetorical verve to defend the claim that rights must be taken seriously and if we do so, and understand them appropriately, they point our communities in the best possible direction for the future.

When I speak of the age of right, I refer to a historical period during which rights became the central element in legal, political, and moral language; not only that, rights also made, or seemed to make, a positive difference in the way legal, political, and moral decisions were taken. Dworkin happened to live the golden age of rights and embraced it whole-heartedly highlighting the strengths and achievements that could be reached in their name. It nonetheless seems to me high time to evaluate the contribution of rights in a more balanced light—I am not going to suggest that rights do not make any difference, but what I would like to stress is that they do not seem to make as much difference as they trumpet. They are but another element in the moral horizon of political societies. Moreover, rights no longer seem to provide compelling arguments to decide cases, perhaps precisely because of their success—their scope has widened beyond imagination, so each of the rights protected by constitutions or international treaties pull in competing—at times conflicting—directions. Rights frame disagreement as much as they frame agreement.

The period I am thinking about spans from 1948 to 1989, from the Universal Declaration of Human Rights (UDHR) to the fall of Berlin's wall. The starting point is obvious—the international community declared universal rights of all human beings at the end of the most devastating global confrontation. The ending point is more controversial, and it will become more apparent later on why I regard it as such. In fact, I should say that it is better described as both the highest point and the beginning of a decline for rights. The decline includes various phenomena amongst which we can cite: the reversal of fortune of a liberal agenda of rights with the return of conservative forces mining the march of rights and at times siding with religious groups to counter liberal reforms in the name of rights. I'd like to suggest that Ronald Dworkin's death is one of the lowest points in the decline of the age of rights.

Dworkin was born in 1931, and was 17 when the UN approved the UDHR. He was coming of age at exactly the right time, or perhaps the rights' time. His early maturity was characterized by the American experience of rights protection, and in particular he witnessed the very activist, and liberally minded, Warren Court (1953–69) while it tried to enhance equality and freedom in the US through a judicially enforced bill of rights. The decline, of the age of rights corresponds to the decline of the model of rights' protection as conceived in America. The American model as shaped by the historical events since 1948 has three fundamental dimensions: (a) politics, (b) law, and (c) morality. At the political level, what pushed forward the American conception of rights was a liberal credo that America wanted to spread throughout the world. The Supreme Court happened to be the voice of that liberal credo, and the Warren court in particular was the prime interpreter of it. The liberal credo was at the beginning a unifying credo in the US, especially when compared and contrasted with the Communist credo. At the legal level, we have already hinted at it, the institution that did most of the work in spreading the liberal credo was the Supreme Court; this informs the second tenets of

Dworkin's faith in rights, and the conviction that judges are there to uphold them. Finally, at the moral level, rights have become the moral lingua franca in which we cast any claim of injustice within and beyond the state. Its success as a discursive practice is not always matched at the practical level—they do not always redress the injustices they address. Moreover, their success as an argumentative tool shows major weakness at the philosophical level since it is a real problem to explain the universality, force and coherence of rights at the moral level. Dworkin did more than anyone else to show why we'd better believe in the moral truth of rights and why they always point us in the best direction. His task was really Herculean and in many ways he single-handedly engaged in a gigantic philosophical task—to explain the independence and the unity of the department of value.

Whether Dworkin was successful in that task is beyond my focus here. What matters is that without him, rights lose their hero and are likely to appear in a dimmer light, incapable of withstanding the charges of their critics. I will endeavour to show to what extent the age of right as I define it has benefited from Dworkin's argument and why it is now in trouble, if not at the last stop of that journey. Following the three pillars described above, I will focus on rights as part of a liberal agenda in the next section; I will then explain the role and function of courts in enhancing the protection of rights; and I will then discuss Dworkin's attempt to provide a unitary and independent foundation to the whole domain of value within which rights play a central role.

Liberal Rights

The age of rights was a response to World War II (WW2), the most brutal war of all times. Human rights were declared as the bedrock of any decent society in the world. To declare them was a first big step; the aim was to provide a common basis for all the nations, a foundation for peaceful mutual relations. But at the very same time, the world was divided into two blocs vying for ultimate power and for two opposite views of power: the western bloc stood for the ideals of liberal democracies and free markets, whereas the eastern bloc represented authoritarian states and a state-run economy. In this climate, each bloc needed to find and fund an ideology through which it could claim moral superiority. The western bloc naturally embraced a liberal agenda based on first generation rights that aimed at protecting the autonomy and dignity of the individual. The eastern bloc resisted the ideology of individual rights and instead focused on the idea of a strong collectivity based on the idea of equality.

Ronald Dworkin's coming of age coincided with the Universal Declaration of Human Rights (UDHR 1948). His formative years as a young boy in America were marked by the looming presence of the war. The UDHR ushered in a new chapter in his life, which he embraced whole-heartedly by becoming the greatest advocate of rights at home and abroad, and universally. However, his conception of rights was partisan—he represented better than anyone else a left-wing liberal position, which he incessantly defended for over 50 years. Indeed, one of his long-standing political and philosophical battles was to reconcile mainstream liberal views with left-egalitarian positions. While the success of liberal rights is beyond dispute, their egalitarian dimension is often the source of bitter disagreement. Dworkin's left egalitarian sensitivity must have been accrued by the seminal case of the Supreme Court in *Brown v. Board*,[1] where school segregation between white and black children was ruled to be unconstitutional. Another seed of his vision was planted: courts could be the agent of the implementation of a left-wing liberal manifesto.

However, the left wing liberal manifesto is based on the tension between liberty and equality. Some even insist that to reconcile liberty and equality is a conceptual impossibility. Isaiah Berlin, one of Dworkin's main philosophical mentors, strenuously defended the idea that sometimes values conflict in a way that cannot be reconciled. Human beings, and human societies, have different goals that cannot be reduced to one single formula. If a society pursues the maximization of liberty in one of its many guises, it is conceptually impossible to maximize at the same time, and to the same extent, equality. This is the gist of pluralism, which goes hand in hand with a modest conception of liberty, namely negative liberty—that is freedom from interference of the state in one's own private decision about what makes a life worth living. In response to Berlin, Dworkin argued that negative liberty is not the only way of conceiving of liberty. An alternative may be the following: liberty is 'freedom to do whatever you like so long as you respect the moral rights, properly understood, of others'.[2] You can see in this reply a very powerful, albeit largely rhetorical, move that combines Dworkin's conception of liberty and equality with moral rights. For Dworkin, an appropriate understanding of rights is what can help us mediate conflicts between political values. In fact, moral rights mark the boundaries between, and provide the glue for, a harmonious view of all political values. For example, when the state wishes to raise taxes in order to improve on the medical care of more vulnerable people, one may describe this situation as a conflict between liberty and equality. Rich people would stand for their liberty not to be interfered with their property, while poor people would claim for better medical care in the name of equality. According to Dworkin, the state is justified to impose taxes on rich people without infringing liberty, because what they own in excess is not rightfully theirs. Here, the conflict between values is not so much resolved but displaced at the level of moral rights—in this sense Dworkin wants to focus all our disagreement on whether or not we are entitled to some things in the name of rights. For Dworkin, political conflicts in a community are solved by appeal to arguments that feature moral rights very prominently if not exclusively.

Dworkin puts moral rights at the centre of his liberal agenda, just like individual rights are at the centre of the US liberal agenda, and more generally of the agenda of western liberal democracies. Moreover, moral rights are not mere aspirations, but they have a clear and sizeable legal impact by way of constitutional interpretation. Dworkin encapsulates a legal constitutional development that is already clear from *Brown v. Board*, the first major decision of the Supreme Court presided over by Chief Justice Warren (1953–69). This court is often perceived as one of the most activist as well as the most liberal. The court was very active in three areas in particular: (a) whenever an enumerated right—such as free speech—was at stake, (b) whenever political conflict would prevent social progress, and (c) whenever minorities were clearly discriminated. In each of these three areas, rights are deeply interwoven with the liberal agenda of the court. Rights are both means of the court to advance the agenda, and ends in themselves of that agenda.

One right above all, the right to free speech, comes to be regarded as the core principle of any democracy, the individual right par excellence. For liberals, free speech is the guarantee of a properly working political system where serious and genuine disagreement is played out in public and is supposed to lay bare truths and dispose of wrongs and mistaken ideas. Free speech is particularly useful for liberals when applied to politics and political officials. The Warren Court was central in advancing that thesis in *New York Times Co. v. Sullivan*,[3] where it was held that a public official could only win a libel suit against the press if he could prove that the statement was made with 'actual malice' and not simply showing that the statement was incorrect. While Dworkin praised the result of the case, which makes it more difficult for the press to be bullied into burying some news for fear of being sued, Dworkin also criticized Brennan's leading opinion that seemed to give priority to an instrumental reading of free speech rather than a constitutive one. The instrumental argument is the one that links democracy and free speech and argues that the latter promotes the former, and that is why the right is valuable. Dworkin suggests that free speech should also be conceived as a constitutive right given that it sustains the idea that each one of us has moral agency and is therefore, capable of choosing which opinions are worth being followed and which ones are not. To insist on moral agency and responsibility puts the individual at the centre of the picture and the state is distrusted as a benign gatekeeper who decides which opinions can be heard and which ones cannot. By denying the access of some opinions to the general market of ideas, the state would deny the dignity and personhood of human beings who are not regarded as being capable to elect autonomously what to believe in. Dworkin suggested that Brennan's original instrumental reading could be expanded to include the constitutive reading of free speech—in other words the right of free speech ought to be regarded as both a means and an end. The discussion on free speech also shows that disagreement is possible within the liberal camp, even if the goal is common.

Another fundamental tenet of the liberal camp is the fight for sexual and reproductive deregulation. This is a field within which, there was little hope for progress from within politics, and probably explains why the court felt so keen to intervene and give a new surprising grounding to the whole debate—the right to privacy emerged as one of the core un-enumerated rights from the jurisprudence of the court. In *Griswold v. Connecticut*,[4] the Supreme Court planted the seeds for many other great liberal decisions in the fields of sex and reproduction. The case itself made it unconstitutional to prohibit contraception between married couples. But the great legacy of the case is to announce a core un-enumerated right which will be at the centre of very many other decisions, including *Roe v. Wade*.[5] Liberals in the Court thought that the right to privacy—understood as the right to make one's own decisions about sex and reproduction unencumbered by the judgment of the state—was central to the Constitutional enterprise, even if it were not explicitly mentioned in the list of enumerated rights in the text. Conservatives since then heavily criticized the liberal activism of the court, in particular when it essentially made up from scratch rights that were not even remotely mentioned. Dworkin makes a case against conservatives suggesting that the very distinction between enumerated and un-enumerated rights is bogus. For Dworkin, the Constitution is couched in very sweeping moral language that is there to be interpreted; clauses referring to the equal protection of the law, or to due process call for a great deal of further instantiation, and judges are there to bring the constitutional enterprise forward and cast the best possible light on the text. It nevertheless remains clear that if some rights are explicitly mentioned and others are not, then this must be evidence of the constitutional choices of the framers that are not fully catered for in Dworkin's viewpoint. It seems unavoidable to suggest that Dworkin, as an advocate of liberal rights, had a great stake in protecting the status of the right to privacy.

Indeed, as mentioned above, the right to privacy is again at the core of the most important judicial victory for the liberal camp, that is *Roe v.*

Wade—which established the right to abortion on the basis of the right to privacy. A woman should be allowed to make up her own mind about as private a matter as pregnancy, and the state is not justified in preventing women from choosing not to abort their pregnancy. If *Roe v. Wade* was the victory of a great battle for liberals, it did not amount to the winning of the war on sexual reproduction and liberation. Conservative forces took *Roe v. Wade* as the principal example of what can go wrong when the court advances too aggressively a political agenda. The decision backfired and the last 40 years were spent to undo the decision that is heralded by Ronald Dworkin as one of the greatest. This is certainly true from a liberal viewpoint, but it also entailed a very deep political polarization between liberal and conservatives, between right and left wing. It also raises the question of how far can a court go when attempting to protect a right that is very controversial from both a constitutional and political viewpoint.

The right to privacy contributed to further victories for liberals, in particular the overruling of Bowers, which gave constitutional approval to law criminalizing homosexual sex in private. In *Lawrence v. Texas*,[6] the Supreme Court led by the most Dworkinian of justices, Justice Kennedy, found the Texas statute criminalizing homosexuality unconstitutional on the basis of the right to privacy. At first sight, one may claim that free speech and privacy are co-extensive, and can be reduced to, negative liberty—but Dworkin explains why this is not the case: a political community is genuinely liberal if it treats its individuals as fully fledged moral members. To do so, individuals have to take part in the political process, they have to have a stake in the political process, and they have to be independent from the political process even if they are subject to its decisions. The first two conditions are easy to grasp. An individual that cannot voice her concern in the political process is not a member of the community. And also an individual who does not see his interest represented in the political process, can hardly accept the final decision of the community since his viewpoint has never been accounted for.

The third condition is more difficult to grasp, since it is hard to understand how one can possibly be independent and bound at the same time. Or to put it differently, how is it possible that individual freedom can be furthered by collective self-government? Dworkin suggests that an individual endowed with self-respect and dignity understands that a political community is a common endeavour where responsibility for decision on important policies is given to an ultimate authority. He compares that situation with a musical orchestra, where individual musician endowed with self-respect understand that for the orchestra to work they have to rely on the choices of the musical director. It is not the case that their independence is curtailed or limited; in such a situation, their independence is compatible with the idea of being directed. Dworkin suggests that in political matters, it is even more so the case. People can accept that moral independence exercised on question of private life is compatible with having issues of justice decided by a collective body when individual interest compete and collide and the community requires a common standard for all that compromises between divergent interests. Of course, in Dworkin's view, competition and clash of interests can always be interpreted in a way that dispel a fundamental conflict of values and the compromise to which Dworkin aspires is always couched in terms of rights.

We have already seen, however, how divisive some liberal positions could be, in particular in relation to sexual and reproductive freedom. The gap that was being excavated between liberal and conservative was to widen progressively in the 1970s and in the 1980s. What seemed to keep the country together was in those years the fact that the US had a foreign common enemy, who was particularly inimical to the idea of individual rights from the liberal point of view. The fall of the Berlin wall in 1989 gave rise to the all-encompassing crisis of liberal values in the west. Liberal western democracies based on individual rights had won the cold war, but they were likely to become victim of their own success. Once its competing ideology was gone, the liberal dogma was much more likely to show all its weaknesses and internal contradictions.

The fall of the Berlin wall, made Isiaha Berlin's idea of value pluralism even more popular and widespread. But value pluralism was the biggest threat for a harmonious liberal recipe based on moral rights. Not that Berlin's ideas are illiberal. To the contrary, he is a very committed liberal and believes that value pluralism—the idea that values are objective *and* incommensurable—is the heart of liberalism. For Berlin, liberalism should promote diversity as far as possible. Every individual should be protected in the free pursuit of what he thinks best for the purpose of his self-development and flourishing. The society should refrain as far as possible from imposing any overarching set of norms that would stifle diversity and promote one homogeneous and harmonious position as to what is a good life. Value pluralism has a great explanatory power, and highlights the appeal of liberalism as committed to diversity, but it also underlies a major challenge for liberalism in so far that it recognizes that some moral disagreement is the stuff of tragic conflict and there is no way in which all values can be made to cohere in a harmonious whole. The challenge is to be able to accept tragic conflicts, while devising a method to cope with them without polarising the society.

In the post-Berlin-wall world, human rights spread their wings in liberal democracies. The rights revolution swept the whole world and in two decades most countries adopted constitutionally entrenched rights with judicial review. These included all eastern European Countries, as well as most commonwealth countries including the UK itself. However, the spread of human rights documents and the introduction of judicial review has not always been an unequivocal success. In some countries, human rights are used as an instrument to fuel social and political conflicts. Societies are being divided along moral, political and, religious lines and human rights advocates are not capable of mediating these conflicts in a way that does not leave moral or political residue.

Polarization became even starker with 9/11, which brought a new form of global division along national identity lines, based in particular on religious difference. Religious Identity is a strong form of belonging coupled with a strong set of beliefs that can be hard to square with other equally strong beliefs. Rights in this environment are not always suited to help mediate between the concerns of liberal polities and those of religious communities. On sexual morality and reproduction, for example, old divisions resurface and liberalism's commitment to diversity can hardly be squared with its commitment to sexual freedom. Value pluralism asks us to understand and accept other world-views, the problem arises when other world-views want to impose themselves on the rest of the society on the ground that they are the only ones to hold the truth about moral matters.

Dworkin himself had to acknowledge that liberal democracies, starting with the US, had received a massive blow in the last 10 years or so and came to ask whether Democracy is possible in these circumstances of deep moral and political division. The return of religion-fuelled deep-seated divisions and promoted confrontation rather than compromise. Despite his bleaker look at present-day liberal societies, Dworkin insisted that societies need a common ground, one big idea that can be shared and from which disagreement can be started and articulated. The big idea he has in mind is that of dignity and it has two major implications. Firstly, dignity means to recognize the special and intrinsic value of everyone's life. Second, everyone has personal responsibility to make decisions concerning how to live the best possible life. Unfortunately, this optimistic minimal common ground seems to ride roughshod over the fact that sometimes some world-views are simply incompatible with others. It is not necessarily a holistic incompatibility all the way through, but it surfaces on important decisions that need to be taken collectively—such as the nature of marriage, the permissibility of euthanasia and other moral dilemmas that cannot find an answer that will appease everyone. Dworkin's hope to find a common ground defies the widespread belief that, perhaps, the only thing there is in common is the fact of unbridgeable pluralism.

Courts

Moral rights need their advocates and, more importantly, they need institutions who are likely to implement them and argue for them. Post-war America found in the Warren Court a formidable bastion in defence of a liberal view of rights. The US Supreme Court judicial activism is the second important pillar of what I call the age of rights. Not only rights were declared in bills of rights, but they were also effectively protected by the intervention of courts. At the same time, post-war Europe, in particular Italy and Germany were cutting their teeth with a brand new set of constitutional instruments inspired by the American experience and completed with strong power for their respective constitutional courts. Constitutional courts that are composed by elites of a country tend to be progressive and liberal, and so they naturally advance a mainstream liberal agenda on free speech, decisional privacy, sexual freedom, and procreation.

Needless to say, courts became for Dworkin the place where it all happens. A liberal agenda can be carried forward in the name of rights, since rights are trumps against policies that are shaped by the aggregation of interests. Rights are not purely instrumental, they are constitutive and they resist most forms of consequentialist (or instrumentalist) thinking. Courts have the power to argue in favour of rights and against legislation that does not take rights seriously. Judges can engage in detailed arguments of principle and can apply them to the facts of the case to help carry forward the constitutional ethos. Courts, however, are not fully trained in moral arguments and Dworkin's liberal agenda aims at convincing judges that they should reason with principles that are embedded in rights.

But first, Dworkin had to overcome an important hurdle—HLA Hart's influential book, *The Concept of Law*, offers an understanding of law that does not have a place for morally oriented principles. The building block of law is the notion of rules; legal rules do not invite judges to engage in moral reasoning. They invite them to interpret legal materials carefully and to apply rules to the facts by religiously respecting the words crafted by the legislator. Hart's Positivism does not rule out altogether the possibility for judges to engage in moral reasoning—sometimes rules are crafted in a way that explicitly requires them to draw some moral lines; so for instance the unfair contract terms legislation requires judges to establish the meaning of unfairness. However, the link between law and morality is purely contingent and does not arise if rules are crafted in a technical and precise way. As we all know very well, Dworkin attacks precisely on that point and suggests that the law is not made only of precise rules, the dimension of which is one of validity. The law is made of principles that are an integral part of any legal practice; principles are different in kind from rules to the extent that they behave differently since they do not prescribe a precise set of actions. By arguing that principles are a constitutive part of the law, Dworkin also suggests that there is a necessary link between law and morality and that judges have an obligation to bring morality to bear whenever the law is unclear or incomplete. In particular, judges have to determine the moral rights and obligations of all parties to litigation in a way that reflect sophisticated moral arguments. Morality requires judges to take rights seriously.

There is another reason for Dworkin to provide a competing theory of law to Hart's. A positivist sometimes has a hard time defending his liberal views and arguing that the law can well be contrary to his own liberal convictions and still be fully valid. Dworkin probably found Hart's position unsatisfactory when faced with Lord Devlin's arguments on prohibiting homosexuality on grounds of immorality. Hart, as a positivist, was not entitled to say that the law could not interfere with individuals' private choices as a matter of principle. Dworkin thought that this was a basic weakness of the positivist position that could not properly advance a liberal agenda even if it wanted to. Dworkin's alternative answer to the debate on homosexuality is to argue that as a matter of principle, and basic rights, no individual can be coerced to behave against one's own private or sexual preferences. No law could be considered as binding if it infringed those basic rights.

Dworkin's move allows him to have a direct weapon against conservative moralist like Devlin. If legislation is not compatible with moral rights, then it cannot be regarded as valid law. Devlin on the other hand is simply expounding a conventional understanding of the law based on the orthodox doctrine of parliamentary supremacy. Parliament can do whatever it wishes, and in moral matters it is perfectly allowed to follow common sense. A positivist has to allow for the fact that law may be bigoted and conservative. Dworkin is unsatisfied with that position and his theory of law incorporates as much as possible his moral position. What Dworkin did not realize though is that to subordinate the law to moral substantive views is a double-edged sword— sometimes it may go in a favourable direction, but at other times, it may just go against one's moral preferences. Positivists in that case can distance themselves from the law and criticize from an external viewpoint. A moralist like Dworkin can only resort to internal criticism of the law.

The role of the court, for Dworkin, is to bring moral rights to bear on the interpretation of law. In some cases, like *Riggs v. Palmer*, it is particularly easy to see the appeal of that position. Someone who kills a member of the family in order to inherit his property as stipulated in the will is deemed to forebear his moral right to inheritance because of his wrong-doing. Legislation could not foresee this wicked case, and was therefore, silent about it. The judge was faced with a gap, the positivist says. And in the case of a gap, the judge is empowered to use his discretion; the wider the gap, the wider the discretion of course, but in these cases it helps to guide discretion according to common sense and morality. In this case, nobody disputes what is the morally right answer; it's a dead easy case. But Dworkin builds on this case the idea that law has no gaps, and no discretion. The judge has a general duty to decide cases on the basis of the best moral interpretation, whenever the law does not provide a clear answer. Moral rights fill every gap of the law, because moral rights underpin the whole legal enterprise.

So the job of the courts is not only to mechanically interpret rules, but it is also—if not chiefly—about balancing moral principles underlying the law. Principles—we are told—have a dimension of weight rather than validity. They do not apply in an all-or-nothing fashion, but require instead that each policy be evaluated in light of competing moral principles that lie beneath it. If the policy produced displays appropriate concern for all underlying principles, then legislation is sound. Otherwise it will have to be invalidated in the name of its incompatibility with an important moral concern that has been largely overlooked. It is not clear whether this is the 'real' way courts proceed, but Dworkin tried to persuade us that that was the case for the whole of his career. His passionate defence of the court reached a pinnacle when he described them as a forum of principle, a place where moral deliberation can take place in a controlled and judicious way.

Dworkin's American audience was bound to be more sympathetic to Dworkin's claim than a British audience. The reason was simple, America already displayed a great degree of moral deliberation on the basis of the rights contained in the bill of rights. But Britain lacked a formal, modern, bill of rights on the basis of which all law could be scrutinized. And for a long time, Britain resisted the temptation to bring into the law such a mammoth bill that would alter the relation between parliament and the courts. Britain was very happy that other, less liberal, countries adopt a written constitution with judicial review; but a standard British understanding of the law was that it naturally tended towards fairness without having judges to step in to redress the balance.

Having noticed the erosion of that fairness in the 1980s, during Thatcher's government—when the west was battling for its economic deep concerns, Dworkin came to realize, as many other people did, that Britain had vanquished its true liberal commitments that it had inherited from its constitutional history and his great liberal philosophers such as Locke and Mill. He decided to plea for a Bill of Rights for Britain.[7] Soon thereafter, in the 1990s, a new left wing liberal movement led by Tony Blair campaigned in favour of bringing rights home. Home here means the place where they originally belong, but it also means away from the Strasbourg's court, which was increasingly intervening in British affairs to redress some basic infringements. So in 1998, the Human Rights Act (HRA) comes into force and is the centrepiece of the New Labour constitutional reform that attempts to bring Britain in line with other Western Democracies. Of course, the point of the HRA is not so much to have a substantive impact, but to alter the separation of powers between parliament and the courts and to this effect, the supreme court of the UK is also created independently from the House of Lords where the previous highest judicial formation was sitting.

It is not clear why courts are trusted with a special constitutional power that would bring back rights into one's country-legal culture. This idea travelled the world and spread nearly everywhere, but there is no empirical evidence that judicial review based on rights has the effect of restoring, or ushering in, a new age of rights. In the words of one of Dworkin's mentors, Justice Learned Hand, 'I often wonder whether we not rest our hopes too much upon constitutions, upon laws, and upon courts. These are false hopes; believe me these are false hopes. Liberty lies in the hearts of men and women; when it dies there, no constitution, no law, no court can save it; no constitution, no law, no court can even do much to help it. While it lies there it needs no constitution, no law, no court to save it.'[8] It is not clear whether the HRA 1998 can restore the spirit of liberty that was seemingly lost under the Thatcher's era. It does not seem to be the case if we judge from the massive backlash against the bill in the British media, not to mention its crusade against Strasbourg.

And perhaps, there is a small grain of truth in the muddled waters of British media. The golden age of liberty in the UK was not secured by courts, but by parliament. So why would it be sensible to hand to a bevy of judges issued from the very same social background the keys of the interpretation of rights? Recent studies show that the rationale for shifting power from parliament to courts through the incorporation of a bill of rights is not so much a concern for universal justice, but a preservation of the control of the society by a bien pensant elite that is losing its grip through the representative mechanism. Ran Hirschl shows this mechanism very well in the case of Israel for example; the bill of right empowers a bevy of judges from a secular Ashkenazi elite to prevent the loss of control of the Knesset.[9] The problem is that judicial institutions themselves have to open up and become more representative. The slippery slope is only slowed down, but the grip on a liberal understanding of society is a concrete possibility.

Dworkin had to struggle himself with the curse of judicial power when it eventually became dominated by conservative minded judges appointed by President Bush.[10] Dworkin was horrified by the prospect of a reversal of liberal fortune and in the last ten years, he began to attack the Supreme Court and in particular its republican judges. Abortion, Euthanasia, gay marriage, and many other liberal crusades are all in the hands of a bevy of conservative judges who are not going to abide by a liberal agenda anymore. Perhaps the greatest blow was given during the *Bush v. Gore* litigation, when the Supreme Court had to step in to virtually determine the outcome of the presidential election—obviously in favour of the Republican candidate. Having chanted the greatness of the Supreme court as a forum of principle, it became difficult for Dworkin to start firing bullets against it, while preserving its image and legitimacy. Either the court is a forum of principle, or it is the locus of politics by a random bunch of unelected people who may happen to have liberal views but may just as well happen to be very conservative.

Rights in the hand of left liberal judges will advance a left liberal agenda. However, in the hands of conservative judges they will only entrench privileges and inequalities. The problem of principles is that they can always go one way or another. Dworkin would no doubt welcome disagreement, but would be deeply upset about outcomes that are not in line with his political views. How upset can one be before starting to think that the constitutional pact is not for everyone anymore? Is it enough to claim that constitutional rights provide a common ground for everyone, when the constitution allows for major inequalities and discrimination? Can there be a common foundation that is truly common?

Moral Lingua Franca

From 1948 to today, rights became the lingua franca of any talk of justice at the national and international level. The number of declarations, charters, bills of rights enacted in the last 65 years is astounding. Some experiments have had great success while others are of limited impact, but what is clear is that at an abstract level everyone agrees that the language of rights is the most popular way of casting claims against actual or perceived wrongs. To this extent at least, we live in the age of rights. But there is a discrepancy between the language of rights and the practice of rights both at the national and at the international level. At the national level, the language of rights fuels disagreement rather than contribute to the understanding of society as a common venture. It is not hard to understand this: if every individual can attempt to fit his claims in the language of rights, then any denial would be perceived as a major setback. Setbacks, however, are inevitable as individual interests cast in the language of rights will inescapably conflict one against another. At the international level, the language of rights is even more controversial as any firm understanding of what human rights could require is inescapably tainted with accusation of imperialism and lack of cultural sensitivity. Few wrongs command universal agreement in principle—say for instance torture—but even then they are violated at times despite all prohibitions.

The language of rights may be omnipresent, but it suffers from conceptual imprecision since it applies to many different objects. Dworkin, for example, addresses many different types of rights—legal, political, moral rights of which human rights are but one species. Moreover, there does not seem to be a common structure to rights, even if they all have the same point or purpose for Dworkin—legal, political, and moral rights are all grounded on the ethical notion of dignity. In Dworkin's theory, political rights are trumps against collective national goals. However, human rights are not simply trumps against national sovereignty. That would yield a far too thin conception of human rights for Dworkin. Human rights require a precise attitude on the part of everyone, and in particular on the part of the state—people must be treated as deserving full respect in the name of their human dignity. Legal right is the narrowest term and it applies to those rights recognized by the state in legislation or constitutions to which we attach a number of institutional consequences such as the possibility for a court to strike down other norms. So as you can see, the structure of rights varies greatly, but their foundation is the same—dignity as entailing ethical independence and moral responsibility.

Dworkin put his great rhetorical vigour in defence of an understanding of rights that has a common philosophical foundation. His inner citadel—the ultimate idea for which he stands—is that the department of value through which we judge all human actions and achievements has a deep unshakable unity and is completely independent from other fields of knowledge; it has its own internal standards of truth. Dworkin's position argues against two major ideas about values: firstly, he argues that values do not depend on any other deeper thought or action. Second, he is squarely opposed to the idea that values are fundamentally incommensurable and at times conflict in an inescapable way. The best understanding of rights can recompose them in a wholly harmonious way without leaving moral residue. The impression though is that conflicts are always resolved in the direction of a left liberal agenda, Dworkin's agenda. How is it possible to convince someone who's not a left-liberal that her rights have been respected and her moral viewpoint has been taken into account properly? Dworkin is firmly aware of the fact that we all disagree about issues of principles, but he's still confident that there is one best moral argument that is capable to display the deep unity of the department of value.

I find it hard to believe that the department of value is unitary, and harmonious in the way Dworkin sees it. This is the case for both morality and law. It is hard to believe that for each hard question there is one clear and final answer as to which values take priority over another. More importantly it is hard to believe that someone will be convinced to accept the idea that if we disagree it is just because I know the objective truth about moral values and you do not. Dworkin eventually accepts this basic intuition and acknowledges in *Justice for Hedgehogs* that 'the best answer on some occasion is that nothing is any better to do than anything else'.[11] We reach the paradoxical core of Dworkin's position according to which on occasion the right answer is that there is no right answer. The moral truth Dworkin accidentally stumbles across is that on occasion values conflict and it is not possible to discern one clear ranking between the two. Dworkin muddles the water by suggesting that his opponents escape the question by appealing to answers that are external to the department of value. His opponents would claim for example that the question of truth in morals is not to be investigated from within the department of value, but requires a higher—detached–meta-ethical view that would help to explain and track truth in a way that is independent from substantive questions of value. But this clearly misses the point since value pluralists can say that value conflict as a matter of truth about values without having to search for higher metaphysical or meta-ethical truths. So how would Dworkin arbitrate between the objective truth pluralist hold and that of monists? One of them is right, and the other wrong—but is there an *internal* answer to morality that tells us who wins? The answer must surely be found at a higher level.

The department of value covers all the fields of practical philosophy and goes from ethics, through morality to politics. According to Dworkin there is deep unity across the department of value. The department of value is to be distinguished from the department of science, where the conception of truth functions in a completely different way from truth in the field of value. The truth of moral judgments comes from within—when we are searching moral truth we are trying to figure out what we really believe in. Seeking for truth in the department of science is a different endeavour insofar that it attempts to understand and describe pre-existing natural order that is external to, and independent from, human behaviour. In the department of value, Dworkin holds, dignity is the all-encompassing foundation, and common ground, that provides the basis to understand ethical questions about goodness of life as well as moral obligations between people, to end up with the duties that the state has towards individuals.

When applied to law, Dworkin's position is appealing for judges, but puzzling when it comes to the explanation of conflicts of rights. In some cases, rights pull in two opposite direction—freedom of religion allows individuals and groups to organize their lives on the basis of their beliefs. But what if their belief requires them to treat some people better than others simply because they happen to share the same beliefs? Is it possible to discriminate between people on the basis of one's freedom of religion? The requirements of liberty and equality are not so easily recomposed in this case. It is possible to suggest intricate alternatives as to how to cope with this situation, but in one way or another something of value must be sacrificed. If it is decided that freedom of religion allows for the discrimination of people, then equality can end up being undermined. If it is decided on the other hand that no belief can justify preferential treatment in the running of a community, then freedom to live according to one's beliefs can also be undermined. I don't believe there is one answer that leaves no moral residue that is one answer that satisfies all the parties and shows a harmonious coherent realm of value. Sometimes it is necessary to choose between two equally important values, and the identity of the society will be shaped precisely by the kind of choices we make. The society as a whole has responsibility to choose between clashing values, and some values will be given preference over others.

Who's the ultimate authority when it comes to decide clashes between conflicting rights? And more importantly even, on what basis can any ultimate authority decide conflicts in a way that preserve the harmony of the department of value. Dworkin believes in a unitary foundation, a common ground that we all share. We have already explored his idea of dignity with its emphasis on ethical independence and moral responsibility. Dworkin believes that rights have the same core and are the fundamental element of any polity that is committed to a proper understanding of value. Judges have a special role in that they have to hold other institutions to their overarching ethical commitment. Rights are those trumps that prevent institutions from taking decisions that go against the foundation of dignity, which is the bedrock of any liberal democratic country.

Dworkin came back to the same point over and over again. If appropriately interpreted, liberty and equality do not conflict but are clearly compatible. This runs against the wisdom of value pluralist according to whom values at times are inescapably in conflict. The bottom line for Dworkin is the notion of hope, a deeply religious notion.[12] Given that we can choose between interpreting values in a way that conflict or cohere, then he hopes that we will do everything to show that values are always compatible.[13] The hope that no tragedy would ever occur in our societies flies in the face of the fact that tragedy occurs and that we need a vocabulary to account for those tragedies that involve dramatic conflict of interests. Greek tragedy provides majestic examples—think of Antigone's obligation to bury the corpse of her brother pitting her against the will of the ruler of the city, Creon, who has decreed that those who fought against the city forfeit their right of burial.

One major challenge for rights at the international level is to escape the charge of imperialism and steer away from the deflating perils of relativism. Human rights are either the by-product of western ideology or they collapse into meaningless cultural difference. Either way, human rights are defeated. Dworkin is a relentless advocate of a common foundation of all types of rights including human rights. This foundation is anything but relativistic: we'd better believe in dignity and what it means for each one of us. This is not to say that different legal and political systems will make different choices about what rights to entrench in their constitutions; this is very much a matter of their constitutional history and independence. But in any case, those choices always bring us back to the basic fact that all political rights have the same ultimate foundation. Moreover, that foundation has nothing western or imperialistic. If we think long and hard enough, dignity understood as ethical independence and moral responsibility is truly something that we could all embrace as a foundation of our department of values. The problem with this argument at the international level is that it smacks as deeply western and perhaps even simply left-liberal. Here we have an individualistic conception of human nature that puts all the stress on the individual ability to author his own life and to make decisions that steer his boat in the direction that the individual wishes for himself. Most cultures do not have such a strong commitment with individualism.

There remains a much deeper philosophical problem—some people, even and perhaps especially in the west, do not believe that the department of value has a special independence as Dworkin would like us to believe. In addition to that most philosophers believe that even if values have an objective dimension, it does not mean that they exist independently from our thoughts or actions. Dworkin develops his posthumous argument in an interesting direction, somehow what I had always suspected. Dworkin acknowledges a deep religious attitude even if he does not believe in god.[14] To have a religious attitude means to reject all forms of naturalism,[15] which according to Dworkin either equates with nihilism (values are only illusory) or with the idea that values exist but don't have independent existence since they are based on people's thoughts or reactions. Dworkin is a profound religious atheist in that he believes in the objectivity of values and in their complete independence. The department of value is completely self-standing and values have no other foundation but themselves. Dworkin stretches this metaphor to the idea that we have faith in the existence of the department of value. If you cannot see that, you simply lack that faith.

Human rights, however, do not depend on the existence of god. This is also very clear for Dworkin. He's not simply articulating a classic thesis of the religious foundations of human rights. It is not an issue of having rights simply because we have been created in the image of a god that is source of all good and evil. In order to know whether god is good, we need an independent premise to our reasoning. Here Dworkin's argument is distinctively Humean. Dworkin would like to show that religion itself has two distinctive tasks that can be presented as distinctive department of knowledge. One is the science part of religion that tells us several things about the origin and existence of the world and the way in which god has shaped it. The other part of religion is the department of value and concerns the way in which human should behave. Dworkin argues that even for religious people, there is no connection of cause and effect between the department of science and that of value. We are entitled to believe or not to believe in the existence of god and in his omnipotence; however, god's omnipotence in the natural world does not warrant his inherent goodness or evil. In order to know that, we need an independent premise that is internal to the department of value and therefore independent from the faith in the existence of god. People who display a religious attitude have independent faith in the existence of objective, independent values and this does not require faith in the existence of god. So both religious people and atheists share more than we think when it comes to values. In effect they both share a faith in values (in their objectivity and independence), according to Dworkin.

Dworkin's religious attitude of hope and faith is what is making the hard work in the construction of the domain of value. Faith is what explains the independence of the department of value and hope explains its inner harmony. We can also suggest that, for Dworkin, rights are based on the same premises. To believe in the foundation of human rights is to suggest that we have faith in a universal commitment to treat human beings in a certain way—that is, with full respect that flows from a proper understanding of human dignity. Moreover, to believe that rights can always be composed in a harmonious whole relies on the hope that we can always prevent tragedies and promote happy endings.

***

The age of right as I defined it owes much to Ronald Dworkin who embraced it and interpreted in the best possible light he could. Rights became the quintessential tool to bring forward a left wing liberal reform of the society. Through rights implemented by national supreme courts, many liberal battles have been won in matters of individual independence, sexual and reproductive morality, and equality between different people. To win battles, however, does not mean to promote a society that is cohesive and harmonious; on the contrary, American society, and the west in general grew more and more divided especially in the last twenty years. Rights can advance agendas but they cannot achieve moral and political unity. Dworkin, like a Greek tragic hero, is rolling the rock of rights up against the mountain of disagreement and polarization.

Dworkin's work is monumental in scope and ambition. A modern hero of liberal democracies, he never gave up the fight for justice in the name of rights. Dworkin never gave up hope and faith that a better society could be fashioned in the image of the objective realm of moral values he believes in. Part of his optimism was due to the historical period within which he grew up. The American model of judicial review of rights had made important advancements towards a more liberal and more equal polity at home, and inspired many other liberal democracies to move on with their own liberal agenda.

But any hero has his own Achilles' heel. Dworkin's is the over-inflated confidence in what rights can achieve. Rights are a moral element of a much wider universe. Also, rights can have varying gravitational pulls—and they can hardly all go in one direction—harmoniously and without clashing one with another. This basic point requires an argument that cannot be made from within the department of value, as Dworkin would like us to believe. Either value pluralists are right or Dworkin is right; but what would help deciding this disagreement? Would we need a court of principle to establish the winner?

Exit Hercules: with Dworkin passes away the most articulate, energetic, passionate advocate of rights in the twentieth century. The beauty of his speech and the force of his convictions will inspire many people, and will most probably remain unequalled. It is in this spirit that I argued that the golden age of right through which Dworkin lived and which he interpreted so well is now coming to a close. Exit Hercules from the stage. Just like in a Greek tragedy, the light goes off and it all just look like a dream. A very noble dream.

Notes and References

1. *Brown v. Board*, 347 US 483 (1954).
2. Ronald Dworkin. 2006. *Justice in Robes*. Cambridge: Belknap Press of Harvard University Press. p. 112.

3. *New York Times Co. v. Sullivan*, 376 US 254 (1964).
4. *Griswold v. Connecticut*, 381 US 479 (1965).
5. *Roe v. Wade*, 410 US 113 (1973).
6. *Lawrence v. Texas*, 539 US 558 (2003).
7. Ronald Dworking. 1990. *A Bill of Rights for Britain: Why British Liberty Needs Protection*. London: Chatto & Windus.
8. Irving Dilliard (ed.). 1954. *The Spirit of Liberty: Papers and Addresses of Learned Hand*. New York: Knopf. pp. 189–90.
9. Ran Hirschl. 2004. *Towards Juristocracy: The Origins and Consequences of the NewConstitutionalism*. Cambridge: Harvard University Press. pp. 21–4.
10. Ronald Dworkin. 2007. 'The Supreme Court Phalanx', *New York Review of Books*, 30 August <http://www.nybooks.com/articles/archives/2007/sep/27/the-supreme-court-phalanx/?pagination=false> accessed 24 April 2013.
11. Ronald Dworkin. 2011. *Justice For Hedgehogs*. Cambridge: Belknap Press of Harvard University Press. p. 24.
12. See Ronald Dworkin. 2001. 'Do Liberal Values Conflict?' in Mark Lilla, Ronald Dworkin, and Robert Silvers (eds), 'The Legacy of Isaiah Berlin'. *New York Review of Books*. p.90 'Perhaps, after all, the most attractive conceptions of the leading liberal values do hang together in the right way. We haven't yet been given reason to abandon that hope.'
13. Ronald Dworkin, *Justice in Robes* (See endnote 1) p. 116.
14. Ronald Dworkin, *Religion without God* (forthcoming Harvard University Press).
15. Ronald Dworkin. 2013. 'Religion Without God', *New York Review of Books*. April 4. <http://www.nybooks.com/article/archives/2013/apr/04/religion-with-out-god/?pagination=false> accessed on 24 April 2013.

14

Revamping Associative Ol

*George Pavlakos**

Ronald Dworkin was a defender of the idea
obligation to obey the law of the state we live
tions are moral obligations that extend over
within a political community and are associate
way. Dworkin was probably the first philosoph
of political morality as *associative*, but others,
soon joined him.

The paper argues for an interpretation o
account of political obligations, which does
dependent on the coercive institutions of the
on a distinction between two candidate explan
play in the determination of political obligation
facts are the sole *grounds* of political obligation
stitute the existence-conditions of these. On thi

* This research was partially supported by the Gra
of Sciences through a project on 'The Role of the Pr
Decision-Making Process of Courts' (grant ID: 15
efited from an earlier exchange with Dr Tria Gkouv:
explanation.

PART IV

DIGNITY, CONSTITUTIONS, AND LEGAL SYSTEMS

depend on facts about the coercive institutions of the state. The alternative interpretation considers social facts merely as contributing factors to the existence of political obligations—the way in which they contribute is by triggering background moral reasons, which ultimately ground political obligations. In this, the second interpretation, political obligations do not depend for their existence on facts about coercive institutions of the state.

If the argument succeeds two intriguing results come to light. First, at a more abstract level, it allows us to conceive of associative obligations outwith particular forms of social organization—you and I can partake of an associative relation not just when we satisfy some membership criteria set by convention or practice, but when we become the subjects of a common set of normative reasons which govern our interactions. Second, with respect to Dworkin's own account of law, a surprising albeit welcome conclusion is in the offing—among Dworkin's seminal contributions to legal theory has been the idea that the truth of legal propositions is grounded on moral principles. However, no sooner we demonstrate that such principles are not a mere consequence of, but the gauge for associative relations, the possibility of a non-statist understanding of law is rendered conceivable in an attractive manner. A key effect of such a move is the realization of the fact that domestic political communities can be bound by international obligations independently of their consent or otherwise involvement in the production of those obligations. What is more, such obligations will turn out to include duties of justice and fraternity in contrast to the view defended by Dworkin and Nagel that such duties obtain only among citizens of the same state.

Law and Political Obligation

A driving theme in Dworkin's thought has been the relatively uncontroversial idea that coercion through the law ought to be justified, '[…] a conception of law must explain how what it takes to be law provides a general justification for the exercise of coercive power by the state'.[1] This explanatory task he set to himself drives Dworkin's seminal contributions to legal philosophy. Perhaps if pressed to name Dworkin's most original contribution one would have to point at *interpretivism* which is an account of the meaning and content of evaluative, and in particular, legal concepts. Famously interpretivism's main claim is that the meaning of legal concepts cannot be fixed by reference to any plain, that is, non-normative, facts (for example, facts about social practices, the psychology of their participants and so on) because the instances of applications of such concepts remain throughout sensitive to evaluative argument. Instead interpretivism instructs us to refer to moral reasons in order to determine the content of the law. But reference to *any* moral reasons would not suffice either; what we are looking to refer to are reasons of political morality, that is, reasons concerning the exercise of government.

No less influential has been Dworkin's claim that there exists a *general political obligation* of those living in a political community to obey its laws, even if they have no reason to do so other than the fact that these are the laws of the community. Also this claim is a consequence of the general constraint to justify state coercion. To understand how, we need to remind ourselves that Dworkin understands law as an instance of justified coercion; but if that's what it is, then it generates genuine (moral) duties which in turn support a general obligation to obey the law. But the said obligation is merely a conceptual requirement that follows from the requirement of the justification of coercion. What does not follow from it is that any institutional fact that purports to impose duties will *actually* succeed imposing a genuine obligation. Rather, a certain relation must hold between moral standards of legitimate government and the duty-imposing practices of a community, in order for the obligation to obey the law to take hold. Notice, however, that because legal concepts are interpretive, no institutional action that operates outside standards of legitimacy will be capable of contributing to the content of the law; conversely, any such actions that succeed to explain why the law is what it is, will ipso facto generate genuine obligation (for otherwise they would not be contributing to the content of the law). As a result, what may count as the law of a political community is conditioned on the normative standards that generate political legitimacy; this is why, in Dworkin's account, when something qualifies as law, then the question about its capacity to obligate becomes redundant.

In a nutshell, the connecting narrative between those two key elements of Dworkin's theory runs somewhat like this: to pin down the evaluative facts, which determine the content of legal (qua *interpretive*) concepts, one needs to enquire into conditions of legitimacy that generate the obligation to obey the law. Thus, whatever grounds the content of the law also grounds the obligation to obey it. Or, what is a consequence of the above—in order to determine the content of the law we need to enquire of the conditions under which it generates an obligation to obey it.

The key, therefore, to understanding the various parts of Dworkin's political philosophy as elements of a unified story[2] is his account of the conditions that legitimize coercive government, which function at the same time as grounds of the content of the law and of the obligation to obey it. Such conditions we are told are moral reasons governing the life of a political community (principles of political morality). Which specific norms count among those principles and how we can locate them are among the central questions that are in need of an answer.

A correct understanding of the relevant principles of political morality requires clarity about the content and nature of legitimacy that is on the cards. Dworkin submits that legitimacy is achieved when the institutions and the structure of the state generate decisions to which political obligation attaches: 'A state is legitimate if its constitutional structure and practices are such that its citizens have a general obligation to obey political decisions that purport to impose duties on them' (Dworkin 1986: 191).

In turning to specify the content of political obligation Dworkin rejected early on some standard accounts and proposed a fresh understanding of this concept. Such standard accounts of political obligation seem to require some form of control on behalf of agents over the obligations that become binding on them—whether it be under some variant of the consent theory or any of the available scenarios of fair play, agents are assumed to have 'authorized' the responsibilities they incur through participating in a social practice. This is clearer in the case of consent within the context of social contract theories but applies, mutatis mutandis, to accounts of fair play to the extent to which those assume that people have the opportunity to reject the benefits involved in the participation to a practice.[3] A further result of 'voluntaristic' accounts of legitimacy is that they amount to a fair degree of relativism when it comes to specifying the principles that govern patterns of collective action—I am alluding here to the danger inherent to entrusting the force of legitimating reasons to contingent facts (consent) or even the particular views of a collective about what counts as benefit, that deserves respect by everyone who is part of the scheme.[4]

In the place of such accounts Dworkin advances the idea of associative obligation to describe the special responsibilities that a social practice attaches to membership in some social group. In calling upon the idea of associative duties Dworkin aims to model political obligations after those other responsibilities that attach to agents in virtue of their membership in social groups (*associative obligations*). It would seem that, although non-political associations differ from political ones both in size and degree of proximity between their members, they may still offer a good place for basing an account of the core features of political obligation. Let me offer a brief conspectus of some of their key features.

First, non-voluntariness—associative obligations attach to agents independently of their capacity to exercise control over them. Dworkin speaks characteristically of the fact that associative practices/relations, even those that appear to be the result of choice (for example, friendship), *attract* obligations of which we are rarely aware until some later moment when some instance of application arises (Dworkin 1986: 197). This captures accurately the way in which members of a political association incur obligations between one another. At the same time it preserves the valuable intuition that obligations are not independent of particular relations or interactions between agents, as some ideas of a natural duty to support justice would have it. A key consequence of non-voluntariness is that political obligation takes hold on citizens not as piecemeal approval of individual obligations but, instead, as a general scheme of principle which ought to be presumed as forming a shared conception of legitimacy among the members of a political community (208–15).

Second, the moral pedigree of associative obligations—associative relations seem to fit our best understanding of how conventional facts, which are parts of larger social practices, interact with practice-independent moral principles. Dworkin has defended throughout his work, but most prominently in *Justice for Hedgehogs,* the view that social facts cannot, on their own, determine the content of associative obligations.[5] Rather obligations that attach to associative relations are only partly grounded on the social facts of the relevant practice. Conventional practices, including law-making ones, are parasitic on underlying and independent moral facts which are the ultimate determinants of the content of the relevant obligations.[6]

It should be pointed out that the associative account of legitimacy has the further advantage of demonstrating the superiority of the interpretivist explication of the law over most other positivist legal theories. In contrast, most of the other standard accounts of legitimacy (fair play, consent) are compatible with positivist accounts of the law—they can be added as an extra layer on top of a positivist story that identifies the content of the law independently of its merit or demerit, but delegates the question of the obligation to obey the law to a different level. Thus prominent positivists are happy to identify the law independently of any conditions that generate an obligation to obey it.[7]

Political Association Curtailed

In a surprising move Dworkin (and more recently Nagel)[8] have sought to limit the scope of associative obligations to domestic political communities and their legal practices. A quick explanation for adopting this stance is the overstated focus on the coercive apparatus of the state. Recall that the early concern of Dworkin, what in fact I called a driving idea of his entire legal philosophy, was a concern to provide justification for state coercion. It would seem that this emphasis of coercion misleads both philosophers to think that questions of justification and legitimacy arise only with respect to the coercive imposition of laws that are created and managed by a centralized government.[9] To this Nagel adds the further condition that coercion be imposed 'in the name' of its addresses (Nagel 2005: 121). It is through this further claim, Nagel thinks, that our coercive institutions become subject to justification from associative principles of political morality. But if the demand for justification arises only on the occasion of coercion exercised by sovereign institutions, then political morality becomes operative only within domestic political communities. In other words, we can be associated in the salient moral sense, only when we are coerced centrally and 'in our name'. It comes then as little or no surprise that Dworkin and Nagel, when turning to discuss associative relations (and concomitant political obligations) beyond the state, reject the possibility of such relations among persons who are situated in different communities. Let me discuss briefly why this is a surprising conclusion before I turn to point out two instances of the detrimental results of this conclusion.

First off, Dworkin explicitly commits to the view that the state is no more than a personification and should not be taken to constitute a distinct 'party' in the associative relation (Dworkin 2013: 9–10)—rather, in looking for associative relations we are looking at relations between individuals while the state serves more the purpose of a shortcut for conceptualizing collections of individuals. If that is true, then it seems surprising to require the presence of the state as a distinct agent for the determination of associative obligations. Instead, it would be far more consistent with Dworkin's reductive conception of the state to also conceive the building blocks of the associative relation in a manner that does not involve facts about the state.

Yet, there might be another reason why the scope of the associative bond should be confined to the domestic realm, notwithstanding the reduction of states to collections of individuals. Frequently (both in *Law's Empire* and in *Justice for Hedgehogs*) Dworkin speaks of associative relations as designating a *special relation* that is manifested through an acceptance or appreciation of the responsibility toward those others to whom we are related (2011: 320–1).

The obvious way to interpret 'specialty' in a manner that would restrict the scope of the associative bond would be to narrow it down to instances of proximity, which require the presence of specific psychological or other attitude-based responses of affinity, kinship, or even tribal allegiance between those associated with one another. Now, such a move would be reversing the order of explanation between associative obligations and feelings of responsibility—it is because we 'care' about others in a special way that we incur the relevant obligations. On this explanation, one first needs to develop a special psychological proximity with someone before they recognize any responsibility toward them. Helpfully, Dworkin has warned time and again against such interpretations, mainly with an eye to rebutting the argument against the extension of the associative bond from the context of small substantive relationships (family, friendship) to more impersonal, 'at-arms-length' interactions between agents (political communities) (Dworkin 1986: 201). He contends that the criterion for an associative relation should remain normative, not psychological or otherwise empirical, arguing that the *feeling* of a 'special' bond does not explain our being in association with others but rather it is the outcome of the normative pull on us exercised by the principles that ground the associative bond (Dworkin 2011: 314–15).[10]

In addition to surprise, the confinement of associative obligations to domestic political communities leads to a couple of disturbing results. On the one hand, it makes it very difficult to escape a statist understanding of international law with an eye to setting it free from the caveats imposed by narrow sovereign interests. This is what Dworkin set out to do in his posthumously published *A New Philosophy of International Law* with very modest results. A key requirement for undermining the standard statist understanding of international law is to remove state consent from the grounds or the validity of international law obligations. Dworkin's anticipated argumentative move in that paper was to replace state consent with associative obligation, as the ultimate ground of the norms of international law. However, this move was not available to Dworkin because of his earlier commitment to the 'domestic' nature of associative relations. If no associative relation can take hold between agents who are not co-citizens, then there is little hope to detect associative obligations at the international level.

Dworkin's second best solution has been to invoke a rather cumbersome conceptual construction in order to ground the force and validity of international law on domestic associative relations. He argues that states incur international obligations when these would enhance their own legitimacy vis-à-vis their own citizens. But why should an obligation, say, owed to an immigrant non-national (I), who has not yet entered state X's territory, become binding on X if there was no obligation in the first place to justify X's decisions to immigrant I? Dworkin would reply that because X has an obligation to justify its decisions to its own citizens, therefore X should incur any other 'external' obligation that is likely to enhance its legitimacy vis-à-vis its own citizens. It is easy to detect the problematic character of this hybrid solution—in it the associative bond between the members of a political community makes it the case that a set of non-consent based obligations attach to the community even toward actors who are not members of the domestic association. Puzzlingly, such obligations remain associative only for the members of the domestic community, but not for those outside it. We never learn whether these actors acquire rights corresponding to the said obligations, or whether they themselves become the bearers of duties toward those living in other communities, and so on.

What is probably the most disturbing consequence of the 'domestication' of associative obligations is a refusal to extend political obligations of justice and fraternity beyond the boundaries of domestic political communities. Following Dworkin's understanding of associative obligations, Thomas Nagel, in a much discussed—and criticized—paper, states that obligations of distributive justice are associative and as such they materialize only among agents who are subject to a coercive legal system that enforces the law 'in their name' (Nagel 2005: 129–30). Thus, Nagel accepts that he himself stands in the right associative relationship with the New Yorker who irons his shirt but not with the Brazilian who grows his coffee (141). And with that he draws a normative atlas of the world which excludes ex ante any investigation into the justification of claims of re-distribution when these are not accommodated under the common umbrella of coercive government.

On the Site and the Scope of Associative Obligations

We must do better. It is not productive, as in the case of Dworkin, to propagate a progressive, non-statist understanding of international law and at the same time accept as a default position that political obligations obtain only between fellow citizens. It is also very disappointing, as in the case of both Nagel and Dworkin, to consider restrictions on autonomy and choice caused by fellow citizens as sufficient for imposing duties of justice but decline to recognize such duties when the exact same type of restriction is directed at actors beyond the boundaries of our institutional coercive order.

In this section I wish to review this impasse and suggest that the associative account of political obligations can reach beyond or across boundaries of states. Authors working in the field of global justice have already criticized the limitations imposed by Nagel on an important class of political obligations (principles of justice). Yet those accounts—beyond rejecting the premise of Nagel about the requirement of coercive imposition—have not sought to clarify the independent value of the associative account. They have not assessed whether the element of coercive imposition is a necessary component of the associative account, or whether that account could be refined with an eye to explaining the obtaining of political obligations beyond the state.

A second limitation of these accounts is that they hardly refer to the details of the associative account of political obligations. This is not surprising, because Nagel himself merely points in the direction of Dworkin, without supplying much detail. Yet this is regrettable, for Dworkin's account, aside of being the original locus of exposition, is also richer and can offer important insights into the nature of political association, if updated appropriately.

In what follows I shall argue that coercive imposition as a factual condition is a necessary element of one among many possible sites of political obligation (that is, the site of the nation state). However the scope of political obligations should not be confused with any of their particular sites. Rather, in order to determine the scope[11] of political obligations we need to look into what grounds them, that is, what determines their existence and content. Ultimately I will suggest that the idea of associative relations, if refined, has the resources to offer a plausible account of the grounds of political obligations which escapes the limitations imposed by a narrow focus on facts of coercive imposition.

Grounds and Triggers

In attacking Nagel's account of global justice, many theorists located its weakness in the central assumption of its author that the site of the nation state is identical to the scope of obligations of global justice. Cutting through the thickets of subscripts, here is a succinct reconstruction of the criticism, 'the site-scope identity is a substantive thesis, not an analytical truth and therefore its demonstration requires substantive argument'. In other words, there is no conceptual argument that can establish that it is part of the meaning of the concept of political obligation that its normative ambit encompasses only those who are subject to the coercive institutions of the same state. If such argument were available, there would exist little disagreement about the scope of standard instances of political obligations, such as obligations of justice. But the disagreement is deep and pervasive, which suggests the need to employ substantive arguments about the existence conditions and the content of political obligations (one hastens to add, in the manner suggested by Dworkin's interpretivism).

What would be then the associative version of the existence conditions or grounds of political obligations? There are two possible candidate versions for such an account—a less appealing version might contend that facts about coercive government *ground* political obligations. I argue below, by pointing to Dworkin's own writings that this is not what the associative account recommends. A second more promising version says that on the associative account what grounds political obligations are not the social facts of coercion but the principles of political morality, which *justify* coercive imposition.[12]

This interpretation can be extrapolated from Nagel's claim that obligations of justice apply only to coercive institutions which act *in the name of their citizens*, 'Justice, on the political conception, requires a collectively imposed social frame work, enacted in the name of all those governed by it, and aspiring to command their acceptance of its authority even when they disagree with the substance of its decisions' (Nagel 2005: 140).

The second interpretation makes space for a distinction between *a ground* and *a trigger*, each representing a distinct mode of explanation. A trigger merely activates or calls upon an item (fact, property, and so on) which might then perform a more robust explanation (for example, to operate as ground) with respect to the phenomenon under investigation. In contrast a ground—using the parlor of metaphysics—is an item (fact, property, and so on) which generates a full explanation of the existence of the phenomenon under investigation. Here is a first suggestion how this distinction may operate in the context of the explanation of political obligations: if coercive facts are triggers then they do not directly explain the existence of political obligations. They merely 'tease out' other facts (in the present context, background moral principles) which actually do the grounding work with respect to the obligations at hand. In particular, coercive facts can 'tease out' moral principles in virtue of their capacity to impact on the autonomy of the actors involved, and through that invite an onus of justification.

The short conclusion from the second variant of the associative account might run like this: what marks the capacity of coercive institutional facts to function as triggers is the onus of justification that is attached to them as a result of the impact those facts have on the autonomy of agents. It turns out thus, that the relevance of coercion is not one of a ground but of a trigger—coercive facts trigger those moral principles which can justify the impact those facts have on the autonomy of actors. But if that is true, then other instances of social fact, which have an impact on the autonomy of agents, will trigger the same principles of political morality which can justify the said impact.

In what follows I shall try to demonstrate that Dworkin's analysis of associative relations lends support to the interpretation that takes institutional coercive facts as mere triggers of political obligations. Resting on this conclusion, I will suggest that any other social fact or event that has an impact on autonomy in the appropriate way may function as a trigger of the same moral principles. Following up on this premise I will further suggest that such autonomy-restrictive facts are not confined within the site of states but can arise beyond and across states. This will lend support to two conclusions: first, that we do not need the consent of states to account for the validity of international law obligations; second, that obligations of justice do materialize beyond the boundaries of the nation state.

Scope before Site

I begin by investigating whether Dworkin's associative story licenses the conclusion that coercive social facts have the capacity to determine obligations in Dworkin's account. We saw that a striking advantage of representing political obligations as associative is that, while they remain connected to actual instances of human interaction (social practices), at the same time their existence cannot be suspended, as would be the case with any conventional arrangement which remains subject to revocation. The later aspect is present because of the background moral principles which are attached to the practice independently of the mental attitudes of the participants. Using the parlor of site and scope that I introduced earlier we can now take a closer look at Dworkin's argument. In doing so I will consider the early and the later phase of Dworkin's work alike.

In *Law's Empire* Dworkin argued that the bare facts of a practice determine something like the locus or the *site* of the associative relation, 'The question of the communal obligation does not arise except for groups defined by practice as carrying such obligations: associative communities must be bare communities first' (1986: 203). But this might be going too fast—indeed the bare facts of a social relation may delineate a 'space' (that is, *site*) which is opened up for normative contestation, but it does not follow from that they can settle the *scope* of the associative relation or of the obligations that this generates. They cannot settle *who may count as a 'member' of the associative relation and/ or which persons fall under the scope of the obligations, which govern the relation.*

Dworkin actually seems to allow room for a distinction between site and scope, 'But not every group established by social practice counts as associative: a bare community must meet [...] conditions [...] before the responsibilities it declares become *genuine*' (1986: 204). The interpretivist approach offers plenty of resources to substantiate the view that bare social fact, though necessary for activating normative concerns, is not sufficient for determining any of the aspects of the obligations at play. In particular, it appears that the judgment about 'when bare social facts are 'upgraded' into a genuine associative relation' relies on a 'moral' reading of facts and conventions in the light of background moral principles that pre-date any particular configuration of bare fact. In *Justice for Hedgehogs* we read, '[associative] obligations are genuine because convention does not create but only focuses and shapes the more general principles and responsibilities it assumes' (2011: 314).

And a little later:

> So convention strengthens as well as shapes role (i.e. associative – clarification added by GP) obligations. The expectations they nourish cannot be dismissed as mere predictions with no moral force, because they are supported not just by the practices themselves but by the more basic responsibilities the practices refine and protect [...] Reciprocal interaction between background responsibility and social convention explains a further and crucial feature of these obligations. Role conventions do not impose genuine associative obligations automatically: the conventions must satisfy independent ethical and moral tests. (Dworkin 2011: 315)

What provides more conclusive evidence is Dworkin's contention that social practices cannot generate ex nihilo new obligations but have the capacity to merely *clarify* genuine obligations that pre-exist them, 'Once we recognize that role practices clarify genuine but indeterminate responsibilities that flow from the internal character of the relationships on which they build, we have a basis for interpreting them in the way we interpret anything else' (316). Further these obligations derive from the internal nature of the associative relation and form background principles against whose backdrop conventional practices are to be justified:

> It is the internal character of these relationships, not the fact that some assignment of special responsibility is evidently needed, that drives the responsibilities that the community's conventions recognize and shape. So we must find a justification of the role those conventions play [...] The best justification, I believe, describes a repeated feedback loop between a special responsibility we have to people in certain relationships with us, just in the nature of the case, and a set of social practices that progressively reduces the uncertainties inherent in that kind of responsibility. (Dworkin 2011: 311–12)

He further states that, 'Reciprocal interaction between background responsibility and social convention explains a further and crucial feature of these obligations. Role conventions do not impose genuine associative obligations automatically: the conventions must satisfy independent ethical and moral tests' (315).

It is safe to read into these contentions the view that the bare facts or the *site* of a social relation cannot determine the *scope* of the associative relation at hand. For it is the pre-existing background moral principles which actually determine the existence and the scope of the associative bond. Notice also that the conclusion about normative inertness applies to any type of bare social fact, including facts of coercive imposition by an institutionalized organization.

If the site of bare fact fails to determine the scope of the associative relation it is because of the nature of the explanatory relation that pertains between social facts and political obligations. On a charitable reconstruction of Dworkin's account, social facts *cannot ground* political obligations. For, the grounding explanation requires that some other normative fact figure amongst the grounds of said political obligations. The salient normative facts are those background principles of political morality which, on Dworkin's story, are needed in order to classify a set of social facts and events as generative of an associative relation. Not to put too fine a point on it, the inability of bare social facts to ground political obligations is manifested through their failure to demarcate the scope of associative relations. In either case, it is background principles of political morality that perform the respective tasks, for example, to demarcate the range of persons who stand in an associative relationship and ground the political obligations that pertain among those persons.[13]

Yet, a further crucial question arises: can Dworkin's account provide enough support to the claim that facts of social interaction (for short social facts) can *trigger* the principles that determine the scope of the associative bond, by actually grounding political obligations? Substantiating the triggering function is decisive for otherwise the Dworkinian account would fail to relate social facts to the background principles which generate political obligations. That said, Dworkin's account is incomplete in this respect. One must zoom into his construction in order to retrieve the details of the triggering function of social facts. A good starting point is his account of how associations create obligations—Dworkin thinks that political association produces political obligation in the same way in which any other association produces obligations. Political association merely mirrors the same structure of the production of obligations that is common to all associative relations. Here is a succinct reconstruction: political, as all other associative relations, are entangled in a paradox—they threaten to curtail the autonomy of their members by imposing joint patterns of action on them (usually designated through collective actions/decisions). But at the same time, they facilitate freedom and autonomy by creating such joint patterns of action (Dworkin 2011: 312; 320–1).

For the part that they facilitate freedom (by creating joint patterns of action which can co-exist with everyone's freedom) associative relations become sources of obligation—obligations of friendship, familial obligations, or political obligations, such as, obligations of justice and the obligation to obey the law. Up to this point there is not much to go by with respect to an explanation of the triggering function of social facts, for the grounding of additional 'joint pathways' of freedom is the task of background principles of political morality, as submitted earlier.

Yet there is a further dimension: for the part that they pose a risk to freedom associative relations—and the standards they produce—become answerable to a set of normative standards that are presumed to flow out of the principles which instantiate the freedom of autonomous agents in its various aspects. It is precisely at this point that the triggering function of the factual interactions among agents comes at play. In virtue of their capacity to direct the agency of persons, facts of social interaction *trigger* normative standards that control the quality of the direction imposed by the social facts on persons' agency.

The triggering function of social facts is of key significance in two respects. First, it recommends that any socially imposed pattern of action is subject to a formal normative standard—it ought to co-exist with the freedom of every agent whom it purports to direct. Notice two crucial by-products of this recommendation: on the one hand, it appeals to a set of foundational normative principles which instantiate the freedom of persons *not merely as isolated individuals* but also during their mutual interactions, by seeking to create patterns of action in which the freedoms of those involved can co-exist with one another.[14] On the other hand, the account rejects some unrestricted version of universalism. It does not focus on some notion of the person in general in order to extract principles of freedom. It is interested in establishing conditions of *co-existence* for the freedom of agents who engage in *concrete* instances of interaction. Notwithstanding the fact that the account departs from a general notion of freedom, which admittedly is universal, it is indexed to the problem of enabling patterns of action that can co-exist with the freedom of everyone involved.

Second, it abstracts from any particular instantiations of a trigger. Even granting the contention that state coercion is the paradigmatic case of a triggering social fact, it need not be the sole one. Any instance of social fact or event, which threatens to limit freedom and, thus, poses the problem of a pattern of action that can co-exist with the freedom of everyone involved, has the capacity to trigger the relevant background principles. I shall turn next to discuss in more detail the conditions under which interactions among agents may pose the problem of a pattern of action that can co-exist with the freedom of everyone involved.

Political Association Revisited

I have tried to suggest the plausibility of an interpretation of Dworkin's associative account of political obligations, which does not make political obligation dependent on coercive institutions of the state. This interpretation relied on the possibility of distinguishing between two candidate explanations of the role social facts play in the determination of political obligations. In the former, social facts are the *grounds* of political obligations, in the sense that those constitute the existence conditions of these. On this account political obligations depend on facts about the coercive institutions of the state. The alternative interpretation considers social facts merely as contributing factors to the existence of political obligations—the way in which they contribute is by triggering the *actual* grounds of political obligations, for example, background principles of political morality which ultimately ground political obligations. In this, the second interpretation, political obligations do not depend for their existence on facts about coercive institutions of the state. I argued further that apart from its strong normative appeal, the second interpretation is also more faithful to Dworkin's argumentation. Let me take some stock.

The argument in favour of the second interpretation relied on Dworkin's account of the role social facts play in determining associative obligations more generally. There I demonstrated that the *triggering* capacity of social facts is the result of their structure—irrespective of the particular form they assume, ultimately they are inclined to direct the agency of those who interact in virtue of the trajectories those social facts create. Specifically, they generate an onus of justification by directing the agency of those involved, an onus that can be discharged only through meeting the standards of background moral principles which describe general features of agential freedom. This is precisely what the *triggering* function consists in—in activating background moral principles, and effecting their involvement in the determination of the relevant associative obligations.

This line of reasoning also put the account of associative relation in a fresh light. I argued that the range of persons who become members of an associative relationship (that is, the *scope* of the association) cannot be inferred from any specific configuration of social facts (that is, *site* of the association) but needs to be directly determined by the obligations that obtain on the occasion of (any) set of social facts, which has the capacity to trigger moral principles of freedom. Any such set of social facts can become an appropriate site for the associative relation. To put it succinctly scope determines site, not the other way round.

This is enough said as far as goes the metaphysics (that is, the enquiry into what 'counts as') of an associative obligation in general. But now we must revert to associative obligations of the political kind in order to flesh out some details about our preferred interpretation. For, recall that compatible as it may be with Dworkin's own account, the interpretation favoured herein leads to (partly radically) different outcomes. There are, in particular, two main differences. First off, in conferring priority of the site over the scope of political associative relation, it is no longer defensible to confine such relations to those who live under the same coercive institutional structure (that is, the state). As a result, second, the full range of political obligations (including those of *justice*) can transcend the boundaries of states and materialize among persons, even in the absence of a single institutional coercive structure that mediates their interactions.

Political Association beyond the Established Borders

No sooner has the triggering function been attributed to the class of all social facts that produce a limiting effect on freedom, than coercive institutions are divested of any special role in the grounding of political obligations. Thus triggering facts will end up including any pattern of joint action which engages the agency of plural persons, for example, my transactions with those who manufacture my clothes in some remote country; the pattern set up by the New York headquarters of a multi-national corporation which has created an outpost in a remote country; or, even, a decision of the UN security council to freeze the accounts of those suspect of terrorist activity. Such patterns of joint action trigger those precise principles that can render the course of action specified in the pattern compatible with the agency of everyone who is engaged in the pattern.

Perhaps we are going too fast—surely, one would object, you do not want to include in political relations those associative relations pertaining to friendship, family, and so on. But if you divest institutional coercive facts from their specific ability to trigger the principles that ground political obligations, then there would be no easy way to avoid confusion. There is something to be said in response—the triggering function consists in teasing out normative principles (or reasons) which aim to secure consistency of action. A key assumption of this line of reasoning is that the agency-directing patterns are answering to a standard of freedom as independence from domination by others. Without putting too much detail in this claim, suffice it to say that it concerns the plausible and widely accepted idea that an agent can remain free only if she can act for reasons that she has independently of the incentives and acts of others.[15] It follows that socially constructed patterns of action, which purport to direct the agency of those engaged by them, are in danger of collapsing into coercion, exploitation and so on. For that reason each and every agency-directing arrangement comes under an onus of justification. Justification, in turn, is performed by the normative reasons[16] which outline the general features of a 'well-functioning' pattern, in the sense of a pattern that succeeds to direct the actions of everyone involved in the 'proper' manner, that is, through laying down a course of action that can co-exist with everyone's freedom as independence.[17]

Thus far there is no difference between political and other associative contexts. The difference comes next, when we turn at the kind of justification, or the type of pattern that is required to become available in different contexts. I shall confine my discussion of the differences to the angle of the political association. There is a standard assumption that political association sets a threshold that is higher than that of other associative relations. Thus Nagel postulates for political associations a higher degree of density and Dworkin the presence of a special bond. In a sense their contention is surprising because it aligns the political association with a class of other associations from which it needs to distinguish itself—family, friendship and other such 'thick' relations surely require a higher degree of density in respect of the bond between their members, but are not on the face of it political. The confusion arises because Dworkin and Nagel wish to keep political associations separate from yet another class of relations that tend to resemble them closely but which, in their view, are not political: that is, those pertaining between people living in different communities, who are subject to disparate coercive institutional orders. But in relying on the density or specialty of the relation to deliver this task, they focus on a feature that disjoins rather than unites associative relations—density/specialty, if it were rendered the key element of associative relations, would always select the least inclusive relation as approximating the ideal of an associative relation. Thus, expressed in terms of density, family and friendship would turn out consistently to be 'more associative' than citizenship and so on.[18]

The account I have suggested proposes a fresh start by reversing the earlier picture. It identifies in political relations a characteristic that is key *to all associative relations*, that is, the formal requirement for consistency of action. The requirement is to uphold moral principles that determine the structure of patterns which enable each to act in a way that can co-exist with the freedom of everyone else, when freedom is construed as independence from one another's choice. Notice that on this picture the political relation turns out to be the most fundamental[19] associative relation, which is instantiated when collective agency-direction is on the cards, be it informal—that is, absent any antecedent institution—or as in the standard case of agency-direction through state institutions. The implicit thought is that even those relations which display denser connections among their participants (for example, family, friendship) are political in a deeper, fundamental sense.

What differentiates these associative relations (what adds layers of 'density' as it were)[20] lies downstream of the fundamental political relation, in a manner that does not negate but presuppose it. For, these other associations do not aim to replace consistency of action as the relevant standard but rather to uphold it through reference to reasons that are indexed to particular contexts, roles, or properties of agents.[21]

Proto-legal Obligations

Elsewhere[22] I have called those fundamental political relations *proto-legal*. Proto-legal relations, in instantiating patterns of agency-direction, trigger normative reasons which set out conditions under which those patters can be rendered compatible with the freedom of everyone involved in them. In that sense proto-legal relations are like legal relations because they track the conditions of what has come to be known as *external freedom* but without being dependent on the existence of coercive institutions, which are typically considered to be the hallmark of the law.

In 'mediating' between law and the idea of political association the concept of proto-legal relation can generate appealing explanations of the emergence and role of political and legal obligations. Here is how. Proto-legal *relations* occupy the space of Dworkinian associative relations, but without the fixation on a specific site of social organization—they are instances of social interaction which trigger normative reasons capable of specifying normative conditions of co-existence of the freedom of everyone who is involved in the relation. In the manner outlined earlier, such normative reasons ground obligations, for short proto-legal obligations, whose subjects range over those who are involved in the relation.

Proto-legal *obligations* occupy the space of Dworkinian political obligations and can be employed to explain the production of additional obligations when law-making institutions are involved, as it were, further downstream. Crucially in this picture, proto-legal obligations make their appearance much earlier than any action taken by law-making institutions, in other words, their creation does not require some institution to act. But their nature is not crucially different from that of obligations for which we usually reserve the label 'legal'—they demand, on a par with legal obligations, to be enforced in the name of everyone who is involved in the relation, not just the few who on some occasion happen to avail themselves of it.

This should not come as a surprise. Enforceability should not be confused with enforcement. While the latter concept requires for its instantiation the actual existence of coercive institutions, the former is tied up to a normative requirement, which lies in the core of political association—the requirement that freedom can be realized only if we are acting together for its sake—*we can only be rendered free together*. When collective or joint freedom becomes our starting point, not an end-point, then the normative reasons that instantiate it ground obligations in the *name* of a collective 'we-subject' and not in the *names* of aggregated individuals. However, and that shouldn't be too hard to picture, if the obligation is imposed in the name of some collective we-subject, a kind of 'polis', then the claim to uphold it is not merely second-personal, limited to the binary relation between claimant and addressee, but omnilateral. It becomes a claim that involves a we-subject which assumes the responsibility for upholding it. This can be represented in a triangular structure involving a claimant, an addressee and the 'public' or 'omnilateral' we-subject. If that is not the textbook depiction of the structure of legal obligation, then what is!

Illustrating enforceability as a triangular normative relation precisely captures the political significance of the law (its publicity, omnilaterality) without holding the political relation hostage to a pre-occupation with any particular set of social institutions and their configuration under some rule of recognition. To that extent, recasting political obligations (and the relations that trigger them) as proto-legal has the clear advantage of demonstrating the *continuity* between the normative tasks undertaken by political obligations and narrowly confined legal obligations. Further it demonstrates that the task law is invited to accomplish has actually begun much earlier—it has begun in all those occasions of interaction, in which coexistence of freedom is at stake.

In this picture *law narrowly confined* is only a 'by-product' of proto-legal relations and the obligations generated by them. Saving a lot of detail for another occasion, here is a succinct description: when a proto-legal relation takes hold it generates obligations which very roughly can be categorized into two types—on the one hand, enforceable obligations which describe general characteristics of patterns of action which guarantee that everyone involved is acting in a way that can coexist with the freedom of everyone else. These obligations are self-standing and all institutions can do is 'repeat' them by coupling them with the possibility of coercive force. On the other hand, the set of proto-legal obligations will typically include an obligation to set up institutions which produce more norms that specify additional 'pathways' of action which can co-exist with the freedom of everyone involved. Here we can imagine, downstream of the proto-legal relation, an array of institutional actors which can generate further freedom-combining course of action. Crucial is to point out that not only the particular products of institutional action, but also the abstract (proto-legal) obligation for the establishment of law-creating institutions aim to realize the system of collective freedom. To speak with Kant the abstract proto-legal obligation stands for an obligation to enter a *rightful condition* which, far from addressing humanity as a whole, is canvased against a more modest background of proto-legal relations.

International Law and Justice

I reverted to proto-legal relations in order to capture the transformation of political associative relations from relations that are tied down to a particular site of social organization—that of the nation state and its coercive institutions—to such relations as arise in any interaction between agents which comes under the constraint of achieving consistency of action.

The key advantage of thematising associative relations as proto-legal is the prospect of offering appealing explanations of international law and justice. Recall Dworkin's recent efforts to undermine a statist conception of international law in favour of a moralized one (Dworkin 2013). In particular, he was interested to show that the binding force of international law is not conditioned by the consent of states but rests on independent normative principles that are not left at the disposal of individual states. Yet, in order to argue for this idea in international law, he would have to point at some form of international associative relation which would ground the requisite principles. For, as we know from the domestic case, Dworkin explains legal obligations against the backdrop of principles that pertain to the associative relation between citizens. However, this option is not available once he steps outside of the domestic realm: here, as we saw, there is no room in Dworkin's account for any supra-, inter-, or trans-national associative relations. Accordingly the prospect of developing, in terms of associative obligations, a moralized conception of international law is curtailed.

Contrariwise, political associative obligations understood as proto-legal are capable of grounding directly enforceable (proto-legal) obligations between agents across and beyond the established, institutionalized forms of political association. This dispenses with cumbersome constructions, such as Dworkin's, which ultimately must ground international law on the domestic political community.

The account of political association in terms of proto-legal relations has a further, far from negligible, advantage. It exports the full range of political obligations into the international realm. Of particular importance is this consequence for obligations of distributive justice. Both Dworkin and Nagel decline to allow obligations of distributive justice to take hold beyond the nation state.[23] Their thought is that obligations of justice are strictly political and to that extent require the existence of robust associative relations, of the kind we encounter only at the domestic level. Once we leave the boundaries of the state justice dissolves, for those whom we encounter are no longer fellow citizens but, at most, human beings who might need our help or charity.[24] Naturally were the current community of states to develop into a world state, equipped with a coercive apparatus for imposing decisions in the name of everyone, then obligations of justice would anew acquire 'global' status (Nagel 2005). However, in Nagel's words, not only is the current world far removed from such a state of affairs, but also we do not incur any obligation to take things forward with an eye to a world state.

If, however, what is distinctively political about associative relations is their capacity to track normative conditions of external freedom, under which a pattern of interaction can be rendered compatible with the freedom of all those partaking in it, then there is little to recommend a confinement of political obligations (including those of justice) to fellow citizens only. Rather, we should say that where agents—as a condition for engaging in non-wrongful exchanges—are confronted with a demand to realize together one another's freedom, their actions should become answerable to the full range of principles which determine the features of appropriately freedom-enhancing patters of action—such principles ground obligations which claim force in the name of everyone, much in the way political obligations do at home.

Notes and References

1. Ronald Dworkin. 1986. *Law's Empire*. London: Fontana Press. p. 190.
2. Dworkin's account is non-centralist, in the sense that it does not rely on any master-idea or master-concept for explaining legal phenomena. On a non-centralist account the correct application of the concept law is the one that is favoured by the theory, whichever it may be, that gives the best account of the relationships between specific values that apply to the alternative interpretations of the relevant social facts. For an in-depth analysis of non-centralism, see S.L. Hurley. 1989. *Natural Reasons*. New York: Oxford University Press. p. 11.
3. Granting this opportunity must be incorporated in the account of fair play for otherwise agents would incur obligations simply by receiving what they do not seek.
4. For an in-depth discussion see Dworkin 1986: 192–5; John Horton. 2010. *Political Obligation*, 2nd ed. Hampshire: Palgrave. Chapter 6.
5. Ronald Dworkin. 2011. *Justice for Hedgehogs*. Cambridge Mass.: Harvard University Press.
6. See endnote 5 and for a very informative recent reconstruction of Dworkin's views Nicos Stavropoulos. 2014. 'Legal Interpretivism', *The Stanford Encyclopedia*

of Philosophy. Edward N. Zalta (ed.), available http://plato.stanford.edu/archives/sum2014/entries/law-interpretivist/.

7. Famously, Joseph Raz distinguishes the question about the content of the law from the one about the obligation to obey the law and points at separate criteria for answering each of them. See instead of other places, Joseph Raz. 1999. *Practical Reason and Norms,* 2nd ed. New York: Oxford University Press.

8. Thomas Nagel. 2005. 'The Problem of Global Justice', *Philosophy and Public Affairs.* 33 (2).

9. See Ronald Dworkin. 2013. 'A New Philosophy for International Law', *Philosophy and Public Affairs.* 41(1). p.17.

10. It is true that in *Law's Empire* Dworkin identifies several conditions for the legitimacy of associative obligations, many of which smack of psychologism. All of that is set aside in *Justice for Hedgehogs.* In this book he points out that the background legitimating principles—in whose light a social practice can qualify as associative—are moral facts which are related to fundamental aspects of agential autonomy. He also adds that the associative obligations generated by practices simply clarify those background moral principles. But admittedly his discussion remains abstract without much detail (that is, there is no list of such moral principles or a method for working them out or making them explicit, if indeed they are implicit in the meaning of autonomy and dignity.

11. 'Scope' refers to the range of subjects on whom the obligation becomes binding. See for a detailed discussion, Arash Abizadeh. 2007. 'Cooperation, Pervasive Impact and Coercion', *Philosophy and Public Affairs.* 35(4). p. 320.

12. It is more accurate to say that social facts cannot be the sole grounds of political obligations, even though they need to feature among the facts that ground those obligations. Their real shortcoming is that they cannot determine their own contribution to the explanation of an obligation given that such facts are bereft of normative relevance. Instead, we would need to refer to some other kind of fact which can render intelligible the role of social facts in the determination of the content of obligations. In as much as it will turn out that normative facts (e.g. moral reasons) are responsible for determining the contribution of the various grounds to the content of political obligations, I shall consider them to be the ultimate determinants of the grounding relation and, as a consequence, the *grounds proper* of political obligation. To that extent I will omit some of the complexity pertaining to different types of grounds and shall refer as 'grounds' only to whatever turns out to be an ultimate determinant in the above sense. For refinements of the grounding relation between social facts and obligations (albeit applied to legal obligations more narrowly) see the seminal text by M. Greenberg. 2004. 'How Facts Make Law', *Legal Theory.* 10. Reprinted in Scott Hershovitz (ed.). 2006. *Exploring Law's Empire: The Jurisprudence of Ronald Dworkin.* Oxford: Oxford University Press.

13. It is apposite to remark that the judgment about whether a collection of bare facts constitutes the site of an associative relation *depends* on the antecedent judgment

about its scope, which in turn is determined by the normative principles that are activated by the said bare facts.

14. Once the requirement has been formulated like this, two alternatives present themselves for consideration: co-existence of plural freedoms can be understood either as *co-incidence* of self-enclosed, pre-existing individual freedoms; or it may be taken to point at irreducible patterns of joint freedom which possess *independent value*, in that they help to realize the freedom of each agent. In the last part of the chapter I will suggest a way for exploring the latter alternative.

15. This, broadly speaking Kantian, view has informed a number of recent influential accounts with most prominent among them being, Arthur Ripstein. 2009. *Force and Freedom*. Cambridge, Mass.: Harvard University Press; A.J. Julius. 2017. 'Independent People', in S. Kisilevsky and M. Stone (eds), *Freedom and Force: Essays on Kant's Legal Philosophy*. Hart Publishing; A.J. Julius. *Reconstruction*, Princeton University Press. Forthcoming, MS available at http://www.ajjulius. net/reconstruction.pdf.

16. What is more, as indicated earlier, in the light of those principles the social pattern becomes the site of an associative relation.

17. See the next section of the chapter.

18. I am not claiming that either Dworkin or Nagel would endorse this outcome; I am only saying that they are reluctantly drawn into that conclusion even as they must fight against it. Dworkin makes an explicit effort to re-interpret the elements of 'density' in a passage of *Law's Empire* (1986: 197–8) that argues against extending the criteria of physical proximity or acquaintance between agents to apply to the case of the political association.

19. In terms of degrees of universality, the scope of political obligations is second only to some unrestricted cosmopolitan obligations (the latter can be portrayed as being indexed to the thinnest possible associative relation, for example, humanity). Obligations pertaining to family relations and friendship are far more restricted in scope and emerge downstream of political obligations.

20. A rough and ready proposal for a criterion of degrees of density is to explain them in relation to a concept of 'authorization' of agency-directing patterns through reference to reasons with variable scope. In doing so we still regard the denser patterns as aiming to realize freedom as independence for everyone involved, yet the freedom-upholding reasons that support them may remain dependent on some test of pedigree or membership (as in the case of family).

21. It is very interesting how both Dworkin and Nagel, in taking political associations to generate a special bond which sets them apart from cosmopolitan accounts, have to struggle to distinguish them from non-political associations. This forces them to revert to a formalistic criterion—namely the fact that coercion is exercised in the name of the community. But 'in the name of' is arguably a substantive requirement: it can be instantiated even in the absence of any explicit claim that coercion is exercised in the name of the collective. As in cases in which we join our efforts to pursue an aim, or we are involved in interactions that aim to become exchanges between more of us. When we do these things

we are acting in the name of everyone (involved), whether it be the case that we proclaim it or not.

22. George Pavlakos. 2016. 'The Proto-Legal Relation: A Normative Compass in a Globalised World', in E-M Mbonda & T Ngosso (eds), *Théories de la justice Justiceglobale, agents de la justice et justice de genre* (Louvain: Presses Universitaires de Louvain); *idem.* 2016. 'From a Pluralism of Grounds to Proto-legal Relations: Accounting for the Grounds of Obligations of Justice', *Ratio Juris* 29.

23. Conversely, they are happy to concede the existence of international standards governing the justification and conduct of war as well as those corresponding to the most basic human rights. For an explicit statement see Nagel (2005).

24. In that respect Dworkin and Nagel side with Rawls's account of international justice in John Rawls. 1999. *The Law of Peoples*. Cambridge, Mass.: Harvard University Press.

15

Dworkinian Dignity

Rights and Responsibilities of a Life Well Lived

Erin Daly

'Without dignity our lives are only blinks of duration. But if we manage to lead a good life well, we create something more.'
—Ronald Dworkin, *Justice for Hedgehogs*[1]

Human dignity is the most slippery of ideas. When we think we understand it as a fundamental value, it squirms out of our hands like a right. When we seize on it as an end-value, as a goal in and of itself, it slithers away like a means to accomplishing some other goal. Just as we start to see it as the cornerstone of civic and political rights, it reappears in another guise, as the measure of a second, third, or fourth generation right. And if we think it is a single thing, that an individual can hold onto and be sure of, it becomes infinitely divisible—shared among all human beings equally and allocable to cultural or political communities without losing its essential form. In each person's hands, it is always the same, but invariably unique. Few legal scholars or philosophers have been able to take the full measure of the idea of human dignity, though Ronald Dworkin has come close.

By the end of Dworkin's life, dignity had become central to his thinking—the basis for the 'one big thing' that the hedgehog knows. The unity of value, it turns out, is human dignity. It grounds the twin obligations of government—the obligation to 'show equal concern for the fate of every person over whom it claims dominion' and the obligation to 'fully respect the responsibility and right of each person to decide for himself how to make something valuable of his life'.[2] As Dworkin said shortly before his death, 'I'm talking about dignity. It's a term overused by politicians, but any moral theory worth its salt needs to proceed from it' (Jeffries 2011).[3] Dignity, in other words, is not only the value that distinguishes the hedgehog from the fox; it is the value that distinguishes Dworkin from consequentialist or relativist or subjectivist philosophers with whom he is often contrasted. As Thomas Nagel wrote shortly after Dworkin's death, 'Most of Dworkin's work is a defense and exploration of this domain of objective value—an attempt to show that it makes sense to seek objectively right answers to difficult questions of law, or morality, and even of how to live' (Nagel 2013).[4] Dworkin defends not only the 'metaphysical independence of value' (2011: 9), but the metaphysical independence of a *particular* value; and that value is dignity. Indeed, dignity is so powerful a force in Dworkin's view that it can stand up to the pointlessness and meaninglessness of the universe: 'Even if there is no eternal planner, *we* are planners—mortal planners with a vivid sense of our own dignity and of good and bad lives that we can create or endure' (217).

Early Invocations: Dignity as Afterthought

Dignity has not always been at the forefront of Dworkin's thinking. In *Taking Rights Seriously*, he barely mentions it (and it does not even appear in the index). When he does turn his attention to it, however, it plays an essential role in understanding why we should take rights seriously. Even though rights are costly and inefficient for a government to respect, the *point* of rights is two-fold: first, to respect human dignity and, second, to assure equal respect to each person. But he explains dignity only in the following cursory way: the 'idea' of dignity, 'associated with Kant, but defended by philosophers of different schools, supposes that there are ways of treating a man that are inconsistent with recognizing him as a full member of the human community, and holds that such treatment is profoundly unjust' (Dworkin 1977: 198).[5] So Dworkin's early thinking seems to recognize the importance of dignity but not its complexity; it is a concept so obvious in significance for Dworkin that it does not even merit investigation or examination. Indeed, without adumbrating the meaning of dignity at all, Dworkin says that violations of dignity, or equality, are 'special moral crimes, beyond the reach of ordinary utilitarian justification' (199). While it is true that Dworkin speaks only of men, it must be assumed that violating the dignity of a woman is equally unjust and just as much of a moral crime as violating the dignity of a man.

A few points about this summary disposition are worth noting here. First, in this articulation, dignity is a sort of super-right—it is the justification, or the embodiment of all other rights. To take all rights, or any rights, seriously is to take dignity seriously and to take dignity seriously is to take all other rights seriously. Only the right to equal treatment is on par with dignity as a foundational right. Second, dignity and equality are two separate, independent, though equal values. They are distinct here, and not obviously interrelated except that they are the twin justification of rights. Third, dignity's significance seems to lie primarily in its negative, in the importance of not violating it. It is not described in Dworkin's work as a positive or affirmative interest—as the interest that ensures that humans are able to develop their full personality or live in a certain way or receive the respect they are due just by virtue of being born human; rather, dignity must be protected because *failing to do so* is inconsistent with treating a person as a full member of the human community, because *failing to do so* is profoundly unjust. And yet, lastly, hints of dignity as it will be developed in later years are evident in incipient form here. Dworkin offers that dignity attaches to every person in equal measure, and he places dignity at the heart of the human experience in both its individual and its social dimensions. Moreover, he suggests that dignity, as both the embodiment of and the justification for all other rights, represents the limits of what the majority can do to the minority (1977: 205). Dignity has political and legal as well as moral significance.

Combining all of these definitional crumbs does not exactly add up to a loaf of bread, but it does tell us something about the implications of recognizing, or rather failing to recognize, the value of human dignity. Even early on, it *is* important, even though we don't yet know exactly what 'it' is. To infringe on a 'relatively important right must be a very serious matter' because it means 'treating a man as less than a man' (199). But this makes dignity almost tautological—to respect one's dignity is to treat a person *as a person*; to give him (or her) less than the amount of respect that is due is to violate his or her dignity because it treats him or her as less than a person. All well and good, but this tells us nothing about how much respect is due, or why a person's measure lies in his or her dignity. It just says that it does.

Cursory though it was, Dworkin's thinking in the 1970s was very much consistent with global understandings of dignity as a legal concept. We all knew—we had all known since the Universal Declaration of Human Rights in 1948 and the two Covenants of the 1960s—that dignity was important—indeed, foundational.[6] But we couldn't really articulate what dignity was (other than to say that it had something to do with personhood and that it was tied to equality, but it wasn't the same thing). Nor could we explain why it was important to protect (other than to say that violating a person's dignity was a very serious matter, as the Nazis had proven beyond a shadow of a doubt). This is the umbrella you take with you just in case you need it, but you don't give it much thought, and you hope you won't need to rely on it.

Even in *Justice for Hedgehogs*, where dignity finds itself at the core of the Dworkinian way of life, it remains ill-defined, it is under-investigated, and perhaps even under-appreciated. Dignity, 'whatever it turns out to mean' (2011: 15)—is the obscenity of philosophical concepts—it resists definition but we know it when we see it.[7] It looks like people 'holding their heads high as they struggle for all the other things they want' (2011: 13–14). It is in the 'otherwise mysterious phenomenology of shame and insult' (14). Even in the culmination of his work, dignity defies even Dworkin's extraordinary capacity for analytic elucidation.

The Responsibilities of Dignity

As Dworkin's thinking evolved on the nature of rights, the obligations of government, and the obligations that each person owed not only to others but also to himself, his conception of dignity evolved too. By the end of his life, dignity became for Dworkin not so much a matter of rights, or even of value, but of responsibility. Human dignity embodies each person's *responsibility* to live well. The gift of human dignity imposes on us the obligation to protect and nurture it. And this is, he says artfully, a matter of performance.

For many philosophers and legal theorists, dignity has always had both internal and external aspects. It is who we are and how we want to be perceived by others, it attaches to our individual personhood and to our status in society. It is simultaneously subjective and objective—the classical sense of dignity, as attaching to high office or sovereignty, implies an objective measure of human dignity, while the modern sense connotes what is at the core of each person's being and what is most important in each person's life (Hennette-Vauchez 2011).[8] There is in this sense a profound contradiction at the heart of dignity—we have it inherently, inalienably, and individually and yet we can be treated without it and it can be violated and we can be left failing to measure up. Most people who have acknowledged this conundrum have simply accepted dignity's chameleon nature and allowed dignity to have both these qualities. And so too does Dworkin. Dignity is at the heart of both ethics (how we live) and morality (how we treat others), in Dworkin's taxonomy. And even in the latter context, dignity has a two-fold aspect: it requires *respect* for the importance of other people's lives and *equal concern* for their lives. As Nagel writes, 'Dworkin believed that these complementary values enabled him to dissolve all the traditional tensions within moral and political theory—between morality and self-interest, between liberty and equality, between the right and the good' (Nagel 2013: 57).

In Dworkin's construct, as elsewhere, these different aspects of dignity can't be balanced against each other, neither one can be compromised for the sake of the other (Dworkin 2011: 265). They must both be fully recognized. But dignity explains the relationship between the self and the other, between the obligation to treat the self well and the same obligation with respect to others. If the self is *subjectively* important (I think therefore I am), it must also be objectively important (265) (we all think and therefore we all are) and if the value you find in your own life is truly objective, it must be the value of humanity itself. (If I am, then so is everyone else, equally so.)

Dworkin puts this in Kantian, not Descartian terms; citing Kant he says that we 'cannot adequately respect our own humanity unless we respect humanity in others' (2011: 14) explaining on this basis that morality is the condition for ethics. And although Dworkin does not dwell on it, this precept is as equally true backward as it is forward—once we respect our own humanity, we must recognize the equal (and equally worthy of respect) humanity of others.

Equality imposes up on us the obligation of morality—we treat everyone with equal concern and respect because each person is equally entitled to concern and respect because in some important way, we are all each other's equals. This obligation is as central to governance as it is to personal morality, as understood by Dworkin. But a moment's inspection of this proposition reveals its untruth—people are not equal in physical attributes, capabilities, resources, opportunities, or in other ways that meaningfully contribute to the quality of the lives we lead. Why should we treat the concert violinist and the person who is tone-deaf equally? The one way in which each human being *is* equal to every other is in the matter of dignity. It is thus dignity that gives meaning to equality—that creates the obligation of equal concern and respect. And conversely, to Dworkin, equality gives meaning to dignity—the principle of equality of resources, he says, 'presumes only that we treat people with equal concern when we allow each to design his own life' (2011: 363). Because we have dignity, we should treat people equally; because we are equal, we should each be able to 'design' our own lives. One of the conjoined twins describes who we are (ethics) while the other describes how we should treat each other (morality).

This orientation toward responsibility puts dignity in tension in some way with the concept of law, which is about how norms are created and ultimately how force or the threat of force is used to compel people to do certain things. Law is what takes up the slack when personal responsibility or ethics or morality fail. In the yin and yang of social and political relations, personal responsibility, and law occupy mutually exclusive though perhaps interdependent spaces. So to say that dignity is a matter of responsibility is almost to say that dignity and law do not mix. But not quite.

Dignity and Law

The fact that dignity means both that each person is important and that each person is equally important has not only moral and ethical significance but legal significance as well. If dignity as understood this way is true, then the law *must* recognize it. The law *must* treat each person with equal concern and respect, and it must ensure that people treat each other in the same way. This is something of a leap, but perhaps a logical one: if dignity is so important to who we are as individuals, the law—the political community we create to govern us—should respect this core attribute of humanity. It is what all humans share, and perhaps the only thing that all humans share, so our institutions of government—the structures we create that enhance our freedom by limiting our autonomy—should respect the core of our common humanity. Indeed, one could say that a system of governance that does not respect both the fundamental equality of each member and some degree of personal freedom or autonomy is necessarily unjust and perhaps illegitimate.

Kenneth Simons encapsulates Dworkin's analysis this way:

> Respect for human dignity, he says, entails two requirements: (1) self-respect, that is, taking the objective importance of your own life seriously; and (2) authenticity, that is, accepting a 'special, personal responsibility for identifying what counts as success' in your own life and for creating that life 'through a coherent narrative' that you have chosen. According to Dworkin, these two principles of dignity do triple duty. First, as a matter of personal ethics, they provide guidance about what we should do in order to live well. Second, they elucidate the rights that individuals have against their political community. And third, they account for the moral duties we owe to others. (Simons 2010: 715)[9]

As so understood, dignity imposes on government the obligation of good faith to respect both its equality and its personal freedom aspects (Guest 2013).[10] These are the rights that individuals have against their political communities.

Examining them in turn, we begin with equality. Equality is not difficult to understand, at least at a conceptual level, even though it gets complicated down in the weeds. It means that being born human puts you on the same level, with the same opportunities, as everyone else, that no one starts off with disadvantages or advantages that cannot be overcome. It prohibits a caste system, it prohibits slavery, and it may require some affirmative actions on the part of government to rectify social inequalities such as differences in family wealth. Nagel writes that 'the equality that morality requires of a political system', in Dworkin's view, 'is the equality in the resources that people need to exercise their individual responsibility for their lives' (Nagel 2013: 57).

But the content and boundaries of personal freedom are much harder to pin down, particularly in the context of a legal regime which, by definition, is only effective if it limits personal freedom to some extent. So the question is, to what extent? Where must the boundary lie between the coercive state and individual autonomy? Dworkin wrestles with this and seeks to define dignity in such a way as to mark its outer bounds. But it's not clear whether even as capacious and creative a mind as his can give dignity the form it needs to do the work assigned to it.

Dworkin tells us that the protective shell that dignity provides is significant, but not unlimited. To understand its form, its essential content, it may be helpful to start not with dignity itself but with law. Government can, as it were, impose swimming lanes, to ensure the orderly conduct of social life (Guest 2013: 176–7). But it can't limit personal freedom in core matters; it can not dictate, for instance, 'personal choices in religion, and personal intimacy, and beliefs in political and moral ideals' (176). Dworkin seems to suggest that what distinguishes these choices from other choices is in the nature of autonomy. This has some intuitive appeal: we can generally tolerate the restriction on our freedom imposed by swimming lanes in part because these restrictions allow us to do better what we all want to do and we can easily see that such rules prevent anarchy and the chaos that anarchy produces. But in fact it is not clear why one's impulse to swim wherever one pleases is less meaningful than one's impulse to love a certain god or a certain person or associate oneself with a particular political party. Why is political, moral, religious, or intimate autonomy more important than swimming (or personal movement or artistic) autonomy? In *Sovereign Virtue*, Dworkin explains this, but not in general terms of dignity.[11] In *Life's Dominion*, he explains it somewhat, in largely decisional terms. But so be it. Let's accept that it is so and explore further the relevance of autonomy.

For Dworkin, autonomy is a mental exercise.[12] 'A person's dignity,' he says plainly in *Life's Dominion*, 'is normally connected to his capacity for self-respect' (1993: 221). It represents the ability to decide, to act, to control one's life, to define one's self, to choose to live well. This is the meaning of dignity in the phrase 'death with dignity'. To have dignity at death is not to defy or avoid death, but to control it to the extent of one's ability; here, it means to control how, though not if, one dies. Indeed, for Dworkin, dignity lies at the heart of the arguments both for and against euthanasia. Here he defines dignity as 'respecting the inherent value of our own lives' (238) and then explains that 'because we cherish dignity, we insist on freedom, and we place the right of conscience at its center, so that a government that denies that right is totalitarian no matter how free it leaves us in choices that matter less' (239). He further explains, 'Whatever view we take about abortion and euthanasia, we want the right to decide for ourselves, and we should therefore be ready to insist that any honourable constitution, any genuine constitution of principle, will guarantee that right for everyone' (239).

And, again in the context of abortion, the decisional aspect of dignity trumps the life aspect of the fetal dignity. Dworkin believes that procreative autonomy is central to dignity and that conception of dignity is central to the just form of government outlined in the American Bill of Rights, 'The most important feature of [Western political] culture is a belief in individual human dignity: that people have the moral right—and the moral responsibility—to confront the most fundamental questions about the meaning and value of their own lives for themselves, answering to their own consciences and convictions' (166). In *Life's Dominion*, he goes further in his insistence that this mental form of dignity underlies all that is true and good: 'for both religious and secular abolitionists, the cruelest aspect of slavery was its failure to recognize a slave's right to *decide* central issues of value for himself' (166–7; emphasis added). Whether he is correct that abolitionists hated most the denial of the slave's power to decide (and whether he is correct by implication that slaves hated this aspect of slavery the most), it is beyond dispute that this aspect of dignity is what Dworkin himself finds most important—the ability to decide important matters for oneself, to design one's own life.

Autonomy-laced dignity is why we can be *influenced* by others, but should not be dominated by them (Dworkin 2011: 212). It explains why lying is morally wrong—because to lie to someone is to intentionally limit the control he or she has over information.[13] If I lie to you about where I was, I've expanded the control I have over the situation—I can hide, have an affair, plan a surprise party for you, or anything else without subjecting myself to consequences from you—and I've limited your ability to make an informed decision about my whereabouts, I've impaired your ability to act *responsibly* and *authentically* for yourself because I've distorted the bases on which you might rest your decisions and actions. This is a zero-sum game—the expansion of my autonomy diminishes yours. Intentionality is central in Dworkin's conception of autonomy not because the consequences are any different but because, to *intentionally* make a decision for another expands one person's autonomy at the expense of the other's.

Episodically, he ventures across the threshold into a more objective or communal understanding of dignity as when, for instance, he considers the rights of people living with dementia whose capacity for self-respect, or self-reflection of any kind, is long gone. Here, he says, we must consider whether 'people have a right not to suffer *indignity*, not to be treated in ways that in their culture or community are understood as showing disrespect' (Dworkin 1993: 233)[14] and he further explains that in 'one sense, dignity is a matter of convention, because the systems of gesture and taboo that societies use to draw the boundary between disadvantage and indignity differ' (236). But even here, he circles back to the individual, the subjective, the *mental* landscape, 'A person's right to be treated with dignity... is the right that others acknowledge his genuine critical interests: that they acknowledge that he is the kind of creature, and has the moral standing, such that it is intrinsically, objectively important how his life goes' (236). What is important is the intrinsic value *to each person* of *his* own life. But Dworkin seems to be saying that such dignity is not fully recognized unless it is recognized by others. I cannot live well—as if my life is important—unless others recognize the value of my life's project. Thus, the subjective experience of my own dignity—my own ethical stance, how I live my life—becomes an objective right, a right that I can claim against others, be they governmental authorities or caretakers, 'the right that all people have—that their society recognizes the importance of their lives, expressed through whatever vocabulary it has—is not itself a matter of convention' (236). So, the reason that even a person with severe dementia, who has lost the capacity for self-respect, is entitled to be treated with dignity is because 'what happens to him then affects the value or success of his life as a whole. That he remains a person, and that the overall value of his life continues to be intrinsically important, are decisive truths in favor of his right to dignity' (237).

This mental conception of dignity—characterized throughout Dworkin's writing by words like 'recognize', 'appreciate', and 'acknowledge'—also explains why death is acceptable, but killing is not; why, in the rampant hypothetical cases Dworkin tosses out about fat men on trolley tracks and kids nearly drowning and paraplegic violinists, there is always a difference in whether a decision has been made and who makes it. Letting death happen does not violate the victim's dignity, whereas killing him does. This is what Dworkin sometimes calls the double effect.[15] The latter is impermissible because it represents one person making a decision *for* the other person, *deciding* that the other person should die, whereas in the former situation, the death is the same, but no one is asserting the authority over, or limiting the autonomy of, another person. An accidental death produces a loss of life, but not a loss of dignity. This is why, in the South African case that invalidated the death penalty, the Court suggested that capital punishment is unconstitutional not only because it takes a life—after all, lives are lost all the time—but because it represents a *loss* of the person's dignity[16]—one person or entity has made a deliberate choice *for* the other. That is an assertion of dominance by the decision-maker over the victim that dignity precludes. Each person must be allowed to decide *for* him or herself.

This approach once again brings Dworkin in line with Kant who famously posited the anti-objectification principle that individuals can never be used as *means* to another person's ends. Dworkin makes the most of this, arguing that it's true even if the other person's goal is to benefit the other person or to save more lives or to save the concert violinist. Viewed in this way, Dworkin's œuvre reveals him as a philosopher as much as a legal theorist. His life's work is a prolonged investigation of the 'self' and of its instantiation, one's life. As he spirals in towards dignity, he focuses his attention on why the self is important and how to express that importance through how one lives. Dignity encapsulates that importance. If it *is* fundamentally important, then one can make claims against others—against the person who would throw us on the trolley tracks, against our community that would otherwise treat us 'as a mere object at the full disposal of [their] convenience' (1993: 237) and against the government, in the form of rights—to protect the dignity—the value, the important quality—of the self. Claiming these rights against others enables each one of us to live well, with self-respect and authenticity and a full appreciation of the importance of our own lives.

Sadly, or paradoxically, or perhaps just curiously, Dworkin lived and wrote and thought in the two countries that have perhaps the strongest, longest commitment to constitutional democracy (written or unwritten, but commitment nonetheless), but the weakest jurisprudence of dignity of almost any modern constitutional democracy. Looking at the constitutional law of the United States and the United Kingdom, one can barely discern any appreciation for the dignity of human life as an abstract concept or more pragmatically in the quotidian experience of people.

During Dworkin's lifetime, the only case from the Roberts Court in the United States to make any kind of serious contribution to our understanding of constitutional dignity was *Edwards v. Indiana*,[17] a case involving the right to self-representation of a defendant with diminished mental capacity. In the majority opinion, holding that Indiana could deny Edwards his right to self-representation, Justice Breyer wrote that 'a right of self-representation at trial will not "affirm the dignity" of a defendant who lacks the mental capacity to conduct his defense without the assistance of counsel. To the contrary, given that defendant's uncertain mental state, the spectacle that could well result from his self-representation at trial is at least as likely to prove humiliating as ennobling.'[18] While the sentiment here may be admirable, as the Court tries to protect Edwards from the humiliation that he would bring on himself if the state did not stand in his way, the idea of dignity as protecting a person's *nobility* has little purchase in rights theory; it is a sort of secular version of sacredness, and in that sense it protects what is special about every human being, as does the Universal Declaration of Human Rights, but it has little explanatory power nor legitimacy as a tenet of American constitutional law.[19]

Justice Scalia's dissent inverts this understanding of human dignity, drilling down to its core in a quintessentially Dworkinian way, 'there is little doubt that the loss of "dignity" the right is designed to prevent is *not* the defendant's making a fool of himself by presenting an amateurish or even incoherent defense. Rather, the dignity at issue is the supreme human dignity of being master of one's fate rather than a ward of the State—the dignity of individual choice'.[20] If dignity is to be a linchpin of a right in the American Constitution, Justice Scalia says, it is to be understood in the individualist sense of being master of one's fate—the right to control the course of one's own life, to 'define one's own concept of existence, of meaning, of the universe, and of the mystery of human life', as the joint opinion said in *Casey*.[21] Soaring sometimes into the spiritual realm, Scalia's concept of dignity, like Dworkin's, is nonetheless firmly rooted in the cognitive, mental experience of the individual as he tries to manage the course of his own life.

Either way, the *Edwards* Court gives us no more. Brief though it is, this incidental back-and-forth between majority and dissenting justices in *Edwards* in fact constitutes one of the most thoughtful investigations of human dignity to be found anywhere in Supreme Court jurisprudence, until after Dworkin's death.

Taking Dignity Rights Even More Seriously

Because Dworkin drew mainly on the case law from the United States, there was, for him, little to draw on in constitutional case law to illustrate his thinking. A global scope provides abundant examples of how people make claims against each other and against their government based on an acknowledgment of the importance of their own lives. It can enrich our understanding of dignity by revealing its dimensions beyond the mental self. In short, in the case law of other countries, we can see Dworkin's theory come to life.

The turn that most of the world's constitutions and many active and engaged constitutional courts have taken in recent decades illustrates and perhaps even demonstrate the correctness of Dworkin's big idea—that law is a part of morality, that it cannot be understood separate from morality, and that human dignity is the one big idea that animates the development of the law. Indeed, just as Dworkin was zeroing in on the idea of human dignity as the central value, so too were constitution drafters and jurists around the world.

In the last 40 years, human dignity has appeared in the constitutions of almost all of the countries of the world, and very few are currently amended or rewritten without attention to human dignity. Often it is a foundational value, as in South Africa; sometimes it is eternal, as in Germany. Where it is not explicit, courts have interpreted it into the fabric of the constitutional system, as in India and Israel. And courts around the world are increasingly taking seriously claims based on human dignity. The constitutional jurisprudence of courts in Latin America have been particularly attentive to such claims, but courts in Asia, Africa, Europe, and elsewhere have likewise acknowledged the fundamental importance of human dignity not only as a philosophical tenet but as a constitutional principle with legal consequences. As a result, a robust global jurisprudence of dignity has emerged from the case law of these disparate nations, with new cases, giving new meaning to dignity, being decided every day.

Many of the cases, particularly from Germany and elsewhere in Europe, reflect the individualist, cognitive version of dignity that Dworkin himself thought was most salient. Some of these cases arise out of factual situations that echo Dworkin's concerns—the Italian constitutional court invalidated a civil oath that included a reference to God on the ground that it violated the freedom of conscience that is an essential part of human dignity.[22] In Israel, the Constitutional Court protected the right to conscientiously object to military service as an incident of the right to dignity.[23]

Moreover, the cases typically protect the aspect of dignity that is primordially linked to equality, as Dworkin recognized. This linkage emanates from the Universal Declaration of Human Rights[24] and has been repeated in constitutions throughout the world.[25] In some countries, discrimination itself is not defined in terms of differentiation or disparate treatment, but turns on whether the different treatment affects the dignity of one group or the other.[26] As one Israeli jurist has written in almost Dworkinian terms, 'the Basic Law protects against a violation of the principle of equality when the violation causes degradation, that is, an insult to the dignity of a human being as a human being.'[27] The Czech Constitutional Court has explained that 'equality under Article 1 of the Charter is not understood in the abstract, but in relation to the dignity and the rights of an individual'.[28] This dignity-derived obligation of equal concern and respect that courts have recognized at times imposes affirmative burdens on government. As the Indian Supreme Court has said, 'The aim of the Constitution, is to equip each member of the weaker sections with the ability to compete with other citizens with dignity on an equal playing field'[29]—reflecting Dworkin's view that that what is important is 'equality in the resources that people need to exercise their individual responsibility for their own lives' as Nagel wrote (2013: 57).

Perhaps the most interesting cases that channel Dworkin's views are the cases that understand dignity as the instantiation of the full development of the personality. In a number of cases, the Colombian Constitutional Court has acknowledged that dignity represents the human desire to 'live as one wishes'.[30] In Germany, it is the right to self-determination, in Hungary (under the 1989 constitution), it was the right to the full development of the personality. As such, it has grounded not only the rights that Dworkin was concerned about—the right to choose to terminate a pregnancy, the right to die with dignity—but also right to information, to travel, to choose a name, to privacy, and to protect one's reputation, among other things. The German Constitutional Court has written that dignity 'protects the individual human being not only against humiliation, branding, persecution, outlawing, and similar actions by third parties or by the state itself'.[31] And again in Dworkinian mode, courts have protected the dignity rights of deceased people because 'It would be inconsistent with the constitutional mandate of the inviolability of human dignity, which underlies all basic rights, if a person could be belittled and denigrated after his death'[32] echoing Dworkin's view that it is the sum of a person's life that is the measure of his dignity.

In one case, the German court invalidated a provision of the Air Transport Security Act that would have allowed the government to shoot down a passenger plane if it had reason to believe that the plane would be used by hijackers as a weapon. As in the South African death penalty case, the court found that the determinative constitutional injury was to dignity, not just to life. The Court held that the law 'ignores the status of the persons affected as subjects endowed with dignity and inalienable rights' and instead treats the persons as objects to be acted upon to accomplish the state's goals, even the laudable goal of protecting more innocent lives.[33] This channels the Kantian principle that prohibits objectification—when one person uses another as a means to accomplish his or her own ends. In Latin America, this is called 'cosificar'—to make into a thing—which is likewise prohibited by the principle of human dignity. It is on this principle that some courts have found rape to be not only a physical violation but a violation of a person's dignity;[34] an Israeli court found the same principle to apply to pornography.[35] Emphasizing Dworkin's notion of intentionality, the German court in the transport security case explained that the difference between the hijackers and the passengers was that the former had chosen their fate, exercising their own autonomy, while the latter had not; to kill the hijackers would therefore not be a violation of their dignity, while to kill the passengers would be.

Intentionality therefore plays an important role in some of the cases, just as it does in Dworkin's thinking. Encapsulating Dworkin's idea of authenticity and self-respect as conditions for living well, the Canadian Supreme Court has written:

> Individuals are afforded the right to choose their own religion and their own philosophy of life, the right to choose with whom they will associate and how they will express themselves, the right to choose where they will [live] and what occupation they will pursue. These are all examples of the basic theory underlying the Charter, namely that the state will respect choices made by individuals and, to the greatest extent possible, will avoid subordinating these choices to any one conception of the good life.[36]

In South Africa, Canada, and finally the United States, constitutional courts have recognized the dignity-based interest in marrying whom one chooses, as an incident of living as one wishes. In *Fourie*, the South African Constitutional Court wrote that 'the capacity to choose to get married enhances the liberty, the autonomy and the dignity of a couple committed for life to each other'.[37] In the United States, it would take until a few months *after* Dworkin's death for the Supreme Court to recognize the dignity interests in marriage for both opposite-sex and same-sex couples[38] and a few years after that for the Court to announce firmly that the United States Constitution protects the right to marry the person of one's choice, regardless of gender.[39] When it finally did so, it rooted the right in the human dignity interests that lie at the intersection of due process and equal protection.

The Court had held in the past that certain interests related to autonomy, privacy, intimate decisions, and the like—including the right to marry, the right to choose whether and when to bear children, and decisions relating to how to raise children—were grounded in the constitutional protection for liberty, which encompasses a right to privacy. It has never been clear exactly why these are the interests that are constitutionally protected, but the jurisprudence clearly aligns with Dworkin's understanding: 'In addition these liberties extend to certain personal choices central to individual dignity and autonomy, including intimate choices that define personal identity and beliefs,'[40] the court explained. Thus, when the Court refers to the importance of the decision of whom to marry, it refers to autonomy ('the right to personal choice regarding marriage is inherent in the concept of individual autonomy'[41]) and when it refers to autonomy, it refers to dignity: 'There is dignity in the bond between two men or two women who seek to marry and in their autonomy to make such profound choices.'[42]

Likewise, the Court's equal protection jurisprudence recognized, at least in retrospect, that laws that made irrational classifications on the basis of sex 'denied the equal dignity of men and women'[43] and reflected that 'many persons did not deem homosexuals to have dignity in their own distinct identity'.[44] These discriminatory laws were repealed 'as society began to understand that women have their own equal dignity'[45] and the Court was doing the same now with respect to same sex couples.

While *Obergefell* was the landmark decision that recognized the constitutional right to marry for all, several preceding cases had laid the groundwork for expanding the rights of gays and lesbians, specifically on the basis of the need to recognize their human dignity. In *Lawrence v. Texas*, the Court had invalidated a statute that sought to criminalize sexual activity when engaged in by people of the same sex; the Court said: 'It suffices for us to acknowledge that adults may choose to enter upon this relationship in the confines of their homes and their own private lives and still retain their dignity as free persons.'[46] And in *Windsor v. United States*, the Court found that a federal law defining marriage as between a woman and a man was unconstitutional.

In this triad of cases, the Court maintained that the rights to liberty and equality fuse into the protection of human dignity. In this sense, it was consistent not only with the vast global case law on the right to dignity but also with Ronald Dworkin's precept that human dignity underlies government's obligation to assure equal concern and respect for everyone.

What mattered here was the government's decision to single out a group based on an immutable characteristic in a way that stigmatizes and therefore ostracizes, with no discernable reason for doing so other than a bare desire to harm, or exclude, people in that group. This violates the fundamental antisubordination principle that derives from the idea that if each of us is equal in dignity, then no one can be subordinated to another. It is the principle of equality applied to the value of dignity. The salient harm is to the person's dignity. Dignity, on this account, is essential to a person's ability to live well, in the Dworkininan sense, with authenticity and self-respect.

In this way, *Windsor* takes dignity beyond where Dworkin left it, recognizing not only its subjective and cognitive aspects, but its social and experiential dimensions as well. Noting the expressive impacts of both state and federal laws, the Court acknowledged that what the law says about a group of people affects not only how members of that group feel but how they are perceived in society: while a state law allowing same-sex marriage 'dignifies' couples,[47] a prohibition on same sex marriage 'tells those couples, and all the world, that their otherwise valid marriages are unworthy of federal recognition'.[48] This subordination continues into the next generation where, the 'humiliation' of the discriminatory law, the Court says, affects both how those children feel inside and how they relate to others in their community.[49]

This construct is consistent with cases from other countries, which protect both individual and social interests for the simple reason that people are both individual and social animals. They touch, as Dworkin would have us see, on both ethics and morality.

Likewise, in the Mexican case allowing adoption by same-sex couples, the court emphasized not only the decisional right of choice in family matters, but the social meaning of family. The court said that the issue was 'the right to be *considered* as a human, as a person, that is, as a being with dignity'.[50] Similarly, in a Brazilian case allowing stem cell research to find cures for diseases, the court said that the benefit was not just because some people's diseases may be cured but because such cures would enable those people to live together in society with others which would enhance their human dignity.[51] And cases that protect against embarrassment and humiliation recognize that how we are seen by others, and how we relate to others, is another aspect of human dignity.

The communal or collective aspect of dignity is often closely tied to its material aspect—a dimension of human dignity that goes beyond Ronald Dworkin's focus but is well recognized in the cases. As the Peruvian constitutional court wrote in a case about the provision of medicine for HIV/AIDS, 'For this court, ensuring well-being at a level of a dignified life is a collective obligation, as much for the society as for the particular individual, and the state.'[52] The German Constitutional Court has held that social security benefits must be sufficient to permit a person to live in a social state with dignity. There is no absolute amount that defines the *existenzminimum*, but rather it depends on what the people within their society need. Likewise, the Colombian Constitutional Court has insisted that a public housing plan must provide 'dignified housing' for all. The Indian Supreme Court in particular has considered human dignity in this way. It has insisted that the right to life which is enshrined in the constitution is a right to live in dignity and 'all that goes along with it, namely the bare necessaries of life such as adequate nutrition, clothing and shelter over the head and facilities for reading, writing, and expressing oneself in diverse forms, freely moving about and mixing and commingling with fellow human beings.'[53] This is suggestive of Dworkin's views about equality, but in his view, the resources are necessary to enable each person to exercise his personal responsibility for his own life, whereas in the cases, the goal is often to enable each person to live comfortably in society with others. Dworkin is more interested in the consequences of dignity—what meaning or significance it has or produces, than in the nature of dignity itself. But courts must look head on into dignity; it's what the constitutions require, it's the legal term that must be interpreted and applied and given precedential not just consequential meaning. Perhaps this is the difference between a philosopher's stance and the obligations of a constitutional court, duty-bound to establish rules for the regulation of society, identifying, as it were, where the swimming lanes should or should not be laid down.

Notes and References

1. Ronald Dworkin. 2011. *Justice for Hedgehogs*. Cambridge: Harvard University Press. p. 423.
2. *Justice For Hedgehogs*: For instance, in arguing for a refined understanding of liberty, Dworkin writes: 'I do not endorse any general right to freedom. I argue, instead, for rights to liberty that rest on different bases. People have a right to ethical independence that follows from the principle of personal responsibility. They have rights, including rights to due process of law and freedom of property, that follow from their right to equal concern.' But the right to equal concern, in turn, rests on a recognition of equal human dignity. Similarly, 'law is branch of political morality, which it itself a branch of a more general personal morality, which is in turn a branch of a yet more general theory of what it means to live well', which, in turn, grows from the root of dignity. In one of his most important books, *Life's Dominion*, he writes: 'Dignity is a central aspect of the value we have been examining throughout this book: the intrinsic importance of human life.' Ronald Dworkin. 1993. *Life's Dominion: An Argument about Abortion, Euthenasia, and Individual Freedom*. New York: Alfred A. Knopf. p. 236.
3. Stuart Jeffries. 2011. 'Ronald Dworkin: "We Have a Responsibility to Live Well"', *The Guardian*. 31 March. Available http://www.theguardian.com/books/2011/mar/31/ronald-dworkin-morality-dignity-hedgehogs
4. Thomas Nagel. 2013. 'Ronald Dworkin: The Moral Quest', *New York Review of Books*. November 21. pp. 56–7.
5. Ronald Dworkin. 1977. *Taking Rights Seriously*. Cambridge: Harvard University Press.

6. See UN General Assembly, Universal Declaration of Human Rights, 10 December 1948, p. 217 A (III), available at: http://www.refworld.org/docid/3ae6b3712c.html [accessed 31 December 2013], Preamble: 'Whereas recognition of the inherent dignity and of the equal and inalienable rights of all members of the human family is the foundation of freedom, justice and peace in the world...'; UN General Assembly, International Covenant on Civil and Political Rights, 16 December 1966, United Nations, Treaty Series, vol. 999, p. 171, available at: http://www.refworld.org/docid/3ae6b3aa0.html [accessed 31 December 2013], Preamble: 'Recognizing that these rights derive from the inherent dignity of the human person...'; UN General Assembly, International Covenant on Economic, Social and Cultural Rights, 16 December 1966, United Nations, Treaty Series, vol. 993, p. 3, available at: http://www.refworld.org/docid/3ae6b36c0.html [accessed 31 December 2013], Preamble: 'Considering that, in accordance with the principles proclaimed in the Charter of the United Nations, recognition of the inherent dignity and of the equal and inalienable rights of all members of the human family is the foundation of freedom, justice and peace in the world, Recognizing that these rights derive from the inherent dignity of the human person...'

7. *Jacobellis v. Ohio*, 378 US p.184 (1964) (Stewart, J. concurring).

8. Stephanie Hennette-Vauchez. 2011. 'A Human Dignitas? Remnants of the Ancient Legal Concept in Contemporary Dignity Jurisprudence', *International Journal of Constitutional Law*. 9(1): pp.32–57.

9. Kenneth W. Simons. 2010. 'Dworkin's Two Principles of Dignity: An Unsatisfactory Non-Consequentialist Account of Interpersonal Moral Duties', *Boston University Law Review*. 90.

10. Stephen Guest. 2013. *Ronald Dworkin*. 3rd Edition. Stanford: Stanford Law Books. p. 174. Mistakes may justifiably be made but government may never act in contempt of persons' dignity.

11. Ronald Dworkin. 2000. *Sovereign Virtue: The Theory and Practice of Equality*. Cambridge: Harvard University Press. p. 354: 'Free speech and democracy are connected not instrumentally but in a deeper way, because the dignity that freedom of speech protects is an essential component of democracy rightly conceived.'

12. Rarely, does Dworkin invoke dignity's other attributes. One example is in *Sovereign Virtue*, where he mentions that most people 'would attempt to buy [unemployment insurance] coverage that would at least enable them to sustain life with some dignity—provide food, decent shelter, and a minimum level of medical care for themselves and their family' (355). But there is no elaboration or adumbration of the concept of dignity here. Later, he refers to dignity medically as the absence of pain, the opposite of appalling circumstances. Americans, he says, 'disagree about whether ... people must never kill themselves, even to avoid terrible pain or crippling indignity, and even when they will soon die anyway. Some think it degrades life to end it prematurely, even in those circumstances;

others think it degrading not to die in dignity when further life would be appalling' (453). Again, no explanation of when pain crosses the dignity line.

13. Lying 'place the other at a lower level' and impairs 'their ability to exercise responsibility for their own lives' (Guest 2013: 172).

14. He explains, 'Every civilized society has standards and conventions defining these indignities, and these differ from place to place and time to time'. What or why these are, or how they relate to his idea of dignity are not explored.

15. 'It is permissible to let someone die when that is the necessary consequence of rescuing others' (Dworkin 2011: 293 et seq). See also Stephen Guest, 'Dignity is not compromised by competition harm, and so this explains the double-effect cases because dignity is only compromised when it requires that I alone make the decision' (2013: 169–70).

16. *S v. Makwanyane and Another* (CCT3/94) [1995] ZACC 3; 1995 (6) BCLR 665; 1995 (3) SA 391; [1996] 2 CHRLD 164; 1995 (2) SACR 1 (6 June 1995).

17. *Indiana v. Edwards*, 554 US p.164 (2008). See generally Erin Daly. 2011. 'Human Dignity in the Roberts Court: A Story of Inchoate Institutions, Autonomous Individuals, and the Reluctant Recognition of a Right', *Ohio North University Law Review*. 37: p. 381.

18. *Indiana v. Edwards*, 554 US pp. 164, 176 (2008).

19. Dignity in this sense is mentioned in *Planned Parenthood v. Casey*, 505 US at pp. 833, 852 (1992) ('That these sacrifices have from the beginning of the human race been endured by woman with a pride that ennobles her in the eyes of others and gives to the infant a bond of love cannot alone be grounds for the State to insist she make the sacrifice.') However, it does not figure prominently in Supreme Court decisions before Casey or since.

20. *Indiana v. Edwards*, 554 US p.164, 186–7 (2008) (Scalia, J., dissenting).

21. *Planned Parenthood v. Casey*, 505 US pp. 833, 851 (1992).

22. Sent. 334/96 (Italy 1996). See Erin Daly. 2012. *Dignity Rights: Courts, Constitutions, and the Worth of the Human Person*. Philadelphia: University of Pennsylvania Press. p. 33 et seq. Much of the research in this chapter is derived from cases discussed in this book.

23. *Zonenstein v. Military Advocate* (High Court of Justice, Israel, 2005) ISR-2002-3-005 HC 7622/02.

24. Universal Declaration of Human Rights, Article 1: ' All human beings are born free and equal in dignity and rights.'

25. See, for example, Bolivia Constitution 2009, Article 9, Section 2, 'To guarantee the welfare, development, security and protection, and equal dignity of individuals, nations, peoples, and communities, and to promote mutual respect and intra-cultural, inter-cultural and plural language dialogue.' Czech Republic, 1993, Amended 2002, Charter Of Fundamental Rights And Basic Freedoms, chapter 1 General Provisions, Article 1: 'All people are free, have equal dignity, and enjoy equality of rights.'

26. *R. v. Kapp* [Canada 2008] 2 SCR 483, 2008 SCC 41, paras. 19–25; *Minister of Home Affairs v. Fourie*, 2006 (3) BCLR 355 (CC), p. 72 (S. Afr.).

27. HCJ 4541/94, 49(4) PD 94 [1995] (Isr.)., cited in Ariel L. Bendor and Michael Sachs, 'Human Dignity as a Constitutional Concept in Germany and in Israel,' *Israel Law Review*, pp. 44, 30 (2011): pp. 1, 30.

28. 'Fine Property Situation', Pl US 38/02, at III.2.A.b (9 March 2004).

29. *EV Chinnaiah v. State of Andhra Pradesh & Ors* (2005) 1SCC 294, p. 88.

30. Sentencia T-088/08, para. 3.5.5 (Constitutional Court of Colombia)

31. Air Transport Security Case, Zitierung: BVerfG, 1 BvR 357/05 vom 15.2.2006, Absatz-Nr. (1–154), http://www.bverfg.de/entscheidungen/rs20060215_1bvr035705en.html, para. 119; in English at http://humanities.princeton.edu/files/AviationCase.pdf.

32. Bundesverfassungsgericht [BVerfGE], [Federal Constitutional Court, First Division], 24 February 1971, 30 BVerfG 173 (FRG).

33. Air Transport Security Case, Zitierung: BVerfG, 1 BvR 357/05 vom 15.2.2006, Absatz-Nr. (1-154), http://www.bverfg.de/entscheidungen/rs20060215_1bvr035705en.html, in English at http://humanities.princeton.edu/files/AviationCase.pdf at p. 4.

34. Aborto en Caso de Violacion, Inseminacion Artificial o Trasferencia de Ovulo no Consentida-Supone la relativización del principio de dignidad humana (S.V. C-355/06) (Colombia); *Mohamad Bin Senik v. Public Prosecutor* [2005] 4 MLJ 164 (High Court Malaysia—Seremban).

35. HCJ 5432/03, *Shin v. Council for Cable TV and Satellite Broadcasting* [2004] IsrSC 58(3) p. 65.

36. *R. v. Morgentaler* [1988] 1 SCR 30, p. 158 (opinion of Wilson, J.).

37. *Minister of Home Affairs v. Fourie*, 2006 (3) BCLR 355 (CC), 10 (S. Afr.).

38. *Windsor v. United States* 570 US 133 S.Ct. 2675, 2706-08 (2013) (Scalia, J., dissenting).

39. *Obergefell v. Hodges*, 576 US ___, 135 S. Ct. 2017 (2015).

40. *Obergefell v. Hodges* at 10.

41. *Obergefell v. Hodges* at 12.

42. *Obergefell v. Hodges* at 13.

43. *Obergefell v. Hodges* at 21.

44. *Obergefell v. Hodges* at 7.

45. *Obergefell v. Hodges* at 6.

46. *Lawrence v. Texas*, 539 U.S. 558, 567 (2003).

47. *Windsor v. United States* at pp. 2681, 2693.

48. *Windsor v. United States* at p. 2694.

49. *Windsor v. United States* at p. 2694.

50. Acción de Inconstitucionalidad 2/2010 (Mexico 2010).

51. AD 3510 (Brazil 2008).

52. *Meza Garcia v. Ministry of Health*, Exp. N. pp. 2945–2003-AA/TC, Resolution & 2 (20 April 2004) (Peru Constitutional Tribunal).

53. *Francis Coralie v. Union of India* (1981) AIR 746, 1981 SCR (2) 516.

16

Ronald Dworkin's Judge

Philosopher Master of Rights

Salman Khurshid

Any attempt at describing the work of Ronald Dworkin is a daunting task, given that his writings are replete with political theory, sociology, and philosophy, not to mention his profound experience of constitutional courts as well as jurisprudential thought.[1] Having early in life assumed the mantle of a leading legal philosopher of the twentieth century, Dworkin's work has naturally been the subject of close study across the world and particularly in his native United States. Fortunately India can count itself as part of the academic universe that has been drawn to and inspired by Dworkin.[2] Much of his later writings published, namely, *A Matter of Principle*,[3] *Law's Empire*,[4] and *Justice in Robes*,[5] have expanded the canvas far beyond judicial decision making into philosophical explorations of social institutions. Interestingly, Dworkin has elsewhere discussed the idea of judge as philosopher.[6] In this paper I hope to concentrate on the idea of a judge that emerged in Dworkin's early work, *Taking Rights Seriously*, and was fortified over several decades.

A sojourn into the work of Ronald Dworkin on how judges decide hard cases shows that it is not just another theory about the process of judicial decision making and the nature of law. He disagreed vigorously with his teacher and predecessor at Oxford as Professor of Jurisprudence and the leading jurisprudent of the positivist school, H.L.A. Hart, whose seminal work, *The Concept of Law*,[7] had clear echoes of Wittgenstein's[8] linguistic theory. For Hart, law is about rules of human conduct that have a strong normative element induced by a combination of a higher rule (Kelsen's Grundnorm)[9] as well as the citizen's habitual and conscious acceptance of the rule. Coercion and sanction associated with enforcement might well contribute to the normative (Kelsen 1967) impact but ultimately it is popular acceptance that really matters. Language inevitably plays an important dimension of a person's understanding of the meaning of the rule whilst at the same time contributing to its core content. An echo of this might be found in the popular legal theories of interpretation of statutes,[10] particularly for judges who believe that interpretation can at best be an attempt to discover what the legislature wished to legislate but perhaps failed to express accurately, rather than to use the opportunity to legislate by judicial pronouncement or 'filling the gaps'[11] as it were. But both categories of Judges here, the strict constructionist as well as activist, may[12] yet not pass muster as Ronald Dworkin's Judge Hercules. Obviously to some extent both traditions must deal with language and what was described by H.L.A. Hart (1961) as the uncertain and somewhat vague penumbra of meaning (with the core idea being clear in the umbra). Irrespective of the material that a judge considers relevant to his task the constraints and limits of language are inevitably felt. Words used in a statute as indeed in past judicial decisions have a natural meaning or an intended meaning susceptible to purposive interpretation.

In his remarkable landmark inaugural lecture at Oxford as Professor of Jurisprudence, 'Hard Cases' (1977), Dworkin boldly questioned the very basis of the then presiding theory of justice by examining closely how judges in the common law world decide cases irrespective of what they say they do. Of course it is presumptuous to construct a theory of decision making that departs from the intuitive understanding of judges themselves but that indeed is ironically a different concern. For Dworkin, curiously the judge may well have far greater freedom to be creative than is considered permissible under the alternative model by strict constructionists and scholars who believe it is a judge's job to apply law and not make law. Yet as we will see it is not mere discretion exercised with or without rules of guidance as external constraints that provides Dworkin's judge his dramatic power. In a particular case his judge may well come to the same conclusion as a judge who does not subscribe to Dworkin but as we will see later, for entirely different reasons. The contrasting approaches would inevitably give different answers in many if not most cases. But the thesis is of course to be tested on hard cases (ones that in popular perception make bad law!)

Principle and Policies: Competing Justifications of Judicial Decisions

In laying out the landscape of judicial decision making Dworkin examines the contrasting backdrop of legislation and adjudication in the following manner. Although Dworkin's exposition of the judicial process has several philosophical arguments, reduced to its core elements the following suggest themselves:

1. There is an essential difference between arguments of Principles and Policy.
2. Principles are largely the working materials for a judge while Policies dictate the content of responsive legislation. It may well be that the two are not water tight compartments and there may well be a degree of overlap, consciously or unwillingly.
3. A good judge gleans Principles from a comprehensive study and absorption of the institutional history of his or her society by which he arrives at the institutional morality of society as opposed to popular morality of the times that can be best assessed through referendum and periodic electoral choice. It is another matter that Dworkin's theory of democratic choice makes the latter more complex than it is often assumed.
4. The fact that the judge makes a mistake does not undermine Dworkin's thesis because there is an inherent method for weeding out mistakes and periodically reaffirming the unadulterated history (Dworkin 1977: 82).

Of the several models available to Dworkin, in particular the judge under Hart's thesis, he narrowed down the field by first putting the choice in the context of a fundamental distinction between principles and policy based decisions. A valid distinction here also reflects upon the relationship between the judge and the legislator.

> In fact, however, judges neither should be nor are deputy legislators, and the familiar assumption, that when they go beyond political decisions already made by someone else they are legislating, is misleading. It misses the importance of a fundamental distinction within political theory, which I shall now introduce in a crude form. This is the distinction between arguments of principle on the one hand and arguments of policy on the other.

Arguments of policy justify a political decision by showing that the decision advances or protects some collective goal of the community as a whole. The argument in favour of a subsidy for aircraft manufacturers, that the subsidy will protect national defense, is an argument of policy. Arguments of principle justify a political decision by showing that the decision respects or secures some individual or group right. The argument in favour of anti-discrimination statutes, that a minority has a right to equal respect and concern, is an argument of principle. These two sorts of argument do not exhaust political argument. Sometimes, for example, a political decision, like the decisions to allow extra income tax exemptions for the blind, may be defended as an act of public generosity or virtue rather than on grounds of either policy or principle. (Dworkin 1977: 82–3)

Dworkin's analysis of theories of adjudication can thus be seen from intuitive, descriptive, conceptual, and democratic dimensions. The latter two are significant for an understanding of the thesis whilst the first two show the points of reference. He lays the ground for examining them as follows:

Theories of adjudication have become more sophisticated, but the most popular theories still put judging in the shade of legislation. The main outlines of this story are familiar. Judges should apply the law that other institutions have made; they should not make new law. That is the ideal, but for different reasons it cannot be realized fully in practice. Statutes and common law rules are often vague and must be interpreted before they can be applied to novel cases. (Dworkin 1977: 82)

The real issue is not about how a statute is perceived and enforced by a judge but how to respond when it begins to fade at the edges or is unclear. Of course some judges resort to indicating that where a statute is unclear the legislature must step in. Yet that logic is less persuasive in the matter of conflicting or unclear precedents. On the other hand, policy issues do not encounter similar constraints or compulsions. In other words whilst consistency is an ingredient of a judicial decision, it may at best be a desirable element in legislation and policy making.

The doctrine demands, we might say, articulate consistency. But this demand is relatively weak when policies are in play. Policies are aggregative in their influence on political decisions and it need not be part of a responsible strategy for reaching a collective goal that individuals be treated alike. It does not follow from the doctrine of responsibility, therefore, that if the legislature awards a subsidy to one aircraft manufacturer one month, it must award a subsidy to another manufacturer the next. In the case of principles, however, the doctrine insists on distributional consistency from one case to the next, because it does not allow for the benefit in question. (Dworkin 1978: 88)

Dworkin highlights this as significant difference between adjudication and other forms of rational decision making, such as reasonable political policy based on a degree of consistency. We will return to this a little later.

Two Judges and Their Jurisprudence

Drawing from intuition and experience of how judges in the common law system approach difficult legal problems, Dworkin arrives at the following conclusions:

> We might therefore do well to consider how a philosophical judge might develop, in appropriate cases, theories of what legislative purpose and legal principles require. We shall find that he would construct these theories in the same manner as a philosophical referee would construct the character of a game. I have invented, for this purpose, a lawyer of superhuman skill, learning, patience and acumen, whom I shall call Hercules.
>
> Hercules must suppose that it is understood in his community, though perhaps not explicitly recognized, that judicial decisions must be taken to be justified by arguments of principle rather than arguments of policy. He now sees that the familiar concept used by judges to explain their reasoning from precedent, the concept of certain principles that underline or are embedded in the common law, is itself only a metaphorical statement of the rights thesis. He may henceforth use that concept in his decisions of hard common law cases. It provides a general test for deciding such cases that is like the chess referee's concept of the character of a game, and like his own concept of a legislative purpose. It provides a question, what set of principles best justify the precedents, that build a bridge between the general justification of the practice of precedent, which is fairness, and his own decision about what that general justification requires in some particular hard case. (Dworkin 1977: 105–6)

Let us now look at the alternative model also widely accepted amongst judges but which in the ultimate analysis often runs into stiff opposition on grounds of unwarranted judicial activism in departure from democratic norms (Sathe 2001).[13]

> Let us imagine another judge, called Herbert, who accepts this theory of adjudication and proposes to follow it in his decisions. Herbert might believe both women have a background right to abort fetuses they carry, and that the majority of citizens think otherwise. The present objection argues that he must

resolve that conflict in favor of democracy, so that, when he exercises his discretion to decide the abortion cases, he must decide in favor of the prohibitive statutes. Herbert might agree, in which case we should say that he has set aside his morality in favor of the people's morality. That is, in fact, a slightly misleading way to put the point. His own morality made the fact that the people held a particular view decisive; it did not withdraw in favor of the substance of that view.

Herbert did not consider whether to consult popular morality until he had fixed the legal rights of the parties. But, when Hercules fixes legal rights he has already taken the community's moral traditions into account, at least as these are captured in the whole institutional record that it is his office to interpret.

Of course, Hercules' techniques may sometimes require a decision that opposes popular morality on some issue. Suppose no justification of the earlier constitutional cases can be given that does not contain a liberal principle sufficiently strong to require a decision in favor of abortion. Hercules must then reach that decision, no matter how strongly popular morality condemns abortion. He does not, in this case, enforce his own convictions against the community's. He rather judges that the community's morality is inconsistent on this issue: its constitutional morality, which is the justification that must be given for its constitution as interpreted by its judges. (Dworkin 1977: 125–6)

The real strength of Hercules comes from this understanding of not submitting to majoritarian choice every time there is a hard case.

It is not a coincidence that the two judges Dworkin speaks of he named Hercules and Herbert. The former is obviously a larger than life adjudicator able to scan the centuries for spontaneous responses of society to real life, actual situations whilst the latter as his name suggests is less ambitious philosophically/intellectually, though no less talented, but wedded to the positivist school of Herbert Lionel Hart. The first uncovers what is not apparent to ordinary people and judges, creating or developing law as lawyers call it but which can be said to exist in a virtual reality whilst the latter looks for extant rules and where they run out without providing an answer judge Herbert simply legislates much as elected public representative would do, though perhaps with different and greater constraints.

Although Dworkin wrote with the United States and United Kingdom experience in mind, his thesis is remarkably and equally apposite for understanding the judicial history of Independent India as indeed the challenges that the judges face under contemporary conditions of deeply contested moral positions.

Notably Dworkin speaks of 'rights that people have' as though rights precede constitutional or legislative entitlements. But of course these constitutional rights are not rights in the manner of Natural Law rights or indeed any rights ordained by religions. Dworkin's rights are to be found in what he describes as institutional morality of society, largely but not entirely evidenced in the Constitution and periodic legislative enactments. Curiosity, in addition to the text of the Constitution as well as extant legislation, the judge seeks the substance and contours of rights in judicial history itself or what is familiar to common law as binding precedents or stare decisis. It might be thought that binding precedents are just a matter of good policy to ensure certainty in the guidance of law for the citizens to order their lives in compliance. But for Dworkin it is more, for it has an element of an imperative–deductive logic to arrive at rights that exist in the sense that they are part of a seamless whole. His work on Democracy and testing the Rights Thesis on the anvil of democracy provide the ultimate validation of his arguments.

Prima facie the architecture of the Indian constitution seems to contradict Dworkin's distinction between Policy and Principles.[14] The Fundamental Rights Chapter III of the Constitution is strictly binding on the State whereas the Directive Principles of State Policy not only telescope the distinct features but also are not directly enforceable. Yet in *Minerva Mills*[15] the Supreme Court was able to build on the Directive Principles to make them relevant to the enforceable content of Fundamental Rights. Essentially, therefore, there is immediate counter intuitive posture of the court to the concept of rights and the ambit of a right. The temptation to treat this as a mandate for utilitarian calculus seemed to work especially when left wing judges like Krishna Iyer, P.N. Bhagwati, O Chinnappa Reddy, D.A. Desai dominated the Court. Of course that has not prevented the Supreme Court from creatively amplifying the reach of Articles 14 (equality) and 21 (right to life and liberty) far beyond what might have been imagined by the Founding Fathers and recognized by the judges of the early years after Independence. But interestingly creative reading of Chapters III and IV have thus far obviated any conflict between Fundamental Rights and Directive Principles but it cannot be said that such a conflict can never arise. Similarly the court has had little difficulty in comfortably accommodating the words 'Secular' and 'Socialist' introduced into the Preamble by the 42nd Amendment by holding that they make explicit what was already part of the original intent of the Constitution. It is a moot question how the Court will react if an attempt was made to delete the two words by a fresh amendment.

Part III of the Constitution of India contains the Fundamental Rights and Article 13 makes any law that takes away or abridges rights therein void. Part IV has the Directive Principles of State Policy, not stricto senso enforceable by any court, but the principles therein laid down are nevertheless fundamental in the governance of the country and it 'shall be the duty of the State to apply these principles in making laws'. Although indicated to be unenforceable it can only be to the extent of direct enforcement because being fundamental to governance they are indirectly enforced by courts as in *Minerva Mills*[16] and *Waman Rao*.[17]

Furthermore, the concept of 'basic structure' that was conceived is both interesting and challenging. The concept emerged in the majority view (7–6) in *Kesavananda Bharati*[18] and in effect is similar to Dworkin's exercise of discovering legal rights that too can be said to exist but are not apparent. The issue entailed the extent to which the Constitution can be amended using the provisions available such as Article 368, including that Article itself. Chief Justice Sikri summed up the position:

> Every provision of the Constitution can be amended provided in the result the basic foundation and structure of the Constitution remains the same. The basic structure may be said to consist of the following features:
>
> 1. Supremacy of the Constitution
> 2. Republican and Democratic form of government
> 3. Secular character of the Constitution
> 4. Separation of powers between the legislature, the executive, and the judiciary
> 5. Federal character of the Constitution
>
> The above structure is built on the basic foundation, that is, the dignity and freedom of the individual. This is of supreme importance. This cannot by any form of amendment be destroyed.[19]

Curiously the wafer thin majority upheld the *Golakhnath*[20] view distinguishing constituent power from constitutional power and crafted an edifice of Constitutional jurisprudence with far reaching impact on India. Although at that time many people saw that decision to be conservative and opposed to what was described as 'social revolution', over the years it has come to be seen as a critical bulwark against majoritarianism.

An interesting point for students of the American Constitution is the fact that unlike that where the 27 amendments (enforced out of 33 proposed by Congress) have sought to strengthen the citizen against the State, the over 100 amendments have in many cases given the State greater rights against the citizen, not to mention Fundamental Duties. For example, the Fundamental right to property in the original Constitution was removed from that chapter and placed in Article 300A by the 42nd Amendment. As a consequence the US Supreme Court has not had to grapple with an issue such as in *Kesavananda Bharti*.[21]

Jurisprudentially, would it be correct to say that much as the Supreme Court has ventured to add wholesome dimensions to the rights under Articles

14 and 21[22] and thus improved constitutional architecture, it has done so by virtually substituting itself for the functus officio Constituent Assembly, an act permissible only if we subscribe to the theory that judges are entitled to legislate and in fact actually do so where considered necessary? However, if we follow Dworkin faithfully that is not only impermissible but also a clear departure from ordinarily understood democratic norms. The judges are neither authorized by a popular electoral mandate nor remotely equipped to legislate, not to mention the absence of any post hoc accountability. We have encountered writings on democracy that speak of Elected Dictatorships;[23] it would be much worse to have to deal with Unelected Judicial Dictatorship![24] This is a dilemma that needs to be addressed.

However, the Dworkin camp would neither be defeated nor puzzled by the above account of how the Indian Supreme Court has acted. It would also not be immobilized by the theory of binding precedents in common law, seeking support from developments like the House of Lords Practice Direction of 26 July 1966[25] unshackling the UK highest court from the self-imposed prohibition on departure from the binding force of previous judgments. Dworkin therefore, relies on institutional morality distinct from prevailing popular morality.

A good positivist judge such as Herbert approaches a case with source materials available such as legislation and precedents. He might look at popular morality, not necessarily his own predilection, to fill the gaps through interpretation and thus create the law going forward although the parties before him would obviously be bound. The objection that arises is that this is unfair to the parties who could not have known that to be the law. Hercules on the other hand would not be stumped by the gap but would examine the history of his society over a long period, in the process refining his understanding of the precedents and applying that to the facts on hand. Although not explicitly so available to Hercules, his investigations will take him to the conclusion that the appropriate logical fit of the history provides a right answer. In other words the hidden deductive legal solution as to what rights parties before Hercules could be said to have always had would be enunciated. There is no fresh arrangement of rights and duties but exposition of logically existing equilibrium. The fact that in his attempt to find the right answer even Hercules may falter and end up giving the wrong answer is not fatal to the thesis. Just as in scientific investigation the answer at any given moment is the best and therefore at that moment, the right answer, fortifies the thesis. Further information that could in either case lead to the conclusion that the right answer was different does not undermine the exercise.

As a graduate student at Oxford in the 1970s, I had the privilege to hear Professor Dworkin expand on his thesis in his Oxford lectures (Dworkin

1977). He often used a simple but telling example. Pointing to a painting on the wall he described the scene of a valley with a road and a stream, with mountains in the background. He then said to a group of students to describe what the picture looks like beyond the frame of the painting. Varying imaginative descriptions were offered. He would ask each one to be justified by deductive logic. There would always be the possibility of having the artist on hand to tell us what he might have painted if the canvas was larger. Consulting contemporaneous notes and rough drawings of the artist might have been of some help. Ultimately, Dworkin said there could be only one right option consistent with the existing picture and it did not matter that we get it wrong to begin with. Our attempt has to be to arrive at the actual picture that the artist would have painted if he had to continue beyond the limited canvas. In modern day syntax one might say that beyond the actual picture there is the virtual picture that can bring to life with some effort.

Some years later in 1980, I brought Dworkin face to face with Justices Krishna Iyer and Bhagwati at Oxford in what was the first such meeting he had with Indian Supreme Court judges. The two top judges had already established themselves as advocates of the rights of underprivileged and marginalized sections of society. But as it transpired their structure of rights was focused on intuition of fairness as justice supported by a broad socialist philosophy. Dworkin, on the other hand, was looking at a holistic structure or seamless web of rights and thus the conversation remained inconclusive.[26]

There is another test that must be passed by a judicial decision in a hard case and that might be called the test of democracy.

The Democratic Test and Fairness

The familiar story, that adjudication must be subordinated to legislation, is supported by two objections to judicial originality. The first argues that a community should be governed by men and women who are elected by and responsible to the majority. Since judges are, for the most part, not elected, and since they are not, in practice, responsible to the electorate in the way legislators are, it seems to compromise that proposition when judges make law. The second argues that if a judge makes new law and applies it retrospectively in the case before him, then the losing party will be punished, not because he violated some duty he had, but rather a new duty created after the event. (Dworkin 1977: 84)

This is a double edged test that must satisfy the democratic understanding that only persons answerable to the electorate can freely change the contour of rights and expectation, and furthermore to be told suddenly that arrangement of rights is quite different from what was assumed must be fair and just.

> But suppose, on the other hand, that a judge successfully justifies a decision in a hard case, like Spartan Steel, on grounds not of policy but of principle. Suppose, that is, that he is able to show that the plaintiff has a right to recover its damages. The two arguments just described would offer much less of an objection to the decision. The first is less relevant when a court judges principle, because an argument of principle does not often rest on assumptions about the nature and intensity of the different demands and concerns distributed throughout the community. On the contrary, an argument of principle fixes on some interest presented by the proponent of the right it describes, an interest alleged to be of such a character as to make irrelevant the fine discriminations of any argument of policy that might oppose it. A judge who is insulated from the demands of the political majority whose interests the right would trump is, therefore, in a better position to evaluate the argument. (Dworkin 1977: 85)

Whilst the Principle-Policy dichotomy might be said to be a significant procedural part of Dworkin's thesis and the test of Democracy used to validate that position, there is a substantive dimension as well.

Dworkin's model of judicial decision making is also referred to as the Rights Thesis. In the final analysis Hercules J. works within a structure of interwoven and interdependent rights as the landscape of his effort. This may well be because as Dworkin observes his model is situated in the common law and democracy. It is thus informed by the basic position of Rawls in his *Theory of Justice*. No serious discussion on equality can take place without coming to terms with Affirmative Action or as some scholars call it, Reverse Discrimination. It is surely this understanding of justice in social institutions that provides the base of the Rights thesis.

> The right thesis, that judicial decisions enforce existing political rights, suggests an explanation that is more successful on both counts. If the thesis holds, then institutional history acts not as a constraint on the political judgment of judges but as an ingredient of that judgment, because institutional history is part of the background that any plausible judgment about the rights of an individual must accommodate. Political rights are creatures of both history and morality; what an individual is entitled to have, in civil society, depends upon both the practice and the justice of its political institutions. So, the supposed tension between judicial originality and institutional history is dissolved: judges must make fresh judgments about the rights of the parties who come before them, but these political rights reflect, rather than oppose, political decisions of the past. When a judge chooses between the rule established in precedent and

some new rule thought to be fairer, he does not choose between history and justice. He rather makes a judgment that requires some compromise between considerations that ordinarily combine in any calculation of political right, but here compete. (87)

Thus, it might be that despite two jurisdictions adhering to the Hercules model the archival material might be different as indeed their respective histories. I am not venturing to argue that there are universal values that are common to most liberal systems. But other writings of Dworkin touch upon something similar to common human values. Clearly Equality is a basic paradigm without which much of Dworkin's analysis becomes vulnerable. He therefore devoted *A Matter of Principle* to the study of equality.

The theory of Mistake is the last but crucial part of Dworkin's thesis. Inevitably some decision stands out against the trend. *ADM Jabalpur*,[27] decided by the Supreme Court during the Internal Emergency declared by the then Prime Minister Indira Gandhi is clearly one such decision. Both before and after the Emergency justification of such a severe curtailment of individual liberty is not to be found in the judgments of the Court. It is interesting though that *ADM Jabalpur*[28] was a culmination of decisions of the Court that placed welfare of society above individual rights although directed at land reform legislation. The diminishing protection to property rights albeit in the interest of social transformation eroded the jurisprudential cage that protects all rights and thus ended up conceding to the State suspension of Habeas Corpus. The judgment continues to hold ground, not having been over ruled but at least one former Chief Justice has expressed regret in retirement and another Bench of two judges wondered if a judgment can itself violate Fundamental Rights. On the other hand as though to redeem itself the Supreme Court subsequently set out to justify the panorama of rights from *Maneka Gandhi v. Union of India*[29] to *Francis Coralie Mullin v. Administrator, Delhi*.[30]

Let us examine the Herculean effort in the light of the example of *Naz Foundation*,[31] a remarkable judgment of the Delhi High Court presided by the then Chief Justice A.P. Shah. The case involved a challenge to Section 377 of the IPC that imposes criminal culpability upon persons of different sexual orientation for indulging in carnal intercourse against the order of nature.[32]

Essentially the question was the right of an individual to live their life in a particular manner even if society found that distasteful. The court overruled all objections of the State and private objectors to quash the section to the effect of consensual conduct. When the matter travelled to the Supreme Court, an activist judge, Justice G.S. Singhvi overturned the High Court on the ground that this was in the realm of Parliament. Two important takeaways stare us in the face. First, that the impressive jurisprudence of the Supreme Court on Fundamental Rights developed post the internal emergency of 1976 did not persuade the Bench to see LGBT orientation to be on par with the rights of an individual. Secondly, that such matter are best left to judgment of Parliament and public representatives. A closer examination of the analysis tools used by the justices is very revealing.

The High Court had concluded that equality, inclusiveness, dignity of the individual is an anti-thesis of some persons being treated as deviants or of different sexual orientation. Citing *John Vallamattom v. Union of India*[33] (para 79) the court endorsed the view that prohibition on discrimination (in that case gender) implies the right to autonomy and self-determination. The court took on the argument of morality as a ground for restriction on fundamental rights. The court relied on *Gobind v. State of M.P.*[34] to hold that it is a promise of the Constitution that there is a realm of personal liberty which the government may not enter.

Chief Justice A.P. Shah took the core idea to its logical conclusion. Popular morality or public disapproval of certain acts is not a valid justification for restriction of fundamental rights under Article 21. Popular morality, as distinct from a constitutional morality derived from constitutional values, is based on shifting and subjecting notions of right and wrong. If there is any type of 'morality' that can pass the test of compelling state interest it must be 'constitutional morality and not public morality'.

Thus the High Court zeroed in on rights under Articles 14, 15, 19, and 21 as gathered into a constitutional bouquet by *Maneka Gandhi*[35] and the judgments that followed but was not willing to subject them to anything short of constitutional morality. Autonomy became the short hand description of the bouquet. What followed was the striking down of Section 377 of the IPC that made consequences of that autonomy a criminal offense (paras 129–31). Curiously it is this analysis that the Supreme Court missed entirely in reversing the judgment. To begin with, the Supreme Court proceeded to consider the presumption of constitutionality of legislation although it is just a tool of convenience rather than a profound principle of law. Looking at the doctrine of sever-ability and technique of reading down statutes to uphold them it then proceeded to flag the fact that despite many opportunities Parliament has refrained from amending the statute, particularly in spite of a recommendation of the Law Commission to that effect. After a comprehensive survey of the history of Section 377 the court held that 'from these cases no uniform test can be culled out to clarify acts as "carnal intercourse against the order of nature" ... identity and orientation'.[36]

A significant universal principle that can be derived from the High Court judgment but was entirely missed by many conservative religious groups that spontaneously rejected the judgment was the element of autonomy they can claim for themselves. Since the Directive Principles of State Policy include the aspiration of a Uniform Civil Code for the country and in recent years the clamour for it has grown the Court is bound to consider the issue in entirety. The inherent tension between religious practice of communities and rights and duties of an individual citizen under the Constitution will need to be resolved. Once again the question will arise whether Directive Principles will prevail over Fundamental Rights or indeed as Dworkin says, the latter will trump the former. For advocates of free choice and preferred diversity there can be no better argument than autonomy upheld by the High Court. The parting observation of the Chief Justice merits close scrutiny:

> If there is a constitutional tenet that can be said to be underlying theme of the Indian Constitution, it is that of 'inclusiveness'. This court believes that the Indian Constitution reflects this value ingrained in Indian society, nurtured over several generations. The inclusiveness that Indian society traditionally displayed, literally in every aspect of life, is manifest in recognising a role in society for everyone. Those perceived by the majority as 'deviants' or 'different' are not on that score excluded or ostracized ... In our view, Indian Constitutional law does not permit the statutory criminal law to be held captive by the popular misconceptions of who the LGBTs are.[37]

There can indeed be no better and clinching example of an Indian judge following the Dworkin aspiration, both in adherence to the Rights Thesis as well as distinguishing popular morality from constitutional morality.

Although for the present the petitioners in *Naz Foundation*[38] remain unsuccessful, it is not because the larger principle enunciated by the High Court has been negative but only that its application in that particular case has been denied. The battle between diversity and uniformity is still to be joined. To the extent that the contest remains focused on issues of gender justice it is one thing but uniformity beyond quite another. Any aspect of a community's Personal law if looked at in isolation will undoubtedly appear less acceptable than being seen as part of the whole alternative system and practice. Plural societies the world over will need to resolve similar problems and courts examine the extent to which the initiative of reform must remain with the judiciary.

Interestingly the Supreme Court too relied upon *Gobind v. State of M.P.*[39] a case of 2005 (para 23) to prepare ground for restricting the ambit of autonomy and holding it like other rights not to be absolute.

Individual autonomy, perhaps the central concern of any system of limited government, is protected in part under our Constitution by explicit Constitutional
guarantees. 'In the application of the Constitution our contemplation cannot
only be of what has been but what may be.' Time works changes and brings
into existence new conditions. Subtler and far reaching means of invading privacy will make it possible to be heard in the street what is whispered in the
closet. Yet, too broad a definition of privacy raises serious questions about the
propriety of judicial reliance on a right that is not explicit in the Constitution.
Of course, privacy primarily concerns the individuals. It therefore relates to
and overlaps with the concept of liberty. The most serious advocate of privacy
must confess that there are serious problems of defining the essence and scope
of the right. Privacy interest in autonomy must also be placed in the context of
other rights and values.[40]

How the Supreme Court could have arrived at that conclusion despite
its consistent endeavour over the past few years to expand the contours of
freedom leaves one puzzled.

In *Kharak Singh v. U.P.*[41] the Supreme Court laid the foundation of the
right to privacy, not explicitly provided in Chapter III. Upon the base of
privacy was developed the concept of autonomy.

The case involved a challenge to surveillance of domiciliary situation of the
targeted citizen. The entire court struck down most of the impugned regula-
tions though Justice Subba Rao, writing a separate judgment went further to
strike down the entire regulation being ultra vires having held that the word
'liberty' in Article 21 was comprehensive enough to include privacy also. His
Lordship said that although it is true that our Constitution does not expressly
declare a right to privacy as a fundamental right, but the right is an essential
ingredient of personal liberty, that in the last resort, a person's house where he
lives with his family, is his castle that nothing is more deleterious to a man's
physical happiness and health than a calculated interference with his privacy
and that all the acts of surveillance under Regulation 236 infringe the fundamental right of the petitioner under Article 21 of the Constitution. As regards
Article 19(1)(d), he was of the view that the right also was violated. The right
under that sub-Article is not mere freedom to move without physical obstruc-
tion and observed that movement under the scrutinizing gaze of the police-
men cannot be free movement, that the freedom of movement in Clause (d)
therefore must be a movement in a free country, that is, in a country where
he can do whatever he likes, speak to whomsoever he wants, meet people of
his own choice without any apprehension, subject of course to the law of
social control and that a person under the shadow of surveillance is certainly
deprived of this freedom. He concluded that surveillance by domiciliary visits

and other acts is an abridgment of the fundamental right guaranteed under Article 19(1)(d) and under Article 19(1)(a).

Despite referring to the above judgments in *Naz Foundation*[42] the higher aspirations were given a quiet burial by the Supreme Court, brushing off judgments from other countries by stating 'we feel that they cannot be applied blindfolded for deciding the constitutionality of the law enacted by the Indian Legislature'.[43] In the process, a powerful argument made by the High Court was side stepped; closing the door, at least for the present to what might have been a landmark decision of modern jurisprudence :

> Thus popular morality or public disapproval of certain acts is not a valid justification for restriction of the fundamental rights under Article 21. Popular morality, as distinct from a constitutional morality derived from constitutional values, is based on shifting and subjecting notions of right and wrong. If there is any type of 'morality' that can pass the test of compelling state interest, it must be 'constitutional' morality and not public morality. This aspect of constitutional morality was strongly insisted upon by B.R. Ambedkar in the Constituent Assembly. While moving the Draft Constitution in the Assembly [Constitutional Assembly Debates: Official Reports Vol. VII: November 4, 1948, p. 38] Ambedkar quoted Grote, the historian of Greece, who had said: 'The diffusion of constitutional morality, not merely among the majority of any community but throughout the whole, is an indispensable condition of government at once free and peaceable; since even any powerful and obstinate minority may render the working of a free institution impracticable without being strong enough to conquer the ascendancy for themselves.'[44]

The refusal by the Supreme Court to tread upon promising territory of Articles 14, 16, and 21 of the Constitution explored by Chief Justice P.N. Bhagwati and his colleagues in a series of judgments in 1970s and 1980s is a great opportunity missed for developing Indian constitutional law profoundly. Nevertheless, the powerful arguments of the High Court remain unanswered. Herbert indeed could have done none better. Hercules' effort went in vain to await another day. And it was not even a hard case as we might imagine. The question remains whether this will now stand in the way of another attempt by Hercules, this time in the Supreme Court, to reopen the issue. Given that the Supreme Court functions in the incredible structure of 31 judges sitting in Benches of 2, 3, 5 (Constitution Bench), 7 judges and/or more, there is no reason to believe that this is indeed the last word. Although the Review was dismissed,[45] under Curative jurisdiction[46] the petition for a review was accepted and will entail a full court hearing.[47] We do not really know what the other judges think and now that the two judges on the Bench have also retired. Dworkin fortunately thought of this as well as part of the Mistake Theory. Is that an escape from an intractable problem or indispensable ingredient of the thesis?

Dworkin approaches the matter thus:

> Hercules' technique encourages a judge to make his own judgments about institutional rights. The argument from judicial fallibility might be thought to suggest two alternatives. The first argues that since judges are fallible they should make no effort at all to determine the institutional rights of the parties before them, but should decide hard cases only on grounds of policy, or not at all. But that is perverse; it argues that because judges will often, by misadventure, produce unjust decisions they should make no effort to produce just ones. The second alternative argues that since judges are fallible they should submit questions of institutional right raised by hard cases to someone else. But to whom? There is no reason to credit any other particular group with better facilities of moral argument; or, if there is, then it is the process of selecting judges, not the techniques of judging that they are asked to use, that must be changed. So this form of skepticism does not in itself argue against Hercules' technique of adjudication, though of course it serves as a useful reminder to any judge that might well be wrong in his political judgments, and that he should therefore, decide hard cases with humility. (Dworkin 1977: 130)
>
> He will construct the first part of this theory of mistakes by means of two sets of distinctions. He will first distinguish between the specific authority of any institutional event, which is its power as an institutional act to affect just the specific institutional consequences it describes, and it is gravitational force. If he classifies some event as a mistake, then he does not deny its specific authority but he does deny its gravitational force, and he cannot consistently appeal to that force in other arguments. He will also distinguish between embedded and corrigible mistakes; embedded mistakes are those whose specific authority is fixed so that it survives their loss of gravitational force; corrigible mistakes are those whose specific authority depends on gravitational force in such a way that it cannot survive this loss. (121)

Clearly then Dworkin's thesis essentially replicates scientific enquiry where the search for the right answer leads to the best answer at any given moment in time (though colloquially it might be called the right answer). It is the constant and consistent search of the right answer that ensures the best answer on the given material, analysis, and understanding of history. However, for a scientific enquiry to be meaningful there has to be a natural existing correlation between phenomena that investigation unravels. Similarly the search for a consistent value system in Dworkin's model seems implicitly based on liberal democracy with a nodal point of equality. Every other value flows from that basic premise.

It is arguable that a moral system has greater consistency than an immoral or amoral system. In other words, telling truth is more likely to exhibit consistency than telling untruths. Perhaps the nature of Dworkin's arguments converges his thought with the work of John Rawls in *A Theory of Justice*.[48] Not surprisingly therefore, the two provided the two points of reference of liberal thought in the twentieth and twenty-first centuries. The extent to which modern day judges in democratic societies are able to accomplish their task of delivering justice assisted by the works of Ronald Dworkin and John Rawls will in many ways transform the world we live in. That India shares that destiny will be an interesting enterprise for successive generation if appellate judges of the country keep the following caveat in mind when deciding hard cases:

> Hercules' technique encourages a judge to make his own judgments about institutional rights. The argument from judicial fallibility might be thought to suggest two alternatives. The first argues that since judges are fallible they should make no effort at all to determine the institutional rights of parties before them, but should decide hard cases only on grounds of policy, or none at all. But that is perverse; it argues that because judges will often, by misadventure, produce unjust decisions they should make no effort to make just ones. The second alternative argues that since judges are fallible they should submit questions of institutional rights to someone else. But to whom? There is no reason to credit any other group with better facilities of moral argument; or, if there is, then it is in the process of selecting judges, not the techniques of judging that they are asked to use, that must be changed. So this form of skepticism does not in itself argue against Hercules' technique of adjudication, though of course it serves as a useful reminder to any judge that he might well be wrong in his political judgments, and that he should therefore decide hard cases with humility. (Dworkin 1977: 130)

The Rights Thesis makes a profound distinction between the 'rights people have' and the 'right thing to do' in the given circumstances. Without properly understanding that rights become vulnerable to contrary opinions. Thus Hercules not only searches for the right but also consciously considers himself bound not to bypass that right on any competing consideration. It is thus, that Rights become the cornerstone of justice as we understand it. The conundrum of Rights versus the right thing to do was most recently reflected in two decisions of the Supreme Court, *Shreya Shinghal*[49] and *National Anthem* case in *Shyam Narayan Chouksey v. Union of India*.[50] In the latter, the Court ruled that at the end of public screening of films the audience must stand to the rendering of the National Anthem. Yet 30 years ago he Court had accepted that Jehovah's witnesses[51] need not stand to show respect to the national anthem, placing individual preferences above society. Justice Dipak

Misra was obviously looking at what is good for cohesion in society rather than a rights perspective.[52]

[I]t is clear as crystal that it is the sacred obligation of every citizen to abide by the ideals engrafted in the Constitution. And one such ideal is to show respect for the National Anthem and the National Flag. Be it stated, a time has come, the citizens of the country must realize that they live in a nation and are duty bound to show respect to National Anthem which is the symbol of the Constitutional Patriotism and inherent national quality. It does not allow any different notion or the perception of individual rights, that have individually thought of have no space. The idea is constitutionally impermissible.[53]

It is important to keep in mind that the court was conscious of the Fundamental Duties of citizens included as Article 51A of the Constitution by the 42nd Amendment. On the other hand, in *Shreya Shingle v. Union of India*,[54] Justice Rohinton Nariman struck down Section 66A of the Information Technology Act, 2000[55] entirely on a rights perspective.

Chilling Effect and Overbreadth

Information that may be grossly offensive or which causes annoyance or inconvenience are undefined terms which take into the net a very large amount of protected and innocent speech. A person may discuss or even advocate by means of writing disseminated over the internet information that may be a view or point of view pertaining to governmental, literary, scientific or other matters which may be unpalatable to certain sections of society. It is obvious that an expression of a view on any matter may cause annoyance, inconvenience or may be grossly offensive to some. A few examples will suffice. A certain section of a particular community may be grossly offended or annoyed by communications over the internet by 'liberal views', such as the emancipation of women or the abolition of the caste system or whether certain members of a non-proselytizing religion should be allowed to bring persons within their fold who are otherwise outside the fold. Each one of these things may be grossly offensive, annoying, inconvenient, insulting or injurious to large sections of particular communities and would fall within the net cast by Section 66A. In point of fact, Section 66A is cast so widely that virtually any opinion on any subject would be covered by it, as any serious opinion dissenting with the mores of the day would be caught within its net. Such is the reach of the Section and if it is to withstand the test of constitutionality, the chilling effect on free speech would be total. (Para 87)[56]

Thus clearly both models operate across the judicial landscape in India.[57] It is high time judges reflect on their techniques and decide which ones and to what extent they are compatible with the essential idea of rights that exist independent of the view that it would be right to grant them.[58] Following Dworkin might be difficult but promises to protect us from the unintended excesses of utilitarianism in times of homogeneity perceptions versus pluralism.

Interestingly two important judgments of the Indian Supreme Court in recent months have specifically noticed the work of Dworkin. A Constitutional bench of nine judges[59] delivered a land mark judgment recognizing Privacy as a Fundamental Right, something that was repeatedly assumed to exist but was not specifically endorsed in the light of two judgments of Eight and Six judges respectively that had held otherwise. In his far reaching exposition on behalf of Chief Justice J.S. Khehar and four other judges, Justice Chandrachud looked at the close link between Privacy and Dignity, the Right to Life with dignity under Article 21, and the need to read together the different Fundamental Rights under Chapter III. In the process, Justice Chandrachud dwelt briefly upon the thesis of Dworkin but essentially to support the view that there are certain Rights that are prior to the Constitution, in effect endorsing the theory of Natural Rights. However, it has been argued here that for Dworkin, rights flow essentially from the Original Contract between individuals and sophisticated reading of the institutional history of the society they belong to. Natural Rights are largely instinctive and a priori whilst Dworkin's rights thesis attributes them to a Herculean analysis.

[45] The concept of natural inalienable rights secures autonomy to human beings. But the autonomy is not absolute, for the simple reason that, the concept of inalienable rights postulates that there are some rights which no human being may alienate. While natural rights protect the right of the individual to choose and preserve liberty, yet the autonomy of the individual is not absolute or total.[60]

[46] The idea that individuals can have rights against the State that are prior to rights created by explicit legislation has been developed as part of a liberal theory of law propounded by Ronald Dworkin.[61]

Dealing with the question whether the government may abridge the rights of others to act when their acts might simply increase the risk, by however slight or speculative a margin, that some person's right to life or property will be violated, Dworkin says:

But no society that purports to recognize a variety of rights, on the ground that a man's dignity or equality may be invaded in a variety of ways, can accept such a principle... If rights make sense, then the degrees of their importance cannot be so different that some count not at all when others are mentioned... If the Government does not take rights seriously, then it does not take law seriously either.[62]

The term 'natural law' needs to be understood. It refers to combination of moral theory with legal theory, although the core claims of the two are logically independent. It is largely different from the *laws of nature*, that is, laws that science can observe. According to natural law moral theory, the moral standards that govern human behaviour are, in some sense, objectively derived from the nature of human beings and the nature of the world. While being logically independent of natural law legal theory, the two theories intersect. However, the majority of the article will focus on natural law legal theory.

According to natural law legal theory, the normative power of legal standards necessarily derives, at least in part, from considerations—the moral worth of propositions. There are several natural law legal theories. The conceptual jurisprudence of John Austin provides a set of necessary and sufficient conditions for the existence of law that distinguishes law from non-law in every possible world. Classical natural law theory such as the theory of Thomas Aquinas focuses on the overlap between natural law, moral, and legal theories. Similarly, the neo-naturalism of John Finnis is a development of classical natural law theory. In contrast, the procedural naturalism of Lon L. Fuller is a rejection of the conceptual naturalist idea that there are necessary *substantive* moral constraints on the content of law. Ronald Dworkin's theory in response to and critique of H.L.A. Hart's *legal positivism* may well be thought to be part of this tradition, as indeed Justice Chadrachud has assumed. However a closer examination would reveal that it arrives at many conclusions similar to natural law but has a distinctly different process for arriving there.

Justice Sikri and Justice Bhushan who were not members of the Constitutional Bench had considered the concept of Dignity in another matter, *Binoy Vishwam*,[63] where counsel had exerted to persuade the Bench that the issue of dignity could be examined independently of Privacy to be examined by the Constitutional Bench. Ultimately, the Bench of two judges declined to accept that view but not without looking at Dignity in considerable detail. In the process Justice Sikri looked at Dworkin's thesis as being rooted in the social contract, noted with approval arguments made to secure the Right to Dignity in Article 21 of the Constitution but was unable to go further in view of the reference pending before the Constitutional Bench. But he did describe the matter as 'hard case' drawing upon Dworkin.

[Counsel] made an additional submission, invoking the principle of right to live with dignity which, according to him, was somewhat different from the Right to Privacy. He submitted that although dignity inevitably includes privacy, the former has several other dimensions which need to be explored as well. In his submissions, the test to identify whether certain data collected about individuals is intrusive or merely expansive is to consider whether it causes embarrassment, indignity, or invasion of privacy. Thus, the concept of dignity is quite distinct from that of privacy. Privacy is a conditional concept. One has it only to the extent that one's circumstances allow for it, as a matter of fact and law. While it is widely accepted that a situation may occur where a person may not have any Right to Privacy whatsoever, dignity is an inherent possession of every person, regardless of circumstance. In that sense, Dignity is an inherent dimension of equality, the basis of John Rawls *Theory of Justice*. The Social Contract theory propounded by Rousseau remains the ground on which John Rawls developed the model of the Original Position in which the contours of the compact are conceived. Anything that reduces the personality of the participant, such as diluting the human element and substituting it with a number or biometric data, virtually destroys the model. Dignity is an immutable value, held in equal measure at all times by all people, a quality privacy does not share. No court has ever held that a person can be stripped entirely of his/her dignity. The concept of dignity is deeper than that of privacy and its boundaries do not depend upon the circumstance of any individual and thus the State cannot legitimately fully infringe upon it. He pointed out that in *M. Nagaraj and Ors. v. Union of India and Ors*[64] this Court has, thus, elucidated the concept of Right to Dignity in the following manner:

20. This Court has in numerous cases deduced fundamental features which are not specifically mentioned in Part III on the principle that certain unarticulated rights are implicit in the enumerated guarantees....

26. It is the duty of the State not only to protect the human dignity but to facilitate it by taking positive steps in that direction. No exact definition of human dignity exists. It refers to the intrinsic value of every human being, which is to be respected. It cannot be taken away. It cannot give [*sic*: be given]. It simply is. Every human being has dignity by virtue of his existence. The constitutional courts in Germany, therefore, see human dignity as a fundamental principle within the system of the basic rights. This is how the doctrine of basic structure stands evolved under the German Constitution and by interpretation given to the concept by the constitutional courts.[65]

For the present there might be no great difference in practical terms but the test would arise in application of the two contrasting models to emergent facts such as challenge to Death Sentence. The nine judges model would require a search for pre-Constitutional right to life without the State claiming the right to terminate it. Of course it is entirely possible that just as the Court overruled *ADM Jabalpur*[66] it might overrule *Bachan Singh*[67] that left the hangman's noose dangling around 'rarest of rare cases' on a correct reading of precedents as in the present case. The trouble with that model is the ease with which judges might differ on the content of natural rights, particularly in a plural society. On the other hand, Dworkin's analysis of institutional morality combined with social contract model is more likely to bring us closer to the right answer.

Notes and References

1. Ronald Dworkin. 1978. *Taking Rights Seriously*. Cambridge: Harvard University Press.
2. Upendra Baxi, 1 Int I Cons Law 557 (2003); Abhishek Sudhir, *Discovering Dworkin in the Supreme Court of India-A comparative excursus.*
3. Ronald Dworkin. 1985. *A Matter of Principle*. Cambridge: Harvard University Press.
4. Ronald Dworkin. 1985. *Law's Empire*. Cambridge: Harvard University Press.
5. Ronald Dworkin. 2006. *Justice in Robes*. Cambridge: Harvard University Press.
6. Ronald Dworkin. 2000. 'Must Our Judges be Philosophers? Can They be Philosophers?' *New York Council for Humanities*, Scholar of the year lecture.
7. H.L.A. Hart. 1961. *The Concept of Law*. Oxford: Oxford University Press.
8. Ludwig Wittgenstein. 1953. *Philosophical Investigations*. New York: Macmillan.
9. Hans Kelsen. 1967. *Pure Theory of Law*. Berkeley: University of California Press.
10. G.P. Singh. 2016. *Interpretation of Statutes*. Gurgaon: LexisNexis.
11. *Census Commissioner v. R. Krishnamurthy*, (2015) 2 SCC 796.
12. Interesting contrast of the two in Indian Supreme Court judgment *Abhiram Singh v. CD Commachen* CA 37/1992 decided on 2 January 2017.
13. S.P. Sathe. 2001. 'Judicial Activism: The Indian Experience', *Washington University Journal of Law & Policy.* 6: (029).
14. Chapters III and IV of the Constitution of India.
15. *Minerva Mills Ltd. v. Union of India*, (1980)3 SCC 625.
16. (1980) 3 SCC 625.
17. (1981) 2 SCC 362.
18. (1973) 4 SCC 225.
19. (1973) 4 SCC 225 at p. 366, para. 292.
20. *Golaknath v. State of Punjab*, AIR 1967 SC 1643.
21. *Kesavananda Bharati v. State of Kerala* (1963) 4 SCC 225; I R Coelho (2007) 2 SCC 1.
22. Article 14. The State shall not deny to any person equality before the law or the equal protection of the laws within the territory of India.

Article 21. No person shall be deprived of his life or personal liberty except according to procedure established by law.

23. Melik Kaylan. 2014. 'The New Wave of Elected Dictatorships around the World', *Forbes*. Washington. 31 July.
24. David Pannick. 1987. *Judges*. Oxford: Oxford University Press.
25. Lord Gardiner LC made announcement in House of Lords on his own behalf and other Lords of Appeal in Ordinary.
26. The Supreme Court has taken note of Ronald Dworkin's work in several cases:
    Sahara India Real estate corp. Ltd v. Securities and Exchange Board of India (2012) 10 SCC 603; *Santosh Kumar Satishbhushan Bariyar v. State of Maharashtra* (2009) 6 SCC 498; *State of UP v. Jeet S. Bisht* (2007) 6 SCC 586; *Madras Bar Association v. Union of India* (2014) 10 SCC 2; *S.R. Bommai v. Union of India* (1994) 3 SCC 1; *Indra Sawhney v. Union of India* (1992) Supp (3) SCC 217.
    Several High Courts too have referred to Dworkin's ideas: *Baichung Bhutia v. Soumik Dutta* 2014 SCC Online Del 4339; *Swatanter Kumar v. Indian Express Ltd.* (2014) SCC Online Del; *Mohd. Farooq Abdul Gafur and Anr. v. State of Maharashtra* 14 SCC 641; *Vinaya v. State of Kerela* 2002 SCC Online Ker 76; *Harrisons Malayalam Ltd. v. State of Kerela* 2007 SCC Online Ker 430; *Sartaj v. State of UP* 2010 SCC Online All 1273; *Ranga Reddy District Sarpanches Association and others v. Governmentt of A.P. and others* 2004 SCC Online AP 61.
27. AIR 1976 SC 1207.
28. The court held that if the right to enforce personal freedom through a writ of habeas corpus is suspended by the Emergency provision, it cannot be said that the enforcement can be restored by resorting to 'any other purpose' under Art 226 by which the High Courts have writ jurisdiction. Justice H.R. Khanna dissented in a celebrated pro-liberty judgment.
29. (1978) 2 SCR 621.
30. (1981) 1 SCC 608.
31. (2014) 1 SCC 1.
32. Article 377. Unnatural offences: Whoever voluntarily has carnal intercourse against the order of nature with any man, woman, or animal shall be punished with imprisonment for life, or with imprisonment of either description for term which may extend to ten years, and shall also be liable to fine. Explanation: Penetration is sufficient to constitute the carnal intercourse necessary to the offense described in this section.[3][4]
33. (2003) 6 SCC 611.
34. AIR 1975 SC 1378 (para. 36).
35. 1978 2 SCR 621 (para. 75, 79).
36. *Suresh Kumar Koushal v. Naz Foundation*, (2014) 1 SCC 1.
37. *Naz Foundation v. Govt. of NCT of Delhi*, (2009) 111 DRJ (DB).
38. *Naz Foundation v. Govt. of NCT of Delhi*.
39. AIR 1975 SC 1378.
40. AIR 1975 SC 1378.
41. (1964) 1 SCR 332.

42. (2014) 1 SCC 1.

43. (2014) 1 SCC 1 p. 78.

44. (2014) 1 SCC 1 p. 19.

45. (2014) 3 SCC 220.

46. Curative jurisdiction was developed by the Supreme Court in *Rupa Ashok Hurra v. Ashok Hurra* (2002) 4 SCC 388, whereby a party dissatisfied with dismissal of Review petition can file a curative petition on limited grounds certified by a Senior Advocate. The matter is then circulated to the judges who heard the case and are still on the Bench and such other senior most judges as to make the number five.

47. (2016) 7 SCC 485.

48. John Rawls. 1971. *A Theory of Justice*. Cambridge: Harvard University Press.

49. *Shreya Singhal v. Union of India*, (2015) 5 SCC 1.

50. (2016) SCC Online 1449.

51. *Bijoe Emmanuel v. State of Kerala*, (1986) 3 SCC 615.

52. See Ronald Dworkin. 2000. 'The Threat to Patriotism', *New York Review of Books*, 28 Feburary.

53. (2016) SCC Online 1449.

54. (2015) 5 SCC Online 1.

55. Information Technology Act, 2000 CHAPTER 11—OFFENCES Section 66-A. Punishment for sending offensive messages through communication service, etc.

    Repealed 1[66-A. Punishment for sending offensive messages through communication service, etc. Any person who sends, by means of a computer resource or a communication device:

    (a) any information that is grossly offensive or has menacing character; or

    (b) any information which he knows to be false, but for the purpose of causing annoyance, inconvenience, danger, obstruction, insult, injury, criminal intimidation, enmity, hatred or ill will, persistently by making use of such computer resource or a communication device; or

    (c) any electronic mail or electronic mail message for the purpose of causing annoyance or inconvenience or to deceive or to mislead the addressee or recipient about the origin of such messages, shall be punishable with imprisonment for a term which may extend to three years and with fine.

    Explanation: For the purposes of this section, terms 'electronic mail' and 'electronic mail message' means a message or information created or transmitted or received on a computer, computer system, computer resource or communication device including attachments in text, image, audio, video and any other electronic record, which may be transmitted with the message.]

56. *Justice K.S. Puttaswamy v. Union of India and Others*, Writ Petition(Civil) No. 494 of 2012, decided on 24 August 2017.

57. See unreported Order of Justice Markandey Katju re Bail of Dr Binayak Sen Vol. 26 (2000).

58. The most glaring example of this shows up in the dramatic range of positions taken by the Supreme Court in matters of Bail. It would come as a surprise to constitutional scholars that the Supreme Court has to deal with Bail in a routine manner. The locus classicus on Bail is the judgment of Krishna Iyer J in.*State of Rajasthan v Balchand.*,(1977) 4 SCC 308, 'bail is the rule and jail an exception'. This was most recently reaffirmed in *Sanjay Chandra v CBI (2012) 1 SCC 40 yet* every day Bail petitions are refused giving prosaic reasons such as 'renew application after six months'.
59. *Justice K.S. Puttaswamy v. Union of India and Others*, Writ Petition(Civil) No. 494 of 2012.
60. *Justice K.S. Puttaswamy v. Union of India and Others* p. 37, part G.
61. *Justice K.S. Puttaswamy v. Union of India and Others* p. 38.
62. *Justice K.S. Puttaswamy v. Union of India and Others* p. 39.
63. *Binoy Vishwam v. Union of India*, Writ Petition(Civil) No. of 247, decided on 9 June 2017.

    The case was a challenge to the mandatory requirement of the bio- metric Adhaar card for filing of income tax returns and turned on Fundamental Rights chapter of the Constitution.
64. (2006) 8 SCC 212.
65. (2006) 8 SCC 212.
66. *ADM Jabalpur v. Shivakant Shukla*, AIR 1976 SC 1207.
67. *Bachan Singh v. State of Punjab*, AIR 1980 SC 898.

17

A Dworkinian Reading of the Indian Constitution

Suhrith Parthasarathy

The Indian Constitution, on last count, comprises 449 articles and 12 appended schedules. More than any other written constitution, the document, by virtue of its sheer prolixity and the nature of its country's democracy, is inherently prone to incongruities. It also happens to be a text of substantial political significance. For one, it outlines a set of individual rights that even a democratically elected Parliament cannot abrogate. Determining the import of these rights, therefore, attains enormous importance. But for all its exhaustiveness, the Constitution is not of much help in telling us how its language ought to be interpreted, and how its various incongruities ought to be demystified. Do its words encompass, for the most part, criterial or purely natural-kind concepts, whose interpretation is defined by certain agreed benchmarks? Or do they, as Ronald Dworkin would have observed, comprise interpretive concepts (Dworkin 2010),[1] whose defence must draw on values beyond themselves? (Dworkin 2011: 7).[2]

The Constitution's prime aim, one would imagine, is to effectuate into justiciable principles those ideas contained in its Preamble. But the attempted crystallization of the philosophies underpinning the Preamble, namely, Justice (social, economic, and political), Liberty (of thought, expression, belief, faith, and worship), and Equality (of status and of opportunity), has only resulted in further abstractions. Article 14, for instance, which seeks to provide a right to equality, says the State shall not deny to any person equality before the law or the equal protection of the laws within the territory of India. It, however, offers no explicit clues on what equality means—on whether it guarantees merely formal equality, which would give individuals a right to be treated equally without discrimination, or whether it guarantees a more substantive equality, which would demand that the State treat its people with equal concern. The attempted crystallization also doesn't rid the Constitution of its innumerable contradictions (Seervai 1991: 172–260).[3] When a person's right to religion conflicts with another's right to free expression, for instance, which right must prevail? The Constitution doesn't give us any overt answers. It leaves judges with the task of adjudicating these cases in the hope that there is a right answer to be found within its language.

What we need, therefore, is a working model of interpreting the Constitution, which nonetheless maintains a basic fidelity to the text (Fleming 2012: 23).[4] Judges of India's Supreme Court and its various high courts have devised different theories—some have sought to maintain a false fidelity by being parsimonious in their interpretation, relying solely on what they call the text of the document;[5] others have sought to flex the meaning of a word by looking beyond its plain text, into the purported intention of the Constitution's drafters,[6] and, at times, into the fundamental ethos of political morality;[7] some others have supplied meanings to imbue their own sense of right and wrong into the Constitution's interpretation.[8] This variance is really only symptomatic of incoherence in constitutional theory. And this incoherence often has a tricking effect on the law's inner morality. How might we set this right? For Dworkin, the answer lies in seeing law as an interpretive concept; an argument over a difficult constitutional case, where two different interpretations are plausible is often a disagreement over the correct interpretation of the Constitution itself (Nagel 1986).[9] So, for Dworkin, it is always important we ask ourselves how the Constitution is to be interpreted.

In answering this question, Dworkin arrives at what he terms a 'moral reading' (Dworkin 1996: 8; Fleming 2012: 25).[10] This, he says, is a construal which endeavours to make the Constitution the best it can be (Dworkin 1996). The various abstractions of the Constitution, such as the right to free speech, the right to equality, are by all accounts moral principles about political decency and justice, and are, therefore, says Dworkin, deserving of a moral interpretation. The failure of American judges, he says, is not as much in an eschewal of the moral reading as it is in an inability to recognize the moral reading as the best way to interpret the Constitution. If one identifies this theory as a rational strategy to construe the Constitution, it would, he says, help bring political morality into the heart of public law. But he tempers his argument by appealing to a requirement, simultaneously, for a constitutional integrity (Dworkin 2010: 95–6).[11] This demands not, as the popular misconception suggests, that judges read their 'own convictions into the Constitution' (Dworkin 1990),[12] but that they read the abstract moral clauses of the Constitution in a manner that is both consistent with the structural design of the Constitution as a whole, and of past judicial practice.

In this essay, I argue that Dworkin's theory, founded predominantly in the framework of the American Constitution, carries enormous significance in the Indian context too, especially in its application to our rights-jurisprudence. Indian courts have often interpreted the Constitution by drawing upon values beyond those at stake in a concerned dispute. But they have, at times, been at fault in failing to supply cohesion to the document. The courts' interpretation of the term 'personal liberty' in Article 21, perhaps, best exemplifies this manufactured dichotomy. In recognizing rights, as inherent in Article 21, beyond those expressly guaranteed by the Constitution, judges have appealed to a larger morality. But the basis for such an interpretation, provided as it was by the seminal decision of the Supreme Court in *Maneka Gandhi v. Union of India*,[13] remains flawed.

The decision in *Maneka*, no doubt, provoked an extraordinary growth in human rights jurisprudence in India. But by engaging purely with a general principle of liberty to locate within Article 21 a multitude of rights, the court mired constitutional reading with an often-unsolvable confusion. The result has been the creation of an illusory conflict between liberty and equality, which I hope to elucidate in this essay. Had the judges in *Maneka*, for example, appealed to a more Dworkinian conception of liberty and equality, where the two are seen as not so much conflicting as complimentary ideals, and located, in the process, new rights and liberties not otherwise elucidated in the Constitution, by appealing to a unity of value, the document may have been infused with a bolt of coherence.

For Dworkin, individual rights to distinct liberties must be recognized only when the fundamental right to treatment as an equal can be shown to require these rights. He argues that if this proposition is taken to be true, 'then the right to distinct liberties does not conflict with any supposed competing right to equality, but on the contrary follows from a conception of equality conceded to be more fundamental' (Dworkin 2013a: 328).[14] So when he says that a moral reading of the Constitution is the best way to interpret the document, what he is really advocating is a unity of value, embedded chiefly in the basic principle of equality. 'It would be flaccidly circular to appeal to liberty to defend a conception of liberty,' writes Dworkin in *Justice for Hedgehogs*, his penultimate and most comprehensive book. 'So political concepts must be integrated with one another. We cannot defend a conception of any of them without showing how our conception fits with and into appealing conceptions of the others' (Dworkin 2011: 7). A Dworkinian interpretation of rights is, therefore, predicated on the general claim that if one accepts equality of resources as the best conception of distributional equality, liberty becomes an aspect of that equality rather than an independent political ideal potentially in conflict with it (Dworkin 2002: 121).[15]

Now, needless to say, to defend this interpretation in the Indian context, we must first show that our Constitution is animated by these principles that Dworkin considers foundational. It could quite plausibly be argued that this is not the case in India, that its Constitution, in fact, recognizes liberty and equality as independent values, that the clashes between the two will have to be somehow resolved, even if the consequences are undesirable. But while it might require a separate essay altogether to disprove this proposition, it might, at this juncture, suffice to say that a bare reading of the Constitution's text admits of no such clash. Identical importance is after all accorded to both the right to equality and the various freedoms—such as the right to free speech, to form associations, to travel freely, to personal liberty and so forth—and neither one is made subject to the other. To therefore avoid any clash between these rights, it might be helpful to see liberty and equality as values that depend on each other, as Dworkin recommends—to see that the policies of the government treat every person's fate 'as equally important and respect their individual responsibilities for their own lives' (Dworkin 2002: 330). Even if such an approach might, on the face of it, appear to occasionally disregard liberty, a closer examination will reveal that it, in fact, espouses a deeper commitment to liberalism. Its effect is to provide a unified morality to the Constitution that recognizes each of us as equal beings, as attracting the equal concern of the state.

Dworkin's Moral Reading of the Constitution

Morality, when used in the context of the law, and in the context of interpreting the law, often assumes the undertones of a bad word. As lawyers, one is expected to argue only on what the law is. Positivists (Raz 1995)[16] theorize that this law can scarcely be a product of morality or such other similar values, which are contingent and precarious, but is always a matter of social fact (Greenberg 2012: 225–6).[17] The English jurist John Austin, one of the earliest proponents of positivism, put it this way, 'The existence of law is one thing; its merit and demerit another. Whether it be or be not is one enquiry; whether it be or be not conformable to an assumed standard, is a different enquiry' (1995).[18] To the legal positivists, therefore, what the law is depends primarily on historical matters of fact—it depends on what the community in question, as a matter of custom and practice, accepts as law (Dworkin 2011: 401). Under the Hartian theory (Hart 1994),[19] for example, if an unjust law were to meet a community's accepted test for law (if the law were to be accorded, for instance, legislative sanction, which the judiciary holds to be paramount) then the unjust law really is law (Dworkin 2011: 401). And where there are gaps in the law, in hard cases, as Dworkin describes them, Hart and other positivists believed that judges are not bound by the law, but were, on the contrary, performing an exercise of lawmaking. For positivists, the meaning of legal rules depends primarily on the processes through which they are enacted (Eisgruber 2012: 13–14),[20] and this demands, in most cases, a separation of law from morality.[21]

Through the twentieth century, this form of legal positivist thinking came to represent the dominant school of jurisprudence, and has provided the grounding—the departing point, even—for Dworkin's philosophy. In the course of his half-a-century as a legal philosopher, Dworkin sought to prove—and I would submit demonstrated with unerring brilliance—that law is, in fact, but a branch of a larger system of values. In *Justice for Hedgehogs*, the culmination of his life's work, which comprises the richest and most comprehensive account of his views on the law, Dworkin argues for law as morality (Dworkin 2011: 7). Law includes, he writes, 'not only the specific rules enacted in accordance with a community's accepted practices but also the principles that provide the best moral justification for those enacted rules' (401). Specifically, the law, according to him, is a branch of political morality, which is itself a branch of a more general personal morality, which is in turn a branch of a yet more general theory of what it is to live well (5). We can picture this, as I wrote elsewhere, 'as a network, in which our most fundamental values are the nodes with the densest connections to other values and principles' (Parthasarathy 2013).[22] Laws, like other political conceptions, are defensible only when they fit well with moral and ethical principles that are mutually complimentary, and every effort should be made to interpret the law to supply it with the best possible conception.

The philosophical basis[23] for this argument lies in what Dworkin calls the one big idea—the unity of value. There are, he writes, relying on what he called the 'Hume principle' (Dworkin 2013b: 26–7),[24] defended, as it was, by the great eighteenth-century Scottish philosopher David Hume, objective truths about value (Dworkin 2011: 151). *This*, to him, was an 'obvious, inescapable fact' (24). But the truths, he argues, were to be arrived at by making the 'best sense' of value, by interpreting *ethics* and *morality* as fundamental knobs of a larger, unified system of values.

Here, picture values as comprising the structure of a tree (24). At the base, providing the foundations, are the ethical and moral judgments that we make. The former, Dworkin says, borrowing from Bernard Williams's conception, concerns claims about what people should do to live well—a responsibility that we have to make our lives valuable. A moral judgment, on the other hand, as Immanuel Kant would have it, concerned how we treated others. These two fundamental conceptions are not only objectively ascertainable, but also mutually complimentary, according to Dworkin. 'A person can achieve the dignity and self-respect that are indispensable to a successful life', writes Dworkin, 'only if he shows respect for humanity itself in all its forms' (20). Our values are grounded by reference to other values and principles, and therefore, the best interpretation of any value would strive towards a construal that achieves, at the least, a tenuous balance.

While the foundations rest on the unity of these values, human dignity, which can be considered as a branch of this tree, naturally derives from the twin theories of ethics and morality. Dignity, for Dworkin, includes both a right to respect as an equal, and a right to ethical independence (Guest 2013: 11). And *human rights*, which we now understand as both inherent and inalienable, are really only formulations of dignity: when the state violates either your right to respect as an equal or your right to ethical independence, it is principally trampling upon your human rights. Dworkin terms this duty of government to show an abiding respect for dignity, in respecting both your right as an equal and your right to ethical independence, as a principle of 'equal concern'. Respecting equal concern, therefore, represents the best interpretation of *democracy*. The role of the law, in all of this, to Dworkin, is to enforce these principles; as a subset of these larger values, the law is an interpretive concept—to decide what it encompasses one must not only consider the plain language of the statute or the rules or the constitution, as the case may be, and precedent—how courts before have interpreted the law—but also the principles in which the law is entrenched—a formation, which Dworkin terms, 'law as integrity' (Nagel 1986).

For Dworkin, integrity demands that a nation's political decisions are a product of a principled consistency (Eisgruber 2012: 15–16). It requires, as Stephen Guest puts it, that the 'law cohere in a way that is distinct from justice', that 'law should always be created, or interpreted to form an integral whole'. Integrity, Dworkin writes, is a political ideal in and of itself, which fits and explains the features of a democratic constitutional structure—in his book *Law's Empire*, he puts it thus: 'A community of principle, which takes integrity to be central to politics, provides a better defence of political legitimacy than the other models. It assimilates political obligations to the general class of associative obligations and supports them in that way' (Dworkin 2010: 176–225).

So when Dworkin says the Constitution must be read morally, what he means is that any interpretation of a provision of the Constitution mustn't damage or destroy the values that it underpins. Dworkin's theory doesn't shun any previously understood process of construal; on the contrary, he urges judges faced with a difficult case to find what he terms the 'best' interpretation of the Constitution, a reading that would both fit the historical record (Brown 2012: 49)[25] and make the finest moral sense of the document as a whole (Nagel 1986). An interpretation, according to him, not only must 'fit the practices and history it claims to interpret—but also provide a justification for those practices' (Dworkin 2013c).[26] There are various interpretations that may fit coherently into the practices and history of a concerned provision. The second requirement, however, which demands a justification for the interpretation is harder to fit: here, Dworkin says, legal positivism fails as a theory. 'We cannot identify law', he writes, 'without assuming some justification, however weak, in political morality' (Dworkin 2013c). To be clear, Dworkin calls judges to consider the text of the Constitution in the context of its history. But the interpretation, he says, needn't necessarily appeal to the moral judgment of the framers, but must rather appeal to the morality of the present-day (Brown 2012).

To illuminate his theory by way of illustration, Dworkin refers to the 1954 US Supreme Court judgment in *Brown v. Board of Education*.[27] The decision in *Brown*—celebrated as one of the finest delivered by the top court—says Dworkin, could not have been arrived at, except by employing a moral reading. The court's ruling that the equal protection law of the American Constitution outlawed racial segregation in public schools ran directly counter with what the framers thought. At the time when the American Constitution was drafted, racial segregation was not only being practiced, but was thought to be socially and morally acceptable. The framers could not have imagined, when drafting the equal protection clause, that the Constitution would outlaw racial segregation in schools, but their job was to draft a Bill of Rights in abstract language, allowing the courts and the legislatures of their times to interpret the terms that they used in line with the thinking of their day,[28] without fundamentally damaging or destroying the constitutional structure.[29] For an originalist, for someone who believes that the Constitution ought to be interpreted in a manner which merely fits with the intent of the framers, the court's approach in *Brown* ought to have been to rebuff the challenge to racial segregation in public schools. This is because the framers never saw such segregation as being opposed to the legal demands of the equal protection clause. But had the majority in *Brown* taken such a view the court would have had to make a basic concession—that the equal protection clause simply could not partake moral progress. It is therefore that Dworkin argues that the court got its decision in *Brown* correct, by bringing to the centre of the interpretive exercise a search for those principles that are intended to guide society through time. These principles were not restricted to what the framers thought of a certain policy, but they asked a more fundamental question: on what moral basis did the framers draft the provisions of the Constitution? In answering this question the court will, therefore, have to eschew the pure diktats of originalism and look towards a broader theory that demands, as Rebecca Brown put it, a reconciliation between moral intuition and law (Brown 2012: 55).

Now, it's important here to note that Dworkin did recognize that in any Constitution certain provisions are couched in direct, non-abstract, terms, and are therefore, undeserving of a moral reading. In the Indian context, take, for instance, Article 58 of the Constitution, which prescribes qualifications for election as President. It provides, among other things, that no person shall be eligible for election as President unless he completes the age of 35. Such a provision would, according to Dworkin, deserve a decidedly non-moral construal. It has to be read as providing a definite qualification as opposed to comprising some general principle of disability (Dworkin 1990: 14). Other provisions, however, such as the fundamental rights contained in Part III of the Constitution or, for that matter, the power of Parliament to amend the Constitution contained in Article 368, are unequivocally moral provisions—to read these provisions in any other manner would neither fit nor justify the Constitution as a moral document.

However, many of these clauses, which doubtless represent distinctly moral values, are replete with abstractions, making their meanings occasionally abound with incoherence. As a result, there are particularly thorny questions that can come up for judgment. Consider some of these questions: can the state interfere in the functioning of temples, which perform a distinctly religious function, when the temple discriminates between members of different castes?[30] Can speech, which offends, be censored in the interest of a perceived morality?[31] Can the State insist that a minority educational institution, whose administrative independence is protected by the Constitution, be barred from denying admission on grounds of religion?[32] Can the speech of one person, which curtails the right of another person to trade, be justifiably restricted?[33] To solve these conundrums, some argue, we must accept a basic gradation of rights. But the Constitution, in most cases, doesn't tell us explicitly about its preference for one value over another. It does not outwardly advocate the discrimination between the enforcement of different rights of different people. Yet, these conflicts exist and have often proved hard to solve.

Equally, there are other cases where a bare reading of a simple provision of the Constitution gives rise to a potential anomaly. For example, Article 368, which gives Parliament power to amend the Constitution, does not prescribe any limitations thereof, hypothetically permitting lawmakers to fundamentally alter the document's most significant provisions.[34] There are other cases, where a crude reading of a provision—on purely textualist grounds—can curtail a person's most basic liberties, impinging the spirit of democracy.[35] It is in these cases—which Dworkin might have described as hard cases[36]— where the courts are required to read the provisions of the Constitution by looking beyond the mere text of the document, by looking, occasionally, past the history of its drafting and the purported intentions of the framers. The court will have to glean the interpretation, in such cases, by looking at those principles, which will ensure that the reading fits the overall scheme of the Constitution. For example, when the court concludes that Parliament has a plenary power to amend the Constitution, and it can remove altogether any provision of the document, howsoever basic it might be, the judgment may well be justified through a purely textual interpretation. But the question to be asked is this: would such an interpretation fit with the overall scheme of the Constitution? Likewise, it might be easy for the court to conclude that the right to life or personal liberty can be curtailed by Parliament by enacting any piece of legislation, regardless of whether such a law is just, fair, or reasonable. In thus ignoring *due process* the court's interpretation may be in consonance with a bare reading of Article 21, but it might not fit with the kind of moral reading that Dworkin advocates. For Dworkin, in hard cases, to ensure that any interpretation respects the fidelity of the Constitution and the values that it stands for, the courts must apply an interpretive strategy that would make the document the best it can be, by finding the law from within the Constitutional scheme as opposed to gleaning it from the outside. Or as James E. Fleming put it, to ask: 'Which interpretation provides the best justification, which makes our constitutional scheme the best it can be, which does it more credit, or which answers better to our best aspirations as a people?' (Fleming 2012: 26–7).

'Equal Concern' in the Indian Constitution: Searching for a Dworkinian Interpretation

Unlike courts in several other democratic polities, the power of judicial review inheres in India's Supreme Court through constitutional design. But the limits of this power have been the subject matter of much debate. The Supreme Court has used its authority to not only strike down legislation, when found *ultra vires* the Constitution, but has also controversially invalidated constitutional amendments,[37] which, in the view of the court, infract the 'basic structure' of the Constitution. The adoption of this approach shows that the judiciary already recognizes, albeit implicitly, that the Constitution does rest on a particular moral theory—that the document's several abstract provisions represent distinct principles, which demand an interpretation that requires the courts to bring political morality into the heart of their functions. But in spite of this recognition, of a need to infuse into constitutional interpretation a moral understanding, the courts have in the hardest of cases failed to fully appreciate what it takes to treat rights as trumps without disturbing constitutional clarity. Some of the Supreme Court's decisions, for example its ruling that Articles 14, 19, and 21—which respectively provide the rights to equality, freedom and life, and personal liberty—represent a collective whole, appear, on the surface, to appeal to a larger unified system of values. But the court in striving to enlarge the rights contained in these articles is often at fault in viewing the rights to a multitude of liberties as an extension of a general right to liberty. Such an argument, I would submit, is circular and ultimately defeatist. A moral reading of the Constitution demands not the creation of a set of non-delineated liberties, but a respect chiefly for equal concern.

In this part, I will begin with a discussion of the decision in *A.K. Gopalan v. State of Madras*,[38] perhaps, the first case where a significant issue of Constitutional importance was argued before the Supreme Court. I will then submit that the evolution of the law from *Gopalan* to *Maneka Gandhi v. Union of India*,[39] resulting in an unforeseen enlargement of fundamental rights, while laudable, in fact, produces an incoherent constitutional theory. Through this discussion, I hope to make a case for a Dworkinian interpretation of the Indian Constitution by submitting that liberty ought to, in all cases, be derived from equality, as opposed to being seen as a *sui generis* value.

The Limitation of Equal Concern in *A.K. Gopalan v. State of Madras*

In its early halcyon years, the Supreme Court was quite content with reading the Constitution along narrow, positivist lines. In *A.K. Gopalan v. State of*

Madras[40] the Preventive Detention Act of 1950 was challenged on grounds that some of its provisions abrogated, inter alia, the petitioner's rights guaranteed by Article 21 (Khosla 2012: 108).[41] The petitioner in *Gopalan* sought to compare the provisions of Article 21 to the 5th and 14th Amendments of the US Constitution, where the provision, inter alia, is 'that no person shall be deprived of his life or liberty or property except by *due process of law*'. Article 21 of the Indian Constitution, on the other hand, states: 'No person shall be deprived of his life or personal liberty except according to *procedure established by law*' (emphasis mine).

It was reasoned before six judges of India's Supreme Court that the omission of the word 'due' made no difference to the interpretation of Article 21. As was the practice in the US, where due process of law envisioned the promise of both a substantive and procedural due process, the word 'law' used in Article 21, the petitioner contended, included in its purport certain fundamental principles of natural justice. Chief Justice Harilal Jekisundas Kania, whose opinion, along with those of Justices Sudhi Ranjan Das, Bijan Kumar Mukerjea, M. Patanjali Sastri, and Mehr Chand Mahajan,[42] represents that of the majority, rebuffed these arguments and wrote:

> No extrinsic aid is needed to interpret the words of Article 21, which in my opinion, are not ambiguous. Normally read, and without thinking of other Constitutions, the expression 'procedure established by law' must mean procedure prescribed by the law of the State. If the Indian Constitution wanted to preserve to every person the protection given by the due process clause of the American Constitution there was nothing to prevent the Assembly from adopting the phrase, or if they wanted to limit the same to procedure only, to adopt that expression with only the word 'procedural' prefixed to 'law'.[43]

Life and personal liberty, the court held, could be whittled down so long as Parliament chooses to do so by validly enacted law. In arriving at this conclusion, the judges relied on two forms of interpretive techniques, both of which were a feature of the Supreme Court's early years—'textualism' and 'original intent' (Mate 2010: 232–3).[44] Although their approach in comparing the provisions of the Indian Constitution to governing laws of other countries may not have been in keeping with a pure textualist's method,[45] their ultimate interpretation was unquestionably in furtherance of such seemingly conservative values.

To read the words 'procedure established by law' in Article 21 in such a manner as to exclude a commonly understood *due process* analysis may ensure a fidelity to the text of the specific provision, as well as to the precise intent of the drafters.[46]But does it ensure a greater fidelity to the Constitution as a whole, answering to our deepest value systems? Due process, as Dworkin argues, is an intrinsic requirement of any Constitution, which seeks to protect certain foundational liberties. The right to due process flows, not necessarily from the words of the Constitution, but from the duty of the government to treat 'each person's life as of distinct, objective and equal importance' (Guest 2013: 183), or to treat people, as *equality* demands, with equal concern. In his dissent in *Gopalan*, Justice Fazl Ali did not quite go this far, but he nonetheless invoked a more natural-rights conception to hold that were 'law' in Article 21 meant to mean a law enacted by legislature then the objective of providing a right to life and personal liberty as a fundamental right would be rendered nugatory (Seervai 1991: 975–1010).[47] Fundamental rights, he held, are limitations on legislative power; if mere authority of law could negate the rights under Article 21, the right has the effect of placing no restriction on legislative power at all (Seervai 1991: 972–3).

Additionally, the majority in *Gopalan* read the term 'personal liberty', narrowly, differentiating its scope from the freedoms enumerated in Article 19(1).[48] Its purport was restricted to the Dicey-ian view, which understood the expression to mean a person's right not to be subjected to imprisonment, arrest or, other physical coercion in a manner contrary to the permits of the law. Article 19, the court effectively ruled, operates in a field where a citizen is not under physical restraint by operation of the law. The freedoms conferred by Articles 19(1) (a) to (g), available solely to citizens, were found to be of a nature, which could not be enjoyed substantially by a person who had been imprisoned in accordance with the procedural postulates of Article 21. A contrary reading, under which 'personal liberty' would include those freedoms conferred by Article 19 (such as the freedom of speech and expression and the freedom to move freely throughout India,) would have led, in the opinion of the court, to an absurd result where Article 21 conferred on non-citizens those freedoms, which were expressly denied to citizens by Article 19 (Seervai 1991: 991).

Maneka Champions Fundamental Rights, but Denies Both Equal Concern and Constitutional Coherence

The majority decision in *Gopalan* has since been set aside, first, in the *Bank Nationalization Case*,[49] and later in *Maneka Gandhi v. Union of India*.[50] But, while, as a result of this overruling, today, on paper, India's people have a greater set of civil and political and, even, social and economic rights, the approach by the courts in delineating these rights has been confused, constitutionally infidel, and ultimately, from a remedial perspective, unfulfilling. For the purposes of our discussion, although the Supreme Court has interpreted Article 21 in a variety of ways in different cases, the decision in *Maneka*, which is widely regarded as revolutionary (Khosla 2012: 109), needs to be considered closely.

This was a case that reached the Supreme Court after the petitioner's passport was impounded 'in public interest', with the government refusing to furnish the petitioner any reasons for its order. Aggrieved by this, the petitioner challenged Section 10(3) of the Passports Act, 1967, as violating Articles 14, 19(1)(a), 19(1)(g), and 21 as well as the order impounding her passport on the grounds that various fundamental rights of hers were infracted. Five separate opinions were delivered by the court: one each by Beg C.J., Chandrachud J., Bhagwati J. (on behalf of himself, Untwalia and Fazal Ali, JJ), Krishna Iyer J., and Kailasam J. (who rendered a dissenting opinion). Ultimately, rather spuriously, by way of the opinions of Chandrachud, Bhagwati, and Krishna Iyer, the court, in view of a statement made by the Attorney General, promising to give the petitioner a post-decisional hearing, disposed of the writ petition without a pronouncement of a final order, with the passport retained in the custody of the registrar of the court (Seervai 1991: 1004). But in arriving at this conclusion, each of the judges rendered substantial opinions, of which Bhagwati's judgment is generally considered as laying down the law.

Bhagwati seemed to recognize a throng of principles, in what is today regarded as a significant decision. However, as Madhav Khosla points out, the judgment remains deeply muddled: 'It dodges the arguments in *Gopalan*, is rich in rhetoric, and remains unclear on its "all for one, one for all" thesis that Articles 14, 19 and 21 interact.'[51] But generally, the takeaways from *Maneka* are as follows:

1. The approach of the court should be to expand the reach and ambit of fundamental rights rather than attenuating their meanings;
2. The term 'personal liberty' in Article 21 has many attributes, and includes such varieties of rights that go beyond those specifically delineated in Article 19(1),[52] including the right to go abroad;[53]
3. The word 'law' used in Article 21 ought not to be interpreted as merely a validly enacted law, but as a just, fair and reasonable law;
4. That any law curtailing the rights under Article 21 is also susceptible to the checks of Articles 14 and 19; and
5. That Article 14 is the antithesis of arbitrariness:[54] 'The principle of reasonableness, which legally as well as philosophically, is an essential element of equality or non-arbitrariness pervades Article 14 like a brooding omnipresence', wrote Bhagwati, 'and the procedure contemplated

by Article 21 must answer the test of reasonableness in order to be in conformity with Article 14'.

Such a holding, in theory, seems to not only incorporate a *due process* analysis, but also seems to provide an illusory coherence to the Indian Constitutional structure, interpreting the document, seemingly on Dworkinian terms, along moral lines. But the findings in *Maneka*, well intentioned as they were, compromised constitutional fidelity and caused, in the process, an acute confusion in the processes of judicial review.

Let us consider, at first, the assertion that the right to personal liberty contained in Article 21 includes freedoms delineated in Article 19(1), such as freedom of speech and expression, freedom to form associations or unions, freedom to move freely throughout India, and such other freedoms, which are not expressly outlined there. In deciding thus, Bhagwati largely affirmed the majority opinion rendered by Subba Rao C.J., in *Satwant Singh Sawhney v. D. Ramarathnam*,[55] where it was held, by ignoring earlier binding precedent, that '"liberty" in [the Indian] Constitution bears the same comprehensive meaning as is given to the expression "liberty" by the 5th and 14th Amendments to the US Constitution and the expression "personal liberty" in Art. 21 only excludes the ingredients of "liberty" enshrined in Art. 19 of the Constitution.' Therefore, Article 21, it was held, takes in the right of locomotion and to travel abroad. Subba Rao C.J. had effectively appealed to a more general right to liberty, which he found inherent in Article 21, and located therein such other liberties, which were a part of this universal, more expansive, right. He had, in other words, engaged in an analysis, confirmed by *Maneka*, which Dworkin would have doubtless termed as a flaccidly circular argument: as an appeal made to liberty to defend a conception of liberty (Dworkin 2011: 7).[56]

In his book, *Taking Rights Seriously*, Dworkin posits that liberty as traditionally conceived by its champions, including such luminaries as Isaiah Berlin and Jeremy Bentham, supposes the absence of constraints placed by government upon what a man might do if he wants to (Dworkin 2013a: 320). Under such a conception (Constant 1969: 118–72),[57] as Bentham, has for instance, argued, any law would be an infraction of liberty, which is conceived essentially as a *license*. Some of these infractions would be deemed necessary, but this theory would rubbish any claims to pretend that these are not infractions as reactionary and conservative (Dworkin 2013a: 321). 'In this neutral, all embracing sense of liberty as license', writes Dworkin, 'liberty and equality are plainly in competition. Laws are needed to protect equality, and laws are inevitably compromises on liberty' (321). For example, when the US Supreme Court in *Brown*[58] struck down racial segregation in schools, some saw the measure as a violation of the people's right to freedom of association (Bork 1990: 147).[59] It was effectively, in their opinion, a violation of a liberty to uphold a specious concept of equality. Dworkin argues, on the contrary, that liberty being a derivative of a more general right to equal treatment, which demands, among other things, that people be treated with equal concern, was not infracted by the judgment, as there is no general right to liberty, except such liberty which is rooted in equal concern. Both the right to free speech, and the right, say, to eat vanilla ice cream, are rooted in modern-day conception in a general right to liberty, but to argue merely that a violation of the former is unjust because it has a special impact on liberty, as such, while a violation on the latter has no such special impact is, according to Dworkin, an illegitimate argument (Dworkin 2013a: 325). But if we hold that there is no general right to liberty, why do we, in a democracy, place such importance on rights such as the right to free speech, the right to freedom of association, the right to practice any religion of our choice? Because, writes Dworkin, these rights are rooted in political morality: 'individual rights to distinct liberties must be recognized only when the fundamental right to treatment as an equal can be shown to require these rights'. 'If this is correct, then the right to distinct liberties does not conflict with any supposed competing right to equality, but on the contrary follows from a conception of equality conceded to be more fundamental' (325).

Let us, here, pause to take an example from the Indian context. If, the term 'personal liberty' in Article 21 derives from a general right to liberty, and includes those rights that are specifically enumerated in Article 19(1) as well as such other rights that are not delineated therein, it would mean that Article 21 is so wide as to include the right to do what one wants. The right to own property, which was once recognized in Article 19(1) (f) would, therefore, be inherent in Article 21. But, this right was not only excluded by way of the 44th Constitutional Amendment, from Part III, but has also been held by the Supreme Court to be outside the purview of the Constitution's basic structure.[60] Given, however, that the 44th Amendment does not alter Article 21 to clarify that the right to 'personal liberty' does not include within its ambit the right to property, it can only be reasonably deducted by reading the decision in *Maneka* that, notwithstanding the 44th Amendment, only a just, fair, and reasonable law can curtail the right to property.[61] If all freedoms comprised in Article 19(1) are contained within 'personal liberty' then there is nothing to deny that the right to property is inherent in Article 21. Such a conception, therefore, is dangerous, and also unintelligible. One of the reasons for guaranteeing only personal liberty was because the framers saw no general right to liberty. Any particular liberty demanding of constitutional protection as a right under Part III would therefore have to flow from a more general commitment to equal concern, which is at the centre of Dworkin's theory of moral reading. The principles set out in the US Constitution, taken together, Dworkin argues, mandate that 'the government must treat all those subject to its dominion as having equal moral and political status; it must attempt, in good faith, to treat them all with equal concern and it must respect whatever individual freedoms are indispensable to those ends' (Dworkin 1990: 8).[62] This thesis of 'equal concern and respect' is really at the root of Dworkin's work, and represents the bedrock on which his entire theory of constitutional interpretation rests (Dworkin 2013a: 326–7); it also represents the starting point for any analysis on the depth and content of individual rights, which are nothing but those liberties that place restrictions on government's power, or 'rights as trumps', as Dworkin put it. This principle of equal concern, for Dworkin therefore, embraces something more than formal equality. 'Government must treat those whom it governs with concern, that is, as human beings who are capable of suffering and frustration,' Dworkin writes, 'and with respect, that is, as human beings who are capable of forming and acting on intelligent conceptions of how their lives should be lived' (326). Hence, the principle demands a respect for two foundational notions: the individual right to ethical independence, and the individual duty to ethical responsibility.

But if all rights can be identified and derived from equality, it begs the question: why then did the framers bother with defining a specific set of freedoms and liberties? The answer, I submit, lies in the particular nature of these rights, which the framers wanted protected at all costs, over and above the more general protection offered to them under Article 14. For example, even if the right to freedom of speech and expression did not emanate out of a conception of equality, in a given case, the framers found the value in such a right to be of such overriding importance that the right can only be curtailed if the grounds specifically enlisted in Article 19(2) of the Constitution are fulfilled.

The primary conclusion in *Maneka*, in rooting new rights in the term 'personal liberty' and not in a general principle of equal concern is, therefore, circular. Decisions, which have, since, followed *Maneka,* have found inherent in Article 21 a wide spectrum of rights, including the rights to livelihood,[63] health,[64] a clean environment,[65] privacy,[66] food,[67] and so forth. But was such a reading required to protect these rights, which would have in the given cases, where necessary, been justifiable as extensions of equality? Recognizing new rights, it cannot be denied, has a value of its own—such an approach, as Madhav Khosla argues, 'can play a vital expressive role. It can help to change social meanings about certain guarantees, and push the state towards delivering social services'.[68] But finding these rights to be contained in Article 19 or Article 21 is one thing; to use these articles as a flow of reference, as a creator of these various rights presents a false dichotomy.

As we've seen, especially over the last decade or so, the thoughtless expansion of Article 21, by using *Maneka* as the basis, has come at a heavy cost. For instance, in upholding Sections 499 and 500 of the Indian Penal Code, which collectively criminalize defamation, the Supreme Court fashioned a 'right to reputation.'[69] 'Reputation being an inherent component of Article 21, we do not think it should be allowed to be sullied solely because another individual can have its freedom,' Justice Dipak Misra wrote, for the court. There are several other such instances where the court has used Article 21 as a weapon to restrict other liberties guaranteed under the Constitution, by creating what is really a false dichotomy (Bhatia 2016).[70] This has resulted in a gradation of rights, which the Constitution doesn't really demand—some liberties are seen as fundamental while others are seen as violable. One of the ways to solve this conflict is by using Dworkin's moral interpretation. By reading the Constitution as a moral document, by trying to see what construal best fits our conceptions of democracy, it would allow us to recognize those rights that further the cause of equal concern. We can achieve this by striving to discover whether individual freedoms are indispensable to the achievement of equality.

It might be argued that the above argument was precisely what Bhagwati, J., sought to make in *Maneka*—that any law curtailing a person's life or liberty must be answerable to the equality tests of Article 14. But such a statement is only trite. All laws, regardless of whether they impinge Article 21, by virtue of Article 13(2),[71] must confirm to Article 14, as well as all other provisions comprised in Part III of the Constitution.[72] It was the founders' belief that the life or personal liberty of a person can never be abridged except by way of a validly enacted law. But it cannot be argued that it wasn't their belief that such validly enacted law needn't confirm to the principles of equality contained in Article 14. What we need therefore, is not an approach, which creates deceptive conflicts between rights—between, for instance, the right to property of one person and the right to equality of another, or between the right to religious freedom of one person and the right to be free from discrimination of another—but an approach that facilitates a unity of value. Under such a theory of interpretation, conflict between liberty and equality would rarely, if ever, accrue; on the contrary, a right to liberty would ensue only when equal concern demands its presence.

When we hold—as India's Supreme Court has—that liberty is a value unto itself, and that it isn't derivable from equality, and therefore, that the terms 'personal liberty' and 'freedom' include a wide spectrum of liberties, guaranteed as rights under Articles 21 and 19, placing limitations on such rights, even in circumstances where equal concern (and democracy) demand the imposition of such limitations, becomes an insurmountable challenge. In a piece published in 2013,[73] I lent on the example of the right to freedom of the press to highlight this false dichotomy. In *Sakal Papers v. Union of India*,[74] widely regarded as an influential decision, the Supreme Court, even in the tranquil, pre-*Maneka* days, recognized that the freedom of the press is contained within the more general right to freedom of speech and expression. The court was tasked, here, with determining the validity of legislation, which sought to regulate the number of pages in a newspaper on the basis of its price. The government sought to defend its law as one aimed at preventing unfair competition amongst newspapers. The court was, perhaps, quite justified in annulling the legislation as one that infringed the petitioner's most fundamental freedoms, especially their right to freedom of trade. But in finding press freedom to be implicit in the right to freedom of speech and expression, guaranteed by Article 19(1) (a), and in therefore effectively holding that a law cannot be sustained merely because it seeks to suppress monopoly when it interferes with a person's right to own press, the court set a dangerous precedent. It should have seen that the best interpretation of the right to press freedom ought not to be limited to an examination of an individual's right to own business. On the contrary, it demands a reading along democratic lines—what interpretation, it should have asked, would most benefit the public's right to access information free from political force. In this case, the legislation was arguably invalid because it interfered with the public's right to access information, and not because the law impinged a company's right to own press. Freedom of the press cannot be interpreted in a manner that entails a repression of that freedom by private interests.[75] It includes within its gamut, not merely the overt rights of the owners of newspapers and television channels, but also the rights of the collective—the right of each individual in a democracy to be informed.[76] Dworkin, as Gautam Bhatia has written, would have argued that 'part of what it means for government to accord equal concern and respect to every citizen is to ensure that she has an equal opportunity of shaping the moral environment of society, the moral environment in which we all live' (Bhatia 2013).[77]

Assume today that Parliament enacts a law, recommended as it happens by the Telecom Regulatory Authority of India, restricting the rights of politicians to own media. The law when challenged as unconstitutional would naturally be assailed on grounds of it violating the politicians' fundamental rights under Articles 14, 19, and 21. Article 14 because the law, the argument would go, is arbitrary and makes an unreasonable classification. Article 19 because it violates the right to freedom of the press (as an extension of the right to freedom of speech and expression) and the right to own business. Article 21 because the term 'personal liberty' post-Maneka captures all those freedoms contained in Article 19 and more. At the first and third level, the Court, based upon established precedent, might even hold that the law is not unreasonable, but is on the contrary well thought through and is just, fair and rational, and therefore, in consonance with Articles 14 and 21. At the second level, however, because the reasonable restrictions contained in Article 19(2) do not include such measures which are made in the interest of the general public, and because the right of a person to own media has now been seen as an extension of the right to freedom of the press contained by interpretation in Article 19(1)(a), a law restricting the ability of a person, including corporations,[78] to own media would be struck down as an unconstitutional infraction of Article 19. The consequence—an illusory liberty of the powerful would be protected at the cost of suppressing the liberty of the masses. The decision contrary to appealing to equal concern would violate every recognized tenet of the principle, which, as Dworkin argues, is fundamental to our functioning as a constitutional democracy. To Dworkin, every supposed claim of infringement of the right to free speech requires an individual analysis of the particular facts of the case, to determine whether equal concern compels the enforcement of such a right (Bhatia 2016). Therefore, in *Sakal Papers*, the court could have, at the least, in principle held that even if Article 19(2), which enunciates the specific restrictions that may be placed on free speech, was not directly applicable to the facts of the case, the right under Article 19(1) (a) never accrued to the petitioners given that the enforcement of any supposed right to free speech of theirs would run counter to equal concern, and hence, democracy.

Recognizing rights in abstract to emanate out of Articles 19 and 21, as the Supreme Court advocated in *Maneka*, can, therefore, in a given case be injurious to democracy. After the 44th Constitutional Amendment, with the removal of Article 19(1) (f), the right to property has been considered, by implication, to be outside the scope of Part III, to be unenforceable under the writ jurisdiction of the Supreme Court. The abstract statement by the courts that the right to personal liberty in Article 21 includes a broad spectrum of liberties has not been taken to its logical conclusion to find inherent within the provision the right to property. Such an extension would have no doubt infracted *equal concern*, but this failure in extending the right has also meant that the right to property when mandated by *equal concern* has gone unprotected. This is a consequence, therefore, both of reading several abstract rights into Article 21 and also of a general 'doctrinal looseness'—as Abhinav

Chandrachud describes it—in Article 14 analysis (Chandrachud 2011: 202).[79] Post *Maneka,* Article 14, the equal protection clause of the Indian Constitution, is seen as an antithesis to arbitrariness forcing courts to look not as much at the reasonableness of a given classification as the old doctrine demanded, but into whether the state's action—whether in enacting a law or in implementing a law—is 'arbitrary'.[80] As a consequence of the proposition, courts have been willing to uphold statutes on the grounds that the legislation is un-arbitrary and therefore, just, fair, and reasonable, allowing a law to simultaneously pass the tests both of Articles 14 and 21.[81] In a given case even where *equal concern* might have demanded the implementation of a right that the law has been passed with the full and proper consideration of Parliament has been found to accord sufficient justification. *State of Tamil Nadu v. Ananthi Ammal,*[82] a 1994 Supreme Court ruling, is a classic example. Here, the Tamil Nadu Acquisition of Land for Harijan Welfare Schemes Act, 1978, was under challenge as a statute in violation of Articles 14, 19, and 300A.[83] Given that the right to property had by now been considered to be outside the scope of Part III, at an abstract level, the court restricted its analysis to the particular provisions of Articles 14 and 19. The main ground on which the statute was assailed was that it differed fundamentally from another statute, the Land Acquisition Act of 1894, thereby giving the state the power to use different mechanisms, and apply different methods of calculating compensation, in acquiring a person's land based on the object for which the land was being acquired. While no general right to property can be claimed under Part III of the Constitution, a reading that would have recognized such a right in cases where equal concern demands its presence would have allowed the court in *Ananthi Ammal* to recognize the obvious—that a statute to acquire land cannot fundamentally differ from another statute, which is also used to acquire land, purely on the basis of the reasons for such acquisition. To recognize otherwise would, as the Supreme Court has previously held,[84] have the effect of putting the cart before the horse. While no general right to property can be gleaned from Part III of the Constitution, such a right should nonetheless be enforced, as fundamental, when demanded by the larger principles that govern the basis for the Constitution as a moral document.

The Supreme Court's decision in *Maneka* has had an unquestionably dramatic effect on the interpretation of the Constitution. On the face of it, its eschewal of textualism appears to appeal to Dworkinian principles. But by rooting further abstraction into Article 21, and by providing a 'doctrinal looseness' to Article 14 analysis (Chandrachud 2011: 105), the court has infused a confusion that continues to damage constitutional interpretation. Any provision must be construed in a manner that removes any inherent abstractions in it through a gleaning of the larger values on which it is based. To impart the Constitution with further abstraction through the process of interpretation can be, as we have seen, distinctly damaging.

***

What we need in India is a truer Dworkinian interpretation—a reading that would strip the Constitution of its abstractions by appealing to a principle of equal concern and to a more unitary value built on political morality, as opposed to purely positivist law. Constitutional law, as Dworkin argues, can make a genuine advance only when 'it isolates the problem of rights against the state and makes that problem part of its own agenda' (Dworkin 2013a: 183). A moral reading of the Constitution, which Dworkin argues makes the Constitution the best it can be (Dworkin 1990), demands that judges apply their minds to a hard case in a polygonal fashion by bringing political morality to the centre of its interpretive role. It doesn't require, as commonly misconceived, that judges apply their own personal moralities to the task of adjudicating. But on the contrary, it requires that they identify the core standards that drive the Constitution and read its provisions in a manner that coalesces these standards into a unitary value.

To this end, viewing liberties as *sui generis* and self-serving tenets might seem outwardly appealing, but is ultimately defeatist. Regardless of the truth that we want to attach to Dworkin's statement that there is no general right to liberty, it fits our constitutional structure better to root liberties, as he suggested, in equal concern—to see liberties as 'only one consequence of the more general right to ethical independence in foundational matters' (Dworkin 2011: 376). This, as the preceding discussion shows, can often result in the creation of more rights in practice than have been found to exist conjecturally. The proposition would, of course, also demand more of the judges—they would have to analyze the facts of each case to determine whether equal concern demands the presence of a right to a particular liberty. But it would also make our Constitution better, answering, as James Fleming demanded, to our 'best aspirations as a people' (Fleming 2012).

Notes and References

1. Ronald Dworkin. 2010. *Law's Empire* (3rd Reprint). Delhi: Universal Law Publishing.
2. Criterial concepts, for Dworkin, are those 'that can be explicated through some neutral analysis that makes no assumption about their value or importance'. See

Ronald Dworkin. 2011. *Justice for Hedgehogs*. Cambridge, Mass.: Belknap Press of the Harvard University Press.

3. H.M. Seervai. 1991. *Constitutional Law of India* Vol. 1. Bombay: N.M. Tripathy Pvt. Ltd.

4. James E. Fleming. 2012. 'The Place of History and Philosophy in the Moral Reading of the American Constitution', in Scott Hershovitz (ed.), *Exploring Law's Empire: The Jurisprudence of Ronald Dworkin*. Oxford: Oxford University Press.

5. *A.K. Gopalan v. State of Madras*, AIR 1950 SC 27.

6. *A.D.M. Jabalpur v. Shivkant Shukla*, AIR 1967 SC 1207.

7. *Maneka Gandhi v. Union of India*, AIR 1978 SC 597; See also, *Golak Nath v. State of Punjab*, AIR 1967 SC 1643.

8. *Bachan Singh v. State of Punjab*, (1982) 3 SCC 24.

9. Thomas Nagel. 1986. 'Reading the Law', *London Review of Books*. 8(16). 18 September.

10. Ronald Dworkin. 1996. *Freedom's Law: The Moral Reading of the American Constitution*. Oxford: Oxford University Press.

11. Also see Stephen Guest. 2013. *Ronald Dworkin (Jurists: Profiles in Legal Theory)*. Stanford: Stanford University Press. p. 78. Integrity, according to Dworkin, means that law should always be 'created, or interpreted, to form an integral whole'. There is, perhaps, no greater testament to Dworkin's theory of law as integrity than Justice H.R. Khanna's historic dissent in the Habeas Corpus case, *ADM Jabalpur v. Shivkant Shukla*, where he pithily observed in conclusion:

> [J]udges are not there simply to decide cases, but to decide them as they think they should be decided, and while it may be regrettable that they cannot always agree, it is better that their independence should be maintained and recognized than that unanimity should be secured through its sacrifice. A dissent in a court of last resort to use ins words, is an appeal to the brooding spirit of the law, to the intelligence of a future day, when a later decision may possibly correct the error into which the dissenting judge believes the court to have been betrayed.

12. Ronald Dworkin, *Freedom's Law*, Nagel 1986, *Reading the Law*.

13. AIR 1978 SC 597.

14. Ronald Dworkin. 2013a. *Taking Rights Seriously*. New York: Bloomsbury.

15. Ronald Dworkin. 2002. *Sovereign Virtue*. Cambridge, Mass.: Harvard University Press.

16. Joseph Raz. 1995. *Ethics in the Public Domain: Essays in the Morality of Law and Politics*. Oxford: Clarendon Press.

17. Mark Greenberg. 2012. 'How Facts Make Law', in Scott Hershovitz (ed.), *Exploring Law's Empire: The Jurisprudence of Ronald Dworkin*. Oxford: Oxford University Press. Scholars such as Joseph Raz, as Greenberg notes here, put the point epistemically: the content of the law 'can be identified by reference to social facts alone, without resort to any evaluative argument'.

18. John Austin. 1995. *The Province of Jurisprudence Determined*. W.E. Rumble (ed.) Cambridge: Cambridge University Press.

19. H.L.A. Hart. 1994. *The Concept of Law*. 2nd Edition. Oxford: Oxford University Press.

20. Christoper L. Eisgruber. 2012. 'Should Constitutional Judges be Philosophers', in Scott Hershovitz (ed.), *Exploring Law's Empire: The Jurisprudence of Ronald Dworkin*. Oxford: Oxford University Press.

21. A theory of 'soft positivism' allows morality a role in interpreting the law, but only when some other law, usually a founding law such as a constitution, permits such a function (Hart 1994: 265). The moral virtue of positivism, as Dworkin argues, is in its pronouncement of the limits of state requirements. Ideology, morality demands, ought not to be infused into an interpretation of the law (Guest 2013: 29–30).

22. Suhrith Parthasarathy. 2013. 'The Hedgehog: What interpreters of the Indian Constitution Can Learn from the Late Legal Philosopher Ronald Dworkin', *The Caravan*. 1 March.

23. As the title of the book indicates, Dworkin's theory is, in many ways, a riposte to Isaiah Berlin's philosophy, derived as it was from the ancient Greek poet Archilochus's proposition: 'The fox knows many things, but the hedgehog knows one big thing.'

24. Ronald Dworkin. 2013b. *Religion without God*. Cambridge, Mass: Harvard University Press. According to the Hume principle, one cannot support a value judgment, an ethical or moral or aesthetic claim, as Dworkin describes it, purely through some 'scientific fact about how the world is or was or will be'. This principle, he argues, contrary to being philosophically sceptical, speaks to the independence of morality.

25. Rebecca L. Brown. 2012. 'How Constitutional Theory Found Its Soul: The Contributions of Ronald Dworkin', in Scott Hershovitz (ed.), *Exploring Law's Empire: The Jurisprudence of Ronald Dworkin*. Oxford: Oxford University Press.

26. Ronald Dworkin. 2013c. 'Law from the Inside Out', *New York Review of Books*. 7 November.

27. 347 U.S. 483 (1954).

28. Incidentally, when the Constituent Assembly was debating the contents of the Indian Constitution, some members wanted the document to clarify that the phrase 'religious instruction', used in what is now Article 28, is distinct from the study or research into religion, the chairman of the assembly, B.R. Ambedkar said: 'the courts will decide when the matter comes up before them.' [*See*: Constituent Assembly Debates, VII, p. 884; *See also*: Ronojoy Sen. 2010. *Articles of Faith: Religion, Secularism and the Indian Supreme Court*. New Delhi: Oxford University Press. p. 92. Ambedkar was indirectly alluding to the abstractions of the Constitution, which deserved to be interpreted in a manner that fit the morality of the times.

29. Here, Dworkin differentiates a Constitution from an ordinary statute. See Dworkin *Law's Empire*, 'The Constitution is foundational of other law, so Hercules' [Dworkin's reference to the ideal judge] interpretation of the document as a whole, and of its abstract clauses, must be foundational as well. It must

fit and justify the most basic arrangements of political power in the community, which means it must be a justification drawn from the most philosophical reaches of political theory' (2010: 380).

30. *Sri Venkataramana Devaru v. State of Mysore* AIR 1958 SC 255.
31. *Ranjit D. Udeshi v. State of Maharashtra* AIR 1965 SC 881.
32. *TMA Pai Foundation v. State of Karnataka* (2002) 8 SCC 481.
33. In re *Vengan and Ors. v. Unknown* AIR 1952 Mad 95; *Damodar Ganesh v. State of Bombay* AIR 1952 Bom 459.
34. In the Fundamental Rights Case (AIR 1973 SC 1461), however, by interpretation, the Supreme Court by a narrow 7:6 majority ruled that Parliament cannot amend the Constitution in a manner that destroys or damages the document's 'basic structure'.
35. *A.K. Gopalan v. State of Madras*, AIR 1950 SC 27.
36. Not every case of constitutional conflict is a 'hard case' however. For Dworkin, 'hard cases' refer only to those disputes where 'no settled rule dictates a decision either way', and where, therefore, 'it might seem that a proper decision could be generated by either policy or principle'. In other words, they encompass cases where there exists a particularly knotty controversy over deciding what the law really is, where an application of differing value judgments could plausibly result in contradictory identifications of the law.
37. *Kesavananda Bharati v. State of Kerala* AIR 1973 SC 1461.
38. AIR 1950 SC 27.
39. AIR 1978 SC 597.
40. AIR 1950 SC 27.
41. Madhav Khosla. 2012. *The Indian Constitution*. New Delhi: Oxford University Press.
42. It must be noted here that Mahajan, J., was the only judge to, however, hold that Articles 20 to 22 comprised a separate code of its own, which required an analysis completely distinct from the rest of Part III.
43. Chief Justice Kania's opinion in *A.K. Gopalan v. State of Madras*, AIR 1950 SC 27.
44. Manoj Mate. 2010. 'The Origins of Due Process in India: The Role of Borrowing in Personal Liberty and Preventive Detention Cases', *Berkley Journal of International Law*. 28(1).
45. But as Mate suggests, 'borrowing is not just used by those who seek to challenge the status quo on such issues as fundamental rights. Rather, both sides of an interpretive approach may use borrowing when there is a debate over an ambiguous area of law' (2010).
46. There is an oft-quoted anecdote involving the great US Supreme Court Justice Felix Frankfurter, who reportedly advised BN Rau, a leading member of the Indian Consitutent Assembly, on one of his visits to America, to drop the due process clause from the Indian Constitution—the clause found inclusion in earlier drafts of the document—as it was 'undemocratic' and imposed an 'unfair

burden' on the judiciary. See, Granville Austin. 1966. *The Indian Constitution: Cornerstone of a Nation.* New Delhi: Oxford University Press. p. 103.

47. Some scholars, including H.M. Seervai have been critical of Fazl Ali, J.'s interpretation as well as those of other benches, which impliedly overruled the majority ruling in *Gopalan.*

48. Article 19(1) of the Constitution upholds certain fundamental freedoms such as the right to freedom of speech and expression, the right to freedom of association and so forth, which are, however, subject to reasonable restrictions ingrained therein.

49. *RC Cooper v. Union of India,* AIR 1970 SC 564.

50. AIR 1978 SC 597.

51. Madhav Khosla. 2012. *The Indian Constitution.* New Delhi: Oxford University Press. p. 112.

52. This conclusion, as Seervai has pointed out, has the absurd result of granting non-citizens a wider set of rights than those granted to citizens under the Constitution.

53. As held previously in *Satwant Singh Sawhney v. D. Ramarathnam, Assistant Passport Officer, Government of India and Ors.,* AIR 1967 SC 1836.

54. A reassertion of a view expressed in *E.P. Royappa v. State of Tamil Nadu,* AIR 1974 SC 555, which is generally considered to have created a new doctrine of equality analysis.

55. AIR 1967 SC 1836.

56. While Subba Rao's methods in locating a right to travel abroad in the facts of the case at hand may have been periphrastic, he was quite justified in arriving at the conclusion that the petitioner therein did, in fact, enjoy such right. The reasoning for locating such a right should have, however, been grounded in equality and not a general right to liberty, as I shall argue.

57. See for example, Benjamin Constant. 1969. 'The Liberty of the Ancients Compared with That of the Moderns', in Isaiah Berlin's, *Two Concepts of Liberty.* Oxford: Oxford University Press.

58. 347 US 483.

59. Robert H. Bork. 1990. *The Tempting of America: The Political Seduction of the Law.* New York: Macmillan; see generally, Brown (2012: 66).

60. *Kesavananda Bharati v. State of Kerala* AIR 1973 SC 1461. See also *Indira Gandhi v. Raj Narain* AIR 1975 SC 2299.

61. See the discussion later in the chapter on, *State of Tamil Nadu v. Ananthi Ammal* AIR 1995 SC 2114.

62. See also, Brown (2012: 51–2).

63. *Olga Tellis v. Bombay Municipal Corporation* AIR 1986 SC 180.

64. *Consumer Education and Research Center v. Union of India* AIR 1995 SC 922.

65. *M.C. Mehta v. Union of India* AIR 1987 SC 965.

66. *Rajagopal v. State of Tamil Nadu* AIR 1995 SC 264.

67. *PUCL v. Union of India,* (2004) 12 SCC 104.

68. Madhav Khosla. 2010. 'Making Social Rights Conditional: Lessons from India', *International Journal of Constitutional Law*. 8(4). p. 739.

69. *Subramanian Swamy v. Union of India*, W.P. Cri 184 of 2014, 5 SCC 75.

70. Gautam Bhatia. 2016. 'Judicial censorship: A Dangerous, Emerging Trend', *Legally India*. 2 May. Available at http://www.legallyindia.com/blogs/judicial-censorship-a-dangerous-emerging-trend. It has to be noted here that some of these conflicts are genuine; a clash between right to privacy and the right to free speech, for example, has been an issue in many comparative states, but even those can be solved by reading the Constitution in a manner that seeks to arrive at the best fit.

71. Article 13(2) states: The State shall not make any law which takes away or abridges the rights conferred by this part and any law made in contravention of this clause shall, to the extent of the contravention, be void.

72. Even in *Gopalan*, the judges did not hold that the concerned preventive detention law was not susceptible to an Article 14 test; it just so happened that the law was not assailed on grounds of an Article 14 violation.

73. Suhrith Parthasarathy. 2013. 'The Broken EstateHow political ownership curtails press freedom', *The Caravan*. 1 December. Available http://www.caravanmagazine.in/perspectives/broken-estate.

74. AIR 1962 SC 305.

75. *Justice Black in United States v. Associated Press* 326 US 1.

76. See generally, Dissent of Mathew J. in *Bennett Coleman v. Union of India* AIR 1973 SC 106.

77. Gautam Bhatia. 2013. '*Sakal Papers v. Union of India*—I: Why do we have the freedom of speech?', *Indian Constitutional Law and Philosophy*. 2 August. Available at http://indconlawphil.wordpress.com/2013/08/02/sakal-papers-v-union-of-india-why-do-we-have-the-freedom-of-speech/ [accessed on 26 November 2013].

78. *Bennett Coleman v. Union of India* AIR 1973 SC 106.

79. Abhinav Chandrachud. 2011. *Due Process of Law*. New Delhi: Eastern Book Company.

80. *Maneka Gandhi v. Union of India* AIR 1978 SC 597.

81. *State of Tamil Nadu v. Ananthi Ammal* AIR 1995 SC 2114.

82. *State of Tamil Nadu v. Ananthi Ammal* AIR 1995 SC 2114.

83. Article 300A, a consequence of the 44th Constitutional Amendment, which removed the right to property from Part III, says that no person shall be deprived of his property save by authority of law.

84. *P. Vajravelu Mudaliar v. Special Deputy Collector*, Madras, AIR 1965 SC 1017.

18

A Dworkinian Right to Privacy in New Zealand

Mark Bennett and *Petra Butler*

Ronald Dworkin was one of the previous half-century's most vocal and influential champions of liberal values in law and politics. He forcefully brought those values to bear on such controversial moral and political issues as distributive justice, civil disobedience, abortion, euthanasia, freedom of speech, and affirmative action.[1] However, Dworkin said surprisingly little about one of the key contemporary debates, namely, what level of control people should have over the access of others to themselves, information about their lives, and an inherent freedom to live one's life according to one's personal preferences. Dworkin has not squarely answered this question in relation to privacy in the sense of individual control over how and when others can access them and their information; his analysis of the right of privacy has focused on the US constitutional idea that people have a 'private realm' where the state ought not constrain their decisions, 'some sphere private to himself in which he is solely responsible'.[2] The question of what rights we have to privacy has become pressing in the face of the intensified facility that the now-ubiquitous internet allows governments, businesses, and individuals to access, aggregate, and disseminate data and images concerning ourselves.[3] The clash between economic interests of business, the security interests protected by governments, and the privacy of individuals, is surely one of the most important social and political issues of this century.

In his recent book *Justice for Hedgehogs*[4] Dworkin restates his position. He clearly identifies his view of what is of ethical and moral value, and how this value should be given effect to in political life through rights. However, neither there or in his other work does Dworkin address how privacy fits within that framework—whether our interests in the protection of privacy are matters of principle because they flow from the fundamental liberal values of equality and autonomy, in the particular way he characterizes these values; or whether some of these interests are better thought of as flowing from general social goals. This question is crucial, because it determines whether we see privacy protections as principled limitations on freedom of speech, or as merely policy-based limitations that will yield to speech rights except in the most pressing of social interests.

This chapter considers how Dworkin's work might allow us to answer our pressing questions of privacy within his framework of liberal value and politics. It first briefly presents that framework, primarily with reference to its concise restatement in *Justice for Hedgehogs*. It then asks where privacy fits within that framework—do privacy protections flow from Dworkin's basic liberal values, so as to ground rights that have a special status in our political and legal debates, or are privacy protections better seen as matters of policy? Finally, we examine how the emerging jurisprudence of privacy rights in New Zealand might be analyzed within the Dworkinian framework.

Dworkin's Liberal Framework

The Unity of Value

Justice for Hedgehogs' central claim is that human value is itself 'one big thing'; there is a unified scheme of value that runs through ethics and morality, which we should give effect to in our politics and law.[5] Dworkin's one big thing is dignity; this has long been the foundation of his value theory, with an early article referring to the value of 'liberty as dignity, that is, the status of a person as independent and equal rather than subservient'.[6] From dignity, Dworkin implies two principles of justice that governments must respect if they are to be legitimate, 'equal concern for the fate of every person over whom it claims dominion', and full respect for 'the responsibility and right of each person to decide for himself how to make something valuable of his life' (Dworkin 2008: 2). We will sketch the main planks of Dworkin's account below.

Ethics and Morality

Dworkin first examines the idea of dignity in the context of his discussion of ethics— 'how we ought to live ourselves'—as opposed to morality—'how we ought to treat others' (Dworkin 2008: 191). The unity of value means that the ethical search for a 'good life' is continuous with morality (191). 'We need a statement of what we should take our personal goals to be that fits with and justifies our sense of what obligations, duties, and responsibilities we have to others' (193). Ethics must refer to morality. Dworkin therefore proposes a distinction between the good life and living well, and argues that living well means striving for a good life subject to respecting moral constraints required by respect of human dignity (195). The simple view of the 'good life' means the satisfaction of our drives, but 'living well' requires creating 'a life that is not simply pleasurable but good in [a] critical way' (196). This responsibility is ours because we are self-conscious creatures that understand that it is important to live well in the sense of showing care for our existence (196).

The other side of the unity of value is that our convictions about our moral responsibilities to others are integrated with our account of what it is to live well (255). This is because the ethical elaboration of the ultimate principle of human dignity leads to moral principles. Dworkin argues that the first ethical principle of self-respect 'entails a parallel respect for the lives of all human beings. If you are to respect yourself, you must treat their lives, too, as having objective importance' (255). Dworkin terms this universal recognition of the importance of human lives 'Kant's principle': 'Your reason for thinking it objectively important how your life goes is also the reason you have for thinking it important how anyone's life goes: you see the objective importance of your life mirrored in the objective importance of everyone else's' (260). This moral concern for the lives of others sits alongside the moral equivalent of the ethical demand of authenticity—taking responsibility for one's own life—which in its moral guise requires that we 'endorse the values that structure [our lives]' by making our own decisions about morality and acting according to them.

A relevant application of these principles for our purposes is Dworkin's chapter on 'harm'. Here he examines what kinds of harm that we cause to others are contrary to our dignity, and what harms are not (285–7). Dworkin believes that the second principle of dignity is most important for this question; 'you have a personal responsibility for your own life, a responsibility you must not delegate or ignore, and Kant's principle requires you to recognize a parallel responsibility in others' (287). These parallel responsibilities must somehow be reconciled, and this can only be done by distinguishing between

two different kinds of harm that we might suffer due to other people leading their own lives 'with their own responsibility for their own fates' (287).
'Bare competition harm' is the harm that we suffer when someone else takes
an opportunity—in education, employment, sport, or love—that we would
have liked to have (287–8). This is an inevitable kind of harm that in part
defines our personal responsibility to live well—we must take others into
account and treat them as morality and ethics require if we are to live well.
'Deliberate harm' is intentional hurt, which infringes our ability to take effective responsibility for our lives (288). Deliberate harm is contrary to the second principle of dignity, which means that we must have 'a moral immunity
from deliberate harm by others' (288). We consider below whether such harm
can include harms to our privacy.

Politics and Law

With this view of value in place, Dworkin turns to his account of rights
and their relationship with law. For Dworkin, rights should act as trumps
in political debate and reasoning—they place constraints on the decisions
that politicians can make to make individuals or society as a whole better
off (229–30). Except in extreme circumstances, arguments of policy yield
to rights (Dworkin 1985: 377). The content of these rights flows, as can be
predicted, from Dworkin's unified scheme of value based on human dignity
(Dworkin 1977: 272–3), so that (Dworkin 2008: 330), 'A political community has no moral power to create and enforce obligations against its members
unless it treats them with equal concern and respect; unless, that is, its policies
treat their fates as equally important and respect their individual responsibilities for their own lives. [...] The principles of dignity[...] state very abstract
political rights: they trump government's collective policies.'

As Dworkin observes, we disagree about what concrete rights flow from
the idea of human dignity—what exactly equal concern and responsibility for
our own lives demands the government to do for us, or refrain from doing
to us, in the name of rights (330).[7] Equality obviously rules out apartheid,
discrimination, and genocide—just as the traditional list of liberal rights is
required by the responsibility principle (336). Beyond this, we must return to
the guiding moral principles to work out more difficult questions about the
implications of dignity for politics.

Indeed, it was his insistence on the importance of adopting the correct
framework of argument that is involved in particular political controversies
that dominated many of Dworkin's public interventions.[8] Sometimes his
criticism was directed towards setting the moral justification of constitutional

rights on the wrong kind of foundation, which led to the weakening of those rights.[9] More often it was directed at getting right the nature of the rights-based argumentation.[10] Within Dworkin's framework, the 'rights-based strategy' for privacy is more powerful than the 'goal based strategy'.[11] Competing rights require government to decide which right is more important from the perspective of fundamental values.[12] Rights can also be limited 'internally' or 'inherently'[13] by showing that the values underlying the right are not affected in certain situations putatively covered by the idea of right.[14] But Dworkin was adamant that in the case where arguments of policy are 'dressed up' as arguments of right to be balanced against a genuine right, the image of balancing those rights will be 'profoundly misleading'.[15]

Dworkin applies this idea of rights to the liberal ideal of liberty. There he claims that the protection of liberty derives from dignity, in the sense that governments should let their citizens be free to make their own ethical decisions, but coerce them to protect other's ability to make decisions and enjoy equal respect without interference (Dworkin 2008: 365–8). Government should not deny people the ability to make their own ethical decisions, so long as their actions do not affect the 'life, security, or liberty of others' (369). It must also not restrict freedom in the service of upholding controversial ethical values (369). But 'ethical independence is not jeopardized when a matter is not foundational and government's constraint assumes no ethical justification. Government relies on moral rather than ethical arguments when it pressures me to conserve scarce resources, forces me to pay taxes, and forbids me to drive carelessly' (369). These laws do not deny us our responsibility to define our own ethical choices about how to live (369). Instead, they are the moral limits on our ethical lives, defined by the 'opportunities and resources people are rightfully entitled to have' (371).

Dworkin also discusses the well-established claim that political rights are not 'absolute' but limited (373). He accepts this—previously he argued that policy should be trumped by any competing rights unless the community would 'suffer a catastrophe'[16]— but notes that 'the character and justification of these limits differs, depending on which of the justifications for the right... is in play' (Dworkin 2008: 373). The arguments that flow from Dworkin's foundational principle of dignity may not apply, or may not apply to the same degree, for all kinds of expression or speech: 'the justification they offer is not engaged at all on certain occasions' (374).

The brief chapter on law re-states Dworkin's view that morality is interdependent with law in that the law of a community, including the moral principles that best justify the community's enacted rules, so that a judge's obligation is to interpret the law as she finds it in light of the justifying moral principles (402).[17] But here he develops the theme of unity, by characterizing law as the institutionalized branch of political morality (405). Legal rights are political rights that 'are properly enforceable on demand through adjudicative and coercive institutions' without further law-making (407); disputes in legal philosophy should thus focus on the political morality concerning the sources and interpretation of the political rights that are enforced by the state (409). Difficult legal questions are answered by our fundamental values, so that lawyers and judges are 'working political philosophers of a democratic state' (414).

If we accept Dworkin's vision of law and the account of value set out above, what follows for the protection of privacy?

A Dworkinian Right to Privacy

Dworkinian Privacy

On Dworkin's framework, it is clearly of the greatest importance whether we characterize privacy protections as a matter of principle and rights rather than as a matter of policy or social goals. If so, then the competition between freedom of speech and privacy is not one of right versus policy goal or social interest—with the right trumping the goal—but of right versus right—to be resolved by reference to the underlying account of dignity.[18]

However, Dworkin's wide-ranging discussions of how liberal ideals apply to the key political controversies of our times do not include a detailed analysis of how to understand the protection of privacy. There are fleeting mentions of a possible right to privacy in *Taking Rights Seriously*, but these are presented as illustrations of how rights reasoning should proceed rather than as Dworkin's own view.[19] He said much more about the 'privacy' jurisprudence of the US Supreme Court in relation to the due process clause, arguing in *Freedom's Law* that the Supreme Court's privacy jurisprudence could only be justified on the assumption that 'decisions affecting marriage and childbirth are so important, so intimate and personal, so crucial to the development of personality and sense of moral responsibility, and so closely tied to religious and ethical convictions protected by the first amendment, that people must be allowed to make these decisions for themselves, consulting their own conscience' and that the Constitution recognized 'the special intimacy of a person's connection to her own physical integrity' (Dworkin 1996: 50–1). These arguments are about privacy in the sense what decisions we ought to be able to make ourselves. However, we are further interested in privacy as a right telling us what access to information about themselves a person should be able to control.

It might be thought that the lack of discussion in regard to access and control of information results from the relevant political controversies only exploding into the mainstream since the rise of the internet to the mainstream in the early twenty-first century (Nissenbaum 1998: 119),[20] during which time Dworkin was less focused on contributing to political debates as to systematising his thoughts into *Justice for Hedgehogs*, as well as setting out further arguments about democracy and law.[21] However the sixties itself was a time of technological change and significant comment on the 'death of privacy',[22] and important debates on the justification of privacy occurred in the legal and philosophical literature in the 1970s.[23] Still, given that much of Dworkin's concrete applications of his liberalism were made in discussions of prominent legal decisions, the lack of progress in—and use of—the US privacy tort[24] may offer another explanation for this gap.

So the question is how Dworkin's detailed account of privacy might have played out, if he had turned his mind to it. What would a Dworkinian account of the right to privacy look like, and what effect would it have on our understanding of that right in the law, particularly in New Zealand? However, it is not a case of speculating as to what exactly he would have said—rather, we attempt to look at present arguments concerning privacy protection through the Dworkinian framework set out above, with reference to the way that judges and commentators have reasoned about these things in the development of new remedies concerning certain invasions of privacy.

Privacy has in general two strands. One strand may be defined as 'relating to those things or aspects of one's life that you, as an individual in a social world, would have a reasonable expectation of exerting control over in terms of dissemination or disclosure should you wish to'.[25] The state of privacy obtains if, in N.A. Moreham's words, a person 'is only seen, heard, touched or found out about if, and to the extent that, he or she wants [these things]' (2005: 628).[26] The other strand is related to first but captures the idea that a right to privacy protects one's ability to do what one deems important to fulfil one's personality.[27] The state of privacy is obtained if one has full autonomy. However, the moral right we have to privacy protection is not to total control over access to us—the scope of the right is limited by reference to the value that it is grounded in.[28] The protection of privacy by law can take many forms, calibrated to prevent different kinds of interference;[29] the immediate question is what Dworkin's scheme of value would require as a matter of morality and political rights.

The first point is that we must put to the side wider policy considerations justifying various protections of privacy.[30] To characterize privacy protections as a matter of Dworkinian rights, we must focus on deontological justifications of privacy, not consequentialist accounts that look to benefits to individuals or society that are not matters of right.[31] We seek a way of making sense of the value inherent in Dworkin's principles of morality as applied to the question of the protection of privacy. Can the protection of privacy be justified as necessary conditions of (a) respect for the objective importance of the lives of all—equal concern and respect—or, (b) responsibility for deciding how to live our lives, and respect that responsibility in others. If we can find such a justification for the protection of privacy, then it stands a chance of surviving integration with the general political principle of liberty, which is clearly at stake to some extent in the form of freedom of speech when we place limitations on what people can say or publish in the name of privacy protection.

Privacy and Harm

Harm is an important aspect of our enquiry, for as noted above, harms are actions that impair our dignity and are contrary to morality, but when done by other individuals as private citizens rather than the state (Dworkin 2008: 288). Our ability to take responsibility for our lives is compromised when others deliberately harm us, by interfering 'with our control over our bodies or property for any reason whatsoever' (288). In such cases, the law should protect us from harm, and it can be said we have a moral right that others' freedom to commit such harms is limited.

Can invasions of privacy be characterized in this way? An obstacle to this is that Dworkin's ideas of deliberate harm seems focused on harm to our physical bodies and our property or wealth; it is not clear that he would accept that deliberate harm includes the harm that is often identified in invasions of privacy. That is the harm of others deliberately interfering with our control over ourselves and our assigned resources (288–9). Schauer has noted the view that the harms that others' speech can cause us do not affect our ability to control our lives in the same way that other kinds of actions of others do—'the apparent harms of speech are lesser in degree or different in kind, individually or categorically, than the harms ensuing from other kinds of conduct'.[32] The same might be said of the harms that flow from a lack of control over information concerning, and access to, our lives.

However, Dworkin does not definitively state the content of deliberate harm, and it is arguable that we can extend the idea of 'control over our body' to control over intimate and personal information about our body and lives. Thus, it may be that Dworkin would agree that deliberate harm to our privacy involves some kind of (adapting his words) 'general transfer of control over the integrity' of our selves—if not our bodies—which, especially when that transfer is to 'those who do not have [our] interests at heart', which would leave our 'dignity in shreds' (Dworkin 2008: 289). He discussed such non-physical harm in the context of pornography, there noting that limiting harm to only bodily or financial harm would mean that harm could not justify much of existing American law (Dworkin 1981: 178). On the other hand, he observed that defining harm as extending to any mental distress or annoyance would justify too much interference in our lives—as any conduct whatsoever has the potential to annoy or distress someone (178). In addition, when contemplating academic freedom, Dworkin argues that there is no right against being harmed by speech that insults, embarrasses, or lowers our esteem in the eyes of others or our own self-respect.[33]

However, while these arguments concerning non-physical harm are suggestive of Dworkin's position on privacy protections, the details of his arguments should not detain us, dealing as they do with different situations. Instead, the important point is that Dworkin resolves the question about whether non-physical distress should be considered harm by reference to the fundamental value of human dignity. If dignity is subverted by individual or state actions, then this is a harm against which rights should protect us. Whether this is the case is of prime importance within the Dworkinian framework of rights, determining how we should think about the relationship between privacy and other rights such as freedom of speech, which we will return to later.

Privacy and Dignity—Autonomy

Our question thus becomes: Can we say that privacy protections might be considered by Dworkin as matters of principle—moral requirements that must be respected by other individuals and the state and protected by rights?

What is striking in the legal and philosophical literature is the prominence of arguments justifying privacy protections on the basis of dignity and autonomy.[34] One of the foremost experts on the common law's protection of privacy, Nicole Moreham, has identified the justification for the protection of privacy squarely in the way that it upholds the dignity of the individual (Moreham 2008: 234).[35] Her idea of dignity develops Kant's idea that people must be recognized and treated as 'ends in themselves' whose lives have their own intrinsic value, and that people are not treated simply as means for the achievement of our own ends (235). Moreham argues that invasions of privacy take away a person's autonomy to decide when others can 'access' them; 'an intruder who looks at, listens to or finds out about another against his or her wishes is disregarding that other's choices about when and by whom he or she is accessed' (236). Chris Hunt also notes this Kantian, dignitarian approach to the value of privacy:

> It is apparent that both physical intrusions into privacy (arising from the actions of a peeping tom) and informational intrusions into privacy (arising from the tabloid disclosure of personal information) offend this elementary principle of dignity; in each case the wrongdoer is treating the victim as simply a means to an end (that is, to his own titillation, for the tom, and to boosting magazine sales, for the tabloid) rather than as an end in himself. (Hunt 2011: 204)

Grounding privacy protections by reference to dignity is not a recent development in the common law world. In 1890, Warren and Brandeis, in one of the most influential US law review articles ever published, argued that the principle that justifies the protection of personal writings from unauthorized publication is 'not the principle of private property, but that of inviolate personality.'[36] Discussing this claim at mid-century, the legal scholar Bloustein argued that:[37]

> [T]he principle of 'inviolate personality' to posit the individual's independence, dignity and integrity; it defines man's essence as a unique and self-determining being. It is because our Western ethico-religious tradition posits such dignity and independence of will in the individual that the common law secures to a man 'literary and artistic property'—the right to determine 'to what extent his thoughts, sentiments, emotions shall be communicated to others'. (Bloustein 1964: 971, citing Brandeis and Warren 1890: 198)

The idea of dignity is thus connected to the idea of autonomy, in terms of the prevention of people from being under the control of others, in terms of access to themselves.[38] It is clear that unwanted access undermines our choices about how we wish to be accessed (Hunt 2011: 206).

But further, privacy can also be seen as a necessary condition for the existence of autonomy—our capacity to regard our own decisions as meaningful and important—in the sense that people cannot have a conception of themselves as autonomous individuals, nor the space to formulate plans for their lives, if they do not have a certain freedom from the access of others. The philosopher Jeffrey Reiman's contribution to a key 1970s debate in *Philosophy and Public Affairs* identified the value of privacy in this way:

> Privacy is a social ritual by means of which an individual's moral title to his existence is conferred. Privacy is an essential part of the complex social practice by means of which the social group recognizes—and communicates to the individual—that his existence is his own. And this is a precondition of personhood. To be a person, an individual must recognize not just his actual capacity

to shape his destiny by his choices. He must also recognize that he has an exclusive moral right to shape his destiny. And this in turn presupposes that he believes that the concrete reality which he is, and through which his destiny is realized, belongs to him in a moral sense. (Reiman 1976: 39)[39]

On these accounts, privacy rights are justified to the extent that the level of control they give us over the autonomy to live our life as we see fit, as well as other people's access to us and information about us are required if we are to be able to be responsible for our lives—to have the autonomy to control over informational and physical access to us.[40]

In all of these statements, we can find Dworkin's idea of ensuring people are allowed to take responsibility for their lives, and are not affected by the control or will of others in ways that prevent them from making their own choices about how to live their lives. The arguments above present privacy protections as both (a) essential to the 'Kantian principle' of recognizing the objective importance of others' lives and (b) as foundational of our autonomy—our responsibility to make our own decisions about how we ought to live. In the space of this short discussion, and in light of the lack of explicit analysis in his own work, we will not attempt to provide an analysis of what Dworkin's view of privacy protections should be given his account of value. However, it is clear that the foundational value and basic principles of Dworkin's ethical/moral system are the same as those being used to explain why privacy protections are important. A Dworkinian account of privacy as a matter of principle, to be protected by rights, is at least arguable.

Yet although we might phrase the protection of privacy in the language of dignity and autonomy, we must remember that in Dworkin's framework there are legitimate limits on our autonomy drawn from morality—our ability to choose our own path is limited by what is necessary to protect others' ability to choose their own path. Our control over access to information about ourselves rubs up against others' freedom to gain and publicize that information through freedom of speech. In order to show that Dworkin's moral and political philosophy should recognize a right to privacy, it must be shown that privacy protection prevents harms to our dignity, and that these protections do not unjustifiably limit freedom of speech.

Applying Dworkin's Framework

The difference that the Dworkinian framework makes is that—if it is found that there is a right to privacy protection due to its basis in the value of dignity—the clash between freedom of expression and privacy will be on the basis of rights versus rights, rather than on the basis of the right to freedom of expression being limited by the policy goal of privacy protection. We need to specify what kind of 'value' or 'interest' they are, rather than just saying that they are recognized human values. What is crucial is whether the values are those identified as basic moral principles that the state must treat as political rights if it is to be legitimate.

If privacy is not a matter of principle to be protected by rights, its place in the Dworkinian framework is clearly weakened. On the 'rights as trumps' view propounded by Dworkin, actions falling under the scope of freedom of expression should not be compromised by individual or societal consequences unless the failure to achieve those consequences would be a catastrophe. A right of freedom of expression would win out over a social interest in privacy except in the most exceptional circumstances. Just such a situation been identified in the United States experience with the First Amendment protection of freedom of speech;[41] as one American constitutional scholar observed: 'there is a clear pattern. Speech almost always wins' (Gewirtz 2001: 140).[42]

In contrast, if privacy is a right, then it would sit on an equal level with freedom of expression. In the event that there was a seeming clash between these rights, the conflict would be resolved through a balancing exercise. It may be that this balancing exercise would be difficult where the consideration 'on both sides of the equation'[43] is dignity and autonomy.[44] It may be that autonomy would be found to be better protected overall through allowing the privacy protection and limiting freedom of expression. Or it could be that the putative right to freedom of expression is not actually implicated—the particular expression is outside the scope of the moral right to freedom of expression justified by reference to autonomy.[45] An example is the jurisprudence of the German Constitutional Court. In Germany the right to privacy is enshrined in the Basic Law and is anchored in the respect and protection of dignity.[46] The Court balances the person's right to privacy with freedom of expression and favours the right to privacy in cases where self-determination is threatened.[47]

Because of Dworkin's general prominence and the dominance of liberal justifications in US constitutional scholarship, there are analyses that follow something like a Dworkinian approach to privacy.[48] Yet, as observed above, there is no wholly Dworkinian analysis, for the simple reason that Dworkin himself did not provide one.

The Right of Privacy in New Zealand's Legislation and Jurisprudence

New Zealand provides an interesting paradigm for the study of privacy since unlike any other common law country New Zealand has no supreme bill of rights protected by strong judicial review. The New Zealand Parliament is the final arbiter what privacy its citizen enjoy. Privacy protection in New Zealand law was thoroughly examined in a 2011 Law Commission review. This major review commenced in 2006, and its long gestation and the number of resulting publications indicate the intricate nature of privacy. In its stage one analytical paper, *A Conceptual Approach to Privacy*[49] and study paper *Privacy Concepts and Issues*,[50] the Commission explored the general concept of privacy. The Law Commission when conceptualizing privacy found that the right to privacy embodied two values.[51] The first of these core values is the autonomy of humans to live a life of their choosing. The second is the equal entitlement of people to respect.

The Commission elaborated that privacy can be seen as informational, as well as local (or spatial). It is interesting to note that the notion of self-determination is not part of the Law Commission's notion of privacy. In particular, the Law Commission does not seem to import the notion of self-determination into 'autonomy'. The Law Commission described informational privacy as being concerned with control over access to private information or facts about oneself. The Commission considered that not all personal information could be regarded as private but conceded that opinions might differ as to exactly which facts count as private. On the other hand, the Law Commission defined local or spatial privacy as that which is concerned with control over access to one's person and to private spaces, typically the home, but in other places as well.[52] While it was clear that the commission saw privacy as a matter of principle, as a moral right,[53] it did not think it was an absolute trump in Dworkin's sense.[54]

In the Law Commission's subsequent reports, however, the focus was on specific issues, namely public registers, penalties, and remedies, and a review of the Privacy Act 1993, with little reference to the overall concepts. This approach was in line with the Commission's earlier pronouncement in its initial scoping process: 'We are saying nothing more profound than that our approach to privacy protection should be piecemeal and particularised, not generalised. Where there are demonstrable problems and abuses, intervention should be made, but not otherwise.'[55]

However, the Commission repeated the Issues Paper observation that 'Privacy is not an absolute right or value; it can justifiably be overridden in particular circumstances by other rights and interests.'[56] This may be accurate on a Dworkinian approach, but it is not clear as there is ambiguity about whether privacy is a moral or legal right, whether the suggestion is that privacy might not be a right but only a value, and concerning how 'justifiable overriding' of privacy is therefore going to proceed. In effect, the Law Commission did not take a 'rights-focussed', Dworkinian style approach to its enquiries. Although it obviously had the values underlying privacy protections at the forefront of its analysis, and provided reasoning that might be interpreted in a roughly Dworkinian manner—for example the discussion of visual surveillance of a private dwelling[57]—it refrained from undertaking an explicit and strict rights-based analysis.

At present, there is a patchwork of privacy protections from various sources of law in New Zealand.[58] The law is comprehensive in its protection of data, evolving in the area of information privacy and spatial privacy but incomplete in the area protection of autonomy or self-determination.[59] The latter, however, is a key concept of Dworkin's idea of ensuring people are allowed to take responsibility for their lives, and are not affected by the control or will of others in ways that prevent them from making their own choices about how to live their lives.[60] Overall the following picture of privacy protection shows that if we regard privacy as a right based on dignity and autonomy in the Dworkinian sense, it has only been partly implemented in New Zealand. The closest acknowledgment of the notion that privacy also protects the autonomous self was in the judgment of *Brooker* where McGrath J considered privacy as 'an aspect of human autonomy and dignity'.[61] Justices John Joseph McGrath and Edmund Walter Thomas (both dissenting) afford privacy such an importance within the New Zealand legal framework in *Brooker* that it has the value of a right equal to freedom of expression.[62]

International Commitments

New Zealand has ratified the International Covenant on Civil and Political Rights (ICCPR)[63] and United Nations Convention on the Rights of the Child (UNCROC).[64] Rather than fully incorporating the conventions into domestic law, however, they were incorporated in different pieces of legislation with the result that not all their protections are fully implemented; this includes a stand-alone right to privacy. Privacy values may be taken into account by the courts and the executive 'only' as part of New Zealand's obligations under international law[65] and as 'so far as its wording allows legislation should be read in a way which is consistent with New Zealand's international obligations'.[66]

The New Zealand Bill of Rights Act 1990

One of the purposes of the New Zealand Bill of Rights Act 1990 was to affirm New Zealand's commitment to the ICCPR. However, a general right to privacy was excluded because it was seen as inappropriate to 'attempt to entrench a right that is not by any means fully recognized now, which is in the course of development, and whose boundaries would be uncertain and contentious'.[67] Therefore, as it stands, the Bill of Rights itself does not recognize privacy as a right of the same standing as those it does expressly protect. However, notwithstanding the lack of a general right to privacy, four aspects of the Bill of Rights Act indirectly protect the right to privacy.

First, New Zealand's international commitments protect privacy interests. The Long Title provides that the Bill of Rights Act 'affirm[s] New Zealand's commitment to the [ICCPR]'. The Long Title was designed to be used as an interpretive aid to 'ascertain the intention of Parliament'.[68] The commentary in the White Paper notes that while the ICCPR is binding on New Zealand only under international law, the courts could make reference to the ICCPR in interpreting and applying the Bill of Rights Act and, in particular, 'in considering what restrictions on the rights conferred by the Bill are justified'.[69] Thus, the right to privacy in article 17 of the ICCPR will be directly relevant when considering the scope of limitations to the right to freedom of expression in Section 14 of the Bill of Rights Act.

Second, Section 28 provides that rights not expressly included in the Bill of Rights Act are not taken to be abrogated merely by their absence. The equivalent provision in the White Paper was described as ensuring that 'the fact that an existing right is only partially incorporated by the Bill does not thereby destroy any wider ambit that that right otherwise has'.[70] Such recognition accords with the commitment to the ICCPR expressed in the Long Title. Thus, Section 28 can be seen as recognizing that the right to privacy in the ICCPR may be given effect in New Zealand.[71] However, due to a lack of jurisprudence it is unclear at this point in time whether a right recognized via Section 28 has the same weight as a right enumerated in the Bill of Rights Act under Section 5 of the Bill of Rights Act or whether a right recognized via Section 28 is seen similar to a social value (which also can be taken into account under Section 5).[72]

Third, protection of the right to privacy can be achieved through Sections 5 and 6 of the Bill of Rights Act. Those provisions allow for privacy considerations to play a part in the interpretation of legislation and development of the common law.[73] Section 5 allows for a limitation of a right if that limitation is demonstrably justified in a free and democratic society. The test developed by the courts to determine whether a limitation is demonstrably justified[74] allows for the consideration of other rights (enumerated in the Bill of Rights Act) but also for the consideration of social values or 'rights' not included in the Bill of Rights Act. Therefore, the rights and freedoms in the Act may be subject to reasonable expectations of privacy as far as those expectations are 'demonstrably justified in a free and democratic society'. It should be noted that this is a lesser threshold for the violation of rights than Dworkin's view that rights should trump (non-rights) social goals except in cases where the breach is needed to avoid a catastrophe.[75]

Moreover, the Bill of Rights Act allows for privacy protections to be embraced through Section 6 of the Bill of Rights Act. Section 6 mandates that the courts have to interpret legislation and the common law in light of the rights in the Bill of Rights Act.[76] Since, as mentioned above, privacy can be 'imported' into the Bill of Rights Act via Section 28 of the Act, it would be open to the courts to interpret legislation and develop the common law in light of privacy. However, it is at this point in time unclear how much weight the courts will afford rights incorporated into the Bill of Rights framework via Section 28. They may even in effect do so without reference to Section 28, as is arguably the case in the *Hosking* case discussed ahead.

Fourth, the right to privacy also plays an important role in assessing whether there has been a breach of one's right to be free from unreasonable search and seizure 'whether of the person, property, or correspondence or otherwise'.[77] The White Paper specifically acknowledged that this freedom is an aspect of the privacy of the individual.[78] The importance of the privacy aspect in regard to Section 21 of the Bill of Rights Act is pointed out by Elias CJ in *Hamed v. R* when stating, 'The right [to be free from unreasonable search and seizure] protects privacy. [...] It describes a "right to be let alone"'[79] protecting 'people, not places'.[80] Her Honour unequivocally clarified that 'Section 21 guarantees reasonable expectations of privacy from state intrusion.'[81] Elias CJ further pointed to the influence of human dignity on the citizen's right to privacy when she observed that, 'The values protected by Section 21 are not simply property-based, as were the common law protections which preceded it. Rather, they provide security against unreasonable intrusion by State agencies into the personal space within which freedom to be private is recognised as an aspect of human dignity'.[82]

The degree of intrusion into privacy may determine what constitutes 'search and seizure' and whether a search is 'reasonable'.[83] While the absence of a right to privacy in the Bill of Rights Act has not been fatal to its recognition by the courts, it has acted as a restraint on the development of the right. In particular, the use of international law principles, justified limitation, and Section 28 have not yielded a strong and unequivocal statement of privacy protections being a matter of rights that gives them a special role in our law, governmental action, and our political debate. If privacy should be considered a right in the Dworkinian sense, this is not clearly reflected in the Bill of

Rights. And even if we accept that privacy is a right, the Section 5 'reasonable justification' structure is a further divergence from the Dworkinian 'rights as trumps' framework, for it provides a lesser threshold of justification than the catastrophe requirement imposed by Dworkin. The effect of these features of the Bill of Rights on judicial acknowledgment and development of the right to privacy is explored further below.

The Privacy Act 1993

The Privacy Act 1993 was enacted to 'promote and protect individual privacy'[84] and was heralded as an 'important milestone in the evolution of human rights legislation'.[85] The Act protects individuals' private information, rather than other facets of privacy.[86] For reasons of scope, this paper will discuss some key features rather than setting out the mechanisms of the Act exhaustively.

The Act protects personal information held by an 'agency', which includes natural and legal persons from the public and private sector,[87] but excludes the news media in connection with their news-gathering activities, the Governor-General, Members of Parliament, courts, and certain other bodies acting in a judicial capacity.[88] The Act also only protects the private information of living natural persons, rather than corporate entities or individuals who are deceased.[89]

One of the most significant aspects of the Privacy Act is its formulation of Privacy Principles.[90] The Privacy Principles govern the responsible collection, use and disclosure of personal information. Where any 'agency' breaches a Privacy Principle, or has not complied with a code of practice, an individual may make a complaint to the Commissioner on the basis that there has been an interference with his or her privacy.[91] In this way, the Privacy Act diverts first instance privacy concerns from the judicial system. For a complaint to be successful, however, the complainant must also show that the breach caused (or may cause): loss or injury; adverse effect on his or her rights or interests; or significant humiliation, loss of dignity or injury to feelings.[92] The threshold is high: mere misuse or dissemination of personal information is insufficient for a complaint to be upheld. If the complaint is not settled, civil proceedings may be commenced before the Human Rights Review Tribunal,[93] which has wide powers to award remedies, including declarations, injunctions, and damages.[94]

Although the Privacy Act creates substantive obligations for both state and private actors, its greatest purpose is to serve as an educative tool 'to change both practices and perceptions regarding the handling of personal information'.[95] As such, the ambit of the Act is limited to just that—protection of information, rather than other kinds of privacy. Nevertheless, aspects of the moral right to privacy are protected by the Act.

Other Legislation

Further domestic legislation recognizes elements of the value of privacy in piecemeal form. The Broadcasting Act 1989, 'fills the gaps' caused by the exclusion of news media from the scope of the Privacy Act, providing for the maintenance of programme standards and the establishment of the Broadcasting Standards Authority. The Act applies to state-owned media, as well as private television and radio, and requires broadcasters to maintain standards consistent with individuals' privacy and develop codes of broadcasting practice.[96] The Act establishes a complaints regime with reference to breaches of codes of practice: if a broadcaster fails to maintain standards consistent with individual privacy, it may be required to pay the complainant compensation.[97] Although the Act itself is silent as to what 'privacy' means, the Authority has developed principles with which to measure allegations of breach of privacy.[98] In the course of the development of those principles the Privacy Commissioner was consulted to ensure compliance with the Privacy Principles encapsulated in the Privacy Act.[99]

Section 216H of the Crimes Act 1961 makes everyone liable to imprisonment if they intentionally or recklessly make an intimate visual recording of another person. The Summary Offences Act 1981 prohibits the intimidation of any person, which occurs where a person threatens or follows another, deprives them of their property, loiters near their home or work, or confronts them in public with intent to intimidate them.[100] The offence protects freedom of movement and prevents unlawful interference with the home, reflecting article 17 of the ICCPR. Moreover, the Trespass Act 1980 protects the rights of occupiers of private property by making it an offence to trespass after being warned to leave; and the Harassment Act 1997 recognizes privacy of one's physical body, personal space, and home life by prohibiting the physical harassment of another, such as by stalking, though such behaviour must be repetitive in nature. Another example is the right to quiet enjoyment from unwanted or unauthorized intrusion into personal space or personal affairs embodied in Section 38 of the Residential Tenancies Act 1986. An affirmation of the privacy concept of freedom from intrusion can also be found in the Search and Surveillance Act 2012.[101]

The Defamation Act 1992 reformed the common law of defamation and enshrined a right to reputation in legislation (the right to reputation being linked in the ICCPR and elsewhere to the right to privacy). The 1992 Act provides civil remedies for those who are defamed. Protection is, however, limited as there are several defences to a claim in defamation, including honest opinion and truth.

As well as the examples outlined above, there are a myriad of other legislative provisions in particular areas which take privacy into account.[102]

Protection of Privacy in Common Law

The way in which New Zealand law conceives of the value of privacy cannot be ascertained only by examining the protection of the citizens' privacy within public and criminal law contexts. The full picture can only be gained through considering how citizens' privacy interest or rights as against the interests or rights, especially information interests, of other citizens or their agencies is protected. In New Zealand, this 'horizontal' regulation of privacy and expression—and the key Dworkinian question of whether these are rights or mere interests—are increasingly being answered by the common law.

Tort of Interference with Privacy

The New Zealand Court of Appeal in *Hosking v. Runting* recognized a tort of invasion of privacy.[103] The plaintiffs in Hosking were in a relationship and had children together. One of the plaintiffs was a well-known New Zealand television host who attracted significant media attention. The couple objected to photographs of their children (that had been taken in public) being published in a magazine owned by Pacific Magazines NZ Ltd, the second defendant. The couple advised Pacific Magazines that they did not consent to the taking or publication of the photos, but Pacific Magazines refused to cancel publication. They applied for an injunction restraining publication on the basis of a tort of invasion of privacy which, they submitted, did not require proof of damage.[104]

In confirming the existence of the tort and determining its elements, the majority of the Court of Appeal identified the two fundamental requirements which must be met for the tort to be successfully made out.[105] First, there must be facts in existence in respect of which there is a reasonable expectation of privacy. Second, the publicity given to those private facts must be considered highly offensive to an objective reasonable person.[106] Rather than formulating all the boundaries to this cause of action in a single decision, Gault P and Blanchard J considered it was more appropriate for the tort of privacy to develop incrementally as the courts applied the law to particular circumstances.[107]

The Court in *Hosking* did, however, recognize a defence to an invasion of privacy where disclosure of the relevant private facts was 'justified by a legitimate public concern in the information'.[108] Further, on the facts of Hosking, the Court held that the plaintiffs failed to make out their claim since the photos were not taken in circumstances in which there was a reasonable expectation of privacy.[109] We will expand on this brief summary of the decision in *Hosking*, as there were a number of individual judgments handed down, and a closer analysis demonstrates the difference that using a Dworkinian framework makes.

Hosking was applied in *Brown v. Attorney-General*[110] and *Andrews v. Television New Zealand Ltd.*[111] The incremental approach continued in 2012 when the High Court had to decide in *C v. Holland* whether a tort of intrusion upon seclusion should form part of the law of New Zealand.[112] The Court found that privacy concerns were undoubtedly increasing with technological advances, including prying technology through, for example, the home computer. Therefore, the Court held that the affirmation of a tort of intrusion upon seclusion was commensurate with the value already placed on privacy and, in particular, the protection of personal autonomy. Since the similarity to the *Hosking* tort was sufficiently proximate, the tort of intrusion upon seclusion could be seen as a logical extension of, or adjunct to, it.[113]

Privacy as a Fundamental Value that Limits Other Rights

Privacy has been conceptualized by the New Zealand courts as a fundamental value. But rather than treating privacy as a 'trump card'—as a 'right' in the Dworkinian sense—the courts consider it a value to be balanced against other important values. The exclusion of privacy from the enumerated list of rights in the Bill of Rights seems to be behind this position: there seems to be a recognition that certain privacy protections are required if human dignity is to be upheld, but a reluctance to speak of a right to privacy. Thus, although judicial treatment of privacy as a fundamental value can be found in case law, particularly in relation to unreasonable search and seizure (prohibited by Section 21 of the Bill of Rights Act),[114] it may be that positive gains could be made from confirmation of its place among other fundamental rights and freedoms in the Bill of Rights Act.[115] These gains would not be confined to the practical—enhanced privacy protections were required for autonomy and equal respect—but also theoretical, at least according to the above interpretation of Dworkin's jurisprudence of dignity.

Entick v. Carrington establishes a common law rule that there must be some lawful basis for police entry onto property for the purpose of preventing or detecting crime.[116] There is no general right of entry onto private property; there must be implied (or express) licence to enter, which also applies to the general public.[117] An implied licence 'is an invention of the common law to reflect the balance between respect for an individual's right to privacy and the public interest in enforcement of the criminal law'.[118] In the already cited Supreme Court decision of *Hamed v. R* Elias CJ unequivocally affirmed that Section 21 protects 'personal freedom and dignity from unreasonable and arbitrary state intrusion'.[119] For Elias CJ and Tipping J that meant that private conversations and conduct are protected from state interference even in public places.[120] The Court of Appeal had observed in an earlier case that the 'main aim of Section 21 of the Bill of Rights is to protect privacy interests',[121] and had deemed evidence seized as a result of an unreasonable search to be inadmissible.[122] Privacy interests were also considered in the 2006 decision *Avowal Administrative Attorneys Ltd v. District Court at North Shore*, where Avowal was investigated for tax avoidance.[123] Avowal claimed a right to privacy in respect of the Commissioner of Taxation's statutory powers of entry onto premises and obtaining of information pursuant to Section 16 of the Tax Administration Act 1994. Avowal argued that the Commissioner's powers had to be read in accordance with Section 21 of the Bill of Rights Act and the common law right to privacy. Baragwanath J observed that two competing interests had to be balanced: privacy and the collection of revenue for the public good. The incursion into privacy was held to be justified because it was reasonable for the Commissioner to enquire into Avowal's conduct because it was in the business of tax mitigation.[124]

Privacy concerns have to be weighed when search warrants are issued. General warrants have been held invalid for a long time to safeguard privacy and property.[125] In *Dotcom v. Attorney-General* the High Court had to decide whether a warrant issued under the Mutual Assistance in Criminal Matters regime had to meet the requirements that are demanded by New Zealand law in the light of Section 21 Bill of Rights Act.[126] The Court found that the warrant in the particular case did not adequately state the alleged offence and was, therefore, too general.[127]

The right to privacy in the home has also been upheld in cases such as *Choudry v. Attorney-General*, where the Court of Appeal refused to imply into legislation that conferred powers on the Security Intelligence Service an incidental power of entry onto private property.[128] Furthermore, several of the judges in *Brooker v. Police* considered that the common law recognized that people were entitled to feel secure and enjoy tranquillity in their homes, identifying this right to residential tranquillity as an element of the right to privacy.[129]

Additionally, the courts have taken privacy matters into account in respect of judicial discretion to allow the media access to court records of criminal proceedings under the search rules;[130] and recognized the right to privacy as an important discretionary factor when deciding whether or not to grant permanent name suppression where a case does not reach the stage of public prosecution.[131]

A Closer Analysis of *Hosking v. Runting*

The decision in *Hosking v. Runting* demonstrates the difference that a Dworkinian analysis that considered certain privacy protections as a matter of principle—yielding privacy rights—would make, compared with an approach that takes the Bill of Rights' exclusion of privacy from the enumerated rights seriously and treats privacy as merely an interest.[132] The other main question—how to formulate the requirements of the privacy tort—is equally required to a Dworkinian analysis, and Moreham (2008) has provided a clear account of what a dignity-based tort of privacy might look like.

Anderson and Keith JJ's decisions illustrate how treating privacy as an interest rather than a right can lead to lesser protections of privacy. Keith J emphasizes that in deciding whether to develop the common law to protect certain privacy interests, we must consider that such protections act as limits on the right of freedom of expression,[133] that there is no general right to privacy, and that the question is thus one of privacy interests versus expression rights.[134] Anderson J notes that the case in front of them does not present anything that could be regarded as a moral right to privacy, so that 'An analysis which treats that value as if it were a right and the Section 14 NZBORA right as if it were a value, or treats both as if they were only values when one is more than that' is in error.[135] His subsequent analysis proceeds on this basis, with the relatively Dworkinian result that the right of expression trumps the relevant privacy interests at stake.[136] Anderson and Keith JJ's decisions thus sit relatively well with Dworkin's framework, developing the common law so as to uphold matters of principle in the face of matters of mere policy or interest[137]—although the Bill of Rights framework of 'reasonable limits' allows for greater consideration of interests than Dworkin's 'trumps except in catastrophe' analysis. The obvious avenue of criticism of their positions is their view that no moral right to privacy is involved in the relevant situation.

This criticism, and the subsequent difference that conceiving of privacy as a right makes, is seen most clearly in the decision of Tipping. Although he often speaks – imprecisely from a Dworkinian perspective—about the competition between 'values' of privacy and expression,[138] he argues that the lack of express recognition of the right to privacy in the Bill of Rights should not inhibit the development of the common law.[139] Tipping J's reluctance to speak in terms of a right to privacy continues through the key parts of his decision—where 'privacy values' are considered as limits to expression rights, and a proportionality analysis is applied.[140] This might be explained, again, by reference to the structure of rights/interests set out in the Bill of Rights. However, Tipping J ultimately states that we have a moral right to privacy, because 'It is of the essence of the dignity and personal autonomy and well-being of all human beings that some aspects of their lives should be able to remain private if they so wish.'[141] He also notes that the value of privacy around the world has often been accompanied by 'the terminology of rights'.[142] Although this 'rights' terminology is generally eschewed in favour of 'values'—and the standard 'reasonable limitation' methodology for interest/policy limits applied—the substance of Tipping J's decision seems to treat privacy as a moral right that constitutes an 'internal' limit on the right of freedom of expression. Indeed, the core analysis considers, in Dworkinian fashion, the underlying moral values of privacy and free expression and how and whether they are implicated in the present situation.[143] Like Keith J, Tipping J does seem to be doing something analogous to Dworkin's framework, though constrained by structure and language imposed by the Bill of Rights. The difference between them is their assessment of whether certain protections of privacy amount to moral rights.

The main majority decision of Gault P and Blanchard J is perhaps the least expressly Dworkinian in the case. They note that privacy was deliberately excluded from the enumerated rights in the Bill of Rights,[144] and consider the development of the law primarily in terms of justifying a limit on freedom of expression.[145] Yet there is a lack of clarity when deciding the ultimate question of 'how the law should reconcile the competing values'.[146] The key question for Dworkin—and in a different form under the Bill of Rights—is what kind of values we are dealing with in competition with each other. Is it a matter of moral rights versus social policy interest, or rights versus rights? While Gault P and Blanchard J do not take the American approach that they see as allowing expression rights to trump privacy interests,[147] that would be the Dworkinian approach, and the Bill of Rights analysis would still give greater protection for rights than mere interests. But it is not clear that either of these frameworks plays out in their decision.

A further example of this is the 'legitimate public concern' exception, of which Gault P and Blanchard J observe that 'A matter of general interest or curiosity would not, in our view, be enough to outweigh the substantial breach of privacy harm the tort presupposes. The level of legitimate public concern would have to be such as outweighs the level of harm likely to be caused.'[148] This statement raises a number of questions. Is 'harm' part of the justification of a privacy right, or is it a matter of social policy interest? What kind of weighing is going on here? Is it the limitation of expression rights by privacy rights, or merely privacy interests? If the decision were phrased differently, it could be read as a Dworkinian examination of how the liberal values underlying privacy and expression protections play out in a particular situation, and the subsequent judgment of whether people have a moral and legal right to the particular privacy protection at stake—or, on the contrary, whether people have a moral and legal right to expression in the relevant circumstances.

As Katrine Evans noted at the time, it makes a difference to legal decision-making whether we regard privacy as a matter of moral right.[149] Evans notes that unlike English judges, who have explicitly recognized privacy as a moral right (aided by the inclusion of privacy as an enumerated right in their human rights legislation), the majority judges in Hosking 'were certainly feeling towards a similar conclusion, but arguably needed to articulate rather more clearly the weight to be given to privacy'.[150] Again this might not only have benefits for the practical protection of privacy in situations where it rubs up against freedom of expression, but it would have benefits from the perspective of the Dworkinian structure of rights. It would require an explicit examination of the value of the rights to privacy and freedom of expression, considering whether, how, and to what degree the values that underlie these rights—whether Dworkin's dignity or otherwise—are furthered or diminished by a particular legal rule.[151] While it has been argued that resolving conflicts between privacy and free expression cannot be done through reference to rights,[152] on a Dworkinian view the examination of what legal rule will give effect to the moral right that upholds human dignity is both possible and necessary. Tipping J's decision shows how such an analysis of the relative the weight of the dignity concerns can yield clear outcomes in particular cases.[153]

It should be remembered that Dworkin would regard getting right our account of how privacy and freedom of expression work as a matter of morality and/or social goals not only as a matter of correct moral reasoning: it is also a matter of correct legal analysis. While his account of law in general is controversial, it is often accepted as a plausible account of the development of the common law in difficult cases or new situations. It has also found some supporters in the 'common law constitutionalism' account of law. Furthermore, the Bill of Rights itself, to the extent that sets out the framework of rights that act as the justifying principles of our political-legal order, acts as a legislative restatement of the judicial duty to interpret statutes and develop the common law so as to better fulfil our deeply-held values. Despite the difference in threshold for the abrogation of rights, the Dworkinian framework is useful for judges in thinking through our privacy jurisprudence, and is detectable in key decisions such as *Hosking* and *Holland*. Time will tell if a Dworkinian right of privacy becomes entrenched and developed in our common law of privacy.

***

Privacy was a frontier of law's empire that Dworkin did not map out, but it is increasingly discussed dues to the quickly changing technological and social landscape. The law—both legislation and the common law—is struggling to keep up. Dworkin would insist that it matters fundamentally whether we have moral rights to privacy, because a number of privacy protections act are limitations on values that are a matter of principle and rights—in this chapter we have focused on freedom of expression, and shown the difference that the use of a Dworkinian framework would make to our understanding and development of the law. The analysis of the legislation and jurisprudence shows that New Zealand has comfortably embraced one strand of Dworkin's privacy value— information privacy. Information privacy is strongly protected, for example, by the Privacy Act 1993. However, the interconnectedness of privacy and dignity has not gone unnoticed in New Zealand either. While for many years the common law did not recognize a right to physical privacy, more recent New Zealand jurisprudence suggests a tentative shift towards the inclusion of such a privacy right based on dignity and autonomy, that is, the second strand of privacy in the Dworkinian sense. That development can be observed where an unfettered adherence to a right, especially freedom of expression, would deny the other party their dignity. Whatever the reality, the Dworkinian insistence on privileging our moral rights in political and legal decision-making, and his elaboration of the idea of dignity and application of it in pressing controversies, constitutes an important resource for thinking through the privacy controversies that will likely plague us for years to come.[154]

Notes and References

1. Ronald Dworkin. 1977. *Taking Rights Seriously*. Cambridge, Mass.: Harvard University Press; Dworkin. 1985. *A Matter of Principle*. Oxford: Oxford University Press; Dworkin. 1996. *Freedom's Law*. Oxford: Oxford University Press; Dworkin. 1993. *Life's Dominion: An Argument About Abortion, Euthanasia, and Individual Freedom*. New York: Knopf.

2. See, for example, Ronald Dworkin. 1981. 'Is there a right to pornography?', *Oxford Journal of Legal Studies*. 1(2). p. 191. Ruth Gavison observes that the US Supreme Court's privacy decisions do not focus on privacy as 'freedom from unwanted publicity': Ruth Gavison. 1992. 'Too Early for a Requiem: Warren and Brandeis Were Right on Privacy vs. Free Speech', *South Carolina Law Review*. 43(3): 454–5.

3. See Daniel Solove. 2011. *Nothing to Hide: The False Tradeoff between Privacy and Security*. New Haven: Yale University Press; Dan Jerker B. Svantesson. 2012. 'Systematic Government Access to Private-Sector Data', *International Data Privacy Review*. 2(4): 268–76; Christopher Kuner, Fred H. Cate, Christopher Millard, and Dan Jerker B. Svantesson. 2017. 'Data Protection and Humanitarian Emergencies' *International Data Privacy Law*. 7(3): 147–8.

4. Ronald Dworkin. 2011. *Justice for of Hedgehogs*. Cambridge: Belknap Press.

5. Ronald Dworkin. 2008. *Justice in Robes*. Cambridge: Harvard University Press. p. 1. See also Dworkin (2008: 327–8): 'Ethics studies how people best manage their responsibility to live well, and personal morality what each as an individual owes other people. Political morality, in contrast, studies what we all together owe others as individuals when we act in and on behalf of that artificial collective person.'

6. Ronald Dworkin. 1974. 'Did Mill Go Too Far?' *New York Review of Books*.

7. See also Dworkin. *Taking Rights Seriously*. 198–9.

8. Dworkin *Taking Rights Seriously*, Chapters 7–13; Dworkin *A Matter of Principle* Parts 3, 5, and 6; Dworkin *Freedom's Law* Parts I and II; Dworkin *Life's Dominion*.

9. Dworkin *Freedom's Law*. Chapter 8.

10. Dworkin *Freedom's Law*. Chapter 9.

11. Dworkin *Taking Rights Seriously* p. 274; Dworkin *A Matter of Principle*. p. 336.

12. Dworkin *Taking Rights Seriously*. pp. 193–4.

13. See Alon Harel. 1997. 'What Demands Are Rights: An Investigation into the Relation between Rights and Reasons', *Oxford Journal of Legal Studies*. 17(1): p. 101; Andrei Marmor. 1997. 'On the Limits of Rights', *Law and Philosophy*. 16(1): p.1; Frederick Schauer. 1982. *Free Speech: A Philosophical Enquiry*. Cambridge: Cambridge University Press. Chapters 7 and 13.

14. Dworkin *Taking Rights Seriously*. p. 200.

15. Dworkin *A Matter of Principle*. p. 377.

16. Dworkin *A Matter of Principle*. p. 375. See also p. 387 requiring 'emergency or great risk'.

17. Dworkin's essay 'Law's Ambitions for Itself' sets out his view succinctly.

18. See for example the balancing that is required in the jurisprudence of the German Constitutional Court in regard to the German Basic Law's protection of freedom of speech (Article 5) and the right to privacy (Article 2(1) in conjunction with Article 1) BverfGE NJW 2005 pp. 3271–3273; and ECHR Article 8 (privacy) and Article 10 (freedom of speech) [2004] EMLR 379; (2005) 40 EHRR 1.

19. Dworkin *Taking Rights Seriously* pp. 117–19 and pp. 160–1.
20. Helen Nissenbaum. 1998. 'Protecting Privacy in an Information Age: The Problem of Privacy in Public', *Law and Philosopy*. 17; Lisa Austin. 2003. 'Privacy and the Question of Technology', *Law and Philosophy*. 22.
21. Dworkin. 2008. *Is Democracy Possible Here? Principles for a New Political Debate*. Princeton: Princeton University Press; Dworkin *Justice in Robes*.
22. Daniel Solove. 2009. *Understanding Privacy*. Cambridge: Harvard University Press. p. 4.
23. L. Henkin. 1974. 'Privacy and Autonomy', *Columbia Law Review*. 74: 1410; J.J. Thomson. 1975. 'The Right to Privacy', *Philosophy and Public Affairs*. 4: 295; T. Scanlon. 1975. 'Thomson on Privacy', *Philosophy and Public Affairs*. 4: 323; J. Rachels. 1975. 'Why Privacy is Important', *Philosophy and Public Affairs*. 4: 323; Jeffrey H. Reiman. 1976. 'Privacy, Intimacy, and Personhood', *Philosophy and Public Affairs*. 6: 26; R. Gavison. 1980. 'Privacy and the Limits of Law', *Yale Law Journal*. 89: 421; W. Parent. 1983. 'Privacy, Morality and the Law', *Philosophy and Public Affairs*. 12: 269.
24. See for example Harry Kalven. 1966. 'Privacy in Tort Law—Were Warren and Brandeis Wrong?', *Law and Contemporary Problems*. 31: 326; Diane L. Zimmerman. 1983. 'Requiem for a Heavyweight: A Farewell to Warren and Brandeis's Privacy Tort', *Cornell Law Review*. 68: 291; Danielle Citron. 2010. 'Mainstreaming Privacy Torts', *California Law Review*. 98: 1085. Compare with Ruth Gavison. 1992. 'Too Early for a Requiem: Warren and Brandeis Were Right on Privacy vs. Free Speech', *South Carolina Law Review*. 43: 437.
25. Mark Hickford. 2007. *A Conceptual Approach to Privacy*. NZLC M19.
26. N.A. Moreham. 2005. 'Privacy in the Common Law: A Doctrinal and Theoretical Analysis', *Law Quarterly Review*. 121.
27. See Dworkin *Freedom's Law* pp. 50–1; 27 BVerfGE 1 (1969) (*Microcensus Case*).
28. Jeffrey H. Reiman. 1995. 'Driving to the Panopticon: A Philosophical Exploration of the Risks to Privacy Posed by the Highway Technology of the Future', *Santa Clara Computer & High Technology Law Journal*. 11(1): 33.
29. See Daniel J. Solove. 2006. 'A taxonomy of privacy', *University of Pennsylvania Law Review*. 154(3): p. 477; Hickford (2007: 12–13).
30. See Dworkin (2011: 373) with respect to the protection of freedom of speech.
31. Chris D.L. Hunt. 2011. 'Conceptualizing Privacy and Elucidating its Importance: Foundational Considerations for the Development of Canada's Fledgling Privacy Tort', *Queen's Law Journal*. 37: 176 esp. pp. 202–3 and David Lindsay. 2005. 'An Exploration of the Conceptual Basis of Privacy and the Implications for the Future of Australian Privacy Law', *Melbourne University Law Review*. 29(1): 144.
32. Frederick Schauer. 1993. 'Phenomenology of Speech and Harm', *Ethics*. 103(4): 641.
33. Ronald Dworkin. 1996. 'We Need a New Interpretation of Academic Freedom', *Academe*. 82(3): 14.

34. This literature has been well summarized in a number of places, including N.A. Moreham, Chris D.L. Hunt, and Hickford. See also *Ingo v. Münch/Philip Kunig, Kommentar zum Grundgesetz Vol 1* (6th edition, Beck, München, 2012), Article 2.

35. N.A. Moreham. 2008. 'Why Is Privacy Important? Privacy, Dignity and Development of the New Zealand Breach of Privacy Tort', in Jeremy Finn and Stephen Todd (eds), *Law, Liberty, Legislation: Essays in Honour of Joh Burrows QC*. Wellington: LexisNexis.

36. Samuel D. Warren and Louis D. Brandeis. 1890. 'The Right to Privacy', *Harvard Law Review*. 4(5). 15 December. pp. 193–220.

37. Edward Bloustein. 1964. 'Privacy as an Aspect of Human Dignity: An Answer to Dean Prosser, *New York University Law Review*. 39. pp. 962–1007.

38. Hickford, citing Jeffrey Reiman. 2004. 'Driving to the Panoptican: A Philosophical Exploration of the Risks to Privacy Posed by the Information Technology of the Future', in Beate Rössler (ed.), *Privacies: Philosophical Investigations*. Stanford: Stanford University Press. p. 201.

39. See also Reiman (1995: 42).

40. Hickford (2007), Chapter 5; also see Moreham (2005: 636–41).

41. For consideration of privacy protections as a limitation on freedom of expression, see William L. Prosser. 1960. 'Privacy', *California Law Review*. 48(3): 422–3; Eugene Volokh. 2000. 'Freedom of Speech and Information Privacy: The Troubling Implications of a Right to Stop People from Speaking About You', *Stanford Law Review*. 52: 1049; Paul Gewirtz. 2001. 'Privacy and Speech', *Supreme Court Review*. 139; Frederick Schauer. 2001. 'Free Speech and the Social Construction of Privacy', *Social Research*. 68(1): 221; Samantha Barbas. 2010. 'The Death of the Public Disclosure Tort: A Historical Perspective', *Yale Journal of Law & the Humanities*. 22(2): 171; Neil Richards. 2011. 'The Limits of Tort Privacy', *Journal of Telecommunication and High Technology Law*. 9: 357.

42. See Justice Alito's dissenting opinion in *Snyder v. Phelps* 562 US (2011) (*Westborough Church case*) for whom privacy is at the heart of the decision and which trumps freedom of expression (IV & VI) and which might indicate a starting shift in the value that privacy is allocated.

43. *Bartnicki v. Vopper* 121 S Ct at p.1766 Breyer J, cited in Gewirtz 2001: 157.

44. Geoffrey Gomery. 2007. 'Whose autonomy matters? Reconciling the competing claims of privacy and freedom of expression' *Legal Studies*. 27(3): 404.

45. For example see Gewirtz 2001: 172–3, including the claim that 'Freedom of the press is not fundamentally about the freedom to disclose private matters or to invade the private sphere', and Gavison 1992: 457, 460 and 462–4.

46. See 27 BVerfGE 1 (1969) (*Microcensus Case*).

47. See an overview of the German position: Petra Butler. 2013. 'The Case for a Right to Privacy in the New Zealand Bill of Rights Act', *New Zealand Journal of Public and International Law*. 11: 213, 232–3. See also Elspeth Reid. 2012. 'Rebalancing Privacy and Freedom of Expression' *Edinburgh Law Review*. 16: 253.

48. See for example Gewirtz 2001.
49. Mark Hickford. 2007. *A Conceptual Approach to Privacy.* NZLC M19.
50. Law Commission, *Privacy Concepts and Issues* (NZLC SP19, 2008).
51. *Privacy Concepts and Issues* [4].
52. *Privacy Concepts and Issues* [3.21].
53. Hickford, *A Conceptual Approach to Privacy*, pp. 6, 9, and 15.
54. Hickford, *A Conceptual Approach to Privacy*, p. 65.
55. *Privacy Concepts and Issues* [16].
56. Law Commission, *Review of the Privacy Act 1993: Review of the Law Of Privacy Stage 4* (NZLC R123, 2011) [2.15]
57. Law Commission *Invasion of Privacy: Penalties and Remedies* (NZLC IP14, 2009) [3.33–3.49].
58. *Invasion of Privacy: Penalties and Remedies*, [5] and [11].
59. The omission is evidenced, for example, by the discussion of privacy in *Hosking v. Runting* (discussed later) where self-determination as a privacy value was not discussed; the Attorney-General's Section 7 Report in regard to the Privacy (Information Sharing) Bill 2011 which extended the information sharing between Government departments. The Report discusses very briefly Section 21 of the Bill of Rights Act 1990, the right to be free from unreasonable search and seizure. The Report concludes (without any analysis) that the right is not infringed by the extensive sharing of information between departments.
60. This has been discussed in detail later in the chapter.
61. *Brooker v. Police* [2007] NZSC 30; [2007] 3 NZLR 91 at [123]
62. Petra Butler. 2013. *The Case for a Right to Privacy in the New Zealand Bill of Rights.* 11 New Zealand Journal of Public and International Law. p.244.
63. The ICCPR was signed by New Zealand on 12 November 1968 and ratified on 28 December 1978, United Nations, Treaty Series, vol. 999, p. 171 and vol. 1057, p. 407.
64. The United Nations Convention on the Rights of the Child was signed by New Zealand on 1 October 1990 and ratified on 6 April 1993.
65. Law Commission, *A New Zealand Guide to International Law and its Sources* (NZLC R34, 1996) 24; and *New Zealand Air Line Pilots' Association Inc v. Attorney-General* [1997] 3 NZLR 269 (CA) 289.
66. *Rajan v. Minister of Immigration* [1996] 3 NZLR 543 at p. 551; *Tavita v. Minister of Immigration* [1994] 2 NZLR 257 (CA) at p. 266. See also *Ashby v. Minister of Immigration* [1981] 1 NZLR 222 (CA) where the Court held that some international obligations were so important that the executive had to take them into account when making decisions. *Hosking v. Runting* [2005] 1 NZLR 1 (CA), at [6] per Gault and Blanchard JJ.
67. Department of Justice, *A Bill of Rights for New Zealand: White Paper* (1985) [10.144].
68. *A Bill of Rights for New Zealand: White Paper* [10.144].
69. *A Bill of Rights for New Zealand: White Paper* [10.13].
70. *A Bill of Rights for New Zealand: White Paper* [10.179].

71. See for example the view of Thomas J (dissenting) in *Brooker v. Police* [2007] NZSC 30, [2007] 3 NZLR 91 [229].
72. See in regard to a full discussion in regard to the operation of Section 5: Andrew Butler and Petra Butler. 2006. *The New Zealand Bill of Rights Act 1990: a commentary*. Wellington: Lexis Nexis. Chapter 6.
73. Explicitly in regard to common law, see *Hamed v. R* [2011] NZSC 101, [2012] 2 NZLR 305 at [37] per Elias CJ.
74. See in regard to the test *R v. Hansen* [2007] 3 NZLR 1 (SC) at [104].
75. See above discussion in the section 'Politics and Law'.
76. See Elias CJ in *Hamed v. R* [2011] NZSC 101, [2012] 2 NZLR 305t [37] where her Honour states the courts' duty: 'Indeed, the New Zealand courts would fail in their obligations under ss 3 and 6 of the Bill of Rights Act if they do not ensure that the common law is consistent with the Act.'
77. New Zealand Bill of Rights Act 1990 [Bill of Rights Act], Section 21.
78. New Zealand Bill of Rights [10.144].
79. *Hamed v. R* [10] citing *Olmstead v. United States* 277 US 438 (1928) 478 per Brandeis J.
80. *Hamed v. R* [17].
81. *Hamed v. R* [10].
82. *Hamed v. R* [11].
83. *Hamed v. R* [10] per Elias CJ, [163]–[164] and [172] per Blanchard J and [222]–[223] per Tipping J. However, it needs to be noted that no clear majority position as to what constitutes a search emerges from *Hamed*: see *C v. Holland* [2012] NZHC 2155, [2012] 3 NZLR 672 at [22].
84. Privacy Act 1993, Long Title.
85. Tim McBride. 1994. 'NZ's Privacy Act 1993—Part 1', PLPR 2.
86. McBride states that focus of the Privacy Act is on protecting personal information as this is the only type of breach to which the complaint jurisdiction applies. In addition, the Act only applies to natural persons: Section 2(1).
87. Section 2(1).
88. Radio New Zealand and Television New Zealand, as state-funded media organisations, are not exempted in respect of Privacy Principles 6 and 7 which relate to individuals seeking to access or correct personal information: Section 6.
89. Privacy Act, Section 2(1).
90. Privacy Act, Section 6.
91. Privacy Act, Section 66.
92. Section 66.
93. Usually, the Director of Human Rights Proceedings will commence proceedings: Section 82. However, if the Director chooses not to do so, complainants may commence proceedings themselves: Section 83.
94. Section 85.
95. McBride, 'NZ's Privacy Act 1993 – Part 1'.
96. Broadcasting Act 1989, Sections 4 and 21(2).
97. Section 13(1) (d).

98. See for instance the discussion in *Andrews v. Television New Zealand Ltd* [2009] 1 NZLR 220 (HC) [55].

99. When the Broadcasting Standards Authority develops codes of broadcasting practice with broadcasters that relate to privacy, it must consult with the Privacy Commissioner: see Broadcasting Act, Section 21(4).

100. Summary Offences Act 1981, Section 21(1)(d). See *Brooker v. Police*, per McGrath J at [123] where in regard to the Summary Offences Act 1981 his Honour observed: 'Privacy is "an aspect of human autonomy and dignity". Although, as a police constable, the complainant is a public official, in her private life she is entitled to enjoyment of the rights of an ordinary citizen. Her privacy interest in the present appeal is her right to be free from unwanted physical intrusion into the privacy of her home.'

101. See especially Search and Surveillance Act 2012, Section 46(1)(c): 'Except as provided in Sections 47 and 48, an enforcement officer who wishes to undertake any 1 or more of the following activities must obtain a surveillance device warrant ... (c) observation of private activity in private premises, and any recording of that observation, by means of a visual surveillance device.'

102. For example Accident Compensation Act 2001, Sections 159, 160, and 246; Arbitration Act 1996, Section 14H; Armed Forces Discipline Amendment Act (No 2) 2007, Section 68; Births, Deaths, Marriages, and Relationships Registration Act 1995, Section 75 G; and Evidence Act 2006, Section 69.

103. *Hosking v. Runting.*

104. The plaintiffs also brought a claim based on intentional infliction of emotional distress. However, that tort did not neatly fit the facts of the claim. A particular difficulty was that the plaintiffs needed to show that harm was intended by Pacific Magazines (or that it was reckless as to harm occurring). The publication of the photos would not necessarily result in harm or distress.

105. *Hosking v. Runting* [117] per Gault P and Blanchard J, and [249]–[256] per Tipping J.

106. *Hosking v. Runting* [117].

107. *Hosking v. Runting* 118].

108. *Hosking v. Runting* [129].

109. *Hosking v. Runting* [164].

110. *Brown v. Attorney General* [2006] DCR 630.

111. *Andrews v. Television New Zealand Ltd.*

112. *C v. Holland.*

113. *C v. Holland* [86].

114. Though the Bill of Rights Act is not entrenched or supreme law, it is accepted as one of New Zealand's constitutional documents: see for instance Anna Adams 'Competing Conceptions of the Constitution: The New Zealand Bill of Rights Act 1990 and the Cooke Court of Appeal' [1996] NZ L Rev 368; and Paul Rishworth. 1995. 'Affirming the Fundamental Values of the Nation: How the Bill of Rights and the Human Rights Act Affect New Zealand Law', in Grant

Huscroft and Paul Rishworth (eds) *Rights and Freedoms: The New Zealand Bill of Rights Act 1990 and the Human Rights Act 1993*. Brookers: Wellington. p.71.

115. Compare Elias CJ in *Hamed v. R*, [37] where her Honour states the courts' duty: 'Indeed, the New Zealand courts would fail in their obligations under Sections 3 and 6 of the Bill of Rights Act if they do not ensure that the common law is consistent with the Act.'

   This obligation stated so clearly by Elias CJ authorises (if not instructs) the courts to develop (at least) the common law in light of privacy.

116. *Entick v. Carrington*.

117. See *Robson v. Hallett* [1967] 2 QB 939; and *Howden v. Ministry of Transport* [1987] 2 NZLR 747 (CA) at p.751. On the scope of implied licence, see also *Tararo v. R* [2010] NZSC 157, [2012] 1 NZLR 145.

118. *Police v. McDonald* [2010] NZAR 59 (HC) [35].

119. *Hamed v. R* [10].

120. *Hamed v. R*, [12] per Elias CJ and [222] per Tipping J.

121. *R v. Williams* [2007] 3 NZLR 207 (CA) [236] per William Young P and Glazebrook J.

122. *R v. Shaheed* [2002] 2 NZLR 377 (CA).

123. *Avowal Administrative Attorneys Ltd v. District Court at North Shore* [2010] 2 NZLR 794 (HC).

124. *Avowal Administrative Attorneys Ltd v. District Court at North Shore* [105].

125. *Leach v. Money* (1765) 19 State Tr 1002; *Chic Fashions (West Wales) Ltd v. Jones* [1968] 2 QB 299; *Auckland Medical Aid Trust v Taylor* [1975] 1 NZLR 728 (CA) at 733 per McCarthy P; and *Dotcom v. Attorney-General* [2012] NZHC 1494, [2012] 3 NZLR 115 [28] per Winkelmann CJ.

126. *Dotcom v. Attorney-General*, [31] et seq.

127. *Dotcom v. Attorney-General* [50]–[51].

128. *Choudry v. Attorney-General* [1999] 2 NZLR 582 (CA).

129. *Brooker v. Police* [11] per Elias CJ, [60] per Blanchard J, [129] per McGrath J and [218] per Thomas J.

130. *Mafart v. Television New Zealand Ltd* [2006] NZSC 33, [2006] 3 NZLR 18 [7]; and *R v. Mahanga* [2001] 1 NZLR 641 (CA) [32].

131. *Forrest v. A and B* [2009] NZAR 697 (HC).

132. See the analysis of Katrine Evans. 2004. '*Hosking v Runting*: Balancing Rights in a Privacy Tort', *Privacy Law and Policy Reporter*. 11(2): 34. Available at http://www.austlii.edu.au/cgi-bin/sinodisp/au/journals/PLPR/2004/28.html. Also, see generally the analysis of Ursula Cheer. 2007. 'The Future of Privacy: Recent Legal Developments in New Zealand'. *Canterbury Law Review*. 13: p. 169.

133. *Hosking v. Runting* [178].

134. *Hosking v. Runting* [184].

135. *Hosking v. Runting* [265].

136. *Hosking v. Runting* [266–7].

137. *Hosking v. Runting* [208]–[222].

138. *Hosking v. Runting* [224] and [229]–[230].
139. *Hosking v. Runting* [226].
140. *Hosking v. Runting* [235–7].
141. *Hosking v. Runting* [239].
142. *Hosking v. Runting* [241].
143. *Hosking v. Runting* [233]–[243].
144. *Hosking v. Runting* [87].
145. *Hosking v. Runting* [111–116] and [130]–[135].
146. *Hosking v. Runting* [116].
147. *Hosking v. Runting* [73].
148. *Hosking v. Runting* [134].
149. Evans, '*Hosking v. Runting*: balancing rights in a privacy tort'.
150. Evans, '*Hosking v. Runting*: balancing rights in a privacy tort'.
151. See in particular *Hosking v. Runting* [109]–[135].
152. Hunt, 'Conceptualizing Privacy and Elucidating its Importance: Foundational Considerations for the Development of Canada's Fledgling Privacy Tort', pp. 208–9: 'It would be largely impossible for courts to balance privacy and expression based solely on deontological considerations; each party would simply assert its dignity and autonomy, and respect for the party's personhood would compel the court to vindicate its right to privacy or its right to speech'.
153. *Hosking v. Runting* [233]–[243].
154. See in regard whether a right to privacy embedded in the New Zealand Bill of Rights Act 1990 would strengthen privacy Petra Butler. 2013. 'The Case for a Right to Privacy in the New Zealand Bill of Rights Act', *New Zealand Journal of Public and International Law*. 11: 213.

Afterword

The law, its definition, its description as a command, or as a provision of standards that provides rights and duties, or as timeless rules awaiting discovery by judges, the historical significance of its origin, the moral implications as well the political considerations, and most importantly, its interpretation, has been the subject of jurisprudential thought, since time immemorial. From the professional approach[1] to jurisprudence, which embraced a technical scheme in resolving jurisprudential issues, to Sociological Jurisprudence propounded by Roscoe Pound, where a judge was considered as one 'responding to social and personal stimuli' (Dworkin 1978: 16), the discussion of the role of the judges in the legal system, their function within the web of interpretation, and whether they can step outside this web and formulate new rules has been the central issue. It is this aspect of jurisprudence that Ronald Dworkin has discussed in detail in his various celebrated articles and books which include *Taking Rights Seriously* as well as, *Law's Empire*. While many have strived to wear a number of hats, whether it is of a legal philosopher attempting to answer questions that have left the greatest thinkers baffled or of a jurist concocting a legal formula that is applicable to practical problems; no one has worn these hats with the deftness as Dworkin has. It is these facets that are being explored in the book *Dignity in the Legal and Political Philosophy of Ronald Dworkin*. I endeavour to capture this persona of Dworkin in the first instance.

The Legal Philosopher: The Ineluctable Presence of Morality

Being one of the finest thinkers, Dworkin created his own jurisprudential road when he paved it with the essential asphalt of morality. The difference between law and justice is rooted in an understanding of morality. Justice is a notion, which is the upshot of the best and correct theory of moral rights (16). A person's picture of justice is his own, painted by his own interpretation, which draws its inspiration from his personal convictions. This justice can be realized in a Dworkinian State only when individuals have a right to equal concern and respect. They possess this right not because of any significant contribution, achievement, merit or excellence on their part but simply by virtue of being human beings. Dworkin upholds the value of equality and the prominence it ought to have in a society however for him within a scheme of contemporary liberalism, it is an imperilled model.[2] On the other hand, the 'Law' defends the use of what he calls 'coercion on the part of the State', as the law appertains to and is inferred by the past political decisions.[3]

The Jurist: Interpretation Is the Solitary Verse of a Legal Song

Through the relationship between interpretation and law and his philosophical avowal of law always providing answers if interpreted correctly, Dworkin paved the way for a whole new genre of legal thinking which continues to enthral many. The legal propositions are not a reflection of legal history and neither they are historically evaluated rules but are a result of the interpretation of legal history. He draws a comparison with artistic interpretation and urges lawyers and judges to apply this parallel when conflicted with legal propositions that do not seem relatively straightforward.[4]

Dworkin's rather intriguing 'artistic hypothesis' though might be critiqued as being impractical or far-fetched which Dworkin himself suspected, provides a novel insight on which the edifice of his legal interpretation is built. The 'tabula rasa' is not the judicial ideal,[5] it is inconceivable for the judges to have no prior thought or opinion, for even interpretation requires the knowledge of the proposition, as then only one is able to decipher as to what is an addition and what is plain interpretation. Interpretation however isn't simple. Whether it's a painting, where the colours are primary and the strokes, a few or a piece of music composed of basic notes or plain lyrics, each person trying to interpret the painting or the song will see and hear a different piece of art, much of which will be a reflection of their theoretical beliefs about the nature, coherence, other formal properties of art, or by a consideration of what the painter or musician intends to portray. Applying this analogy of Dworkin in legal interpretation, it is safe to say, that he attempts to show that each judge interprets a legal proposition differently, being guided by the primary aim of giving it the best possible explanation satisfying its objectives. However, two interpretations will seldom be identical. Devising a new model for interpretation in perhaps an extremely creative way, Dworkin provides an instance of a group of novelists who are engaged in a single project, starting with one novelist writing the first chapter of the book, it is followed by each novelist, reading the previous chapter written by the other author, interpreting it and writing a new chapter, and so on till the novel is created as a single amalgamated whole. It is this ingenuity of Dworkin's approach to interpretation that can be seen applicable to Indian cases. Each judge is like a novelist in the chain.[6] Whether it's the opinion of the lower courts, or the judgments of the higher courts given in the past, when a Judge has to decide the matter at hand with the distinctive set of facts, varied parties as well as the question of law specific to the case, while interpreting the proposition of law as well as the precedents, he devises a scheme which is applicable to the particular case at hand, in order to meet the ends of justice. Each case is no doubt unique, so the Judge is required to treat the case as a new chapter of the book, drawing inspiration while interpreting the previously decided applicable cases and laws drafted by the elected representatives. It is this aspect which may be termed as a creation, so if the interpreted scheme was a sculpture, then the laws would be the clay and the precedents; water, what sculpture has to be made however is left to the judge's discretion.

Role of Judges When Grappling with Daunting Cases

Striving to provide a satisfying answer regarding judicial independence in interpretation, when confronted with hard cases, the duty of the judges he expounds, primarily resides in attempting to identify the rules in order to discern the rights of the parties, whether they uncover new laws, or shed a new light to an existing law, it should be generated by fundamental moral principle and not policy.[7] This principle is the moral rule, which guides the judges in distinguishing between the correct and the erroneous. It is only these principles which when weighed can steer one towards the right answer at any given stance, especially when one is confronted with a 'hard problem'. While it is an easy claim to speak of judges as 'free standing moral agents' as being the guardians of democratic virtues and values,[8] it is a task of a particular complexity when the case in front of a judge is a hard one. Situations arise many a times when a judge is torn between various legal options, without the legal system guiding his way. The judge in these circumstances has a certain discretionary power. Though this discretion is not absolute, like a field confined within a boundary where the runner has the freedom to sprint within it, the judge is like a runner with the freedom to choose within the boundary of the legal limitations. His is not an absolute freedom and has certain moral obligations; his choice in Dworkin's world would be guided by principle while striving for optimal solution.

Though Dworkin many a times has tried to tackle this concept, what constitutes as a hard case is peculiar to societies and countries. Matters overlaid with religious disputes continue to be those where even the most equipped guardians in our country are irresolute about their next move. However, certain concerns are deemed to be hard consistently around the world where the legislators or the judges are inevitably in a quandary; these may range from problems that have moral tones for example, LGBT human rights or those which deal with the whole gamut of social issues like bigamy, extra marital relations, euthanasia, abortion, privacy, death penalty, and even sentencing in certain types of criminal cases, to those involving two or more conflicting interests leaving the decision maker more often than not, perplexed. While Dworkin provides a solution to these cases by inventing a hypothetical adjudicator, a nonpareil guardian, an ideal judge—Hercules, it only acts as an apotheosis of his 'best interpretation' philosophy. Hercules takes the policies drafted by the lawmaker in the given instance and being guided by 'principle', prefers to apply that policy which provides a better justification.[9] It's the application of the statute to the particular case that gives the full meaning to the definite words of the statute, that defines the limits of the otherwise unlimited meanings and that compels the reader to understand the underlying tones of the rules.

In *National Legal Services Authority v. Union of India*,[10] came before us an issue, to which the 'Dworkin's Principle' fits like a glove. The traumatic experiences faced by the members of the transgender community in our country were brought to our consideration; questions regarding the legal right of their sex orientation and their right to determine their identity. Since they were neither categorized as 'male' or 'female' they were subject to discrimination and were deprived of rights, which are essential to human beings. It was necessary to define and understand the term 'transgender' as now is used, for it has become an umbrella term that is used to describe a varied array of identities and experiences, who strongly identify with the gender opposite to their biological sex; male and female. Identifying as male and female is the most characteristic feature of a person, however gender identity is an innate and inexplicable sensation of individuality, 'this may not correspond with the sex ascribed at birth, including the personal sense of the body which may involve a freely chosen, modification of bodily appearance or functions by medical, surgical, or other means and other expressions of gender, including dress, speech, and mannerisms'. Being guided by the morally circumscribed principles and by interpreting our Constitution, which provides the right to live with dignity inherent in the fundamental right to life, the interpretation in this case is archetypal of the Dworkinian Model. It was Dworkin who aptly said, 'We have a responsibility to live well.'[11] This takes us to the central theme of the book at hand, namely, human dignity as the core value of human rights and Dworkin's perception about this fundamental principle.

Taking Human Dignity Seriously

Let me first discuss certain aspects of human dignity in general. Insofar as concept of human dignity is concerned, it dates back to thousands of years. Historically, human dignity, as a concept, found its origin in different religions which is held to be an important component of their theological approach. Later, it was also influenced by the views of philosophers who developed human dignity in their contemplations.[12] Jurisprudentially, three types of models for determining the content of the constitutional value of human dignity are recognized. These are: (a) Theological Model, (b) Philosophical Model, and (c) Constitutional Model. Legal scholars were called upon to determine the theological basis of human dignity as a constitutional value and as a constitutional right. Philosophers also came out with their views justifying human dignity as core human value. Legal understanding is influenced by theological and philosophical views, though these two are not identical. Aquinas, Kant, as well as Dworkin discussed the jurisprudential aspects of human dignity. Over a period of time, human dignity has found its way through constitutionalism, whether written or unwritten.

Theological Model

Amritasya Putrah Vayam
[We are all begotten of the immortal.] This is how Hinduism introduces human beings.

'Every individual soul is potentially divine.'
—proclaimed by Swami Vivekananda

Hinduism does not recognize human beings as mere material beings. Its understanding of human identity is more ethical-spiritual than material. That is why a sense of immortality and divinity is attributed to all human beings in Hindu classical literature.

Professor S.D. Sharma, sums up the position with following analysis:

Consistent with the depth of Indian metaphysics, the human personality was given a metaphysical interpretation. This is not unknown to the modern occidental philosophy. The concept of human personality in Kant's philosophy of law is metaphysical entity but Kant was not able to reach the subtler unobserved element of personality, which was the basic theme of the concept of personality in Indian legal philosophy.[13]

It is on the principle that the soul that makes the body of all living organisms; its abode is in fact an integral part of the Divine Whole—*Paramaatman*—that the Vedas declare unequivocally:

Ajyesthaaso Akanisthaasa Yete; Sam Bhraataro Vaavrudhuh Soubhagaya (No one is superior or inferior; all are brothers; all should strive for the interest of all and progress collectively.)
—Rig Veda, Mandala-5, Sukta-60, Mantra-5

Even in Islam, tradition of human rights became evident in the medieval ages. Being inspired by the tenets of the Holy Koran, it preaches the universal brotherhood, equality, justice, and compassion. Islam believes that man has special status before God. Because man is a creation of God, he should not be harmed. Harm to a human being is harm to God. God, as an act of love, created man and he wishes to grant him recognition, dignity, and authority. Thus, in Islam, human dignity stems from the belief that man is a creation of God—the creation that God loves more than any other.

The Bhakti and Sufi traditions too in their own unique ways popularized the idea of universal brotherhood. It revived and regenerated the cherished Indian values of truth, righteousness, justice, and morality.

Christianity believes that the image of God is revealed in Jesus and through him to human kind. God is rational and determines his goals for himself. Man was created in the image of God, and he too is rational and determines his own goals, subject to the God as a rational creation. Man has freedom of will. This is his *dignitas*. He is free to choose his goals, and he himself is a goal. His supreme goal is to know God. Thus, he is set apart from a slave and from all the creations under him. When a man sins, he loses his human dignity. He becomes an object.[14]

Philosophical Model

The modern conception of human dignity was affected by the philosophy of Kant.[15] Kant's moral theory is divided into two parts: ethics and right (jurisprudence). The discussion of human dignity took place within his doctrine of ethics and does not appear in his jurisprudence.[16] Kant's jurisprudence features the concept of a person's right to freedom as a human being.

According to Kant, a person acts ethically when he acts by force of a duty that a rational agent self-legislates onto his own will. This self-legislated duty is not accompanied by any right or coercion, and is not correlative to the rights of others. For Kant, ethics includes duties to oneself (for example, to develop one's talents) and to others (for example, to contribute to their happiness). This ability is the human dignity of man. This is what makes a person different than an object. This ability makes a person into an end, and prevents her from being a mere means in the hands of another.

Professor Upendra Baxi in his First Justice H.R. Khanna Memorial Lecture[17] on the topic 'Protection of Dignity of Individual under the Constitution of India', has very aptly remarked that dignity notions, like the idea of human rights, are supposed to be the gifts of the West to the Rest, though, this view is based on the prescribed ignorance of the rich traditions of non-European countries. He, then, explains Eurocentric view of human dignity by pointing out that it views dignity in terms of personhood (moral agency) and autonomy (freedom of choice). Dignity here is to be treated as 'empowerment' which makes a triple demand in the name of respect for human dignity, namely:

1. Respect for one's capacity as an agent to make one's own free choices.
2. Respect for the choices so made.
3. Respect for one's need to have a context and conditions in which one can operate as a source of free and informed choice.

To the aforesaid, Professor Baxi adds:

> I still need to say that the idea of dignity is a meta-ethical one, that is, it marks and maps a difficult terrain of what it may mean to say being 'human' and remaining 'human', or put another way the relationship between 'self', 'others', and 'society'. In this formulation the word 'respect' is the keyword: dignity is respect for an individual person based on the principle of freedom and capacity to make choices and a good or just social order is one which respects dignity via assuring 'contexts' and 'conditions' as the 'source of free and informed choice'. Respect for dignity thus conceived is empowering overall and not just because it, even if importantly, sets constraints state, law, and regulations.

Professor Jeremy Waldron[18] opines that dignity is a sort of status-concept: it has to do with the standing (perhaps the formal legal standing or perhaps, more informally, the moral presence) that a person has in a society and in her dealings with others. He has ventured even to define this term 'dignity' in the following manner:

> Dignity is the status of a person predicated on the fact that she is recognized as having the ability to control and regulate her actions in accordance with

her own apprehension of norms and reasons that apply to her; it assumes she is capable of giving and entitled to give an account of herself (and of the way in which she is regulating her actions and organizing her life), an account that others are to pay attention to; and it means finally that she has the wherewithal to demand that her agency and her presence among us as human being be taken seriously and accommodated in the lives of others, in others' attitudes and actions towards her, and in social life generally.

Kant, on the other hand, has initially used dignity as a 'value idea', though in his later work he also talks of 'respect' which a person needs to accord to other person, thereby speaking of it more as a matter of status.

Constitutional Value

The most important lesson which was learnt as a result of Second World War was the realization by the governments of various countries about the human dignity which needed to be cherished and protected. It is for this reason that in the U.N. Charter, 1945, adopted immediately after the Second World War, dignity of the individuals was mentioned as of core value. The almost contemporaneous Universal Declaration of Human Rights (1948) echoed same sentiments.

Article 3 of the Geneva Conventions explicitly prohibits 'outrages upon personal dignity'. There are provisions to this effect in International Covenant on Civil and Political Rights (ICCPR) (Article 7) and the European Convention of Human Rights (Article 3) though implicit. However, one can easily infer the said implicit message in these documents about human dignity. The ICCPR begins its preamble with the acknowledgment that the rights contained in the covenant 'derive from the inherent dignity of the human person'. And some philosophers say the same thing. Even if this is not a connection between dignity and law as such, it certainly purports to identify a wholesale connection between dignity and the branch of law devoted to human rights. One of the key facets of twenty-first century democracies is the primary importance they give to the protection of human rights. From this perspective, dignity is the expression of a basic value accepted in a broad sense by all people, and thus constitutes the first cornerstone in the edifice of human rights. Therefore, there is a certain fundamental value to the notion of human dignity, which some would consider a pivotal right deeply rooted in any notion of justice, fairness, and a society based on basic rights.

Aharon Barak, former Chief Justice of the Supreme Court of Israel, attributes two roles to the concept of human dignity as a constitutional value, which are:

1.   Human dignity lays a foundation for all the human rights as it is the central argument for the existence of human rights;
2.   Human dignity as a constitutional value provides meaning to the norms of the legal system. In the process, one can discern that the principle of purposive interpretation exhorts us to interpret all the rights given by the Constitution, in the light of the human dignity. In this sense, human dignity influences the purposive interpretation of the Constitution. Not only this, it also influences the interpretation of every sub-constitutional norm in the legal system. Moreover, human dignity as a constitutional value also influences the development of the common law.

Within two years of the adoption of the aforesaid Universal Declaration of Human Rights that all human beings are born free and equal in dignity and rights, India attained independence and immediately thereafter Members of the Constituent Assembly took up the task of framing the Constitution of this Country. It was but natural to include a Bill of Rights in the Indian Constitution and the Constitution Makers did so by incorporating a Chapter on Fundamental Rights in Part III of the Constitution. However, it would be significant to point out that there is no mention of 'dignity' specifically in this Chapter on Fundamental Rights. So was the position in the American Constitution. In America, human dignity as a part of human rights was brought in as a Judge-made doctrine. Same course of action followed as the Indian Supreme Court read human dignity into Articles 14 and 21 of the Constitution.

Dworkin's Rather Quixotic Dignity

The above discussion of human dignity as constitutional value aptly demonstrates that under the Indian Constitution this concept is evolved by the Supreme Court while undertaking interpretative process predicated on Articles 14 and 21 of the Constitution. How Dworkin perceives interpretative process adopted by a Judge some reflection thereof has already been captured in the beginning. To recapitulate briefly, Dworkin, being a philosopher–jurist, was aware of the idea of a Constitution and of a constitutional right to human dignity. In his book, *Taking Rights Seriously*, he noted that everyone who takes rights seriously must give an answer to the question why human rights viz-a-viz the State exist. According to him, in order to give such an answer one must accept, as a minimum, the idea of human dignity. As he writes, 'Human dignity ... associated with Kant, but defended by philosophers of different schools, supposes that there are ways of treating a man that are inconsistent with recognizing him as a full member of the human community, and holds that such treatment is profoundly unjust.'[19]

Talking particularly about certain hard cases involving moral overtones, he specifically discussed the issues pertaining to abortion and euthanasia with emphasis that both supporters and critics accept the idea of sanctity of life. Thus, the concept of human dignity stands on both sides of arguments. 'Dignity—which means respecting the inherent value of our own lives—is the heart of both arguments.'[20]

Decisions regarding death—whether by abortion or by euthanasia—affect our human dignity. In Dworkin's opinion, proper recognition of human dignity leads to the recognition of the freedom of the individual. Freedom is a necessary condition for self-worth. Dworkin adds, 'Because we cherish dignity, we insist on freedom.... Because we honour dignity, we demand democracy' (Dworkin 1994: 239).

In his book, *Is Democracy Possible Here?*[21] Dworkin develops two principles about the concept of human dignity. First principle regards the intrinsic value of every person, namely, every person has a special objective value which is not only important to that person alone but success or failure of the lives of every person is important to all of us. The second principle, according to Dworkin, is that of personal responsibility. According to this principle, every person has the responsibility for success in his own life and, therefore, he must use his discretion regarding the way of life that will be successful from his point of view. Thus, Dworkin's jurisprudence of human dignity is founded on the aforesaid two principles which, together, not only define the basis but the conditions for human dignity. Dworkin went on to develop and expand these principles in his book, *Justice for Hedgehogs* (2011).

An ideal state for Dworkin cannot be fathomed without a few essentials; interpretation of law where principle is the guiding light in the dark and where equality is the norm which is realized by 'taking rights seriously' however it is notion of dignity which is at the heart of the Dworkinian way of life. Equality gives colour to dignity and dignity enables equality to realize its full meaning. To be treated equally we ought to be given an equal path in order to walk in life with dignity. While we may belong to different caste, religion, race, economic backgrounds, and so on, it is the podium of dignity, which makes us stand together, in the same way, rubbing shoulders; being equal. When speaking of rights, it is impossible to envisage it without dignity. In his pioneering and all inclusive *Justice for Hedgehogs*, he proffered an approach where respect for human dignity, entails two requirements; first, self-respect, namely, taking the objective importance of one's own life seriously; this represents the free will of the person, his capacity to think for himself and to control his own life and second, authenticity, namely, accepting a 'special, personal responsibility for identifying what counts as success' in one's own life and for creating that life 'through a coherent narrative' that one has chosen.[22] According to Dworkin, these principles form the fundamental criteria supervising what we should do in order to live well (Simons 2010: 715). They further explicate the rights that individuals have against their political community,[23] and they provide a rationale for the moral duties we owe to others. This notion of dignity, which Dworkin gives utmost importance to, is indispensable to any civilized society. It is what is constitutionally recognized in our country and for good reason. Living well is a moral responsibility of individuals; it is a continuing process that is not a static condition of character but a mode that an individual constantly endeavours to imbibe. A life lived without dignity, is not a life lived at all for living well implies a conception of human dignity which Dworkin interprets includes ideals of self-respect and authenticity. This constitutional value of human dignity has been beautifully illustrated by Aharon Barak, as under:

> Human dignity as a constitutional value is the factor that unites the human rights into one whole. It ensures the normative unity of human rights. This normative unity is expressed in the three ways: first, the value of human dignity serves as a normative basis for constitutional rights set out in the constitution; second, it serves as an interpretative principle for determining the scope of constitutional rights, including the right to human dignity; third, the value of human dignity has an important role in determining the proportionality of a statute limiting a constitutional right.[24]

By perfectly explaining the notion of Dignity as applicable when interpreting a Constitution, Barak however pointed out the weakness in Dworkin's model of dignity. Dworkin was not interpreting any Constitution when he formulated his conception; his model was not to fit a constitutional scheme but was a more philosophical one. Hence, applying it to a country governed by a constitution whether written or unwritten was more of an impracticality (Barak 2015: 103).

Notwithstanding the above critique, the Dworkinian 'Dignity' can be considered to be an exemplar in the context of the judgment of the Supreme Court of India in the case of *Jeeja Ghosh v. Union of India*.[25] The Court, in a way, adopted his approach to the principle of human dignity, reading the same into the Constitutional provisions, albeit, by following the path which the Court had tread on earlier as well. We have a written Constitution which guarantees human rights that are contained in Part III with the caption 'Fundamental Rights'. Right to life is given a purposeful meaning by this

Court to include right to live with dignity. It is the purposive interpretation, which has been adopted by this Court to give a content of the right to human dignity as the fulfilment of the constitutional value enshrined in Article 21. Thus, human dignity is a constitutional value and a constitutional goal.

Dworkin's notion, a philosophical one albeit, is an ideal. While considered by many to be unviable, it does bring the moral element to the fore and throws light on its importance more on an individual level as it focuses on persons taking their own as well as the lives of others seriously. His theory is a hard one to ignore, through the plinth of morality, he made 'dignity in life' and 'interpretation in law' pillars, that constitutions around the world have tried to incorporate in one form or another, whether it is the independence of judiciary in interpretation and the value it continues to hold in society or the constitutional shape that his philosophical dignity has moulded into.

The BOOK *Taking Dignity Seriously: The Role of Dignity in Professor Ronald Dworkin's Legal and Political Philosophy*, through various articles, impeccably captures the impact and the essence of Dworkin's theories. It's a commendable effort of Salman Khurshid, Lokendra Malik, and Professor Veronica Rodriguez-Blanco to put together some of the most significant works of writers portraying the prominence and relevance of Dworkin. The assemblage of the articles ranging from his unparalleled perception on interpretation, his supreme godly adjudicator, and primarily his central notion of dignity, this book aptly encapsulates Dworkin's role through the lens of legal thinkers, lawyers, scholars, jurists, professors of law, and philosophy.

A.K. Sikri
Hon'ble Judge, Supreme Court of India

Notes and References

1. Ronald Dworkin. 1978. *Taking Rights Seriously*. Cambridge, MA: Harvard University Press.
2. Ronald Dworkin. 2002. *Sovereign Virtue: The Theory and Practice of Equality*. Cambridge, MA: Harvard University Press.
3. Ronald Dworkin. 1988. *Law's Empire*. Cambridge, MA: Harvard University Press. p. 97.
4. Ronald Dworkin. 1982. 'Law as Interpretation', *Texas Law Review*, 60. pp. 527–50 (at p. 528).
5. Richard A. Posner. 1993. *The Problems of Jurisprudence*. Cambridge, MA: Harvard University Press. p. 125.
6. Posner 1993. p. 6.
7. Posner 1993. p. 1.

8. Upendra Baxi. 2003. 'A Known but an indifferent judge: Situating Ronald Dworkin in contemporary Indian jurisprudence', *International Journal of Constitutional Law*. 1(4):557–89 (at p. 565).

9. Baxi 2003. p. 1.

10. (2014) 5 SCC 438.

11. Ronald Dworkin. 2011. *Justice for Hedgehogs*. Cambridge, MA: Harvard University Press.

12. Though western thinking is that the concept of human dignity has 2,500 years old history, in many eastern civilizations including India, human dignity as core human value was recognized thousands of years ago.

13. S.D. Sharma. 1988. *Administration of Justice in Ancient Bharat*. New Delhi: Harman Publishing House.

14. Based on the approach of Thomas Aquinas (1225–74) in his work *Summa Theologia*.

15. See Toman E. Hill. 1980. 'Humanity as an End in Itself', *Ethics*. 90(1). p. 84.

16. See Dietmar von der Pfordten. 2009. 'On the Dignity of Man in Kant', *Philosophy*. 84(3). pp. 371–91.

17. Professor Upendra Baxi. 2015. 'Protection of Dignity of Individual under the Constitution of India', in Lokendra Malik and Manish Arora (eds), *Justice H. R. Khanna: Law, Life and Works*. New Delhi: Universal Law Publishing (an Imprint of LexisNexis). p. 368.

18. Jeremy Waldron. 2012. 'How Law Protects Dignity', *The Cambridge Law Journal*. 20 March. 71(1). pp. 200–22.

19. Waldron 2012. p. 1.

20. Ronald Dworkin. 1994. *Life's Dominion: An Argument About Abortion, Euthanasia, and Individual Freedom*. New York: Vintage Books. p. 238.

21. Ronal Dworkin. 2006. *Is Democracy Possible Here? Principles for a New Political Debate*. Princeton: Princeton University Press.

22. Kenneth W. Simons. 2010. 'Dworkin's Two Principle of Dignity: An Unsatisfactory Nonconsequentialist Account of Interpersonal Moral Duties', *Boston law Review*. 90. p. 715.

23. See footnote 12.

24. Aharan Barak. 2015. *Human Dignity: The Constitutional Value and the Constitutional Right*. Cambridge: Cambridge University Press, p. 103.

25. Writ Petition (C) No. 98 of 2012.

About the Editors and Contributors

Editors

Salman Khurshid is a practising advocate in the Supreme Court of India. He is a senior Indian National Congress leader who was the cabinet minister in the UPA-2 government headed by Prime Minister Dr Manmohan Singh. He held the portfolios of law and justice, minority affairs, and external affairs. He belongs to Farrukhabad in Uttar Pradesh.

Khurshid holds a BA (Honours) degree from St. Stephen's College, University of Delhi. He did his BCL at Oxford University, UK, and also taught law for a few years at Trinity College, Oxford. He is a well-known educationist who was the president of Delhi Public School Society for many years. He is a prolific author and public intellectual. *At Home in India* (2014), *The Other Side of the Mountain* (2015), and *Triple Talaq* (2018) are some of his prominent books. He has appeared in many landmark cases in the Supreme Court including the famous *Triple Talaq* case.

Lokendra Malik is a practising advocate of the Supreme Court of India. Before entering legal practice, he taught law at the Indian Institution of Public Administration (IIPA), New Delhi, India. He has earned his BA LLB and LLM degrees from Chaudhary Charan Singh University, Meerut and did his PhD in Law at Kurukshetra University, Haryana, India. He has also been awarded the prestigious LLD (post-doctorate) degree from the National Law School of India University, Bengaluru, in the area of Indian Constitutional Law. Public law is his main area of interest. As a professor of law at IIPA, he taught senior civil servants. He is associated with a number of prestigious academic bodies such as Indian Law Institute, IIPA, and Dr Zakir Hussain Study Circle. He is also a member of Berkeley Comparative Equality and

Anti-Discrimination Law Study Group, established by the University of California, Berkeley, USA. He has published many books on different topics pertaining to law and governance from reputed publishers.

Veronica Rodriguez-Blanco is the inaugural Chair in Moral and Political Philosophy (Jurisprudence) at the University of Surrey Centre for Law and Philosophy, UK. She studied law and legal philosophy at Oxford and Cambridge and is the author of numerous articles in peer-reviewed journals. She is also the author of the monograph *Law and Authority under the Guise of the Good*.

Contributors

James Allan holds the oldest named chair at the University of Queensland. He is a native-born Canadian who practised law at a large firm in Toronto and then at the Bar in London before moving to teach law in Hong Kong, New Zealand, and then Australia. He has had sabbaticals at the Cornell Law School and the University of San Diego School of Law in the US, and at Osgoode Hall Law School and the Dalhousie Law School in Canada (where he was the Bertha Wilson Visiting Professor of Human Rights). Allan has published widely in the areas of constitutional law, legal philosophy, and bill of rights scepticism. He was elected to the Mont Pelerin Society in 2011.

T.R.S. Allan is professor of Jurisprudence and Public Law at the University of Cambridge and Fellow of Pembroke College, Cambridge, UK. He is a Fellow of the British Academy. He is the author of *Law, Liberty, and Justice*, *Constitutional Justice* (Oxford University Press, 2001), and *The Sovereignty of Law* (Oxford University Press, 2013). He has regularly published journal articles and book chapters on legal and constitutional theory.

Pritam Baruah teaches law at Jindal Global Law School, India. His research and teaching interests are in legal philosophy and constitutional theory. Currently his research focuses on how constitutional courts reason with constitutional values, particularly dignity, liberty, and democracy. He has previously taught legal theory and constitutional law at the National University of Juridical Sciences, Kolkata, India; held visiting professorships in constitutional law at the University of Ottawa, Canada and the China University of Political Science and Law; and practiced law at the Supreme Court of India. Baruah was a commonwealth doctoral scholar at University College London, Felix scholar at the University of Oxford, UK and has an undergraduate degree in law from NALSAR University of Law, India. He was one of the founding conveners of the UCL Legal Philosophy Forum, UK and is executive director of the Center for Legal Philosophy at Jindal Global Law School.

Mark Bennett teaches at Victoria University of Wellington School of Law, New Zealand. His interests include legal philosophy, property, and trusts. After completing undergraduate studies in law, classics, and sociology at Victoria University of Wellington, Bennett was a Frank Knox Memorial Scholar at Harvard Law School, US, where he took an LLM. He subsequently completed a doctorate at the University of Toronto Faculty of Law, Canada, supported by a Connaught Scholarship. Bennett's work has been published in journals such as the *Australian Journal of Legal Philosophy*, the *Indigenous Law Journal*, *The Journal of Equity*, *Law and Philosophy*, and the *Victoria University of Wellington Law Review*.

Alexander Brown is a reader in political and legal theory at the University of East Anglia (UEA), UK. He is the author of *A Theory of Legitimate Expectations for Public Administration* (2017), *Hate Speech Law: A Philosophical Examination* (2015), *Ronald Dworkin's Theory of Equality: Domestic and Global Perspectives* (2009), and *Personal Responsibility: Why It Matters* (2009).

Petra Butler teaches at the Victoria University of Wellington School of Law, New Zealand, and is the co-director of the Centre for Small States at Queen Mary, University of London, UK. Butler specializes in public and private comparative law, private international law with an emphasis on international commercial contracts, domestic and international human rights, and business and human rights. She has published extensively in those areas, including with Andrew Butler, *The New Zealand Bill of Rights Act 1990: A Commentary* (2015). Petra advises public and private clients in her areas of expertise and has been involved in New Zealand's high profile human rights cases in recent years. She is a member of a number of advisory boards of human rights NGOs and has been awarded a number of fellowships. She was the Wilmer Cutler Pickering Hale and Dorr LLP scholar-in-residence in 2015.

Jonathan Crowe teaches law at Bond University, Australia. His research examines the philosophical relationship between law and ethics, looking at issues such as the nature and foundations of legal obligation and the role of ethics in legal reasoning. He is the author or editor of five books and more than seventy book chapters and journal articles. His work has appeared in numerous leading international and Australian journals, including the *Modern Law*

Review, the *Oxford Journal of Legal Studies, Law and Critique*, the *Melbourne University Law Review*, the *Sydney Law Review*, and the *Australian Journal of Legal Philosophy*.

Erin Daly teaches law at Widener University Delaware Law School in Wilmington, Delaware, US. She is the author of *Dignity Rights: Courts, Constitutions, and the Worth of the Human Person* (2013) and the co-founder of the Dignity Rights Project, which advances the dignity rights of people around the world through education, litigation, and advocacy. She is also the co-author of *Reconciliation in Divided Societies: Finding Common Ground* (2006) (with Jeremy Sarkin) and *Global Environmental Constitutionalism* (2015) (with James R. May), and the co-editor and author of many articles, chapters, and books on comparative constitutionalism. She also serves as the director of the Global Network for the Study of Human Rights and the Environment.

James E. Fleming is the Honorable Paul J. Liacos Professor of Law at Boston University School of Law, US. His books include: *Fidelity to Our Imperfect Constitution: For Moral Readings and Against Originalisms* (2015); *Ordered Liberty: Rights, Responsibilities, and Virtues* (2013), *Constitutional Interpretation: The Basic Questions* (2017, with Sotirios A. Barber); and *Securing Constitutional Democracy: The Case of Autonomy*. He is working on a book on perfectionism and the appropriate scope of the enforcement and promotion of morals and public values. Fleming is president of the American Society for Political and Legal Philosophy. He is a former faculty fellow in Princeton University's Program in Law and Public Affairs and in Harvard University's Safra Center for Ethics. He edited symposia on Ronald Dworkin's *Justice for Hedgehogs* and *Religion without God* in *Boston University Law Review*.

Imer B. Flores is professor-researcher at the Legal Research Institute and the Law School of National Autonomous University of Mexico (UNAM). He is also a member of the National System of Researchers (SNI) of the National Council of Science and Technology (CONACYT), Mexico. He has been visiting professor and scholar at American and International Studies, Ramapo College of New Jersey (as Fulbright scholar); Harvard Law School, Harvard University; Honors College, University of Houston; and Georgetown University Law Center (USA); and Center for Transnational Legal Studies (in the UK). He has been advisor and consultant for the Economic Commission for Latin America and the Caribbean of United Nations, for the United States Agency for International Development, and for the Commonwealth

Secretariat in the redrafting process of the Constitution of Sri Lanka. He has an LLB (graduated with honours) and a S.J.D. (graduated with honours) from Law School of UNAM; and an LLM from Harvard Law School, Harvard University.

Barbara Baum Levenbook teaches philosophy at North Carolina State University. Her articles on legal philosophy have appeared in *Legal Theory*, *Law and Philosophy*, *Philosophy Compass*, *Oxford Studies in the Philosophy of Law*, *The Canadian Journal of Philosophy*, and in law reviews. She has also published articles in social and political philosophy, in normative ethics, and in its intersection with metaphysics. She has contributed and continues to contribute to several philosophical anthologies, and is the author of an article in *Philosophy of Law: An Encyclopedia*, edited by Christopher Gray. She is a contributing editor to *Jotwell*, Jurisprudence section, and holds a BA and an MA in philosophy from the University of Rochester and a PhD in philosophy from the University of Arizona (in the US).

Linda C. McClain is Paul M. Siskind Research Scholar and teaches law at Boston University School of Law, where she teaches family law, feminist legal theory, and gender and law. Among her books are: *The Place of Families: Fostering Capacity, Equality, and Responsibility* and *Ordered Liberty: Rights, Responsibilities, and Virtues* (with James E. Fleming). Her book-in-progress, *Bigotry, Conscience, and Marriage: Past and Present Controversies,* is under contract with Oxford University Press. Her scholarship addresses the respective roles of the institutions of civil society and government in fostering persons' capacities for democratic and personal self-government, and the relationship between constitutional rights and responsibilities. She is a former Laurance S. Rockefeller Faculty Fellow at the University Center for Human Values, Princeton University, USA and faculty fellow in Harvard University's Safra Center for Ethics (USA). She had the good fortune to study with Ronald Dworkin while getting her LLM at NYU School of Law, USA.

Suhrith Parthasarathy is a lawyer and writer based in Chennai, India. In 2013, he established an independent law office, and appears regularly in the Madras High Court. His interests include constitutional law, taxation, and jurisprudence. He also teaches a course on law and journalism at the Asian College of Journalism, Chennai, and is a regular columnist and op-ed writer for *The Hindu* newspaper. His articles have appeared in a number of dailies and magazines including, *The Indian Express*, the website of *The New Yorker*, *The Caravan Magazine*, *The New York Times*, and the *Economic and Political*

Weekly, among others. Parthasarathy is presently working on a book on the history of the Supreme Court of India. He is a graduate in law from the National University of Juridical Sciences, Kolkata, and in journalism from Columbia University, New York.

George Pavlakos teaches law and philosophy at the School of Law, University of Glasgow, Scotland. From 2007 to 2016 he was a research professor and director of the Centre for Law and Cosmopolitan Values at the University of Antwerp, Belgium. His personal research awards include two Alexander von Humboldt Fellowships, an FWO-Odysseus grant, a J.E. Purkyne Senior Research Fellowship (Czech Academy of Sciences) and a Fernand Braudel Senior Fellowship (European University Institute, Florence, Italy). He publishes in legal philosophy and theory with an emphasis on those aspects of the law that raise foundational questions in metaphysics, metaethics, and substantive political philosophy, often engaging with their practical implications on the legal doctrine. His published work includes the monograph *Our Knowledge of the Law* (2007) and he has recently co-edited *Reasons and Intentions in Law and Practical Agency* (2015). He is also general editor of the book series *Law and Practical Reason* and joint general editor of the journal *Jurisprudence*.

David A.J. Richards is Edwin D. Webb professor of law at New York University School of Law (US) where he teaches constitutional law and criminal law. He also conducts seminars with Carol Gilligan (Resisting Injustice) and another with James Gilligan (Retributivism in Criminal Law Theory and Practice). He is the author of twenty books, including *The Deepening Darkness: Patriarchy, Resistance, and Democracy's Future* (with Carol Gilligan, 2009); *Fundamentalism in American Religion and Law* (2010); *The Rise of Gay Rights and the Fall of the British Empire* (2013); and *Why Love Leads to Justice: Love across the Boundaries* (2016).

Isabel Trujillo teaches legal philosophy at the University of Palermo, Italy, where she is also director of the International PhD Program in Human Rights. Prior to joining the Department of Law at Palermo, she has worked at the University of Ferrara and at the University of Rome Tor Vergata (Italy). Trujillo holds a PhD from the Sapienza University of Rome. She teaches and writes about jurisprudence, the philosophy of international law, global justice, legal ethics, and human rights. Her publications include *Francisco de Vitoria. Il diritto alla comunicazione e i confini della socialità umana* (1997), *Imparzialità* (2003, translated into Spanish by UNAM in 2007), *Giustizia globale* (2007),

Etica delle professioni legali (2013), and together with Francesco Viola, *What Human Rights Are Not (Or Not Only)*, and *A Negative Path to Human Rights* (2014).

Allen W. Wood is Ruth Norman Halls Professor at Indiana University and Ward W. and Priscilla B. Woods Professor Emeritus at Stanford University (US). He has also held professorships at Cornell and Yale University and has held visiting appointments at the University of Michigan, University of California at San Diego (US) and Oxford University (UK). He received the BA degree from Reed College and PhD from Yale University (US). He is the author of a dozen books, including *Hegel's Ethical Thought* (1990), *Kant's Ethical Thought* (1999), *Fichte's Ethical Thought* (2016), and *Karl Marx* (1981, 2nd edition, 2004), and has also edited a dozen other volumes. He is co-general editor of the Cambridge Edition of the *Writings of Kant* in English translation. He was editor in-chief of the *Philosophical Review* for many years in the 1980s and 1990s, and serves on the editorial boards of a dozen journals, including *Ethics*, *Kant-Studien* and *Kantian Review*, and the editorial board of the *Stanford Encyclopedia of Philosophy*.

Lorenzo Zucca teaches law and philosophy at King's College, London, UK. His research interests are in jurisprudence, constitutional theory, EU constitutional law and human rights. He is the author of *Constitutional Dilemmas: Conflicts of Fundamental Legal Rights in Europe and the USA* (2007) and articles on European human rights law and theory. His last book is entitled *A Secular Europe: Law and Religion in the European Constitutional Landscape* (2012). Some of his prominent books are, *A Secular Europe: Law and Religion in the European Constitutional Landscape* (2012), and *Law, State and Religion in the New Europe* (2012).

Index